MCSE Complete:
Electives

SYBEX®   SAN FRANCISCO ▸ PARIS ▸ DÜSSELDORF ▸ SOEST ▸ LONDON

Associate Publisher: Guy Hart-Davis

Contracts and Licensing Manager: Kristine O'Callaghan

Acquisitions & Developmental Editors: Neil Edde, Linda Lee

Compilation Editor: Malka Geffen

Editors: Suzanne Goraj, Ronn Jost, Valerie Perry, Margaret Jane Ross

Technical Editors: Jim Cooper, Matthew Fiedler, Joshua Konkle, Darin McGee, Rob Sanfilippo, Scott Warmbrand

Book Designer: Maureen Forys, Happenstance Type-O-Rama

Graphic Illustrators: Michael Gushard, Tony Jonick, Michael Parker

Electronic Publishing Specialist: Grey Magauran

Project Team Leader: Shannon Murphy

Proofreaders: Bonnie Hart, Laura Schattschneider, Laurie Stewart, Theresa Mori, Nancy Riddiough

Indexer: Nancy Guenther

Cover Designer: Archer Design

Cover Illustrator/Photographer: FPG International

Library of Congress Card Number: 99-63824
ISBN: 0-7821-2584-0

Manufactured in Canada

10 9 8 7 6 5 4 3 2 1

Trademarks

SYBEX has attempted throughout this book to distinguish proprietary trademarks from descriptive terms by following the capitalization style used by the manufacturer.

The author and publisher have made their best efforts to prepare this book, and the content is based upon final release software whenever possible. Portions of the manuscript may be based upon pre-release versions supplied by software manufacturer(s). The author and the publisher make no representation or warranties of any kind with regard to the completeness or accuracy of the contents herein and accept no liability of any kind including but not limited to performance, merchantability, fitness for any particular purpose, or any losses or damages of any kind caused or alleged to be caused directly or indirectly from this book.

Microsoft, the Microsoft Internet Explorer logo, Windows, Windows NT, and the Windows logo are either registered trademarks or trademarks of Microsoft Corporation in the United States and/or other countries.

SYBEX is an independent entity from Microsoft Corporation, and not affiliated with Microsoft Corporation in any manner. This publication may be used in assisting students to prepare for a Microsoft Certified Professional Exam. Neither Microsoft Corporation, its designated review company, nor SYBEX warrants that use of this publication will ensure passing the relevant exam. Microsoft is either a registered trademark or trademark of Microsoft Corporation in the United States and/or other countries.

ACKNOWLEDGMENTS

This book incorporates the work of many people, inside and outside Sybex.

Guy Hart-Davis and Linda Lee defined the book's overall structure and adapted its contents, and Malka Geffen compiled all the material for publication in this book.

A large team of editors, developmental editors, project editors, and technical editors helped to put together the various books from which *MCSE Complete: Electives* was compiled: Neil Edde and Linda Lee handled developmental tasks; Suzanne Goraj, Ronn Jost, Valerie Perry, and Margaret Jane Ross all contributed to editing; and Jim Cooper, Matthew Fiedler, Joshua Konkle, Darin McGee, Rob Sanfilippo, and Scott Warmbrand provided technical edits.

The *MCSE Complete: Electives* production team of electronic publishing specialist Grey Magauran and project team leader Shannon Murphy worked with speed and accuracy to turn the manuscript files and illustrations into the handsome book you're now reading.

Finally, our most important thanks go to the contributors who agreed to have their work excerpted in *MCSE Complete: Electives*: James Chellis, Gary Govanus, Robert King, Lance Mortensen, Rick Sawtell, and Joseph L. Jorden. Without their efforts, this book would not exist.

CONTENTS AT A GLANCE

TABLE OF CONTENTS

INTRODUCTION

MCSE Complete: Electives is a one-of-a-kind book—valuable both for the breadth of its content and for its low price. This thousand-page compilation of information from five Network Press books provides comprehensive coverage of all the elective MCSE exams.

If you've purchased this book, you are probably chasing one of the Microsoft professional certifications: MCP, MCSE, or MCT. All of these are great goals, and they are also great career builders. Glance through any newspaper and you'll find employment opportunities for people with these certifications—these ads are there because finding qualified employees is a challenge in today's market. The certification means you know something about the product, but more importantly, it means you have the ability, determination, and focus to learn—the greatest skill any employee can have!

You've probably also heard all the rumors about how hard the Microsoft tests are—believe us, the rumors are true! Microsoft has designed a series of exams that truly test your knowledge of their products. Each test not only covers the materials presented in a particular class, it also covers the prerequisite knowledge for that course. This means two things for you—that first test can be a real hurdle and each test *should* get easier since you've studied the basics over and over.

▶ Is This Book for You?

MCSE Complete: Electives was designed to be a portable exam review guide that can be used either in conjunction with a more complete study program (book, CBT courseware, classroom/lab environment) or as an exam review for those who don't feel the need for more extensive test preparation. It isn't our goal to "give the answers away," but rather to identify those topics on which you can expect to be tested and to provide sufficient coverage of these topics.

Perhaps you've been working with Microsoft networking technologies for years now. The thought of paying lots of money for a specialized MCSE exam preparation course probably doesn't sound too appealing. What can they teach you that you don't already know, right? Be careful, though. Many experienced network administrators have walked confidently into test centers only to walk sheepishly out of them after failing an MCSE exam. As they discovered, there's the Microsoft of the real world and the Microsoft of the MCSE exams. It's our goal with this book to show you where the two converge and where they diverge. After you've finished reading through this book, you should have a clear idea of how your understanding of the technologies involved matches up with the expectations of the MCSE test makers in Redmond.

Or perhaps you're relatively new to the world of Microsoft networking, drawn to it by the promise of challenging work and higher salaries. You've just waded through an 800-page MCSE study guide or taken a class at a local training center. Lots of information to keep track of, isn't it? Well, by organizing this book according to the Microsoft exam objectives, and by breaking up the information into concise manageable pieces, we've created what we think is the handiest exam review guide available. As you read through the book, you'll be able to identify quickly those areas you know best and those that require more in-depth review.

NOTE

The goal of the Exam Notes series, on which *MCSE Complete* is based, is to help MCSE candidates familiarize themselves with the subjects on which they can expect to be tested in the MCSE exams. For complete, in-depth coverage of the technologies and topics involved, we recommend the *MCSE Study Guide* series from Sybex.

▶ How Is This Book Organized?

This book has five parts and two appendices.

Part I: TCP/IP for NT Server 4   Covers objectives for exam 70-059.

Part II: Internet Information Server 4   Covers objectives for exam 70-087.

Part III: Exchange Server 5.5   Covers objectives for exam 70-081.

Part IV: SQL Server 7 Administration   Covers objectives for exam 70-028.

Part V: Internet Explorer 4 Administration Kit   Covers objectives for exam 70-079.

Appendix A   Answers to the Exam Questions section of each unit.

Appendix B   A comprehensive glossary of terms.

As mentioned above, this book is organized according to the official exam objectives list prepared by Microsoft for the 70-059, 70-087, 70-081, 70-028, and 70-079 exams. The parts coincide with the different exams, and the chapters coincide with the broad objectives groupings, such as Planning, Installation and Configuration, Monitoring and Optimization, and Troubleshooting. These groupings are also reflected in the organization of the MCSE exams themselves.

Within each chapter, the individual exam objectives are addressed in turn. And in turn, the objectives sections are further divided according to the type of information presented. For each objective, you'll find all the critical information you need to know, followed by key procedures. Each part ends with a selection of questions similar to those you'll encounter on the actual MCSE exam. Answers and explanations are provided in Appendix A so you can gain some insight into the test taking process.

In Appendix B, the glossary, you'll find the most important terms and concepts related to each objective brought together in a comprehensive glossary. You'll understand what all those technical words mean within the context of the related subject matter.

For a more comprehensive collection of exam review questions, check out the MCSE Test Success series, also published by Sybex.

▶ How Do You Become an MCSE?

Attaining Microsoft Certified Systems Engineer (MCSE) status is a challenge. The exams cover a wide range of topics and require dedicated study and expertise. This is, however, why the MCSE certificate is so valuable. If achieving the MCSE were too easy, the market would be quickly flooded by MCSEs and the certification would become meaningless. Microsoft, keenly aware of this fact, has taken steps to ensure that the certification means its holder is truly knowledgeable and skilled.

To become an MCSE, you must pass four core requirements and two electives. Most people select the following exam combination for the MCSE core requirements for the most current track:

Client Requirement

70-073: Implementing and Supporting Windows NT Workstation 4.0 *or*

70-098: Implementing and Supporting Microsoft® Windows 98®

Networking Requirement

70-058: Networking Essentials

Windows NT Server 4.0 Requirement

70-067: Implementing and Supporting Windows NT Server 4.0

Windows NT Server 4.0 in the Enterprise Requirement

70-068: Implementing and Supporting Windows NT Server 4.0 in the Enterprise

Electives

Some of the more popular electives include:

70-059: Internetworking Microsoft TCP/IP on Microsoft Windows NT 4.0

70-087: Implementing and Supporting Microsoft Internet Information Server 4.0

70-081: Implementing and Supporting Microsoft Exchange Server 5.5

70-026: System Administration for Microsoft SQL Server 6.5

70-027: Implementing a Database Design on Microsoft SQL Server 6.5

70-028: System Administration for Microsoft SQL Server 7

70-088: Implementing and Supporting Microsoft Proxy Server 2.0

70-079: Implementing and Supporting Microsoft Internet Explorer 4.0 by Using the Internet Explorer Administration Kit

TIP

The source books for *MCSE Complete: Electives* are part of a series of MCSE Exam Notes books, published by Network Press (Sybex). These cover the core requirements and your choice of several electives—the entire MCSE track!

NOTE

You can also check out *MCSE Complete: Core Requirements,* which will help you prepare for some of the most popular core requirement exams. These include: Implementing and Supporting Windows NT Workstation 4.0 *or* Implementing and Supporting Microsoft Windows 98, Networking Essentials, Implementing and Supporting Windows NT Server 4.0, and Implementing and Supporting Windows NT Server 4.0 in the Enterprise.

▶ Where Do You Take the Exams?

You may take the exams at any one of more than 800 Sylvan Prometric Authorized Testing Centers around the world or through Virtual University Enterprises (VUE).

For the location of a Sylvan testing center near you, call (800) 755-EXAM (755-3926). Outside the United States and Canada, contact your local Sylvan Prometric Registration Center. You can also register for an exam with Sylvan Prometric via the Internet. The Sylvan site can be reached through the Microsoft Training and Certification site or at http://www.slspro.com/msreg/microsoft.asp.

To register for an exam through VUE, call 888-837-8616 (North America only) or visit their web site at http://www.vue.com/ms/.

NOTE

At the time of this writing, the exams are $100 each.

When you schedule the exam, you'll be provided with instructions regarding appointment and cancellation procedures, ID requirements, and information about the testing center location.

▶ How Microsoft Develops the Exam Questions

Microsoft's exam development process consists of eight mandatory phases. The process takes an average of seven months and contains more than 150 specific steps. The phases of Microsoft Certified Professional exam development are listed here.

Phase 1: Job Analysis   Phase 1 is an analysis of all the tasks that make up the specific job function based on tasks performed by people who are currently performing the job function. This phase also identifies the knowledge, skills, and abilities that relate specifically to the certification for that performance area.

Phase 2: Objective Domain Definition   The results of the job analysis provide the framework used to develop exam objectives. The development of objectives involves translating the job function tasks into a comprehensive set of more specific and measurable knowledge, skills, and abilities. The resulting list of objectives, or the objective domain, is the basis for the development of both the certification exams and the training materials.

NOTE

The outline of all Exam Notes books is based upon the official exam objectives lists published by Microsoft. Objectives are subject to change without notification. We advise that you check the Microsoft Training & Certification Web site (www.microsoft.com\train_cert\) for the most current objectives list.

Phase 3: Blueprint Survey   The final objective domain is transformed into a blueprint survey in which contributors—technology professionals who are performing the applicable job function—are asked to rate each objective. Based on the contributors' input, the objectives are prioritized and weighted. The actual exam items are written according to the prioritized objectives. The blueprint survey phase helps determine which objectives to measure, as well as the appropriate number and types of items to include on the exam.

Phase 4: Item Development   A pool of items is developed to measure the blueprinted objective domain. The number and types of items to be written are based on the results of the blueprint survey. During this phase, items are reviewed and revised to ensure that they are

- ▶ Technically accurate
- ▶ Clear, unambiguous, and plausible
- ▶ Not biased toward any population, subgroup, or culture

- ▶ Not misleading or tricky
- ▶ Testing at the correct level of Bloom's Taxonomy
- ▶ Testing for useful knowledge, not obscure or trivial facts

Items that meet these criteria are included in the initial item pool.

Phase 5: Alpha Review and Item Revision During this phase, a panel of technical and job function experts reviews each item for technical accuracy, then answers each item, reaching consensus on all technical issues. Once the items have been verified as technically accurate, they are edited to ensure that they are expressed in the clearest language possible.

Phase 6: Beta Exam The reviewed and edited items are collected into a beta exam pool. During the beta exam, each participant has the opportunity to respond to all the items in this beta exam pool. Based on the responses of all beta participants, Microsoft performs a statistical analysis to verify the validity of the exam items and to determine which items will be used in the certification exam. Once the analysis has been completed, the items are distributed into multiple parallel forms, or versions, of the final certification exam.

Phase 7: Item Selection and Cut-Score Setting The results of the beta exam are analyzed to determine which items should be included in the certification exam based on many factors, including item difficulty and relevance. Generally, the desired items are answered correctly by 25 to 90 percent of the beta exam candidates. This helps ensure that the exam consists of a variety of difficulty levels, from somewhat easy to extremely difficult.

Also during this phase, a panel of job function experts determines the cut score (minimum passing score) for the exam. The cut score differs from exam to exam because it is based on an item-by-item determination of the percentage of candidates who would be expected to answer the item correctly. The experts determine the cut score in a group session to increase the reliability.

Phase 8: Live Exam Once all the other phases are complete, the exam is ready. Microsoft Certified Professional exams are administered by Sylvan Prometric.

Tips for Taking an MCSE Exam

Here are some general tips for taking an exam successfully:

▶ Arrive early at the exam center so you can relax and review your study materials, particularly tables and lists of exam-related information.

▶ Read the questions carefully. Don't be tempted to jump to an early conclusion. Make sure you know exactly what the question is asking.

▶ Don't leave any unanswered questions. They count against you.

▶ When answering multiple-choice questions you're not sure about, use a process of elimination to get rid of the obviously incorrect questions first. This will improve your odds if you need to make an educated guess.

▶ Because the hard questions will eat up the most time, save them for last. You can move forward and backward through the exam.

▶ This test has many exhibits (pictures). It can be difficult, if not impossible, to view both the questions and the exhibit simulation on the 14- and 15-inch screens usually found at testing centers. Call around to each center and see if they have 17-inch monitors available. If they don't, perhaps you can arrange to bring in your own. Failing this, some have found it useful to quickly draw the diagram on the scratch paper provided by the testing center and use the monitor to view just the question.

▶ Many participants run out of time before they are able to complete the test. If you are unsure of the answer to a question, you may want to choose one of the answers, mark the question, and go on—an unanswered question does not help you. Once your time is up, you cannot go on to another question. However, you can remain on the question you are on indefinitely when the time runs out. Therefore, when you are almost out of time, go to a question you feel you can figure out—given enough time—and work until you feel you have got it (or the night security guard boots you out!).

▶ You are allowed to use the Windows calculator during your test. However, it may be better to memorize a table of the subnet addresses and to write it down on the scratch paper supplied by the testing center before you start the test.

Once you have completed an exam, you will be given immediate, online notification of your pass or fail status. You will also receive a printed Examination Score Report indicating your pass or fail status and your exam results by section. (The test administrator will give you the printed score report.) Test scores are automatically forwarded to Microsoft within five working days after you take the test. You do not need to send your score to Microsoft. If you pass the exam, you will receive confirmation from Microsoft, typically within two to four weeks.

▶ Contact Information

To find out more about Microsoft Education and Certification materials and programs, to register with Sylvan Prometric, or to get other useful information, check the following resources. Outside the United States or Canada, contact your local Microsoft office or Sylvan Prometric testing center.

Microsoft Certified Professional Program—(800) 636-7544   Call the MCPP number for information about the Microsoft Certified Professional program and exams, and to order the latest Microsoft Roadmap to Education and Certification.

Sylvan Prometric testing centers—(800) 755-EXAM   Contact Sylvan to register to take a Microsoft Certified Professional exam at any of more than 800 Sylvan Prometric testing centers around the world.

Microsoft Certification Development Team—Web: http://www .microsoft.com/Train_Cert/mcp/examinfo/certsd.htm   Contact the Microsoft Certification Development Team through their Web site to volunteer for participation in one or more exam development phases or to report a problem with an exam. Address written correspondence to: Certification Development Team; Microsoft Education and Certification; One Microsoft Way; Redmond, WA 98052.

Microsoft TechNet Technical Information Network — (800) 344-2121   This is an excellent resource for support professionals and system administrators. Outside the United States and Canada, call your local Microsoft subsidiary for information.

How to Contact the Publisher

Sybex welcomes reader feedback on all of their titles. Visit the Sybex Web site at www.sybex.com for book updates and additional certification information. You'll also find online forms to submit comments or suggestions regarding this or any other Sybex book.

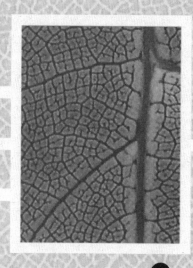

PART i
TCP/IP FOR NT SERVER 4

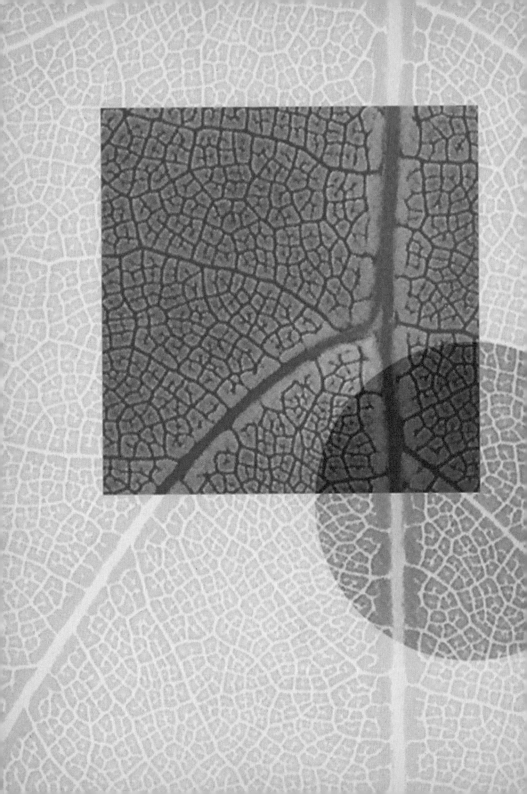

Chapter 1

PLANNING

I f you are *really* fortunate, you get to plan your own implementation of TCP/IP. If you are like most people, you get to work on a network that other people laid out, and you get to implement the corporate strategy. Some people are "lucky" enough to come in and clean up a network that someone implemented without planning. That is always a joyous occasion.

For the purpose of this chapter, it is assumed that your corporate network has no TCP/IP implementation strategy and you are the one responsible for a WAN (wide area network) rollout of the new protocol. This chapter lays out some of the things to think about in your rollout.

Adapted from *MCSE Exam Notes: TCP/IP for NT Server 4* by Gary Govanus

ISBN 0-7821-2307-4   352 pages $19.99

▶ Given a scenario, identify valid network configurations.

TCP/IP is an acronym for Transmission Control Protocol/Internet Protocol. It is most commonly thought of as the protocol of UNIX and the Internet. Calling TCP/IP a protocol is like calling an encyclopedia a book. TCP/IP is really made up of a multitude of different protocols that combine to provide communications between two computers. The types of communications that each of these protocols provides depends on the purpose of the communication.

UNIX is the greatest operating system ever designed by a committee that never met. When the operating system was originally written, it was published and other people tried it and liked it. Like most blossoming technologies, users wanted more. In this case, the developers of UNIX simply provided the code and the wherewithal for the users to write the utilities they wanted. When the utilities were written, the new version of UNIX was re-posted, people used it, they wanted more, and the evolution continued.

The Internet is unique because it is a multinational entity without an owner, or even an official governing body. There is no Internet CEO who decides what goes where and who can do what. Instead, there are a variety of committees, task forces, and advisory groups that make up the standards that govern the Internet and computer communication. The process is much more democratic than you might believe.

The Internet and TCP/IP are both constantly changing. The change to TCP/IP will start with something called a Request For Comment or RFC. When an RFC is published, it is given a unique number and made available to anyone who would like to subscribe. When an RFC is distributed, anyone can comment, from someone who deeply understands the inner workings of the protocol to a novice who may just have an idea. After the subject has been kicked around awhile, the RFC begins to take a more solid format, and at this time the task force or authority responsible for the RFC will assign it a designation that lets the world know where this RFC is in the standards process.

So how do you create an RFC? The process starts when someone formalizes a topic by writing a document that describes the issue, and mails it to Jon Postel (Postel@ISI.EDU). Postel acts as a referee for the proposal. Anyone wishing to take part in the discussion then comments on the topic. The proposal itself may go through multiple revisions. Should it be generally accepted as a good idea, it will be assigned a number and filed with the RFCs.

An RFC goes through five stages, which don't appear to be formal, but they generally include the following:

Draft standard stage: This is the first stage. It can be likened to an early discussion stage. This is where things are really loose and the community is just trying to get an idea of what should be placed in the RFC.

Proposed standard stage: Once the RFC has been roughed out, it then moves to the more formalized proposed standard stage. At this stage the Internet community works out the details of the standard.

Experimental stage: Once the details are worked out, the feasibility of the procedure must be determined; this is where the experimental stage comes into play.

Standard stage: Once all the preparation and testing have been completed, the document has earned the right to be called a *standard*.

Obsolete or historic stage: Like most things in computing, even standards have a shelf life. After a standard has done its job and technology has moved on, the standard can be moved to the obsolete or historic category.

In addition to these five stages of a standard, the following five classifications can be associated with each RFC:

Classification	Comments
Required	This RFC must be implemented.
Recommended	The Internet community recommends that this standard be implemented.
Elective	You can implement this standard if you want to, but you don't have to.
Limited	This standard is only to be implemented in very specific circumstances.
Not Recommended	Isn't it nice to know that even the esteemed members of the Internet community sometimes come up with ideas that go over like the proverbial lead balloon?

So, when someone talks about an RFC for the Ethernet standard, you know that the RFC has reached the stage where it is pretty much written in stone. This particular standard is the way things are going to be for a while. If the standard is for something such as the Ethernet 802.2 frame type, the standard is required. That means anyone making use of the Ethernet 802.2 frame type must follow the information in the RFC, or the new product simply will not work.

If you are interested in looking at an RFC, go to the InterNIC FTP site at ds.internic.net. Look for the index of RFCs in the RFC directory. RFCs are numbered, so if you miss the index file, you may end up with an RFC that is of little or no interest to you.

If you do not have access to the FTP server, you can also request RFCs through e-mail. The process is automated and you can access it by sending e-mail to mailserv@ds.internic.net and including the following line in the text of your e-mail:

document-by-name RFCxxxx (replace the "xxxx" with the actual number)

If you are looking for the RFC index, use this text:

Document-by-name rfc-index

RFCs are fascinating things. Besides being tremendous technical resources available on just about any topic that relates to the Internet, an RFC is like a cyber sleeping pill. If you think studying for your TCP/IP will put you to sleep, just try an RFC on for size!

All this information is really fascinating, but don't sweat it for the test. You need to know about RFCs for your working life, but testing will not be impacted. I have found RFCs to be particularly useful in social situations where you are confronted by someone you may not want to spend time with. You may get a reputation as being somewhat boring, but your real friends will know what a witty and charming person you are. As for the others, heck, you didn't want to talk to them anyway!

The DOD Model and the TCP/IP Suite

To understand the TCP/IP suite, you must first understand how communication occurs between two computers. One reference point that is used to describe communications is the Open System Interconnect (OSI) seven-layer model. Because TCP/IP was originally written to specifications laid out by the Department of Defense (DOD), there is a special four-layer DOD model used as a reference. Figure 1.1 shows how the seven layers of the OSI model equate to the four layers of the DOD model.

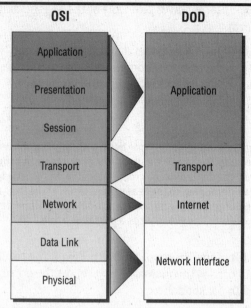

FIGURE 1.1: The OSI model and the DOD model compared

By the time you have reached this stage in your MCSE testing, you have passed the Networking Essentials test. The seven layers of the OSI model are described in that courseware, so you should be familiar with it. Knowing how the four layers of the DOD model map to the seven layers of the OSI model is important for testing purposes. Knowing what each of the different protocols are responsible for will help you understand material later in the book.

The Network Interface Layer

The bottom layer of the DOD model is the *Network Interface layer*. This layer specifies how the computers will put signals on the physical network. The standards set at the Network Interface layer are specifications for technologies, such as Ethernet and Token Ring.

The Internet Layer

One step up the ladder is the *Internet layer*. The protocols at the Internet layer are responsible for the addressing and delivery of packets from one computer to another. The protocols at the Internet layer allow you to access the Microsoft home page from anywhere in the world.

These are the common Internet layer protocols of the TCP/IP suite and the tasks they perform:

Internet Protocol (IP): IP is responsible for the addressing and routing of datagrams from one computer to another. IP also handles the delivery of datagrams from one host to another.

NOTE

Communications between computers is done by the transmission of binary digits (1's and 0's). In order for the sending and receiving computers to know what these digits represent, the digits must be grouped together in some logical format. The naming of this grouping changes at various levels of the DOD model. At the Internet layer, the grouping is referred to as a datagram. Upper layers of the DOD model may refer to this grouping as a packet or frame.

Internet Control Message Protocol (ICMP): This is the tattletale protocol. ICMP carries the messages that report the errors that have occurred in packet delivery.

Address Resolution Protocol (ARP): Each host is identified by several addresses. The first address is the Media Access Control layer or MAC address. This is the Network Interface layer address that is specific to the network interface card (NIC) in the computer. An MAC address will take the format of 00-60-08-02-4D-D1. The Internet layer address, or IP address, takes the form of 207.98.156.52. It is up to the Address Resolution Protocol to resolve or equate the IP address (207.98.156.52) to the MAC address of 00-60-08-02-4D-D1.

The Transport Layer

The *Transport layer* of the DOD model is responsible for transporting the data from one computer to another. If you think of this transmission like a phone call, it would be up to the Transport layer to dial the phone and make sure the connection stayed open from the time you said "Hello" until the time you said "Good-bye."

These are the TCP/IP protocols at the Transport layer:

Transmission Control Protocol (TCP): TCP is a reliable method of delivering data from one host to another. It uses a connection-oriented communication method to perform packet delivery and error detection. TCP will perform data recovery if a packet is damaged in transit. It provides a guaranteed delivery of the information.

User Datagram Protocol (UDP): UDP is a connection-less method of delivery. A UDP packet makes a best effort to deliver a packet. If the packet is damaged in transit, it is up to the application to discover the problem and ask for a retransmission.

The Application Layer

Finally, we reach the Application layer of the DOD model. Don't get carried away by the term "application"; this term does not describe programs, such as Excel or Word. The protocols at the Application layer describe processes that are used in the background to print, copy files, resolve names and addresses, and so on. Only the most sophisticated of end users will recognize their existence and function.

Some of the Application layer protocols and applications include the following:

File Transfer Protocol (FTP): FTP works to transfer files to and from hosts.

Telnet: This utility allows a takeover of the host. You can create a Telnet session to issue commands to a remote computer.

Domain Name Service (DNS): DNS is a name resolution system that will equate a name, such as www.microsoft.com to an IP address, such as 207.68.156.52.

Windows Internet Name Service (WINS): WINS is a name resolution system that resolves the Windows NetBIOS names to a physical address.

Simple Network Management Protocol (SNMP): SNMP provides the resources for proactive network management. It provides information on the stability of the resources and workstations on your network.

Dynamic Host Configuration Protocol (DHCP): DHCP provides the dynamic addressing and configuration of workstations on a TCP/IP network.

Planning Considerations

For the sake of planning an efficient network utilizing TCP/IP there are several areas that need to be addressed, primarily the following ones:

▶ Proper use of an addressing scheme for a TCP/IP network. This includes knowing how many addresses your network will require.

▶ Proper use of DHCP servers throughout the network.

▶ Proper use of Hosts and LMHOSTS files in a TCP/IP environment.

▶ Proper use of DNS in the network environment.

▶ Proper use of WINS servers throughout the network.

▶ Proper use of SNMP in the network environment.

Configuration of an Addressing Scheme for a TCP/IP Network

Before you can start planning how to deploy IP addresses across your network infrastructure, you have to know how many addresses your system will actually need. Each host or network component is identified by a unique IP address. Here's a good rule of thumb to follow: if a network interface card is installed, it needs at least one IP address. Some network cards can have multiple IP addresses.

An IP address is made up of two parts, a network address and the host address. In addition to knowing how many hosts or network components you have on your network, you also have to know how many physical network segments your network contains.

TIP

A host is defined as any component on your network that communicates using IP. Hosts can be workstations, servers, printers, routers, bridges, and so on. If a host has more than one network interface card (NIC), each card must have its own unique IP address. If a host has multiple NICs, Microsoft refers to that host as being multihomed. This term will come up often in this book.

An IP address is a 32-bit long number that is divided up into four 8-bit fields. These fields are called *octets*. Each octet is separated by a period and each octet represents a decimal number in the range of 0 to 255. An example of an IP address is 207.68.156.52. The IP address, 207.68.156.52, is assigned to Microsoft on the World Wide Web.

NOTE

The assignment of actual IP addresses to each network component will be discussed in Chapter 2, "Installation and Configuration." At this point, we are simply interested in the number of physical network segments your network has, and the number of hosts.

So, how do you find this addressing information? Usually, by locating the wiring diagrams of your network. For some of you, this may be unfamiliar territory. Many administrators have heard of the term documentation, but they are so busy running the network that documenting their work is a dream not a reality. You know who you are! You also knew all along that someday this was going to come back and bite you. It just happened!

If you are one of those administrators smugly sitting back with a grin on your face, knowing exactly where to get an up-to-date map of your network that shows every workstation on the network, with every network segment and router labeled, congratulations. The rest of us are very envious. That up-to-date map is exactly what you are going to need.

When you have the documentation it is simply a matter of counting the number of physical network segments and the number of hosts on each segment. As you are counting, use the following tips:

▶ Unpopulated segments between routers count as a network segment.

▶ Each network card in a host needs its own IP address. If you have a multihomed server or a multihomed router with five network cards in it, that multihomed router or multihomed server will require at least five IP addresses.

▶ As you are busy counting, plan for growth. The numbers you come up with at this stage of the process will be important later, so make sure you take into account the new expansion project that will add 50 more users to a segment.

To illustrate, look at Figure 1.2. This is a map of small network that is spread out over three buildings. Each building has its own server and each of the buildings is connected by a router.

As you see, there are five physical network segments. Each network segment needs a current maximum of seven host addresses (one for the server, one for each workstation, and one for each side of the router). Because this is a high-level network overview, we don't care which network exists in which building. We are only interested in the five physical network segments.

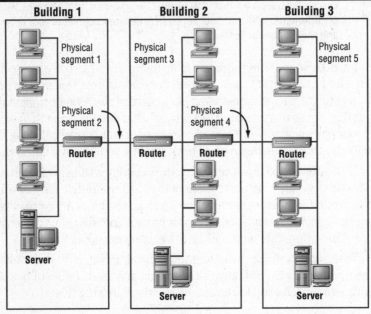

FIGURE 1.2: Map of a small network

After you conclude this stage of the planning, you should have a diagram that shows the number of physical network segments and the number of hosts on each segment. To move on to the next step, you should be able to say with confidence that your network will have x number of segments with a maximum of y number of hosts on each segment. Remember to take into account growth.

DHCP Servers in the Network

How big is your network? If you look at Figure 1.2, my example shows six network segments with a maximum of six hosts on a segment. Two of the segments are unpopulated, so I would have to assign no more than 36 (6x6) unique IP addresses. That does not sound like too much work, does it? Your numbers may differ considerably. You may be looking at the assignment of several hundred (or thousand) unique IP addresses. That does sound like a lot of work, doesn't it?

Dynamic Host Configuration Protocol (DHCP) can come to the rescue. You can configure one or more DHCP servers to provide automatic addressing and gateway information for every host. When a DHCP server provides an address to a host, it is said the host is *leasing* the DHCP address.

Some systems on a segment may not be able to take advantage of DHCP. Because the system (usually a server or a router) needs to maintain the same IP address all the time, it must have a permanent or static address, not a leased address. In that case, the address must be manually configured.

When you configure a server to provide DCHP addresses, you give the server a block of addresses to assign. This block is referred to as a *scope of addresses*. DHCP can also provide the appropriate subnet mask and information about the gateway that serves that segment. Host computers are then configured to go out and look for a DHCP server when the host boots. Using a process called BOOTP, the host asks the DHCP server for information. The DHCP server then gives the host an IP address with the appropriate subnet mask and the IP address of the gateway. From the administrator's point of view, configuring DHCP servers saves you the trouble of going to each of the hosts and manually entering an IP address.

Clients accessing a DHCP server do not need to be on the same side of a router or even on the same subnet as the DHCP server. While BOOTP does not travel well across routers or subnets, you can configure a DHCP relay agent. A *relay agent* simply listens for a BOOTP request, then forwards the request directly to the DHCP server. The computer acting as the DHCP relay agent needs to be running either Windows NT Workstation or Windows NT Server, and the relay agent does needs to be on the same subnet as the host computers.

NOTE

Configuring a computer to be a BOOTP relay agent will be covered in Chapter 2.

HOSTS and LMHOSTS Files in a TCP/IP Environment

Have you ever wondered how TCP/IP manages to turn the IP address of 207.68.156.52 into a somewhat user-friendly name, such as www.microsoft .com? Actually, there are several ways of handling the transformation.

In the early days of the Internet, when there were just a few computers on the network, system administrators manually kept track of where things were by updating a text file called the HOSTS file. The format of the HOSTS file wasn't anything special. As a matter of fact, if your workstation is running Windows 9*x*, you have the following HOSTS.SAM file located in your C:\Windows directory:

```
# Copyright (c) 1998 Microsoft Corp.
#
# This is a sample HOSTS file used by Microsoft TCP/IP
stack for Windows98
# This file contains the mappings of IP addresses to
host names. Each
# entry should be kept on an individual line. The IP address
should
# be placed in the first column followed by the corresponding
host name.
# The IP address and the host name should be separated by at
least one
# space.
#
# Additionally, comments (such as these) may be
inserted on individual
# lines or following the machine name denoted by a '#' sym-
bol.
#
# For example:
#
102.54.94.97  rhino.acme.com   # source server
38.25.63.10  x.acme.com    # x client host
127.0.0.1  localhost
```

The HOSTS file can be edited with any text editor. It is saved without an extension, in a location where the operating system will find it. In the case of Windows, that would be the C:\Windows directory. On some systems, especially UNIX-based servers, the HOSTS file is stored in the ETC directory. Notice the use of the # (pound) sign. In a HOSTS file, the pound sign serves only one purpose—to designate what follows as a comment that should be ignored.

The HOSTS file resolves IP addresses to host computer names. If someone were to type in the name, `rhino.acme.com`, the system would know to find host address 102.54.94.97. When a new system would come online, or the system administrator would find a new IP address that needed to be accessed quickly, the administrator would make a new entry in the local HOSTS file.

TIP

An explanation of the HOSTS file was included to make the discussion of the LMHOSTS file easier to understand. The HOSTS file is common in the IP world, but for testing purposes, the LMHOSTS file is the one you want to focus on. There will be a few questions on the HOSTS file, but the LMHOSTS file is an exam writer's favorite.

In the world of Windows NT, the HOSTS file is still being used, but another file, the LMHOSTS file, helps with NetBIOS name resolution. NT uses LMHOSTS to map IP addresses to NetBIOS computer names. The LMHOSTS file is located in the <drive letter>\<system root>\System32\Drivers\etc directory and looks like this:

```
#LMHOSTS file for PSCONSULTING. Created 4/16/98
210.47.26.50     Bobbi
210.47.26.51     Cris
210.47.26.52     Denise
210.47.26.53     Brandice
210.47.26.54     CJ
210.47.26.55     PSCONSULT  #PRE  #DOM:PSDOM
210.47.26.56     PSService  #PRE
#BEGIN_ALTERNATE
#INCLUDE \\PSCONSULT\SYSTEM32\DRIVERS\ETC\LMHOSTS
#INCLUDE \\PSSERVICE\SYSTEM32\DRIVERS\ETC\LMHOSTS
#END_ALTERNATE
```

So, you have noticed that this file looks a little different from the traditional HOSTS file. Notice the use of the # (pound) sign. In an LMHOSTS file, the pound sign serves two purposes. On the first line, it designates a comment line. In the rest of the file, it serves to set off key words.

NOTE

For testing purposes, you should know that the LMHOSTS file resolves Net-BIOS computer names to TCP/IP addresses. There will be a more complete discussion of the LMHOSTS file and keywords in Chapter 2, "Installation and Configuration."

DNS in the Network Environment

Another way of statically maintaining a name to address resolution service is to use DNS, or Domain Name Service. If your network is not connected to the Internet, configuring one of the servers on your network to be a DNS server will provide a single point of administration for host name resolution. If your network is hooked to the Internet, DNS management is usually handled by your Internet service provider (ISP). You just point your workstations to the ISP's DNS server or any DNS server on the Net.

Microsoft DNS provides resolution of computer host names to IP addresses for systems that cannot take advantage of dynamic name resolution provided by WINS. In other words, it is DNS that makes the name microsoft.com equate to an IP address of 207.68.156.52.

NOTE

For the Planning section on the exam, you will need to know that DNS provides name resolution for computers that are not capable of using WINS name resolution. These include Macs or UNIX workstations on your network. We will discuss how to implement DNS in Chapter 2, "Installation and Configuration."

WINS Servers in the Network

Windows Internet Name Service (WINS) provides name and address resolution for computers with NetBIOS or Windows names. Unlike DNS or the HOSTS and LMHOSTS files, WINS is dynamic. When a Windows-based computer named \\ntserver comes online it can register that name with a WINS server. Then, whenever a client needs to find the \\ntserver computer, the client can query the WINS server for the location. Notice that the NetBIOS name can be different from the DNS name.

Because your network may have multiple subnets, it is possible to have multiple WINS servers on your network. In this case, the multiple servers can be configured to exchange their databases so the information on all WINS servers is consistent.

A computer that is configured to provide the DNS service can also be configured to provide WINS name resolution.

NOTE

WINS implementation is a very common exam question. If the scenario-based questions mention nothing but Windows, Windows 9x, and NT-based computers, you can almost be certain the answer will revolve around WINS. The implementation of WINS will be covered in Chapter 2, "Installation and Configuration."

SNMP in the Network Environment

Simple Network Management Protocol (SNMP) provides the means for proactive network management. Implementing SNMP on routers, servers, and just plain computers can provide SNMP managers the opportunity to query the network to find out what is happening.

NOTE

SNMP consists of several parts, including the SNMP agent and the SNMP manager. An SNMP agent can be configured to send a message when it comes up or goes down, for example. In order for the agent to be effective, there must be an SNMP manager to receive the message and process it.

Microsoft does not have applications that serve as an SNMP manager; however, there are several third-party vendors that provide this capability.

TIP

For exam purposes, it is important to know that SNMP exists and that NT systems can be SNMP agents.

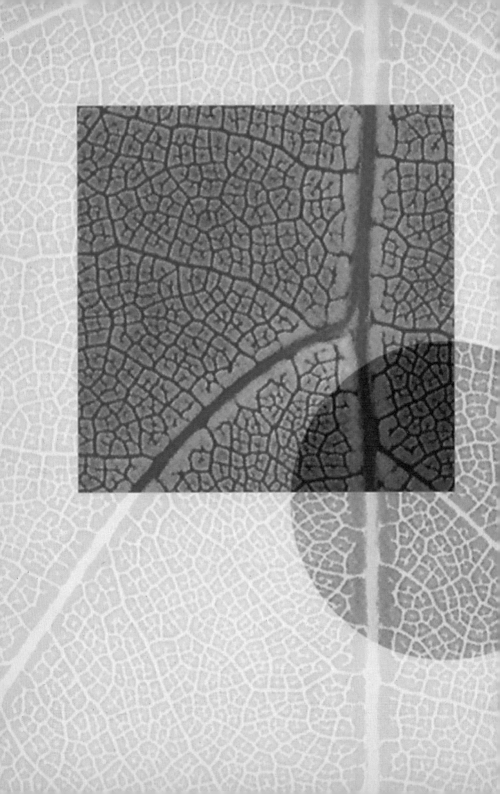

Chapter 2

INSTALLATION AND CONFIGURATION

This chapter covers everything from the installation of the protocol to making sure that every workstation can find every other workstation on the network. Before we can configure our network, we must know what services will be needed. Some of these services were discussed in Chapter 1, "Planning." Here, we'll look at how to apply that information to a real network.

If you are not a TCP/IP expert, make sure you dedicate some time to this chapter. Because this chapter contains the most material, the exam writers spent the most time with it. You are going to find lots of questions on the exam about subnets and host ids as well as all the services.

Adapted from *MCSE Exam Notes: TCP/IP for NT Server 4*
by Gary Govanus

ISBN 0-7821-2307-4   352 pages $19.99

▶ Given a scenario, select the appropriate services to install when using Microsoft TCP/IP on a Microsoft Windows NT Server computer.

What kinds of services are we talking about here? There are all kinds of services that can be installed on an NT Server to make life using TCP/IP just a little bit easier. Some of these services have been discussed in Chapter 1, "Planning," and others will be elaborated on in later chapters. This objective will stress how to utilize these services in a TCP/IP environment and how the services can all work together.

NOTE

For some hints on other areas, you can start by looking at *MCSE: TCP/IP for NT Server 4 Study Guide,* 3rd Edition by Todd Lammle with Monica Lammle and James Chellis (Sybex, 1998).

When you select Control Panel ≻ Network and click the Services tab, there are all sorts of services that can be configured for TCP/IP. These are some of the most notable ones:

- ▶ An NT Server can be configured for either a Dynamic Host Configuration Protocol (DHCP) client or a DHCP server.

- ▶ You can configure the server to aid intranet or Internet browsing by becoming a Domain Name System (DNS) server.

- ▶ If you want to allow your system to be used to host Web pages or allow access to files via the File Transfer Protocol (FTP), you can install and configure the Internet Information Server (IIS).

- ▶ If you have a large contingent of TCP/IP users, many times it will include UNIX hosts. These hosts need to print and the NT Server can be configured to provide Microsoft TCP/IP printing.

- ▶ The Network Monitor Tools and Agent service will allow the system administrator to capture and view packets on the network. The Network Monitor will also allow you to do some rudimentary network management and performance monitoring, including judging the impact of some of the TCP/IP services.

- ▶ One of the reasons that system administrators decide to use TCP/IP is because it is a routable protocol. One of the network services available to NT Server is the Routing Information Protocol or RIP. RIP is a distance vector protocol that can dynamically update its route tables.

▶ For the network that needs more proactive management, Simple Network Management Protocol (SNMP) can be installed. Using SNMP, an NT Server can become an agent, providing a third-party Network Management package with information on the health of the server and the health of the network.

▶ Some networks need more than DNS to resolve names. In the case of the Windows network, you can add Windows Internet Name Service (WINS) to the NT Server. WINS will provide NetBIOS computer name resolution to IP addresses.

Dynamic Host Configuration Protocol (DHCP)

One of the biggest challenges of using TCP/IP is the management of IP addresses, subnets, and gateways. Each TCP/IP host must have a unique IP address and this can involve some serious management time. Each host will reside on a subnet and if more than one subnet exists on the network, each host will need to know how to get to the next segment. To cross to a different subnet, each host must know the address of the gateway. For the network that uses manual configuration of IP addressing, there are many areas where a sudden case of "fat fingered typing" can screw up communication.

Installing DCHP will allow you to automatically assign IP addresses, subnet masks, WINS Server(s), and default gateways, making the process all but foolproof. There are still some "gotchas" to the process, but we will look at those later in this objective.

Domain Name System (DNS)

DNS is one of the foundations of the Internet. When a browser requests http:\\www.microsoft.com something has to resolve that name to an IP address and finally to a hardware address. The DNS will resolve the name to an IP address and provide the information to get the packets to the right destination.

Internet Information Server (IIS)

IIS is the subject of a completely different test, so not much space will be devoted to it in this part of the book. You will need to install IIS if you want to make file transfer available to users via the File Transfer Protocol (FTP).

FTP is one of the more visible protocols in the TCP/IP suite. If you want to transfer files reliably between foreign hosts (computers running NT Workstation and UNIX, for example) one common method would be FTP. Because FTP makes use of TCP, it provides for a reliable connection. FTP also offers several layers of security. You can require the systems trying to access the file to log on to the FTP site or you can allow anonymous access to the site so anyone can access the files. This security can be divided so one folder allows anonymous access and a subfolder requires a more stringent authentication.

TCP/IP Printing

More and more networks are diversifying. The days of a network that serves one operating system are a thing of the past. Now, the network may host Windows 3.11 clients, Windows 9*x* clients, Windows NT Workstations, UNIX systems, OS/2 systems, and Macintosh systems.

Installing TCP/IP printer support accomplishes several goals. TCP/IP printing allows workstation clients to print to a printer that has its own IP address, UNIX systems can access printers configured as part of the NT network, and non-UNIX systems can print to printers on the UNIX network.

Network Monitor Tools and Agents

Network Monitor Tools and Agents will allow you to capture and analyze network packets that have been sent to and from the host computer. This utility is really kind of a subset of the Network Monitor service included with Microsoft's System Management Server or SMS. Network Monitor Tools and Agents can be installed without installing all of SMS.

Once the data has been captured, you can create a graphical representation of the current network activity or just get the numerical overview of the total network activity during the capture period. If you need a more granular breakdown of statistics, you can use the Session Stats screen, which displays communication information between two particular computers during a specific session. The Station Stats window shows all network activity for that particular workstation.

NOTE

Network Monitor Tools and Agents will be covered in Chapter 4, "Monitoring and Optimization."

Routing Information Protocol (RIP)

TCP/IP supports two different types of routing packets from one network to another network—static routing and dynamic routing. *Static routing* is the manual configuration of route tables. *Dynamic routing* means the routing protocol determines where the links are between networks and maintains its own route table. If you decide not to use static routing, NT Server supports RIP.

Simple Network Management Protocol (SNMP)

For a large network, having SNMP running is not an option, it is a necessity. SNMP allows network administrators to be proactive in troubleshooting problems on the network. In addition, SNMP allows for the gathering of statistics so you can manage the growth of the network.

By default, Windows NT will allow you to configure your servers and workstations as SNMP agents. An additional product, such as SMS or Hp OpenView, is necessary to take full advantage of SNMP.

Windows Internet Name Service (WINS)

When you install a Windows 32-bit product, you have to provide a name for the computer. That name is referred to as the *computer name* or *NetBIOS name*. Somehow, this NetBIOS name needs to be resolved to an IP address or to a network hardware address. WINS is the service that makes this possible. If your network is going to have many computers on it, WINS is a service you will need to provide fast name resolution.

Installing WINS is very important when your network consists of a majority of Windows computers.

▶ On a Windows NT Server computer, configure Microsoft TCP/IP to support multiple network adapters.

This objective is rather deceiving. While it is important to know how to configure an NT Server with multiple network cards to support TCP/IP, the real reason for the objective is to lay some groundwork for information yet to come. In this objective, we are going to define some terms and develop some concepts that will be used throughout the book and on the test.

The simple act of installing another network card takes on some larger proportions when you are using TCP/IP. In effect, you are creating another network segment and each time you create another network segment, you are creating another TCP/IP subnet. When you create a new subnet, you need to assign the subnet a new network number. How are the systems on this new network segment going to receive IP addresses? If you use DHCP, you will have to configure a DHCP scope and server for this segment or configure one of the computers on the segment to be a DHCP relay agent. What about name resolution, will there have to be a WINS Server involved for the subnet? If so, make sure the server can handle the increased workload. See what I mean, just adding a new network card to a server has all sorts of ramifications that will be covered later in this chapter.

When you add a second network card to a server, you are creating a router. Obviously, this is not a dedicated router because this computer has server stuff to do besides its job as a router. Adding a second network card to a server also gives the computer some new names. It suddenly becomes a multihomed computer or perhaps a multihomed system.

A *multihomed computer* is any computer that has two or more IP addresses. A *multihomed system* is any multihomed computer that has two or more network cards bound to separate physical networks.

TIP

The terms multihomed computer and multihomed system will show up on the test, so it is important that you know how to differentiate between the two.

NOTE

A network card can have multiple IP addresses assigned to it.

To turn a computer running NT Server into a router, you must perform the following tasks:

► Install a second network card.

► Connect the card to another physical segment.

► Assign the card a network address, a host address, and a subnet mask.

► Enable IP routing.

Once you have enabled IP routing, the server/router will be aware of only the subnets to which it is physically attached. If you want the system to know about all the subnets on your network, you will either have to manually configure the route table or enable the Routing Information Protocol (RIP).

Once the network card has been installed and plugged into your network, it is time to configure the card to communicate using TCP/IP. Because we haven't gotten around to talking seriously about things such as DHCP, IP addressing, and subnets yet, some assumptions must be made. The first assumption will be that you have two network cards in your server, you must add support for the TCP/IP protocol, and configure the first network card to have an IP address of 210.47.26.33 with a subnet mask of 255.255.255.224. In addition, the system will point to a gateway at 210.47.26.1. The second card will be on a different subnet, so its card address will be 210.47.26.65 using a subnet mask of 255.255.255.224. It will also point to the gateway at 210.47.26.1. IP routing will be turned on.

The first thing to do is check that TCP/IP support is loaded on the computer. TCP/IP is the default protocol of NT, but if you didn't install the operating system yourself, it is always best to check.

1. Select Start ➣ Settings Control Panel ➣ Network ➣ Protocols and if TCP/IP support is already loaded, your screen should look like the one shown here:

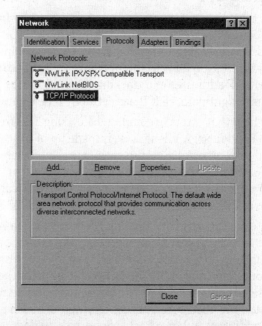

2. Highlighting TCP/IP Protocol and clicking the Properties button will give you access to the screen to configure the cards with the assigned TCP/IP addresses.

3. To add IP information, from the Microsoft TCP/IP Properties screen, click the IP address tab and then highlight the adapter you want to configure. Click the Specify an IP Address radio button. Enter the appropriate IP address, subnet mask, and gateway information.

4. Repeat step 3 for any other adapters that need to be configured.

5. To enable IP forwarding or routing, from the Microsoft TCP/IP Properties screen, click the Routing tab.

6. Click the box marked Enable IP Forwarding.

7. Click OK to close the Microsoft TCP/IP Properties window.

8. Click OK to close the Network window.

▶ Configure scopes by using DHCP Manager.

Two of the greatest time-savers for administrators who use TCP/IP have been Microsoft's 32-bit operating systems and DHCP. Prior to Windows NT and Windows 95, configuring a DOS-based computer to run a TCP/IP stack was not a job for the faint of heart. Manually configuring workstations with IP addresses and tracking those addresses to prevent duplication was a nightmare. DHCP has certainly relieved much of that strain.

Any host that wants to communicate using TCP/IP must have a unique IP address. An IP address is made up of 4 bytes and each byte is referred to as an *octet*. Because each byte is 8 bits, an IP address is 32 bits long. To simplify matters, we refer to IP addresses in their decimal equivalency. In the last section, we configured a network card to have the IP address of 210.47.26.33 with a subnet mask of 255.255.255.224.

There are two ways of assigning IP addresses: manually, as we did in the last section, and dynamically. Using the dynamic approach, you can configure one server on a subnet to "lease" IP addresses to any host that needs one. You can specify the range of IP address the server can assign and reserve certain addresses for particular computers. You can even make sure the hosts receive other information, such as gateway or WINS Server addresses. When a host is done with an address, it returns the address to the server. The next time the host comes up, it will ask for and receive an IP address. It may not be the same address the host had before shutting down, but in most cases that doesn't matter.

The choice between manual assignments or dynamic assignments is not an either/or type solution. You can, and probably will, do both. Some systems do not do well getting their addresses from a DHCP server. For example, if you want to host an intranet, it will make sense for the host server to have a static IP address, one that will never change.

How does DHCP work? The process is really quite simple. You configure an NT 3.5 server or better to be a DHCP server. You then provide the DHCP server with a "scope" of valid IP addresses. Don't let the word "scope" throw you, a scope is just a list. You also configure the DHCP server to pass out all that other information you want the systems to know about, things such as the IP address of the gateway and the IP address of the WINS Server. You then set the lease period so that it can loan addresses out for a period of time. By default, the IP lease is three days.

Placement of a DHCP server can be important. If your network uses routers, check to make sure the routers comply with Request for Comment (RFC) 1542. If the router complies with RFC 1542, it will pass requests for DHCP assignments from one subnet to another. If the router does not meet those specifications, there should be a DHCP server on each network segment, or you will have to configure systems to act as DHCP relay agents.

TIP

DHCP configuration, what a great concept for repeated test questions! You must have a DHCP server on each subnet or there must be a computer configured as a DHCP relay agent. DHCP relay agents will be discussed during the objective on IP routing.

Now that the server is configured, what about the client? When you configure an NT Server, NT Workstation, or Windows 9x to use TCP/IP, by default it will go out and look for a DHCP server. What this means to the administrator is simple: configure the OS, select the TCP/IP protocol, copy the files, and it's a done deal. Now, if the computer is moved from one network segment to another, nothing must be done to reconfigure the machine to continue running TCP/IP.

When a workstation is turned on, it recognizes the need for an IP address. At this point, the workstation broadcasts a lease request, called a DHCPDISCOVER message. The client has no idea about the IP address of the DHCP server. This means the DHCPDISCOVER message is a *broadcast message*, so every client on the subnet will receive the packet. If nothing responds to the request, the workstation will send the lease request four more times, at 9 seconds, 13 seconds, 16 seconds, and then a random number of seconds. If the client still doesn't get an answer, it will continue to issue lease requests every 5 minutes.

When a DHCP server receives a lease request, it answers by sending back an IP lease offer or a DHCPOFFER packet. The offer packet is also sent as a broadcast message because at this point the client does not have an IP address. The DHCP offer will contain an IP address and subnet mask, the hardware address of the DHCP client, the IP address of the DHCP server and the duration of the lease.

Back at the client side, the client receives the DHCPOFFER packet. If you have multiple DHCP servers on a subnet, the client may receive multiple offers. The client accepts the first offer it receives by sending back a packet called the DHCPREQUEST packet. The DHCPREQUEST packet tells the successful DHCP server that the workstation is taking it up on its offer. All the other servers realize the IP address it offered can be returned to the scope to be used by another workstation.

The process has not been completed. The DHCP server still needs to verify the successful lease. The server sends back an acknowledgment in the form of a packet known as a DHCPACK. This confirms the address and other configuration information. Once the client receives the DHCPACK, the client can initialize TCP/IP and the communications begin.

What if the client is unsuccessful in its lease, or it is trying to renew a lease that has expired and the number has been reassigned? In that case, the DHCP server will send out a DHCPNACK. When a client gets a DHCPNACK, it knows it is back to square one, and it starts the process over again.

Once the client has acknowledged the configuration information, it can keep that address until the system shuts down or the address is released manually. Like all leases, this one does have to be renewed. The default lease period is three days. After 50 percent of the time is up, the client will attempt to renew its lease. If the DHCP server is up and working, the client gets a new lease on the address. However, if the DHCP server is down, the client can still keep using the address because the lease will not expire for another 36 hours. DHCP clients also attempt to renew their leases on start-up by broadcasting their last leased IP address. If the address hasn't been given out, it will be reassigned.

DHCP addresses are configured using DHCP Manager. DHCP Manager is installed when DHCP is installed on the server and one installation can manage several DHCP servers. Addresses can be grouped in ranges. Some of the address can be excluded and you can use DHCP Manager to choose the duration of the lease. If network traffic is an issue, you may want the lease to be unlimited in duration.

Taking Care of DHCP

All of these addresses and ranges are stored in database files stuck in the %systemroot%\system32\dhcp directory. Like all database files, these files can become corrupted. Table 2.1 describes the databases and what they are responsible for.

TABLE 2.1: DHCP Databases

FILENAME	DESCRIPTION
DHCP.MDB	An actual DHCP database. Do not even think about trying to open this database and looking inside!
DHCP.TMP	Temporary database created while the DHCP service is running.
JET.LOG and JET*.LOG	Logs of all the transactions written to the DHCP databases. Logged transactions include active leases, lease releases, and lease renewals. These files are used to reconstruct the database in the time of tragedy.
SYSTEM.MDB	The template file for the DHCP database. It contains the information needed to rebuild the structure of the database, if needed.

By default, these databases are backed up to the %systemroot%\system32\dhcp\backup\jet directory every 60 minutes. If you ever have to restore DHCP from these files, the first try should be simply stopping and restarting the DHCP Server service. When you restart the service, it can detect the files that are corrupted and will automatically restore them.

If that fails, you can stop the DHCP Server service and manually copy the contents of the %systemroot%\system32\dhcp\backup\jet directory to the %systemroot%\system32\dhcp folder and then restart the DHCP Server service.

If the DHCP database gets larger than 30MB, it will have to be compacted. This is done by using the JETPACK.EXE utility.

Installing DHCP

To create a DHCP scope, DHCP must be installed on an NT Server. DHCP requires NT 3.5 or greater. To install DHCP on an NT 4 Server:

1. Select Start ➤ Settings ➤ Control Panel ➤ Network.

2. From the Network window, click the Services tab.

3. Click Add and the server will build a list of available services.

4. From the Select Network Service window, choose Microsoft DHCP Server and click OK.

5. Provide the NT Setup screen with the location of the NT files and click Continue.

6. Click OK on the nag screen requiring adapters within the server to have a static IP address.

7. Click Close to close the network dialog box.

8. At this point you will be prompted to restart the computer. Click Yes and when the computer restarts, log on as Administrator or as a member of the Administrator group.

Creating a DHCP Scope

Now that the server is a DHCP server, you can open DHCP Manager from the Administrative Tools menu. DHCP Manager lets you create the IP address scopes on multiple DHCP servers. To configure a scope on a machine running DHCP service:

1. Choose Start ➤ Programs ➤ Administrative Tools ➤ DHCP Manager.

2. Because the configuration will take place on this server, choose the Local Machine from the list of DHCP servers.

3. From the DHCP Manager menu, choose Scope ➤ Create.

4. Enter a Start Address and an End Address as well as the subnet mask for the network.

5. If you have addresses with the range that need to be excluded, enter the address range in the Exclusion Range section. You can have multiple ranges excluded.

6. From the Lease Duration section of the Create Scope (Local) window, make whatever changes are necessary. The default lease is three days. You can choose an unlimited lease duration, although this not recommended.

7. Give the range a name and comment, if appropriate.

8. Click OK.

9. You will be prompted to activate the new scope. Click Yes.

10. Click OK to close the DHCP Manager Servers screen.

Configuring NT Workstation

To configure an NT Workstation to get its IP address from a DHCP server:

1. Select Start ➢ Settings ➢ Control Panel ➢ Network.

2. From the Network window, choose the Protocols tab.

3. Highlight TCP/IP Protocol and click Properties.

4. Make sure the Obtain an IP address from a DHCP server option is selected.

NOTE

In most cases TCP/IP support utilizing DHCP is installed as the default protocol on an NT Workstation computer. This section shows you how to check the default settings.

Compacting the DHCP Database

The DHCP database needs to be compacted when it reaches a size greater than 30MB. Follow these steps to compact the database:

1. Stop the DHCP Server service.

2. Open a command prompt window and change into the \%system-root%\system32\dhcp\ folder.

3. The syntax for using JETPACK.EXE is jetpack dhcp.mdb tempfilename.mdb.

4. Restart the DHCP Server service.

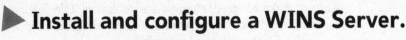

Install and configure a WINS Server.

- ▶ Import LMHOSTS files to WINS.
- ▶ Run WINS on a multihomed computer.
- ▶ Configure WINS replication.
- ▶ Configure static mappings in the WINS database.

During the early days of Windows networking, it was knocked for not being extensible to the enterprise. After all, Windows networking revolved around the NetBEUI protocol, and while NetBEUI is a great little protocol, the fact that you can't route it definitely limits its use in a wide area network (WAN) implementation. Windows networking also worked with computer names to find things. This is part of the NetBIOS name resolution, and again, it just wasn't usable on a WAN.

The proper configuration of Windows Internet Name Server or WINS Servers can make name resolution a much faster process and helps gives legitimacy to NT in the enterprise. The discussion of WINS starts the process of address resolution.

In a Windows NT environment running TCP/IP, a computer can be identified in a variety of ways. If you remember all the way back to Chapter 1, the book opened with a discussion of the seven layers of the OSI model or the four layers of the DOD model. The Application layer (the first one in each case) dealt with how information was put onto the wire and how that information was addressed to find its way back to the sending computer. This hardware level address is a unique hexadecimal number assigned by the network card manufacturer. This address, also called the Media Access Control or MAC address, is the final destination for communications destined for a computer. Everything else—IP address, NetBIOS computer name, DNS name—must be resolved to this MAC layer address.

Address Resolution

Resolving an IP address to a MAC address is done by a TCP/IP protocol called the Address Resolution Protocol (ARP). Once a packet ends up at the proper subnet, it is up to the ARP to resolve the IP address to a MAC layer address and get the packet to its final destination.

Other resolution methods, such as WINS and DNS have a variety of ways of resolving computer or host names to an IP address. In this way, if you send a command to www.microsoft.com, DNS will resolve the name www.microsoft.com to an IP address and direct the packet to that IP address. Once the packet arrives on the appropriate subnet, it is up to ARP to get it to the right host. WINS does the same thing, sort of. Instead of taking the global approach of DNS, WINS takes a somewhat smaller approach, resolving computer names to IP addresses. It is up to WINS to resolve the computer name you find in Network Neighborhood to the MAC address that represents the system.

WINS

WINS is a semi-dynamic system. It is semi-dynamic because in a large Windows environment, most of the information in the database will come dynamically from the client. Other information on non-WINS clients, such as UNIX or LAN Manager computers, can be added to the database manually or by importing a copy of an LMHOSTS file. The process starts with the designation of a WINS Server. A WINS Server will maintain a database of all active computer names that it knows about complete with addresses.

Here is the way NetBIOS and WINS work. In a small (non-routed) environment, any time a computer needs to know a resource's NetBIOS it asks by using the broadcast method, meaning every computer on the net- work gets the message. NetBIOS names are assigned when you install the Windows operating system. The names can be up to 15 characters in length. Now, if you know anything about computers, you know that 15 is a strange number for computers to use; usually, everything is in multiples of eight. The NetBIOS name is no different. You have the ability to assign a name up to 15 characters, but the protocol reserves the 16th character to indicate what service will be registering the name. The Computer Browser service or Net Logon are examples of these services.

The problem with NetBIOS arises whenever you decide that you need to route information. Broadcast messages do not get routed. This means that you would be able to resolve NetBIOS names for all computers on your subnet and not see anything else on the network. Because you prob- ably will want to see things such as shares on the other side of the router, this is not acceptable. So, your friends in Redmond came up with WINS.

When computers want something, they have two ways of asking for it: by means of a broadcast request or a directed request. When a computer uses a *broadcast request*, it sends the request out to every other computer on the network. It would be kind of like standing up in the middle of a crowded room and yelling at the top your lungs, "I need to talk to my editor!" That might be effective, unless everyone else in the room started yelling, also.

Given the limitations of NetBIOS, it became obvious that for a computer to access resources on a computer, it had to issue a directed request to that computer. Now, that term, "directed request," sounds a lot fancier than it really is. A *directed request* means that your computer resolves the NetBIOS name to an address and then sends its request directly to that address. In this case, if I needed to talk with my editor, I would resolve the name to an address by looking up her information in the phone directory. Once I had her address, I could direct my message to her, by either calling or sending her snail mail. No one else would be bothered and the system would use a whole lot less cable bandwidth.

So, how does a computer resolve a NetBIOS name to an IP address? Well, first it looks to itself. When computers "hear" about other computers, they put the computer name and IP address in NetBIOS name cache—they simply store the information in memory. Next, the computer will send out a broadcast request looking for the name. Then, the host will use WINS to try and resolve the name. If all of these systems fail, the computer will read (parse) the LMHOSTS file, parse the HOSTS file, and finally ask DNS if it knows where the other computer is.

Specifically, how does NetBIOS name resolution work over TCP/IP? It would seem to be incompatible. There are two RFCs written that address the subject: RFC1001 and RFC1002 address the four different modes that NetBIOS uses for name resolution. These four modes are defined for the entire world using RFCs. Microsoft has taken one of the modes and "enhanced" it, so Microsoft TCP/IP actually uses five modes for resolution.

Each of the five modes starts out just like our example above. It first checks name cache. If the name and address are stored in memory, why go any farther? Once it has been shown that name cache does not have the answer, then modes begin to take the path less traveled.

The modes include B-mode, P-mode, M-mode, H-mode, and Microsoft Enhanced B-mode. Don't let the funky names scare you off; as you can see, it is pretty easy to remember what each mode does:

▶ **B-mode** is broadcast mode.

▶ **H-mode** is hybrid mode.

▶ **M-mode** is mixed mode.

▶ **P-mode** is peer mode (ask all your friends).

Using B-mode, Microsoft Enhanced B-mode Methods, and P-mode

The first mode that will be used for name resolution is a B-mode method. A computer using B-mode will try and resolve NetBIOS names to IP addresses using only broadcast methods. As you can tell, this is probably not going to be a very efficient means of name resolution. Microsoft recognized this and enhanced the standard.

In Microsoft Enhanced B-mode, the system will try a broadcast and if that doesn't work, the computer will then parse the LMHOSTS file and the HOSTS file to see if the name is in there. Again, it is an enhancement over B-mode, but somehow I find it difficult to believe that many companies would make sure that every computer in the organization is going to be listed in an LMHOSTS file or a HOSTS file. That just doesn't sound too realistic. If you do not have a WINS Server configured, this is the mode your Windows computer will come back to by default.

P-mode is higher up on the elegant scale. With P-mode, or peer-to-peer mode, the computer sends a directed datagram to a WINS Server for assistance. This would be similar to a person who will call and ask directions every time he or she wants to go somewhere.

In all three cases, the systems configured to use these methods use only one way of finding out the IP address. Not very flexible, are they?

TIP

Modes can be manually configured by editing the registry parameter HKEY_LOCAL_MACHINE\SYSTEM\CurrentControlSet\ Services\NetBT\Parameters.

M-mode and H-mode   This is the good stuff. H-mode and M-mode are preferable to the B-mode and P-mode types because they can use more than one resolution method. For example, M-mode will try a B-mode (broadcast) method first. If that doesn't work, it will try a P-mode (peer) method, looking for a WINS Server.

H-mode will do the B-mode and P-mode thing, but it reverses the M-mode order. Working with H-mode, the computer will use the P-mode method first. In other words, the host goes directly to the WINS Server and asks if it knows where this resource is before it tries to broadcast a request. If a WINS Server is configured, the system will default to H-mode for NetBIOS name resolution.

In order for this system to work, workstations need to know that a WINS Server is there. For clients running Microsoft's Windows products, this is done by providing the WINS Server's address during the configuration of TCP/IP. During the section on DHCP, it was mentioned that IP addresses can be configured dynamically or manually. The same is true of providing a client with the WINS address. This can be done manually or dynamically as part of the DHCP process.

For those clients that are not running Windows, Microsoft TCP/IP includes WINS proxy agents. The proxy agent acts like a quasi-WINS Server. It will listen for name registration requests or name queries. When it "hears" one, it checks its cache for the information. If the information is in cache, the proxy agent responds. If the information is not in cache, the proxy agent sends the request on to the WINS Server. The WINS Server will handle any name resolution requests and send the information back to the proxy agent. The proxy agent then sends the information on to the non-WINS client requesting the service. It is important to note that non-WINS clients can send a name registration request to the WINS Server through the proxy agent, but the name will just be verified. The name registration requests will not be added to the WINS Server database.

If you have non-WINS clients on the network and want to install a WINS proxy agent, here are some guidelines:

- ▶ A WINS proxy agent can be any computer running NT Server, NT Workstation, Windows 9x, or Windows for Workgroups (WFW). The WFW computers must be running the 32-bit version of Microsoft TCP/IP.

- ▶ The WINS proxy agent must be configured as a WINS client, not as a WINS Server.

- ▶ The proxy agent must be on the same subnet as the non-WINS clients.

- ▶ You should have a maximum of two proxy agents per subnet.

WINS Server Installation and Configuration

WINS Server has to be installed on a computer running Windows NT Server, version 3.5 or higher. The computer can be a backup domain controller (BDC) or a member server. Microsoft suggests that the WINS Server not be a Primary Domain Controller (PDC) because the PDC may become overworked. Because the WINS client computers will be looking to the WINS Server for guidance, it is important they know where to find the server. The server should be configured with a static IP address.

Theoretically, one WINS Server could provide name resolution for an entire network. This could pose a problem for the network if the only WINS Server were to go down, so it is recommended that you have two WINS Servers. Microsoft recommends that if your network grows to over 10,000 clients you should add a primary and secondary WINS Server for each 10,000 clients.

If you have a large network, and there are a lot of name resolution requests, your WINS Servers will be awfully busy. There may be a time when the load of handling WINS resolutions is all that the server can take, so you can have a server dedicated to nothing but WINS.

WINS is installed through the Network option of the Control Panel. Just like DHCP, installation is done through the Services tab. Once the service has been installed another new icon appears on the Administrative Tools menu, this time it is the WINS Manager. WINS Manager allows you to configure the time lines for maintaining certain lease parameters. For example, you can choose how long a computer can go before renewing its name with the WINS Server. The default is six days.

Import LMHOSTS to WINS

A WINS Server has two ways of gathering information about a network, statically and dynamically. When a WINS *client* (a machine running some form of Windows operating system) begins the boot process, it sends its computer name and address in a direct broadcast to the WINS Server. That is how WINS dynamically learns about its network each time a Windows client starts: it registers its computer name with the WINS Server.

What about those computers on your network that are not WINS clients? These are things such as UNIX computers that have host names but do not use NetBIOS. How can these machines take advantage of the resolution provided by a WINS Server? Because these foreign hosts do not run NetBIOS, they cannot register dynamically on boot up, so the registration has to be done manually.

In Chapter 1, "Planning," we briefly looked at the role of the LMHOSTS file. We will examine the LMHOSTS file in more depth later in this chapter. For the sake of the WINS Server, it has to import an LMHOSTS file into its database to learn about all the hosts registered with the file.

Each host can have an LMHOSTS file that contains different information. Fortunately, there can be a "master" LMHOSTS file that other systems can refer to; it acts like a clearinghouse of host information. A copy of this LMHOSTS file is imported into the WINS database to provide a comprehensive list of foreign clients on the network. Notice the key word, "copy." The file must be copied and renamed for the process to be truly successful. If you try and import an LMHOSTS file into the WINS database, the system will tell you the file was imported successfully, but nothing shows up in the database. Copying the file and giving it another name solves the problem.

TIP

In the LMHOSTS sample file shown in Chapter 1, "Planning," you may have noticed the different tags in the file—things such as #PRE to pre-load the information in the hosts cache. When an LMHOSTS file is imported into a WINS Server, all tags except the domain tag, #DOM, are ignored.

WINS on a Multihomed Computer

Earlier in the chapter, there was a discussion of multihomed computers and multihomed systems. To review, a multihomed computer is a computer with a network card that has up to 25 IP addresses assigned to it. A multihomed system is a multihomed computer with more that one network card and more than one IP address. Why would someone create a multihomed system? Think of an Internet service provider that hosts Web sites for each of its clients. Each client may have a different base IP address, but the NT Server computer can only have a finite number of network cards.

A multihomed computer is created by manually adding more than one TCP/IP address to any network card. Once the multihomed computer has been created, if it is to take part in WINS resolution, it should be added to the static addresses on the WINS Server. When you use WINS Manager to configure static addresses in the WINS database, you can choose what type of system they represent. In addition to the multihomed computer there are the following system types:

▶ *Unique* is a unique name in the WINS database. There can be only one address per name. The unique name is the WINS client's computer name.

> ▶ *Group* indicates a normal group for which the IP addresses of the individual clients are not stored. A *normal group* is the name to which broadcasts are sent and is the domain name used for browsing purposes. A normal group name does not have an IP address associated with it and can be valid on multiple networks and registered with multiple WINS Servers. When a WINS Server receives a request for the group name, the WINS Server returns the limited broadcast address 255.255.255.255, which the WINS client will then use to broadcast to the network.

> ▶ *Internet Group* is a group that contains the IP addresses for up to 25 primary and backup domain controllers for the domain. The Internet group name is another instance of the domain name being registered; however, this instance is used for the domain controllers in the domain to communicate with each other.

The static addresses will be added to the database, though only one will show up in the Static Mappings–(Local) window; that is all the system needs. If it receives a request for a computer with the name of the multihomed computer, it sends the request to the primary address listed.

WINS Replication

Why is there a need for replication of the WINS database? Microsoft recommends a WINS Server for each of the 10,000 clients. One of the reasons you will replicate WINS Servers is to cut down on traffic from each of those 10,000 clients to a single server.

Client-to-server communication is a chatty event. When a client starts up, it sends a NetBIOS name registration message for each service that it initializes to its primary WINS Server. For example, the sample server used as part of the preparation for this book is running six services, so when this system comes online, six name registration messages will be sent to the primary WINS Server. These messages are directed packets, meaning that each packet is sent directly to the WINS Server's IP address. If the WINS Server does not answer, the client will then send out the packets to the address 255.255.255.255 or a broadcast. Every host on the network will receive the packet and have to deal with it, even if the host is not a WINS Server.

If the client's name is not registered in the WINS database, the server will respond with a positive name registration response. The positive name registration response contains the Time To Live, or TTL. If the name is already taken, the WINS Server responds by querying the previously registered computer to see if it is still online. If the computer is still online, the client requesting the name gets a negative name registration response. If the previously registered computer does not respond, the WINS Server takes that to mean the system is offline, and issues the name to the system currently making the request.

When a computer shuts down, if it closes properly, it sends a name release request for each of the services to the WINS Server. Again, six services, six different name release requests. When the server receives the request, it will respond with a positive name release response. The WINS Server checks the name as inactive and the name then becomes available.

WINS Renewal   If the computer has been up for awhile, say half the TTL, it will attempt to renew its name. The computer sends a name refresh request to the server, one for each service. If the server is up and working, it will respond with a name refresh response, one for each service. If the client cannot get in touch with the primary WINS Server it will try the secondary WINS Server. If it does not get the name refresh response, it will continue to use the assigned NetBIOS name because its lease has not expired.

WINS Redundancy   As you can see, there is an awful lot of communication going on just to assign, refresh, and release names. Performance may dictate that you have more than one WINS Server on a network, but that would not be the only reason. The primary reason for WINS is to allow computers to browse the network for services by using computer names. If the only WINS Server on the network goes down, computers will be limited in how many computer names can be resolved to IP addresses by the contents of the local LMHOSTS file. To prevent that from becoming a problem, you can configure a secondary WINS Server and have the WINS Servers exchange databases.

Data exchange at the WINS Server level is done through a push and pull relationship. One of the servers must be configured to push its information to its partner while the other system is configured as a pull partner. Either the push partner or the pull partner can be configured to start the replication process.

The replication works something like this. The push partner has a new computer come online and register. Therefore, the WINS database has changed. The push partner sends a message to the pull partner, informing it the database has changed. The pull partner has to ask to have changes sent to it. When the push partner receives the request for changes, it will send information on just the changes or additions.

Push partner replication is usually configured across fast WAN or LAN links. This is done because push replication is triggered by the number of changes that occur to the database. More changes are made during the busy times of day so push replication should take advantage of the links that can handle the traffic.

If the push partner replication should use the faster WAN links, what about pull partner replication? Pull partner replication can be scheduled or it will occur whenever the pull partner starts up, otherwise the Administrator can force a replication. This form of replication can use slower links because it is usually a time-based process. The pull partner can be configured to request updates at certain start times or intervals. This way, the pull partner can request the changes during periods of low traffic.

By default, replication is a one-way process (see Figure 2.1).

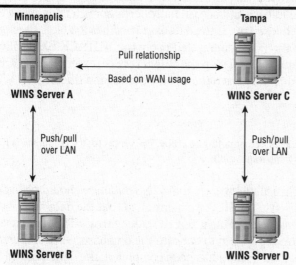

FIGURE 2.1: Replication across WAN links

In Figure 2.1, WINS Server A is configured as a push partner to WINS Server C. This way, systems in Tampa will have a copy of the Minneapolis database. In order for Minneapolis to have a copy of Tampa's database, each server must be configured to be a push/pull partner of the other. When properly configured, all the systems in Tampa will know about all the systems in Minneapolis and vice versa.

TIP

For purposes of the exam, it is important to know that push partners start the process based on the number of changes and pull partners are based on time. There many be several scenario-based questions on the exam, so remember push uses fast links, pull uses slower links.

Backing Up and Restoring a WINS Server Database   Replication is a way to control WAN/LAN traffic. It is also a way of providing fault tolerance for the database. Like it or not, even the most stable database can become corrupted and sometimes restoring from a good backup is the only way to correct a corrupted database. Although it is not specifically covered in the objectives, it is important to know how to compact the WINS database and to configure the WINS databases to get backed up.

The WINS database is named wins.mdb and is located in the %systemroot%\system32\wins directory. Like most databases generated by NT, it is a JET database and occasionally needs some tender loving care before it can be backed up. If the database becomes too large (greater than 30MB), it should be compacted using the JETPACK.EXE utility. To compact the database, you stop the WINS service, execute JETPACK from the same directory the database resides in, and then restart WINS.

NOTE

JETPACK.EXE is a command-line utility. The syntax for the command is JETPACK wins.mdb temp name mdb.

In addition, like all databases, the WINS database should be backed up. When we discussed DHCP, we mentioned that the databases were backed up automatically. This is not the case with a WINS database. You have to configure the system to back up the database. Once configured and the first manual backup has been completed, the database will be backed up every 24 hours to a directory you specify. The backup can be a complete backup. If you have a corrupt database, all you have to do to restore from backup is to stop and start the WINS service. When the WINS Server restarts, it will recognize the corruption and immediately restore from backup. You can also restore from choosing a menu option in WINS Manager, or as a last resort, restores can be done manually.

TIP

It may be important for you to remember that you can restore the WINS database simply by stopping and starting the WINS service.

Static Mappings in the WINS Database

A static mapping is placed in the WINS database to reserve or hold a computer name for a specific computer. It is used primarily for non-WINS clients, allowing WINS-enabled clients to resolve the IP address to the computer name. Non-WINS clients are computers running UNIX or LAN Manager 2.2c for OS/2.

One of the benefits of adding the non-WINS computers to the database is you will no longer need to maintain an entry in the LMHOSTS file for that computer. WINS clients will be able to resolve computer names to IP addresses for the non-WINS enabled clients. The reverse, however, is not the case. You will still need to have some sort of HOST/LMHOST file to resolve names to addresses at the UNIX host.

NOTE

To make maintenance of the static mappings in the WINS database easier, a copy of the LMHOSTS file can be imported into the database.

Static mappings are added to the WINS database using WINS Manager. Before starting WINS Manager, you will need the name of the computer, its IP address, and the type of system you are defining. Types include the following:

- ▶ *Unique* is a unique name in the WINS database that permits only one IP address per name. The unique name is the WINS client's computer name.

- ▶ *Group* indicates a normal group for which the IP addresses of the individual clients are not stored. A *normal group* is the name to which broadcasts are sent and is the domain name used for browsing purposes. A normal group name has [1Eh] in the 16th byte field at the end of the name in WINS Manager. A normal group name does not have an IP address associated with it and can be valid on multiple networks and registered with multiple WINS Servers. When a WINS Server receives a request for the group name, the WINS Server returns the limited broadcast address 255.255.255.255, which the WINS client will then use to broadcast to the network.

▶ *Domain name* allows you to specify a group with NetBIOS names that have 0x1c as the 16th byte. A domain name group stores up to 25 addresses for its members. For registration after the 25th address, WINS overwrites a replica address or the oldest registration. Choosing this option will provide you with additional options to add multiple addresses to the list.

▶ *Internet group* is a group that contains the IP addresses for up to 25 primary and backup domain controllers for the domain. An Internet group has a 0x1c as its 16th byte, which appears as a [1Ch] at the end of the name WINS Manager. The Internet group name is another instance of the domain name being registered; however, this instance is used for the domain controllers in the domain to communicate with each other.

▶ *Multihomed* is similar to a unique name in that it is the WINS client's computer name; however, it can have up to 25 addresses and is for use by multihomed systems. A *multihomed system* is a system with more than one network interface and more than one IP address.

NOTE

When you open Show Database from the WINS Manager Mappings menu option, you will be presented with a detail screen that shows what computer name has been mapped to which IP address. Immediately following the computer name, there is a hexadecimal identifier, which points to the type service being mapped. This is referred to as the 16th bit.

The proper configuration of Windows Internet Name Service is accomplished through several steps, starting with the installation and configuration. Once the server has been installed and configured, you can decide how the WINS Server will gather information—by a dynamic method, a static method, or both.

Installing and Configuring a WINS Server

1. Select Start ➤ Settings ➤ Control Panel ➤ Network.

2. From the Network window, click the Services tab.

3. Click Add, and the server will build a list of available services.

4. From the Select Network Service window, choose Windows Internet Name Service and click OK.

5. Provide the NT Setup screen with the location of the NT files and click Continue.

6. Click Close to close the network dialog box.

7. At this point you will be prompted to restart the computer. Click Yes and when the computer restarts, log on as Administrator or as a member of the Administration group.

Once the WINS Server has been installed and the computer restarted, you can check on how hard the service is working by using the WINS Manager.

Starting WINS Manager.

1. Select Start ➤ Programs ➤ Administrative Tools.

2. Click WINS Manager.

Using WINS Manager to Configure the WINS Server. From WINS Manager, select Server ➤ Configuration ➤ Advanced. Notice that in the WINS Server Configuration window you can configure the Renewal Interval, the Extinction Interval, the Extinction Timeout, and the Verify Interval. Each is set in terms of hours.

Table 2.2 shows what each of the configuration parameters controls.

TABLE 2.2: WINS Server Configuration Parameters

INTERVAL	DESCRIPTION
Renewal Interval	The default time period before the WINS Server releases the client name. If the client does not renew within this time period, it will have to register again.
Extinction Interval	The number of hours that a released name or non-renewed name will remain in the database before it is determined to be extinct.
Extinction Timeout	The amount of time an extinct record will remain in the database before it is purged.
Verify Interval	How often this WINS Server waits before verifying the material stored in other WINS databases.

WINS Servers should work in pairs and should trade databases. This is done through the pull parameters and push parameters.

NOTE

For more information on this subject, see the section, "Configuring WINS Replication," later in this chapter.

Some advanced WINS configuration options allow you to maintain logging and detailed events. You can set up the server to Replicate Only With Partners, Backup on Termination, and set Migrate On/Off. Replicate Only With Partners means that an administrator cannot ask a WINS Server to pull or push replication to an unlisted WINS Server partner. Backup on Termination causes the WINS database to be backed up if the WINS service is stopped unless the system is shutting down. Migrate On/Off specifies that static, unique, and multihomed records in the database are treated as dynamic records when they conflict with a new registration or replica.

Installing a WINS Proxy Agent

Proxy agents are not mentioned in the objectives, but the Microsoft exam writers have an interesting way of bringing other things into the exam. It will help to know about proxy agents.

A WINS proxy agent can be any computer running NT Server, NT Workstation, Windows 9x, or Windows for Workgroups, if the Workgroup computer is running the 32-bit version of TCP/IP. The proxy agent must be configured as a WINS Server and cannot be the WINS Server. The proxy agent must reside on the same subnet as the non-WINS clients. There can be two proxy agents per subnet.

WARNING

Configuring an NT system to be a proxy agent requires you to edit the registry. There have been cases where editing the registry has given Microsoft an excuse not to provide tech support.

To configure an NT system to be a proxy agent, follow these steps:

1. Select Start ➢ Run.

2. Type **Regedt32** in the Open box and click OK.

3. Browse to the registry key HKEY_LOCAL_MACHINE\SYS-TEM\ CurrentControlSet\Services\NetBT\Parameters.

4. Double-click the EnableProxy value entry.

5. In the DWORD Editor box Data window type 1.

6. Click OK and close the Registry Editor.

7. Restart the computer.

Configuring an NT Server to Be a WINS Client

Any Windows-based computer on the network that is not a WINS Server or a WINS proxy agent can be configured to be a WINS client. There are two ways of providing the client information about the location of the WINS Server, either manually or dynamically using DHCP.

To configure the client manually, follow these steps:

1. Select Start ➢ Settings ➢ Control Panel ➢ Network.

2. Choose the Protocols tab ➢ TCP/IP ➢ Properties.

3. From the Microsoft TCP/IP Properties window, click the tab marked WINS address. This will bring up the WINS Address window.

4. In the area marked Primary WINS Server, enter the IP address of the designated WINS Server.

5. In the area marked Secondary WINS Server, enter the IP address of the backup WINS Server.

6. Click OK to close the TCP/IP Properties screen and Network icon.

7. When prompted to restart the computer, click Yes.

To configure a DHCP server to provide the scope to assign the WINS Server address, follow these steps:

1. Click Start ➢ Programs ➢ Administrative Tools ➢ DHCP Manager.

2. Highlight the appropriate scope under Local Machine in the DHCP server's frame.

3. From the DHCP Manager menu, choose DHCP Options ➢ Scope.

4. From the Unused Options frame, scroll down to 046 WINS/ NBT Node Type.

5. Click Add, then select Value.

6. In the Byte text box, type **0x8**.

NOTE

Using 0x8 will configure the client to use a method of accessing the server called hybrid node or h-node. The different broadcast modes will be explained during the objective on LMHOSTS file and NetBIOS resolution.

7. From the Unused Options list box, select 044 WINS/NBNS Server.

8. Click Add.

9. Click Value.

10. Click Edit Array and in the New IP Address box type in the address of the target computer.

11. Click Add.

12. Click OK to close the IP Address Array Editor of the DHCP Options: Scope menu and click OK to close the DHCP Options: Scope menu.

13. Close DHCP Manager–(Local).

Importing LMHOSTS File into WINS

In Chapter 1, "Planning," there was a copy of the LMHOSTS file on one of the server computers for PSCONSULTING. For simplicity, this will be the file imported into the WINS Server. Before beginning, be sure to copy the LMHOSTS file to a file with another name, something really creative like LMHOSTS.BAK.

To import a file into a WINS database follow these steps:

1. Click Start ➢ Programs ➢ Administrative Tools ➢ WINS Manager.

2. From the menu, choose Mappings ➢ Static Mappings. This will open the Static Mappings–(Local) window.

3. From the Static Mappings–(Local) window, click Import Mappings. This opens the Select Static Mapping File browse window. Browse to the path of the file to be imported. In this case, it is D:\winnt\system32\drivers\etc\lmhosts.bak. Click Open.

4. You should receive a message from WINS Manager saying the static mapping file has been successfully imported into the database.

5. Click OK to close the window.

6. Click Close to close the Static Mappings–(Local) window.

Running WINS on a Multihomed Computer

A *multihomed computer* is a computer that has multiple IP addresses added to a network card. To add addresses to an existing network card, follow these steps:

1. Click Start ➢ Settings ➢ Control Panel ➢ double-click Network.

2. Choose the Protocols tab ➢ TCP/IP Protocol and click Properties.

3. Click the Advanced button and you will open the Advanced IP addressing window ➢ Add.

4. Provide the appropriate IP address and subnet mask.

Configuring WINS Replication

To configure a WINS Server as a push/pull partner with another server, complete the following procedures:

1. Click Start ➢ Programs ➢ Administrative Tools (Common) ➢ WINS Manager.

2. To add the IP address of the WINS Server that will be used as a replication partner, choose Server from the menu ➢ Add WINS Server, then enter the computer name or IP address of the WINS Server to be added.

3. To configure replication, highlight a partner in the WINS Server frame, then choose Server from the menu. Choose

Replication Partners to open the Replication Partners–(Local) window.

4. Highlight the computer selected for replication and choose Push Partner, Pull Partner, or both in the Replication Options frame.

5. Click OK to close the window or Replicate Now to force replication.

To customize the push/pull relationship, you can follow these steps:

1. Click Start ➤ Programs ➤ Administrative Tools (Common) ➤ WINS Manager.

2. To add the IP address of the WINS Server that will be used as a replication partner, choose Server from the menu, then choose Add WINS Server. Enter the computer name or IP address of the WINS Server to be added.

3. To configure replication, highlight a partner in the WINS Server frame ➤ Server ➤ Replication Partners to open the Replication Partners–(Local) window.

4. Highlight the computer selected for replication and choose Push Partner, Pull Partner, or both in the Replication Options frame.

5. Click Configure next to the push partner. For the push partner, you can select the number of changes that will be necessary before a replication is initiated. Click OK to close the window.

6. Click Configure next to the pull partner and you can configure a start time and a replication interval. Times can be set using either the AM/PM format or the 24-hour military clock. Click OK to close the Window and exit WINS Server Manager.

Backing Up and Restoring the WINS Database   Although this is not specifically covered in the objectives, there are some questions on how to restore a corrupted WINS database. Before you can restore, you have to back up the database. Backups occur once every 24 hours.

To configure the system to back up, start WINS Manager:

1. Select Start ➤ Programs ➤ Administrative Tools (Common) ➤ WINS Manager.

2. Click Mappings from the menu then select Backup Database.

3. Enter a new directory name or choose from the list of directories already present on the drive. Click OK. Notice that a backup is done immediately.

To restore a WINS database using the menu options, you follow these procedures:

1. Select Start ➤ Programs ➤ Administrative Tools (Common) ➤ WINS Manager.

2. Click Mappings ➤ Restore Local Database.

NOTE

The option, Restore Local Database, will be grayed out unless the database is corrupted.

To restore a WINS database manually you would follow these steps:

1. Manually stop the WINS service by clicking Start ➤ Settings ➤ Control Panel.

2. Click Services ➤ Windows Internet Name Service ➤ Stop.

3. Delete the JET*.log, WINSTMP.MDB, and the SYSTEM.MDB files from the %systemroot%\system32\wins directory.

4. From the Windows NT Server CD, make a new copy of SYSTEM.MDB to the %systemroot%\system32\wins directory. This is the database template file.

5. After you have located a good copy of the WINS.MDB file, copy it to the %systemroot%\system32\wins directory and restart the WINS service. The WINS.MDB file is the actual WINS Server database file.

▶ Configure subnet masks.

Of all the objectives on the test, the topic of subnets is the topic the exam writers spent the most time with. In one way or another, you will be seeing lots of questions on subnetting, including topics such as:

▶ How many subnets will you need?

▶ Given an address and a subnet mask, how many subnets are possible?

▶ Given an address and a subnet mask, how many hosts can reside on each subnet?

▶ Given a network address and a subnet mask, what are the network addresses and the range of IP addresses per network?

▶ Given an address and a subnet mask, what is the host address and what is the network address?

The questions will come up in a variety of formats. As part of this section, we will cover all the basics of subnetting and provide you with some tools that may make the experience of testing a little less stressful.

NOTE

Much of the discussion on subnets revolves around conversion of binary numbers into decimal equivalents and decimals back to binary. If you are uncomfortable with doing this manually, the Windows scientific calculator is available during the test.

Communication at any level revolves around a sender and a receiver. For the communication to carry on for any period of time, the sender will become the receiver and the receiver will become the sender. In each case, both parties must have a way of finding each other.

Addressing Basics

Computer communication is very similar to the mail service as a familiar means of facilitating communication. For example, when someone sends me a letter, they have my name, home address, city, state, and zip code. When the mail carrier picks up the letter from the sender, it checks the city, state, and zip code to find out if the letter is to be delivered locally or if it out of the local postal zone. If the letter is out of the local postal zone, the letter is forwarded to a regional center, which forwards it to another regional center, which sends it to a local center, which delivers the letter.

In IP communications, the process works this way. Assume that your computer wants to request some information from an FTP server. You enter in the appropriate IP address for the FTP server and press Enter. What happens behind the scenes? The sending computer formats the data to be sent in something called a *packet* or *datagram*. Don't let the fancy terms scare you, just think of it as putting a letter in an envelope.

This packet has a source address (the sender) and a destination address (the recipient), as does your envelope. When your computer is ready to send out the packet, it looks at the destination address to determine if the packet is destined for the local network or somewhere else. If the packet is destined for the local network, the computer sends it on its way. If it is destined for somewhere else, the computer sends the packet to the designated gateway and lets the gateway handle it.

The packet addresses are a little more complex than a familiar mailing address. First of all, the packet address is an IP address. Similar to the way your address is made up of several parts, so is an IP address. Your address consists of a street address to identify your house, and a city, state, and zip code. An IP address consists of the network address the host resides on and a host address to identify the computer on the network.

IP Addressing

Network addresses are interesting things. If you have a network that is not connected to the Internet, it really doesn't matter what network address you give each network segment. Just make sure everything is unique and life is good. I like to refer to this approach as the 1.2.3.4 method of network addressing. You start numbering the first machine at 1.2.3.4 and slowly increment by one for each new host you install on the subnet. Things become a little more complicated when you decide to hook your system to the Internet. Every computer on a network must have a unique address. It doesn't matter if the network is the three-work-station configuration at the corner insurance office or the Internet. Everything has to be unique. At the Internet level, you just cannot pick yourself a block of addresses and go. You or your company must be assigned addresses. This assignment is done by the Internet Network Information Center, affectionately known as the InterNIC. It is up to the InterNIC to determine what address block you can use. There are three ways to apply. You can go to the InterNIC Web site at `http://inter-nic.net`; you can call Network Solutions at 703-742-4777 or send them an application at the following address:

> Network Solutions
> InterNIC Registration Services
> 505 Huntmar Park Drive
> Herndon, VA 22070

or you can send e-mail to hostmaster@internic.net.

Applications are available from the Web site.

Part i

NOTE

Actually, depending on the size of your organization, you can also ask your Internet service provider to cut through the paperwork for you. The ISP may have a block of addresses you can rent. The problem with renting a block of addresses from an ISP is the ISP owns the addresses. If you decide to change ISPs, you have to reconfigure your entire network addressing scheme.

When you receive your assignment, it will be in the form of an IP address. The typical IP address looks like 205.46.15.198. The funny looking address uniquely identifies a host on a network. The address is actually made up of two parts, a network address and a host address.

This IP address is made up of 4 bytes. Because each byte is made up of 8 bits, each byte is also referred to as an *octet*. Each octet is expressed as the decimal representation of a binary number. To translate a decimal number to a binary number, we need some kind of translation table. The number we are going to translate is the first number of the octet, 205. Look closely at Table 2.3 to see how to translate this number from binary to a decimal.

TABLE 2.3: Binary to Decimal Translation of 205

	Bit 8	Bit 7	Bit 6	Bit 5	Bit 4	Bit 3	Bit 2	Bit 1
Decimal value	$2^7 = 128$	$2^6 = 64$	$2^5 = 32$	$2^4 = 16$	$2^3 = 8$	$2^2 = 4$	$2^1 = 2$	$2^0 = 1$
Binary value of byte	1	1	0	0	1	1	0	1
Decimal conversion	128	64	0	0	1	1	0	1

If you look at the decimal value of the byte, using the bit binary values, you have 128+64+8+4+1 = 205. To us, it is 205, to your computer it is 11001101. See how it works? Pretty simple, huh?

If all the bits are set to 1, you have a maximum value of 255. There are some rules to IP addressing and one of those rules states that an address cannot have all the bits set to all 1's or all 0's. That means there are no network (or host, for that matter) addresses of 255 or 0. In addition, there is a reserved address, 127.0.0.1, which is called a *loopback address*. A loopback address is an address used for testing the local machine.

The InterNIC has divided IP network addresses into five classes. Microsoft TCP/IP recognizes the first three classes, so those are what we will concentrate on, but you should know about all five. Table 2.4 gives you a breakdown of the classes.

TABLE 2.4: InterNIC Address Classes

CLASS	VALUE OF FIRST BYTE	BINARY RANGE	DECIMAL RANGE
A	First bit must be 0.	00000001–01111111 Note: A value of zero for the network address is not permitted.	1 to 127 Note: 127 is reserved for testing.
B	First 2 bits must be 10.	10000000–10111111	128 to 191
C	First 3 bits must be 110.	11000000–11011111	192 to 223
D	First 4 bits must be 1110.	11100000–11101111	224 to 239

Note: This range of network addresses is reserved for multicasts and is not available for host addressing.

E	First 5 bits must be 11110.	11110000–11110111	240 to 247

Note: This range of addresses is reserved for experimental purposes and is not available for host addressing

Because the Class D and Class E network addresses are reserved, we will ignore them for the rest of the book.

TIP

For the exam, know the class limits. If you can remember the value of the first byte, you will be fine. There can be several questions based on the class of a specific address.

The IP addressing scheme takes into account that some networks are very large, some are medium sized, and some are small. A Class A address uses the first octet to represent the network address and the last three octets to represent hosts. Looking at the table above, with only 127 numbers available for a Class A address, there aren't many given out. They were designed for a large organization with lots of hosts.

A Class B address fulfills the needs of a medium-sized organization. The first two octets designate the network and the last two octets designate the number of hosts. The Class C address uses the first three octets to designate the network and the last octet to designate the host. There is a formula to determine the number of networks or the number of hosts. The formula is 2 raised to the number of bits for varying minus 2. You subtract 2 to take into account that you cannot use 0 and you cannot use 255. So, in the case of a Class A address, 1 bit is used to designate the network and 7 bits are left for "varying" in the first octet. Given the formula, $2^7 - 2 = 126$ networks. Now, I like math as much as the next person, but I figure formulas like that are the reason God created calculators. Table 2.5 shows how the addresses break down.

TABLE 2.5: IP addressing scheme

CLASS	IP ADDRESS	NUMBER OF NETWORKS	NUMBER OF HOSTS
A	NET.host.host.host	126 Network = 7 bits $2^7 - 2 = 126$	16,777,214 Hosts =24 bits $2^{24} - 2 = 16,777,214$
B	NET.NET.host.host 16,384 Network = 14 bits $2^{14} - 2 = 16,384$	126 Network = 7 bits $2^7 - 2 = 126$	65,534 Hosts=16 bits $2^{16} - 2 = 65,534$
C	NET.NET.NET.host	2,097,152 Network = 21 bits $2^{21} - 2 = 2,097,152$	254 Hosts=8 bits $2^8 - 2 = 254$

TIP

For exam purposes, parts of this chart should be memorized, or at least known cold. You should know which octets are used to designate the network and which octets designate the host for each of the three classes. Memorizing the number of networks and hosts is not necessary, but you should recognize the trend; Class A has few networks and lots of hosts and Class C has lots of networks with a few hosts.

You have heard the old question, "What's in a name?" The 90s' version could be, "What's in an IP address?" When I just pinged Microsoft, I returned an IP address of 207.46.130.17. From the information you have seen so far, you should be able to determine that this is a Class C address because the first octet is greater than 191 and less than 224. Because it is a Class C address, you know that this host is on network number 207.46.130.0 and the unique host number is 0.0.0.17. You also know this is one host out of a possible 254.

Subnets and Subnetting

When you applied to the InterNIC for your IP address, you were returned a number like 207.46.130.0 and a subnet mask of 255.255.255.0. You were told that you could have 254 different hosts on that network. At this point, it is very important we define the term "network." That is one of those terms that gets thrown around and has different meanings depending on its context. I can look in my lab and see an NT Server hooked up to a couple of NT Workstations and that is a network. I can drive down the street to the IS headquarters of a major bank and start talking about the nationwide network. In terms of this section, a network should really be defined as a network segment. Each NT Server that has a network card in it has a network number assigned to that card. Each network card may define its own network segment. Look at Figure 2.2 and you will see that even in this extremely simple design, there are four networks.

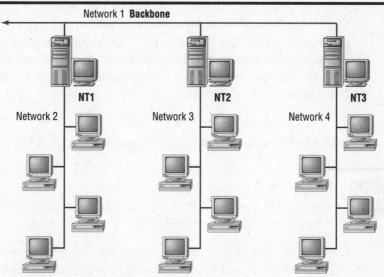

FIGURE 2.2: Simple network infrastructure

As you look at the structure of your network, you will see that you have multiple network segments. Depending on the type of network you have

(Ethernet versus Token Ring), you may only have 50 hosts on any network segment. Does this mean that you will have to apply for a separate IP address for each network segment? After all, each network must have its own unique address. That would be really wasteful. You would have an address that could use up to 254 hosts and you are applying it to a segment that has only 50 hosts, wasting 204 addresses. With the explosive growth of the Internet, everybody wants an IP address, so they are in short supply. Wasting them like that would be criminal. There has got to be a better way. It's called subnetting.

NOTE

With the popularity of the Internet, there is a shortage of IP addresses. There is a new IP addressing scheme in the works called IP version 6, or IPv6. The new IP is going to be incompatible with the old IP. In addition, the next generation will have a 128-bit source and destination address. A valid IP address in the future will look something like 1543:B24E:9853:574C:3336:43C7:4B3E:7C36.

When we take an IP address and subnet it, we are taking an address that is designed for one unique network with 254 hosts (in the case of a Class C network) and giving ourselves more unique network numbers with a fewer number of hosts per network segment.

This is how it works. In a Class C network, we know the first three octets are destined for the network number and the last octet is determined to be the host. So, in binary, it would look something like this, with 1's determining the network and 0's determining the host:

11111111.11111111.11111111.00000000

That would give us the default Class C subnet of 255.255.255.0.

NOTE

Each class has its own default subnet; for Class A it is 255.0.0.0, for Class B it is 255.255.0.0, and Class C is 255.255.255.0.

To give us the opportunity to have more networks and fewer hosts, IP will let us "borrow" bits from the host address to use as a network address. We can use the formula of $2^x - 2$, where x is the number of borrowed bits, to determine the number of networks. Using $2^x - 2$ with the number of remaining bits will give you the number of hosts per segment.

Before, our subnet in binary was 11111111.11111111.11111111.00000000. Let's change that to 11111111.11111111.11111111.11110000. To figure out what our new custom subnet mask would be, let's take the numbers we used earlier and plug them into the chart. The conversion of this subnet is Table 2.6.

TABLE 2.6: Subnet Conversion

	Bit 8	Bit 7	Bit 6	Bit 5	Bit 4	Bit 3	Bit 2	Bit 1
Decimal value	$2^7 = 128$	$2^6 = 64$	$2^5 = 32$	$2^4 = 16$	$2^3 = 8$	$2^2 = 4$	$2^1 = 2$	$2^0 = 1$
Binary value of byte	1	1	1	1	0	0	0	0
Decimal conversion	128	64	32	16	0	0	0	0

To convert this back to decimal, we add 128+64+32+16=240 so our new subnet mask is 255.255.255.240. Using the formula, we see that we have $2^4 - 2 = 14$ subnets available and also 14 hosts available per subnet for this Class C address.

If our subnet had been 11111111.11111111.11111111.11100000, our subnet mask would have been 255.255.255.224 and we would have had the ability to have six subnets with 30 hosts each on the subnet. To keep you from having to do the math and conversion each time, look at the tables below to see what the subnet is and how many subnets and hosts you can get for each subnet. Table 2.7 will show Class A addresses.

TABLE 2.7: Summary of Subnet Mask Effects on a Class A Address

Number of Bits Used in the Subnet	Subnet Mask	Number of Networks	Number of Hosts
2	255.192.0.0	2	4,194,302
3	255.224.0.0	6	2,097,150
4	255.240.0.0	14	1,048,574
5	255.248.0.0	30	524,286
6	255.252.0.0	62	262,142
7	255.254.0.0	126	131,070
8	255.255.0.0	254	65,534

Can a Class A network be subnetted down further? Certainly. You can continue to subnet a Class A down to the next to last bit of the last octet. The number of networks will continue to grow and the number of hosts per network will continue to decline.

NOTE

Take a close look at the relationship between the number of networks as the numbers of bits used for the subnet increases. In each case the number of networks is doubled plus two. If you look closely at the number of hosts, you will notice that from bottom to top, it increases by the same margin. If you can remember that a subnet of 192 has two networks, and can also recall the formula, you have the rest of the network section figured out. If you can remember a Class A has 65,534 hosts with a subnet mask of 255.255.0.0, you can fill out the rest of the hosts section. For those of you who have math phobia, remember, you do have access to the calculator.

Table 2.8 outlines Class B addresses.

TABLE 2.8: Summary of Subnet Mask Effects on a Class B Address

Number of Bits Used in the Subnet	Subnet Mask	Number of Networks	Number of Hosts
2	255.255.192.0	2	16,382
3	255.255.224.0	6	8,190
4	255.255.240.0	14	4,094
5	255.255.248.0	30	2,046
6	255.255.252.0	62	1,022
7	255.255.254.0	126	510
8	255.255.255.0	254	254

Again, the Class B address can be subnetted down into the next octet. The number of networks will continue to increase and the number of hosts per subnet will continue to decrease.

Finally, Table 2.9 will look at the effects of subnetting a Class C address.

TABLE 2.9: Summary of Subnet Mask Effects on a Class C Address

NUMBER OF BITS USED IN THE SUBNET	SUBNET MASK	NUMBER OF NETWORKS	NUMBER OF HOSTS
2	255.255.255.192	2	62
3	255.255.255.224	6	30
4	255.255.255.240	14	14
5	255.255.255.248	30	6
6	255.255.255.252	62	2
7	255.255.255.254	Not allowed	Not allowed
8	255.255.255.255	Not allowed	Not allowed

TIP

Be sure you know how to use the information in Tables 2.7, 2.8, and 2.9, and how to re-create the tables. In an exam situation, you may be given a question that asks which subnet mask you would apply to a Class C network if you had 11 subnets, each with no more than 12 hosts. In that case, the subnet would be 255.255.255.240 because it has a maximum of 14 subnets with 14 hosts. The majority of questions about subnetting revolve around Class B and Class C addresses.

You will notice in Table 2.9 that there are some "N/As" showing up for bits 7 and 8. If you pay close attention to the number of hosts, every time a bit is added, the number of hosts is reduced by the formula of $(x/2-1)$. Don't let the math frighten you. The first subnet, 255.255.255.192, has a potential total of 62 hosts. The next subnet, 255.255.255.224, has $(62/2-1)$ or 30 hosts. When you get to bit 6, 255.255.255.252, there are only two hosts per subnet. The next step would have $(2/2-1)$ or 0 hosts. We have just subnetted the network down as far as it can go.

Determining Network and Host Addresses

If you are given an IP address, we have just shown how to determine the appropriate subnet mask to provide you with the number of network addresses and host addresses. The host addresses must be assigned to the appropriate network address, otherwise, systems on the subnet will not be able to communicate. The next step in the process is to take the network address assigned, with the appropriate subnet mask applied, and break it down into subnets and host addresses.

The sample address from Microsoft was 205.46.15.76. Because this is a Class C address, if the default subnet mask of 255.255.255.0 was used, the network address would be 205.46.15.0 and the host address would be .0.0.0.76. Let's assume when Microsoft was assigned this address, they were going to use this address on a network with four subnets and 25 hosts on each subnet. Looking at Table 2.9, we find that the subnet mask that meets all of those criteria is 255.255.255.224, using the first 3 bits of the last octets for a network address and the remaining 5 bits for host addresses.

Using the 3 bits of the last octet gives us six choices for the network number. These would be the binary choices:

- ▶ 00000000 – Invalid address because the network portion contains all 0's
- ▶ 00100000 = 32
- ▶ 01000000 = 64
- ▶ 01100000 = 96
- ▶ 10000000 = 128
- ▶ 10100000 = 160
- ▶ 11000000 = 192
- ▶ 11100000 – Invalid address because the network portion contains all 1's

To convert the binary choices to decimal, remember we are dealing with only three places from the octet. The conversion chart shows us the opening three places have values 128, 64, and 32.

Using the original network address of 205.46.15.0 and applying a subnet mask of 255.255.255.224 means these would be our network numbers:

- ▶ 205.46.15.32
- ▶ 205.46.15.64
- ▶ 205.46.15.96
- ▶ 205.46.15.128

► 205.46.15.160

► 205.46.15.192

Now that we have determined the network numbers, we must determine the host addresses by applying the last 5 bits of the octet. Using the binary representation for the first network, our range of host addresses would be between 00100001 and 00111110. Converting those binary numbers to decimal we find the network 205.46.15.32 has hosts ranging from 205.46.15.33 to 205.46.15.62. Applying the same principal to the next subnet, we would have addresses ranging from 01000001 to 01011110. Remember, the first three positions are the network address and the last five are the host address. Network number 205.46.15.64 would be made up of hosts 205.46.15.65 to 205.46.15.126. You can use the same procedure to find the host addresses on any subnet, using any subnet mask. Use the binary method to define the network portion of the address and then use the binary method to determine the host portion of the address.

TIP

For exam purposes, it is very important you know how to figure out host address ranges. If a host address is on the wrong subnet, it will not be able to communicate with the rest of the subnet. In other words, even though host addresses 205.46.15.62 and 205.46.15.65 are close in proximity, they must be on different subnets to communicate.

You can use the same method to back engineer an IP address. For example, given the sample address of 205.46.15.198 and a subnet mask of 255.255.255.224, what is the network address and what is the host address? In looking at the information above, we know that the highest available network address is 205.46.15.192. This host must reside on that network. If the network address is 192, the host address must be 0.0.0.6.

Case Study Review The exam writers will pound you with subnet and addressing questions. So, let's start at the beginning with a made-up case study and see how we can apply the principals we discussed in this section.

First of all, remember, the exam writers would concentrate on these questions:

► How many subnets will you need?

► Given an address and a subnet mask, how many subnets are possible?

▶ Given an address and a subnet mask, how many hosts can reside on each subnet?

▶ Given a network address and a subnet mask, what are the network addresses and the range of IP addresses per network?

▶ Given an address and a subnet mask, what is the host address and what is the network address?

We can keep these points in mind as we approach the case study. Let's begin.

For our sample company, Brandice has been named the head of the Information Technology department for the company she works for. Her task is to come up with a TCP/IP addressing scheme for the network based on the following criteria:

1. Brandice's predecessor had applied to the InterNIC for an IP address. The company network received the addresses of 203.45.16.0 with a default subnet mask of 255.255.255.0.

2. When Brandice asked for a map of the computer network, she was told the company currently has the corporate headquarters, with 15 employees. There are two remote offices with 10 employees each.

3. Each employee has a computer. Here are some additional details:

   ▶ At the home office, there is a server with two network interface cards (NICs). There are two laser printers hooked directly into the network, each using a (NIC). Each printer should be assigned an IP address.

   ▶ At each of the remote offices, there is a server with two network cards. There is one laser printer hooked directly into the network with a NIC. Each printer should be assigned an IP address.

   ▶ There is a router that contains three network cards connecting the three offices.

While Brandice was rummaging around her new office, she found the network map that is shown in Figure 2.3.

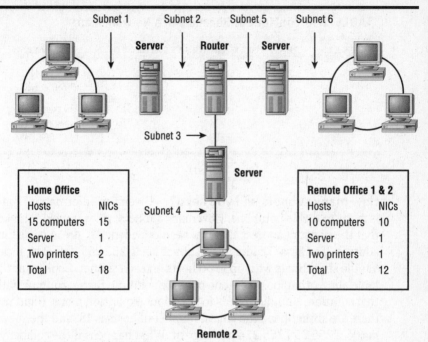

FIGURE 2.3: A network map

Looking at the network map and using the information above, Brandice devised the chart shown in Table 2.10.

TABLE 2.10: Summary of a Network Map

SUBNET	# OF HOST ADDRESSES NEEDED	COMMENTS
1	18	15 computers 1 server NIC 2 printers
2	2	1 server NIC 1 router NIC
3	2	1 server NIC 1 router NIC
4	12	10 computers 1 server NIC 1 printer NIC

TABLE 2.10 continued: Summary of a Network Map

SUBNET	# OF HOST ADDRESSES NEEDED	COMMENTS
5	2	1 server NIC 1 router NIC
6	12	10 computers 1 server NIC 1 printer NIC

How many subnets will you need?   Given this information, Brandice is ready to tackle point one: How many subnets will you need? You know that the network address that has been provided; 203.45.16.0 is a Class C address. If a Class C address is a subnet using 255.255.255 .224, it can handle six subnets with up to 30 hosts on each subnet. Looking at the table above, that looks like one possible solution. Before running with that solution, Brandice needs to ask about expansion plans. Right now there are six subnets, the largest number of hosts is 18, and the subnet mask of 255.255.255.224 works great. What happens if the company decides to add another branch office? All of a sudden, the network map goes to heck in a hand basket. For the sake of this example, we will say that the company is frozen at current levels and will never expand.

Brandice's other choice was to add another NIC to the servers and subdivide the current networks. Then she could use the 255.255.255.240 subnet mask, giving her 14 subnets with 14 host addresses per subnet.

Given an address and a subnet mask, how many subnets are possible? Given an address and a subnet mask, how many hosts can reside on each subnet?   Let's tackle both of these questions at the same time. If you are curious about how the address can be subnetted, here is a recap in Table 2.11 showing the subnet mask for a Class C address, the number of possible subnets, and the number of possible hosts.

TABLE 2.11: Subnet summary for Class C

SUBNET MASK	NUMBER OF NETWORKS	NUMBER OF HOSTS
255.255.255.192	2	62
255.255.255.224	6	30

TABLE 2.11 continued: Subnet summary for Class C

SUBNET MASK	NUMBER OF NETWORKS	NUMBER OF HOSTS
255.255.255.240	14	14
255.255.255.248	30	6
255.255.255.252	62	2

Given a network address and a subnet mask, what are the network addresses and the range of IP addresses per network?

We now know our assigned network address and the subnet mask we are going to use, 255.255.255.224. A subnet mask of 224 means we are going to be using the first 3 bits of the last octet for a network number and the last 5 bits of the octet for the host ID. This means our network numbers can be determined by using Table 2.12.

TABLE 2.12: A Network Conversion

128	64	32	NETWORK ID
0	0	0	Not allowed, all 0's
0	0	1	203.45.16.32
0	1	0	203.45.16.64
0	1	1	203.45.16.96
1	0	0	203.45.16.128
1	0	1	203.45.16.160
1	1	0	203.45.16.192
1	1	1	Not allowed, all 1's

What about host addresses? In the case of host addresses, we are using the last five places in the octet. Because there are 30 possible hosts for each, Table 2.13 will demonstrate first address, last address, and the addresses you cannot use. We will use the first network, 203.45.16.32, for the example of host addresses.

TABLE 2.13: Host Addressing

16	8	4	2	1	ADDRESS	EXPLANATION
0	0	0	0	0	Not allowed, all 0's	
0	0	0	0	1	203.45.16.33	Network address 203.45.16.32 plus the host address of 0.0.0.1 = 203.45.16.33.
1	1	1	1	0	203.45.16.62	Network address 203.45.16.32 plus the host address of 0.0.0.30 = 203.45.16.62.
1	1	1	1	1	Not allowed, all 1's	

Table 2.14 shows the network address, the starting host address, and the ending host address for the six subnets.

TABLE 2.14: Subnet Summary

NETWORK ADDRESS	STARTING ADDRESS	ENDING ADDRESS
203.45.16.32	203.45.16.33	209.45.16.62
203.45.16.64	203.45.16.63	209.45.16.92
203.45.16.96	203.45.16.97	209.45.16.126
203.45.16.128	203.45.16.129	209.45.16.158
203.45.16.160	203.45.16.161	209.45.16.190
203.45.16.192	203.45.16.193	209.45.16.222

Given an address and a subnet mask, what is the host address and what is the network address?   Another aspect of the testing revolves around being able to break down a given IP address into the two components of a network address and a host address. Here is an example.

CJ is working at a computer that has an IP address of 187.26.36.210. The subnet mask is 255.255.240.0. What is the network address and what is host address for this computer?

Actually, this is just reverse engineering of the scenario above. First of all, looking at the address you know it is a Class B address. Class B addresses range from 128 to 191. The default subnet mask for a Class B address is 255.255.0.0. This means that the first 4 bits of the third octet are used for the network address and the last 4 bits of the third octet are used for the host address.

Table 2.15 shows the possible network addresses given this subnet.

TABLE 2.15: Class B Subnet Addresses

128	64	32	16	NETWORK ADDRESS
0	0	0	0	Not allowed, all 0's
0	0	0	1	187.26.16.0
0	0	1	0	187.26.32.0
0	0	1	1	187.26.48.0
0	1	0	0	187.26.64.0
0	1	0	1	187.26.80.0
0	1	1	0	187.26.96.0
0	1	1	1	187.26.112.0
1	0	0	0	187.26.128.0
1	0	0	1	187.26.144.0
1	0	1	0	187.26.160.0
1	0	1	1	187.26.176.0
1	1	0	0	187.26.192.0
1	1	0	1	187.26.208.0
1	1	1	0	187.26.224.0
1	1	1	1	Not allowed, all 1's

If you look at the network address given, you will see it is 187.26 .36.210. Looking at the table, you will see the network address must be 187.26.32.0. If that is the network address it means the host address must be 0.0.4.210.

If you have followed the logic of these examples, you shouldn't have any problems with the subnetting portion of the exam.

Supernetting

Another way of handling IP addressing is called supernetting. *Supernetting* actually steals addresses from the network to apply them to hosts.

Supernetting bypasses the concepts of Class A, Class B, and Class C networks, replacing these concepts with the general term, "network prefix." The routers will work with the network prefix to determine where the network address stops and the host address begins.

An example of a supernet address would be something like 208.95.46.32 with a subnet mask of 255.255.240.0. In this case, the supernet borrowed 4 bits from the network number and applied those bits to the host numbers.

TIP

For testing purposes, it is not necessary to understand the concept of supernetting, but it is wise to know that it exists.

▶ Configure a Windows NT Server computer to function as an IP router.

▶ Install and configure a DHCP relay agent.

One of the main reasons for making TCP/IP the default protocol on an NT Server is because TCP/IP is a routable protocol. NetBIOS helps with computer name resolution; it is easy to install and configure, but it is not routable. That limits the size of the network on which it can be used. Not only is TCP/IP routable, but it is also flexible enough for you to decide how you want it to route. You can create static route tables for security or you can configure a protocol that will update and maintain its route table without any user intervention.

In its simplest form, routers route. A router will route a packet from one location to another until it gets to its destination address. It does not matter if the packet is destined for a server on the other side of the building or the host of a Web page on the other side of the world, a router is what gets the packet from one location to another.

If you are used to working on a small network, you may not think you have a router. If you have access to the Internet from your desktop, you have a router. If your file server has more than one network card in it, you have a router. A router can be a very sophisticated (read expensive) piece of equipment dedicated to the task of routing packets or it can be a file server that has two network cards in it. In either case, it is a router. Microsoft also calls routers *gateways* so the terms are synonymous.

Here is how a router works. When a router receives a packet, the packet is kicked up to the Internet layer and handed off to IP. IP looks at the packet, specifically at the Time To Live (TTL) portion of the packet. The Time To Live is a number that represents the number of routers this packet will be allowed to cross. Each time the packet crosses a router, IP will decrement the TTL, usually by a unit of 1. If the TTL hits zero, it is obvious to the router that this little packet has lost its way and the packet is trashed or discarded. The router also looks at the size of packet. Some routers can handle large packets, others can't. If the router is hooked to other routers that can't handle large packets, the router breaks up the packet into fragments, adds new headers to each fragment, and sets a flag. The new packet also acquires a fragment ID and a fragment offset, all so the packets can be put back together in the right order on the other side.

IP now has to calculate a new checksum for each fragment. After the router has done all this, it checks for the hardware address of the next router and sends the packet on its way to the next step in the journey. The next router follows the same routine.

How does the router know where to send the packet? Each router maintains something called a *route table*. This table contains information on everything the router needs to know to do its job. This table can be updated or changed dynamically or statically. In this case, as in most cases, "dynamically" means the router does all the work and "statically" means *you* do all the work.

How does the router get the packet in the first place? When your computer sends out the packet, the computer checks the destination IP address. The computer is looking to see if the IP address is on the same subnet as your computer; that's why proper addressing is so important! If the destination system is on your subnet, the computer sends the packet directly to the destination. If the destination is not on your subnet, the packet goes to a gateway/router.

Determining Local versus Remote Subnets   When a computer wants to send a packet to another host, it puts the remote host's IP address in the destination address area of the packet. The system must then decide where to send the packet. If the destination address is on the same subnet as the sending host, the packet is sent directly to the receiving computer. However, if the host address is on a different subnet, the packet is automatically forwarded to the subnet's gateway for its trip around the network.

How does the computer determine if the destination address is local or remote? It uses a process called ANDing. This process comes from Boolean logic. ANDing takes the destination address and converts it to binary. It then applies the subnet mask and begins to work its magic to see if the two network addresses work.

ANDing works like this. It compares two numbers, a 0 AND any value is always 0. A 1 AND another 1 is always 1.

Let's take a closer look at how this works. Earlier in this chapter, under the subnetting objective, we worked with a network address for a Class B address. We worked with the address of 187.26.36.210. Let's see how the Boolean ANDing process will determine the network address. Table 2.16 shows how the octets are handled in binary.

Judging from this, the network address that we arrived at in the earlier example matches, so we must be right.

TABLE 2.16: ANDing 187.26.36.210, Subnet of 255.255.240.0

IP ADDRESS/SUBNET	1	2	3	4
187.26.36.210	10111011	00011010	00100100	11010010
255.255.240.0	11111111	11111111	11110000	00000000
Result	10111011	00011010	00100000	00000000
	187	26	32	0

NOTE

Yes, I know, I didn't describe how I converted the IP address to binary. Actually, I used the scientific calculator that is available in Windows. This calculator is available to you during the exam.

Now let's try ANDing another IP address to see if it is on the same subnet. Let's say that the computer at 187.26.36.210 was sending a message to a computer at 187.26.30.16. Judging from the fact both are Class B addresses, it's possible that their hosts could reside on the same subnet. The ANDing process will find out if the target host is on the right network.

Table 2.17 will show the ANDing process for this address, and yes, I am going to use the calculator again!

TABLE 2.17: ANDing 187.26.30.16, Subnet Mask 255.255.240.0

IP Address/Subnet	1	2	3	4
187.26.30.16	10111011	00011010	00011110	00010000
255.255.240.0	11111111	11111111	11110000	00000000
Result	10111011	00011010	00010000	00000000
	187	26	30	0

Through ANDing we have determined that these two computers are on separate subnets. Therefore, the sending computer would send the packet on to the gateway for transport through the network.

NT Server as a Static Router

To be configured as a static router, the NT Server has to have at least two network interface cards (NICs) installed. As you begin to plan the configuration, remember that you have to configure a static router so that its route table contains an entry for the routes to all of the other subnets on your network. A route table entry consists of a destination network address, the subnet mask, and the address of the gateway to reach that network address.

When a static router receives a packet, it has to determine where to forward the packet based on the destination network address. These destination network addresses are found in the route table. The router makes these decisions for the packet:

▶ If the destination network is listed in the route table, and the router is connected directly to that network, the router forwards the packet directly to the host.

▶ If the destination network is listed in the route table, and the router is not directly connected to the network, the router forwards the packet to the router specified in the router table.

▶ If the route table does not have an entry for the destination network, the router gets rid of the packet by forwarding it to the default gateway. The default gateway can handle the problem.

Before you can configure the route table, you have to know how the network is laid out. This is one of those times when you really hope your documentation is up to date.

Planning a Route Table   Figure 2.4 shows a relatively small network with four servers, each with two network cards. Any time a server has more than one network card, it becomes a multihomed computer; it also becomes a router. For the sake of this diagram, don't think of the servers as servers, think of the computers as routers.

Table 2.18 shows how the route table would have to be configured. Each server knows about the networks it is directly connected to without entries having to be made in the route table. This condition accounts for the N/A settings in Table 2.18.

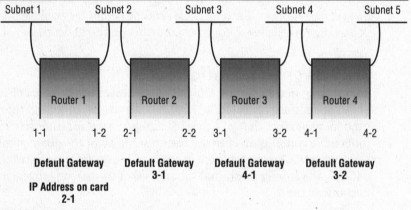

FIGURE 2.4: Design of a small network

TABLE 2.18: Route Table Worksheet

DESTINATION SUBNET	ROUTER 1 TO:	ROUTER 2 TO:	ROUTER 3 TO:	ROUTER 4 TO:
Subnet 1	N/A	Adapter 1-2	Adapter 2-2	Adapter 3-2
Subnet 2	N/A	N/A	Adapter 2-2	Adapter 3-2
Subnet 3	Adapter 2-1	N/A	N/A	Adapter 3-2
Subnet 4	Adapter 2-1	Adapter 3-1	N/A	N/A
Subnet 5	Adapter 2-1	Adapter 3-1	Adapter 4-1	N/A

In the case of the route table worksheet for your company, the adapter number would be replaced by the IP address and subnet mask.

Static Routing Implementation

To utilize your server as a static router, it must have at least two properly configured network cards attached to different network segments or subnets. Each card must have the appropriate IP address and subnet mask, and have IP forwarding enabled from the Routing tab for Microsoft TCP/IP Properties page.

Once that has been accomplished and tested, you can start configuring your route table using the route command. The syntax for the route command is

> **route** [**-f**] [**-p**] [*command* [*destination*] [**MASK** *netmask*] [*gateway*] [**METRIC** *metric*]]

-f clears the route tables of all gateway entries. If this parameter is used in conjunction with a command, the tables are cleared before the command is run.

-p enables persistent routes. (Route table changes are carried over automatically after restarting your computer.)

command can be one of the commands shown in Table 2.19.

TABLE 2.19: Commands Used with the Route Command

COMMAND	PURPOSE
print	Prints a route.
add	Adds a route.
delete	Deletes a route.
change	Modifies an existing route.

destination is the host or network to which you want to route.

MASK specifies that the next parameter be interpreted as the *netmask* parameter.

netmask is the subnet mask value to be associated with this route entry. If not present, this parameter defaults to 255.255.255.255.

gateway is the gateway to the destination.

METRIC specifies that the next parameter be interpreted as the *metric* parameter.

Metric associates a cost/hop count for the destination specified by the route entry. Generally, this specifies the distance in the number of hops from the destination. If not specified, the metric is set to 1 by default.

The gateway must be on the same logical network as your computer. Otherwise, the route will not be added.

Default Gateways   In a TCP/IP configuration, you can add default gateways for each network card. On a computer on which multiple default gateways are defined, all remote network traffic that does not match an entry in the route table is passed over the first default gateway defined. Because one default gateway is used, you should configure only one card to have a default gateway. This reduces confusion and ensures the results you intended. If you add a second gateway to the same network, the entry is added to the route table and is used if the first gateway goes down.

Example of Adding a Static Route   At the command prompt, type the following:

```
route add 199.199.41.0 mask 255.255.255.0 199.199.40.1 metric 2
```

It is important to note that in the sample above, the entry in the route table would be volatile. It would only last until the computer was restarted. If the computer was restarted, the entry would be lost. To make sure the entry is persistent, this would be the command:

```
Route -p add 199.199.41.0 mask 255.255.255.0
199.199.40.1 metric 2
```

Each router would have to be updated with the appropriate routes. Any time that a new router was added to the network, entries would have to be made in the route table of each router. As you can see, deciding to go with a static route table in a large network would be a considerable task and one that would be ongoing.

NT Server with Dynamic Routing

With dynamic routing, the work involved in building and maintaining a route table is eliminated because the routers automatically exchange information about the known routes. Windows NT uses the Routing

Information Protocol for dynamic routing. The only configuration that needs to be done on the host is to point the host to the default gateway, in this case, the network card in the router serving the subnet.

While this may seem like a great solution after imagining the horror of configuring and updating the route tables of 100 different routers, RIP does have some problems. By default, any entry in the route table is given a time-out value of three minutes. If the route is not confirmed every three minutes, it is discarded. If a router goes down, it may be a while (at least three minutes) before anyone knows it.

The biggest problem with RIP in a WAN environment is network traffic. RIP broadcasts the entire contents of its route table to all the other routers on the system, once every 30 seconds. If you have multiple routers and slow WAN links, much of your bandwidth is going to be taken up by RIP broadcasts.

RIP is a service that is installed through the Network icon in Control Panel.

DHCP Relay Agent Installation and Configuration

Earlier in this chapter, DHCP was discussed as a way to dynamically assign IP information to workstations throughout the network. This is a great solution as long as the DHCP server is on the same subnet as the DHCP client. DHCP requests are not routable, so if a client exists on one subnet and the DHCP server resides on another subnet, there has to be some kind of intermediary configured. The intermediary is the DHCP relay agent.

When a client on a subnet that does not contain a DHCP server broadcasts a request for an IP address, the DHCP relay agent gets the request. It forwards the request to the DHCP server on the other subnet. The request to the server contains the address of the client so the DHCP server returns the information back directly to the requesting host.

There is some information that the DHCP relay agent must have. It must have the IP address of the DHCP server so it knows where to forward the requests. The DHCP server must have a scope defined for each subnet that it will service using the relay agent.

In the following sections, we will perform the following tasks using a sample network:

▶ Configure IP forwarding.

▶ Design a static IP route table.

▶ Write the routing commands for each router.

▶ Demonstrate how to configure a DHCP relay agent.

After the static routing has been configured, we will install the Routing Information Protocol (RIP) to provide dynamic routing.

Figure 2.5 below shows the sample network that will be used as part of this section. It consists of three servers, each with two network cards. As you look at the illustration, pay close attention to the IP addresses of each card. Each server has two cards, each card connects to a different subnet, and the addressing scheme reflects this.

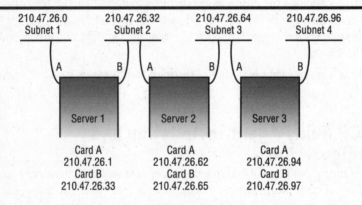

Subnet Mask 255.255.255.224

FIGURE 2.5: Sample network

Configuring IP Forwarding

Each network card in our example must be configured to forward IP packets. To accomplish this, follow these steps:

1. Click Start ➢ Settings ➢ Control Panel.

2. From the Control Panel window, double-click Network.

3. From the Network window, select the Protocols tab ➢ TCP/IP ➢ Properties.

4. From the Microsoft TCP/IP Properties window, click the Routing tab and click in the box, Enable IP forwarding.

5. Click OK to close the Properties window.

6. Click OK to close the Network window.

7. Agree to restart the computer by clicking Yes.

Designing a Static IP Route Table

The next step in the process is to have an idea of what goes where and how it gets there. You may have a complete set of documentation for your network (yes, there truly are networks out in the real world that are completely documented. At last count, there were at least two), or you may just use a sketch. Whatever form your documentation comes in, some is better than none. Table 2.20 is the route table for our sample network. Because each router knows about the networks it is connected to, you do not have to add the information to the route table. These entries are marked with N/A in the table below.

TABLE 2.20: A Routing Worksheet for a Sample Network

DESTINATION SUBNET	ROUTER 1 FORWARDS TO:	ROUTER 2 FORWARDS TO:	ROUTER 3 FORWARDS TO:
Subnet 1 (210.47.26.0)	N/A	210.47.26.33	210.47.26.65
Subnet 2 (210.47.26.32)	N/A	N/A	210.47.26.65
Subnet 3 (210.47.26.64)	210.47.26.62	N/A	N/A
Subnet 4 210.47.26.96	210.47.26.62	210.47.26.94	N/A

Routing Commands for Each Server

When you decide to use the static form of routing, you are faced with several ways you can enter data into the route table. If you use the *route add* command, you can configure all the commands to run in a batch file at start-up; you can add the commands manually each time the server starts back up; or you can enter the commands once, using the –p parameter to enable persistent routes. With persistent routes, the route table will reinitialize on start-up. There are pluses and minuses to each approach, even the approach where you enter all the information manually each time the system starts up. This is usually referred to as job security.

I, on the other hand, work for myself. My job is really secure, I wouldn't have the heart to fire me. I also recognize that I am basically a lazy person. So I have immediately ruled out entering the commands each time the server comes up. That leaves a batch file and the persistent switch. If I have to write a batch file, I still have to type in all the commands, plus save them in a batch file format, put the batch file somewhere that it will start every time the server starts up, and test it. The persistent switch means all I have to do is enter the commands once and if the computer gods smile on me, that should be it, unless someone clears the route table. If someone clears the route table, I believe I could make a strong case for torture. So, I will opt for the persistent method.

On server 1, my commands would be: To get to subnet 3 (210.47.26.64):

route −p add 210.47.26.64 mask 255.255.255.224 gateway 210.47.26.62

   To get to subnet 4 (210.47.26.96):

route −p add 210.47.26.96 mask 255.255.255.224 gateway 210.47.26.62 metric 2

On server 2, my commands would be: To get to subnet 1 (210.47.26.0):

route −p add 210.47.26.0 mask 255.255.255.224 gateway 210.47.26.33

   To get to subnet 4 (210.47.26.96):

route −p add 210.47.26.96 mask 255.255.255.224 gateway 210.47.26.94

On server 3, my commands would be: To get to subnet 2 (210.47.26.32):

route −p add 210.47.26.32 mask 255.255.255.224 gateway 210.47.26.65

   To get to subnet 1 (210.47.26.0):

route −p add 210.47.26.0 mask 255.255.255.224 gateway 210.47.26.65 metric 2

TIP
The metric parameter is added to indicate that the network is another hop or router away.

Installing and Configuring a DHCP Relay Agent

Configuration of the DHCP relay agent is a two-step process. The first step is to install the DHCP Relay Agent service on the NT Server that will act as the agent. The agents can then be configured, using the Microsoft TCP/IP Protocol Properties dialog box with the IP address of the computer running Windows NT Server DHCP, so the agent will know where to forward requests from clients for available IP addresses. Installing the service and configuring the agents are done using the Network icon in the Control Panel.

1. Click Start ➤ Settings ➤ Control Panel.

2. Select Network ➤ Services tab ➤ Add.

3. Under Network Services, click DHCP Relay Agent, then click OK.

4. In the message that appears, type the full path to the Windows NT Server DHCP files and click Continue. The DHCP service is installed.

5. Click Close. Configuration and binding information is checked.

6. You will get an error message as part of unattended setup. It requires a DHCP server IP address be listed. Click Yes to add the server address. This opens the Microsoft TCP/IP Properties window.

7. Click the DHCP Relay tab, click Add, and then type in the address of the DHCP server.

8. Click OK and agree to restart the computer by clicking Yes.

Installing and Configuring Routing Information Protocol

The installation of RIP is done from the same place as the installation of a DHCP relay agent, the Network Services tab.

1. Click Start ➤ Settings ➤ Control Panel.

2. Double-click Network, then click the Services tab and click Add.

3. Under Network Services, select RIP for Internet Protocol, then click OK.

4. Provide a complete path to the NT system files in the dialogue section of the Windows NT Setup window and click Continue.

5. Click Close to shut the Network window and the bindings will be checked.

6. Agree to restart the computer when prompted by clicking Yes.

▶ Install and configure the Microsoft DNS Server service on a Windows NT Server computer.

▶ Integrate DNS with other name servers.

▶ Connect a DNS server to a DNS root server.

▶ Configure DNS server roles.

Talk about simple yet elegant, the Domain Name System or DNS really fits the bill! When the Internet was young and the number of hosts few, systems connected to the Internet relied on a text file to resolve host names to IP addresses. This text file, called the HOSTS file, will be discussed further in the next objective.

As the Internet continued to grow, and it became more and more obvious that some type of system was needed to regulate and locate host names, DNS was born.

DNS is a static, distributed, hierarchical database system of millions of registered, unique domain names. Each domain name needs to be unique within its section of the database. Some of the top-level domain databases commonly used are included in Table 2.21.

TABLE 2.21: Some of the Major Domains

TOP-LEVEL DOMAIN	DESCRIPTION	EXAMPLES
.com	Commercial	Microsoft.com Psconsulting.com Compaq.com
.gov	Governmental	Whitehouse.gov Senate.gov

TABLE 2.21 continued: Some of the Major Domains

TOP-LEVEL DOMAIN	DESCRIPTION	EXAMPLES
.mil	Military	Army.mil Navy.mil
.edu	Education	Umich.edu UMN.edu
.net	Network services	InterNIC.net
.se	Sweden	www.stockholm.se
.au	Australia	www.smh.com.au

The top level of the domain database hierarchy is *<root>*, which is usually represented by a trailing period in the domain name. The trailing period is so common, it's ignored. The Internet is broken down by domain names. Domains are then broken down to the host level by a fully qualified domain name (FQDN). A FQDN starts at the host level and works its way back all the way through the DNS hierarchy, left to right, smallest to biggest. For example, my registered domain name is psconsulting.com. As part of psconsulting.com, I have an NT Server host that is named mail. The FQDN for that server would be mail.psconsulting .com. As long as all the host names within a domain are unique, all FQDNs are unique.

TIP

The InterNIC is also in charge of registering domain names. You can check and see if the domain name you want is already taken by using the WHOIS site at the InterNIC. The URL is http://www.internic.net/cgi-bin/whois. Your ISP can register your name for you. If your network is not connected to the Internet, you can still use DNS, you just don't have to worry about a unique domain name.

At this point in the discussion, I should probably issue a few disclaimers to make sure there is no confusion. There is absolutely no connection between what Microsoft calls a domain and what the InterNIC calls a domain. These are two completely different things. Microsoft calls a grouping of computers in your company a domain. The InterNIC takes a much broader view of things. It groups hosts from multiple companies together by the type of DNS name the company uses. For example, .com would be a domain.

Also, while DNS and WINS serve similar functions, the two should not be confused. WINS resolves NetBIOS computer names and DNS resolves host names. There are some other differences. For example, WINS maintains a single dynamic database while DNS has distributed, static databases. The WINS name space is flat while the DNS name space is hierarchical. WINS operates at your network level. While DNS can be configured to operate at your network level, it was designed to work at the Internet level. When configured to work at the local network level, DNS can also communicate with other DNS servers on the Internet to provide Internet level resolution.

NOTE

Throughout this discussion of DNS you will come across the term BIND. It stands for the UNIX-based Berkeley Internet Name Domain servers that provide name resolution at the Internet level.

Microsoft DNS Server Service on a Windows NT Server Computer

Before you run right out and install DNS, it would probably be a good thing to figure out where you are going to put it and what you are going to have to do with it after you get it installed.

DNS on NT runs as a server service. Therefore, it must run on an NT Server. DNS is also one of those server services that have been patched a couple of times, so it would probably be a good idea to reapply the latest NT Service Pack (SP #3 or greater) as well as any DNS related patches. If you are running NT on an Intel platform, there is at least one additional patch available at Microsoft's post-SP3 FTP site. The URL is `ftp://ftp.microsoft.com/bussys/winnt/winnt-public/fixes/usa/nt40/hotfixes-postsp3/dns-fix`. There were two files in this site; one is for the Alpha installation of NT and the other is for an installation on an Intel server. If you are installing on an Intel system, the filename is dnsfix_i.exe.

After the DNS Server service is installed, you will notice there is another new utility on the Administrative Tools (Common) menu, DNS Manager. You start the configuration of DNS by defining the computer as a DNS server in DNS Manager. Once you have defined the server, you will notice that immediately under the server is the word Cache. See Figure 2.6 below.

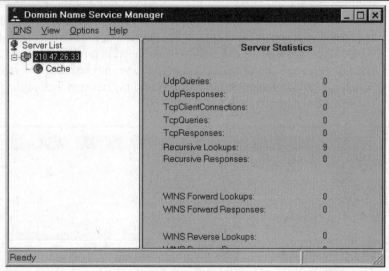

FIGURE 2.6:   Domain Name Service Manager

When you first create a DNS server, it is a caching-only server. As a caching-only server, it will not maintain any of the DNS database, it will just help resolve names by contacting other DNS servers. Does this sound like too much middle management? Not really, because once the names have been resolved, the DNS caching server stores the queries in memory as part of cache. Each entry has a TTL (doesn't everything?). If you want to see the entries in your cache, simply go to the Domain Name Service Manager and click Cache. You will be presented with a listing of all the information stored in memory.

Besides the information that the DNS server has been able to ascertain for itself, it also caches entries in a file called cache.dns. This is just a text file that contains information on where DNS should go to find top-level servers to resolve names to IP addresses. Figure 2.7 shows all the Root servers stored in cache for name resolution.

NOTE

DNS Manager can manage up to 15 servers.

Earlier in this objective, we mentioned that DNS used a static database. That means you or someone like you is the person responsible for adding information to the database. However, before information can be added to the database, you have to tell DNS just what it controls. This is called a DNS Zone. A DNS Zone is the portion of the DNS name space whose database records exist and are managed in a particular zone file. For example, one server may manage the zone that handles the .com, .edu, and .gov name space while a server on my network will manage the psconsulting.com name space.

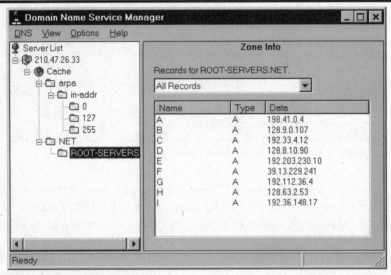

FIGURE 2.7: DNS cache

When you create the first DNS Zone, it will be the Primary Zone. The Primary Zone is where the zone file is stored. The zone file is nothing more than a text file that contains all the records for the zone the DNS server manages. It is usually named after the zone with an extension of .dns. When you enter information into the zone file, you are creating DNS entries for your network. This can be done using any text editor or a graphical utility. In the case of DNS, you can use DNS Manager to add the information called *resource records* to the DNS database.

There are many different types of resource records that can be added to a DNS database. Each record has a type designator assigned to it and each record provides a different service. Table 2.22 provides a summary of some of these records.

TABLE 2.22: DNS Record Types

RECORD TYPE	RECORD NAME	DESCRIPTION
SOA	Start of Authority	The SOA record is always the first record in the database files. This record indicates the server is an "authority" on host names.
NS	Name Server	This record points to another DNS name server. If the local DNS name server cannot resolve the name, it will forward the request to other servers.
A	Address	An A record maps the host name to the IP address.
CNAME	Canonical Name (Alias)	An *alias* is just an alternative name to a host.
PTR	Pointer	This record maps the IP address to the host name. It is the reverse of an A record.
MX Record	Mail Exchanger	An MX record dictates where to send e-mail for any specific domain name.
RP	Responsible Person	If you use the InterNIC's WHOIS utility, you will see that each domain name has a responsible person listed. This is where it gets that information.

After you create the zone, you will notice that several records are added for you. Look at Figure 2.8 and you will see that an SOA record and an NS record were created for my server.

After you have created the zone, your DNS server is fully configured. You can now add records to the database or integrate DNS into the network with other name services.

DNS Integration with Other Name Servers

Actually, this section is misnamed. It should be called, "Integrate DNS with WINS," because that's what it's all about.

WINS and DNS are sort of the same, but sort of different. Both services resolve names to IP addresses, but the types of names and the way the resolution occurs is really different. The databases themselves are also very different.

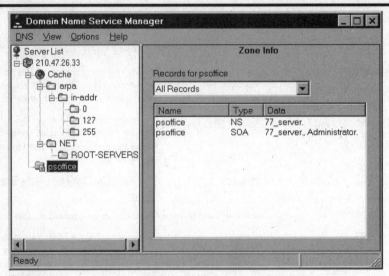

FIGURE 2.8: Domain Name Service Manager with default zone records

DNS works with host names. On a Windows-based machine, by default, the host name is the computer name. On non-Windows machines, such as those UNIX boxes that are popping up all over the place, there is no such thing as a NetBIOS computer name; there is just the host name. Somehow, it has to be possible to meld the best of both worlds.

You can configure a DNS server to use a WINS Server to resolve just the host name portion of the FQDN. Here is how it would work. Suppose the DNS server for psconsulting.com received a request for ntmail.psconsulting.com and the DNS server did not have an entry for the host name, ntmail. At that point, DNS would ask the WINS Server for the IP address of the WINS client, ntmail. If WINS had the client information, it would pass the information back to the DNS server, which would then forward the information to the client.

One of the benefits of configuring DNS and WINS to work together is making DNS appear to be almost dynamic. Because many companies are now relying on DHCP to assign IP addresses, that means host names will change from one IP address to another. In a DNS environment, where the address table is static, this can lead to chaos. Because WINS is a dynamic system, it will help resolve the host name with the current IP address, whether the client is using DHCP or a permanent address.

TIP

The only way DNS and WINS can work together in this manner is if the host name and the NetBIOS computer names are the same throughout the network.

Integrating WINS and DNS is done through the Zone Properties page of the DNS Zone. When completed, the WINS integration creates a WINS resource record in the Primary Zone file. This is a record that cannot be added manually.

DNS Server Connection to a DNS Root Server

Now that a DNS server has been installed, perhaps it's time to look at how these things all work together. Earlier in this section, it was mentioned that the DNS is a distributed database. This is "geek" for there are several databases stored on the Internet that you probably don't know about, nor do you have to. DNS knows about these databases and knows how to find them, that's all that matters.

The structure of the DNS database is very similar to a DOS file system. It starts out at the root and branches out from there. Remember, the root name of this database is a null character or "", but it is designated by a period. Figure 2.9 gives a simplified view of the structure.

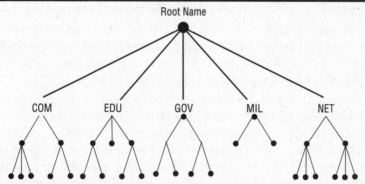

FIGURE 2.9:   Representation of the DNS database system

In the DNS system, each root of the domain (for instance the part of the database that handles the commercial or .com domains) is divided into subdomains. Each domain and subdomain has a domain name that shows the position in the domain database. So, for example, psconsulting is my domain name, which resides in the .com database.

Because I now have my "own" domain name, I can divide it up further if I so choose. I may name part of my domain .corp so references to that section of the DNS tree would be corp.psconsulting.com.

In addition to all these domain names, remember that each host has a unique name on the Internet. I may configure a server to handle all my incoming and outgoing Internet mail, so I will call the server something really creative like mail.corp.psconsulting.com. In the course of daily events, you decide to send me an e-mail message. While we are not even going to start getting into the inner workings of e-mail, let's just say your computer wants to send a packet to mail.corp.psconsulting.com. As soon as your computer decides to send that packet, it becomes a *resolver*.

A resolver runs on the client that needs information. It doesn't really know how to find the information, but it does have a starting point. When TCP/IP was configured for that client, someone gave it at least one IP address of a DNS server. The resolver simply asks the DNS server if it knows the location of the host, mail.corp.psconsulting.com. The DNS name server may not know where this system is located, but it knows where the root name server resides, so it queries the root name server. The root name server provides the IP address of the domain root server in question, in this case the root server for the .com domain. The root server for the .com domain knows where psconsulting is, so it refers the request to psconsulting. Psconsulting knows where corp is, so it refers the request to corp, which finally resolves the request to the mail host.

This system works really well in the world of the Internet and it can also work well for an intranet, even if it is not hooked up to the outside world. When you design your DNS system, you must make sure your DNS servers know about each other. How do you do that?

Actually, that part is a no-brainer. If you remember, earlier in this section when the DNS server was installed, the file cache.dns was discussed. This file comes complete with all the root server's IP addresses already installed. If your DNS server is connected to the Internet, it should be able to help resolve DNS names with the information provided on installation.

What about if your network is not connected to the Internet and you still want to use DNS? How can you link one server to another? In Domain Manager, you start by creating a new host in your primary zone. To do this, you will need the host name of the DNS server that will be asked for help and its IP address. Once the host has been created, create a resource record of type NS pointing to the new DNS host. Then, when your DNS server has a problem resolving names, it will look to the other DNS server for help.

DNS Server Roles

When DNS is originally installed, it is installed as a caching-only computer. When configured as part of a zone, computers can take on different server roles.

Primary Name Server   The primary name server gets all of its zone data from local files. Any changes to a zone are done at the primary name server level.

Secondary Name Server   A secondary name server gets its information from another name server across the network. This provides for DNS redundancy. If you position the servers carefully, you can also speed up DNS access for remote locations and reduce the load on the primary name server.

Master Name Server   A secondary name server must receive its information from another name server. The information source can be a primary name server or a secondary name server. When you designate a source name server, that server becomes the master name server for the receiving secondary name server.

When a secondary name server starts up, it contacts the master name server and initiates a zone transfer of information for that server.

Installing and Configuring the Microsoft DNS Server Service on a Windows NT Server Computer

To install the DNS Server service, follow these procedures:

1. Select Start ➤ Settings ➤ Control Panel.

2. Double-click Network, then click the Services tab and click Add.

3. Choose Microsoft DNS Server from the Select Network Services window. Click OK.

4. If prompted, provide a complete path to the setup files in the dialogue window of the Windows NT setup screen and ➤ click Continue.

5. Click Close to exit the Network window and begin the check of the bindings.

6. Agree to shut down and restart the computer when prompted by clicking Yes.

To reapply Service Pack 3 to patch DNS Server service, follow these procedures:

1. Locate where the file NT4sp3_I is stored and click the file name to begin the extraction and installation process.

NOTE

The filename may change. This was the latest NT 4.0 Service Pack at the time this book was written.

2. From the Welcome screen, click Next to install the Service Pack.

3. Click Yes to agree to the license and this will take you to the Service Pack Setup menu.

4. Make sure the radio button that will allow you to install the Service Pack is selected. Click Next.

5. Choose whether you want to create an uninstall directory or not, then ➤ click Next.

6. Click Finish to complete the installation.

7. After the Service Pack setup is complete, you will be prompted to restart the computer. Click OK.

To install the DNS Service Pack, follow these steps:

1. Browse to the location where you stored the file dnsfix_i.exe.

2. Double-click the file to install the patch.

3. Remove any diskettes from the drive and click OK to restart your computer.

Once the DNS Server service has been installed, you must define a new server. To define a new DNS server, follow these steps:

1. Click Start ➤ Programs ➤ Administrative Tools (Common) ➤ click DNS Manager.

2. From the Domain Name Service Manager, click DNS ➤ New Server.

3. Enter the name or IP address of the new DNS server.

Before you can enter records into the DNS database, you must also configure a DNS Zone. To create the Primary DNS Zone, follow these procedures:

1. Click Start ➢ Programs ➢ Administrative Tools (Common), then click DNS Manager.

2. From the Domain Name Service Manager, click DNS.

3. Click New Zone. This will open a dialogue window called Creating new zone for IP Address.

4. Choose whether this zone will be a Primary or Secondary Zone type by clicking the radio button next to Primary. Click next.

5. Enter in the zone name. Notice that the zone name is the default name for the zone file. Click Next after entering the name.

6. Click Finish to create the new zone.

Integrating DNS with Other Name Servers

To integrate DNS with WINS, follow these steps:

1. Click Start ➢ Programs ➢ Administrative Tools (Common) ➢ DNS Manager.

2. Click the server that houses the Primary Zone.

3. Highlight the zone name ➢ right mouse button ➢ Properties.

4. Click the WINS Lookup tab.

5. Fill the check box next to Use WINS Resolution and add the IP address of the WINS server.

6. There is another check box available, Settings only affect local server. If this box is not checked, all secondary servers will use the WINS server as well. If any secondary DNS servers are non-Windows servers, this box should be checked.

NOTE

NetBIOS names and host names must be the same throughout the network.

Connecting a DNS Server to a DNS Root Server

When DNS is installed, the addresses of all the DNS root servers are placed in the cache.dns file. If your DNS server is connected to the Internet, the system will take care of the rest.

Configuring DNS Server Roles

The primary name server was created as part of the integration process with other name services. To create a secondary name server, follow these steps:

1. Click Start ➢ Programs ➢ Administrative Tools (Common) ➢ DNS Manager.

2. Highlight the name of the primary domain and click with the right mouse button. Select Properties to bring up the Zone Properties window.

3. Click the Notify tab.

4. Add in the IP address of the secondary server in the dialog box and click Add. Notice that you can add more than one system to the Notify list. This allows the server to service more than one secondary server.

5. Clicking the box, Only Allow Access From Secondaries Included on Notify List, means that only DNS servers on the notify list can replicate this Zone file.

6. Click OK to close Zone Properties and close Domain Name Service Manager.

Configure HOSTS and LMHOSTS files.

Throughout this section, the HOSTS and LMHOSTS files have been mentioned over and over. Just to do a high-level overview, when you think of HOSTS, think of resolving the UNIX or non-Windows–based host names to an IP address. When you think of LMHOSTS, think of manually resolving WINS computer names to IP addresses.

While we have cleared up some of the mysteries of TCP/IP addressing, there seems to be much discussion about these computer names or host names. UNIX host names were put in place to simplify the life of the end user. It is much easier to remember a host named microsoft.com than it is to remember the appropriate IP address.

HOSTS File Configuration

Host names are much more convenient to use than IP addresses, but somehow that host name needs to be resolved to the appropriate IP address. We have already discussed one method of host-to-address resolution in the section on Domain Name System or DNS. Like most things in computing, there is more than one way to approach any task.

The HOSTS file is a simple text file that sits on the local machine. It contains line after line of entries mapping IP addresses to host names. If DNS does the same thing, what is the advantage of a HOSTS file? In a word, speed. The name to address resolution process on your average UNIX computer starts out with the computer checking to see if the requested host name is the host name of the local computer. Kind of a "Check to see if it's me first" kind of thing. If the computer is not requesting local resources, it checks the local HOSTS file to see if the information is there. If the information is not in the HOSTS file, the system then starts the DNS process.

How to Be a Good HOSTS File   The HOSTS file is very similar to the LMHOSTS file in many ways. It is created using any text editor. It is saved in the %systemroot%\ system32\drivers\etc subdirectory with a file name of HOSTS and no extension. The syntax for each entry is

```
IP address <tab> Host Name <tab> Alias Names <tab> #Comment
```

Alias names are alternate names assigned to any host, so they are optional. Comments are also optional.

These are the rules of the HOSTS file:

- ▶ Case doesn't matter, the entries can be all uppercase, all lowercase, or any combination of the two.

- ▶ Each entry can contain up to 255 characters.

- ▶ HOSTS files are parsed (read) from the top down. Put the hosts you will use the most toward the top of the file.

- ▶ HOSTS files do not support any of the tags that the LMHOSTS file uses. The only special characters you can use are the # (pound sign) or the ; (semicolon) to signal a comment.

- ▶ LOCALHOST is an entry created by default; it must be in each HOSTS file.

- ▶ If you create a HOSTS file using WordPad or Notepad, you will probably have to go in and rename the file after you save it.

WordPad and Notepad have a bad habit of adding unwanted extensions to file names.

▶ The HOSTS file must be created in the %systemroot%\ system32\drivers\etc folder.

▶ Because the HOSTS file does not use the #INCLUDE statement like the LMHOSTS file, it is difficult to have a central copy of the file. Users would have to copy the central file down to the workstation every time there was a change and any local entries would be lost.

Troubleshooting a HOSTS File   After you create a HOSTS file, if you have problems, the easiest way of troubleshooting is to look in a mirror. Sorry, but because this is a manually configured file, the only way something can go wrong is if the carbon-unit interface between the chair and the keyboard screws it up. Of course, this makes it somewhat simpler to troubleshoot because you will be intimately familiar with the ways you manage to make those little typos. You know, if it weren't for a spelling checker and a great editor, every time you saw the word "receive" in this book, it would be spelled wrong!

Common things to check:

▶ Is the host name spelled right?

▶ Is the IP address correct?

▶ Is the file named HOSTS? Does it have an extension? (Hint: Type the DIR command at the command line to check. Explorer doesn't show extensions unless asked!)

▶ Is the HOSTS file stored in the right place?

▶ Is the HOSTS file in the right format? Word is a great tool, but not for creating text files. This is why the computer gods created the Edit command.

▶ Do you have duplicate entries in the file?

▶ Is the LOCALHOST listing there?

LMHOSTS File Configuration

An LMHOSTS file has all the charm of a HOSTS file, but it also has an attitude. With an LMHOSTS file, you are resolving NetBIOS computer names to IP addresses rather than host names with the HOSTS file. The

LMHOSTS file is parsed from top to bottom, just like the HOSTS file. The LMHOSTS file is maintained using a text editor, just like the HOSTS file. The LMHOSTS file is saved in the %systemroot%\system32\drivers\ etc directory and should be saved without an extension. The LMHOSTS file does have some special tags that can be embedded to provide advanced functions.

This is the syntax of the LMHOSTS file:

```
IP_address<tab>computer_name<tab>#PRE<tab>#DOM:Domain_
name<tab>#Comments
```

In the LMHOSTS file the pound sign (#) does double duty. It not only serves as a flag that a special tag is coming, but also as a mark that a comment will follow. Only the IP address and the computer name are required.

How to Be a Good LMHOSTS File   The LMHOSTS file can be tweaked to a greater extent than the HOSTS file. For example, let's look at the use of the #PRE tag. Normally, when the system gets a request for name resolution, the first place it will check in the operating system will be memory. If it does not find the information in name cache, the operating system will then parse the LMHOSTS file line by line until it comes to the right computer name.

When the computer first comes up, the operating system checks the LMHOSTS file. When the #PRE tag is found during start-up, the system immediately loads the entry into name cache. Name cache is always better than the LMHOSTS file because the response from memory is always quicker.

You can also share an LMHOSTS file. This definitely simplifies management. Instead of having to maintain several hundred LMHOSTS files, you can create a corporate standard to roll out to all the desktops on installation and then include the commands necessary to refer to a file in a central location. Any changes just have to be made to the shared file and everyone gets the benefit.

The tags and their meanings are covered in Table 2.23.

TABLE 2.23: LMHOSTS File Tags

Keyword	Meaning
#PRE	This keyword is added after an entry so the information will be pre-loaded into name cache. #PRE must be appended for any entries also appearing in the #INCLUDE statements. If #PRE is not present, the #INCLUDE statement will be ignored.

TABLE 2.23 continued: LMHOSTS File Tags

KEYWORD	MEANING
#DOM:*domain*	This keyword is put in after an entry to refer to a group name for the domain. This keyword impacts how the Browser and Logon services work. The #DOM entry must be proceeded by #PRE.
#INCLUDE *filename*	This keyword causes the system to go out and look for a file that may not reside on the host computer. Once this file is located, it will be treated as if it were local. A UNC mapping to the server must be provided before the #INCLUDE section and the #INCLUDE section must be proceeded by #PRE.
#BEGIN-ALTERNATE	This keyword starts a section of multiple #INCLUDE statements. It provides for fault tolerance.
#END-ALTERNATE	This keyword ends a section of multiple #INCLUDE statements. It provides for fault tolerance.

What happens if the server that hosts the shared file is not available? LMHOSTS files also have the ability to provide for fault tolerance. If the primary server that hosts the shared file is not available, the system will look to the tags between #BEGIN-ALTERNATE and #END-ALTERNATE.

The computers that host the master LMHOSTS file need to have the registry edited. The registry parameter, HKEY_LOCAL_MACHINE\ SYSTEM\CurrentControlSet\Services\LanmanServer\Parameters\ NullSessionShares, needs to be edited with the name of the share to which you want to grant null logon privileges. After this has been done, other Windows NT machines can access the LMHOSTS file without authenticating to the computer.

Troubleshooting an LMHOSTS File   Once again, when troubleshooting an LMHOSTS file problem, remember the adage "To err is human." I have also heard that adding a computer changes the adage to a physical law, kind of like gravity, but I have never been able to prove that. Basic troubleshooting skills involve checking the following items:

- Is the computer name spelled right?

- Is the IP address correct?

- Is the file named correctly? It is LMHOSTS without an extension. It is saved in the %systemroot%\system32\drivers\etc directory.

▶ Are the #PRE and #DOM tags entered correctly? All tags must be entered in capital letters.

▶ If you cannot access the LMHOSTS file on a remote machine, has its registry been properly updated?

▶ Is the UNC path in the #INCLUDE statement correct?

▶ Are there duplicate entries?

If you have made it this far in the MCSE track, you can probably handle firing up the Edit command, so I will just show you samples of the HOSTS file and the LMHOSTS file.

Sample of the HOSTS File

```
'#      Host file for portable PC
#       Manually configured IP address 210.47.26.34


127.0.0.1              localhost
210.47.26.50           bobbi
207.46.130.16          microsoft
137.65.2.9             novell
192.9.9.100  sun
## end of file
```

Sample of an LMHOSTS File

```
#LMHOSTS file for PSCONSULTING. Created 4/16/98
210.47.26.50 Bobbi
210.47.26.51 Cris
210.47.26.52 Denise
210.47.26.53 Brandice
210.47.26.54 CJ
210.47.26.55 PSCONSULT     #PRE   #DOM:PSDOM
210.47.26.56 PSService     #PRE
#BEGIN_ALTERNATE
#INCLUDE \\PSCONSULT\SYSTEM32\DRIVERS\ETC\LMHOSTS
#INCLUDE \\PSSERVICE\SYSTEM32\DRIVERS\ETC\LMHOSTS
#END_ALTERNATE
```

▶ Configure a Windows NT Server computer to support TCP/IP printing.

There are printers and then there are PRINTERS. There are the printers that can be hooked directly to a PC and do a pretty nice job of printing your average letter, and then there are printers that hook directly into the network and can do everything but start the morning coffee.

When you start talking about printing in a TCP/IP environment, you can have only so many kinds of printers. You can have a printer that is hooked directly into the network and comes complete with its own IP address. You can have a printer hooked to a UNIX-based host that needs to be shared with computers running Windows NT, and you can have printers hooked to an NT-based system that the UNIX folks want to access.

Three different printing choices offer three different ways to configure the printer. Three different configuration options offer three different utilities. First, for the UNIX user who wants to access a printer on the NT network, you would have the LPDSVC utility. For the Windows NT system that needs to use the printer attached to the UNIX computer, there is the LPRMON utility. Finally, there is the Add Printer Wizard for that printer, which is hooked directly to the network.

NOTE

You will be seeing the terms LPD and LPR in the discussion of UNIX printing. LPD is the Line Printer Daemon, or software piece that makes the TCP/IP printer shareable. LPR is the Line Printer utility that sends information to the printer.

To support TCP/IP printing, the Microsoft TCP/IP printing service must first be installed and the TCP/IP print server has to be started. Beware, some of the management of the print server has to be done through the registry.

Once the print server is up, the TCP/IP printers need to be configured. This is done through the Add Printer Wizard, just as you would configure any other printer. Well, almost like any other printer, with the exception of the printer port; here you have to configure an LPR port.

Accessing Printers with an IP Address

NT can use the Add Printer Wizard to install or connect to a TCP/IP printer that is either hooked directly to the network or connected directly to an NT Server. To attach to a printer hooked to a UNIX host, the LPR command-line utility will allow users to print to the printer. The LPQ utility can be used to view the status of jobs.

LRP and LPQ can both be used to print to printers running on Windows NT.

Installing Microsoft TCP/IP Printing

The first step involved in making printers available to workstations using TCP/IP is to add the TCP/IP Print Service to the NT Server.

To install TCP/IP printing, follow these steps:

1. Click Start ➤ Settings ➤ Control Panel.

2. Double-click Network to open the Network window.

3. From the Network window, click the Services tab.

4. Click Add.

5. From the Select Network Service window, highlight Microsoft TCP/IP Printing and click OK.

6. Provide the path to the Windows NT Setup files and click Continue.

7. Windows NT will copy some files and add the service. Click Close to shut the Network dialog box, and agree to shutting down and restarting the computer by clicking Yes.

Configuring the TCP/IP Print Server to Start Automatically

In order for TCP/IP print services to be available every time the NT Server restarts, the TCP/IP Print Server has to be configured to start automatically. To do this, follow these steps:

1. Click Start ➤ Settings ➤ Control Panel.

2. Double-click Services to open the Services window.

3. Scroll down through the Service window until you see TCP/IP Print Server. By default, the Print Server requires a manual start.

4. With TCP/IP Print Server highlighted, click Startup.

5. In the Startup Type box, click the Automatic radio button and click OK.

6. Click Close to shut the Services window.

7. Restart the system to test the results.

Some TCP/IP parameters can be configured from the registry. The settings, located in the HKEY_LOCAL_MACHINE\SYSTEM\CurrentControlSet\Services\LPDSVC\Parameters, include settings such as the AllowJobRemoval setting that will allow a user using the LPR command to remove a print job from the printer. The AllowPrintResume lets a user send the resume printer command to the Print Server and finally, the MaxConcurrentUsers parameter sets the maximum number of users that can connect to the printer at any one time.

Now that the print server has started, all that is left is to configure the printer and then attach to it.

Configuring a TCP/IP Printer

To create a TCP/IP-based printer, start the Add Printer Wizard.

1. Click Start ➢ Settings ➢ Control Panel.

2. Double-click Printers to open the Printers window.

3. From the Printers window, double-click Add Printer.

4. Verify that My Computer is checked and click Next.

5. In the Add Printer Wizard box, click Add Port. This will bring up the Printer Ports window.

6. Check to make sure LPR Port is highlighted and click New Port.

7. Add Name or address of the server providing lpd:. This should be a host name or an IP address. Then add the Name of the printer or printer queue on that server. Click OK to continue.

8. Click close to shut the New Port window, bringing you back to the Available ports window of the Add Printer Wizard. Make sure the port you just added is checked and click Next.

9. From the Manufacturers window, choose the Manufacturer of your printer. From the Printers window, highlight the model of your printer and click Next.

10. Type in the Printers Name and click Next. This will bring up the window to share the printer. Click Shared, accept the default shared name, and click Next.

11. If you would like to print a test page, now is the time to do it. Make your choice and click Finish.

Printing to TCP/IP-Based Printers

The Add Printer Wizard can be used to access a TCP/IP-based printer or connect to a printer configured with NT. Users can use the LPR utility to print to printers on a UNIX host and the LPQ utility to check the status of print jobs on a UNIX host.

This is the syntax of the LPR command-line utility:

lpr –S *ipaddress* –P *printername* –o 1 filename

The options for the lpr command are case sensitive. The –S *ipaddress* is the IP address of the server, the –P is the name of the print queue, and the –o 1 indicates the type of file, if the file is not a text file. In this case the 1 sends a binary file.

The LPQ utility displays the state of the remote print queue. This is the syntax for the LPQ command-line utility:

lpq –S*servername* –P*printer* –l

–l is for verbose output.

In place of the Server name or printer name, you can substitute the IP address.

▶ Configure SNMP.

One of the really powerful aspects of TCP/IP is the inclusion of SNMP (Simple Network Management Protocol). It is designed to help the network manager be proactive rather than reactive. It helps to show you areas of concern or bottlenecks in your network.

SNMP is made up of two pieces, an SNMP manager and an SNMP agent. It is up to the SNMP manager to request information from an SNMP agent and it is up to the agent to send the information directly to the SNMP manager. Windows NT comes complete with the SNMP agent piece of the puzzle. For the management piece, you will have to look at something such as Microsoft's System Management Server, HP's Open-View, or Intel's LanDesk Manager.

SNMP Basics

SNMP managers get information from SNMP agents using three types of calls or commands. The first is the get operation. In this case the SNMP manager can request or get specific information from the SNMP agent. An example of a get call would be a command sent to a router to get the latest number of TCP/IP packets routed in the last ten minutes.

The next call is the get-next operation. This procedure does exactly what the name implies. I have set up a prescribed number of values that an agent will keep. My SNMP manager will send out a get call to receive the first value and get-next calls to go through the rest of the list. The final operation is a set call. In this case, the SNMP manager can set a parameter for a particular agent. An example of this would be to reset the number of packets routed over a set period of time to 0.

SNMP Communities

Given the information in SNMP basics, you have an SNMP manager asking all these SNMP agents for information about the network. What is to stop an SNMP manager from another network querying your agents and getting information about the network? In some cases, not much.

One way to combat that problem is by creating SNMP communities. In a community, an SNMP agent can only send information to the SNMP manager in the same community. For the sake of diversity, an SNMP agent can be a member of more than one community. By default, SNMP agents belong to the community, public.

MIBs

SNMP agents collect statistics on a set of defined objects. These objects are defined in Management Information Bases, or MIBs. Several types of MIBs are defined, including the Internet MIB II, which defines over 150 objects that are essential to analyze the health and well-being of a computer network. The Microsoft SNMP agents also support the LAN Manager MIB II. This MIB supports 90 different objects including statistics, shares, session information, user information, and logon information. The DHCP MIB monitors DHCP activity and the WINS MIB monitors WINS activity.

MIB objects are organized in a tree similar to the Windows NT registry. Each object has a unique name that consists of its location in the tree and the object name. The InterNIC handles the assignment. Individual organizations can apply for authority over their part of the name space. This means they can design MIBs especially for their products.

How Does SNMP Work?

How does an SNMP manager get information from an SNMP agent?

1. The SNMP manager starts out by sending a request to the SNMP agent by using either the agent's host name or its IP address. The request is either a get, get-next, or set packet for information on an object or a set of objects. Because there is some security in place, the request must also have the SNMP manager's community name.

2. The agent receives the manager's request. It checks the community name to make sure that it is valid and then checks the source SNMP manager's host name or IP address. The agent is *very* particular; it will only accept requests from authorized managers.

3. The agent passes the request off to the DLL (dynamic link library) based on the information requested. If the request is for information from the Internet MIB II object, it will be directed to the TCP.DLL. When the DLL returns the information, the SNMP agent sends it back to the SNMP manager.

Even if you do not have an SNMP manager, it might be a good idea to install the SNMP agent. Performance Monitor uses the SNMP agent to monitor TCP/IP statistics.

NOTE

There is also a quasi-SNMP manager provided with the Windows NT Resource Kit. It's called SNMPUTIL.

Installing SNMP

To install SNMP on a computer, follow these steps:

1. Click Start ➤ Settings ➤ Control Panel.

2. Double-click Network to open the Network window.

3. From the Network window, click the Services tab. Click Add.

4. Scroll down through the Network Service screen until you can highlight SNMP Service. Once it has been highlighted, click OK.

5. Provide the path to set up files and click Continue.

6. At this point, the Microsoft SNMP Properties Agent screen will be brought up.

7. The Contact and Location information shown above are optional and for informational use only. The Services include the following:

   ▶ **Physical:** This option is selected if the agent manages a physical device, such as a concentrator or repeater.

   ▶ **Applications:** This option would be selected if the SNMP agent uses any TCP/IP applications. This selection should always be checked.

   ▶ **Datalink/Subnetwork:** This option should be selected if the agent manages a bridge.

   ▶ **Internet:** Select this option if the agent manages an IP router or gateway.

   ▶ **End-to-End:** Select this option if the agent functions as an IP host.

8. Errors that occur with the SNMP Service will be logged automatically and can be viewed in the System Log in the Event Viewer.

WARNING

After installing SNMP services, it is very important that you reapply the latest Service Pack patches. Several older files are copied during the SNMP installation.

9. After configuring the SNMP Agent screen, you can click the Traps tab.

10. Traps may or may not be required. If you enter and add a community name, it will be sent with the trap message. You must then define a management system for the community you defined. The default community name is public. Trap destinations are the IP address of the SNMP manager.

11. Clicking the Security tab will bring up the following window.

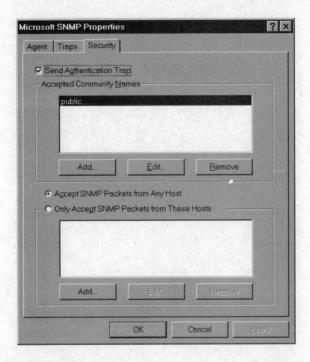

12. When you check Send Authentication Trap, it allows the SNMP agent to send a failed request trap to the SNMP manager when it gets a request for information from an unknown host or manager.

13. Accepted Community Names are the communities the agent belongs to. An agent can belong to multiple communities. Clicking the Add button will allow you to define different communities. Public is the default.

14. Checking the box Accept SNMP Packets from Any Host allows the Agent to accept a request from any SNMP manager in its community.

15. Only Accept SNMP Packets from These Hosts specifies which managers can request information from the agent. To add a manager, click the Add button and provide the IP host or IPX address in the Security Configuration window. Click Add to close the window.

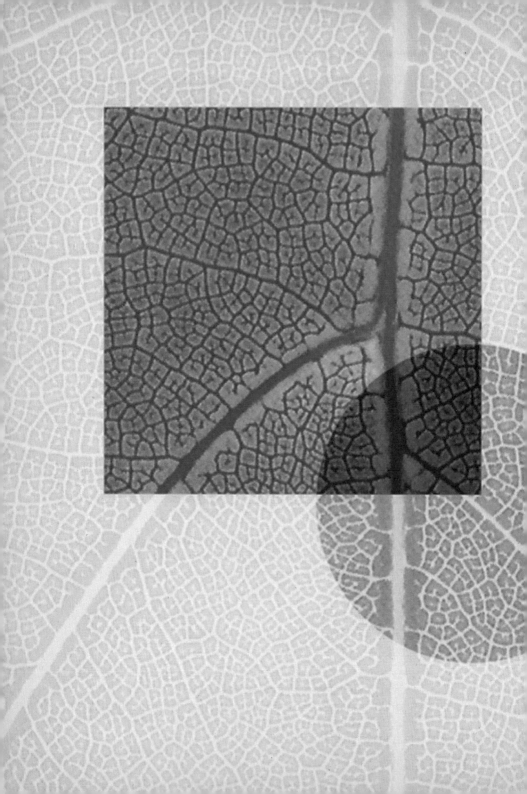

Chapter 3

CONNECTIVITY

This chapter could be subtitled, "What If?" That is what connectivity is all about, isn't it? Consider the following scenarios:

- What if you needed to access resources from a UNIX host and could not do it through "normal" channels?

- What if your network suddenly had an outbreak of laptop computers or work-at-home employees who needed to dial in and access the network?

- What if your network was so big that it spanned the continent and you had domains everywhere; would it still be possible to access resources from one end of the network to another? What if your users needed to use stuff that was on that network, but not readily available? Would you be able to provide them with the access they needed?

Adapted from *MCSE Exam Notes: TCP/IP for NT Server 4* by Gary Govanus

ISBN 0-7821-2307-4   352 pages $19.99

While the information in this chapter is not covered as extensively as the information in Chapter 2, "Installation and Configuration," it is still covered thoroughly. Be especially aware of knowing when to use each of the utilities. Because some of this section is based on the "scenario" concept, I will show where each utility can be used to its best advantage.

▶ Given a scenario, identify which utility to use to connect to a TCP/IP-based UNIX host.

If you are trying to communicate with a UNIX host, there are several ways you can access resources. FTP (File Transfer Protocol), TFTP (Trivial File Transfer Protocol), and RCP (Remote Copy) will allow you to transfer (copy) files between hosts, and Telnet will let you take over a host and establish a terminal session. Command-line utilities, such as REXEC (Remote Execution), will let you remotely execute programs with a semblance of security. RSH (Remote Shell) will let you start processes on remote hosts without having to worry about security. Finally, there are some utilities, such as your favorite browser and HTTP (Hypertext Transfer Protocol), that you probably use so often you don't even think about them using part of the TCP/IP suite. There are even some printer utilities, such as LPR (Line Printer) and LPQ (Line Printer Queue). These various types of utilities will be discussed later in this chapter.

REXEC, RSH, and Telnet utilities allow a user to take over another host and execute applications. For the sake of simplicity, let's call these the execution utilities.

Execution Utilities

When you operate in the UNIX world, security can sometimes be unreliable. UNIX was originally written as an open standard, making it easy to share information. All of the source code for the original operating system was put out on the Internet and anyone who wanted to make a change was free to do so. If there was something about the UNIX version you were using that you didn't like, all you had to do was change it. This was especially appealing when it came to utilities. If you wanted a utility, you simply wrote it or rewrote a current utility to increase the functionality. This led to some really interesting utilities—for example, Vi, which is used to edit files.

Given the open history of UNIX, and the fact that the source code is floating around, securing a UNIX network is a challenge that should not be accepted by the faint of heart. Some of the utilities included with Microsoft TCP/IP have this attitude: basically, let anyone do whatever they want. Others provide for some minor security and even then it is not much. In the case of the execution utilities, REXEC has a security piece, RSH doesn't, and Telnet requires an account. Each of these is discussed below.

Remote Execution (REXEC)   REXEC will run a process on a remote system that is equipped with the REXEC server service. REXEC is password protected so the request for the process will not be handled until the password is verified. If you are familiar with NetWare, this would be similar to the RCONSOLE command. Using RCONSOLE, you can sit at a workstation anywhere on the network, and take over the file server console. You can issue commands that will be run on the server, use any utilities that must be run on the server, and edit files on the server. This is done using a secure password protected connection.

An example of REXEC is shown in Figure 3.1.

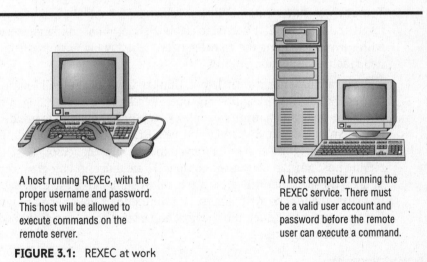

A host running REXEC, with the proper username and password. This host will be allowed to execute commands on the remote server.

A host computer running the REXEC service. There must be a valid user account and password before the remote user can execute a command.

FIGURE 3.1:   REXEC at work

Remote Shell (RSH)   The Remote Shell utility lets a user issue a command to a remote host without logging onto that host. While the system does not require a password, it does require a designated username to exist in the .rhosts file on a UNIX host running the RSH daemon. This command is usually used to execute a program compiler.

An example of RSH is shown in Figure 3.2.

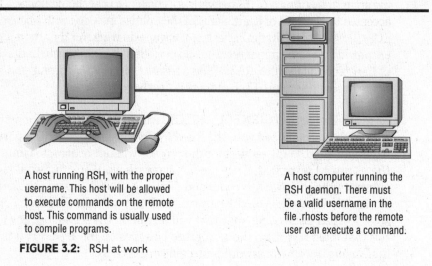

A host running RSH, with the proper username. This host will be allowed to execute commands on the remote host. This command is usually used to compile programs.

A host computer running the RSH daemon. There must be a valid username in the file .rhosts before the remote user can execute a command.

FIGURE 3.2: RSH at work

Telnet   Of the execution utilities, Telnet is probably the best recognized and most used. It is used to establish a terminal emulation session with a system running the Telnet service. Telnet, which requires a dependable connection, utilizes TCP.

If you are unfamiliar with Telnet, think of any tool that will let you take over another workstation and operate it like you were sitting at the remote keyboard. There are a couple of examples that jump to mind, such as PC Anywhere from Symantec and even RCONSOLE from Novell. Just like these two utilities, in order for you to take over the remote host, the remote host must know you are coming. There must be a program running on the host that will allow you to take command of the processor. In this case, the remote system must be running the Telnet Server program. If it does, you can Telnet into the host and execute commands that will run on that computer.

TIP

The Microsoft Windows NT installation CD does not provide for the Telnet Server program. If you check the NT Resource Kit CD, you will find it provides Telnet Server software.

If TCP/IP is installed on the NT computer, the computer has the capabilities of running Telnet. To establish a Telnet session, use the TELNET command with the IP address or host name. Security is provided by having a username and password identical to those used when logging onto the remote system directly. Figure 3.3 shows how you may use Telnet.

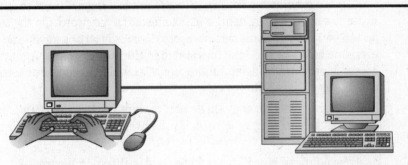

A host running TELNET, with the proper username and password. Host can use a variety of terminal emulations including VT100, VT 52, or TTY. Telnet can be used to connect to libraries to access card catalogs. You can even TELNET into the InterNIC and access the DNS lookup information from the menu options. The command would be TELNET internic.net.

A host computer running the TELNET. There must be a valid username and password created before the remote user can establish a session. Once the user establishes a session, it is as if the user is sitting at this machine. Many hosts will offer menu-driven options to allow users to access information or even place orders.

FIGURE 3.3: Working with Telnet

For the execution utilities portion of the exam, the scenarios may include viewing a document stored on a UNIX computer. In this scenario, look at the utilities presented carefully, but the choice would usually be Telnet. Because Telnet is a TCP/IP utility, your host would use DNS or a HOSTS file to resolve host names. That may also have a bearing on the way you answer the question.

File Transfer Utilities

When it comes to choosing a file transfer utility, you must be aware of the strengths and weakness of each one. Some of these utilities provide more security than others. Some also come with more overhead than others. The utilities that we will be looking at include FTP, TFTP, and RCP.

File Transfer Protocol (FTP)   As is the case in most of the utilities we will be discussing, FTP is a two-sided process. Before you can FTP to a server and download files, the server must be running some kind of FTP server. FTP operates over TCP. TCP, if you remember, is the connection-oriented part of the TCP/IP suite and that brings with it extra overhead, but a more secure transmission.

FTP is a remarkably flexible process. You can require users to authenticate to certain folders using a username and a password. On the same server, you can allow anonymous access, basically letting anyone and everyone have access to the files stored in the public folders. Anonymous access is provided by using "anonymous" as a username and an e-mail address as a password.

FTP can be used to copy single files or multiple files. You can either download files to your system, or, if you have the rights, upload files to the remote host.

An example of how FTP would be used is shown in Figure 3.4.

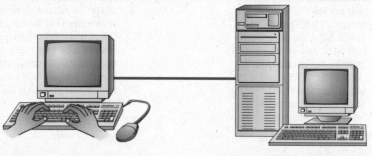

A host connecting to the remote server using FTP, with a username and password. The host can use a variety of methods to connect to the remote host, including a variety of browsers. FTP can be used to connect to another host to upload or download files.

A host computer running the FTP server service. There may be a variety of user-names and passwords created to specify who gets access to which folders. By default an anonymous account is created. The password would be the remote user's e-mail address. FTP is used to provide access to files. An example would be a hardware or software manufacturer that needs to provide patches to their customers.

FIGURE 3.4: FTP at work

Trivial File Transfer Protocol (TFTP) TFTP is FTP without the overhead. Because TFTP uses UDP (User Datagram Protocol) instead of TCP, the inherent overhead in a connection-oriented protocol is removed. This means file transfer will be quicker, though the transfer may not be as reliable.

TFTP requires the TFTP server to be running on the target computer. The TFTP server piece is not provided with Windows NT and must come from a third-party vendor or from an alternate operating system, such as UNIX.

An example of TFTP is shown in Figure 3.5.

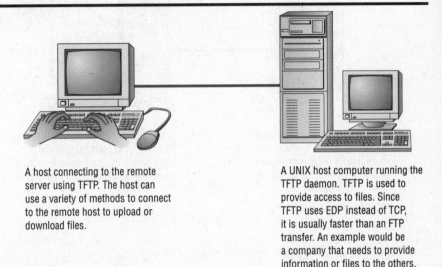

A host connecting to the remote server using TFTP. The host can use a variety of methods to connect to the remote host to upload or download files.

A UNIX host computer running the TFTP daemon. TFTP is used to provide access to files. Since TFTP uses EDP instead of TCP, it is usually faster than an FTP transfer. An example would be a company that needs to provide information or files to the others.

FIGURE 3.5: TFTP at work

For the file transfer utilities, scenarios on the exam would include copying several files to/from a UNIX computer. In this scenario, look at the utilities presented carefully, but the choice would usually be FTP. Because FTP is a TCP/IP utility, your host would use DNS or a HOSTS file to resolve host names.

Remote Copy (RCP)   RCP is the "simplest" of the file transfer utilities. It is a command-line utility used to copy files to or from a remote host.

Printer Utilities

Printer utilities are command-line utilities that will allow a non-UNIX computer to print to a UNIX server. There are two basic utilities: LPQ and LPR.

Line Printer Queue (LPQ)   The LPQ command allows a user to see what jobs are in a print queue on an LPD (Line Printer Daemon) server. It shows the state of the remote queue and also allows the user to manage some of the print jobs in the queue. Figure 3.6 shows how you would use LPQ.

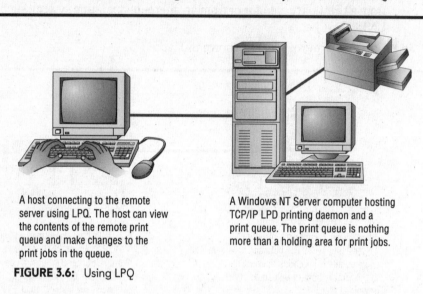

A host connecting to the remote server using LPQ. The host can view the contents of the remote print queue and make changes to the print jobs in the queue.

A Windows NT Server computer hosting TCP/IP LPD printing daemon and a print queue. The print queue is nothing more than a holding area for print jobs.

FIGURE 3.6: Using LPQ

Line Printer (LPR) The LPR utility allows jobs to be sent to a printer that is serviced by a host running an LPD server. You can send text-based files to the printer or jobs that must be sent to a PostScript printer.

Figure 3.7 shows how the LPR utility would be used.

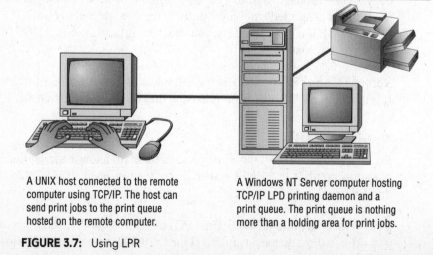

A UNIX host connected to the remote computer using TCP/IP. The host can send print jobs to the print queue hosted on the remote computer.

A Windows NT Server computer hosting TCP/IP LPD printing daemon and a print queue. The print queue is nothing more than a holding area for print jobs.

FIGURE 3.7: Using LPR

For the printing utilities, scenarios on the exam would include viewing a list of documents sent to a UNIX-based print server. In this scenario, look at the utilities presented carefully, but the choice would usually be LPQ. LPQ has command-line parameters in place to provide an IP address of the target computer. If this is not available, LPQ is a TCP/IP utility, so you would use DNS or a HOSTS file to resolve host names.

All of the commands and utilities discussed in this chapter come with options that enhance their functionality. For testing purposes, it is not necessary to memorize syntax, but looking over the following examples will give you a better idea of how to use each command.

Using Execution Utilities

Execution utilities let you execute a command or procedure on a remote host.

Remote Execution (REXEC)   Before using REXEC, have the valid password handy. This is a TCP/IP password-protected utility. This is the syntax for REXEC:

```
REXEC host [-1 username][-n] command
```

Table 3.1 lists the options available for the REXEC command.

TABLE 3.1: REXEC options

Option	Description
Host	Host specifies the host name or IP address of the target computer.
-l username	This option specifies a valid username on the remote system.
-n	-n redirects the input for REXEC to NULL if you don't need to provide input.
Command	Command specifies the command you want to execute on the remote host.

Remote Shell (RSH)   Remote Shell does not require the user to log into the remote host nor does it require a password. This is the syntax for Remote Shell:

```
RSH host [-1 username] command
```

Table 3.2 lists the options available for the RSH command.

TABLE 3.2: RSH options

Option	Description
Host	Host is the host name or IP address of the target system.
-l username	-l username requires a valid username on the target system. The user-name must appear in the .rhosts file located in the user's home directory.
Command	Command specifies the UNIX command that is to be run on the target computer.

Telnet   To establish a Telnet session with a target computer running the Telnet service, the command is TELNET hostname. Host name specifies the IP address or DNS name of the target computer. The user must have a valid username and password configured on the target computer.

Using File Transfer Utilities

File transfer utilities will allow the copying of files from the local host computer or a remote target computer. Some of these utilities require user validation while others do not.

Remote Copy (RCP)   Remote Copy does not require user validation, per se. It does require the username to be contained in the .rhosts file located on the UNIX server running the RCP daemon. This is the command syntax:

```
RCP [-abhr][localhost.][localuser:]source [remotehost.]
[remoteuser:]path/destination
```

Table 3.3 lists the options available for the RCP command.

TABLE 3.3: Remote copy options

Option	Description
-a	-a is the default. It sets the method of transfer to ASCII (as opposed to binary) and specifies the translation of certain characters, includ-ing carriage return/linefeed and linefeed.
-b	-b sets the transfer mode to binary.
-h	-h sets the transfer of hidden files.

TABLE 3.3 continued: Remote copy options

Option	Description
-r	-r recursively copies the contents of all subdirectories of the source to the destination. Both source and destination must be directories. This option is similar to the DOS XCOPY command with the /s parameter.
Localhost	Localhost is the host name or IP address of the source system.
Localuser	Localuser specifies valid usernames on the source system. The localuser name is stored in the .rhosts file.
Remotehost	Remotehost is the host name or IP address of the target system.
Remoteuser	Remoteuser specifies valid usernames on the target system. The remoteuser name is stored in the .rhosts file.
Path/destination	Path/destination is the path where the files are going to be copied.

File Transfer Protocol (FTP)   FTP is probably the best known of all the file transfer protocols. It is common when looking for the latest version of drivers or utilities to be referred to a company's FTP site. This is the syntax for FTP:

```
ftp host command
```

When you establish an FTP session with a remote host, you will be prompted for a username and a password. Once the FTP session has been established, there are a plethora of FTP commands that can be used. A sampling of these commands is listed in Table 3.4.

TABLE 3.4: FTP options

Option	Description
Host	Host is the DNS name or IP address of the FTP server.
Append	Append allows you to add information to a file.
Ascii	Ascii sets the transfer mode to ASCII rather than binary.
Bye	Bye closes an FTP session and exits the FTP program.
Binary	Binary sets the transfer file type to binary as opposed to ASCII.
Cd	Cd changes directory on the FTP server.
Close	Close closes the FTP session.

TABLE 3.4 continued: FTP options

OPTION	DESCRIPTION
Delete	Delete removes a remote file.
Dir	Dir lists the directory of files.
Get	Get retrieves a file.
Help	Help displays the command description.
Lcd	Lcd changes the local directory.
Ls	Ls lists a directory of files.
Mdelete	Mdelete removes multiple remote files.
Mdir	Mdir provides a directory of multiple remote directories.
Mget	Mget downloads multiple files from a remote system.
Mkdir	Mkdir makes a directory on the remote system.
Mls	Mls provides a directory of multiple remote directories.
Mput	Mput puts multiple files in a remote directory.
Open	Open begins an FTP session.
Put	Put uploads a file.
Pwd	Pwd prints a working directory.
Quit	Quit exits the FTP session.
Recv	Recv downloads a file.
Rename	Rename renames a file.
Rmdir	Rmdir removes a remote directory.
Send	Send uploads a file.
Trace	Trace toggles packet tracing.
Type	Type sets the transfer type.
User	User sends new user information.
Verbose	Verbose toggles the verbose mode.

Trivial File Transfer Protocol (TFTP)   This is the syntax for the TFTP command:

```
TFTP [-I] host [GET | PUT] source [destination]
```

The options available for TFTP are listed in Table 3.5.

TABLE 3.5: TFTP options

Option	Description
-I	-I specifies binary image transfer mode. If –I is not present, the file transfer mode is set to ASCII.
Host	Host is the IP address or DNS name of the host computer.
get	The get command transfers a file from a remote host to the local host.
Put	The put command transfers a file from a local host to a remote host.
Source	Source is the path where the file is copied from.
Destination	Destination is the path where the file is copied to.

NOTE
Having problems running TCP/IP - UNIX commands? UNIX is a very case-sensitive operating system. When it doubt, try help by typing command /?.

Using Printer Utilities

The two printer command-line utilities are LPQ and LPR.

Line Printer Queue (LPQ)   This is the syntax for the LPQ command:

```
Lpq -Sserver -Pprinter [-1]
```

The options available for the LPQ command are listed in Table 3.6.

TABLE 3.6: LPQ options

Option	Description
-Sserver	-Sserver is the DNS host name or IP address of the host providing the LPD service.
-Pprinter	-Pprinter is the name of the print queue.
-l	-l specifies that a detailed status should be given.

Line Printer (LPR)   This is the syntax for the LPR utility:

```
Lpr -Sserver -Pprinter [-Cclass][-Jjobname][-oOption][-x]
[-d]filename
```

Table 3.7 lists the options available for the LPR command.

TABLE 3.7: LPR options

OPTION	DESCRIPTION
-Sserver	-Sserver is the DNS host name or the IP address of the host providing the LPD service.
-Pprinter	-Pprinter is the name of print queue.
-Cclass	-Cclass is the job classification for the banner or cover page.
-Jjob	-Jjob is the job name to be printed on the banner or cover page.
-oOption	-oOption specifies the type of file. By default, it is a text file.
-x	-x is a compatibility switch for SunOS 4.1.x or a prior version.
-d	-d is for sending a data file first.

▶ Configure a RAS server and dial-up networking for use on a TCP/IP network.

One of the things that is nice about the Microsoft exams is there is always some overlap. By this time in the MCSE testing process, you have probably already taken some of the tests, so you have probably noticed some of the material presented on the Server test shows up on the Enterprise test and vice versa. This is another of those topics. RAS is a popular topic with Microsoft, so you will see questions on the Server exam, Enterprise exam, Workstation exam, and here on the TCP/IP exam. Some of the material here has been covered in other Sybex books, but it is always good to review.

Sometimes, I really feel like network administrators should just learn to say "no." Now, be honest, haven't you ever wanted to tell the latest "suit" with an idea, "No, we can't do that?"

Ever since networking came out, things have just gotten worse and worse. First, the suits wanted to connect to the mainframe, then they wanted Macs on the network. Then we had to let the UNIX bit-heads on the system, not to mention contending with those people who still insist everything runs better on NetWare.

It is not bad enough that you have to deal with all those different types of systems, but now, laptops are the vogue and everyone wants to dial into the network and connect as if they were sitting right at their desks. Do these people have any clue about the work they are causing?

NT and RAS to the rescue. Remote Access Service or RAS will allow a workstation computer configured to use Microsoft TCP/IP while running Windows NT or Windows 95 to connect to remote systems using the POTS (Plain Old Telephone System). When the client connects, the workstation is treated just like any other client. So users can access the network, check e-mail, get documents; just about anything they would do from their desks they can do from their laptops. This is something you can really use on your network and there is also a lot of testable material here. If you have already taken your NT Server and NT Workstation tests, you already know that RAS is a popular subject with the exam writers. If you have taken previous exams, some of this information may be a review, but we can all use a review at times.

The purpose of RAS is to allow for communications between remote locations, usually utilizing nothing more than telephone lines. However, RAS can be configured to work with ISDN (Integrated Services Digital Network) and X.25 connections. The purpose of this book is not to describe the multiple ways to use RAS, but it is designed to give you a broad overview of the product and get you through the test. So, we will stick to client-to-network communication using Microsoft TCP/IP over a dial-up connection.

In order for RAS to work, you need to create a mini-network. A network is nothing more than the following:

- ▸ Two systems with some information to share
- ▸ A physical communication medium over which to share the information
- ▸ Rules to govern the transmittal of the information

To create the network, we look at the first part of this objective. It discusses the server piece of RAS, how to configure the server so it can "answer" the call when it comes. Once the server is configured, we have one of the two parties to the communication. We know that we will be using the telephone lines so our physical medium already exists. The second party to the conversation joins the network when it calls the server.

That leaves just the rules. When the server answers the call, it must "talk" with the client using that specific set of rules, so we will discuss the part Microsoft TCP/IP plays and how to configure it to work with a dial-up client. In order to hold any kind of discussion, we must have two parties, so we will also show how to configure dial-up networking clients.

RAS Communications

The best place to start is always at the beginning. If you are going to configure a system where your workstations can call in and get information, then there had better be something there to answer the phone. In this case, it will be our NT Server. There are communication products that would allow you up to 256 dial-up connections from a single expansion card. RAS will take advantage of systems like that, as well as a plain old modem hooked off a COM port.

The first question to ask yourself is, "What is the main goal of this communication channel?" In some cases, your main goal may be to provide dial-up service to all those salespeople and executives out there traveling around the countryside. If your company is small, you may not have a lot of salespeople or high-powered executives traveling all over the country selling your company's wares. However, you may have a remote site that needs to communicate with the home office and doesn't need all the power of a T1 line. In that case, an ISDN line may be just the ticket. ISDN stands for Integrated Services Digital Network. ISDN is a faster, better version of what you normally think of as a modem connection. A modem connection is provided by the Public Switched Telephone Network or PSTN, generally referred to as the phone company.

NOTE

Any time you say faster and better, that usually translates into more expensive. Costs vary on ISDN service around the world, but it is safe to say it is more expensive then a standard dial-up line.

Modems modulate and demodulate the signals between two computers, sending the signal over the phone line. Your computer speaks digital. The phone company uses analog. A modem turns a digital signal into an analog signal on the sending end and turns the same signal from analog to digital at the receiving end. Lots of translations are going on in that process, aren't they?

The key word in the definition of ISDN is *digital*. You are now using a phone line that speaks digital so no translation is necessary. The ISDN modem or router just sends digital signals over a line that understands how to deal with 1's and 0's. You have a cleaner, faster communication link. If you are planning on connecting two sites, you may look at installing ISDN service. In some places it may not even be available. In others, it may be prohibitively expensive. In some areas, it may be just the solution you are looking for. When judging cost, keep in mind that ISDN service is really like two phone lines; therefore, you would expect it to cost twice as much as a single phone line. Because there are two channels, you get twice the speed. Because it is digital, and analog modems rarely give you their rated speed, it is usually faster than twice as fast.

You have now gotten over the first hump, but should you use ISDN or a regular phone line? Assuming you are going to be using the dial-up capabilities of the phone company, the phone line has to be dedicated to RAS communications. RAS is very selfish, it doesn't want to share. So, if your system is configured to dial out and notify you if the power goes out, or if you are running a fax server solution using a modem and phone line, you need to add more hardware. RAS requires its own phone line with its own modem.

If you are installing an ISDN device, follow the manufacturer's directions. The ISDN device is slightly more challenging to install than a modem. Make sure you have somewhere to connect to (another ISDN connection) and make sure you have all the paperwork the phone company left for you when they installed the ISDN line. There are some interesting parameters that you will need to configure, things like SPIDs or Service Profile IDs. A SPID identifies the services the ISDN line is providing. The SPID itself looks like a normal 10-digit phone number, except there are two of them.

After all these decisions have been made and all the hardware is installed, the installation of RAS is really anticlimactic. Because RAS is a service, it is installed through the network icon in the Control Panel. It is just a matter of copying some files off the installation CD and linking the RAS with the modem or communication device you already have configured. Part way through the installation process, the system will begin asking you questions about protocols, which is what this section is all about.

RAS Protocols

As far as protocol support, RAS supports the big three—TCP/IP, Net-BEUI, and NWLink. However, it does require some explanation. The explanation even requires some explanation because you are about to be buried in a flow of acronyms.

Transport Driver Interface (TDI)   The first acronym is Transport Driver Interface or TDI. The TDI is a specification to which all Windows NT transport protocols must be written in order to be used by higher-level services, such as RAS.

Point-to-Point Protocol (PPP) and Serial Line Internet Protocol (SLIP)   The next two acronyms deal with *communication framing protocols*, or the set of rules that allows communication devices to negotiate how information will be "framed" or blocked as it is sent over the network. The two framing protocols that RAS can use are Point-to-Point Protocol or PPP and Serial Line Internet Protocol or SLIP. Because SLIP is the grand ol' daddy of framing protocols, it is just an implementation of Internet Protocol (IP) over a serial line. By and large, SLIP has been replaced by PPP.

PPP is a Data Link layer protocol that performs over point-to-point network connections, such as serial or modem lines. PPP can negotiate with any transport protocol used by both systems involved in the link and can automatically assign IP, Domain Name Service (DNS), and gateway addresses when used with Transmission Control Protocol/Internet Protocol (TCP/IP). Cool, huh? This is one protocol that can do DHCP (Dynamic Host Configuration Protocol) as well as communicate.

An Overview of Protocols   Now that terms are defined, we can look at an overview of protocols. When a dial-in client accesses a RAS server, it will use PPP as its Network layer protocol. Think of PPP as the Ethernet or Token Ring of the dial-up world.

NOTE
SLIP is an older version of PPP, and while you can configure a RAS server to dial out using SLIP, in most environments SLIP has gone the way of CP/M.

Once connected to the RAS, PPP supports TCP/IP, NWLink, and Net-BEUI. Each protocol can be bound to a modem, or a modem may have more than one protocol bound to it. Because we are concentrating on TCP/IP, we will look at its pluses and minuses, depending on the job you are configuring the system to do.

TCP/IP Strengths and Weaknesses
Transmission Control Protocol/Internet Protocol is the standard protocol suite of the Internet. TCP/IP is a mature, stable, robust protocol suite

that brings a lot to the table, including routing capabilities and the ability to handle less than perfect phone connections. While it is robust, it is not necessarily the fastest protocol out of the gate.

RAS using TCP/IP will allow the administrator to configure whether the client computer can access just the RAS server or the entire network. In addition, the RAS server controls how the client receives its TCP/IP address.

RAS Security

Once the client computer has called the RAS server and has connected, how do you protect your network against intruders? RAS does have some built-in security features. You can configure the RAS connection security using permissions, encrypted passwords, Point-to-Point Tunneling Protocol (PPTP), and call back. Once you have installed RAS, you can take a look at the Administrative Tools menu and you will see a new utility listed, Remote Access Admin. The Remote Access Admin utility is used to configure communication ports, start and stop the RAS service, and configure user access. This utility also allows you to grant user permissions, which are discussed next.

Permissions   When a user dials in and authenticates to RAS, permissions are the first line of defense for the network. Permissions in RAS are different from other sets of permissions. RAS permissions can only be granted to individual users and cannot be granted to Global Groups or Local Groups. Permissions are granted using the Remote Access Admin utility.

Call Back   One of the ways RAS enforces security is to call back the initiating system before finalizing communication. This way, RAS is sure that the system calling is really what it says it is. Call back features can be set for each user with dial-in access. You cannot set call back authentication for groups of users or for certain modems.

Call back can be configured to be initiated by the caller or it can be preset.

Passwords and Data Encryption   By now, just about everyone in the free world has heard the trials and travails of passing passwords and other information over phone lines and even over the Internet! There are several ways of protecting information sent over phone lines, the most common is some form of encryption.

When the client and the server begin to communicate, they use PPP. To authenticate over PPP, RAS supports three authentication protocols:

▶ Password Authentication Protocol (PAP)

▶ Challenge Handshake Authentication Protocol (CHAP)

▶ Microsoft extensions of CHAP (MS-CHAP)

The default selection is MS-CHAP. When you configure a client to call the RAS, it must encrypt its password via MS-CHAP. Using MS-CHAP ensures that the system on the other end of the phone is at least using Windows 95 or above for an operating system. If the Require Data Encryption button is selected, not only is MS-CHAP used, but the data that is sent over the phone lines is further encrypted.

Suppose you have a diverse environment that is not Microsoft centric. That is the politically correct way of saying you may have some bit-head that wants to dial in from a UNIX box. Because that system cannot use MS-CHAP, something else needs to be provided. You can require encrypted authentication, which sets up the system to run CHAP as well as MS-CHAP.

The final selection you can make involves those systems that do not support encrypted password authentication. In that case, you can check Allow Any Authentication Including Clear Text. This is the free-for-all method of system access.

PPTP

Another security feature mentioned above is PPTP. PPTP is a new NT 4.0 feature. It is Internet-centered and uses a two-step approach to connecting the client to the server. Here are the two steps:

1. Connect the client to the Internet.

2. Use the Internet to create an encrypted link to the RAS server. In some areas, this is called creating a Virtual Private Network or VPN.

NOTE
Using this approach, obviously the RAS server must be attached to the Internet.

If you have a question on the exam where the terms RAS and security are used in the same sentence, start looking for the Point-to-Point

Tunneling Protocol. PPTP supports Virtual Private Networks (VPNs) over a variety of different networks, including ISDN, PSTN, and X.25 networks. If you work within a major company that makes use of IBM systems, VPNs can be configured to work over IBM's System Network Architecture protocol (SNA) and other intranet backbones.

Think of PPTP as the leech of the protocol family. PPTP can leech onto a variety of protocols on a variety of public and private networks to create a secure connection between two hosts. An example of this would be if your network was using NetBEUI or IPX (Internet Packet Exchange Protocol). Either type of packet can be encapsulated or hidden in a Point-to-Point Protocol packet and transported over TCP/IP. When the PPTP session is established, security is negotiated using data encryption and the VPN is established.

RAS and the Internet

With the Internet becoming more and more a part of daily life, one of the big decisions companies have to make is how to connect to an Internet service provider (ISP). If you work for a multimillion-dollar-a-year company with hundreds of employees, a T1 or T3 connection is in your future. Suppose you work for a small company and the company cannot afford a 7-by-24 connection to the Internet. Is there a way that RAS can help you connect to a local ISP using dial-up capabilities? Absolutely!

Let's look at this scenario. You have a small network, where access to the Internet is very limited. You want to be able to provide users logging onto the network the ability to connect to the Internet, but you do not want to provide each workstation with dial-up capabilities of modems and phone lines. You can configure your RAS server to dial up the ISP log onto the ISP system and open an Internet connection for the workstation. There are a couple of "gotchas," though. In order to accomplish this, the RAS server is configured with a blank gateway address. The server is then configured to connect to the ISP using a dial-up connection and you will also have to make some changes to the registry. For the exact settings to the exact keys, be sure to check the Microsoft TechNet CD for the latest information. The article I found on TechNet was entitled, "Configuring Dial-up Networking for ISP DNS."

While the RAS server has a blank gateway address, the RAS client (a Windows 95 or Windows NT Workstation computer) will have the gateway address configured to point to the RAS server network interface card that connects to the local network.

Dial-up Networking

Reaching out and touching someone has never been more popular than it is with computer people. We are constantly hitting dial-up connections to the Internet, dialing in to the office to pick up e-mail or voice mail, or connecting to bulletin boards to download the latest in patches and drivers. Now, regular people are even getting into the act; the Internet isn't just for geeks anymore! Salespeople want to transmit their orders electronically and management types want to be in contact with the office for more than 24 hours a day. What is a tech-type to do?

Dial-up networking (DUN), combined with Remote Access Service (RAS), lets you be the star in everyone's eye. You can configure the CEO's laptop to dial up and access the network from anywhere in the world. Road-warrior salespeople can download orders and upload e-mail as easily as plugging in an RJ11 connector to the wall. If these people work from home, rather than from hotel rooms, ISDN lines can be installed for even faster connections.

Windows NT Workstation supports two of the most common telephone line protocols, Serial Line Internet Protocol (SLIP) and Point-to-Point Protocol (PPP). Each of these line protocols takes the standard LAN protocols (TCP/IP, NetBEUI, and NWLink) and hides or *encapsulates* them within the telephone protocol. SLIP is the older of the two protocols and is rarely used anymore. PPP is the most popular because it supports Dynamic Host Control Protocol (DHCP) as well as static IP addressing.

Windows NT Workstation also supports a procedure called *multilink*. With multilink, multiple lines can call the same destination at the same time for faster throughput.

In addition to the standard line protocols, NT supports Point-to-Point Tunneling Protocol (PPTP). This protocol allows you to "steal" a part of the Internet to create a Virtual Private Network (VPN) between your remote location and the office.

There is a lot to do in this section. This objective is all about configuring, and while the first part gave an overview of the decisions to be made and things to be ordered, this is where the meat of the process lies—actually doing the work.

The test developers approached this section in a logical fashion. The first three areas talk about how to install RAS on the server, how to configure the protocols that the systems will use, and finally, how to lock down security.

The last section takes you away from the server and onto the workstation. The client side configuration is a dial-up configuration, similar to configuring the system to dial into AOL or CompuServe.

Configuring RAS Communications

RAS is a network service and is installed like most of the other network services—from the network icon in the Control Panel. Before beginning to install RAS or any network service be sure to have the NT Installation CD handy, or at least have access to the files it contains. Follow these steps to install and configure RAS:

1. Log onto the computer as Administrator.

2. Open the Control Panel by choosing Start ➤ Settings ➤ Control Panel.

3. Next, double-click the Network icon.

4. Next, open the Services tab by single-clicking it.

5. Because RAS is not installed, click Add.

6. Clicking Add will open the Select Network Service window. This is a selection of all the services available, but not currently installed on your server. Scroll down to Remote Access Service, highlight it with a single click, and then click OK.

7. By clicking OK, you have opened the Windows NT setup screen. This Window is looking for the location of the NT setup files. Provide the appropriate location and click the Continue button. At this point, the Installation Wizard copies the files it needs to the places it needs to put them.

8. The next window you are presented lists all the RAS-capable devices attached to the server. If you have more than one modem attached to the server, the drop-down menu will allow you to select the device for RAS communications. If you haven't installed a modem, you can choose Install Modem or Install X.25 pad from this screen. Once you have chosen your RAS capable device, click OK.

NOTE

RAS is selfish. The communication channel must be dedicated to RAS. If you want to use the channel for something else, you will have to stop RAS and restart it when you are finished.

9. At this juncture, you should see the Remote Access Setup screen shown below. Instead of continuing at this time, click Configure.

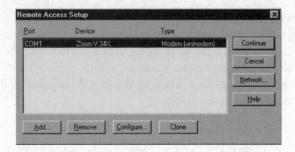

10. Clicking Configure opens the Configure Port Usage screen. This allows you to specify how you want the port to be used. Make your selection from the choices below:

   ▶ **Dial Out Only:** If you are configuring this server to dial into another RAS connection and you only want this machine to dial out, this would be the appropriate selection.

   ▶ **Receive Calls Only:** This is the default selection. If your RAS connection will not be going out looking for work and dialing into other servers, this would be the appropriate selection.

   ▶ **Dial Out and Receive Calls:** This selection provides two-way communication.

11. Click OK to return to the Remote Access Setup screen.

12. You should now be back at the Remote Access Setup screen. Click Continue to open the RAS Server NetBEUI Configuration window.

NOTE

The first protocol that is configured is for the simplest and most basic of network protocols—NetBEUI. We are not interested in NetBEUI here, but it is one of the ways of configuring RAS protocols.

13. The next screen is the RAS Server TCP/IP Configuration screen. You will see there are several decisions you will have to make before continuing.

▶ The first set of radio buttons will allow you to decide how far the TCP/IP client will be allowed to go. The choices are Entire Network or This Computer Only.

▶ You will also have to make some decisions about TCP/IP addressing. Selecting Use DHCP to Assign Remote TCP/IP Client Addresses causes the server to pass the buck to a DHCP server to provide the IP address. Choosing Use Static Address Pool will let this service decide which of the IP addresses to assign to each connecting device.

▶ You can also check the box at the bottom of the screen, which allows the remote client to request a predetermined IP address. After making the appropriate selections, click OK.

14. Next, click OK and close the RAS Installation Wizard.

15. Click Close to close the Network Configuration window.

16. Finally, select Yes to restart the computer.

NOTE

Notice there is a Begin and End selection as well as excluded ranges in the Use Static Address Pool area. For a more complete discussion on TCP/IP addressing, read Chapter 2, "Installation and Configuration."

Installing Dial-up Networking (DUN)

All that stuff up above did the job of getting the server ready to accept phone calls. Some additional work is necessary to configure the client. There are some differences between the way DUN is configured on an NT Workstation, an NT Server, and a Windows 95 client. In this example, DUN will be configured on the Windows NT Workstation. The installation consists of following these steps:

1. Start the installation of dial-up networking by double-clicking on the My Computer icon on the desktop. Then click the Dial-Up Networking icon. This will start the Installation Wizard.

2. The first screen that appears is an information-only kind of screen. It tells you how you can use either a modem or an ISDN line to use dial-up networking. Click Install to get to work.

3. Once you click Install, NT goes out and starts to copy files. It will locate the Remote Access Service device installed in your computer (your modem or ISDN adapter). If you don't like the modem it found, there are choices to install a modem or install an X.25 pad. Click OK to add the RAS device we installed back in Chapter 1, "Planning."

4. This brings up the Remote Access Setup screen. The RAS setup screen shows the modem installed and allows you to add or remove components, configure or clone (copy) a component, or click Continue. Click Continue.

NOTE
We will come back to this screen in the "Configuring Dial-up Networking" portion of this chapter.

5. Windows NT Workstation installs RAS and binds the appropriate protocols. You finally get a message that says DUN has been installed and you need to restart your computer for the changes to take effect. Click Restart.

Configuring Dial-up Networking

The configuration of the dial-up networking client really begins with the configuration of Remote Access Services and the modem. These steps are outlined below.

1. To access the modem configuration options, go into the Control Panel, then double-click Modems.

2. Highlight the modem and then click Properties. Depending on the modem, there may not be much to configure. You can configure default line speed, the volume of the modem speaker, and the way the modem connects.

3. From the Modem General page, you can configure your dialing properties. This specifies how your calls are to be dialed. The Modem Properties–General tab gathers some information, such as the following:

    ▶ Click the Dialing Properties button. Using the appropriate check boxes, you can set your location depending on the area code you are calling from. You will notice that you can create multiple configurations. If you are working with a laptop and travel to different cities, you can configure one dial-up session for each city.

▶ You can specify if you need to dial an access code to get an outside line for either local or long distance.

▶ You can set up the system to use a calling card. For the road warrior, this is an especially nice feature. Hotels, motels, and airports tend to add a surcharge to long-distance calls. This surcharge can take the form of arms and legs. Using a calling card to dial the home office bypasses the motel/hotel/airport long-distance profit center and brings the charges back down to a reasonable price.

▶ You can disable call waiting. There is nothing more frustrating than being in the middle of a large download and having someone call you and activate call waiting. It is usually just enough to disrupt the entire download and cause you to restart it.

▶ You can tell the system to use tone or pulse dialing. While it has been some time since pulse dialing systems were common, this setting still comes in handy on occasion. As most people who travel with laptops can tell you, hotels/motels/airports tend to have less than top-of-the-line phone systems. There are some occasions where the laptop dials faster than the phone system can handle. The best way around the issue is to slow things way down using pulse dialing.

4. Once the modem configuration has been completed, you can configure RAS. To start the RAS configuration, go to the Control Panel, then double-click the Network icon.

5. Click the Services tab.

6. Click Remote Access Service and then click Properties. This returns us to the Remote Access Setup screen.

7. Click Configure. This gives you the opportunity to specify how to use the port the modem is attached to. You can tell the system to use the port to dial out only, receive calls only, or dial out and receive calls. The default is Dial Out Only. Make your selections and click OK.

8. Click Network, which brings up the Network Configuration screen. This network selection lets you choose which network protocols will be used on dial out. Your choices are NetBEUI, TCP/IP, and IPX. TCP/IP and IPX are selected by default. If you opted to receive calls also, you can decide how to handle remote clients dialing in. You can allow clients to use Net-BEUI, TCP/IP, and IPX. Each of these protocols has its own configuration screen.

9. Because this book is about TCP/IP, let's take another look at the configuration screen to receive calls made from clients running TCP/IP protocol. From the RAS Server TCP/IP Configuration screen shown again below, you can opt to let clients dialing in access the entire network or just the host computer. You can set up this computer to assign addresses from the manually configured static address pool or let the subnet's DHCP server provide the address. By checking the box at the bottom of the screen, clients can request a predetermined IP address. Setting dial-up clients to use predetermined IP addresses would allow for auditing of calls and connections. Click OK to close the RAS Server TCP/IP Configuration screen.

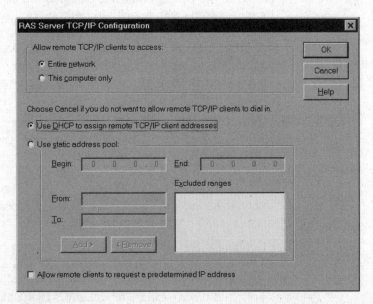

10. Let's take another look at the Network Configuration screen shown above in step 8. You will notice Encryption settings at the bottom of the page. The level of encryption you choose will affect the security of the dial-up session. Allowing any authentication including clear text means everything is out there—there is no encryption at all. Choosing to Require Microsoft Encrypted Authentication and Require Data Encryption means that any communication across the telephone lines will be Encrypted. You can also choose to Enable Multilink, allowing several modems to handle the same phone calls. Make your selections and click OK. If you made changes to the RAS configuration, you must restart the computer. Don't you just hate that?

Creating a Phone Book Entry

At this point DUN is configured and RAS is configured, we just don't have anywhere to call. Now, we must create a phone book entry. Phone book entries are important, not just because they give us somewhere to call, but because this is where RAS security is configured. Phone book entries are part of the configuration information for the user so the other people who use your NT Workstation won't know where you are calling.

To create a new phone book entry, do the following:

1. Double-click My Computer on your desktop, then double-click Dial-Up Networking and click New. This starts the New Phonebook Entry Wizard.

2. You will be asked to name the new phone book entry. Provide a name and click Next.

NOTE

If you know all about phone books, you can check the box that says you would rather edit the properties directly.

3. The Server screen now appears and you can check any or all of the three available options:

   ▶ I am calling the Internet.

   ▶ Send a plain text password if that's the only way to connect.

▶ The non–Windows NT Server I am calling expects me to type login information after connecting or to know TCP/IP addresses before dialing.

4. Make any and all choices and click Next.

5. Enter the phone number and choose to use telephony dialing properties. One slick feature allows you to add alternate phone numbers, so if your ISP has three local access numbers, NT will try each number. Click Next.

6. Now you can choose your serial line protocol. When in doubt, stay with PPP. It's newer and more widely accepted. Click Next.

7. You are now prompted to enter a login script for after the connection. If in doubt, go with the default of None. Again, click Next.

8. Now you are prompted to enter a static IP address. If you are planning on using a DHCP assigned address, leave the entry to all zeros. Click Next. Again, you are asked for some IP addresses, this time for Domain Name Service servers or Windows Internet Name Service servers. When in doubt, leave it to zeros. Click Next.

9. Click Finish.

10. To test the connection, click Dial. This brings up the Connect screen. Here you can add your username, password, domain (if required), and check the box to save your password. Click OK to dial.

▶ Configure and support browsing in a multiple-domain routed network.

You know that when you add a computer to a domain, people can use Network Neighborhood or Explorer to browse for shares or services that are offered to the entire network, even if the network spans multiple domains. What keeps track of where all those computers are located and ways to find the services that are offered? That is what Computer Browser Services provides.

Computer Browser Services maintains something called a *browser list*, which is kind of like the yellow pages. When you need something and you don't know where to find it, you can look in the yellow pages. Around our house, that usually means trying to *find* the yellow pages. This browser list is made available to any client that asks for it.

The term browser seems to be all-inclusive. That is not the case. There are different types of browsers, which are discussed below.

Domain Master Browser

The computer on your desk is part of a massive computer network. Your WAN could have hundreds or thousands of servers, services, and shares available to users. What keeps track of all that information? The Primary Domain Controller (PDC) is not just for authentication and management. It has several other responsibilities, including maintaining a master list of services available for the entire domain. That makes it the Domain Master Browser. Does that sound like a really big job? It can be, which is why the PDC delegates some of its chores. The first delegation goes to the Master Browser.

Master Browser

In any network, there is at least one workgroup. If you have a larger network, you may have several workgroups. If you have several network cards in your file server and you are using the TCP/IP protocol, you will have several subnets in your network. Each of these workgroups or subnets must have a Master Browser. If there are other NT Servers on the subnet or in the workgroup, when that server comes up, it will check in with the Master Browser and tell it what services the newcomer has to offer. Then, when you open your Network Neighborhood, the new server and its services will magically appear. What does the Master Browser do with the list of all services available in its workgroups or on its subnet? It passes that list up to the Domain Master Browser so something knows where everything is in the domain.

Backup Browser

You will never guess what the Backup Browser does. It acts as kind of a backstop for the Master Browser. If you remember, the Master Browser is always trying to keep track of all the services on the subnet or in the workgroup. While the Master Browser is gathering and sorting all that information, the Backup Browser is answering all those "where is" requests floating around the network. The Backup Browser gets its list from the Master Browser.

Potential Browser

The Potential Browser is otherwise known as the Browser Wannabe. This computer is just hanging out waiting to become a browser.

Non-Browser

The name says it all, a non-browser, a true slacker—a computer that cannot act as a browser. Actually, it is probably too busy doing other things to be bothered with answering browser requests.

Browser Elections

How does a Master Browser get to be a Master Browser while a Potential Browser is waiting around with all that potential going to waste? Computer networking is really much more democratic than you may have thought. The systems can actually call for an election.

Here is what happens. You boot your workstation and go into Network Neighborhood looking for the Joke Repository Share. Your computer first looks to the Master Browser and asks for a list of Backup Browsers. Once your computer has the list of Backup Browsers, it will then ask the Backup Browser for the location of the share. What happens if the Master Browser fails? A browser election is held. The election is somewhat weighted. For example, if a computer is running NT Server, it gets more votes than a computer running NT Workstation. If a computer is "just" running Windows 95 it gets fewer votes; you get the picture.

Now that all the computers with NT Server have checked in, there is still a deadlock. NT 4 is higher than NT 3.51, so it gets more votes. If there is still a tie, the Backup Browser will get a higher vote than the Potential Browser. Do you want to feel powerful? You can rig the election. By tweaking the HKEY_Local_Machine\system\CurrentControlSet\Services\Browser\Parameter setting, you can be a political boss. Setting the parameter to Yes means the system will always try to become a browser. No tells the system to sit on the sidelines and watch the elections go by. Auto (which is the default) makes sure the server is at least a potential browser.

Browser elections is one of those behind-the-scenes services that you probably don't think about very often. It just works. Browser services does more than provide information on resources available to your network. It also helps to "load balance" the network by making sure a list of network resources is available on different cable segments and subnets. For your user, this means packets don't have to fly all over the network causing traffic jams at key points. Less traffic usually means quicker response time.

Browsing and Subnets   Every subnet is its own browsing area. That means for each subnet there must be some type of browser hierarchy and at least one NT controller to register the information from the subnet with the Domain Master Browser. This would normally be done with broadcast messages, but there is a problem. If you have multiple subnets, you have routers, and routers do not like broadcast messages at all! A router will usually not allow a broadcast message to pass through the system.

Because broadcasting a message is out, the subnet's Master Browser will use a directed datagram called a MasterBrowserAnnouncement to tell the Domain Master Browser which system rules the roost for the subnet. This announcement is sent out every 15 minutes by default. That way, the Domain Master Browser knows where to send out all the browser lists.

When a Master Browser first boots up, it sends out something called a DomainAnnouncement once a minute for the first five minutes, and then once every 15 minutes after that. If a domain does not respond by sending out a DomainAnnouncement for three consecutive periods, the domain is removed from the Master Browser list. If each period is 15 minutes, and it takes three periods to remove a domain from the Master Browser list, a Domain may be off the network for 45 minutes before the resources are removed from the browser list.

If the Domain Master Browser fails for any reason, the users on the entire network are limited to finding resources on their own subnet if the subnet has a Master Browser. Without a Master Browser, there is no browsing on the subnet at all. To prevent a total meltdown of browsing capabilities, make sure your Domain Master Browser is restored within the three announcement periods or promote the Backup Domain Controller (BDC) to the role of Domain Master Browser.

Windows Browsing and IP Networks—a Match Not Made in Heaven

The problem with browsing is that it is basically a NetBIOS kind of task. While NetBIOS is a great little protocol, it does not necessarily work and play well with the big networks. On the other hand, TCP/IP was made to work and play on a big network and it already has in place a very elegant way of finding host names anywhere on the network. Unfortunately, the way TCP/IP and the way NetBIOS resolve names is *very* different.

Broadcast versus Directed   NetBIOS starts out the resolution process with a broadcast message. A *broadcast message* means that all computers on the network will receive and have to act on that message. In a small network, broadcast messages do not cause a problem. You can imagine the problem that would be caused if 10 percent of the hosts on the Microsoft corporate network all started to browse for resources at the same time and every one sent a broadcast message to every other computer on the network. There would be bedlam! Routers do not let that happen. A router will *usually* not allow a broadcast message to leave the subnet. That is great for the network as a whole because traffic is cut down. It is not so great for browsing the network because it precludes being able to find anything the "normal" way.

Notice I said the router will "usually" not allow a broadcast message to be passed from one subnet to another subnet. Some routers are BOOTP-enabled, which means they can pass broadcast messages. This is great for browsing, but lousy for network traffic. There are ways around the broadcast problem.

The opposite of a packet that is broadcast is a *directed packet*. Take a look at Figure 3.8 below. If a broadcast packet were sent out, and each of the routers were capable of passing the message, each and every workstation on the network would receive the packet, no matter what city the computers were in. On the other hand, if you were sending a directed packet, the packet would be sent directly to the target computer, bypassing everything else.

WINS Resolution and the Domain Master Browser   One of the ways that Windows NT resolves network addresses with direct addressing is by using a WINS Server. In this case, a client comes online and dynamically registers with the WINS Server. The WINS Server gets all the information about the NetBIOS name of the client and the services it offers as well as the IP address of the host. The Domain Master Browser uses the WINS Server to update its database of all the domains listed in the WINS database. By querying the WINS Server, the Domain Master Browser gets information on all the hosts on all the domains. The list has only domain names and IP addresses, not the name of the Master Browser on each subnet.

When a client needs a resource, it sends a directed request to the WINS Server and asks for a list of domain controllers for the domain. WINS will respond with up to 25 domain controllers in the domain. The client can then figure out which domain controller it needs to access the resource and send a directed packet. It is simple, neat, and dynamic, which means not a lot of work for the system administrator. System administrators like that!

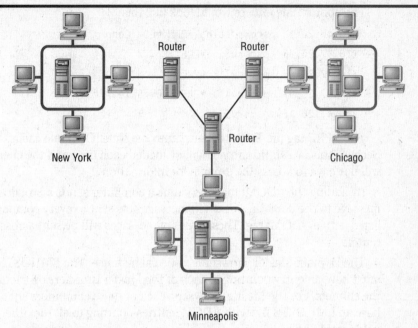

FIGURE 3.8: Map of a wide area network

LMHOSTS and the Domain Master Browser   Just like anything else
in computing, there are several ways to approach the same problem.
When it comes to browsing, one other way of providing name-to-address
resolution is using the LMHOSTS file. The LMHOSTS file is not as neat
and clean as the WINS solution, but it does work just as well. The major
disadvantage of using the LMHOSTS solution is that it is static, not
dynamic. *Dynamic* means the system does the work; *static* means you do
the work. If you are a consultant, static means billable hours. If you are
not a consultant, static usually translates to overtime!

In order to make the LMHOSTS solution work, there must be an
LMHOSTS file on each subnet's Master Browser and in this file there
must be an entry to the Domain Master Browser. Any time there is a
change to the LMHOSTS list, this change must be manually updated in
each LMHOSTS file.

To work across subnets, the LMHOSTS file needs an IP address and
the computer name of the Domain Master Browser. Furthermore, this
information must be properly formatted using the #PRE and #DOM tags.

The appropriate entries would look like this:

```
210.47.26.1    psconsulting #PRE #DOM:Corp
210.47.26.33   pscsrv2      #PRE
210.47.26.65   pscsrv3      #PRE
210.47.26.97   pscsrv4      #PRE #DOM:SalesOff
210.47.26.129  pscsrv5
```

The #PRE tag pre-loads the entry into the NetBIOS name cache. Because this is a static entry, it will be loaded each time and the client will not have to access the domain for information.

By adding the #DOM: tag, every time a computer sends a broadcast message to the domain, a directed message gets sent to every computer listed with a #DOM: tag. These types of messages will be sent across routers.

The Domain Master Browser is a special instance. The LMHOSTS file must have an entry pointing to each of the Master Browsers on each of the subnets. For the Master Browsers, each of these computers should have an LMHOSTS file with #DOM: entries pointing to all the other subnet Master Browsers.

LMHOSTS and Static Mapping

With the LMHOSTS file pointing to WINS Servers, Windows systems are made available by browsing. What about non-Windows systems, such as UNIX hosts? With a UNIX host, you may have to modify both the DHCP scope and the WINS database. In DHCP, if the IP address falls in the middle of a scope, that could cause a problem. Isolating or excluding the static IP address of the UNIX system will solve the problem. How does the system get registered with the WINS Server? All static, non-Windows systems need to be manually entered into the WINS database.

From the discussion above, you know that there are several browser roles. If there is a Primary Domain Controller (PDC), it is the Domain Master Browser. If your network is made up of domains and workgroups, you only have one Master Browser. If your network is a TCP/IP internetwork (a WAN or enterprise network), there may be more than one Master Browser, with the PDC acting as a Domain Master Browser and Master Browsers designated for each subnet. The other browsers are Backup Browsers, Potential Browsers, and Non-Browsers.

Configuring a Computer to Participate in Browser Elections

To configure a computer to participate in the browser elections, you must modify the \HKEY_LOCAL_MACHINE\SYSTEM\CurrentControlSet\ Services\Browser\Parameters\MaintainServerList parameter. Follow these steps to edit this key:

1. Start \%system_root%\system32\regedt32.exe.

2. Select the HKEY_LOCAL_MACHINE hive.

3. Double-click on SYSTEM. This will open HKEY_LOCAL_ MACHINE\SYSTEM.

4. Double-click CurrentControlSet.

5. Double-click Services.

6. Double-click Browser.

7. Double-click Parameters.

8. Click MaintainServerList. At this point, the String Editor screen appears. Here, you can enter three values: Yes, No, or Auto.

   ► **No** means the computer will not be a browser.

   ► **Yes** means the computer will be a Master Browser or a Backup Browser.

   ► **Auto** means the computer can be a Master Browser, Backup Browser, or a Potential Browser.

If your computer is on a network that does not have a PDC (such as a workgroup), you can force a computer to be the Master Browser by changing the key \HKEY_LOCAL_MACHINE\SYSTEM\Current-ControlSet\ Services\Browser\Parameters\IsDomainMaster to TRUE. It is set to FALSE by default, even on a PDC.

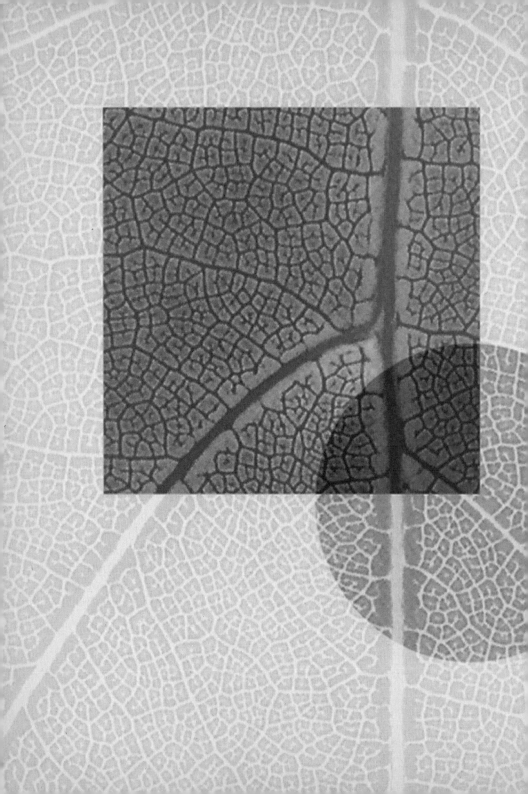

Chapter 4
MONITORING AND OPTIMIZATION

Performance management is a science. You start out establishing a baseline of network operations. When you know how well your network operates normally, you begin to examine areas that could stand improvement. When you begin to make changes, be careful to change just one thing at a time. By changing just one thing, and then reestablishing the baseline, you can determine if your change has had a positive impact on your network. Changing multiple parameters will make the decision difficult because you won't know if everything you did helped or if some of the changes helped and others didn't.

Adapted from *MCSE Exam Notes: TCP/IP for NT Server 4*
by Gary Govanus
ISBN 0-7821-2307-4   352 pages $19.99

Obviously, Microsoft thinks this is an important topic. Unlike Chapter 2, "Installation and Configuration," which had tons of objectives, this chapter is focused on monitoring traffic. If you have taken other Microsoft exams, you know that monitoring performance is a really big thing. Because Microsoft TCP/IP has some tools that allow for advanced monitoring, it takes on an even bigger role.

▶ Given a scenario, identify which tool to use to monitor TCP/IP traffic.

When you look at the tools available for monitoring Microsoft TCP/IP, you will see that some of the tools are simple command-line utilities. Some are processes that run in the background gathering information, some are programs that take that information and put it into a format that the administrator can understand. Some of the utilities that you will be tested on are included with NT, others are included with the NT resource kit, and some are included with the System Management Server or SMS. In this section, we will look at each type of tool.

NOTE

As you prepare for the test, keep in mind that while there are multiple questions about performance management on the exam, all the questions seem to revolve around the same utilities. In several cases, there are multiple questions on the same subject, just phrased slightly differently.

The term *network performance* means many things to many people. For most of your end users, it means never having to say, "The network sure is slow today." When we analyze the term from the aspect of Microsoft TCP/IP, it can only mean communication between two hosts somewhere on the network. This can also be defined as the *communication subsystem*.

If you look closely at the network communication "chain" that connects the two hosts, it will look something like this: The signal will leave the first host (the sender) through the network interface card. The NIC will place the packets onto some form of media, usually a cable. The cable can move the packets at varying speeds, from a "slow" Token Ring network of 4 Mbps (megabits per second), to Ethernet speeds of up to 100 Mbps, to FDDI, with speeds greater than 100 Mbps.

Once on the wire, the packet has to know where to go. This may involve some type of name-to-address resolution using NetBIOS or DNS. If a name is involved, it will be resolved to an IP address and the packet will be examined to see if the packet is destined for a host on the local subnet, or if it is destined for a remote network. If the packet is determined to be for a host on the same subnet, the packet will be directed to that host. This procedure is shown in Figure 4.1.

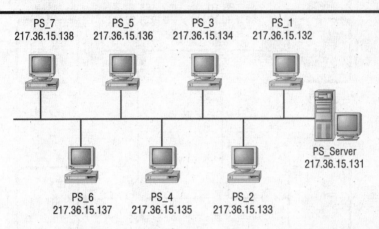

If PS_Server needed to communicate with system PS_6, a packet would be generated and destination address would be checked. Since the address is on the same subnet, the packet would be directed to the appropriate host system without the need of a router or a gateway.

FIGURE 4.1: Communication on a local subnet

If the packet is bound for a remote network, the packet must pass through some kind of a router or a gateway to get directions. The router will take the packet, strip off some information, add some other information and send the packet on its way to the next stop on the trip to the final destination. When the packet reaches the receiving host, it enters the computer through the network card, and finds its way into the CPU. Look closely at Figure 4.2.

In this case, host PS_10 wants to send a packet to host PS_125. PS_10 checks its HOSTS file, or LMHOSTS file, and finds out that PS_125 has a network address of 228.16.25.162. PS_10 recognizes immediately that this system is not on the same subnet. PS_10 checks its configuration and knows that if a target computer is not on the same subnet the packet is sent to the router/gateway for the router/gateway to worry about it. PS_10 then addresses the packet for the router PS_R1 at address 217.36.15.140.

Once the packet has been addressed, PS_10 sends it off. The packet now has two destination addresses—the address of the router and the final destination address of system PS_125.

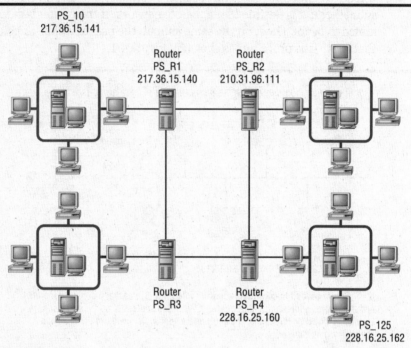

FIGURE 4.2: Map of a small network

When the packet arrives at PS_R1, the router examines the packet and strips off the destination address pointing to PS_R1. When it examines the packet, it finds the IP address of PS_125 and determines the network address that the remote host resides on. Once it has the network address, the router checks its route table to find out how to reach that network. In this case, assume the packet must go through router PS_R2 and onto PS_R4. Once the path to the remote host has been determined, PS_R1 adds the destination address of the next *hop*, or router. In this case it is 210.31.96.111. The packet is then sent on its merry way. When the packet arrives at router PS_R2, the same thing happens. The router strips off its address as a destination, looks at the final destination address, figures out the network number the packet is destined for, and checks the route table to see how to get to that network. It then readdresses the packet and sends the packet on to the next hop, in this case router PS_R4. When the packet arrives at PS_R4, it strips off its address as the destination. The router examines the packet and finds that the address is a local address. In this case, the router knows about the hosts on its network, so it readdresses the packet for the destination of 228.16.25.162 and sends it on its way. Finally, the packet arrives at the final destination; the host PS_125 can now act on the message sent by PS_10. And you wonder why the network slows down sometimes. There is a lot going on here!

If you want to check the performance of the network segment, there are a few places along the way that can act as bottlenecks.

First of all, the network cards. If any network card is defective, it can slow down the process. If the card is *chattering*—flooding the network with packets—it can slow down the entire network, not just communication with another host.

The media that the packets travel on is another potential trouble spot. Each type of media can move packets at a maximum speed. That maximum speed is obtainable only in ideal conditions. For example, if your Ethernet segment has too many hosts on it, collisions may occur. When two packets collide, the two "senders" have to step back and wait to resend their packets. Just like a freeway, a collision is going to slow down traffic flow for everyone.

Once the packet gets to the router, it faces another potential bottleneck. If the router is getting more packets than it can handle, packets may be dropped or lost. Once again, the sender will have to resend the packet and the network will become even more congested. Even if the router is not overwhelmed with work, it still has to examine the packet, determine its destination, readdress the packet and send the packet on its way. Routers have ratings and it is not surprising that a router's rating is based on speed. This means that the faster the router, the better. You can also translate that to mean the better the router, the more expensive.

In looking at this subsystem, it appears there are only a few places to check to see how the network is performing: the NICs, name-to-address resolution, the traffic on the media, and the routers. There are more tools at your disposal than you may think. Here is just a partial list:

- ▶ GUI (Graphical User Interface) Utilities
  - ▶ Network Monitor
  - ▶ Performance Monitor

▶ Command-Line Utilities

   ▶ The ARP command-line utility

   ▶ IPCONFIG

   ▶ NBTStat

   ▶ Netstat

   ▶ PING

   ▶ Route

   ▶ SNMP

   ▶ TraceRT

This is a rather impressive list of tools. It reminds me of the time I went out to my grandfather's machine shop and just stared at the tools. I knew there were a bunch of 'em. I knew they could be used to make wondrous things, because I had seen the things my grandfather had made. I was totally lost when it came to what each tool did, and *how* it was used was beyond me.

These network performance tools are easier to use than your average power tool. You just need to know when to use them, and how they will provide the best possible results. Because the objective includes the word "scenario" I will try and give you appropriate times and ways to use each tool.

TIP

These tools can be used in conjunction with one another. In some cases, one tool is dependent on the presence of another to perform properly. I will point out these areas as we go along.

GUI Utilities

Network Monitor and Performance Monitor are GUI (graphical user interface) utilities; the rest are command-line utilities run for a command prompt. The descriptions are grouped accordingly, starting with the two GUI utilities.

Network Monitor   Network Monitor is one of the most useful tools for performance monitoring. It allows you to actually capture packets and examine them from the inside out. Network Monitor can be configured to act as an SNMP manager to provide you with network usage statistics. Because Network Monitor is such a useful tool, you would probably love to have it installed on your system. Unfortunately, the full version of Network Monitor is not an integral part of NT; it comes as part of System Management Service or SMS. A limited version of Network Monitor is part of NT. The difference between the full version (which ships with SMS) and the limited version of Network Manager, which ships with NT, is that the NT version can only capture information being sent to or from the computer it is installed on. The full version (the SMS version) can access information from any device on the subnet.

TIP

It will pay dividends to understand the inner workings of Network Monitor, even if it is not available on your computer. There will be multiple performance monitoring questions that will revolve around Network Monitor.

The full version of Network Monitor will allow you to view statistics on those processes that are generating the most network traffic. These statistics can be broken down by the device generating the traffic or by the protocol. You can also use Network Monitor to identify routers or even capture, edit, and retransmit a frame.

Network Monitor constantly monitors the *data stream*, or all information going by on the network. You can define filters that tell Network Monitor what types of data you want to capture and save. Once the data has been captured, you can filter it again so that you can further isolate the problem.

Here are some scenarios where Network Monitor may be helpful in monitoring a network:

▶ **Monitoring amounts of network traffic**. A network administrator is not sure how much TCP/IP traffic is going over the system. Network Monitor can capture and view the protocol statistics on the server for a given time period.

▶ **Analyzing network traffic**. If you need to analyze traffic by device or by protocol, you can use Network Monitor's capture filters and display filters to get only the information you are looking for.

▶ **Monitoring specific traffic**. A network administrator wants to monitor specific network traffic going to individual servers. By running Network Monitor on each server, the administrator can see which workstations are generating the most traffic to the servers.

▶ **Planning for expansion**. A network administrator is planning on expanding the network. The administrator wants to plan for growth and check current usage of the cable bandwidth. By installing Network Monitor on a computer, the administrator can monitor the data stream and make an informed estimate of how the expansion will affect the current network.

Performance Monitor   If you had the foresight to install the Simple Network Management Protocol (SNMP) service on computers, you can use Performance Monitor to gather some TCP/IP statistics.

NOTE

If you have already passed the Windows NT Server portion of the Enterprise exam (Exam 70-68), some of the following material will be a review. For more information on monitoring performance of a network, check either *MCSE Exam Notes: NT Server 4 in the Enterprise* by Robert King and Gary Govanus (Sybex, 1998), or *MCSE: NT Server 4 in the Enterprise Study Guide* by Lisa Donald with James Chellis (Sybex, 1997).

Performance Monitor, amazing as it may seem, monitors the performance of computers on your network using *counters*. It gathers this data based on *objects*. An object can either be hardware or software. For example, let's assume we are monitoring the performance of a server. One common method of checking the performance of the server is to track what is happening to the paging file on the server. The paging file is to NT what the swap file was to earlier versions of Windows. When the RAM gets filled, and there is more information to go into memory, Windows NT moves that information to a special file on the system's hard disk called the *paging file*. One of the ways to check how hard the system is working is to see how often the paging file is being accessed. Figure 4.3 shows the Add to Chart window of Performance Monitor.

By selecting both %Usage and %Usage Peak, you can track how often the paging file has been accessed and how often the paging file has reached its maximum size. In this case, the paging file is the object and the counters are %Usage and %Usage Peak. The results of monitoring will be sent to a log file or you can configure Performance Monitor to alert one person or one group of people when a threshold has been surpassed.

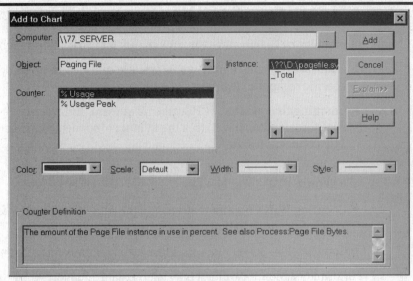

FIGURE 4.3: Preparing to monitor the paging file

Performance Monitor can be used to monitor multiple systems at the same time. Suppose you have five servers on your network and you want to ensure that none of the servers are overworked. In this case, you would configure a Performance Monitor alert for each server. An alert tells Performance Monitor that if a counter for a specific object exceeds a certain level, a message should be sent to a designated user. In this case, you would need to configure the Performance Monitor running on your workstation with an alert for each server.

Performance Monitor is a great tool for tracking information about your network, but all this monitoring, logging, and alerting can take up CPU time. If your workstation is suffering from over-monitoring, increase the monitoring interval or set up a separate workstation to do the monitoring. Increasing the monitoring interval means that you will not check statistics as often. SNMP is not installed on Windows NT computers by default; it is a service that must be configured manually. Once it has been installed, Performance Monitor can be used to monitor TCP/IP statistics for the local computer and any other computer with SNMP installed.

Performance Monitor can manage the following tasks:

▶ Recording the amount of information being handled by the network interface card.

▶ Tracking Internet Control Message Protocol (ICMP) messages that have been sent or received. The system can be even more granular by keeping tabs on error counts for the ICMP protocol.

▶ Counting the rates that IP datagrams are sent and received by a specific computer. It will track IP errors as well.

▶ Counting the rate that TCP segments are sent and received by a specific computer. It will track the number of connections in each TCP connection state.

▶ Counting the rate that UDP datagrams are sent and received. It will track UDP errors as well.

▶ Counting WINS objects that include the rates and statistics for WINS name registration and name resolution.

▶ Counting FTP server requests, logons, and file transfer activities.

Performance Monitor will not only log the data and alert you if there is a problem, it can also chart the data it gathers. If you want to view the information in chart format, Performance Monitor is the tool.

Performance Monitor provides charting and reporting functions necessary to provide a baseline of computer performance. This baseline is necessary to judge the success or failure of any optimization technique.

Suppose you have been monitoring a particular server for a few months and have noticed that you have been receiving more and more page file alerts. To check that you are not imagining things, you take the Performance Monitor information and chart it. You can use the chart function on either current information or by taking information for a Performance Monitor log.

Now that you know you have a problem, you have to solve the problem. You must provide NT Server with more to work with, so you add a lot more memory to the server and adjust the paging file size accordingly. Now, you want to check and find out if your solution actually worked. In this case, you can continue to monitor the paging file and after a week or so, take the statistics that you have gathered and chart them. If you compare the information from the baseline you established before adding the memory, you should see an improvement.

Command-Line Utilities

The rest of the tools discussed in this chapter are command-line utilities.

The ARP Utility   This command-line utility is not to be confused with the ARP protocol. The ARP command-line utility will show what entries are contained in the ARP address resolution table. The address resolution table contains the network card address or MAC address that is routed to each IP address. The ARP command can be used to check that the IP address you *suspect* is mapped to a particular network card actually *is* mapped to the network card. You might consider using ARP if you need to examine the IP address-to-MAC address resolution of outgoing packets from a Windows NT server. Here is an example of the output of the ARP command with the −a parameter, which displays the current address resolution protocol entries:

```
Interface: 209.46.15.148 on Interface 2


Internet Address  Physical Address  Type


209.46.15.130   00-c0-7b-6c-db-c0  dynamic
```

From the information above, you can see the NIC at address 209.46.15 .148 found the gateway at address 209.46.15.130. This gateway had a physical address of 00-c0-7b-6c-db-c0. This entry in the ARP table is dynamic and will expire in just a few seconds.

IPCONFIG   This utility displays all the IP configuration parameters for the host on which the command is issued. This includes manually assigned addresses as well as addresses assigned by DHCP. Issuing the command IPCONFIG without any parameters will display the current TCP/IP configuration values, such as the IP address, the subnet mask, and the default gateway. You would use IPCONFIG if you had just changed the configuration on a host computer and you wanted to ensure the host had registered the change. To display the local system's configuration, you would use the IPCONFIG /ALL command.

An example of the output of an IPCONFIG command is shown below:

```
Windows NT IP Configuration
Ethernet adapter CE31:
IP Address. . . . . . . . . : 210.47.26.35
Subnet Mask . . . . . . . . : 255.255.255.224
IP Address. . . . . . . . . : 210.47.26.34
Subnet Mask . . . . . . . . : 255.255.255.224
```

```
IP Address. . . . . . . . . . : 210.47.26.33
Subnet Mask . . . . . . . . : 255.255.255.224
Default Gateway . . . . . . : 210.47.26.1

Ethernet adapter elpc3r2:
IP Address. . . . . . . . . . : 210.47.26.1
Subnet Mask . . . . . . . . : 255.255.255.224
Default Gateway . . . . . . : 210.47.26.62
```

From looking at the information above, you can see that the computer has two network cards—CE31 and elpc3r2. CE31 has several IP addresses bound to it, 210.47.26.33 through 210.47.26.33. It uses a subnet mask of 255.255.255.224 and points to a default gateway of 210.47.26.1. The card, elpc3r2, is address 210.47.26.1 with a subnet mask of 255.255.255 .224 and its default gateway is 210.47.26.62.

NBTStat   NBTStat helps to figure out what is causing problems with NetBIOS name resolutions. NBTStat will let you view, remove, and correct the dynamic and static entries in the NetBIOS name cache.

Scenarios where NBTStat might be useful include the following:

▶ Oops, someone goofs in the master LMHOSTS file. Somehow, the wrong information has been parsed into the name cache. NBTStat –R purges all the names in the NetBIOS name cache and then reloads the master LMHOSTS file.

▶ You are trying to view a list of all the NetBIOS computer names stored on your computer. In this case, the nbtstat –c command will list the local cached name, the service name, and the status.

Netstat   The Netstat command-line utility will allow you to check the current connections and protocol-related statistics from your host. It shows information about the amount of data that has been transferred as well as the number of packets that have been sent by several protocols including the following:

▶ IP (Internet Protocol)

▶ ICMP (Internet Control Message Protocol)

▶ TCP (Transmission Control Protocol)

▶ UDP (User Datagram Protocol)

The Netstat utility can be used to monitor the statistics of packets coming into a host based on the protocol (IP, TCP, and so on) or based on the topology (Ethernet). In addition, the Netstat utility is one of the ways you can view the host's route table. The command to view the route table would be netstat –r.

Some of the reasons to break Netstat out of your tool kit would be if you need to look at the route table of a local computer or if you have a computer with an Ethernet card. You want to monitor the number of TCP/IP related packets being handled by this network card. This is the output of netstat –r:

Active Routes:

Network Address	Netmask	Gateway Address	Interface	Metric
0.0.0.0	0.0.0.0	209.46.15.130	209.46.15.148	1
127.0.0.0	255.0.0.0	127.0.0.1	127.0.0.1	1
209.46.15.128	255.255.255.192	209.46.15.148	209.46.15.148	1
209.46.15.148	255.255.255.255	127.0.0.1	127.0.0.1	1
209.46.15.255	255.255.255.255	209.46.15.148	209.46.15.148	1
224.0.0.0	224.0.0.0	209.46.15.148	209.46.15.148	1
255.255.255.255	255.255.255.255	209.46.15.148	209.46.15.148	1

Route Table

Active Connections

Proto Local Address	Foreign Address	State
TCP psmain:1025	localhost:1026	ESTABLISHED
TCP psmain:1026	localhost:1025	ESTABLISHED

In the case of netstat –r, it shows both the active connections and the routing information that the server knows about. The first two entries to the route table are 0.0.0.0, or the local network, and 127.0.0.0, or the local computer. The gateway address for the local network is the address of the router connecting the network to the Internet, 209.46.15.130, and the interface address is the address of the NIC in the server.

The third listing of 209.46.15.128 points to the subnet of the local network the server resides on. That network uses a subnet mask of

255.255.255.192 and the gateway address is the address of the NIC in the server, 209.46.15.148.

The fourth listing is for the server NIC, 209.46.15.148. In this case, there is no subnet mask because any communication to this network card from this computer would be internal (the card is in the same computer). The gateway address and the interface address is 127.0.0.1, or loopback.

The next listing, 209.46.15.255, points to the local subnet broadcast address, which is why the subnet mask is 255.255.255.255. This means that if there is a broadcast to all systems on the subnet, this is the address the local computer will use.

The sixth listing, 224.0.0.0, is a multicast address. This is when the host would like to find information from multiple locations, for instance when a host is looking for all the routers on a network; it would send out a multicast packet.

The last address, 255.255.255.255, with a subnet of 255.255.255.255, is a general broadcast address. This means the packet will be sent to anyone and everyone on the system.

You will also notice that under active connections, the system has two TCP sessions opened on port address 1025 and 1026 with a foreign host. The connections have been established.

In all cases, the metric of 1 indicates the destination route is 1 hop away.

PING   When it comes to monitoring or optimization, one of the first tricks to pull out of your bag is the PING command. The PING command tests a physical connection between two devices. It can also be used to ensure that TCP/IP is properly configured on your local computer by using the 127.0.0.1 loopback address.

Here's what happens when you ping 127.0.0.1, or a local loopback address:

```
Pinging 127.0.0.1 with 32 bytes of data:
Reply from 127.0.0.1: bytes=32 time<10ms TTL=128
Reply from 127.0.0.1: bytes=32 time<10ms TTL=128
Reply from 127.0.0.1: bytes=32 time<10ms TTL=128
Reply from 127.0.0.1: bytes=32 time<10ms TTL=128
```

The example above shows that the computer pinged the network address 127.0.0.1 with 32 bytes of data. It received a response in less than 10 milliseconds and each packet had a time to live (TTL) of 128 milliseconds. Just to prove the results weren't a fluke, the ping packet was sent four times.

Here are some scenarios where the PING tool may be useful:

▶ **Communicating with a remote host**. After configuring TCP/IP on a computer, you want to ensure that the computer can communicate with a remote host. To test this communication, you would issue the PING command and the IP address or DNS name of the remote host.

▶ **Testing your complete network**. By starting with a PING command to the local loopback, progressing to the actual host IP address, and moving out one gateway at a time, you can test to make sure the communication channel is open.

▶ **Timing packets**. An end user has called to say the network appears slow. The PING command will also return the amount of time it takes to have to the packet sent to the destination host and returned. This can be a useful tool if you have properly set a baseline for your network.

Route   The route command can be used to display, add, or delete entries to the local route table. From a performance and optimization perspective, it can be used in conjunction with other commands to refine the route tables for a network.

Here are some scenarios where the route command would be useful:

▶ If you are trying to see the complete route table of a local computer, you can use the route print command to display the route table, including the network address, the subnet mask, the address of the gateway, the type of interface, and the metric.

▶ If you have a solid baseline of the network, you can alter the route table (depending on the communication infrastructure) to find which route will be the fastest.

Here is an example of the output of a route print command:

Active Routes:

Network Address	Netmask	Gateway Address	Interface	Metric
0.0.0.0	0.0.0.0	209.46.15.130	209.46.15.148	1
127.0.0.0	255.0.0.0	127.0.0.1	127.0.0.1	1

Active Routes:

Network Address	Netmask	Gateway Address	Interface	Metric
209.46.15.128	255.255.255.192	209.46.15.148	209.46.15.148	1
209.46.15.148	255.255.255.255	127.0.0.1	127.0.0.1	1
209.46.15.255	255.255.255.255	209.46.15.148	209.46.15.148	1
224.0.0.0	224.0.0.0	209.46.15.148	209.46.15.148	1
255.255.255.255	255.255.255.255	209.46.15.148	209.46.15.148	1

You will notice this is almost exactly like the netstat −r command without the local connection information. Because it is nearly the same, I will not explain every entry again.

SNMP   Simple Network Management Protocol (SNMP) allows TCP/IP to send information to other tools so the information can be collated and put into some useful format. SNMP is the piece of the puzzle that provides the facts about what is going on with your network. It is up to utilities such as SMS, Performance Monitor, or Network Monitor to make sense out of the information provided.

NOTE

An SNMP agent is available with NT Server, but it does have to be installed. For more information on the installation and configuration of SNMP, see Chapter 2, "Installation and Configuration."

Here are some scenarios where SNMP would be important:

▶ You want to use Performance Monitor on a workstation to gather information from all the NT Server computers on your network. In order to accomplish this task, SNMP would have to be installed on each server computer.

▶ You want to configure an NT Server computer to use Performance monitor to keep track of all the TCP/IP protocol statistics for that server. In this case, you would have to set up SNMP services for the NT Server computer.

TraceRT   The TraceRT utility is used to trace a route that a packet takes throughout the network. A scenario where using the TRACERT command would be appropriate is if your network includes 10 NT Server computers. Each computer is configured as a static router. You want to verify the path a message takes as it traverses the network. In this case, you would use the TRACERT command.

Here is something Hubert Humphrey could never find—the path from Minnesota to the White House:

NOTE

For those of you too young to remember, Hubert Humphrey was a senator from Minnesota, the vice president under Lyndon Johnson, and a perennial presidential candidate. He was the Democrats' choice to run against Richard Nixon. After that defeat, he never made it out of the convention, where he lost to George McGovern and again to Jimmy Carter.

```
Tracing route to whitehouse.gov [198.137.241.30]

over a maximum of 30 hops:

 1 <10 ms <10 ms <10 ms 209.46.15.130

 2 30 ms 30 ms 30 ms gofast209-46-15.gofast.net [209.46.15.1]

 3 30 ms 30 ms 30 ms 209.46.15.49

 4 40 ms 41 ms 60 ms 206.144.128.57

 5 40 ms 40 ms 60 ms grf-ge030.gofast.net [204.73.51.254]

 6 40 ms 40 ms 40 ms gf-mr-upp-cis.gofast.net
[206.144.128.14]

 7 50 ms 60 ms 40 ms mrnet-GOFAST-2.MR.Net [204.220.29.37]

 8 50 ms 50 ms 50 ms MUXNet-gw.mr.net [204.220.31.254]

 9 60 ms 60 ms 60 ms sl-gw12-chi-12-0-T3.sprintlink.net
[144.228.157.41]
```

```
10 50 ms 60 ms 60 ms s1-bb11-chi-1-2.sprintlink.net
[144.232.0.185]


11 70 ms 60 ms 60 ms s1-bb1-roa-1-0-0.sprintlink.net
[144.232.8.186]


12 70 ms 51 ms 90 ms 144.232.2.198


13 80 ms 90 ms 80 ms s1-bb7-dc-6-1-0.sprintlink.net
[144.232.8.46]


14 90 ms 101 ms 90 ms s1-bb6-dc-4-0-0.sprintlink.net
[144.232.0.10]


15 371 ms 190 ms 170 ms 208.28.7.17


16 80 ms 100 ms 140 ms s1-eop-1-0-T1.sprintlink.net
[144.228.72.66]


17 90 ms 80 ms 80 ms whitehouse.gov [198.137.241.30]


Trace complete.
```

You can see the packet leaves the local network, bounces around from an ISP's ISP, gofast.net. From there, it hits another level of ISP, mr.net. Once it leaves mr.net, it makes the big time, hitting the T3 connection (T3=very fast) at sprintlink. Sprintlink kicks the packet from router to router before it finally ends up at 198.137.241.30, the White House.

Installing SNMP

The information in this chapter revolves around usage. In some cases, services must be installed before other services or utilities can be used. The utilities are presented in the following order, GUI-based utilities first, then the command-line utilities, and everything is in alphabetical order by type. Except SNMP. I know, there always has to be an exception. Because SNMP plays a role in several of the other performance monitors, it is important to get it out of the way first!

SNMP is a Windows NT Server service. To install it on a computer, follow these steps:

1. Select Start ➤ Settings ➤ Control Panel.

2. Double-click Network to open the Network window.

3. From the Network window, click the Services tab. Click Add.

4. Scroll down through the Network Service screen until you can highlight SNMP Service. Once it has been highlighted, click OK.

5. Provide the path to set up files and click Continue.

6. At this point, the Microsoft SNMP Properties Agent screen will be brought up.

7. The Contact and Location information shown above are optional and for informational use only. The Services include the following:

   ➤ **Physical**: This option is selected if the agent manages a physical device, such as a concentrator or repeater.

   ➤ **Applications**: This option would be selected if the SNMP agent used any TCP/IP applications. This selection should always be checked.

   ➤ **Datalink/Subnetwork**: This option should be selected if the agent manages a bridge.

   ➤ **Internet**: Select this option if the agent manages an IP router or gateway.

   ➤ **End-to-End**: Select this option if the Agent functions as an IP host.

8. Errors that occur with the SNMP service will be logged automatically and can be viewed in the System Log in the Event Viewer.

WARNING

After installing SNMP services, it is very important that you reapply the latest patch. Several older files are copied during the SNMP installation.

9. After configuring the SNMP Agent screen, you can click the Traps tab.

10. Traps may or may not be required. If you enter and add a community name, it will be sent with the trap message. You must then define a management system for the community you defined. The default community name is public. Trap destinations are the IP address of the SNMP manager.

11. Click the Security tab.

12. When you check Send Authentication Trap, it allows the SNMP agent to send a failed request trap to the SNMP manager when it gets a request for information from an unknown host or manager.

13. Accepted Community Names are the communities the agent belongs to. An agent can belong to multiple communities.

14. Accept SNMP Packets from Any Host allows the agent to accept a request from any SNMP manager in its community.

15. Only Accept SNMP Packets from These Hosts specifies which managers can request information from the agent.

Installing Network Monitor

Unlike Performance Monitor, which is an integral part of Windows NT Server, Network Monitor (even the version that does not come with SMS) needs to be installed. Follow these steps to install Network Monitor:

1. Select Start ➤ Settings ➤ Control Panel.

2. Double-click Network.

3. Click the Services tab.

4. Click Network Monitor Tools and Agent, then click OK.

5. Provide the path to the NT files and click Continue.

6. Click Close to shut the Network window.

7. Shut down and restart the computer.

Network Monitor will let you capture and interpret network traffic that is sent by or received by the local computer.

Capturing Packets with Network Monitor

To use Network Monitor, start by capturing packets processed by the local computer. Follow these steps to capture packets:

1. Click Start ➤ Programs ➤ Administrative Tools (Common), then click Network Monitor.

2. To begin capturing packets, select Capture from the Network Monitor menu, then click Start. You can also use the F10 key to start the capture.

3. To stop capturing packets, select Capture from the Network Monitor menu, then click Stop. You can also use the F11 key to stop the capture. When you have completed the capture, your screen will look like this:

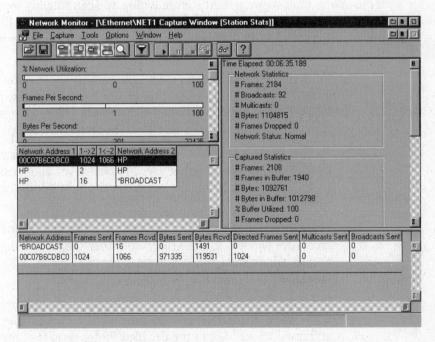

4. To save the captured packets for later review, select File ➤ Save As from the Network Monitor menu and enter a file name and location.

5. Click OK.

Now that you have captured and saved all this data, it is time to use the next piece of Network Monitor, the part that will allow you to manipulate the data. The Monitor tool can allow you to look at the packets captured or just filter out and view those packets that will help in your optimization of the network. Follow these steps to view the captured packets:

1. From the Network Monitor menu, choose Capture ➤ Display Captured Data. You can also use the F12 key.

2. You can display individual packets by highlighting the packet and double-clicking.

Filtering Packets with Network Monitor

If the information shown is a little intimidating, you can simplify your life by filtering out the packets you don't want to look at. For example, if you just want to view all TCP/IP packets, you can create a filter by following these steps:

1. From the Network Monitor menu, choose Display ➤ Filter, which brings up the Display Filter screen. It can be accessed in a variety of ways. In addition to the menu selection, you can use the F8 key, or even the funnel shown on the Taskbar.

2. To filter DNS packets only, the filter needs to be refined. Start by highlighting the line that says Protocol= Any and then click the Operator button under Edit on the right side of the window.

3. The Expression screen will be displayed. At this time, all protocols are enabled for this filter, so rather than disabling dozens of individual protocols to get to the two we want, click Disable All.

4. From the Disabled Protocols window, scroll down and find DNS. When you find the selection, highlight it, click Enable, and it will move back to the Enabled Protocols side of the screen. After this has been completed, click OK to return to the Display Filter screen.

5. You can save the Protocol filter for later use by clicking the Save button on the Display Filter screen and giving the filter a name.

6. From the Display Filter screen click OK.

7. While this screen seems to give a lot of information, there is even more off to the right margin. Slide the bar at the bottom of the screen and you will see several other columns including source address, destination address, and type of address.

8. To display the contents of a particular packet, double-click the packet. You can also use the Window option for the Network Monitor menu to look at information in the packet in detail, summary, or even in hex. Throughout this entire book, we have been talking about packets. Below is an example of some information contained in the average packet. Entire books have been written on the information contained here; suffice it to say, this packet contains all the data it needs to bring information from one spot to another.

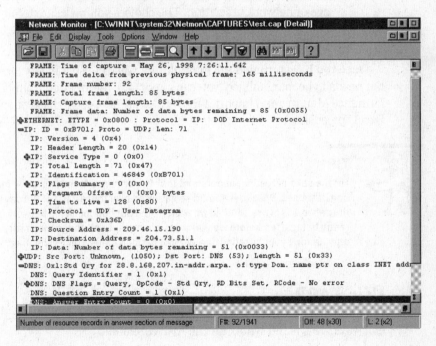

TIP

For the sake of the exam, it is important to remember that Network Monitor comes in two flavors, one from Windows NT and one from SMS. The SMS version can gather information from remote computers. Also, SNMP needs to be installed before Network Monitor can perform adequately.

Creating Charts with Performance Monitor

Follow these steps to create a chart with Performance Monitor:

1. Start Performance Monitor by clicking Start ➤ Programs ➤ Administrative Tools (Common), then click Performance Monitor.

2. To add items to check, click the plus sign (+) on the Performance Monitor Taskbar. This will bring up the Add to Chart screen.

3. Using the drop-down menu from the Object section, you can choose what you want to monitor. For example, you could choose to monitor the network segment total frames received per second, total bytes received per second, and the percentage of network utilization. The choices you make are totally configurable for whatever baseline you want to construct. Clicking Done will start the monitoring process.

Once you have gathered the information, you can use it in raw form, or if it needs to be manipulated, you can export the information from Performance Manager and import it into either an Access database or an Excel spreadsheet.

TIP

For the sake of testing, understand that Performance Monitor is used for setting baselines. Baselines should be gathered over those parts of the day when the network is in use, after all we want to find out how much the network is currently being used before we make any changes. Don't fudge the statistics by only running your baseline during peak periods either, that is cheating.

Using ARP

Depending on the given scenario, the ARP command can be useful in several ways. This is the syntax for the ARP command:

```
ARP -s [ipaddress][ethernet_address][target_address]

ARP -d [ipaddress][target_address]

ARP -a [ipaddress][-N target_address]
```

Table 4.1 explains all of the command-line options.

TABLE 4.1: ARP command-line options

Option	Description
Ipaddress	Specifies the IP address to resolve.
Ethernet _address	Specifies the MAC address to resolve.
Target_address	Specifies the IP address of the network interface card whose ARP table should be changed.
–a	Displays the current ARP table data.
–d	Deletes the host specified by the ipaddress.
–s	Adds the host specified by the ipaddress using the ethernet_address as the MAC address. The MAC address should be 6 hexadecimal bytes separated by hyphens.
–N	Displays the ARP address for the NIC specified by the target_address.

Using IPCONFIG

This is the syntax for IPCONFIG:

```
ipconfig [/all][/release adapter][/renew adapter]
```

Table 4.2 explains the IPCONFIG command-line options.

TABLE 4.2: IPCONFIG command-line options

Option	Description
/all	Displays full configuration information.
/release	Releases the IP address for the specified adapter.
/renew	Renews the IP address for the specified adapter.

Using NBTStat

The NBTSTAT command has the following syntax:

```
Nbtstat [-a remotename][-A IPAddress][-c][-n][-R][-r][-S]
[-s][interval]
```

Table 4.3 explains all the NBTStat command-line options.

TABLE 4.3: NBTStat command-line options

OPTION	DESCRIPTION
Nbtstat –a *remotename*	Lists the remote computer's NetBIOS name table.
Nbtstat –A *ipaddress*	Using the remote computer's ipaddress, lists the remote computer's NetBIOS name table.
Nbtstat –c	Lists the contents of the NetBIOS name cache by IP address.
Nbtstat –n	Lists the local NetBIOS names.
Nbtstat –R	Purges the NetBIOS name cache and reloads the LMHOSTS file.
Nbtstat –r	Lists name resolution statistics for WINS resolution.
Nbtstat –S	Displays workstation and server sessions. All remote computers are listed by IP address only.
Nbtstat –s	Displays workstation and server sessions. All remote computers are listed by name as well as IP address. All name resolution services are used, including HOSTS and LMHOSTS.
Interval	Reshows selected statistics, pausing a specific number of seconds between each display.

The output from an NBTSTAT command is displayed in a table format. Table 4.4 shows what each of the column headings mean.

TABLE 4.4: Table column headings for NBTStat

COLUMN HEADING	DESCRIPTION
IN	Number of bytes received by the local computer.
OUT	Number of bytes sent by the local computer.
IN/OUT	Tells if the connection is inbound or outbound.
LIFE	Remaining Time To Live (TTL) before a computer name is purged.
Local Name	Local NetBIOS name associated with the connection.
Remote Host	Computer name or IP address of the remote computer.
Type	The type of name; it can be either unique or a group name.

TABLE 4.4 continued: Table column headings for NBTStat

COLUMN HEADING	DESCRIPTION
<03>	Each NetBIOS name is 16 characters long. The 16th byte is used to indicate the NetBIOS applications that identify themselves using the NetBIOS computer name.
State	State of the NetBIOS connection.

The possible states of a NetBIOS connection are contained in Table 4.5.

TABLE 4.5: NBTStat connection states

STATE	DESCRIPTION
Connected	A session has been established.
Associated	A connection endpoint has been established and it has been resolved to an IP address.
Listening	The connection end point is available to inbound connections.
Idle	The end point has been opened, but it is not able to accept any connections.
Connecting	The name-to-IP address resolution of the destination is being completed.
Accepting	An inbound session is in the process of being connected.
Reconnecting	A session is attempting to reconnect after a failure.
Outbound	A session is still in the Connecting phase; the TCP connection is now being created.
Inbound	An inbound session is being created.
Disconnecting	The session is in the process of terminating.
Disconnected	The local computer has issued a disconnect and is awaiting the confirmation from the remote computer.

Using Netstat

The Netstat utility has parameters that can be helpful. This is the syntax for the NETSTAT command:

```
NETSTAT [-a][-e][-n][-s][-p protocol][-r][interval]
```

Table 4.6 gives a summary of these parameters.

TABLE 4.6: Netstat options

Option	Description
–a	Shows all connections to the host. Server connections are not shown.
–e	Shows statistics based on the Ethernet adapter. May be used with the -s parameter.
–s	Shows statistics based on the protocol. Default protocols are UDP, ICMP, IP, and TCP.
–n	Shows addresses and port numbers in numerical format rather than computer or DNS name.
–p protocol	Shows connections and statistics by a specific protocol. Can be used with the –s parameter.
–r	Shows the contents of the routing table.
Interval	Refreshes the statistics at this interval, in seconds.

Using PING

This is the syntax for the PING command:

```
PING [-t][-a][-n count][-l size][-f][-I TTL][-v TOS]
[-r count][-s count][[-j host -list][-k host -list]]
[-w timeout]destination -list
```

Table 4.7 explains how each option can be used.

TABLE 4.7: PING options

Option	Description
–t	Pings the specified host until stopped. To stop, press Ctrl+C.
–a	Resolves IP address to host names.
–n count	Number of echo requests to send.
–l size	Specifies the buffer size.
–f	Sets the Don't Fragment flag in a packet.

TABLE 4.7 continued: PING options

Option	Description
–I TTL	Displays Time To Live (TTL).
–v TOS	Displays Type of Service.
–r count	Records the route to count the hops.
–s count	Timestamp for hop counts.
–j host-list	Loose route along a host list.
–k host-list	Strict route along a host list.
–w timeout	Time in milliseconds to wait for reply.

Using Route

This is the syntax for the route command:

```
route [-f] [-p] [command [destination] [MASK netmask] [gate-
way] [METRIC metric]]
```

Table 4.8 explains the options for the route command.

TABLE 4.8: Route options

Option	Description
–f	Purges the route table of all entries. If this parameter is used prior to using a command, the tables are cleared before the command is run.
–p	Enables persistent routes. This parameter will enter the route into the route table and the route will remain after the system has been reset. This parameter will keep the route in the table until route –f is run.
MASK netmask	Specifies that the next entry will be the subnet mask associated with this entry. The default is 255.255.255.255.
Gateway	IP address of the gateway to the destination.
METRIC metric	Associates a cost/hop count with this entry.

In addition to the parameters listed above, there are several commands that can be used in conjunction with the route command. These commands are summarized in Table 4.9.

Part i

TABLE 4.9: Route commands

COMMAND	DESCRIPTION
Print	Prints a route.
Add	Adds a route.
Change	Changes a route.
Delete	Deletes a route.
Destination	The host or network to which you are going to route.

Using TraceRT

This is the syntax for the TRACERT command:

```
Tracert [-d][-h maximum hops][-j host-list][-w timeout] tar-
get_name
```

Table 4.10 explains the options that can be used with TraceRT.

TABLE 4.10: TraceRT options

OPTION	DESCRIPTION
–d	Putting in the –d switch tells the command not to resolve addresses to hostnames.
–h maximum hops	Maximum number of hops to search for target.
–j host_list	Loose source route along host_list.
–w timeout	Wait the timeout number of milliseconds for each reply.
Target_name	The name of the target host for the trace route.

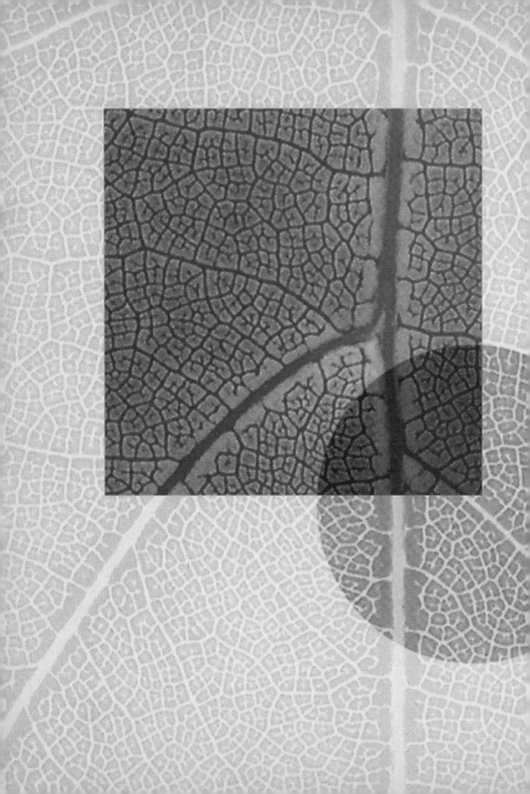

Chapter 5

TROUBLESHOOTING

Effective troubleshooting of TCP/IP is a strange mixture of science and art. On a good day, it's 75 percent art and 25 percent science. *Art* in this context means looking at a problem, immediately recognizing the symptoms, making one small change, and everything works. The *science* comes in when you look at a problem and while maintaining your cool exterior in front of the client you are screaming inside, "I have no clue what is going on here!" At that point, you start at the beginning and test each piece of the subsystem, one step at a time, before you find the piece that fails. This takes a lot longer, is not as exciting, but usually when finished is just as ego gratifying.

TCP/IP problems can be solved the same way; try and find what has changed and take things from the beginning, one step at a time until you see what fails. The trick here is to recognize the infrastructure so you can see what pieces need to be tested. That is some of the material we will cover in this section.

MCSE Exam Notes:
TCP/IP FOR NT SERVER 4
EXAM 70-059
GARY GOVANUS

OBJECTIVE-BY-OBJECTIVE
COVERAGE OF EXAM 70-059

ESSENTIAL INFORMATION
ORGANIZED FOR QUICK
LEARNING AND REVIEW

EXAM TIPS AND ADVICE
FROM EXPERT TRAINERS

Adapted from *MCSE Exam Notes: TCP/IP for NT Server 4* by Gary Govanus

ISBN 0-7821-2307-4   352 pages $19.99

When you get to the troubleshooting part of the exam, the questions are usually straightforward. There are a few of those, "Given the following situation..." kinds of questions, but when you weed through all the excess information and get to the meat of the issue, things usually become clear.

▶ Diagnose and resolve IP addressing problems.

Most IP addressing problems are pretty easy to diagnose. Something isn't able to talk with something else. That is usually the first clue that something is wrong on your network.

Addressing problems often come in two flavors. Something or someone has hosed a network address, or something or someone has hosed a host address. Because every host address is made up of just those two pieces, that pretty much covers it. This is also a fairly insidious problem because Windows NT won't recognize an improper IP address. It will just boot and go on like it's supposed to. It may even be sending the packets out the back of the machine, just like it's supposed too. The only problem is that the packets might as well be falling out on the floor for all the good it's doing.

Network Addressing Problem

In the case of an incorrect network address, you would have two computers on the same subnet with a different network address. If you remember the section on subnets back in Chapter 2, "Installation and Configuration," you recall that some different network numbers can be just a couple of addresses apart. When a host sends a packet, it looks at the destination address of the packet. It ANDs the destination address and if the destination address does not appear to be on the same subnet, the packet is sent to the gateway and out to the rest of the world to bounce around until the TTL expires and the packet is thrown out. Having a workstation with the wrong network address will cause just that sort of thing to happen.

For example, say I am installing a new workstation on someone's desk. I install the workstation and check the next nearest down stream neighbor (for example, the cube next door) to see what IP address that computer is using. I note that the IP address is 210.47.15.30 with a subnet mask of 255.255.255.224. Logically, because the two computers are right next to each other and plug into the same subnet, the two numbers should be close. You use the PING utility to check 210.47.15.29 and find that it has been assigned. You try 210.47.15.31 and don't get a response. You figure the number has got to be unassigned, so you assign it to the new computer. Unfortunately, 210.47.15.30 is on the edge of the subnet. This means 210.47.15.31 is an invalid address and therefore will be accepted by Windows NT, but not used by IP in any worthwhile way.

Symptoms of network addressing problems: The systems will not be able to communicate with other computers on the network.

Solution to the network addressing problems: Use the appropriate network address for the subnet. When in doubt, figure it out.

Host Addressing Problems

While using the wrong network address is common, using the same host address is even more common. Consider this scenario. You have a valid network address and a valid host address; the problem is the host address has already been assigned. This problem rears its ugly head in several ways.

The first exposure is the easiest to troubleshoot. In this case, you assign the same host address to two different Windows NT–based computers on the same network.

Symptoms of a host addressing problem: Windows will recognize the problem at start-up, generate an error message to the screen, and make an entry to the log. The second system to come online will not initialize TCP/IP and will not be able to communicate.

Solution to the host addressing problem: Assign unique host addresses. Documentation is always a good thing here.

NOTE

I am truly sorry, but there will be times when I will have to use vulgar, base, disgusting language to describe how to solve a problem. For those of you with strict sensibilities, I apologize for the use of the word "documentation."

The next exposure to the host addressing problem is when you assign the same host ID to two computers on the same network running different operating systems.

Symptoms of the host addressing problems: Both computers will have trouble communicating across the network. The trick to solving this problem is to be aware of what is happening on your network. This may show up as an intermittent problem (after all, both computers may not be on at the same time). It is difficult sometimes to realize that the dual address is the problem.

Solution to the host addressing problem: Change the IP address of one of the hosts to a valid, unassigned address and see if the problem goes away. Be sure to document the new assignment.

What would happen if a sender tried to send information to a system with a duplicate address?

Symptom of the host addressing problem: The transmission would flat-out fail. The sending hosts seems to work just fine when communicating with other systems on the network; the problem arises when it tries to send a message to the hosts with the duplicate address.

Solution to the host addressing problem: Change the IP address of one of the hosts to a valid, unassigned address and see if the problem goes away. Be sure to document the new assignment.

Finally, what would happen if a system had already been booted up and was happily communicating with other systems on the network and another system with the same IP address was brought online?

Symptom of the host addressing problem: The established session might end unexpectedly and the host systems might freeze up.

Solution to the host addressing problem: Change the IP address of one of the hosts to a valid, unassigned address and see if the problem goes away. Be sure to document the new assignment.

▶ Use Microsoft TCP/IP utilities to diagnose IP configuration problems.

▶ Identify which Microsoft TCP/IP utility to use to diagnose IP configuration problems.

So far, we haven't talked about the utilities that Microsoft provides to work with IP. There are several and they are all helpful. In this section, each will be discussed, as well as when is the best time to break out the utilities and put them through the paces.

In the previous objective section it was shown that there are several reasons why two hosts would not be able to communicate because of addressing problems. There must be other ways to check the communications links.

Using Microsoft TCP/IP Utilities to Diagnose IP Configuration Problems

When Microsoft TCP/IP is installed, it adds several command-line utilities to your troubleshooting arsenal. These utilities are listed below:

- ▶ **PING** is used to check a physical connection between two hosts.

- ▶ **ARP** is not to be confused with the acronym for the Address Resolution Protocol. The ARP utility will allow you to look at the ARP cache on a machine to determine if there are any invalid entries.

- ▶ **Netstat** is designed to check the protocol status and the number of TCP/IP connections.

- ▶ **NBTStat** helps display the status of NetBIOS over TCP/IP. NBT-Stat has several switches that enhance its performance.

NOTE
NBTStat will be discussed in more detail as part of the next objective.

- ▶ **IPCONFIG** is an all-purpose workstation utility. It shows the status of how the workstation is configured. It allows the user to release a DHCP address or renew the lease.

- ▶ **TraceRT** will let you verify the route between the sender and the receiver.

- ▶ **Route** will add routes to the local route table, delete routes, or view the table.

- ▶ **NSLOOKUP** is one of the more powerful TCP/IP command-line utilities used specifically for troubleshooting. It will allow you to access information from DNS servers and display the information it receives. If you wanted to find the computer, education.microsoft.com, you could use the NSLOOKUP command to do so. NSLOOKUP will also return information on the DNS server itself or information on individual domain names. For example, I needed to know how my e-mail was being sent to my ISP. Using NSLOOKUP, I was able to find the records pointing all e-mail to my ISP's server.

NOTE   See Chapter 4, "Monitoring and Optimization," for details on the command-line utilities listed above.

Identifying Which Microsoft TCP/IP Utility to Use to Diagnose IP Configuration Problems

When troubleshooting problems with TCP/IP or any other protocol, the first thing to determine is who or what is affected. If it is one or two hosts, the troubleshooting is much different than if a group of hosts or an entire network segment is down.

As strange as this may sound, it is usually much easier to arrive at the source of a problem if an entire network segment is down than it is to work with just one or two isolated workstations. After all, if 100 workstations cannot communicate, there are very few common points of failure to test. With one or two workstations, the possibilities may seem endless!

For the sake of this discussion, refer to Figure 5.1, which is a very simplified map of a network.

Let us assume that you are at host 210.17.15.10 and you are trying to find the Web site, http:\\www.microsoft.com. Now, because you are a geek (admit it), instead of using the URL, you are going to use the IP address of 207.46.130.17. For some reason, it just doesn't go through and you want to know why.

Now, there is always more than one way to troubleshoot a problem, that is a fact of life. When taking an MCSE test, however, there are exactly two ways of doing everything: the Microsoft way and the wrong way. Here is the Microsoft way of solving this TCP/IP problem.

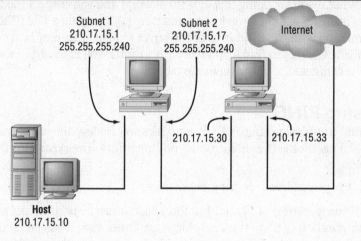

FIGURE 5.1: A simple network map for troubleshooting

First, you determine if TCP/IP is configured right on the host. This can be done by going to the command prompt and using the IPCONFIG /ALL command. This will tell you if your network cards have an IP address, if they have a path to the default gateway, and if the subnet mask is correct. Assuming that all this is correct, while you are the command line, you can use the PING utility to ping 127.0.0.1. That is the local loopback address. A *local loopback* means, is this sucker working? (The term "this sucker" is a highly technical name for the host you are sitting at.)

If the ping to 127.0.0.1 is working, then you begin to branch out. You start by pinging the local gateway on your side of the router or 210.17.15.1. If you can ping that address, you then begin to work farther and farther out the system, one IP address at a time, until you come to Microsoft or to the IP address that will not let you ping it. That *could* be where the problem lies. So, after pinging 210.17.15.1, the next step would be to ping 210.17.15.17. If that system responds, move on to 210.17.15.30.

WARNING

Please keep in mind, this is for Microsoft testing purposes only. PING uses UDP and some routers will not let UDP or PING requests through the system. You may not be able to receive a response to your ping, but the infrastructure may be up and working fine. For testing purposes, this *never* happens.

What if you are doing this in the real world and you suspect the system is in fact working, you just cannot ping it? Try using a TRACERT command with the IP address of the target system. This may be a more realistic test. If you find a problem with a router, you can use the route print command to check the route table.

Using PING

When troubleshooting TCP/IP configuration issues, one of the most useful utilities is the PING command-line utility. The syntax for PING is simply

    Ping ipaddress or **ping** hostname

If the ipaddress is 127.0.0.1 or local host, it can be used to check the configuration of IP on the local computer. Otherwise, it can be used to check the communication link between the host and other machines.

Using ARP

The ARP command will let you view the ARP cached on a machine to detect invalid entries. This command displays and modifies the Media Access Control (MAC) or hardware address translation tables used by the Address Resolution Protocol (ARP).

This is the syntax for ARP:

    arp -a [ipaddress] [**-N** [interfaceaddress]]
    arp -d ipaddress [if_addr]
    arp -s ipaddress *physicaladdress* [interfaceaddress]

Parameters

-a: Displays current ARP entries by querying TCP/IP. If the ipaddress is specified, only the IP and physical addresses for the specified computer are displayed.

-d: Deletes the entry from the ARP cache table that is specified by the ipaddress.

-s: Adds an entry in the ARP cache to associate the ipaddress with the physical or MAC layer address. The physical address is given as 6 hexadecimal bytes separated by hyphens. The IP address is specified using dotted decimal notation. The entry is permanent, that is, it will not be automatically removed from the cache after the timeout expires.

-N [interfaceaddress]: Displays the ARP entries for the network interface specified by interfaceaddress.

Physicaladdress: Specifies a physical address.

Using Netstat

The Netstat utility displays the current protocol status and connections. This is the syntax:

```
Netstat
```

It is also possible to determine the status of the connection by running the Netstat utility and looking at the State column.

The State explanations as shown in Netstat are shown in Table 5.1.

TABLE 5.1: Netstat's state of the protocol

STATE	EXPLANATION
SYN_SEND	Indicates active open. SYN indicates a request to open or establish a communication session.
SYN_RECEIVED	Server just received SYN from the client.
ESTABLISHED	Client received server's SYN and the session is established.
LISTEN	Server is ready to accept connection.
FIN_WAIT_1	Indicates active close. FIN indicates a close connection request.
TIMED_WAIT	Client enters this state after active close.
CLOSE_WAIT	Indicates passive close. Server just received first FIN from a client.
FIN_WAIT_2	Client just received acknowledgment of its first FIN from the server.
LAST_ACK	Server is in this state when it sends its own FIN.
CLOSED	Server received ACK from client and connection is closed.

This is the syntax for Netstat:

netstat –a displays all connections.

netstat –r displays the route table plus active connections.

netstat –n tells Netstat not to convert addresses and port numbers to names.

netstat -e displays Ethernet statistics.

netstat -s displays per protocol statistics for UDP, TCP, and IP.

The following is sample output:

```
C:\>netstat -e
Interface Statistics


  Received Sent
Bytes  3995837940 47224622
Unicast packets 120099 131015
Non-unicast packets 7579544 3823
Discards 0 0
Errors  0 0
Unknown protocols 363054211


C:\>netstat -a


Active Connections


Proto Local Address Foreign Address State
 TCP davemac1:1572 172.16.48.10:nbsession ESTABLISHED
 TCP davemac1:1589 172.16.48.10:nbsession ESTABLISHED
 TCP davemac1:1606 172.16.105.245:nbsession ESTABLISHED
 TCP davemac1:1632 172.16.48.213:nbsession ESTABLISHED
 TCP davemac1:1659 172.16.48.169:nbsession ESTABLISHED
 TCP davemac1:1714 172.16.48.203:nbsession ESTABLISHED
 TCP davemac1:1719 172.16.48.36:nbsession ESTABLISHED
 TCP davemac1:1241 172.16.48.101:nbsession ESTABLISHED
 UDP davemac1:1025 *:*
 UDP davemac1:snmp *:*
 UDP davemac1:nbname *:*
 UDP davemac1:nbdatagram *:*
 UDP davemac1:nbname *:*
 UDP davemac1:nbdatagram *:*
```

```
C:\>netstat -s
IP Statistics

  Packets Received = 5378528
  Received Header Errors = 738854
  Received Address Errors = 23150
  Datagrams Forwarded = 0
  Unknown Protocols Received = 0
  Received Packets Discarded = 0
  Received Packets Delivered = 4616524
  Output Requests = 132702
  Routing Discards = 157
  Discarded Output Packets = 0
  Output Packet No Route = 0
  Reassembly Required = 0
  Reassembly Successful = 0
  Reassembly Failures = 0
  Datagrams Successfully Fragmented = 0
  Datagrams Failing Fragmentation = 0
  Fragments Created  = 0

ICMP Statistics
  Received Sent
Messages  693 4
Errors  0 0
Destination Unreachable 685 0
Time Exceeded 0 0
Parameter Problems 0 0
Source Quenchs 0 0
Redirects 0 0
Echos  4 0
Echo Replies 0 4
Timestamps 0 0
Timestamp Replies 0 0
Address Masks 0 0
```

```
    Address Mask Replies 0 0


  TCP Statistics


    Active Opens  = 597

    Passive Opens = 135

    Failed Connection Attempts = 107

    Reset Connections = 91

    Current Connections = 8

    Segments Received = 106770

    Segments Sent = 118431

    Segments Retransmitted = 461

  UDP Statistics


    Datagrams Received = 4157136

    No Ports = 351928

    Receive Errors = 2

    Datagrams Sent = 13809
```

Using IPCONFIG

The IPCONFIG utility allows the user to see how TCP/IP is configured for a particular computer. In addition, you can use IPCONFIG to release all DHCP address leases, renew all DHCP address leases, or release and renew individual DHCP addresses.

This is the syntax for IPCONFIG:

IPCONFIG: Displays current configuration for the installed network card.

IPCONFIG /ALL: Displays detailed information.

IPCONFIG /BATCH *[filename]*: Provides output of the information from the IPCONFIG request to a file.

IPCONFING /RENEW ALL: Renews the leases for all adapters.

IPCONFIG /RELEASE ALL: Releases the leases for all adapters.

IPCONFIG /RENEW *N*: Renews the lease for the IP address for adapter N.

IPCONFIG /RELEASE *N*: Releases the IP lease for adapter N.

Using TraceRT

The TraceRT utility will verify that a route exists between a sender and a receiver.

This is the syntax for TRACERT:

```
tracert [-d] [-h maximum_hops] [-j host-list] [-w timeout]
target_name
```

tracert −d: Specifies to not resolve addresses to host names.

Tracert −h *maximum_hops*: Specifies the maximum number of hops to search for the target computer; in other words, trace the route to the remote computer over five hops.

Tracert −j *host-list*: Specifies the loose source route along the host list.

tracert −w *timeout*: Waits the number of milliseconds specified by the timeout for each reply.

Tracert *target_name*: Displays the name or IP address of the target host.

Using Route

The route command can be used to view the local route table, as well as add or delete routes from the local route table.

This is the syntax for the route command:

```
route [-fs] [command [destination][gateway]]
```

route −f: Clears the route table.

route −s: If there is a packet with no destination address, it is forwarded to the smart gateway.

route add: Adds a route.

route delete: Deletes a route.

route print: Prints a route.

route change: Changes an existing route.

Diagnose and resolve name resolution problems.

Diagnosing and resolving name resolution problems is not nearly as scary as it sounds. Before you start with the troubleshooting process, there are two very important things to keep in mind. The first is: Where is the name resolution supposed to come from? The second is the ability to realize that sometimes you just have to accept the fact the name cannot be resolved.

Where the name resolution is supposed to come from is the first thing you look for in name resolution. If the name is supposed to be resolved by a DNS root domain server and it still keeps coming back as an unknown address, there is little if anything you can do about it. In this case, the end user will have to accept the fact that the name cannot be resolved. Actually, the majority of these kinds of problems are usually related to the carbon unit interface anyway. It seems some end users have trouble spelling www and other key things. We are getting ahead of ourselves.

When it comes to testing, this section gets attention in an offhanded kind of way. It is another way to point out that WINS works best on all Windows networks and WINS and DNS can work together to resolve name problems.

When a user is having problems resolving a name to an IP address, the first question that should come to mind is: Where is the resolution supposed to come from? If the user is trying to resolve a local printer name using the Windows Network Neighborhood, the troubleshooting steps are much different than if the user is trying to find http:\\www.favoriteweb.com.

Where is the resolution supposed to come from? What are the choices? A DNS server, a WINS Server, an LMHOSTS file, or a HOSTS file. That pretty much covers all the options.

Troubleshooting a DNS Server

If the user is attempting to resolve a host name that should be stored on a DNS server, check first to make sure the DNS server is actually online. After you know the DNS server is online, ask the age-old question, "What have you done to your system recently?" The answer you will get is, "Nothing," but probe deeper. (Remember the laws of computing that state, "end users lie.") Perhaps they were poking around in the Network

Neighborhood properties and changed an IP address. Perhaps someone was poking around on your DNS server and changed an IP address. Perhaps someone was messing with the DNS database and changed the spelling or IP address of a favorite site. If DNS resolution is supposed to go up the directory for resolution, make sure all the pieces are online and working. This can be done by using PING, or if the servers are on the local network, through the network neighborhood.

Finally, if you still can't resolve the DNS question, look very, very closely at what the end-user has typed. It is amazing how often www comes out vvv or something equally as strange.

Troubleshooting a WINS Server

Troubleshooting a WINS issue can be more complicated, simply because there are more places for the WINS Server to get information. DNS is a static database; that means it doesn't change much. WINS is a dynamic database, which means it changes all the time. The WINS database can get information from other WINS databases, from an LMHOSTS file, or from a client on boot up.

When you start troubleshooting name resolution issues, remember the steps the system goes through to resolve the name. With WINS, the host comes up and registers with the WINS Server, if the name is unique. If the name is not unique, the WINS Server does not recognize the computer. Check to make sure the NetBIOS name on the target computer is a unique name.

One of the problems that can come up using WINS is the existence of computers still showing up in the browser, long after they have been shut off. This is especially prevalent in networks with several WINS Servers. Suppose a resource on the network suffers a catastrophic failure. Because the resource did not shut down properly, its name still shows up in the NetBIOS cache. By default, WINS keeps information in cache for at least 15 minutes before checking to see if it is still valid. If it sends out a request and does not get a response, the system still does not remove the resource from the browser. It waits and checks again. When the primary system finally removes the resource from the browser, that change needs to be replicated across the network.

If the backup WINS Server is configured as a pull partner, that replication is usually initiated by a time interval. After the time interval expires, the change is finally replicated out to the backup WINS Server, and the resource is removed from the browser. The interval between the time the resource fails and the time it is removed from the Network Neighborhood can be lengthy. In most cases, this is not a serious problem, unless you are one of the people trying to access the resource. Then it can be an issue. If you suspect, or know, that a resource is not available and it still shows up in the browser, the best way of solving the problem is to force a replication using WINS Manager.

Other issues with WINS can occur if the server is configured to import an LMHOSTS file into the WINS database. If the entry in the LMHOSTS file is not correct, obviously, the entry in the WINS database will not be correct. The LMHOSTS file cannot be directly imported into the WINS database; it must be a copy of the file. If you attempt to import the LMHOSTS file, the system will return a message saying the file was imported successfully, except nothing shows up in the database. This falls under the category of: The operation was a success, except the patient died.

WINS works with DNS to provide resolution of both NetBIOS names and host names. By default, the NetBIOS computer name is used as the host name. If this default is not followed, there may be some confusion. Just one more thing to add to your checklist.

Troubleshooting the LMHOSTS File

The LMHOSTS file is a text-based file. Each entry in this text-based file is manual and any time you have a manual entry, you have the opportunity for a typo. This is the usual reason for problems with the LMHOSTS file. When checking name resolution, be sure to check spelling and syntax.

Resolution using the LMHOSTS file occurs when the file is parsed from the top down. If there is a problem with the resolution for the file, make sure it is the only file that is being parsed. For example, LMHOSTS can reference other files. There is even the opportunity for alternate selections. Make sure you check the syntax of each and every entry in each and every LMHOSTS file.

Troubleshooting the HOSTS File

The HOSTS file is also a text-based file. Each entry in this text-based file is manual and any time you have a manual entry, you have the opportunity for a typo. This is the usual reason for problems with the HOSTS file. When checking name resolution, be sure to check spelling and syntax.

Resolution using the HOSTS file occurs when the file is parsed from the top down. If there is a problem with the resolution for the file, make sure there is only one entry for the host in question. If your HOSTS file is large, there can be duplicate entries.

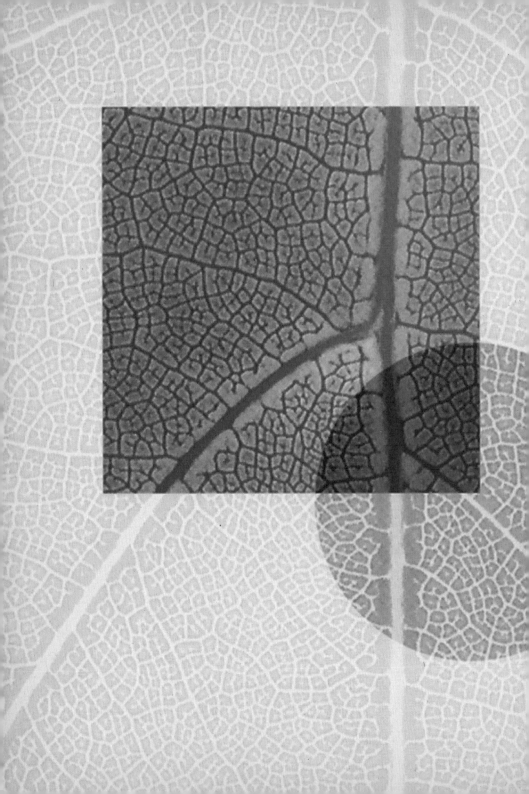

TCP/IP FOR NT SERVER 4 PRACTICE EXAM

Exam Questions

1. Your computer network consists of 35 Windows NT Work-stations, each with one network interface card (NIC). In addition, it has four NT Servers with three interface cards each and four routers, each with three interface cards. How many IP addresses will you need?

   A. 43

   B. 47

   C. 59

   D. 94

2. Two address resolution protocols are

   A. DNS

   B. WINS

   C. DHCP

   D. IP

3. Your network consists of three Windows NT Servers, 100 Windows NT Workstations, and 350 Windows 9x worksta-tions. You are concerned about address resolution of Net-BIOS computer names. Given this scenario, which TCP/IP service should you use?

   A. DHCP

   B. DNS

   C. WINS

   D. RIP

4. What is multilink?

   A. The ability to have two or more modems handling different calls at the same time

   B. The ability of two or more modems to call out at the same time

    C. The ability to use more than one communication channel for the same connection

    D. The ability to have two network interface cards in the same system at the same time

5. The NT Server named NTSRV_1 is assigned five IP addresses to its single network card. It is a

    A. Router

    B. Multihomed system

    C. Multihomed computer

    D. DHCP server

6. When configuring a network card to communicate using TCP/IP, which two entries are mandatory?

    A. IP address

    B. Gateway

    C. WINS Server

    D. Subnet mask

7. Which term(s) would describe a DNS database?

    A. Distributed

    B. Dynamic

    C. Manually configured

    D. Hierarchical

8. TCP/IP protocol properties are found as part of which Control Panel selection?

    A. Modems

    B. Networks

    C. Devices

    D. TCP/IP protocol

9. By default, a DHCP client leases a DHCP address for

   A. One day

   B. Two days

   C. Three days

   D. Four days

10. Your network consists of six subnets. On each subnet, you want IP addresses to be assigned dynamically. You must have either a(n)_____ or a(n) _____ on each subnet.

   A. PDC, BDC

   B. DHCP server, DHCP relay agent

   C. NT 3.51 Server, NT 4.0 Server

   D. Windows 98 Workstation, Windows 95 Workstation

11. Which of the following operating systems can host a WINS Server?

   A. NetWare 3.12

   B. Windows NT 3.5x Server

   C. Windows 98 Server

   D. Windows NT 4.0 Server

12. Your network consists of 10 Windows NT Servers, 100 Windows 9x workstations, 37 Windows NT Workstations, and a smattering of Windows for Workgroups workstations. What type of resolution system should you configure?

   A. DHCP

   B. WINS

   C. DNS

   D. ARP

13. The WINS Server database has become corrupt. The database has been configured so it will be backed up. What is the first way to try to restore the database?

    A. From a tape backup

    B. From the registry backup

    C. From the %systemroot%\system32\backup directory

    D. By stopping and restarting WINS

14. You find that your workstation has an IP address of 129.16.15.24 with a subnet mask of 255.255.0.0. What is the network portion of that address?

    A. 129.0.0.0

    B. 129.16.0.0

    C. 129.16.15.0

    D. 129.16.15.6

15. How many hosts can you have on a network with the address of 205.46.15.0, with a subnet of 255.255.255.240?

    A. 62

    B. 30

    C. 14

    D. 6

16. The InterNIC has assigned you an IP address of 205.46.15.0. What is the default subnet mask for this address?

    A. 255.0.0.0

    B. 255.255.0.0

    C. 255.255.255.0

    D. 255.255.255.255

17. You are troubleshooting a TCP/IP problem and you find that the IP address is an invalid address. Which address below is the invalid address?

    A. 106.34.25.90

    B. 128.4.6.224

    C. 2.128.224.240

    D. 255.23.5.2

18. The dynamic routing protocol that is provided with Windows NT Server is

   A. SAP

   B. RIP

   C. IPX

   D. SPX

   E. NetBIOS

19. What happens to the TTL when a packet crosses a router?

   A. The router adds 1 to the TTL.

   B. Nothing happens to the TTL.

   C. The router subtracts 1 from the TTL.

   D. The router adds a number equal to the metric to the TTL.

20. What two ways can Windows NT establish and maintain a route table?

   A. Volatile

   B. Dynamic

   C. TTL

   D. Static

21. How do you add static routes to a router table?

   A. Using the route command-line utility

   B. Using the Server Manager for Domains graphical user interface

   C. Using the Route Manager graphical user interface

   D. Using the table command-line utility

22. Your company has experienced a sudden growth in the use of laptop computers. Users now want to dial up the company RAS server and access services using encryption. Which protocol(s) should you enable?

    A. PPP

    B. ISDN

    C. SLIP

    D. PPTP

23. You have configured your RAS server to dial up your ISP to establish a connection. What gateway address should you put in the server's TCP/IP configuration for the dial-up connection?

    A. None, it should be left blank

    B. The IP address of the network interface connecting the server to the local network

    C. The IP address of the router that hooks into the ISP

    D. The IP address of the ISP server

24. Which utility is used to configure DHCP scopes?

    A. DHCP Manager

    B. Domain Manager

    C. TCP/IP Manager

    D. User Manager for Domains

25. The first record created in a DNS database is a

    A. SOA

    B. PTR

    C. A

    D. NDS

26. In the DNS database a "zone" is

    A. Another name for the root of the database

    B. The way the database is divided. COM and EDU are DNS Zones.

    C. The part of the database this server manages

    D. A scope of IP addresses

27. You are troubleshooting a host computer that is unable to connect to one particular host on the network. The rest of the computers appear to be communicating without a problem. You have checked the IP configuration running IPCONFIG. You now want to test and see if the local computer can respond to IP commands. The command you would issue is

   A. WINIPCFG

   B. PING *local_ipaddress*

   C. PING *remote_IP address*

   D. PING 127.0.0.1

28. What is the (#) pound sign used for in the HOSTS file?

   A. To designate a comment line

   B. To designate the end of a line

   C. To designate the end of page

   D. To designate a special tag

29. To send a job to a remote TCP/IP printer, you would use which command-line utility?

   A. LPQ

   B. LPR

   C. Add Printer Wizard

   D. The Services tab in the Network dialog

30. The LPR utility sends print jobs in what format, by default?

   A. Text

   B. PCL

   C. PostScript

   D. Binary

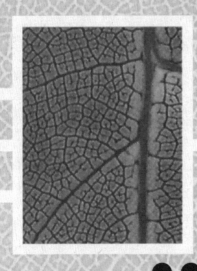

PART ii
INTERNET INFORMATION
SERVER 4

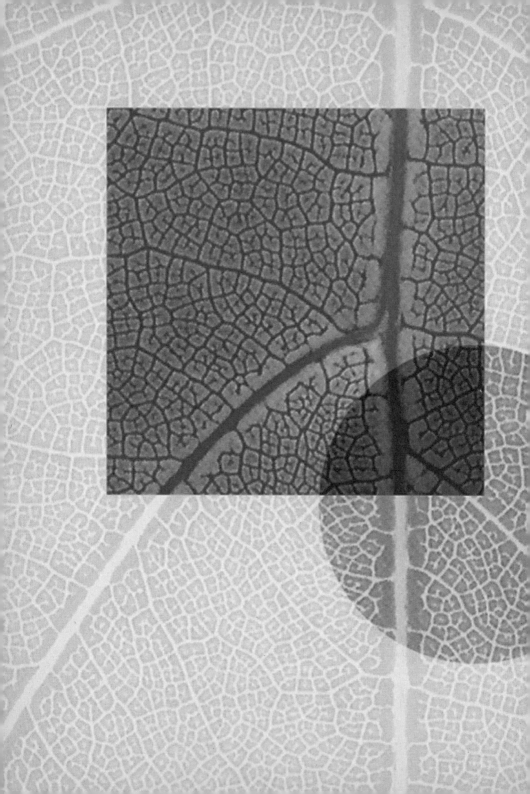

Chapter 6

PLANNING

Planning covers those decisions you should make before you install and implement a Web site based on Internet Information Server. This includes how you will properly secure your Web site, how you will integrate the server with either the Internet or the rest of your network, and which services you need to install to achieve your goals. Planning is the first step in any integration endeavor. For IIS, you must determine which services you will provide and what your security requirements are.

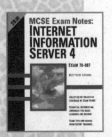

Adapted from *MCSE Exam Notes: Internet Information Server 4* by Matthew Strebe

ISBN 0-7821-2303-1   320 pages $19.99

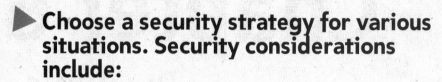

▶ Choose a security strategy for various situations. Security considerations include:

- ▶ Controlling anonymous access

- ▶ Controlling access to known users and groups

- ▶ Controlling access by host or network

- ▶ Configuring SSL to provide encryption and authentication schemes

- ▶ Identifying the appropriate balance between security requirements and performance requirements

Security is critical to Internet service, and often overlooked or incorrectly implemented. Hackers break into Web sites regularly, and penetrate even further into corporate networks either through the Web site or by using information gleaned therefrom. With all this bad press, one might wonder if it's possible to work safely on the Web. It is—if you plan for security from the very beginning.

This objective covers the major security features of both IIS4 and Windows NT itself. IIS4 is an application that runs on and relies upon the security foundation provided by Windows NT. If you don't secure Windows NT, IIS4 will not be secure.

NOTE

NT Network Security by Matthew Strebe, Charles Perkins, and Michael Moncur (Sybex, 1998) is an excellent volume that covers all aspects of security, including firewalls and other protective measures, specific tactics used by hackers, and numerous ways that Internet sites can be compromised.

Access to your Web site and its various areas can be controlled using IIS service security and using NT file system security. IIS service security is implemented by the IIS application, whereas NTFS security is controlled by the operating system.

WARNING

NTFS security is not available on volumes formatted with the FAT file system. For this reason, you should only use the NT file system for storing Internet sites.

You will also need to determine which parts of your site, if any, need to be encrypted when flowing over the public Internet. Connection encryption is performed using the Secure Socket Layer (SSL).

IIS Service Security

When you control access using IIS service security, you are relying upon the IIS service to limit access based on directory location, not user identity. With IIS service security, you can choose to permit:

▶ Read access per directory

▶ Write access per directory

▶ Script execution per directory

▶ Application execution per directory

▶ Directory browsing per Web site

▶ Indexing by Index Server per Web site

These permissions are controlled by IIS. For each access to your site, IIS checks the service permissions for the specified directory in the metabase (a high-speed registry-like construct which will be explained later) and either grants the access or returns an error message, depending upon the service security settings. Figure 6.1 shows the IIS service security settings dialog box.

NOTE

MCSE: Internet Information Server 4 Study Guide by Matthew Strebe and Charles Perkins (Sybex, 1998) contains more detailed information on the topics covered in Part 2 of this book.

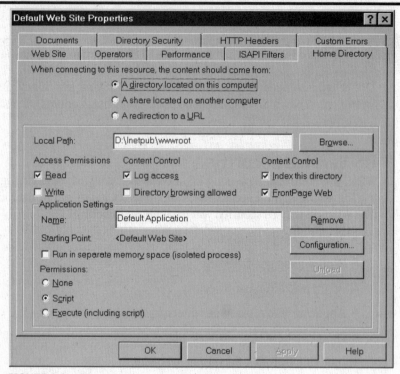

FIGURE 6.1: IIS service security settings

NT File System Security

When you control access using NTFS security, you are relying upon the operating system (Windows NT) to limit access based on the account credentials of the user requesting access. Every resource (file or directory in this case) on an NTFS-formatted volume has an access control list (ACL) containing a number of access control entries (ACEs) which consist of a specific permission and an account that receives that permission. An ACE in the ACL of a resource must specify both the requested access and either the account or a group of which the account is a member in order for a user to be granted access to that resource. Because any number of ACEs may appear in an ACL, and because accounts are normally members of more than one group, conflicting permissions may occur.

Permitted access is always cumulative. If read access is allowed by one group membership, and write access is allowed by another, the account will have read and write access. The special No Access permission will deny access no matter what allowed permissions exist. This permission is used to revoke any cumulative access that occurs due to multiple group memberships.

For example, if user account JANET wishes to gain read access to a file called DEFAULT.HTM, the ACL attached to DEFAULT.HTM must contain an ACE that specifies the JANET:READ permission, or GROUP: READ if JANET is a member of GROUP. However, if an ACE specifying NEWUSERS:NO_ACCESS is encountered and JANET is a member of NEWUSERS, then the account will be denied access no matter what other permissions are encountered.

NTFS permissions are inherited from the permissions assigned to the directory that contains the file when it is created or copied. When files are moved, the ACL does not change, because a move only consists of an update to the file's location in the directory tables; thus the file's permissions may not be the same as those of the containing directory. True moves only occur from one location within a volume to another. When a file is moved between volumes, the file is actually copied to the new location and then deleted from the original location. In this case, the ACL is changed according to the rules for a copy.

You can use NT file system security to control security for your Web site because Web site users are logged onto the server using a standard user account. If the user account has no access to the site files, IIS will return an error message rather than returning the Web site. Figure 6.2 shows NTFS security properly configured to secure a Web site.

TIP

NTFS permissions are the most secure (and easiest) way to secure your Web site. Use NTFS permissions as your primary security method.

Controlling Anonymous Access

Controlling anonymous access is performed by limiting the NTFS security permissions of the IUSR_*computername* account. The IUSR_*computername* account (*computername* is replaced with the name of your computer) is created during the installation of Internet Information Server. When an Internet user attaches to your site using anonymous credentials, IIS logs that user in using the IUSR_*computername* account. The IUSR_*computername* account must have the right to log on locally to the Web server, a right that is granted automatically when IIS creates the account.

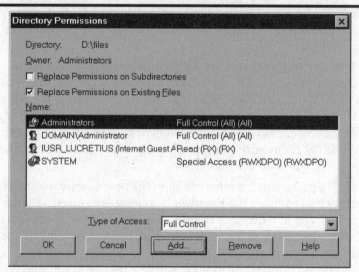

FIGURE 6.2: NT file system security settings

IIS does not change the access control lists of any files or directories when it is installed. This means that by default, the IUSR_*computername* account is not granted access to your Web site. However, the IUSR_*computername* account is a member of the EVERYONE group, so access is provided under those credentials by default. However, if you have removed the default EVERYONE:FULL CONTROL ACE from your NT file system (which is mandatory if you intend to provide any real security), you will have to add the IUSR_*computername* account to provide anonymous access to your site files.

Controlling Anonymous Logon

In addition to the IUSR_*computername* account security, IIS can be configured using IIS service security to grant or deny access to a Web site based on anonymous credentials. For each directory or virtual directory, IIS allows you to choose whether you will accept anonymous credentials, require Basic Authentication, or require Windows NT Challenge/Response authentication. These permissions are generally established per site using the following guidelines:

▶ **Allow Anonymous Access** is used for public Internet sites and informational intranet/extranet sites. Anonymous access does not transmit a password across the network.

▶ **Basic Authentication** is used for membership Internet sites and intranet/extranet sites in a cross-platform network. Basic authentication transmits a clear text (unencrypted) password across the network.

▶ **Windows NT Challenge/Response** is used for intranets/extranets where all clients run Microsoft operating systems and where security is of paramount importance. Windows NT Challenge/ Response transmits a hashed password across the network.

Internet Explorer will automatically attempt to log you on using the highest available security. This means that passwords may be transmitted across your network without your knowledge. For this reason, you should only enable those authentication techniques you intend to allow, and for anonymous sites you should not enable higher security. Figure 6.3 shows the IIS service security settings used to control authentication settings for a Web site.

Part ii

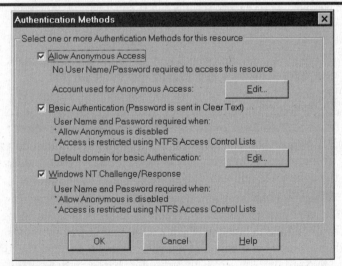

FIGURE 6.3: Controlling authentication

Controlling Access to Known Users and Groups

Controlling access to various accounts is performed using NTFS security, not IIS service-based security. If you want to control access to a Web site based on user account, simply assign NTFS permissions for the files and directories that make up that Web site. Remember that anonymous access is controlled using the IUSR_*computername* account.

When a client's Web browser is presented with content that it cannot access due to NTFS security, it will automatically prompt the user for a logon name and password using the most secure method supported by both the browser and the server. If you have configured security on the site not to accept Basic Authentication, only those users using Internet Explorer will be able to authenticate using NT Challenge/Response. If you've configured the directory to accept only anonymous connections, or if the user fails to log on correctly, IIS will return an access denied error message.

TIP

To require a logon for a Web page, remove the IUSR_*computername* account and any groups it is a member of (like EVERYONE) from the permissions list for the HTML files that make up the site or from the directory they're contained in. Make sure that IIS service security allows either Basic Authentication or NT Challenge/Response authentication, or both.

Controlling Access by Host or Network

Controlling access by host or network is accomplished through IIS service-based security. IIS can determine the IP address of each connected client, and can use the IP address to determine on a host-by-host or network-by-network (IP domain) basis whether or not to complete a transaction with a client. You can restrict or grant access based on either the IP address of a host or the network IP address with subnet mask of an IP domain.

You will use IP-based restrictions to supplement other security procedures. You can block access to any IP host or network of hosts based on either the IP address, a block of IP addresses specified by a net mask, or by the domain name of the host or network. Figure 6.4 shows the dialog box used to grant or deny access to computers based on their IP address.

WARNING

Using the domain name to block access to your site forces your Web server to perform a DNS lookup for every access to the site. This kills performance and is unnecessary since you can simply resolve the domain name to an IP address or domain manually by using the nslookup command at the MS-DOS prompt.

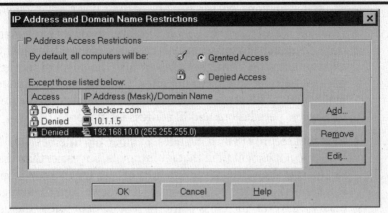

FIGURE 6.4: IP security restrictions

Configuring SSL to Provide Encryption and Authentication Schemes

Secure Socket Layer is an alternative TCP/IP-based connection method that encrypts the communication channel between the host and the client to ensure privacy. SSL is used to encrypt those areas of your Web site that transmit or receive privileged or sensitive information. Because encryption requires considerable compute resources, using SSL will reduce the overall performance of your Web server. You use Certificate Server to generate encryption keys for SSL.

There's no reason to encrypt all communications using SSL. You should only encrypt those portions of your Web site where sensitive or privileged information such as credit card numbers or passwords is transmitted. Since SSL requires considerable processing when it is in use, it reduces the number of users your Web server will be able to handle.

Identifying the Appropriate Balance between Security Requirements and Performance Requirements

Security is always a trade-off. Security is naturally opposed to performance and ease of use because a more secure system is usually harder to use and always requires more compute power than a less secure or non-secure system. Your security requirements will vary greatly depending upon what you want to use your site for.

Most IIS installations will serve in one of three major environments:

▶ **Internet** security is the most difficult to correctly implement because account-based security is generally not used, in order to allow public access. Internet sites are also the target of far more hacking activity than intranet sites. Security must be implemented on an IIS service basis through mechanisms like directory access permissions and IP address restriction.

▶ **Extranet** security (which includes membership Internet sites) is harder to implement than that for intranets, but easier than that for Internet sites. Because the identity of each user is known, you can use NTFS access permissions to lock down your site as necessary. However, the cross-platform requirement forces the use of Basic Authentication, which is less secure than NT Challenge/Response.

▶ **Intranet** security is the most secure, the easiest to implement, and the least likely to require elaborate methods. Since users are already logged into your network, they are already participating in domain security. You can use NTFS access permissions and secure authentication to lock down your intranet site.

Your security requirements will vary depending upon your exact situation. Understanding all the security options available will help you determine what your security requirements are. Understanding the performance impact of the security settings you implement will help you achieve a balance of acceptable performance and acceptable security.

▶ Choose an implementation strategy for an Internet site or an intranet site for stand-alone servers, single-domain environments, and multiple-domain environments. Tasks include:

▶ Resolving host header name issues by using a HOSTS file or DNS, or both

▶ Choosing the appropriate operating system on which to install IIS

This objective is worded strangely, and might lead one to believe that Microsoft thinks you should understand NT security domain concepts as they apply to the Internet. In fact, NT security domains have very little to do with implementing Internet sites beyond their effect on NT file system security. This objective actually concerns Internet domains, interdomain communication, and name resolution.

Name resolution is perhaps the biggest difference between single- and multiple-domain TCP/IP networks. It doesn't have to be a headache—if you install the right services for your enterprise, name resolution is easy and pretty much hassle-free.

Preparing to host Internet sites means preparing a well-structured TCP/IP network. And whether or not you have a large network, you'll probably be attaching your servers to the Internet, which in itself is a large network, so you will have to be familiar with name resolution (which you normally don't need to worry about on smaller networks).

The two name services provided in Windows NT 4 are the Domain Name Service (DNS) used on the Internet and the Windows Internet Naming Service (WINS) used in Windows TCP/IP networks.

Choosing the Appropriate Operating System

Versions of IIS exist for both Windows NT Server and Windows NT Workstation. When installed on Windows NT Workstation, IIS is called Peer Web Services. A similar product for Windows 95 exists called Personal Web Server. Peer Web Services is limited to 10 connections, so it is worthless for all but the smallest intranets. Windows 95 is not a stable operating system and should not be considered for any serious Web site. For any business application, you should only consider installing IIS on Windows NT Server.

Domain Name Service

IP addresses are difficult for humans to remember, and for that reason the Domain Name System (DNS) was established. DNS allows you to use a human-readable name in place of an IP address nearly anywhere an IP address is accepted for input. When the name is provided, DNS will resolve the IP address, and a TCP/IP link can then be established with the target host.

DNS is a distributed database of IP address names maintained for the Internet by InterNIC, a not-for-profit organization dedicated to this task and currently operated by Network Solutions, Inc. For a domain name to be resolved on the Internet, it must be registered with InterNIC. For instance, `microsoft.com` is registered with InterNIC to point to Microsoft's DNS servers. Non-U.S. domain name registration is handled by a local naming authority similar to InterNIC.

Hosts within a domain can be added by the organization without further InterNIC registration. For instance, the four servers named `www.microsoft.com`, `www1.microsoft.com`, `ftp.microsoft.com`, and `support.microsoft.com` need only be registered by the DNS server maintained by Microsoft. The basic process for resolving a DNS name is as follows:

1. Host requests DNS name resolution from its DNS server (statically assigned through the Networking control panel or assigned by Dynamic Host Configuration Protocol [DHCP]) by providing the fully qualified domain name (for example, `support.microsoft.com`).

2. DNS server checks its database. Assuming no matching entry for `support.microsoft.com`, it then attempts to resolve `microsoft.com`. Assuming no matching entry, it resolves `com` to the InterNIC root DNS server.

3. DNS server sends domain name (`support.microsoft.com`) to root DNS server. Root server knows only `microsoft.com` (the only name registered), which it sends back to requesting DNS server.

4. DNS server queries DNS server `microsoft.com` with `support.microsoft.com`. DNS server `microsoft.com` responds with specific IP address.

5. DNS server replies to host with IP address for `support.microsoft.com` and adds entry to its locally cached database. Future name resolution for this address will be provided immediately.

6. Host establishes TCP/IP connection with IP address for `support.microsoft.com`.

Windows Internet Naming Service

WINS is a service similar to DNS that is designed to work with Microsoft's NetBIOS name browser service for Windows networks that span multiple

IP domains. Prior to the use of TCP/IP in Windows networks, computer names were simply broadcast on the network. All computers in the network cached names as they were broadcast, so that after a few minutes each host would have a complete list of names for computers on its network. With protocols like NetBEUI and NWLink/IPX, this system works fine, since all hosts on a network will receive all broadcasts.

With TCP/IP, hosts on different subnetworks do not receive broadcasts because routers do not forward TCP/IP broadcasts. For this reason, computers have no way to resolve names for computers on other networks. WINS solves this problem by maintaining a master list of Windows computer names on a WINS server. Each host knows the IP address of the WINS server and can simply request name resolution if a name is unknown. Unlike DNS, WINS does not rely upon name registration—rather, browser computers automatically discover Windows names when they are broadcast on their respective networks and forward those names to the WINS server for inclusion in the WINS database. For this reason, WINS requires no maintenance once it's properly set up and as long as the database is not accidentally corrupted.

HOSTS Files

HOSTS files are simply text files stored on each client that list computer names and domain names along with their respective IP addresses. A computer can check its HOSTS file to resolve names if a name service is unavailable or unable to do so. HOSTS files are checked before a DNS or WINS resolve is attempted, so you can actually override DNS or WINS registered names if you need to for testing purposes.

HOSTS files are difficult to keep up-to-date because every HOSTS file on every client must be changed each time a new name is added or updated. For this reason, HOSTS files are largely obsolete. HOSTS files remain useful for debugging name resolution issues and for situations where only a small number of computers will ever be addressed.

TIP

Use HOSTS files to check your IIS server's host headers before you actually "go live" on the Internet. From the client you're using to check your Web site, simply list all the domain names your server will respond to and see if your various sites respond the way they should.

Part ii

Resolving Host Header Name Issues by Using a HOSTS File or DNS, or Both

Once you've created your Web site and you want to test it to make sure everything's functioning correctly, it's likely you'll need to see whether or not the host headers feature of IIS is working correctly. There are two ways you can do this:

1. Install the DNS service and add entries for each host name you'll serve. This works only if the domain names will be postfixed with your company's domain name when the server is live on the Internet (e.g.: *yourclient.yourcompany*.com).

2. On the client you want to test from, create a HOSTS file and add entries for each host name you'll serve. This works well in any circumstance, and is easy both to set up and to remove.

The following procedure will show you how to use the HOSTS file to check host header functionality before your server goes live on the Internet:

1. Using a text editor, open the file `c:\winnt\system32\drivers\etc\hosts` on the client you'll be using to browse from.

2. Add an entry to the bottom of the file by typing the current IP address of your server, a tab character, and the domain name you wish to test.

3. Repeat step 2 for each domain name you want to serve.

4. Open your Web browser and enter one of the host names you've set up in step 2. Your computer should resolve to the IP address of your Internet server and open the Web page that matches the site you've set up for host headers.

Choosing the Appropriate Operating System on Which to Install IIS

Install IIS4 on Windows NT Server 4. NT Workstation can support only 10 simultaneous connections, and no other Microsoft operating system is stable enough to function as a Web server.

▶ Choose the appropriate technology to resolve specified problems. Technology options include:

- ▶ WWW service

- ▶ FTP service

- ▶ Microsoft Transaction Server

- ▶ Microsoft SMTP Service

- ▶ Microsoft NNTP Service

- ▶ Microsoft Index Server

- ▶ Microsoft Certificate Server

Internet servers provide a combination of services that in sum create a total Internet environment for users. Different environments require different services, and not all services are necessary in all environments. In fact, WWW service is the only "universal" service that appears on most Internet servers. Other peripheral services like FTP, Mail, and News are niche services that are used on relatively few servers. IIS4 provides all these and other services so you can customize your Internet server to fit your needs exactly.

Understanding the functionality of the different IIS4 components is critical to your success, not only for this objective but for the entire exam. You must understand the functionality of all of the major services of IIS4 if you expect to pass the exam.

WWW Service

World Wide Web service is the premier content formatting service on the Internet—it is single-handedly responsible for the explosion in Internet services, and its presence is so widespread that the term Internet is often confused with the WWW service alone. If you are installing IIS, you're installing it to serve Web pages in addition to whatever else you might be doing.

WWW service allows you to post text documents with codes embedded to change the text's on-screen appearance, to display graphical files, and to link to other text documents. Enhancements to this basic functionality allow scripts, interpreted languages, and compiled code to be embedded in Web pages, and provide a method to return data from clients to the Web server. These enhancements provide a truly interactive multimedia experience. WWW service and its various enhancements can be used to create any client-side interface to a service. For this reason, it's frequently the only service you'll need to provide.

FTP Service

File Transfer Protocol provides an interface through which files can be copied between Internet hosts. FTP provides a login facility and a method to browse directories and either download or upload files. FTP is commonly used whenever a reliable and efficient means to transfer files across the Internet is needed.

Microsoft Transaction Server

Microsoft Transaction Server provides a way to bundle together any number of operations into a single atomic transaction which, once initiated, will either succeed in its entirety or fail without partially succeeding. This functionality is critical for many financial business activities that occur on the Internet. For example, imagine you are transferring money between bank accounts via your Web browser. Imagine that your computer crashes just after the command to subtract money from your checking account is issued, but before the command to add money to your savings account occurs. What happens? Your money is simply lost. With transactions, the entire transaction will succeed or it will fail—either is okay, because you won't lose your money in either case.

TIP

Don't blow a brain cell trying to figure out exactly what Transaction Server does. It's a system integration package that very few people who set up Web sites will ever use, because it requires custom written software. The MCSE exam does not expect you to understand Transaction Server.

Microsoft SMTP Service

The SMTP Service supplied with IIS4 allows you to add "send mail" functionality to your Web sites. The service does not come with any simple way for multiple users to retrieve mail or with a POP service, so it's not very useful as a mail receiver. The primary purpose for this service is to allow you to create forms for customer support and user response that can be mailed to other addresses from your Web server.

Microsoft NNTP Service

The Microsoft NNTP service allows you to create bulletin boards of topical discussion threads. This could be used for customer support or as a public form of e-mail inside your company.

Microsoft Index Server

Microsoft Index Server is used to provide "search engine" functionality for your Web sites. Index Server scans all the Web pages (and any other documents for which a scanning filter exists) on your server and creates a massive index of every word in every document. When a user enters a search phrase, all documents that contain all the words listed in the search phrase are returned in a new Web document. The user can then click on the hyperlink for each matching document to view it directly. Index Server provides a quick way for users to find specific information on your site.

Microsoft Certificate Server

Secure Socket Layer (the protocol used to secure data exchanges between Web browsers and Web servers) uses digital files called keys to encrypt data. Before you can require SSL communications for a directory, therefore, you must create keys for your Web site. But before you can install keys into your Web site you have to have them certified with a certificate authority.

Certificates and certificate authorities assure Web users that your Web site is registered with a responsible organization and is safe to visit. A certificate is a message from that responsible organization (the certificate authority) that identifies your server and resides on your server. Your server can give that message to Web browsers to prove its identity.

Certificate Server allows you to act as your own certificate authority for the purpose of generating SSL keys. Microsoft IIS requires a certificate from a certificate authority before you can require SSL on a directory. If you act as your own certificate authority, however, visitors to your Web site do not get the benefit of knowing that your Web site credentials have been scrutinized by a respected third party (unless you join your Certificate Server to a Certificate Authority Hierarchy). Certificate Authorities matter only if your users care that someone other than yourself has generated your SSL certificate.

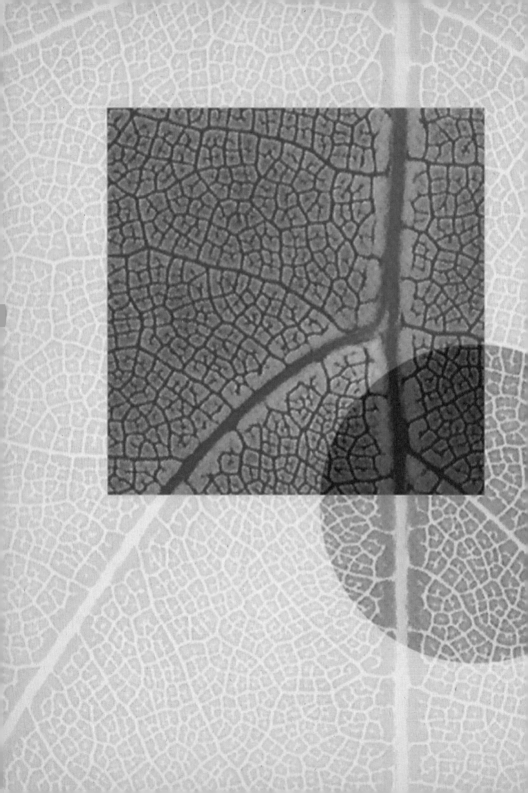

Chapter 7

INSTALLATION AND CONFIGURATION

The objectives in this chapter cover the installation procedures for the most important features of the following services:

- FTP service
- WWW service
- Microsoft Management Console
- Microsoft Certificate Server
- Microsoft SMTP Service
- Microsoft NNTP Service
- Microsoft Site Server Express Content Analyzer
- Microsoft Site Server Express with Report Writer

Adapted from *MCSE Exam Notes: Internet Information Server 4* by Matthew Strebe
ISBN 0-7821-2303-1   320 pages $19.99

Install IIS. Tasks include:

- ► Configuring a Microsoft Windows NT Server 4 computer for the installation of IIS

- ► Identifying differences to a Windows NT Server 4 computer made by the installation of IIS

Installing Internet Information Server is easy; understanding the services provided by each of the available options isn't necessarily so easy. This section shows you the basic installation process, explains the changes made to your system by IIS, and sets the stage for the installation of the remaining services that come with the Option Pack for NT Server 4 or NT Server 5.

IIS4 requires the following hardware and preinstalled software:

- ► At least an Intel Pentium 90MHz with 32MB RAM or a DEC Alpha 200MHz with 64MB RAM and 200MB available hard disk space

- ► Microsoft Windows NT Server 4

- ► NT4 Service Pack 3

- ► Internet Explorer 4

You will also need to obtain the Option Pack for Windows NT Server 4 if your copy of Windows NT didn't come with it. You can download or order the CD-ROM for the Option Pack, Internet Explorer, or Service Pack 3 from Microsoft at www.microsoft.com.

During the installation process, you'll notice a number of components that aren't covered anywhere in this book. That's because these components are for esoteric or very specific applications that are outside the scope of normal Internet site administration. These tools are not critical for IIS administration or exam purposes, but you may use them if you need to develop transaction-based applications for Internet Information Server. Most users will never use the services that are not covered in this volume.

 NOTE

Check the online documentation for information about these additional components.

Configuring a Microsoft Windows NT Server 4.0 Computer for the Installation of IIS

This procedure will install the default components necessary to completely understand the exam objectives and successfully complete the test. As you go through this process, watch the dialog boxes that the wizard raises to see the options.

TIP

You'll need to specify an administration account with administrator equivalence during the IIS4 setup process. Consider setting up a new administrative account used only for IIS remote administration, so that in the unlikely event your IIS administrative account is compromised, the remainder of your network remains secure.

1. Prepare a server by installing Windows NT Server 4, Service Pack 3, and Internet Explorer 4.01.

2. Insert the Option Pack CD-ROM or download the Option Pack from Microsoft's Web site.

3. Browse to the CD-ROM or the location where you've stored the Option Pack and double-click the setup icon.

4. (If upgrading, click OK to acknowledge that Gopher is no longer supported.) Click Next.

5. Click Accept to agree to the end-user licensing agreement.

6. Click Custom (or Upgrade Plus if upgrading) for a custom installation.

7. Check Certificate Server.

8. Double-click Internet Information Server.

9. Check NNTP Service, and ensure SMTP Service is checked.

10. Check World Wide Web Sample Site if it's not already checked and then click OK. This sample site will assist you in sorting out the specific behaviors of IIS, so it's a good idea to install it unless you already know everything you need to know about IIS.

11. Check Index Server if it's not already checked.

12. Check Microsoft Site Server Express if it's not already checked and then click Next.

13. Accept the default file locations and click Next. If the default volume does not have enough room for the IIS site files, select one that does.

14. Accept the default MTS location and click Next.

15. Select Remote.

16. Enter the name of the Administrator or a member of the Administrators group.

17. Enter the password for this account in both the Password and Confirm input boxes and then click Next.

18. Click Next to accept the default Index Server Catalog directory.

19. Click Next to accept the default mail root directory.

20. Click Next to accept the default NNTP root directory.

21. Enter **C:\certserver** (or another location if desired) in the Configuration Data Storage Locations shared directory input box, then click Next and click OK to create the directory.

22. Click OK to create the %systemroot%\System32\Cert-Log directory.

23. Fill out the certificate authority input boxes as appropriate for your organization, then click Next.

24. Click Finish and then click Yes to restart your computer.

Identifying Differences to a Windows NT Server 4.0 Computer Made by the Installation of IIS

The following changes are made to a running Windows NT Server when you install Internet Information Server 4 from the Option Pack as described in the previous section:

1. The Windows NT 4 Option Pack elements are added to the Start ≻ Programs menu, including shortcuts to all the Option Pack administration tools.

2. Directories for components selected during installation are created and populated with the default files for each service installed.

3. The following additional services are installed when you follow the installation procedure in the previous section:

   ▶ Certificate Authority

   ▶ Content Index (Index Server)

   ▶ FTP Publishing Service

   ▶ IIS Admin Service

   ▶ Microsoft NNTP Service

   ▶ Microsoft SMTP Service

   ▶ Protected Storage

   ▶ RADIUS Server/Proxy

   ▶ World Wide Web Publishing Service

4. Several keys are added to the registry and some existing keys are modified. You do not need to understand the purpose or location of these keys to administer IIS or to successfully complete the exam.

5. Two user accounts are created for administrative purposes: the IUSR_ *computername* account used to apply NTFS security to anonymous Internet browsers and the IWAM_*computername* account used to control permissions for Web applications.

▶ Configure IIS to support the FTP service. Tasks include:

▶ Setting bandwidth and user connections

▶ Setting user logon requirements and authentication requirements

▶ Modifying port settings

▶ Setting directory listing style

▶ Configuring virtual directories and servers

FTP provides a simple protocol for transferring files over TCP/IP networks like the Internet. Configuring the FTP service in IIS4 is easy. The Microsoft Management Console does a good job of centralizing and simplifying the administrative functions required for FTP service.

IIS4 creates the default FTP site on port 21 during the installation process. Often, this site will serve your needs perfectly. To use it you need only modify the service parameters for the default FTP site in the Microsoft Management Console to suit your requirements and store your files in the default directory C:\Inetpub\ftproot (or other directory as specified during the installation process).

If you intend to serve more than one FTP site, you should configure the FTP Master Properties in the Microsoft Management Console to suit the majority of your needs. New sites created will automatically inherit those settings, so you'll only need to change them when you want the settings for a specific FTP service to be different.

Opening the Microsoft Management Console

The following procedures will walk you through the steps required to create an FTP site and change all the useful settings for it. For all procedures, you should start by having the Microsoft Management Console open and displaying the IIS4 host:

1. Select Start ➤ Programs ➤ Windows NT Server 4 Option Pack ➤ Microsoft Internet Information Server ➤ Internet Service Manager.

2. Click Close to dismiss the Tip of the Day if it comes up.

3. Expand by double-clicking the Internet Information Server snap-in.

4. Expand the local host computer.

TIP

Instead of right-clicking in the procedures below, you can always select a component and then click the Action toolbar button. This is important to remember while taking the exam because many computers used in testing centers are old and may not correctly respond to right-clicking.

Creating an FTP Site

Creating an FTP site is simple in IIS4. Additional FTP sites are sometimes referred to as "virtual servers" in Microsoft documentation.

1. Right-click the local host and select New ➤ FTP Site.

2. Enter a descriptive name for the site and click Next.

3. Select the IP address you want this FTP site to respond to if different from the default of All Unassigned. Enter the port you want this site to respond to if different from the default of 21. Click Next.

4. Enter the path to the directory containing the files you wish to serve. Click the Browse button to browse to it if desired. If you intend to serve a new directory, you must create the directory before you can enter its name here. Click Next.

5. Check Read Access and Write Access if desired, then click Finish. You've now created an FTP site.

6. Right-click the new site in the scope pane and select Start.

TIP

If you get a message stating that the new site could not be started because it is not correctly configured, you've already got an FTP site or other Internet service running on the port you assigned. Stop and disable the other service or select a new port to run your new FTP site on. FTP sites cannot share the same port the way Web sites can, because no host header functionality for FTP exists.

Setting Bandwidth and Limiting User Connections

Limiting the bandwidth used by Web and FTP sites is useful when a server's primary purpose is not Internet service and you don't want to flood your Internet connection with service traffic, or in situations where you have to pay for bandwidth and you'd like to limit your costs. For FTP sites, it is not possible to limit bandwidth on a per-site or per-service basis, but you can use this procedure to limit the bandwidth of all WWW and FTP services:

1. Right-click your local host server and select Properties.

2. Enter the maximum number of kilobytes per second you want for all combined FTP and WWW traffic.

3. Click OK.

Limiting the number of users of an FTP site is useful when providing FTP service is not the primary function of a server and you don't want FTP use to bog down other services. Limiting users does not limit the amount of bandwidth used, but it does limit memory and compute resources and can also supplement security on sites where more than one or two users is never appropriate. Use the following procedure to limit the simultaneous number of users for a site:

1. Right-click the FTP site and select Properties.

2. Select the FTP site tab.

3. Select Limited To and enter **10** in the input box.

4. Click OK.

Setting User Logon Requirements and Authentication Requirements

Public FTP sites must allow anonymous users to log in. Private sites often don't want anonymous use. You can configure an FTP site to allow either or both. The Allow Only Anonymous Connections setting prevents accounts which may exist on your server (like the Administrator account) from being used over the Internet to gain full control of the site. Use the following procedure to allow or disallow anonymous access to a site and to select which users will be allowed to log into the site via FTP:

1. Right-click the FTP site and select Properties.

2. Select the Security Accounts tab.

3. Check the Allow Anonymous Connection box if you wish to allow public access to the site, otherwise clear the box. Check the Allow Only Anonymous Connections if you wish to ensure passwords are never sent over the network to access this site.

4. Click Add to add specific user accounts or groups to the FTP Site Operators list.

5. Select the account you wish to allow access and click Add.

6. Click OK.

7. Click OK.

Modifying Port Settings

You may want to host multiple FTP sites on your server, or connect certain sites to specific network interfaces on your server—for example, to have one site for internal users and one site for external users. By using a separate IP address for each site, you can have two FTP sites on the same port (e.g., on port 21) if the server has more than one IP address bound to its network interface. Use this procedure to change the TCP/IP properties of your FTP site:

1. Right-click the FTP site and select Properties.

2. Select the FTP Site tab.

3. Enter the port you want this site to respond to in the TCP Port input box.

4. Change the IP address setting as necessary.

5. Click OK.

Setting Directory Listing Style

Use this procedure to change the default MS-DOS directory listing style to the more compatible UNIX directory listing style. The MS-DOS listing style will not work with most FTP client programs because it presents an incompatible directory listing style that these tools cannot parse.

1. Right-click the FTP site and select Properties.

2. Select the Home Directory tab.

3. Select the UNIX listing style for compatibility with all GUI-based FTP utilities.

4. Click OK.

Configuring Virtual Directories and Servers

Virtual directories allow you to serve files that exist in locations outside the ftproot directory structure. The actual location of a virtual directory may be anywhere on your network. (Creating virtual servers is covered under the Create FTP site procedure, above.) Use the following procedure to create FTP virtual directories:

1. Right-click the FTP site and select New ➢ Virtual Directory.

2. Type the name for this directory (for example, **public**) as you want it to show in the FTP directory structure, and press Enter to proceed to the next pane.

3. Enter the local directory pathname or the UNC pathname to the share and the directory you want the virtual directory to point to. You may click the Browse button to browse the local machine or the Network Neighborhood. Click Next when finished.

4. Enter a username and password to be used as credentials to access this site if the directory exists on another computer. You may use the IUSR_*computername* account, but you'll have to set the password here to authorize entry to the site. Click Next. Re-enter the password to confirm and click OK.

5. Check to allow Read Access and Write Access as desired.

6. Click Finish.

You can right-click an FTP virtual directory and select Properties to modify any of these parameters at a later time.

TIP

If you see a red stop sign that says Error in the Scope Pane after you create an FTP virtual root, you most likely incorrectly entered the account name or password for the connecting account.

▶ Configure IIS to support the WWW service. Tasks include:

- ▶ Setting bandwidth and user connections
- ▶ Setting user logon requirements and authentication requirements
- ▶ Modifying port settings
- ▶ Setting default pages

▶ Setting HTTP 1.1 host header names to host multiple Web sites

▶ Enabling HTTP Keep-Alives

The WWW Service is the flagship of IIS. It is the most complex service and the most important, as it forms the backbone of even the simplest Internet sites. The complexity is easy to manage with the Microsoft Management Console, however—the skills you've already practiced for FTP are nearly identical to those needed to administer WWW sites, with just a few more settings thrown in for advanced features like host headers.

The information presented in this section is perhaps the most important information you'll need to know for the test, because it provides the answers to many exam questions. Be sure you understand everything in this section completely. If anything remains unclear to you when you've read through it a few times and practiced the necessary procedures, refer to other sources for additional clarification.

The WWW service serves documents in specially formatted text called Hypertext Markup Language (HTML) to clients called Web browsers, which can display the text and images embedded in the document. HTML is transmitted using the TCP/IP-based Hypertext Transfer Protocol (HTTP).

HTML documents are collected into related sets of files called Web sites. Web sites can be individually secured through both IIS security settings and NTFS security to provide different methods of user authentication and different levels of access per user. You can also change convenience and performance features of the various Web sites on your server to most efficiently handle their particular traffic requirements. Most per-site settings can also be set globally for all sites through the WWW Master Properties dialog box.

Web browsers select a specific Web site on an Internet server by one of three methods:

▶ **By unique IP address**. Each network adapter can respond to multiple IP addresses, and a Web site can be assigned to a specific IP address. This is the most compatible method of hosting multiple Web sites because it works with older browsers that support only the HTTP 1.0 specification. However, since a central authority parcels out Internet IP addresses, more than one may not be available. Use unique IP addresses when multiple IP addresses are available and when you must support legacy Web browsers.

- ▶ **By unique TCP port** on the same IP address. Each Web site can be set to respond to a different TCP port. However, since anonymous browsers expect Web sites to respond to port 80, most users may have a difficult time finding sites on other ports. This method also works with HTTP 1.0 browsers. Avoid using unique TCP ports unless no other method of Web site identification is available.

- ▶ **By the host header** on the same TCP port and IP address. Each Web site can register the host headers (domain names) to which it will respond. HTTP 1.1 clients transmit a host header to the server when they connect, by which the correct site can be identified without a unique TCP port or IP address. This method is the easiest to implement and the most transparent to users, but it only works with HTTP 1.1–compatible browsers. Use host headers whenever you can rely upon clients to use HTTP 1.1– compatible Web browsers. Figure 7.1 shows various host headers assigned to a Web site.

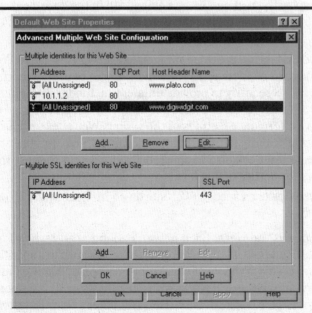

FIGURE 7.1: Multiple host headers for a single Web site

You can individually control the performance features of the various Web sites on your server using the Performance tab of each Web site's

Properties dialog box. Low-level site performance parameters are all configured using the Web site tuning slider, which allows you to set performance
characteristics for low-, medium-, and high-traffic sites. You can also enable
bandwidth throttling to limit the load this site will be allowed to place on
your network connections. This is useful when limited bandwidth is available and you don't want certain sites to "flood the pipe." HTTP Keep-
Alives can be enabled for sites where performance is critical. HTTP
Keep-Alives hold the TCP connection open between requests so that the
user doesn't have to wait to reestablish the connection each time a request
is made. Unfortunately, there's no way for the browser to inform the server
when it actually leaves, so each connection will always remain open for the
timeout period when the browser leaves. This is of no consequence except
on the most heavily loaded servers.

Authentication is controlled on a per-site basis. Through the Directory
Security tab of the Web site Properties window, each Web site can be
individually configured to allow one of the following:

▶ **Anonymous Access**, which allows users to log in without providing an identity. The server automatically uses the account
specified in the Directory Security tab to control NTFS security,
which by default is the IUSR_*computername* account. If anonymous access is allowed, it is automatically used by the Web
browser—a user cannot override anonymous access and provide
logon credentials unless the Web site requires them for access.

▶ **Basic Authentication**, which is the most compatible and widely
used method of authentication. Whenever anonymous access is
disabled or the NTFS security on a file or directory prevents
access, a logon dialog box is displayed. The username and password are transmitted non-securely to the Web browser and the
user is logged in using those credentials.

▶ **Windows NT Challenge/Response authentication**, which is
compatible with Internet Explorer only. Whenever anonymous
access is disabled or the NTFS security on a file or directory prevents access, the Web browser will automatically transmit a one-
way encrypted hash of the account credentials the user used to
log onto their local network. If a matching account exists on the
Web server, the user will be logged in automatically without raising a logon dialog box. Otherwise, a logon dialog box will pop up
on the Web browser and the user must enter a valid account name
and password to gain access to the site.

The functionality of a Web site can be enhanced using ISAPI filters. ISAPI filters are compiled code segments specifically written to enhance the functionality of IIS by modifying data as it flows between the server and the client. For example, a simple ISAPI filter could be used to change all the characters in a Web site to upper case, if you had some reason to do that. When a Web site is transmitted to a client, IIS sends the HTML document to each ISAPI filter in succession for processing. Those ISAPI filters can change the document in any conceivable way. For example, the Active Server Pages ISAPI filter actually interprets programming codes embedded in the HTML document to produce entirely new HTML pages as the pages pass through to the client. You can add, remove, and change the order of ISAPI filters on a global or per-site basis using the ISAPI Filters tab of the site Properties dialog box.

NOTE

The following procedures assume that you have the Microsoft Management Console running and the IIS snap-in expanded.

Creating WWW Sites

Although this procedure is not listed as a task in the Microsoft objectives, it is crucial that you know how to create a Web site for the exam. It also provides a good working site where you can test other necessary procedures without modifying any of your existing Web sites. Use the following procedure to create a Web site:

1. Right-click the local host and select New ➤ Web Site or right-click any existing Web site and select New ➤ Site.

2. Type a description (for example, **test**) for the Web site and press Enter.

3. Select the IP address to which this site will respond, or accept the default of All Unassigned if you will not be using distinct IP addresses to identify sites.

4. Enter the port to which this site will respond, or accept the default of 80 if you will not be using distinct TCP ports to identify sites. Click Next.

5. Enter the path to the home directory for this site or click Browse to browse to it. The directory must already exist.

6. Check Allow Anonymous Access for this site if you do not wish to require logon authentication for the default Web page. (Pages inside the site can require logon authentication through NTFS security.) Clear this checkbox if the site will require logon authentication to access the default Web page.

7. Set the IIS service security settings as necessary to secure this site. For most simple sites, Read and Script permissions are sufficient. For ISAPI Web applications (not filters), allow Execute permission. For HTTP posting, allow Write Access. If you want users to be able to list directories, allow Directory Browsing.

8. Click Finish.

9. Right-click the Web site and select Start.

If you get an error message stating that the Web site could not be started because it is incorrectly configured, you will need to establish a host header to uniquely identify the site because another site already exists on the same TCP port and IP address. Proceed to the next exercise to establish a host header for this site.

Setting HTTP 1.1 Host Header Names to Host Multiple Web Sites

If your Web service is set up in the default state, you will have gotten an error while trying to start the Web site created in the previous procedure. This happens because IIS will not start a Web site with an identity that conflicts with another site. Since neither the IP address nor the TCP port provides a different identity for this site, you must use host headers to make it unique. Use the following procedure to enable host headers:

1. Right-click the Web site and select Properties.

2. Select the Web Site tab.

3. Click the Web Site Identification Advanced button.

4. Click Add.

5. Select All Unassigned in the IP Address pick box.

6. Enter **80** in the TCP port input box.

7. Enter the DNS name assigned to this Web site in the Host Header Name input box (for example, `webtest.footest.com`).

8. Click OK.

9. Click OK.

10. Click OK.

11. Right-click the Web site and select Start.

TIP

You can have more than one host header for a Web site!

You can test host header functionality before you actually assign DNS names to your servers by using the HOSTS file on your Web server. Use the following procedure to test host header functionality:

1. Select Start ➣ Programs ➣ Accessories ➣ Notepad.

2. Select File ➣ Open.

3. Browse to `c:\winnt\system32\drivers\etc\` and open the HOSTS file. There is no `.txt` extension to this file.

4. Move the cursor to the bottom line of this file. It should be directly below the last text entry of the file.

5. Enter the following text, pressing the Tab key where indicated by {tab} rather than typing out the word "tab": `127.0.0.1{tab}webtest.footest.com`.

6. Select File ➣ Exit.

7. Click Yes.

8. Launch Internet Explorer or another HTTP 1.1–compatible Web browser.

9. Enter **webtest.footest.com** in the Address input box.

10. Verify that the correct Web site appears. Close Internet Explorer.

11. Repeat steps 1 through 4.

12. Delete the line containing the text you added in step 5.

13. Repeat steps 6 and 7.

TIP

You can use this handy method to validate any DNS name-based service before you actually assign the DNS names to the server. Just remember to remove entries after you test.

Setting Bandwidth and User Connections

If you serve a wide variety of Web sites, you may want to make sure certain popular Web sites can't bog down your server. This is especially important if you are serving Web sites for other individuals or organizations with content you don't control. Use the following procedure to limit both the number of users and the maximum bandwidth of a specific Web site:

1. Right-click the Web site and select Properties.

2. Select Web Site.

3. Select Limited To in the Connections control group.

4. Enter the maximum number of users in the Limited To input box (for example, **1000**).

5. Select the Performance tab.

6. Check Enable Bandwidth Throttling.

7. Enter the maximum network bandwidth to allow in the input box (for example, **128**).

8. Click OK.

Setting User Logon Requirements and Authentication Requirements

This procedure shows you all features of the different authentication methods. You will rarely need to enable all three methods, but they are all enabled here for practice.

1. Right-click a test Web site and select Properties.

2. Select Directory Security.

3. Click the Edit button in the Anonymous Access and Authentication control group.

4. Check Allow Anonymous Access.

5. Click the Edit button in the Anonymous Access control group.

6. Click Browse.

7. Select the IUSR_*computername* account (even if it's already the account listed).

8. Instead of entering the account password, check the Enable Password Synchronization checkbox. Click OK. Click Yes.

9. Check Basic Authentication. Click Yes.

10. Click the Edit button in the Basic Authentication control group.

11. Click Browse. Browse to the domain in which all authentication accounts are stored. Click OK. Click OK.

12. Check Windows NT Challenge/Response authentication.

13. Click OK.

14. Click OK.

Modifying Port Settings

At some time you may develop Web sites you want to operate from different ports. Some sites use unusual ports as a form of security; however, nothing about an unusual port makes a site more secure, because hackers know how to find it anyway. To modify port settings on a site:

1. Right-click a test Web site and select Properties.

2. Select Web Site.

3. Enter a new port to accept connections on in the TCP Port input box (for example, **8081**).

4. Click OK.

5. Launch Internet Explorer.

6. Enter **http://localhost:8081** in the address-input box. Verify that the correct site appears. Close Internet Explorer.

Setting Default Pages

You can assign the name of the default HTML document opened when no file is specified. This is especially helpful when moving a site that was not created for IIS to your Internet server. Use the following procedure to assign a default document name:

1. Right-click a test Web site and select Properties.

2. Select the Documents tab.

3. Click Add.

4. Enter a new default document name (for example, **index.html**) and click OK.

5. With the new name selected, click the up arrow until this default document name is listed above the other default document names.

6. Click OK.

Enabling HTTP Keep-Alives

HTTP Keep-Alives are performance optimizations that make Web sites more responsive to browsers by keeping the TCP connection open between requests between the browser and the server, thus eliminating the time required to reestablish the connection for each request. Use the following procedure to enable HTTP Keep-Alives:

1. Right-click a test Web site.

2. Select the Performance tab.

3. Check HTTP Keep-Alives Enabled.

4. Click OK.

▶ Configure and save consoles by using Microsoft Management Console.

Microsoft has changed the way IIS is configured in version 4 with a more coherent and easy-to-use tool called the Management Console. Eventually, all Windows NT Server and BackOffice software will use the Management Console to control their functionality. This objective explains the Management Console basics you need to understand for both real-world administration and the exam. You've already become familiar with the Management Console if you've read this chapter from the beginning and performed the exercises in the FTP and WWW service sections.

The Microsoft Management Console (MMC) is a single application used to control the settings of multiple services. Currently, all IIS settings can be controlled through the MMC. Future versions of Windows NT (starting with version 5) will use the MMC to replace current administrative tools like the User Manager for Domains and the Server Manager. For this reason, time spent learning the MMC now with IIS4 is especially well spent.

How can one tool be so flexible as to manage services that aren't even available yet? Through extensions called snap-ins. The MMC controls nothing by itself—every service you want to use the MMC with must provide a special ActiveX control called a snap-in that conforms to the MMC interface specification. Snap-ins can be individually loaded or unloaded from the MMC.

Each snap-in provides a hierarchical view of the settings for whatever services it controls. This display hierarchy is called a namespace. The hierarchy consists first of services which can be controlled. From there, what is displayed is up to the individual snap-in. In the case of IIS, IIS servers in the network are displayed next, then individual Web, FTP, SMTP, and NNTP sites. Inside each site, the directories contained in that site are generally displayed next. Figure 7.2 shows this hierarchy quite clearly.

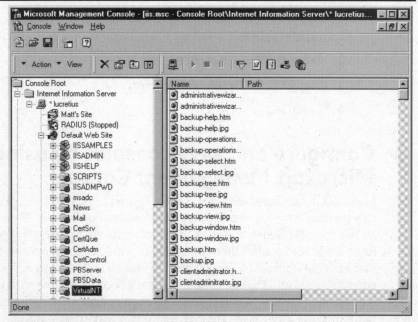

FIGURE 7.2: The IIS namespace in the MMC

The MMC display is split into two panes. The left pane, called the scope pane, displays the browseable hierarchical namespace. The right pane, called the results pane, contains the contents of the currently selected object in the scope pane. For example, if a Web site is selected in the scope pane, its directories are displayed in the results pane. This is the same concept used by the desktop Explorer to display the hierarchical directory structure of your disk on the left and the contents of the currently selected folder on the right.

MMC Settings File Contents

You can load and save various combinations of snap-in settings in files called consoles. Consoles are simply files that describe a set of MMC settings, such as which snap-ins are loaded and what the scope pane displays. For this reason, console files are quite small (usually less than 10K) and are suitable for e-mailing or otherwise distributing as you please to administrators. You can create new empty console files, and then add snap-ins to them to create custom administrative tools for the various services you wish to control. Currently, snap-ins are available for the following services:

- ▶ Internet Information Server

- ▶ Index Server

- ▶ Transaction Server

You can add any or all of these services to an MMC console by loading the snap-in that controls them. Some snap-ins can be extended to provide functionality beyond their default functionality. The IIS snap-in, for example, can be extended to control the SMTP and NNTP services in addition to the default Web and FTP control it provides.

Currently, console files cannot effectively be locked to limit their administrative functionality. Microsoft has announced that future versions will be secured so that you can create individual console files for users of your network. This allows those users to effectively administer the services under their direct authority without affecting services controlled by others. For example, you can currently create a console that has just the IIS snap-in loaded and which displays a single Web site called HumanResources. You can then provide this console file to the HR director at your company to control the HR Web site. In the future, you'll be able to secure the console file so that the HR director cannot use it to control any other Web sites.

Part ii

You've already used the MMC in previous sections of this chapter to control the Web and FTP services, so its behavior with services should be quite clear. Loading and saving consoles is quite easy: simply select Console ➤ Save to save a console, Console ➤ Load to load a console, and Console ➤ New to create a new one. The MMC behaves just like any other multiple document interface Windows application.

For each console, you'll use Console ➤ Add/Remove Snap-in to select the snap-ins you want to load. You can extend certain extendable snap-ins by selecting the Extensions tab in the Add/Remove Snap-ins dialog box and then checking those extensions you want loaded.

Creating, Saving, and Reloading an MMC Console

Creating, saving, and loading MMC consoles is quite easy. Each console is a normal file containing configuration information such as which snap-ins are contained, how windows are laid out, and to what level the hierarchical views are expanded. Use the following procedure to create, save, and reload an MMC console.

1. Select Start ➤ Programs ➤ Windows NT 4 Option Pack ➤ Microsoft Internet Information Server ➤ Internet Service Manager.

2. Select Console ➤ New to create a new empty console file.

3. Select Console ➤ Add/Remove Snap-in.

4. Click Add.

5. Double-click Internet Information Server.

6. Click OK.

7. Expand the Internet Information Server snap-in and the server's icon to display the default Web and FTP sites.

8. Select Console ➤ Save.

9. Browse to the desktop (the topmost setting in the directory pick list). This will store the console on the desktop so you can easily launch it from its desktop icon.

10. Enter iis in the File Name input box. The .msc extension will be added automatically.

11. Click the console window Close box.

12. Select Console ➢ Open.

13. Browse to the desktop and select `iis.msc`.

▶ Verify server settings by accessing the metabase.

You will not directly manipulate the metabase either for the exam or real-world administration purposes. For that reason, this objective is not important—it is a remnant of the beta-test phase of IIS during which IIS settings in the metabase had to be directly manipulated with a command-line utility because the MMC was not yet finished. The command-line utility still ships with IIS, but there's no reason to use it. The metabase is covered here solely for the sake of complete compliance with the Microsoft objectives.

The metabase stores all the IIS settings you can modify with the MMC—for instance, names of Web sites, the ports they run on, the IIS service security settings for the various sites, and any other configurable Web site information. Each time a customer accesses a Web site, IIS accesses the metabase—to determine, for instance, what the security settings for that specific request are before returning it.

The metabase is a speed-optimized registry Microsoft created for IIS because the older method of storing IIS configuration data in the Windows NT registry made IIS too slow to compete with other Web servers. Like the registry, the metabase is a hierarchical database of settings stored as key-value pairs. Unlike the registry, the metabase is optimized for access by IIS directly without going through the operating system services of Windows NT.

Some IIS settings are still stored in the registry for backward compatibility with tools written for IIS, but those settings are only written to the registry for the use of other programs. Whenever IIS checks the value of a setting, the value comes from the metabase.

TIP

The metabase is simply a registry that has been optimized for speed.

Viewing Metabase Settings

Use the following procedure to directly view metabase settings:

1. Select Start ➤ Programs ➤ Command Prompt.

2. Type **cd \winnt\system32**.

3. Type **mdutil enum_all w3svc metadata.txt**.

4. Type **notepad metadata.txt**.

5. Browse through the data displayed in the `metadata.txt` file.

6. Close the notepad.

7. Type **del metadata.txt**.

8. Close the command prompt.

▶ Choose the appropriate administration method.

This objective is about determining when to use the MMC to administer IIS and when to use the HTML service managers to do so.

There are two ways to administer IIS: directly, using the MMC and the IIS snap-in, or through the HTML service managers. HTML service managers are provided for the following services:

- ▶ IIS (WWW and FTP)

- ▶ NNTP

- ▶ SMTP

- ▶ Index Server

The HTML service managers are organized a little differently than the MMC, but they do a remarkable job of simulating its functionality. You can control nearly every IIS setting with the HTML service managers. Despite this functionality, they're rather clunky and slow compared to the MMC because of the additional processing required to format data for transport over the Internet. Because of this additional overhead, you'll rarely use the HTML service managers except when you need to administer a Web site over the Internet.

The HTML service managers are actually just special Web sites served by IIS that contain Active Server Pages scripts and controls that are capable of changing metabase settings. These pages are all organized under the IISADMIN Web site.

Although it's possible to control remote servers using the MMC, a Windows network must exist between the remote server and the administrative computer. Usually this is prevented by firewalls that are configured to block Windows networking protocols because Windows NT domain security is easily hacked from the Internet. In addition, the bandwidth between the server and the administrative computer must be fairly high because the MMC is not optimized for low speed the way the HTML service managers are. Most IIS servers on the Web have the Server, RPC, and Workstation services disabled to prevent hackers from exploiting security holes in the Windows networking protocols and from attempting to log on as the administrator. Without a regular Windows network connection, you won't be able to use the MMC.

Launching HTML Management Web Sites

Use the following procedure to launch each of the various HTML management Web sites:

1. Select Start ➢ Programs ➢ Windows NT 4 Option Pack ➢ Microsoft Internet Information Server ➢ Internet Service Manager (HTML).

2. Click the + symbol to expand the default Web site.

3. Notice the similarities between the MMC and the administration Web site. The left frame simulates the right-click or action menu in the MMC. The right frame simulates the results pane of the MMC.

4. Close Internet Explorer.

5. Select Start ➢ Programs ➢ Windows NT 4 Option Pack ➢ Microsoft Internet Information Server ➢ Microsoft NNTP Service ➢ NNTP Service Manager (HTML).

6. Notice the similarities to the NNTP snap-in for MMC.

7. Close Internet Explorer.

8. Select Start ➢ Programs ➢ Windows NT 4 Option Pack ➢ Microsoft Internet Information Server ➢ Microsoft SMTP Service ➢ SMTP Service Manager (HTML).

Part ii

9. Notice the similarities to the SMTP snap-in for MMC.

10. Close Internet Explorer.

▶ Install and configure Certificate Server.

Secure Socket Layer (SSL) protects the communications between the Web server and the Web browser for purposes such as commercial transactions (e.g., credit card orders) or for accessing confidential information. Secure Socket Layer does not protect your Internet site from intrusion. Instead, it protects the communications between your Internet site and Web browsers from interception and eavesdropping. When a Web browser connects to a directory on your server that has the Require Secure Channel option enabled, an encrypted link is established between the browser and the server, and sensitive information such as passwords and credit card information can then be transferred back and forth.

When you install a key with a signed certificate into the WWW service, you can then require SSL access to WWW service directories. The Require SSL Channel option on the Directory Security tab (which you cannot get to until you install a key) then becomes available. It is clear by default; you can check this option and require all accesses to the directory to be encrypted.

Web servers like IIS require more processing power, more bandwidth, and more time to send encrypted data than they do to send unencrypted data. You should therefore require SSL only on directories that contain sensitive data or Web pages that receive privileged information such as credit card numbers.

Certificates resolve the uncertainty faced by users of Web browsers visiting your site who have no assurance that you are who you say you are. When an individual visits your Web site, that person *can* assume that you are a legitimate business selling software or any other product over the Web, but you could just as well be an impostor with a bogus Web site illicitly set up to capture credit card numbers.

Certificates and certificate authorities assure Web users that your Web site is registered with a responsible organization and is safe to visit. A certificate is a message from that responsible organization (the certificate authority) that identifies your server and resides on your server. Your server can give that message to Web browsers to identify itself.

Microsoft IIS requires a certificate from a certificate authority before you can require SSL on a directory. (The Require SSL option is grayed out in the WWW Service Properties/Directory Properties windows until you install a valid certificate in a key for your Web server.) With IIS4, you can be your own certificate authority by installing the Certificate Server package in the Windows NT 4 Option Pack. If you act as your own certificate authority, however, visitors to your Web site do not get the benefit of knowing that your Web site credentials have been scrutinized by a respected third party (unless you join your Certificate Server to a Certificate Authority Hierarchy).

Installing Certificate Server is easy. In fact, you installed Certificate Server along with IIS, Index Server, and many other Windows NT Option Pack components earlier in this chapter. Once Certificate Server is installed, it starts automatically and is configured to issue certificates.

There are two things you can do to configure the Certificate Server service after you have installed it: you can change the startup options for the service and you can change the account that Certificate Server uses when processing certificates. If you don't need to process certificates often, then configuring Certificate Server to start up manually may be a good idea; you really shouldn't change the account Certificate Server uses, however, unless you have a good reason to do so.

Creating and installing the certificates issued by Certificate Server is performed using the Key Manager, which is covered in the next chapter.

Setting Certificate Service to Start Manually

Since you will rarely actually use Certificate Server once you've created the certificates you need for your site, it's a good idea to use the following procedure to set the service to start manually. You can then start the service whenever you need to issue certificates.

1. Select Start ➤ Settings ➤ Control Panel.

2. Double-click Services.

3. Scroll to the Certificate Authority service and select it.

4. Click Startup.

5. Select Manual.

6. Click OK.

7. Click Stop. Remember to start the certificate service before issuing certificates.

8. Close the Services control panel.

9. Close the Control Panel Window.

▶ Install and configure Microsoft SMTP Service.

The Simple Mail Transfer Protocol (SMTP) is the Internet standard for transmitting and routing mail on the Internet. It is a server-to-server back-end standard. When you check your mail from a client computer, you are using a different mail protocol called the Post Office Protocol (POP) to retrieve your mail from an SMTP server that has received it and is storing it for you. IIS4 does not come with a POP server, so can only be used to generate mail and to receive mail at a single mail drop. The SMTP service is specifically provided to mail-enable Web sites.

You can install the SMTP service simply by checking the SMTP option under the IIS component when you run the Option Pack setup wizard—in fact, if you've followed the installation procedure presented at the beginning of this chapter, you already have SMTP installed. There can be only one mail server per machine—unlike the Web and FTP services, support for more than one mail service is not provided with the SMTP service in Option Pack for NT Server 4.

Once it is installed, you'll notice an SMTP node in the Microsoft Management Console. All mail configuration is performed through this node or through the HTML SMTP Service Manager, which is similar.

As with the other services, you configure settings by right-clicking the service node and selecting Properties. This brings up a dialog box with the following panes:

- ▶ **SMTP Site** controls features that apply to the site in general, such as description, IP address, port, and logging.

- ▶ **Operators** allows you to add NTFS security accounts that are allowed to manage the SMTP service.

- ▶ **Messages** controls the size of messages and connections.

- ▶ **Delivery** allows you to change the undeliverable timings and establish connections to other mail hosts.

- ▶ **Directory Security** allows you to establish authentication methods, Secure Socket Layer connection requirements, IP-based address restrictions, and SMTP relay restrictions.

Browse through the various settings and features of the SMTP service.

Sending and receiving messages using the SMTP service is performed a number of different ways. You can write scripts using VBScript or other programming languages that access the programming interface provided to create mail. You can also simply specify the SMTP service as the SMTP server in your mail client and create messages. Or you can copy properly formatted text files into the SMTP Pickup directory, which the SMTP service will automatically scan and deliver.

The following mail folders are used by the SMTP service for the function indicated:

▶ **Badmail** holds undeliverable mail.

▶ **Drop** receives all mail messages for the domain.

▶ **Pickup** processes outgoing mail messages that are copied into the directory.

▶ **Queue** holds messages awaiting further processing when they can't be delivered immediately.

TIP

Check the online documentation for the SMTP service for more information on its workings.

Limiting the Maximum Size of an E-Mail Message

Use the following procedure to limit the maximum size of an e-mail message and to limit the size of a single session:

1. Start the Microsoft Management Console.

2. Expand the hierarchical view to show the SMTP service.

3. Right-click Default SMTP Site and select Properties.

4. Select the Messages tab.

5. Check the Limit Messages tab.

6. Enter **2048** in the Maximum message size (kilobytes) input box. This limits the size of an individual e-mail message.

7. Enter **8192** in the Maximum session size (kilobytes) input box. This limits the duration of a single transmission session to the size indicated. More sessions will be created as necessary to transmit all queued mail.

8. Click OK.

▶ Install and configure Microsoft NNTP Service.

This objective deals with the Net News Transfer Protocol (also referred to as UseNet News or simply News), which replicates messages from news clients around the network or Internet between all participating news servers. NNTP is often used for support forums or community-based special interest sites because of its convenient, timely, and public dispersion of information between users.

Installing the NNTP protocol is done as part of the regular Option Pack installation and is covered under the first objective in this chapter. As with all other services, configuration is performed through the Microsoft Management Console. There is also an HTML-based NNTP Service Manager you can use for remote administration, but knowledge of its use is not required for testing purposes.

Unlike Web and FTP services, you can only have one NNTP site per server. This site is called the default NNTP site, and it is automatically created when you install the NNTP service.

Newsgroups, or topics of discussion, are managed as directories from the NNTP root by the NNTP service. To create a new topic, you simply create a new directory in the `C:\Inetpub\nntpfile\root` directory (or other root if you've changed the default). When users create groups on your news server, directories to contain their messages are automatically created by the service.

You manage the NNTP service from the Microsoft Management Console by right-clicking on the default NNTP site and selecting an option from the menu presented.

NNTP supports virtual directories exactly the same way that the Web and FTP services do, except that NNTPs contain newsgroups rather than Web or FTP files. You can set NNTP virtual directories to a path on the local machine or to another machine, and you can control whether the group is read-only or writable (allows posting). You can restrict newsgroup visibility so that users without permission to see content can't see the newsgroup listed, and you can indicate whether or not Index Server should index the content of that newsgroup.

You can also set expiration policies for the entire site as well as for individual newsgroups. Expiration policies determine how long messages are kept before being automatically deleted. You can set messages to expire based on their date and their size.

You can enable logging for NTTP the same way you can enable logging for the FTP and Web services.

Creating an NNTP Virtual Directory

Use the following procedure to create an NNTP virtual directory:

1. Start the MMC.

2. Right-click the Default NNTP Site and select New ≻ Virtual Directory.

3. Enter test in the newsgroup name input box.

4. Enter **c:\temp** in the path input box.

5. Expand the Default NNTP Site.

6. Select the Directories node.

7. Double-click the test directory.

8. Check Index news content.

9. Click OK.

10. Right-click the test directory and select Delete.

11. Click Yes.

12. Close the MMC.

▶ Customize the installation of Microsoft Site Server Express Content Analyzer.

This objective is one of several covering Site Server Express, a "lite" version of the commercial Site Server product that is used to manage and maintain Web sites. Site Server Express comprises these components:

▶ Content Analyzer, which analyzes Web pages to map out the structure of a Web site

Part ii

▶ Report Writer, which digests information from IIS logs to create meaningful, concise reports

▶ Usage Import, which is used to import log information for Report Writer from IIS

This objective covers the first component, Content Analyzer.

Microsoft's Site Server Express helps you keep track of your Web pages, informing you of how many pages you are hosting, what the average number of links per page are, how much space is being taken up by images, sound, or video, and how often those pages are being accessed.

The Content Analyzer is the tool you use to manage what is stored in the directories of your Web site (unlike the Microsoft Management Console, which concerns itself primarily with the directories themselves and how the browser connects to them).

If you use a Web browser other than Internet Explorer, if you need to connect to your Web site through a proxy server, or if you need to be able to analyze Web pages protected by passwords, then you will have to specially configure Content Analyzer.

You configure Content Analyzer through the Program Options window, which you get to from the Program Options... item in the View menu. The Program Options window has five tabs:

General allows you to specify which browser to use with Content Analyzer and how to connect to the Web site being analyzed.

Helpers allows you to configure helper applications to be launched when you view or edit any defined object type.

Proxy allows you to configure Content Analyzer to work through a proxy server.

Cyberbolic allows you to change how the cyberbolic view of a Web site behaves.

Passwords allows you to configure any passwords that the Content Analyzer may need to access protected directories on Web sites.

NOTE

Content Analyzer uses Basic Authentication to connect to password-protected resources, so if you want Content Analyzer to map those portions of your Web site you will have to make sure that Basic Authentication is enabled.

Once you've installed and configured Content Analyzer, you can create a Web map to see and browse a graphical view of your Web site. This allows you to quickly identify and fix broken links and other Web site problems. You can create Web maps from two sources:

- Files of sites stored on your network
- URLs of active Internet sites

Content Analyzer can automatically explore your Web site no matter what the source and find the pages it's linked to. You can set constraints to limit how many pages it will add to your site or whether it will explore links to other sites. Figure 7.3 shows the Content Analyzer displaying a cyberbolic view of a Web site.

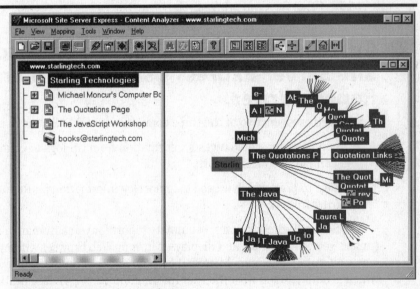

FIGURE 7.3: A cyberbolic Web map

Part ii

Configuring Content Analyzer to Work through a Proxy Server

Use the following procedure to configure Content Analyzer to work through a proxy server if you have one.

1. Select Start ➤ Programs ➤ Windows NT 4.0 Option Pack ➤ Microsoft Site Server Express 2.0 ➤ Content Analyzer.

2. Click Open Web Map.

3. Double-click Sample.wmp.

4. Select View ➤ Program Options.

5. Select the Proxy tab.

6. Select Custom Proxy Configuration.

7. Enter the IP address of your Proxy Server (e.g.: **10.1.1.1**).

8. Enter the port number for the HTTP Proxy Service on that server (e.g.: **8080**).

9. Click OK.

10. Close the Content Analyzer.

▶ Customize the installation of Microsoft Site Server Express Usage Import and Report Writer.

This objective covers two of the three components of Site Server Express:

▶ Report Writer, which digests information from IIS logs to create meaningful, concise reports

▶ Usage Import, which is used to import log information for Report Writer from IIS

Site Server Express creates a summary report for you automatically (unless you tell it not to) and displays it in your Web browser when you create an initial Web map. Microsoft Site Server (the commercial version, which is not included with Internet Information Server 4) has additional reports that can tell you more about your Web site. The summary report is divided into three parts:

▶ **Object Statistics** This part lists the number and size of the objects stored in your Web site, broken down by their type (such as HTML pages, Java classes, image files, and so on).

▶ **Status Summary** This part describes the links in your Web site, separated into on-site and off-site links, and shows the number of good links, bad links, missing links, and unverified links.

▶ **Map Statistics**   This part gives you such miscellaneous information as when the map was made, how "deep" it got, and the average number of links on a page in the Web site.

Report Writer is another major component of Site Server Express.

The logs created by IIS are a gold mine of information on how your server is used. Logs are useful for figuring out how well your server performs over time and what parts of your Web site(s) are the most popular and therefore are consuming the most bandwidth on your server.

Unfortunately, these logs create an enormous amount of information. You can log to an ODBC data source like a Microsoft Access database or an SQL Server, query the data, and then create reports to view any statistics you want, but that process takes a lot of setup effort. Report Writer can perform much of this work for you.

Report Writer is the part of Site Server Express that takes the log data stored by IIS and helps you understand how your site is being accessed. With Report Writer (and Usage Import) you can easily separate out important information from the voluminous amount of data a busy Web site can generate. You can track such data as the most frequently accessed pages, the most common errors, the times of greatest site access, and even where most of your accesses come from. To use Report Writer, you must have IIS4 logging configured to log the information you want. Report Writer can import from any of the logging formats.

The Usage Import tool imports formatted log files into the Jet database format used by Report Writer (the same format used by Microsoft Access). Usage Import is capable of performing reverse DNS lookups to resolve the IP addresses stored in log files to the DNS names of the computers that access your site. Whois queries to determine which organization owns the computer in question, and title lookup opens the HTML page referenced in the log entry to extract the page's title. These operations consume an enormous amount of network bandwidth and time (taking several seconds per entry), so you should only do them when you've got plenty of time and bandwidth to spare. You can automate the Usage Import tool using the Scheduler service. Note that automated Usage Imports that use any of the above resolution tools will take a lot of time, so they should only be scheduled for periods of network inactivity. Figure 7.4 shows the Usage Import tool.

Using Report Writer

1. Select Start ➢ Programs ➢ Windows NT 4.0 Option Pack ➢ Microsoft Site Server Express 2.0 ➢ Report Writer.

2. Click OK.

3. Double-click Summary Reports.

4. Double-click Executive Report.

5. Click Finish.

6. Select File ➤ Create Report Document.

7. Enter **c:\report.htm** in the file name input box.

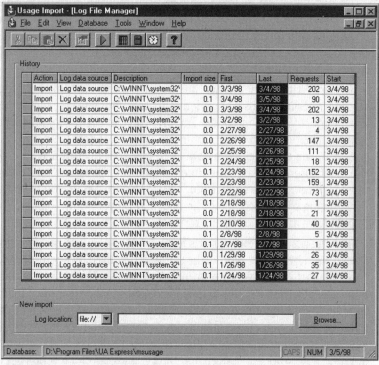

FIGURE 7.4: The Usage Import tool

8. When the report is finished, Internet Explorer will launch automatically. Browse the report using Internet Explorer.

9. Close Internet Explorer.

10. Click Close in the Report Writer dialog box.

11. Close the Report Writer.

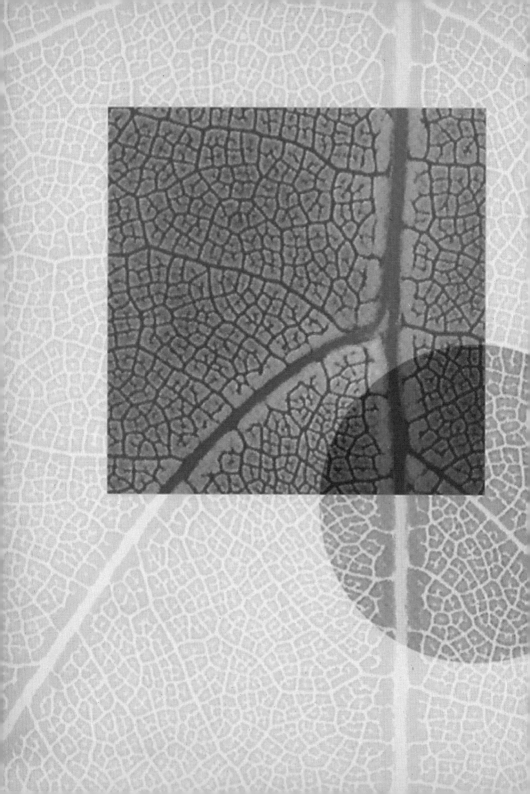

Chapter 8

CONFIGURING AND MANAGING RESOURCE ACCESS

This chapter covers the exam objectives related to configuring and managing resource access with Internet Information Server 4. Since permissions are an important aspect of almost every operating system object, the first three objectives in this chapter concern appropriate permissions for directories, virtual directories, and virtual servers. The next objectives cover writing scripts to manage FTP and WWW services and managing Web sites with Content Analyzer. The next group of objectives deals with configuration issues for Microsoft SMTP Service, Microsoft NNTP Service, Certificate Server, and Index Server. The final set of objectives involves managing MIME types, FTP service, and WWW service.

Adapted from *MCSE Exam Notes: Internet Information Server 4* by Matthew Strebe
ISBN 0-7821-2303-1   320 pages $19.99

▶ Create and share directories with appropriate permissions. Tasks include:

- ▶ Setting directory-level permissions
- ▶ Setting file-level permissions

This objective concerns those things you need to understand about NT file system permissions and Windows networking to properly control access and to support using virtual directories.

NOTE
Refer to Mark Minasi's excellent book *Mastering Windows NT Server 4, Sixth Edition* (Sybex, 1999) for more information about NT file system permissions.

Users identify themselves to Windows NT by providing logon credentials that the system compares to an access control list (ACL) containing individual permission entries maintained for each object the user attempts to access. Permissions are applied to just about every operating system object, but the two most important objects are network shares and file system objects like files and directories.

Your access token is created when you log on. It contains your user identity and the identity of all groups you belong to. The system compares the access token to the ACL of each secured resource (such as a share, file, or directory) you attempt to access. These resources contain ACLs that list each security ID from the user accounts and groups permitted to use the resource. If any of the identifiers in your access token match identifiers in a resource's ACL, you are allowed access as specified by that entry.

Share Permissions

Share permissions control access to shared resources. Directories that have been shared have four levels of permissions that can be assigned to various users and groups. Table 8.1 shows the different share-level permissions that can be assigned and their effects. Keep in mind that the default share permissions assignment is Full Control to the group

Everyone—this is almost never correct. You should usually remove this permission and apply permissions individually for the users and groups who actually need access to this resource.

TABLE 8.1: Share Permissions Properties

PERMISSION	EFFECT
No Access	Prevents access to the shared directory.
Read	Allows viewing of contained files and directories, loading of files, and the execution of software.
Change	Allows all read permissions plus creating, deleting, and changing contained directories and files.
Full Control	Allows all change permissions plus changing file system permissions and taking ownership.

Windows NT does not use share permissions to control access to the Internet host itself. Internet users are logged on locally to the Internet host, so share permissions for that machine usually do not affect them. However, that host may be logged on to other machines and serving data stored in those other machines through the virtual directory mechanism. In that case, share permissions do affect which shares can be accessed. Although share permissions will affect the ability to access those resources, you will normally use file system permissions, rather than share permissions, to secure data on Internet hosts.

Share permissions work regardless of the file system security measures you may have implemented with either the FAT or NT file system, so you can use them on both NTFS and FAT shared volumes. If you have directory permissions set up on an NTFS volume, users will be restricted by both sets of permissions.

TIP

Windows NT selects the most restrictive permission when combining share permissions and file system permissions.

NT File System Permissions

File system permissions complement the basic share-level permissions. The FAT file system does not have a set of file and directory attributes rich enough to implement security on a file or directory basis, so file system permissions are not available for FAT-formatted volumes. The server service in the Windows NT operating system implements share permissions to secure access to file systems that did not implement security.

WARNING

File system permissions are available only for NTFS (New Technology File System) volumes, not for FAT volumes. You cannot properly secure your Web site without using file system permissions. Your Internet site files and system integrity could be compromised unless you use the NT file system and properly configure security for all the Internet publication directories. Only Windows NT computers can read NTFS volumes.

NTFS implements security control over the sharing of information with file system permissions, which are assigned to individual files and directories using file system attribute bits that are stored in the directory tables of the file system. Consequently, file system permissions work even on stand-alone computers. For instance, if Jane creates a directory in an NTFS volume and assigns permissions for only herself, then no one else can access that directory (except administrators who can always take ownership of the directory) even when logged on to the same machine.

NOTE

Since Web users are logged on locally to the Web server, normally only NT file system permissions are effective for security.

File system permissions can also be used to restrict which files are available to a user. Therefore, even though share permissions may allow access to a directory, file system permissions can still restrict it. When both NT file system permissions and share permissions are applied, the more restrictive permissions will take precedence. Table 8.2 shows the effect of NTFS directory permissions.

TABLE 8.2: Directory Permissions

PERMISSION	EFFECT
No Access	Prevents any access to the directory and its files.
List	View filenames; browse directories. Does not allow access to files unless overridden by other file or directory permissions.

TABLE 8.2 continued: Directory Permissions

PERMISSION	EFFECT
Read	Open files and execute applications.
Add	Add files and subdirectories without Read access.
Change	Incorporates Add and Read permissions and adds the ability to delete files and directories.
Full Control	Allows Change and Take Ownership permissions and authority to assign permissions.

Conflicting Permissions

With the myriad shares, groups, files, and directories that can be created in a network environment, some resource permission conflicts are bound to occur. When a user is a member of many groups, some of those groups may specifically allow access to a resource while other group memberships deny it. Also, cumulative permissions may occur. For example, a user may have Read access to a directory because he's a domain user and also have Full Control because he's a member of the Engineers group. Windows NT determines access privileges in the following manner:

- ▶ A specific denial (the No Access permission) always overrides specific access to a resource.

- ▶ When resolving conflicts between share permissions and file permissions, Windows NT chooses the most restrictive. For instance, if the share permission allows full control but the file permissions allow read-only, the file is read-only.

- ▶ When a user is a member of multiple groups, the user always has the combined permissions of all group memberships and any individual permissions assigned to the user account.

NTFS defines access permissions based on file system operations. Because useful permissions usually require more than one file system operation, the file system permissions you can assign are actually combinations of permitted file system operations. Table 8.3 shows the file system operations that are allowed, and Table 8.4 shows the combinations that are formed to create actual permissions. The question marks in the Special Access row of Table 8.4 signify that special access provides a way

Part ii

to create your own combinations of file system operation permissions to create complex special accesses.

TABLE 8.3: File System Operations

Operation	Description
R	Read or display data, attributes, owner, and permissions.
X	Run or execute the file or files in the directory.
W	Write to the file or directory or change the attributes.
D	Delete the file or directory.
P	Change permissions.
O	Take ownership.

TABLE 8.4: Combined Access Permissions

Permission	R	X	W	D	P	O
No Access						
List (Directory only)	X					
Read	X	X				
Add (Directory only)		X	X			
Add & Read (Directory Only)	X	X	X			
Change	X	X	X	X		
Full Control	X	X	X	X	X	X
Special File (or Directory) Access	?	?	?	?	?	?

Each access permission performs a specific set of operations on the file or directory, which can allow or disallow any combination of tasks.

Copying and Moving Files with Permissions

When you copy a file (or a directory) from one directory on an NTFS or FAT partition to another directory on the same or a different partition, the file inherits the share and file permissions and owner of the receiving directory.

Moving a file or directory from one directory to another on the same partition does not change the permissions and owner of that file or directory. However, if you move files across partitions, the permissions change to that of the new directory.

The difference between copying and moving files is that when you copy a file, the original file still resides in its original location. You are essentially creating a new file in the new location that contains the same data as the old file. The new file (the copy) will have the receiving directory's new-file permissions.

When a directory is copied, it receives the directory and default new-file permissions of its new parent directory. As the new files are created within the new directory, they receive the new-file permissions of this directory.

Moving a file or directory within the same partition, instead of copying it, merely changes pointers in the directory structure on the existing FAT or NTFS partition. The file or directory disappears from the old location and appears in the new location but does not physically move on the hard disk. The file and share permissions and ownership of the file or directory remain the same. A file moved between partitions is treated the same as a file being copied because that is actually what happens.

WARNING

Some programs perform a move command by actually copying the file or directory to the new location and then deleting it from the old location. In this case the file obtains new permissions from the receiving directory, just as it would in a regular copy operation. This effect is sometimes called the *container effect*.

Setting Share-Level Permissions

1. Double-click My Computer.

2. Double-click the C: drive in the My Computer window.

3. Right-click a white area (an area where there are no icons or files).

4. Select New Folder in the pop-up menu that appears.

5. Type **Test Share** as the name of the folder. You must do so immediately or the focus will change. If the focus changes

and you can't rename the file, right-click the folder and select the Rename option.

6. Right-click your newly created Test Share folder.

7. Select Sharing.

8. Select Shared As:. The name of the folder will automatically appear as the share name. You can change the share name if you wish. This is the name that users will see when they view the folder through browsing features such as Network Neighborhood.

9. Click Permissions.

10. Click Remove to remove the Everyone: Full Control permission.

11. Click Add.

12. Select Domain Users.

13. Select Read in the Type of Access list box.

14. Click OK.

15. Click OK.

16. Click OK.

17. Click Yes to acknowledge the warning about MS-DOS clients.

Setting Directory-Level Permissions

1. Open the My Computer icon on your desktop.

2. Open the (C:) icon (or the icon for the NTFS partition in your computer) in the My Computer window.

3. Right-click on an empty area of the window and select New ➢ Folder. Type **test** to name the folder and hit Enter. Make sure the folder remains selected.

4. Select File ➢ Properties.

5. Select the Security tab.

6. Click the Permissions button.

7. Select the Everyone group in the Directory Permissions window and then click Remove.

8. Click Add.

9. Click the Show Users button. Select IUSR_*computername*. Click Add. Select Read in the Type of Access list. Click OK.

10. Click Add. Select Administrators. Click Add. Select Full Control in the Type of Access pick list. Click OK.

11. Click OK in the Permissions window and then click OK in the Directory Permissions window. Click OK to close the Properties window.

Setting File-Level Permissions

1. Double-click the test folder you created in the previous exercise.

2. Right-click on a blank area in the test folder window and select New ➤ Text Document. Hit Enter.

3. Right-click on the New Text Document icon and select Properties.

4. Click the Security tab. Click the Permissions button.

5. Notice that the ACL for the file matches the ACL of the containing directory.

6. Select the IUSR_*computername* access control entry and click Remove.

7. Click Add. Select Users. Select Change in the Type of Access pick list. Click OK.

8. Click OK.

9. Click OK.

▶ # Create and share local and remote virtual directories with appropriate permissions. Tasks include:

▶ Creating a virtual directory and assigning an alias

▶ Setting directory-level permissions

▶ Setting file-level permissions

Part ii

This objective concerns the creation and management of virtual directories. Virtual directories allow you to reference directories located on other volumes or machines as subdirectories in your Web site directory by an alias that you assign.

Virtual directories do not actually exist inside your root directory, but they appear to Web browsers as if they do. You can think of them as shortcuts to other locations on your server or other servers.

Virtual directories allow you to share Internet data that exists in directories other than your Web, NNTP, or FTP root directories by creating a "virtual" subdirectory alias that points to the physical location of the data. That data can reside anywhere on your network that is accessible to your Web server. Virtual directories are also useful for redirecting browsers to other directories. For instance, say one of your customers has moved their Web site off of your server. Rather than deleting their files and leaving Web browsers in the dark, you can simply change their virtual directory to redirect browsers to the URL of the new site.

The following can be used to identify the data source for virtual directories:

- ▶ a directory located on a local drive (or mapped network drive) referenced by directory path

- ▶ a share located anywhere on your network referenced by UNC path

- ▶ a redirection to another HTTP server referenced by URL

Virtual directories also give you the ability to control IIS service security inside your Web site. For instance, if you have a directory to which you would like to allow uploads, you can create a virtual directory inside your FTP site that allows writing. The rest of your FTP site remains protected by the IIS service security setting to allow only reading. You can control the following security settings separately for each virtual directory:

- ▶ Read
- ▶ Write
- ▶ Log Access
- ▶ Directory Browsing Allowed
- ▶ Index This Directory
- ▶ FrontPage Web administrable

In addition to those security settings, you can also control the following application settings:

▶ Application name and configuration

▶ Run in Separate Memory Space

▶ None (Permissions)

▶ Script (Permissions)

▶ Execute (Permissions)

NOTE
Virtual directories do not appear in HTTP directory listings or FTP directories. To access a virtual directory from an index list, the browser must know the name and enter it in the address line. You can work around this problem by creating an empty actual directory with the same name as the virtual directory alias.

Virtual Directories on Foreign Domains/Workgroups (Map Drive or Use UNC)

There are two ways to specify that data for a virtual directory should come from a foreign computer:

▶ **Map a drive**, and then specify a normal path. This option requires that you specify a drive using the Map Network Drive setting, and then enter the path to the data as you would for any other volume. Although this solution may seem more natural to those used to working with drive letters, it can potentially cause problems. The drive may for some reason become unmapped, and then your Web site would no longer work. Also, fewer than 26 drive letters are available for mapping, so large Web sites that span many computers would not have enough drive letters to map them all.

▶ **Use the UNC path**. This option does not require any prior setup in the desktop Explorer, and works no matter what your drive letter mappings are. For these reasons, specifying the UNC path is the preferred method of identifying remote computers.

Creating a Virtual Directory and Assigning an Alias

Use the following procedure to create a virtual directory for a Web site. FTP and NNTP virtual directories are created the same way.

1. Right-click the test Web site you created in the previous chapter.

2. Select New ➤ Virtual Directory.

3. Enter **Admin** in the Alias input box and click Next.

4. Click Browse.

5. Browse to `c:\winnt\system32\inetsrv\iisadmin` and click OK. Replace drive letters and pathnames to match your system directory. Click Next.

6. Click Finish.

You have now created a virtual directory that redirects any access to your site's \admin subdirectory to the administration Web site on your server.

Setting Directory-Level Permissions

Setting the IIS service security for a virtual directory is easily accomplished through the Properties panel of the virtual directory. Use the following procedure to change the virtual directory security settings:

1. Expand the test Web site to show the Admin virtual directory you created in the previous procedure.

2. Right-click the Admin virtual directory and select Properties.

3. Click the Virtual Directory Properties pane.

4. Check Directory browsing allowed.

5. Check Write access.

6. Click OK.

These settings were used to show the process of changing the IIS service security settings for virtual directories, not to indicate how a production server should be configured. Using the steps above as a guide, go back through and disallow Directory browsing and Write access.

Setting File-Level Permissions

Setting NTFS permissions for documents inside virtual directories is no different than setting permissions for any file system object anywhere. Use the desktop Explorer to browse to the location where the files or directories are stored, right-click their icon, select Properties, click Permissions, and change their access control list. The exercises in the previous section will walk you through this process if you need a refresher.

▶ Create and share virtual servers with appropriate permissions. Tasks include:

▶ Assigning IP addresses

The information for this objective is exactly the same as the information covered in Chapter 7 under "Create WWW site" in the section "Configure IIS to support the WWW service." That chapter covers the use of host headers and the assignment of IP addresses to Web sites.

▶ Write scripts to manage the FTP service or the WWW service.

Don't panic. You don't have to learn a scripting language to pass the IIS exam. In fact, although you can use scripting to manage services, you probably never will unless you're in the business of setting up Web sites full time. The purpose of this objective is merely to let you know that a scripting facility exists in IIS for the local machine and what functions can be automated through scripting.

NOTE

Refer to the IIS4 online documentation for more information about the Windows Scripting Host.

The Windows Scripting Host is a shell that allows you to use the VBScript and JScript interpreters (the very same ones used by Internet Explorer for browser-side scripting and IIS for server-side Active Server Pages) to control your server at the operating system level. The Windows

Scripting Host is a shell or environment in which scripting languages run to gain access to the local machine's registry, file system, or other system services.

Scripting to Change Service Properties

You can use the Windows Scripting Host to write scripts that change the IIS service properties. For instance, if you implement Index Server on a system that already contains hundreds of Web sites, it might be easier to write a script to loop through all the sites and set the Index of this directory setting, than it would be to simply check the setting for each site. As you can see, you'd have to have a lot of sites in order to save time by writing a script instead of manually changing your sites.

Scripting to Create Web Sites

Creating Web sites is a much more practical purpose for the Windows Scripting Host. It is a relatively easy process to automatically generate customized Web sites with the Windows Scripting Host.

Say, for instance, you are a teacher, and you want to give your students their own Web sites for posting stories and scanned images that parents can browse from home. Setting up each site individually for every student every year would be very tedious indeed. You can use the Windows Scripting Host to create a directory for each student, create the Web site in IIS, create default HTML files for each student (modified to contain their names as the titles), and include default links and images. Students can then modify this default site to customize it any way they want. You can then use another script to remove the IIS Web site and archive the files and directories when the students leave your class at the end of the year.

Using Scripting to Create Web Sites for Internet Server Administration

Use the following procedure to see how scripting can help you administer your Internet Server by creating Web sites:

1. Double-click My Computer and browse to `c:\winnt\system32\inetsrv\adminsamples`.

2. Right-click the file named `mkw3site.vbs`.

3. View the Visual Basic code used to create a Web site.

4. Close the Notepad.

5. Select Start ➤ Programs ➤ Command prompt.

6. Type **cd c:\winnt\system32\inetsrv\adminsamples**.

7. Type **mkw3site.vbs -r c:\inetpub\wwwroot -t test -o 8085**.

8. Close the command prompt.

9. Launch the MMC.

10. Right-click the test Web site and select Properties.

11. Verify that the port is set to 8085.

12. Delete the test Web site.

13. Close the MMC.

▶ Manage a Web site by using Content Analyzer. Tasks include:

- ▶ Creating, customizing, and navigating WebMaps

- ▶ Examining a Web site by using the various reports provided by Content Analyzer

- ▶ Tracking links by using a WebMap

Site Server Express Content Analyzer shows you how the Web pages on your site are related. It does not show you the pages themselves, and thus is similar to the Explorer (versus the Editor) in Microsoft FrontPage. You can use a regular browser to view the pages while using Content Analyzer, and you can specify which browser you will use to do so. You can also specify whether or not the Content Analyzer and Web browser should stay synchronized.

You can configure Content Analyzer to launch a helper application to view or edit any of the defined object types. This way you can use, for example, a text editor to fix a broken link or a paint tool to touch up a graphic image.

Each object type can have up to nine helpers defined for it. One use for this feature is to define several browsers with which to view a single Web page, thereby making sure that the page looks good in more than just Internet Explorer.

In Site Server Express you have two primary views of the Web site—a traditional, hierarchical view in the left panel and a cyberbolic view in the right panel. From this tab you can configure how the cyberbolic view will behave.

If the Web site you are mapping contains password-protected directories and you are accessing it via a URL, you will need to tell Site Server Express what those passwords are. Otherwise Site Server Express will not be able to map the password-protected portions of the Web site.

Creating a Web Map

A Web map is a graphical view of the resources in a Web site. When you create a Web map, Site Server Express traverses all of the HTML pages it can find in the Web site and records those pages as well as all of the objects (graphics, sounds, external pages, etc.) that those pages reference. The information about the Web site is stored in a .wmp file so that the Web site needn't be traversed every time you want to use Site Server Express. Site Server Express can traverse a Web site from URLs or from files. Figure 8.1 shows a cyberbolic Web map created in Content Analyzer.

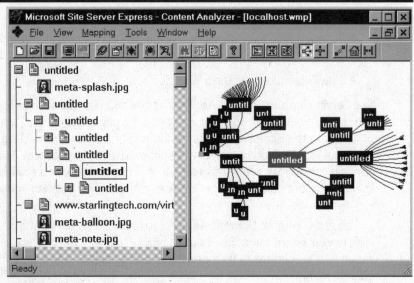

FIGURE 8.1: A cyberbolic WebMap

WebMaps from URLs   If Site Server Express is running on a different computer than IIS4, you will probably connect to the Web site using the

Web site's URL. Site Server Express will use the HTTP protocol to connect to the site and gather its information.

When you create a WebMap, you can set constraints and options to limit how extensive your WebMap will be and hence how much space it will take up and how much of a load it will place on a remote (URL-accessed) Web site. In addition, you can instruct Site Server Express to make a local copy of the Web site.

In order to create a WebMap from a URL, you simply provide the URL path to the home page of the Web site. You can instruct Site Server Express to explore the entire site, to organize the WebMap by directory hierarchy rather than the order in which links are found, and to generate a site report automatically as it creates the WebMap. If you do not want Site Server Express to explore the entire site, you will be able to choose how many pages will be explored. When Site Server Express is done exploring the site, it will ask you for a name prefix for the summary report, and (if you instructed it to generate a report) show you summary statistics for the Web site.

WebMaps from Files   If the Web site is stored locally (either on the same computer as Site Server Express or on another computer in your LAN) you can point Site Server Express to the directory path or UNC path to the Web.

As with creating a URL-sourced WebMap, with a directly accessed Web site you can set constraints and options to limit how extensive your WebMap will be, including whether it will access off-site links and which URLs it will not explore. In addition, you can instruct Site Server Express to explore all of the content of the Web site directories, rather than just the content referenced by hyperlinks. This is an excellent way to find orphaned Web pages.

In order to create a WebMap from files, you must provide the following:

▶ a home page path and filename (this may be a UNC path or a standard pathname starting with a drive letter)

▶ a domain and site root (this may be the Internet name of the Web site)

▶ the location of the CGI Bin directory used by the Web site (specified the same way you specified the home page path and filename)

You can instruct Site Server Express to explore the entire site, to organize the WebMap by directory hierarchy (rather than the order in which links are found), and to generate a site report automatically as it creates the WebMap. If you do not want Site Server Express to explore the entire site, you will be able to choose how many pages will be explored. When Site Server Express is done exploring the site, it will ask you for a name prefix for the summary report and (if you instructed it to generate a report) show you summary statistics for the Web site.

Configuring WebMaps

By clicking the Options... button in the New Map from URL window, you get a new panel with four tabs:

General   From this tab you specify the creation and exploration options of Site Server Express, including:

Ignore Case of URLs   Some operating systems (such as Windows NT) do not differentiate between uppercase and lowercase letters in filenames. Other operating systems (such as UNIX) do. You should set this option to match how the operating system hosting the Web site treats filename case.

Ignore Default WebMaps (URL WebMaps)   You can configure IIS4 (and other Web servers as well) to provide a default Web map to Site Server when Site Server begins to explore a site. Retrieving a locally stored Web map takes considerably less time and generates less Web server load than creating a new Web map. The default Web map may not be current, however, or may not include all of the information you require.

If No Default File, Map All Files in Directory (file WebMaps)   Some links may point to a directory rather than a file, and if directory browsing is allowed for that directory you may want the contents of the directory to be mapped as well.

Verify Offsite Links   Check this option if you want to make sure that links to other Web sites are still valid.

Honor Robot Protocol   Some Web sites have areas marked off-limits to automated Web index creators (commonly called Web spiders or Web crawlers). You can configure Site Server Express to not explore those areas on the site you are indexing.

User Agent (URL-based)   In this field you specify the user agent Site Server Express will use to explore the site. Your choices are Microsoft, Mozilla 2.0, or Mozilla 3.0. (Mozilla is the development name for Netscape Navigator.)

Local Site Root Directory (file-based)   If you move the location of the Web site, you can change this setting to match.

Site Copy   You use this tab to copy a Web site from the Web server to your local hard drive. You must specify the directory location where you want the copy to be stored.

Extensions   From this tab you specify what additional Web sites on your server Site Server Express will explore. The settings are as follows:

None   Site Server Express will only explore from the root you have specified and subroots below it.

All Other Domains   All references to pages or resources on the Web site, including those laterally and closer to the root, will be explored by Site Server Express. For example, if you start exploring at www.mysite.com/mainsite/start/home.html and the page www.mysite.com/mainsite/start/details/summary.html has a reference to www.mysite.com/mainsite/graphics.html, then the graphics domain will be explored as well.

Auto Explore URLs Starting With   This option allows you to specify particular domains (relative URL paths) that Site Server Express will explore.

Restrictions   From this tab you specify which URL paths Site Server Express will not explore.

Using WebMap Summary Reports

Site Server Express creates a summary report for you automatically (unless you tell it not to) and displays it in your Web browser when you create an initial WebMap. Microsoft Site Server (the commercial version, which is not included with Internet Information Server 4) has additional reports that can tell you more about your Web site. The summary report is divided into three parts:

Object Statistics   This part lists the number and size of the objects stored in your Web site, broken down by their type (such as HTML pages, Java classes, image files, and so on).

Status Summary   This part describes the links in your Web site, separated into on-site and off-site links, and shows the number of good links, bad links, missing links, and unverified links.

Map Statistics   This part gives you such information as when the map was made, how "deep" it got, and the average number of links on a page in the Web site.

Searching the Links

A graphic view of your Web links is a neat tool, but the real benefit of Site Server Express is its ability to search your Web site for problems such as broken links, "not found" objects, images without ALT tags, and large objects (which can cause a page to take a very long time to download). The Tools menu gives you the option to do a quick search on the following objects:

- Broken Links
- Home Site Objects
- Images Without ALT
- Load Size over 32K
- Non-Home Site Objects
- Not Found Objects (404)
- Unavailable Objects
- Unverified Objects

When you search on any one of these objects, Site Server Express creates a search results window and lists those objects in it. When you click on the object in the search results window, the tree view and cyberbolic view automatically go to that object. You can then double-click on the object (or its parent if it is a broken link or a not-found object) to view the problem object or HTML page.

Site Server Express makes finding broken links easy. Then it is just a matter of fixing that link with the software you used to create the page, or perhaps just editing the file with a text editor, so that the link points to the correct location. You need to set Verify offsite links if you want Site Server Express to make sure links outside your site are valid, because it does not verify them by default.

NOTE

Site Server Express, unfortunately, does not give you the capability to search for user-defined text, including searching for the content of hypertext links, headings, or titles. If you want to search for these items you must purchase Site Analyst. Site Analyst is a feature of Microsoft Site Server 2 and Microsoft Site Server, Enterprise Edition 2.

Creating, Customizing, and Navigating WebMaps

The following procedure will show you how to create a WebMap from a file location. Creating them from URLs is a similar process.

1. Select Start ➢ Programs ➢ Administrative Tools ➢ Windows NT 4 Option Pack ➢ Site Server Express 2 ➢ Content Analyzer to start the Content Analyzer.

2. Click the New WebMap button.

3. Select File and click OK.

4. Enter the home page path and filename of the default Web site home page (C:\InetPub\wwwroot\index.htm for most installations).

5. Enter the domain site and root (the name of your server).

6. Enter the location of the Scripts directory for the location of the CGI Bin directory (C:\InetPub\Scripts for most installations).

7. Click OK.

8. Click OK in the Generate Site Reports window.

9. Observe the Server Summary report and then close the report (browser) window.

Part ii

10. Select View ➣ Program Options.

11. Click the Cyberbolic tab.

12. Check the Enable Snap Mode option.

13. Uncheck the Show Common Ancestor When Selecting in Tree View option.

14. Click Apply.

15. Click OK.

Examining a Web Site by Using the Various Reports Provided by Content Analyzer

Content Analyzer for Site Server Express does not create various reports, it creates only one: the Site Summary report. You've already seen this report in the previous exercise, but you can use the following procedure to call it up again at any time:

1. Launch Internet Explorer.

2. Point to the file created in the previous procedure. By default this file is `C:\Program Files\Content Analyzer Express\Reports\localhost_summary.html`.

3. View the statistics presented in the HTML file.

4. Close Internet Explorer.

Tracking Links by Using a WebMap

WebMaps make browsing the links in your Web site easy. Use the following procedure to track links using a WebMap:

1. Select Start ➣ Programs ➣ Administrative Tools ➣ Windows NT 4 Option Pack ➣ Site Server Express 2 ➣ Content Analyzer to start the Content Analyzer.

2. Click the Open WebMap button.

3. Select the file you created in the previous procedure and click OK.

4. In the cyberbolic view pane, click the various links to track through the HTML links in your Web site.

5. Right-click on a page with many links and select Links.

6. View the link statistics.

7. Click OK.

8. Close Content Analyzer.

▶ Configure Microsoft SMTP Service to host message traffic.

The Simple Mail Transfer Protocol (SMTP) service provided with IIS4 gives you the ability to mail-enable your Web sites. Using the SMTP service, you can send mail from a Web page and receive e-mail to a general delivery mailbox on your Web server.

The SMTP service provides the function of sending and routing mail. You can use it to create mail messages that are then forwarded to e-mail recipients on the Web. You can also use SMTP to provide a mail relay function and to receive mail to a general delivery directory on your server.

NOTE

The SMTP service provided with IIS4 does not support the use of individual mailboxes for users, nor does it provide a POP3 or MAPI service to allow clients to check their mail. It is provided only to mail-enable Web sites. You'll have to use another product, such as Microsoft Exchange Server or one of the many excellent POP server products for Windows NT, if you want mail for your own Internet users.

The directories listed in Table 8.5 are installed in the `mailroot` directory. These directories manage all of the e-mail handling provided by the SMTP service. The online documentation provides more information about using text files as an interface to the mail system.

TABLE 8.5: Default Mail Folders

Folder	Description
Badmail	Holds undeliverable mail that could not be returned to the sender.
Drop	Receives all incoming mail for the domain. You can choose any directory to be the drop directory except the pickup directory.
Pickup	Processes outgoing text messages that are copied to the directory.
Queue	Holds messages for delivery when they can't be immediately delivered.

Another method of sending mail is to connect to port 25 on the mail host and transmit the text of the message. This is easy using programming languages like Java that can establish socket connections in a single line of code. You can simulate this usage by using the Telnet utility to attach to port 25 and typing in an e-mail message.

SMTP Service Specifics

The Messages panel, accessed by right-clicking on the SMTP service and selecting Properties, allows you to set specific parameters relating to message delivery for the SMTP service. Figure 8.2 shows the SMTP service Properties panel.

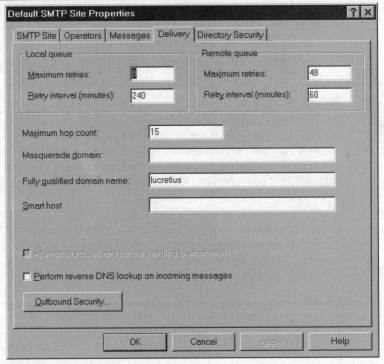

FIGURE 8.2: SMTP Properties

Here you can control the size of messages, the maximum session size, the number of messages per connection, maximum recipients, and undeliverable message handling.

Maximum message size is the preferred limit for the server. A message exceeding this size will still be transmitted as long as it's smaller than the maximum session size.

TIP

Familiarize yourself with the process of SMTP message size limiting.

Maximum session size is the absolute maximum size a message can be. If a message exceeds this size, the connection will be dropped immediately. The connecting mail host is likely to retry the connection up to its retry limit, so setting this value too low will result in a lot of wasted network bandwidth.

Maximum number of outbound messages per connection allows you to specify how many messages will be transmitted per connection. When the number of messages transmitted exceeds the value of this parameter, the existing connection is used, but a new connection is automatically opened. This can improve performance in cases where more than one physical path to the remote hosts exists. By setting a reasonably low number, you can force the creation of numerous simultaneous connections in parallel, which (if the bandwidth exists) will be faster than a single serial connection.

Maximum number of recipients per message specifies how many recipients are permitted per connection. If a message exceeds the number of recipients specified by this parameter, a new connection will be created to handle the additional recipients.

Send a copy of non-delivery reports to allows you to specify an e-mail address that you want copies of non-deliverable messages sent to. This allows you to track the accuracy of the e-mail addresses specified.

Badmail directory allows you to specify the directory where messages that were not deliverable are stored.

Delivery options specify exactly how the connections used to transmit messages are handled. This panel controls retries, maximum hops, domain name settings, and smart host settings. A smart host is a host to which all outbound mail can be transmitted for further delivery.

Part ii

Local/Remote queue Maximum retries specifies the number of times the SMTP service will attempt to deliver a message from the local queue. Once this limit is reached, the message is sent to the Badmail directory and a non-delivery report is generated.

Local/Remote queue Retry interval (minutes) specifies the time between retry attempts.

Maximum hop count specifies the number of SMTP hosts the message can travel through before it is dropped. The primary purpose of this counter is to prevent circular message paths, because most mail is transmitted with very few intervening servers.

Masquerade domain allows you to specify a domain name other than the domain name of the machine transmitting the mail to be placed in the From and Mail From fields of the message.

Fully qualified domain name can be used to specify a domain name other than the local host's domain name.

Smart host can be used to specify another SMTP server that you want all mail from the local host routed to directly. You'll use this option when a less costly path exists, or when you are downstream from an Internet Service Provider that provides an SMTP relay server that you want to use. Often, transmitting to a relay server on a faster pipe will improve performance.

Attempt direct delivery before sending to smart host allows you to specify that the local host is to attempt a direct connection to the receiving host and to transmit to the smart host only if the connection attempt fails. This puts the retry burden on the smart host.

Perform reverse DNS lookup on incoming messages forces the SMTP service to look up the domain name of the transmitting server and make sure it matches the domain name in the From and Mail From fields of the message—thus preventing mail forgery. Unfortunately, reverse DNS lookups put quite a burden on your mail host, and many legitimate mail servers use masquerade domains.

Outbound Security allows you to specify both logon security and encryption settings for remote hosts. Normally, you'll use these settings when you transmit to a smart host or other machine that you control. Most Internet mail hosts do not use encryption or logon security.

> **No Authentication** specifies that no authentication is to be performed.

> **Clear text authentication** specifies that a normal user logon is required to transmit mail.

> **Windows NT Challenge/Response authentication and encryption** specifies that an NT-compatible challenge and response authentication must take place. This setting works only with other Windows NT mail hosts.

> **TLS encryption** specifies that transport layer security encryption is to be used.

Basic SMTP site security is controlled through the Directory Security panel. This panel gives you several options for controlling access to your SMTP server.

> **Anonymous access and authentication control** allows you to specify the authentication required by users who will access the SMTP directories. You can chose from Allow Anonymous Access, Basic Authentication, or Windows NT Challenge/Response as appropriate for your site.

> **Secure communications** allows you to require the level of security that inbound connections must conform to for your SMTP site. Options are Require a secure channel and Require 128 bit encryption. You can also launch the Key Manager by clicking the button on this panel.

> **IP Address and Domain Name Restrictions** allows you to restrict access to the SMTP site by IP address, a block of IP addresses, or by domain name. This restriction works the same way address-based restrictions work for the other services.

> **Relay Restrictions** allows you to restrict the servers you'll let relay mail to your SMTP site. You can grant access to specific hosts, and you can grant relay access to any host that can authenticate successfully.

The SMTP service is configured automatically to support one default domain. You can add aliases to the service so that the SMTP service can handle mail destined for those domain names. There are two types of domains:

▶ **Local domains** route mail to the drop directory on the local host. You'll use local domains when you need to specify another domain name for your mail server.

▶ **Remote domains** route mail to other SMTP hosts. You'll configure remote domains when you need to override your default SMTP site authentication, encryption, and smart host settings for a specific domain.

TIP

Be sure you know how to create remote SMTP domains.

Domain settings are very simple. From the Domain Settings panel you have the following options:

Local/Remote determines whether the alias is local to this host or a remote host.

Default specifies that this is the domain name for the default directory.

Alias specifies that this domain is an alias.

Drop directory specifies the location of the drop directory. You can use any local directory except the pickup directory as a drop directory.

Route domain specifies an SMTP host that all mail for this domain should be routed to.

Allow incoming mail to be relayed to this domain is self-explanatory.

Outbound security allows you to set authentication and encryption settings to attach to this remote domain. These settings can be used to override the SMTP default settings for a specific domain.

Creating a Remote SMTP Domain

Use the following procedure to create a remote SMTP domain that overrides your default security for a specific mail recipient:

1. Launch the MMC.

2. Expand the default SMTP Site.

3. Right-click on the default SMTP Site and select New ➤ Domain.

4. Select Remote in the Domain Type radio button group and click Next.

5. Enter **test** in the Name to be used for the new domain input box and click Finish.

6. Right-click on the test domain and select Properties.

7. Enter **footest.com** in the Route domain input box.

8. Click the Outbound Security button.

9. Check TLS encryption.

10. Click OK.

11. Click OK.

12. Close the MMC.

▶ Configure Microsoft NNTP Service to host a newsgroup.

NNTP is a client/server public bulletin board service. News hosts store a hierarchical database of news messages by newsgroup or topic. Users may post new messages to a newsgroup, create a new newsgroup, or view the messages in a newsgroup using a news client like Internet Mail and News or Outlook Express, which come with different versions of Internet Explorer. Many companies use NNTP to create newsgroups based on projects and clients and then simply refer to these newsgroups to post information or check facts about the project. News is primarily a collaboration tool.

NNTP configuration is performed by right-clicking on the NNTP service in the scope pane of the Microsoft Management Console and setting options in the various panels.

News Site allows you to specify a site description for the MMC, a path header to be used in the path line of each news posting, the IP address and TCP ports the service responds to, connection limitations, and logging options. See the corresponding panels in the sections on WWW, FTP, or SMTP service for more information.

Security Accounts allows you to specify the anonymous account to use for NNTP and the NNTP service operators. See the corresponding panels in the sections on WWW, FTP, or SMTP service for more information.

NNTP Settings allows you to configure how the service responds to NNTP requests.

Allow Client Posting enables posts from clients to this news site. Unless you allow client posting, your news site will be read-only.

Allow Servers to Pull News Articles from This Server allows other news servers to replicate news articles from this server.

Allow Control Messages lets you determine whether control messages should be automatically processed.

SMTP Server for Moderated Groups specifies the SMTP server where moderated messages are forwarded. Optionally, this can be a local directory path on the local machine.

Default Moderator Domain specifies the mail domain for moderated messages. Moderated messages are sent to *newsgroupname@defaultdomain*. You must have e-mail accounts set up on that domain to receive moderated messages.

Administrator Email Account specifies the e-mail account to which non-delivery reports are sent when mail cannot be delivered to a moderator.

Home Directory lets you configure how the service stores the news files.

Directory Location and **Local Path** specify the location of the home directory as per the other services.

Allow Posting is analogous to the Allow Write Access option for the other services. For public news forums, this option is generally left on. For support bulletins, this option is generally turned off.

Restrict Newsgroup Visibility allows you to use NTFS permissions and authenticated logons to restrict the visibility of newsgroups to permitted users. This option creates considerable overhead and should not be used for sites that generally use anonymous access.

Log Access is the same as for other services.

Index News Contents allows Index Server to index newsgroups. This setting is set in the Home Directory for all newsgroups and can be changed for virtual directories.

Secure Communications operates the same as for the other services.

Directory Security is similar to the Directory Security panel for the WWW and FTP services.

Groups allows you to control how newsgroups are set up. This is a complex option so it is discussed separately in the next section.

Controlling Newsgroups

From the Groups tab you configure the topics of discussion as follows:

Create New Newsgroup allows you to create a newsgroup. This option opens a Newsgroups Properties dialog box. Creating a newsgroup immediately creates a directory in the `c:\inetpub\nntpfile\root` directory with the same name as the newsgroup. Posts for that newsgroup are stored in that directory.

Newsgroup Finder allows you to search for newsgroups based on search criteria.

Edit opens a Newsgroup Properties dialog box for the newsgroup you select in the Matching newsgroups list box.

Delete deletes the newsgroup selected in the Matching newsgroups list box. Files and directories from deleted newsgroups are removed the next time the service is stopped.

Part ii

The Newsgroups Properties dialog box has the following controls:

Newsgroup specifies the name of the newsgroup.

Description describes the newsgroup in further detail.

Newsgroup Prettyname can contain Unicode characters for other languages that some news clients support.

Read only allows you to prevent posts to the newsgroup.

Moderation options specify by whom the newsgroup is moderated: Not moderated, Moderated by default newsgroup moderator, Moderated by the e-mail account specified.

Virtual NNTP Directories

As with the other services, you can create virtual directories that appear as newsgroups in your NNTP service. The purpose of virtual directories in NNTP is to make content appear as though it is a normal subdirectory of your NNTP home directory when in fact it is located in another path, on another volume, or on another computer. The process for creating and using virtual directories with NNTP is the same as for Web and FTP sites.

Creating a Normal Moderated Newsgroup

1. Launch the MMC.

2. Right-click Default NNTP Site and select Properties.

3. Select the Groups tab.

4. Click Create New Newsgroup.

5. Enter **testing** in the newsgroup name input box.

6. Enter **A Test Newsgroup** in the Description input box.

7. Select Moderated By and enter your e-mail address in the input box.

8. Click OK.

9. Click OK.

Configure Certificate Server to issue certificates.

Certificate Server allows you to create the digital certificates necessary to establish secure connections over the Internet. You'll use Certificate Server whenever you want to secure your Web sites for commercial purposes.

NOTE

Refer to *NT Network Security* by Matthew Strebe, Charles Perkins, and Michael Moncur (Sybex, 1998) for more information about security and encryption.

Installing Certificate Server is easy. In fact, you installed Certificate Server along with IIS, Index Server, and many other Windows NT Option Pack components in Chapter 6. Everything you need to configure for Certificate Server is completed during the setup phase.

Using Certificate Server is also automatic. You don't need to do anything specific with it to generate SSL keys. The following process should demystify what's going on with Certificate Server, the Key Manager, and SSL:

1. Install Certificate Server.

2. Use Key Manager to generate key requests. These requests are automatically fulfilled by Certificate Server if you have it installed.

3. Insert the key into the Web site. At this point, Certificate Server and Key Manager are no longer necessary unless you want to create additional SSL certificates.

4. Enable SSL security encryption on the Web page using the Management Console.

Using the Key Manager

The use of Secure Socket Layer communications requires keys, and you use the Key Manager to create them and install them in a Web site. You can start the Key Manager from the Directory Security tab of a Web site or the virtual directory Properties window (it will run automatically when you click the Key Manager button if you don't already have a key installed in your Web site).

Part ii

Connecting to Servers and Viewing Keys   You can use Key Manager to manage the keys of several servers. When you start the Key Manager program, you will see the WWW server(s) on the local computer. You connect to additional servers using the Connect to Machine option on the Server menu.

The Key Manager main window has two panels. The left side shows the WWW servers you are connected to and the keys that are configured for those servers. You can expand or collapse the view of a particular server or computer by clicking the plus sign next to the computer or WWW entry.

The right side of the window details a selected key. You can see the key's name, its status, the range of time it is valid for, and the distinguishing information for the key that you entered during key creation (see Figure 8.3).

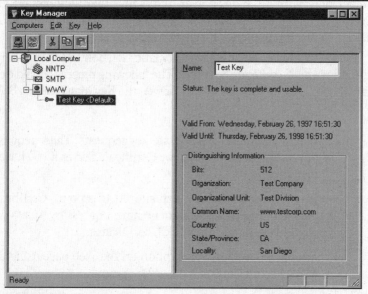

FIGURE 8.3:   The Key Manager program is where you create keys and install certificates for the WWW service.

When you double-click the key or select Properties from the Key menu, you see the Server Connection information for that key. This window specifies how your Web server uses the key. From this window you configure which IP address and port number combinations this certificate will be used for. If the window is empty, the certificate will not be used. You can add an entry that specifies that the key will be used for any port and any IP address, or you can be more specific (limiting the key to a particular port, IP address, or both).

Generating Keys   You generate keys from the Create New Key menu option of the Key menu. (Select a WWW server to contain the key first.) The key name and the password identify the key. The Bits field sets the strength of the key. (Depending on the version of your security DLLs, you may be limited to 512 bits or you may be able to select a more secure length such as 1024 or greater bits.) The key will be either placed in a file you specify or sent automatically to your Certificate Server.

The Distinguishing Information fields in the middle of the window describe your organization. This information, plus the identity of your Web server, is what the certificate authority will be "signing."

If you see a key with a slash through it, the key still requires a certificate. In order to make the key complete and usable, you must send the key to a certificate authority. You can send your request to various certificate authorities, or you can use the Certificate Server software to be your own certificate authority. The certificate authority mentioned in the Microsoft Help information is VeriSign. (You can visit the VeriSign Web site at http://www.verisign.com/microsoft/ for more information.)

If you are using the Certificate Server as your certificate authority, your key will then be complete and usable. You will want to select which IP and port addresses you will use the key for (or you can set it to all ports and IP addresses).

If you are not using Certificate Server for this function, after you submit the request to the certificate authority (usually via e-mail, with other information and perhaps a fee sent by other means) you should receive a file containing a certificate you can install in the key you created. You install a certificate (in the form of a text file) by selecting Install Key Certificate from the Key menu and selecting the file that contains the certificate. You will have to enter the password for the key. After you do so, your key's status will change to complete and usable. You will then be able to require Secure Socket Layer on directories in your WWW service. Instructions for how to install a certificate in your Web site are given below.

Moving, Importing, and Exporting Keys   Once you have installed a key, you can move the key between WWW servers using the cut, copy, and paste options in the Edit menu. You can also export the key to a backup file and import the key from a backup file or a keyset file. (Some

Part ii

security programs that create and manage keys store those keys in key-sets, which are special files on the hard disk.)

Installing a Digital Certificate on Your Web Site

There is no specific method to enable Certificate Server: once it's installed, it's running and enabled. Use the following procedure to install a digital certificate on your Web Site:

1. Right-click the Web site you want to install a certificate on and select Properties.

2. Click the Directory Security tab.

3. Click the Key Manager button.

4. Right-click the WWW service and select Create New Key....

5. Accept Automatically Send the Request to an On-Line Authority and click the Next button.

6. Enter **test key** in the Key Name field.

7. Enter **test** in the Password field.

8. Enter **test** again in the Confirm Password field.

9. Click the Next button.

10. Enter **test company** in the Organization field.

11. Enter **test division** in the Organizational Unit field.

12. Enter the fully qualified domain name that will be used by Web browsers to access the Web site in the Common Name field (e.g., www.footest.com).

13. Click the Next button.

14. Enter your country in the Country field.

15. Enter your state or province in the State/Province field.

16. Enter your city or locality in the City/Locality field.

17. Click the Finish button. (The certificate will be automatically submitted to the Certificate Server on your IIS computer if you installed Certificate Server as instructed in Chapter 6.)

18. Click the Add... button.

19. Accept the Any Unassigned IP Address and Any Unassigned Port options and click the OK button.

20. Click the OK button again.

21. Select Commit Changes Now from the Computers menu.

22. Select Exit from the Computers menu.

23. In the Properties tab for the Test Web site, click the Secure Communications Edit... button again.

24. Check the Require Secure Channel When Using This Resource button.

25. Click the OK button.

26. Click the Apply button.

27. Click the OK button.

▶ Configure Index Server to index a Web site.

Index Server enhances IIS by providing a method to search for documents like Web pages or office documents (or any other document type with an installed content filter) on a server by keyword rather than by name. Index Server creates a database of words contained in documents that are stored on the server. You can then simply enter a plain language search phrase, and Index Server will return a list of documents that satisfy the search phrase. Search phrases are called queries in database and indexing parlance.

NOTE

More detailed information on the operation of Index Server is available in *MCSE: Internet Information Server 4 Study Guide* by Matthew Strebe and Charles Perkins (Sybex, 1998).

Index Server is administered and queried through the Index Server MMC snap-in or through the HTML Index Server manager. The HTML pages you include in your Web site to allow users to query Index Server are called Query HTML pages. Index Server can index any type of document that you've installed a content filter for. Content filters are plug-ins that Index

Server uses to read a specific type of file. Index Server comes with content filters for HTML and for the Microsoft Office applications. Index Server cannot index documents for which there is no installed content filter.

Index Server doesn't necessarily search your entire site. It searches only the virtual directories you specify, which by default is your entire site. This feature allows you to remove virtual directories that you don't want indexed. You specify whether you want a site or virtual directory indexed by checking the Index this directory option in the Home Directory Properties panel.

You may need to have more than one catalog if you have more than one Web site on your server. Each Web site should have its own catalog to prevent documents contained on one site from showing up on queries in another. Queries cannot span more than one catalog. You create a new catalog by right-clicking the Web object in the Index Server snap-in and selecting New ➤ Directory.

Index servers can open an interesting security loophole. Since the index process runs as a system process, it has higher security access to documents on the server than many logged-on users have. Therefore, a query issued to an index server could return fragments of files that the user does not have permission to access—thus alerting the user to the presence of the document and possibly revealing segments of sensitive information.

Index Server prevents this situation by automatically cataloging the ACL for each file it indexes. When a user issues a query, each document that satisfies the query (called a query hit) is checked against the user's permissions. If the user would not normally have permission to view the document, the query is removed from the results list and no indication of the document's existence is revealed.

You can use a single Index Server to index multiple Web sites in your NT security domain by simply sharing the site and creating a virtual root for it on your machine. This requires creating a custom .htx file to return the correct link because the path to the HTTP document will be different between the two machines. The online product documentation discusses this problem and its solution in detail.

Indexing across NT domain boundaries is more complex. To successfully use Index servers in other domains, follow these steps:

1. Establish trust relationships such that the NT domains containing servers to be indexed trust the NT domain in which the indexing server resides.

2. Establish a user account that has the authority to access files on the remote servers. This account must have the 'interactive logon' right to log on locally to each Web server to be indexed.

3. Stop and start the Content Index service to begin indexing the remote machines once they've been configured.

4. Share and set up directories to be indexed as virtual directories on the indexing server.

TIP

Make sure you know the security requirements to allow interdomain Index Server access.

Enabling Indexing from the MMC

Use the following procedure to enable indexing on a Web site from the MMC:

1. Right-click on the Web site and select Properties.

2. Select the Home Directory tab.

3. Check Index this directory.

4. Click OK.

▶ Manage MIME types.

Multimedia Internet Mail Extensions (MIME) are used by Web servers to inform Web browsers what type of information is being sent so that the Web browser can select the proper plug-in to interpret it. For example, when sending audio data to a Web browser, the server must inform the browser that the audio player plug-in should be used or the content will be displayed as garbage on the screen.

MIME types are necessary because not all computers use the same file naming conventions and because filenames are not transmitted from the server to the browser. MIME types consist of File Extension/MIME Type pairs. When a browser connects to your server and requests a file with a specific extension, the Web server checks that extension against its MIME type list and returns the MIME type of data before the data stream begins. The browser then selects the plug-in that handles that type of content and provides the data stream to it.

To add a MIME type to support some new plug-in technology from your server, you must know the correct MIME content type for the plug-in and the file extensions you'll be using to store those files on your server. The producer of the plug-in will provide this information.

MIME types are managed through the IIS default Properties page. By clicking the File Types button from the Web server Properties panel, you can add, remove, and edit MIME types.

Adding MIME Types to Your Web Server

Use the following procedure to add MIME types to your Web server:

1. Right-click on the local Web server and click Properties.

2. Click File Types.

3. Click New File Type.

4. Click New Type.

5. Enter the file extension for the MIME type.

6. Enter the MIME content type.

7. Click OK.

▶ Manage the FTP service.

Chapter 7 covers management of FTP services in detail.

▶ Manage the WWW service.

Chapter 7 covers management of WWW services in detail.

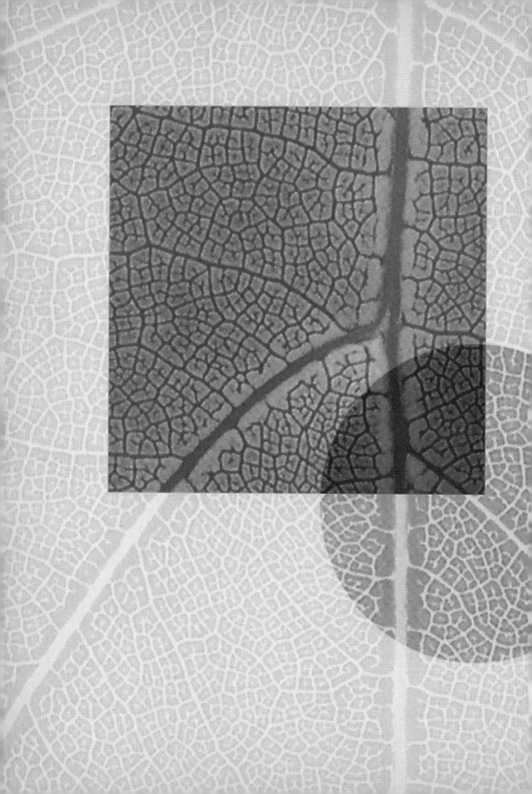

Chapter 9

INTEGRATION AND INTEROPERABILITY

This chapter covers two important aspects of the exam: database connectivity and indexing. Together, these topics make up about 10% of the exam, so they're very important but not as critical to your success on the exam as the topics discussed in earlier chapters.

Adapted from *MCSE Exam Notes: Internet Information Server 4* by Matthew Strebe

ISBN 0-7821-2303-1   320 pages $19.99

▶ Configure IIS to connect to a database. Tasks include:

▶ Configuring ODBC

Databases power modern commerce. Any serious attempt to use the Internet for direct commerce requires live access to these databases and the information they store. IIS supports attaching to databases through the Internet Database Connector (IDC) and, more importantly, through Active Server Pages (ASP).

IIS supports the ODBC (Open Database Connectivity) interface, allowing nearly all database products to function interactively over the Internet.

Windows NT 4 Option Pack comes with Data Access Components and Microsoft Transaction Server. Data Access Components is a suite of ActiveX objects and interfaces that allow the rapid development of Internet-enabled Web clients for databases. Transaction Server provides transaction support to ensure error- and corruption-free database exchanges over the Internet.

There are 5 basic steps to publishing a database on the Web with IIS:

1. Create the database using a traditional database product like MS SQL Server, Access, or FoxPro.

2. Create an ODBC interface to the database.

3. Configure IIS to support a dynamic database client Web site. This may include configuring Transaction Server to support atomic operations.

4. Create the Web site pages and scripts.

Step 1 is beyond the scope of this book—but we will go through a simple procedure to create and use an Access database for data storage.

The ODBC interface is the standard database interface that allows databases to access or link to other software products. ODBC provides a standard method to configure a database as a data source, or publisher of database information. Other software products (like IIS) can then link to those data sources to request (query) information from or store information to the database. Most database products that run under Windows support ODBC, so they can function as database engines for IIS. Figure 9.1 shows the Microsoft Access ODBC driver configured to host a database.

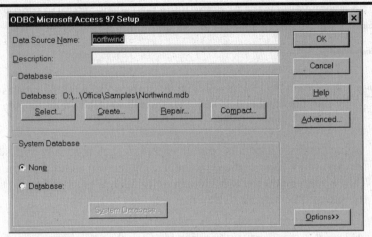

FIGURE 9.1: Microsoft Access ODBC driver configuration

Because IIS controls the services that actually publish your database on the Internet, you will have to tell IIS how you want to deal with the data. You should create a folder to contain the site, create a virtual directory or virtual server to support it, and set the access permissions as appropriate. Remember that ASP scripts must have Execute permission assigned in IIS to function properly.

Creating Site Data Using the Internet Database Connector

The IDC is an add-on to IIS that allows the dynamic publication of databases. Dynamic HTML databases are databases that are updated every time a Web browser requests them, so they contain up-to-the-minute snapshots of the database in question. This method of publication is different from simple static HTML databases, which are published manually whenever the database administrator gets around to it and do not contain changes more recent than the last publication.

IDC works as an extension to IIS, though it's actually an ISAPI application. When a browser requests a dynamic database, IIS reads the .idc file and performs the database connection and query instructions contained within it to create an HTML page. This HTML page contains the results of the database query stored in the .idc file and is formatted according to HTML format instructions contained in an associated .htx file. Since the database is required and a new HTML page is created each time a connection is made, data on the Web site is always in sync with data in the actual database.

TIP

Remember: The .idc file contains the query for retrieving the database information from the database server. The .htx file contains the instructions for formatting the data as HTML.

Some database products contain wizards to automatically create the .idc and .htx files required by the IDC. When you select the Dynamic HTML option in Microsoft's Publish to the Web Wizard in Access, you are creating the .idc and .htx files required by the IDC.

The IDC has no provisions for accepting database input from the Web, however—it is a one-way publication medium. You will have to use CGI scripts, ISAPI applications, or ASP if you want to update a database over the Internet. Figure 9.2 shows Microsoft Access's Publish to the Web Wizard creating a dynamic ASP-based database.

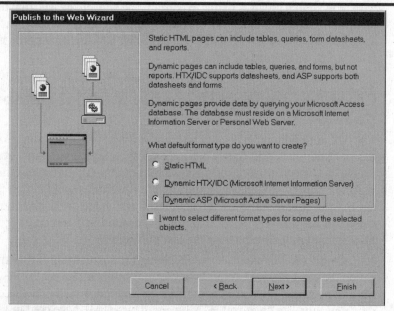

FIGURE 9.2: Microsoft Access's Publish to the Web Wizard

Dynamic HTML databases are convenient for their purpose, but they still don't allow remote users to add or edit the information they provide.

ASP provides this functionality by running code on the Web server to extract information from the remote Web browser and push it into the ODBC-linked database driver running on the Web server. This ODBC driver may simply provide an interface to an existing SQL server, or it may start a database engine to store data into a database file. In either case, the software running on the Web server retrieves the existing client data and stores revised records into the database.

WARNING

The directory containing your `.asp` files must have Execute permission set in the Internet Service Manager, or browsers will simply see your ASP code.

NOTE

For more information on Active Server Pages, refer to *Mastering Microsoft Internet Information Server 4* by Peter Dyson (Sybex, 1997).

Data Access Components

Windows NT 4 Option Pack comes with a set of related services, interfaces, and components called Microsoft Data Access Components (MDAC). These components are provided to ease the development of Internet-based client/server databases for larger databases such as SQL Server and Oracle. The core components of MDAC are:

Microsoft OLE DB, "middleware" that sits between the Web client and the server to translate standard OLE function calls into database-specific calls that a certain back-end database driver (for database engines SQL Server, Oracle, or Access) will understand. Essentially, OLE DB on the server lets you use the remaining components of MDAC to build your database application.

ActiveX Data Objects (ADO), a collection of ActiveX components that provide features to retrieve data from OLE DB–interfaced databases, manipulate that data, and return data to databases. ADOs are pre-built and can be called from VBScripts as well as compiled Visual Basic and Visual C++ applications. These objects essentially allow you to rapidly develop ActiveX-based database applications without having to develop the ActiveX components yourself.

Part iii

Remote Data Service (RDS), essentially a client-side data-caching service that allows clients to grab complete sets of data from a server, manipulate them locally, and return them to the server. This obviates network traffic that would be involved with interactive remote manipulation, thereby speeding the process and reducing network bandwidth requirements.

The online documentation covers these products in more detail for those who would like to build Internet database applications based on these technologies. You won't have to understand anything for the MCSE exam other than what the terms refer to. Unfortunately, the documentation that comes with these products is so jargon-filled and disjointed that unless you already understand ActiveX component-based development and three-tiered database development in detail you probably won't get anything useful out of it.

Microsoft Transaction Server

Microsoft Transaction Server is a middleware component that sits between the Internet-based client and the relational database back end. MTS is a set of programming interfaces to which your database clients must be written. The MTS application itself can be run on Windows NT, or on Windows 95 with DCOM support. If you fail to install DCOM support for Windows 95, installations under Windows 95 will fail. Additional information about MTS is available in the online documentation.

TIP

Remember that MTS can be installed on Windows NT, or on Windows 95 with DCOM support.

Transaction Server provides the ability to create transactions, which are atomic (i.e., base-level indivisible) operations. The entire purpose of Transaction Server is to guarantee that one of two things will happen for every transaction:

▶ The transaction will succeed, and all components of the transaction will be correctly added to the database.

or

▶ The transaction will fail, and none of the components of the transaction will remain in the database.

This sounds simple, but it's critically important to the stability of a database system. Let's say that a banking transaction, such as a transfer between accounts, consists of two operations: a deduction from one account and an addition to another account. Because computers can actually do only one thing at a time, one of these operations occurs before the other. If the completion of the transaction is interrupted for any reason between the two portions of the transaction, the bank computer will be left with a deduction from one account with no corresponding addition to the other. Their database will be corrupt, and you, the client, will be out that much money until the bank figures out what went wrong.

Transaction Server prevents exactly this sort of problem. By packaging a set of functions into a single atomic transaction, you are telling MTS that either all of these functions must occur or none of them can occur—which doesn't really matter, because if they fail they can simply be retried later. Due to the normal delays encountered with Web-based database clients, the opportunity for failure during transactions increases dramatically, to the point that database systems would simply not be possible without the services of a transaction system like MTS.

Database Security

Databases frequently implement security on an object level (tables, queries, stored procedures, forms, and reports may have individual security permissions) to restrict the availability of data that the server will provide. Each database system implements security differently. Some (like MS SQL Server) are well integrated with the operating system and will automatically log you on to the database using your domain credentials. Others (like MS Access) are not built for a specific operating system and so must either log you on as an anonymous database user or ask for credentials when you open a secured database.

For Internet databases, the obvious problem is that users must be logged in correctly. For databases that are tightly integrated with the operating system, you must ensure that users coming in from the Web have properly authenticated with your server or they won't have the security permissions they expect. They'll get access-denied error messages because they're logged in as anonymous Internet users. Perhaps the easiest way to ensure proper authentication is to set security on the directory containing the Web pages that the users are initially greeted with. This will force their browsers either to authenticate behind the scenes (Windows NT Challenge/Response) or ask for credentials (Basic Authentication). Once a user is logged in properly, your database will behave as expected.

TIP

The sorts of errors you'll encounter when Internet users are not logged in correctly vary widely depending upon the database product and the specific application in use. They often show up as either database login failures or object access errors.

Configuring ODBC

1. Select Start ➢ Settings ➢ Control Panel.

2. Double-click the ODBC control panel.

3. Click the System DNS tab.

4. Click Add.

5. Double-click Microsoft Access Driver.

6. Type **northwind** in the Data Source Name input box.

7. Click Select.

8. Browse to `c:\program files\microsoft office\office\samples` or to the location of your Access sample files installation.

9. Select `northwind.mdb` and click OK.

10. Click OK.

11. Click OK to close the ODBC control panel.

Creating Site Files

1. Double-click My Computer and browse to `c:\inetpub\wwwroot\`.

2. Select File ➢ New ➢ Folder.

3. Type **northwind** and press Enter to rename the new folder.

4. Select Start ➢ Programs ➢ Microsoft Access to launch MS Access.

5. Click OK to open more files.

6. Browse to `c:\program files\microsoft office\office\samples` or the location of the Office or Access samples folder on your computer.

7. Double-click `northwind.mdb`.

8. Click OK to dismiss the opening dialog box.

9. Select File ➢ Save As HTML.

10. Click Next.

11. Click the All Objects tab.

12. Click Select All.

13. Click Next.

14. Click Browse.

15. Double-click `default.htm` and then click Next.

16. Click Dynamic ASP and then click Next.

17. Type **northwind** for the ODBC data source name.

18. Delete all the text in the server URL input line.

19. Click Next.

20. Click Browse.

21. Browse through the directory selector to `c:\inetpub\wwwroot\northwind`.

22. Click Select.

23. Click Next to publish locally.

24. Check Yes, I want to create a home page and then click Next.

25. Click Finish. The Access Web Publication wizard will create the site files to attach to your ODBC data source.

26. Close Microsoft Access.

Publishing Data

1. Select Start ➢ Programs ➢ Windows NT 4 Option Pack ➢ Micro-soft Internet Information Server ➢ Internet Service Manager.

2. Expand Internet Information Server and your computer name so that the Default Web Site is visible in the scope pane of the Management Console.

3. Right-click Default Web Site and Select New ➢ Virtual Directory.

4. Type **northwind** in the Alias input line.

5. Click Next.

6. Click Browse.

7. Browse to c:\inetpub\wwwroot\northwind or its equivalent on your system.

8. Click OK, then click Next. Enter a custom port (such as **8081**) or other unique identifier for this Web site.

9. Check the Execute permission in the Access control group.

10. Click Finish.

11. Select the northwind Web site and select Action ➢ Start.

You can now use your Web browser to test the Web site.

▶ Configure IIS to integrate with Index Server. Tasks include:

- ▶ Specifying query parameters by creating the .idq file
- ▶ Specifying how the query results are formatted and displayed to the user by creating the .htx file

Interfacing queries to your Web pages can be as simple or as complex as you want to make it. To allow simple queries of your whole site, all you have to do is provide a link on your Web pages to a sample Web page that was installed when you installed the IIS software—link to /samples/search/query.htm on your own computer and you are done. This section shows you how to customize the way that Index Server queries your Web site.

Index Server, like ASP, is actually a set of Microsoft ISAPI applications. The Index Server DLL (IDQ.DLL) registers two file extensions for use with Index Server: .ida and .idq. Index Server also uses a third file type, .htx. To understand how Index Server works and to customize it for your site, you must know how these files interact. You should understand how the following components work:

- ► Query forms
- ► Internet Data Query (.idq) files
- ► HTML extension (.htx) files
- ► Internet Database Administration (.ida) files

Query Forms

Database queries start from query forms that look just like any other HTML form. Once you install Index Server on your Web site, you can embed the following form to any of your Web pages. The following form uses the sample search pages installed by Index Server in your Scripts directory.

```
<FORM ACTION="/scripts/samples/search/query.idq"
METHOD="POST">

Enter your query:

<INPUT TYPE="TEXT" NAME="CiRestriction" SIZE="60"
MAXLENGTH="100" VALUE=" ">

<INPUT TYPE="SUBMIT" VALUE="Execute Query">

<INPUT TYPE="RESET" VALUE="Clear">

<INPUT TYPE="HIDDEN" NAME="CiMaxRecordsPerPage" VALUE="10">

<INPUT TYPE="HIDDEN" NAME="CiScope" VALUE="/">

<INPUT TYPE="HIDDEN" NAME="TemplateName" VALUE="query">

<INPUT TYPE="HIDDEN" NAME="CiSort" VALUE="rank[d]">

<INPUT TYPE="HIDDEN" NAME="HTMLQueryForm"
VALUE="/samples/search/query.htm">

</FORM>
```

This form has five hidden fields. The information in these five fields is passed on to the .idq file identified in the FORM ACTION field. You should also notice that query forms to the Index Server use the POST method.

This HTML text is not interpreted by IIS or by Index Server—the HTML form listed above instructs your Web browser to display the form to you. When you click the Execute Query button, the form data (the input fields with names, hidden or otherwise) are sent to the Web server with the request that the query.idq file be used to process it.

Part ii

Internet Data Query (.idq) files

When IIS is asked to access an .idq file, it looks up the file extension in the registry and associates it with the IDQ.DLL ISAPI application. If that DLL is not already loaded into the IIS memory space, it is loaded now. Then control passes to IDQ.DLL, along with the location of the .idq file and the query data sent by the Web browser.

The IDQ.DLL application uses the .idq file to guide its processing of the query data. The .idq file contains parameters about the query such as the scope of the search, how many records (maximum) will be returned, how many will be returned in each query result page, what HTML template will be used, and how the results will be sorted.

Paths within the .idq files are from the virtual root of the server and cannot backtrack (i.e., they cannot access directories above the /www-root directory).

The .idq file consists of two sections:

Names defines nonstandard properties that this query may be limited on or display in the result. You can use this feature to index on special properties of documents that are indexed using content filters such as the content filter for Microsoft Office applications. This section is optional.

Query specifies the parameters of the query, such as the scope, columns, restrictions, and template. (These four parameters are required.) Parameters can (and some should) be passed from the HTML query form; for example, %Restriction% takes the restriction value—what you are searching for—from the field named Restriction in the HTML form.

Here is an example of an .idq file having the four required and two optional query parameters:

```
[QUERY]
CiRestriction=%CiRestriction%
CiColumns=filename,size,characterization,vpath,DocTitle,write
CiScope=%CiScope%
CiFlags=DEEP
CiTemplate=/scripts/result.htx
CiSort=%CiSort%
```

To use the preceding `.idq` file, you must place the `result.htx` file in the `/scripts` subdirectory, of course. You can use the `.idq` files to create multiple catalogs simply by creating multiple `.idq` files, each with a separate CiCatalog setting. For example, if one `.idc` had the settings:

```
CiCatalog=C:\Inetpub\Catalog1\
CiScope=\firstroot
```

and another `.idc` was identical except for the settings:

```
CiCatalog=C:\Inetpub\Catalog2\
CiScope=\secondroot
```

then you would have two catalogs: one in the `Catalog1` subdirectory, which allows the user to find files from the `\firstroot` subdirectory, and the other in the `Catalog2` subdirectory, which allows the user to find files from the `\secondroot` subdirectory. Note, however, that the preceding example doesn't keep both catalogs from indexing your entire Web site. It just establishes two directories and allows both to be searched with a restriction on each.

A better use for the CiScope parameter is to limit queries to certain parts of your Web site when the network user is looking for particular information. For example, if you have separate subdirectories for new products, current products, press releases, device drivers, and technical documentation, then you can create specialized `.idq` files for each area of your Web site. That way, browsers of your Web site won't have to wade through extraneous information that just happens to match the search criteria the user types in. This technique is used in Internet search engines that allow you to select whether the search is conducted on the whole site or only on focused sections.

HTML Extension (.htx) Files

IDQ.DLL uses the parameters from the `.idq` page to search its database. It needs another file to tell it how to format the resulting data so that IIS can send it to the Web browser, and `.htx` files are Microsoft's answer to that problem.

The `.htx` documents are almost like programming languages because they must be able to respond to various conditions; for example, no files match your query, one page worth of files match, or many HTML pages worth of files match. Other than the special conditional constructs (e.g., the `%if` statement and `%endif` statement) and the commands to insert data returned from the query (e.g., %filename% and %DocTitle%), the .htx document contains regular HTML-formatted text.

The following .htx file is very simple; it is merely an example of how an .htx file is formatted. You should use the more complicated query sample files installed with Index Server—or edit them to suit the needs of your Web site.

```html
<HTML>
<!-
 <%CiTemplate%>
->
<HEAD>
<TITLE>SEARCH</TITLE>
</HEAD>
<%begindetail%>
 <p>
 <dt>
  <%CiCurrentRecordNumber%>.
  <%if DocTitle isempty%>
   <b><a href="<%EscapeURL vpath%>"><%filename%></a></b>
  <%else%>
   <b><a href="<%EscapeURL vpath%>"><%DocTitle%></a></b>
  <%endif%>
 <dd>
  <b><i>Abstract: </i></b><%characterization%>
  <br>
  <cite>
   <a href="<%EscapeURL vpath%>">http://
<%server_name%><%vpath%></a>
   <font size=-1> - <%if size eq ""%>(size and time
unknown)<%else%>size <%size%> bytes - <%write%>
GMT<%endif%></font>
  </cite>
<%enddetail%>
</HTML>
```

Internet Database Administration (.ida) Files

One more type of file that you should be familiar with to customize Index Server for your Web site is the .ida file type. These files are like .idq files except that .ida files are focused on the overall housekeeping of the Index Server, instead of the actual queries. Furthermore, .ida files accept only four parameters:

CiCatalog specifies where the catalog is located. If it is missing, the default location specified in the registry is used.

CiTemplate specifies the template file (i.e., .htx or .htm file) that will be used to format the data that results from execution of the .ida command.

CiAdministration specifies use of the administrative command, which must be one of the following: UpdateDirectories, GetState, ForceMerge, or ScanDirectories. If nothing is specified, the administrative action will default to GetState.

CiLocale specifies locale information such as the character set or time zone in use.

The administration .ida file for updating the virtual directories that is installed when you install Index Server is as follows:

```
[Admin]
CiCatalog=C:\Inetpub\
CiTemplate=/srchadm/admin.htm
CiAdminOperation=UpdateDirectories
```

The administration .ida file for forcing a master merge that is installed when you install Index Server is as follows:

```
[Admin]
CiCatalog=C:\Inetpub\
CiTemplate=/srchadm/admin.htm
CiAdminOperation=ForceMerge
```

The administration .ida file for forcing a scan of the virtual directories that is installed when you install Index Server is as follows.

```
[Admin]
CiCatalog=C:\Inetpub\
CiTemplate=/srchadm/admin.htm
CiAdminOperation=ScanDirectories
```

The administration `.ida` file for getting statistics on Index Server that is installed when you install Index Server is as follows:

```
[Admin]
CiCatalog=C:\Inetpub\
CiTemplate=/Scripts/srchadm/state.htx
CiAdminOperation=GetState
```

These four administrative files don't seem like much for the results they produce. Most of the work is actually done in the IDQ.DLL program, and the results are formatted using the `admin.htm` and `state.htx` files. You should have no reason to modify the `admin.htm` and the `state.htx` files, but you may want to modify the `.ida` files to customize the functionality of Index Server for your site.

For example, you might want to create `.ida` files that allow you to manage separate master catalogs. You could create two sets of `.ida` files, like those shown in the example, except that the CiCatalog entry for one would point to the `C:\InetPub\Catalog1` and the other set would point to `C:\InetPub\Catalog2`. You could then use these administration pages (using the UpdateDirectories `.ida` command) to limit the virtual directories that each will index. You will end up with two (or more) catalogs that index different portions of your Web site. You can then use specialized `.idq` files (as described in the section on Internet Data Query files) to search these limited catalogs.

Specifying Query Parameters by Creating the .idq File

1. Select Start ➤ Programs ➤ Accessories ➤ Notepad.

2. Select File ➤ Open.

3. Browse to `c:\inetpub\iissamples\exair\search` or the location of the ExAir sample site on your computer.

4. Select All files in the Files of Type box.

5. Double-click `query.idq` in the files list box.

6. Read through the file in detail. In addition to showing actual IDQ variables, this document explains the purpose of each variable in detail.

7. Close Notepad.

Specifying How the Query Results Are Formatted and Displayed to the User by Creating the .htx File

1. Select Start ➢ Programs ➢ Accessories ➢ Notepad.

2. Select File ➢ Open.

3. Browse to `c:\inetpub\iissamples\exair\search` or the location of the ExAir sample site on your computer.

4. Select All files in the Files of Type box.

5. Double-click `query.htx` in the files list box.

6. Read through the file in detail. In addition to showing actual HTX variables, this document explains the purpose of each variable in detail.

7. Close Notepad.

Part ii

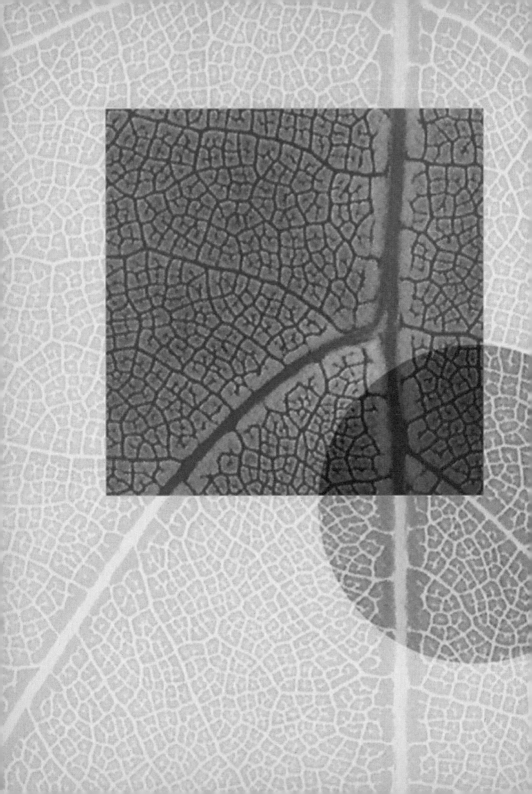

Chapter 10
RUNNING APPLICATIONS

I nternet Information Server by itself is a fast and secure platform for serving HTML files to Web browsers. This chapter will show you how Internet Server Application Programming Interface (ISAPI) and Active Server Pages (ASP) give IIS additional flexibility and power by generating dynamic Web pages.

ISAPI applications are written to a specialized interface in a compiled programming language such as C++. ISAPI applications can perform complex operations on their own or they can be interpreters for scripting languages such as Perl, TCL, Visual Basic, or JScript.

Active Server Pages use an ISAPI Dynamic Link Library (DLL) as a scripting host to implement the VBScript and JScript scripting languages on the server side. These are the same language modules used on the client side in Web

Adapted from *MCSE Exam Notes: Internet Information Server 4* by Matthew Strebe

ISBN 0-7821-2303-1   320 pages $19.99

browsers, although there are some inherent differences between the server and client environments.

▶ Configure IIS to support server-side scripting.

Server-side scripting is the use of scripting languages like Visual Basic or JScript to dynamically create Web pages on demand in the Web server. Also called Active Server Pages, server-side scripting is implemented by the ASP.DLL ISAPI application, which acts as a filter on the output stream to convert .asp files into HTML as they're transmitted to the user.

There isn't anything special you have to do to support server-side scripting, since IIS is configured to support it by default. All you actually need to do is hyperlink .asp files to your Web site. Web sites or virtual directories that contain ASP files must have the Script or Execute permissions set in the Home Directory tab of the Web site's Properties panel. Figure 10.1 shows the Web site Properties panel configured for ASP.

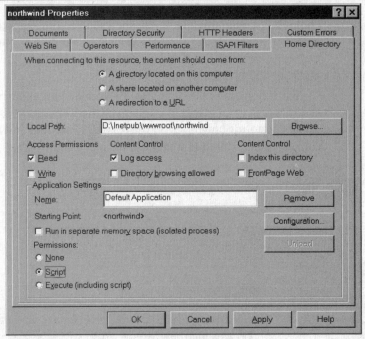

FIGURE 10.1: Scripting is enabled for this Web site

ASPs are HTML pages that contain scripts written in VBScript or JScript, as well as regular HTML text. ASPs have the extension .asp, which is listed in the extensions that are associated with CGI and ISAPI applications. The .asp extension is associated with the ASP.DLL ISAPI application. When a Web browser requests a page with an .asp extension, IIS sends the .asp file to ASP.DLL for processing before transmitting it to the user.

NOTE

Windows NT will only prompt for authentication if you disable anonymous login and secure your Web site files against access by the IUSR_*computername* account.

When IIS is asked to return a file ending in .asp, it recognizes that the ASP ISAPI filter must first process the file. The ASP filter processes the .asp file sequentially until it encounters a scripting language portion of the .asp page. (The special symbols <% and %> surround the scripting language portions of the .asp document.)

ASP.DLL interprets the scripting language portion(s) of the document using the default scripting language for the page, which is VBScript unless the DefaultScriptLanguage registry key is changed or a command such as <%@ LANGUAGE=JScript %> appears at the beginning of the document. The results of the scripted action must either be in HTML code to be viewed on the client browser or be understood by a registered MIME type.

You can also include scripts in .asp files using the SCRIPT LANGUAGE and RUNAT HTML tags. For example, <SCRIPT LANGUAGE= JScript RUNAT=Server> identifies the start of a JScript code segment that will run on the server. A script code segment defined in this manner ends with the </SCRIPT> HTML tag.

You can use ASP scripts to do many of the HTML text generation functions that you can do with CGI executables and ISAPI applications. The primary advantage of ASP scripts, however, is that you can embed them right in with regular HTML text and develop them quickly.

Modifying Scripting Permissions for a Web Site

Use the following procedure to modify scripting permissions for a Web site:

1. Start the MMC.

2. Expand the scope pane to display the default Web site.

3. Right-click on the default Web site and select Properties.

4. Select the Home Directory tab.

5. Select the Execute (including Script) permission.

6. Click Apply.

7. Click Select All.

8. Click OK.

9. Click OK.

10. Close the MMC.

▶ Configure IIS to run ISAPI applications.

ISAPI provides a way for programmers to extend the functionality of IIS. There are two means to do this:

ISAPI applications, which execute when a page with a specific extension is requested by a browser, and which parse the data on that page to return output to the requesting browser. ISAPI applications could be used to implement a scripting language like Visual Basic or Perl.

ISAPI filters, which process all information returned by a Web site. ISAPI filters can be used to implement encryption or translation functions that must be performed on every page returned by a Web site.

ISAPI applications are DLLs that are activated when the WWW service is asked to return a page whose file extension is recorded in the registry as an ISAPI file type. If the recorded entry points to an executable program (i.e., a program that ends in .exe and has %s %s parameters), then IIS starts that program as a CGI executable. If the recorded entry points to a file that ends in .dll, then ISAPI loads the dynamic link library into its own memory space and passes control to it.

Figure 10.2 shows the default ISAPI DLL to extension mappings for ISAPI applications that come with Internet Information Server.

In IIS3, ISAPI DLLs ran in the same memory space as IIS. In IIS4, you can separate each ISAPI DLL into its own memory space. This increases fault tolerance and security, because now a DLL that crashes won't bring down IIS and possibly your server as well. Furthermore, a security violation inside the memory space of a DLL won't provide access to the IIS memory space. Figure 10.3 shows the sample Exploration Air virtual directory configured to run in its own memory space.

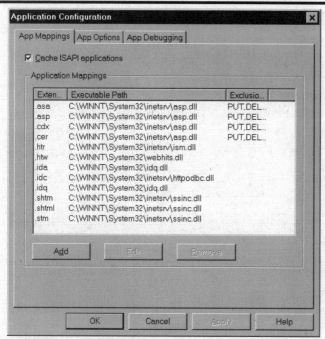

FIGURE 10.2: Default ISAPI DLL extension mappings

Part ii

ISAPI DLLs are usually quite a bit faster than CGI executables because they're optimized to work with IIS. Also, ISAPI DLLs do not have to be loaded and run each time a Web page using them is accessed, because the IIS ISAPI mechanism can use the same copy of the DLL in memory for each access. This arrangement reduces the data transfer time between IIS and the ISAPI DLL and allows the DLL to respond faster than a CGI executable that performs the same function. ISAPI DLLs are more difficult to write, however, because they require a specialized programming environment (most commonly Microsoft C++ with the Win32 SDK, although some people have had success using other compiler environments).

An ISAPI application can do anything that a CGI executable can do, including running scripts. Many scripting languages have been implemented as ISAPI DLLs; one example is Perl, which is currently the most popular server-side scripting language for developing Web pages. (However, JScript and VBScript, which are also implemented by Microsoft as ISAPI DLLs, may soon eclipse Perl.)

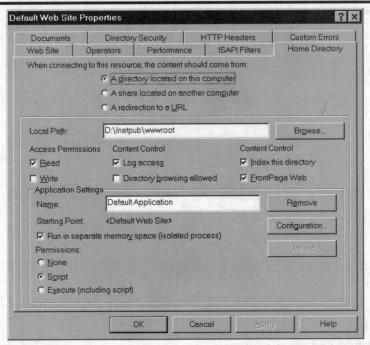

FIGURE 10.3: A Web application configured to run in its own memory space

After you configure IIS to activate the ISAPI DLL when a file with its extension is accessed, you can treat the ISAPI application just like a CGI executable. You interface to an ISAPI application (i.e., pass parameters to it) the same way you interface to a CGI executable (via a URL, from a hypertext link, or from an HTML form).

ISAPI DLLs extend the functionality of the WWW service of IIS. ISAPI DLLs respect the same NTFS restrictions as IIS. For example, if a user is logged on anonymously, the ISAPI DLL will be able to access only resources available to the IUSR_*computername* account. If the user has attached to the WWW service using the Administrator account, then the ISAPI DLL will be able to access any resources that the Administrator account can access.

TIP

Study the NTFS permission environment for ISAPI DLLs carefully.

Because an ISAPI program may access more than the WWW service will normally permit (i.e., it can access directories that are not in the list of home or virtual directories for the WWW service), you must be careful to construct ISAPI programs that access only the data you want accessed. Or you should make sure that the users with permission to run the ISAPI program (including the IUSR_*computername* anonymous user account) have NTFS permissions to access only the files and directories that you determine are safe.

The user of an ISAPI application must have Execute permission for the directory containing the application (.dll) program. The user doesn't need Read access to that directory unless the DLL itself has some reason to read a file in that directory. If the ISAPI application is a script interpreter, however, the user must have NTFS Read permission to the directory containing the script.

Filters extend the functionality of IIS directly by modifying the output of the Web server as it is passed to the browser. Configuring IIS to use an ISAPI filter is a simple matter of installing the filter in a directory with appropriate permissions and using the Internet Service Manager to bind that filter to either the Web server for global filters or to a specific Web site. Using the ISAPI filter, however, requires that you know what the filter does and how it is used. There is no standard as to what filters may do to your IIS server. The whole point of filters is to extend the capabilities of IIS in new and unexpected (to Microsoft programmers, at least) ways. Figure 10.4 shows the default filters set up to process all data served by IIS.

The other use for ISAPI DLLs is to directly extend the functionality of the WWW service of IIS. ISAPI DLLs can be written to preprocess the HTTP requests and to postprocess the HTTP responses of IIS. You can use filters for the following purposes:

- authentication (for other than Windows NT security)

- specialized encryption or compression

- more elaborate access restrictions (such as by Internet name as well as by IP address)

▶ implementation of HTTP commands that IIS does not yet support

▶ additional specialized server-side include commands that execute faster because they do not require file access

▶ additional logging and traffic analyses beyond what the built-in logging features provide

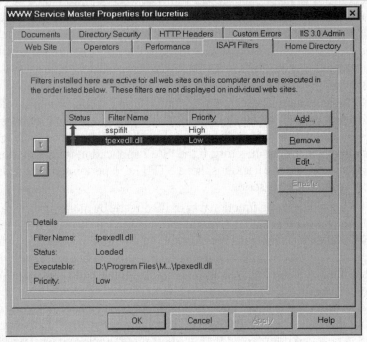

FIGURE 10.4:   Default global IIS filters

When you develop an ISAPI filter, you register which server actions the filter will respond to. It can, for example, preprocess the raw data sent from the client, the headers sent by the client, the data that will be sent to a CGI executable or ISAPI application, the data returned by an application, and final data that will be sent to the Web browser.

To configure an ISAPI filter to work on all Web traffic, install the filter on the WWW Master Properties ISAPI Filters tab.

A correctly written filter will, when initialized by IIS, register which WWW service events it will process. You can apply a filter globally to all IIS-supported services by adding it to IIS, or you can apply a filter to certain Web sites. When you add a global filter, you must stop and start IIS to apply the filter. When you add a filter to a Web site, it will automatically load when a page from that Web site is requested for the first time.

Configuring IIS to Pass Control to a Specific ISAPI DLL

Configuring IIS to pass control to a specific ISAPI DLL based on the requested file's extension is easy:

1. Launch the MMC and right-click on the Web site or virtual directory you want the ISAPI application associated with.

2. Select Properties, and select the Directory tab.

3. Click the Configuration button in the Application Settings control group.

4. Click Add to add the ISAPI DLL executable and the extensions to which it should respond.

The following process shows you how to add filters to specific Web sites:

1. Select the ISAPI Filters tab of the Web site's Properties panel.

2. Click Add.

3. Enter a descriptive name for the filter in the Filter Name input box.

4. Enter the path to the Dynamic Link Library.

5. Click the up or down arrows to increase or decrease the filter's execution priority relative to its peer filters. Filters modify the data stream from top to bottom in the order shown on the ISAPI Filters tab.

Part ii

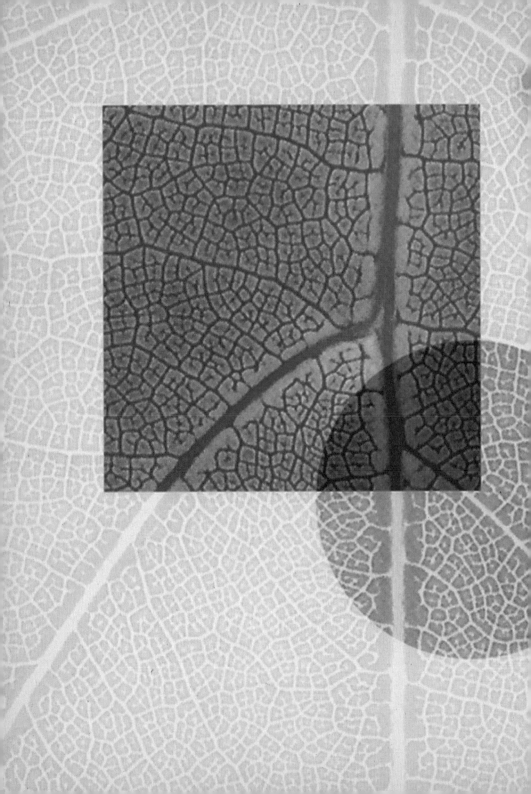

Chapter 11
MONITORING AND OPTIMIZATION

This chapter concerns the monitoring and optimization of Internet Information Server 4. There are several tasks associated with the first objective, which covers maintaining a log for fine-tuning and auditing purposes. The next two objectives deal with monitoring and analyzing performance, with the first testing your knowledge of using Performance Monitor to monitor the performance of HTTP and FTP sessions, and the second analyzing performance issues. The latter group of objectives in this chapter deals with optimizing performance and interpreting performance data. You will need to know how to optimize performance of IIS, Index Server, Microsoft SMTP Service, and Microsoft NNTP Service, as well as how to optimize a Web site with Content Analyzer.

Adapted from *MCSE Exam Notes: Internet Information Server 4* by Matthew Strebe

ISBN 0-7821-2303-1   320 pages $19.99

▶ Maintain a log for fine-tuning and auditing purposes. Tasks include:

- ▶ Importing log files into a Usage Import and Report Writer database
- ▶ Configuring the logging features of the WWW service
- ▶ Configuring the logging features of the FTP service
- ▶ Configuring Usage Import and Report Writer to analyze logs created by the WWW service or the FTP service
- ▶ Automating the use of Usage Import and Report Writer

The logs created by IIS are a gold mine of information on how your server is used. They are also useful for figuring out how well your server performs over time and what parts of your Web site(s) are the most popular and therefore are consuming the most bandwidth to your server.

Unfortunately, these logs create an enormous amount of information. You can log to an ODBC data source like a Microsoft Access database or an SQL Server, query the data, and then create reports to view any statistics you want, but that process takes a lot of setup effort. IIS provides a separate product called Report Writer that can perform much of this work for you.

Report Writer is the part of Site Server Express that takes the log data stored by IIS and helps you understand how your site is being accessed. With Report Writer (and Usage Import) you can easily separate out important information from the voluminous amount of data a busy Web site can generate. You can track such data as the most frequently accessed pages, the most common errors, the times of greatest site access, and even where most of your accesses come from.

The first thing you have to do when working with IIS log data is to get the data you want into the log file you want. You do this through the logging settings of each Web and FTP site, or you can set the default logging characteristics for all of the Web sites and FTP sites in IIS.

Settings you can configure include the type of log file created, which may be:

- ▶ Microsoft IIS Log File Format
- ▶ NCSA Common Log File Format

▶ ODBC Logging

▶ W3C Extended Log File Format

The W3C Extended Log File Format is the default setting and it is also the most flexible format because it allows you to select what goes into the data files.

The more data you put in your log file, the larger and faster your log files will grow. For lightly loaded Web servers, however, the more information you have to work with the better.

Before you can work with the log data, you have to import it into Report Writer. You do this through the Usage Import tool. The Usage Import tool can be found alongside the rest of the Site Server Express tools, in Start ➢ Programs ➢ Windows NT 4.0 Option Pack ➢ Site Server 2.0 Express ➢ Usage Import.

The Usage Import tool has to be configured to retrieve data generated by your Web site. When you first start it up it will ask for the log file format, domain name, and home page location for the Web site. You then may specify the location of the log files to import.

By default, the log files are stored in the LogFiles subdirectory of your Windows NT System32 directory. Each Web site (and FTP site) gets its own subdirectory of LogFiles. The default Web site stores its log files in the W3SVC1 subdirectory.

The W3SVC1 subdirectory (or whichever subdirectory you are using) may contain many log files, depending on how you have set up logging for your Web site. The default setting is to create a new log file every day. When selecting a log file to import, you can select more than one.

The data, when imported, ends up in an .mdb file. This is the same format of database file used by Microsoft Access, so you can use your regular database tools to manipulate it. If you want to generate common Web reports from it, you can use the Report Writer program, described in the next section.

Several reports in the Report Writer tool require more data than is actually stored in the IIS log files. The log files, for example, store IP addresses but not the Internet names of the computers attaching to the Web server. If you want to know the names of the computers connecting to your server, you have to query the DNS server to match the numbers to their names. Usage Import will do this for you, as well as do Whois queries (in order to determine information about the organization responsible for the computer) and title lookup (which connects to each URL referenced in the log file and extracts the title of the HTML page).

These operations can take a great deal of time (up to several seconds for each entry!) and take up significant amounts of Internet bandwidth that could otherwise be used by clients attaching to your Web site, so you should only perform these operations if you really want the reports that are based on them.

One of the nice features of Usage Import (there are too many features to list here) is that you can make data imports happen automatically. If you have a new log file being generated every night at midnight, for example, you might configure Usage Import to import the just-finished log. You use the Scheduler tool to create and schedule the import.

The Scheduler (which you will also use in Report Writer) organizes its activities into Jobs and Tasks. You schedule a job to happen at a specific time, and that job may consist of several tasks, including importing data from the log files.

Once you have the data imported into the .mdb database, you can generate reports using Report Writer (see Figure 11.1). If you try to use Report Writer before importing the data, you will end up with some nice-looking but otherwise useless reports. Report Writer has a number of pre-defined reports you can choose from, divided into detail reports and summary reports.

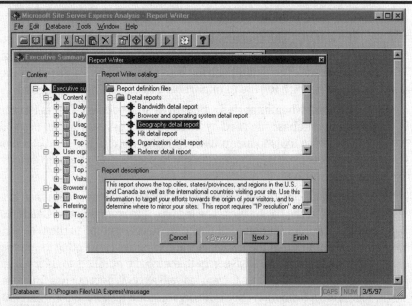

FIGURE 11.1: Report Writer has many forms that make the data generated by IIS's logging feature easier to understand.

The extra data in the log files really doesn't take up a lot more space, and doesn't slow down IIS significantly, but performing IP resolution, Whois queries, and title lookup operations can slow down the reporting process considerably for a WWW site with a lot of log data requirements. Consider performing those operations and running those reports less frequently than regular reports, and do it when bandwidth on the Internet is not at a premium (you could, for example, configure Usage Import to perform such operations at five in the morning on Sundays).

With data from reports, such as the Request detail report, that show the most-accessed pages, you can spend your time optimizing those pages. For instance, the most frequently accessed file on your site might be a logo graphic that occurs in many different Web pages. By reducing the size of that single file and converting it to a monochrome image, you could dramatically reduce the load on your server.

Configuring the Logging Features of the WWW and FTP Services

This procedure guides you through the process of customizing the data reported by the default FTP and Web sites.

1. Start the Microsoft Management Console.

2. Right-click the default FTP site for your computer and select Properties.

3. Click the FTP Site tab.

4. Make sure the Enable Logging button is selected.

5. Click the Properties button.

6. Click the Extended Properties tab.

7. Click the Date, User Name, Bytes Sent, Bytes Received, and Time Taken options.

8. Click Apply, then click OK. Click OK again.

9. Right-click the Default Web site for your computer and select Properties.

10. Click the Web Site tab.

11. Make sure the Enable Logging button is selected.

12. Click the Properties button.

13. Click the Extended Properties tab.

14. Click the Date, User Name, Bytes Sent, Bytes Received, and Protocol Version options.

15. Click Apply, then click OK. Click OK again.

Importing Log Files into a Usage Import and Report Writer Database

Use the following procedure to import log files into a Usage Import and Report Writer database:

1. Click around the sample site a bit using your Web browser (enter **http://localhost/** in the address field) in order to generate some data to import.

2. Start Usage Import by selecting Start ➤ Programs ➤ Windows NT 4.0 Option Pack ➤ Site Server 2.0 Express ➤Usage Import.

3. Click OK to the message that there are no Internet sites configured.

4. Click OK to accept Microsoft IIS W3C Extended Log File Format.

5. Enter the domain name of your computer in the Local Domain field and press OK.

6. Enter **http://*host_name*/** in the Home Page URLs field and click OK.

7. At the end of the Log Location field in the middle of the screen click the Browse... button.

8. Go to the location where your log files are stored on the computer (usually `winnt\system32\logfiles` on the drive where the operating system files are stored).

9. Select the W3SVC1 folder.

10. Select all of the files in the directory (click the first file in the directory then hold down the Shift key on the keyboard and click the last file in the directory).

11. Click the Open button.

12. Select File ➤ Start Import or click the green triangle on the button bar.

13. Click the OK button. Click the Close button.

14. Close Usage Import.

Automating the Use of Usage Import and Report Writer

Use this procedure to automate the use of Usage Import and Report Writer:

1. Start Usage Import by selecting Start ➤ Programs ➤ Windows NT 4.0 Option Pack ➤ Site Server 2.0 Express ➤ Usage Import.

2. Select Tools ➤ Scheduler.

3. Right-click the All Jobs item and select New Job.

4. Check the Active box.

5. Select Every Wednesday at 12:00 A.M.

6. Click OK.

7. Right-click the New Job item and select New Task.

8. Select Import Log File as the Task type.

9. Enter **w3c** in the Log Data Source.

10. Enter the path to your log files in the Log Location field (replace the date with $1. For example, you might enter **c:\winnt\system32\logfiles\w3svc1\ex$1.log**).

11. Click OK.

Configuring Usage Import and Report Writer to Analyze Logs Created by the WWW Service or the FTP Service

Use the following procedure to create a report with Report Writer to analyze logs created by the WWW service or the FTP service:

1. Start Report Writer by selecting Start ➤ Programs ➤ Windows NT 4.0 Option Pack ➤ Site Server 2.0 Express ➤ Report Writer.

2. Accept the From the Report Writer Catalog and click OK.

3. Expand the Detail Reports item.

4. Select Hit detail report and click Next.

5. Accept the Every request you've imported option and click Next.

6. Click Finish.

7. From the Database menu select the Change option.

8. Select the `msusage.mdb` file and click the Open button.

9. Select File ➤ Create Report Document.

10. Enter **defaultweb** in the File Name field and click OK.

11. Click OK.

► Monitor performance of various functions by using Performance Monitor. Functions include HTTP and FTP sessions.

Performance tuning is finding the resource that slows your network the most, speeding it up until something else has the most impact on speed, and then starting over by finding the new slowest resource. This cycle of finding the speed-limiting factor, eliminating it, and starting over allows you to reach the natural performance limit of your network in a simple, methodical way.

Factors that limit performance in a computer are called bottlenecks. For instance, slow memory limits the speed at which a processor can manipulate data, thus limiting the computer's processing performance to the speed that the processor can access memory. If the memory can respond faster than the processor, the processor is the bottleneck. *The* bottleneck in a system is the slowest component, or the component that is causing the other components to wait (even if it is a fast component). Remove that bottleneck (such as by upgrading it) and the next slowest, or heavily loaded, component becomes *the* bottleneck.

System performance is always affected by a bottleneck. You may not notice it because your computer may run faster than the work you perform requires. If you use your computer only for Web service attached to the Internet via a T1 line, the speed of your machine has probably never limited how fast you can work. On the other hand, if you use your computer as an SQL server for a large organization, chances are you've spent a lot of time waiting for the server to catch up to you.

Your connection to the Internet should be your bottleneck in an Internet server. If your server can keep all its connections to the Internet fully loaded, you're getting all the performance you possibly can out of your Internet server.

Performance tuning Internet servers is the systematic process of finding the resource experiencing the most load and then relieving that load. You can almost always optimize a server to make it more responsive. Understanding how Internet Information Server performs and how you can increase its performance is important. Even if you don't need to make your servers any faster, understanding performance tuning can help you diagnose problems when they arise.

If it's not broken, don't fix it. Windows NT, IIS, and Index Server are highly tuned and factory-optimized to work well in most situations. You should perform rigorous performance monitoring only when a problem that is obviously load-related occurs on your server. You should be especially careful not to cause more harm than good with your performance tuning. Avoid changing any settings or options that you don't fully understand.

Performance tuning is a very complex topic and requires a solid knowledge of the NT operating system, since IIS relies so heavily on it. Ferreting out serious performance problems with the Performance Monitor is beyond the scope of this book.

NOTE

If you need additional information about performance monitoring beyond its use with IIS, check out these books from Sybex: *MCSE: NT Server 4 Study Guide* by Matthew Strebe, Charles Perkins, and James Chellis; or *Mastering Windows NT Server 4* by Mark Minasi.

The Performance Monitor is the tool built into Windows NT that monitors all facets of its performance. IIS extends the Windows NT Performance Monitor to include unique specialized performance counters for each of the Internet services and for IIS as a whole. This extension of the Performance Monitor's functionality makes it easy to compare IIS performance counters with Windows NT system counters to find coincidental performance characteristics. Figure 11.2 shows the Performance Monitor running.

Part ii

NOTE

IIS Services such as the HTTP and FTP services will appear in the Performance Monitor only when the services are running. If you don't see the counter object for the service in the Object pick box, close the Performance Monitor, start the service, and restart the Performance Monitor.

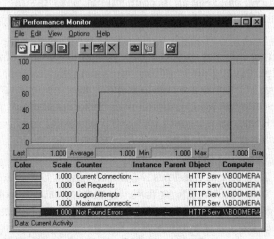

FIGURE 11.2: The Performance Monitor

In the following set of counters, each counter counts from the time the service was started, unless otherwise noted by some sort of rate indicator like per second (/sec), current, or percentage (%).

Per second counters measure the number of counts that occur in one second and provide a good indicator of load relative to earlier loads on the same counter. These counters are good for determining the thresholds at which bottlenecks occur and how often those thresholds happen. These can be considered time period counters because they cover a one-second period of time.

Current counters tell you how many instances of a certain load factor are currently occurring—these counters are especially useful for comparing against processor, disk, and memory counters to identify processes that cause bottlenecks to occur. Try putting them on the same charts as processor, disk, and memory counters to find obvious similarities. Using the Performance Monitor this way will help you determine how and when to upgrade your server. These can be considered instantaneous counters because they cover a moment in time.

Counters that don't have a current or per second indicator simply rate the number of times the measured event has occurred since the service was started. Because there's no indication of how long the service has been running, these counters don't mean much in terms of performance monitoring or optimization—but they are a good source for marketing and usage statistics, or as a metric upon which to base fees for services rendered. These are considered time-independent counters because they cover the entire period of time that the service has been running.

Monitoring the Performance of the Web Service

Use the following procedure to monitor the performance of the Web service:

1. Select Start ➤ Programs ➤ Administrative Tools ➤ Performance Monitor.

2. Select Edit ➤ Add to Chart or click the large + button on the toolbar.

3. Select Web Service in the Object pick box.

4. Select Current Connections in the Counter list box.

5. Click Add. Note that a colored line has begun moving from right to left in the Performance Monitor main window.

6. Select Web Service in the Object pick box.

7. Select Bytes Total/sec in the Counter list box.

8. Click Add.

9. Click Done. You are now monitoring the number of current connections and the total throughput to the IIS Web service using the Performance Monitor.

▶ Analyze performance. Performance issues include:

- ▶ Identifying bottlenecks
- ▶ Identifying network-related performance issues
- ▶ Identifying disk-related performance issues
- ▶ Identifying CPU-related performance issues

Now that the Performance Monitor has armed you with knowledge of the internal workings of the IIS services, it's time to actually compare them with other performance counters to determine the impact of the services on the operation of the server. This comparison is the process of performance analysis.

Since IIS isn't the only software running on your computer, many other factors will affect the computer's performance. However, if your server is primarily an Internet or intranet server, most of the performance-affecting software will be engaged in activities directly related to Internet service. If IIS is merely an add-on to a general purpose server that performs everything from file and print service to light SQL duties, you'll have trouble determining which services impact speed the most. If this is the case, perform your testing at night or when the server is mostly idle.

Generate synthetic (meaning made-up or unreal) loads to put the server under a specific sort of strain. For instance, if you want to measure the impact of HTTP service on a general purpose server, isolate the server from other sources of load and then connect a Web browser to a complex Web page twenty or thirty times. This test will put the server under a known load, and you'll be able to filter out how much that specific factor impacts server performance.

Synthetic loads show you how much a specific service loads your system, but they won't ferret out all your performance problems by themselves. Many performance problems don't show up unless the server is under a full load. For instance, let's say you are running an Internet database that has both an Active Server Pages IIS component and an SQL Server component running on the same machine.

Once the server load reaches a certain point, connections start timing out. But which service is causing the problem? A synthetic load won't tell you unless it's designed to exercise both components the same way a real connection would. Even then, you need to determine whether the bottleneck is caused by network I/O, disk, processor, or memory constraints by using performance counters appropriate to those subsystems. You may not be able to overcome a disk bottleneck if both services compete for time on the same disk array—but moving the SQL Server to another machine attached via a fast network fixes the problem completely.

To analyze performance quickly, select the counters that are most relevant to the aspect of performance that you wish to measure (i.e., Memory Allocated if you suspect you are low on memory, Communication Failed and Session Timed Out if you are diagnosing bad connections, or Requests/Second, Requests Current, and Total Queue Length if your server is heavily loaded) and add to the same graph counters for %Processor Time, %Disk time, and Page faults/sec. Now when you put the server under a synthetic Internet service load, you'll see spikes in these counters that correspond directly to the service counters you added. This measurement gives you a good indication of the relative load IIS is causing on your machine for a specific level of concurrent use.

Many serious performance problems are sporadic. You may have to use the Alerting or Logging features of IIS to track down strange or infrequent problems, or problems that tend to occur when you aren't around. These features are beyond the scope of this book, but you should be able to figure out how to use them with the help file built into the Performance Monitor.

Generating a Small Synthetic Load

To generate a small synthetic load:

1. Double-click the Internet Explorer icon on your desktop.

2. Arrange the positions of Internet Explorer and the Performance Monitor on your desktop so you can see the content windows of both of them at the same time. You may need to make Internet Explorer very small.

3. Type //*computername*/**default.htm** in the Address input line, replacing *computername* with the name of your Internet server.

4. Notice the slight load this action creates on your server. Also notice that the load drops back down after the initial connection once the page is loaded. This example shows the "bursty" nature of HTTP transmissions.

▶ Optimize performance of IIS.

Optimizing the performance of IIS is the most important step to optimizing your Internet server, because IIS generates the majority of traffic (and therefore performance-related problems) on your server.

There are numerous ways to optimize the performance of IIS. Chief among them are:

▶ limiting user connections

▶ enabling HTTP Keep-Alives

▶ bandwidth throttling

Limiting user connections is a simple optimization—by reducing the number of users who can connect to your site, you improve performance for those who are connected because they don't have to compete for bandwidth with as many users. Network traffic to a single server is a "divide by N" problem because the available bandwidth is divided by the number of users connected. If you have a 1500Kbps connection with 100 users attached, you have 1500Kbps/100 (1500Kbps) available for each user. If you limit connections to only 10 users, each user will have 1500Kbps/10 available (150Kbps)—a ten times increase in performance.

Why would you want to limit the number of users to your site? Because with too many users, your server will become so slow that it's worthless to everyone. It's better to be able to fill the needs of some users at least.

HTTP Keep-Alives improve performance by maintaining the connection to the Web browser so IIS can more quickly respond to multiple HTTP requests to the same browser. HTTP Keep-Alives do, however, require more resources when enabled, so there's a performance trade-off. If your computer is resource-limited (for example, if it has only 32 megabytes of RAM), you might want to disable HTTP Keep-Alives. Each open connection takes up some memory, so disabling the Keep-Alives frees up server resources—but also causes subsequent HTTP requests from Web browsers to take longer (a new connection must be negotiated for each request).

Bandwidth throttling lets you determine how much of your network resources you want consumed by each specific Web site. Throttling bandwidth to a Web or FTP site does not make that site perform better. In fact, metering bandwidth impedes performance by restricting load times to a certain level. It can, however, improve the performance of other Web or FTP sites on your server if that site is "hogging" all of the available network bandwidth. Also, if you are using IIS on a server that does double duty as a file server and the IIS traffic is simply not as important as the regular network traffic, you may have to use bandwidth metering to prevent Internet traffic from stealing time away from more important uses of your machine.

Your pipe to the Internet is an automatic bandwidth meter. If you have a 56K leased line, your Internet traffic will never account for more than

56K of network I/O. You don't have to set anything for inherent bottle-necks like this to limit the flow of information to and from your server.

You can also throttle bandwidth globally by enabling bandwidth throttling on the IIS Master Properties page. This will limit the traffic consumed by all IIS services rather than by Web site.

Limiting the Number of Users Who Can Connect to a Web Site

Use the following procedure to limit the number of users who can connect to a Web site:

1. Start the Internet Service Manager.

2. Right-click the site you want to limit and select Properties.

3. Select the Web Site tab.

4. Select Limit To and enter **100** in the Connections input box.

5. Click OK.

Use the following procedure to enable HTTP Keep-Alives:

1. Start the Internet Service Manager.

2. Right-click the site you want to modify and select Properties.

3. Select the Performance tab.

4. Check the HTTP Keep-Alives Enabled option.

5. Click OK.

Use the following procedure to meter bandwidth for a specific Web site:

1. Start the Internet Service Manager.

2. Right-click the site you want to limit and select Properties.

3. Select the Performance tab.

4. Check the Enable Bandwidth Throttling option.

5. Enter the amount of Kbps you want that site to be limited to.

6. Click Apply.

7. Click OK.

Part ii

Optimize performance of Index Server.

Index Server is highly optimized and tuned for near-maximum performance upon installation. However, there are a few things you can do to improve the performance of Index Server in your specific environment.

The Index Server search engine is designed for speed efficiency. When indexed documents change on a server, they are added to a change queue. The change queue is processed in first-in, first-out order very shortly after the documents are stored.

When documents are first indexed, the resulting index of words is stored in RAM in a buffer called a word list. Word lists are not compressed, and they are stored only in RAM, so they can be stored very quickly. When the size of a word list reaches a certain point, it is compressed and stored into a shadow index on the disk. Shadow indexes serve as disk buffers for word lists that have not yet been added to the monolithic master index. Shadow indexes are easy to create but do cause a small amount of disk and processor load. A shadow merge combines all the shadow indexes and word lists into a single shadow index whenever the number of word lists or shadow indexes passes a certain threshold. Shadow merges are generally very fast because the indexes are small.

The master index is the main index for all the documents indexed by the search engine. Every night at midnight (by default) a shadow merge occurs to combine all the word lists and indexes into a single shadow index. Then a master merge occurs to add the shadow index changes to the master index.

All this effort with word lists, shadow indexes, and merges is an important optimization because adding words to the master index is very time-consuming. If every document index were master-merged after each indexing during the day, the load on your server would be tremendous. Word lists and shadow indexes serve as caches for the master merge so that the load-intensive master merge can be delayed until the server is under a light load.

The trade-off for this load optimization is query speed. Every query has to first search all existing word lists, then all shadow indexes, and then the master index each time it is performed. Searching only the master index is much faster, so queries are quicker after a master merge.

The NT Server Performance Monitor utility can be used to determine how your Index Server is loaded using the following objects:

▶ Content Index

▶ Content Index Filter

▶ HTTP Content Index

These objects show you the current state of merges, the number of persistent indexes in your system, and the number and size of word lists. By relating these values to the disk, memory, and processor loads in your system, you can determine how much load Index Server puts on your system. Try staying up one night and monitoring your server's performance during a master merge. You will learn a lot about the indexing load your server is subject to, which will help you make determinations about how to optimize index speed.

If your server spends more time on queries than on merges, you should tighten up the registry values to force merges more often. On the other hand, if your server is spending too much time on merges, you should loosen up the intervals between master merges. Examine the Registry Settings page in the Index Server online documentation very carefully for a complete list of registry keys that can be modified to tune the performance of Index Server.

The following Index Server optimizations are especially effective. You should check out the Index Server online documentation for specific information on how to perform some of these optimizations:

▶ Move a catalog to a different hard disk than the corpus. (The corpus is all the files that are indexed in a catalog.) This optimization splits the I/O traffic during the master merge among two disks and eliminates the need to seek the disk head between the areas containing the corpus and the areas containing the index.

▶ Use the standard Windows NT speed optimizations like striped hard disks or hardware RAID arrays to improve disk I/O speed on servers that hold the corpus.

▶ Increase the amount of RAM in your computer. You can edit registry settings to allow larger word lists in RAM, thus lengthening the time to the next shadow merge.

▶ Create multiple catalogs if you don't need the ability to query everything at once. For instance, you may want to create separate catalogs for office documents and for HTML files, because users will generally know what type of document they are searching for. Smaller indexes mean faster searches.

▶ Narrow the scope of your queries by eliminating virtual directories that don't contain useful query information, such as scripts directories and directories that contain ISAPI applications or Java code.

▶ Change the time that the daily master merge takes place to coincide with the time of day when your server is under the least load. If you are running a public Internet server, this time is most likely in the early morning between 4 A.M. and 9 A.M.; however, if you get browsers from all over the world, there may be no ideal time for this procedure.

▶ Set Index Server to filter only files with known file types. This setting keeps a lot of garbage files out of your query indexes and makes everything run quite a bit faster.

Check out the registry Settings page in the Index Server online documentation for a complete list of the registry settings that you can modify to optimize Index Server.

Index Server installs a number of performance counters that can be viewed using either the NT Server Performance Monitor or a Web browser. The HTML Index Server Manager automatically shows relevant statistics on the main page when you open it.

Adding Index Server Counters to the Performance Monitor

Use the following procedure to add Index Server counters to the Performance Monitor:

1. Select Start ➤ Programs ➤ Administrative Tools ➤ Performance Monitor.

2. Click the + button to add a counter to the Performance Monitor display.

3. Select Content Index in the Object pick list.

4. Select #documents filtered in the Counter pick list.

5. Click Add.

6. Select Start ➤ Settings ➤ Control Panel.

7. Double-click the Services control panel.

8. Select the Content Index service.

9. Click the Stop button. Wait for the service to stop.

10. Click the Start button.

11. Click the Performance Monitor button in the task bar.

12. Notice the indexed documents counter climb. Listen for disk activity on your server.

13. Close the Performance Monitor, the Services control panel, and the Control Panel windows.

▶ Optimize performance of Microsoft SMTP Service.

The steps you take to optimize IIS and the Web service will help you to optimize the other Internet services as well. Metering the bandwidth to greedy Web sites can give your SMTP site room to breathe.

The Mail service, like the Web service, logs access. You configure the log files in the same way you configure the Web service log files, and you can import those log files into a spreadsheet or database tool to analyze them for trends in how your Internet site is being used.

Logging in the Mail service gives you the same four format options as the Web service—Microsoft IIS Log File Format, NCSA Common Log File Format, ODBC Logging, and the W3C Extended Log File Format. As with the Web service, the W3C format allows you to select the data that will be included in the log file.

In addition to log data, the Mail service has counters that you can view in the Performance Monitor. You can use these counters to monitor trends in the behavior of these services and to solve performance problems.

A few things you can do to improve Mail performance include:

▶ Limit the number of simultaneous connections to the Mail service. This gives connected users more bandwidth and processor capacity at the expense of denying connections to other users, making them wait until the site is less busy.

▶ Decrease the connection timeout for the Mail services so that other users can connect and use the (insignificant) bandwidth and (significant) memory taken by idle connections.

▶ Disable logging (only do this if you need every last bit of performance).

▶ Decrease the maximum number of messages per connection in the SMTP service, which will cause it to open more connections and deliver mail faster. You can also decrease the retry interval for local and remote mail delivery—this instructs the SMTP service to try again sooner. Increasing the retry interval has a negative effect on the bandwidth available, though, so don't do it if you are bandwidth-limited. Turn off reverse DNS lookup for incoming messages.

By now, you should have a pretty good feel for the various performance-related features of the various IIS services including SMTP.

Decreasing the Maximum Number of Messages per SMTP Connection

Use the following procedure to decrease the maximum number of messages per SMTP connection, thereby forcing SMTP to open more connections:

1. Launch the MMC.

2. Right-click on the SMTP service and select Properties.

3. Select the Messages tab.

4. Select Maximum number of outbound message per connection.

5. Enter a low value (such as **10**) in the box.

6. Click OK.

▶ Optimize performance of Microsoft NNTP Service.

The performance optimization features discussed for the other services also apply to NNTP. In addition to those methods, you can use the following optimizations that are somewhat specific to NNTP.

Limit the post size to prevent users from hogging space and bandwidth. Large posts take a long time to transmit and take a lot of space on your NNTP server. For most NNTP servers, there's no valid reason why large posts should be accepted.

Limit connection size to prevent NNTP from hogging bandwidth. NNTP allows you to limit the amount of bandwidth a single NNTP connection will be allowed to use. You can do this to prevent NNTP from consuming too much bandwidth at any one time.

Use virtual directories to store newsgroups on different hard disks. Virtual directories allow you to put newsgroups on other volumes and on other servers. If you have the rare occasion to run a disk-limited NNTP server, spread newsgroups onto other disks to improve performance.

Creating an NNTP Virtual Directory on Another Volume

Use the following procedure to create an NNTP virtual directory on another volume. This exercise only works if you have an additional writable storage device mounted as drive D:

1. Launch the MMC.

2. Right-click the default NNTP Site and click New ➤ Virtual Directory.

3. Enter a newsgroup to store in the virtual directory (for example, **hr.policies**) and press Enter.

4. Enter a path located on another physical disk, such as **d:\hr**, and press Enter.

5. Click Yes to create the new directory.

▶ Interpret performance data.

Information for this objective is contained under the Analyze performance objective.

▶ Optimize a Web site by using Content Analyzer.

The Content Analyzer is the tool you use to manage what is stored in the directories of your Web site (unlike the Microsoft Management Console, which concerns itself primarily with the directories themselves and how the browser connects to them). Content Analyzer allows you to easily optimize the content of your Web site rather than the Web server service.

NOTE

There is additional information relevant to this objective in Chapter 8 under "Manage a Web site by using Content Analyzer."

A Web map is a graphical view of the resources in a Web site. When you create a Web map, Site Server Express traverses all of the HTML pages it can find in the Web site and records those pages as well as all of the objects (graphics, sounds, external pages, etc.) that those pages reference. The information about the Web site is stored in a .wmp file so that the Web site needn't be traversed every time you want to use Site Server Express.

Site Server Express can traverse a Web site in two ways:

▶ WebMaps from URLs

▶ WebMaps from files

If Site Server Express is running on a different computer than IIS4, you will probably connect to the Web site using the Web site's URL. Site Server Express will use the HTTP protocol to connect to the site and gather its information.

When you create a WebMap, you can set constraints and options to limit how extensive your WebMap will be and hence how much space it will take up and how much of a load it will place on a remote (URL-accessed) Web site. In addition, you can instruct Site Server Express to make a local copy of the Web site.

In order to create a WebMap from a URL, you simply provide the URL path to the home page of the Web site. You can instruct Site Server to explore the entire site, to organize the WebMap by directory hierarchy rather than the order in which links are found, and to generate a site report automatically as it creates the WebMap. If you do not want Site Server Express to explore the entire site, you will be able to choose how many pages will be explored. When Site Server Express is done exploring the site, it will ask you for a name prefix for the summary report and (if you instructed it to generate a report) show you summary statistics for the Web site.

If the Web site is stored locally (either on the same computer as Site Server Express or on another computer in your LAN), you can point Site

Server Express to the directory path or UNC path to the Web. As with creating a URL-sourced WebMap, with a directly accessed Web site you can set constraints and options to limit how extensive your WebMap will be, including whether it will access off-site links and which URLs it will not explore. In addition, you can instruct Site Server Express to explore all of the content of the Web site directories, rather than just the content referenced by hyperlinks. This is an excellent way to find orphaned Web pages.

In order to create a WebMap from files, you must provide the following:

▶ a home page path and filename (this may be a UNC path or a standard pathname starting with a drive letter)

▶ a domain and site root (this may be the Internet name of the Web site)

▶ the location of the CGI Bin directory used by the Web site (specified the same way you specified the home page path and filename)

You can instruct Site Server to explore the entire site, to organize the WebMap by directory hierarchy (rather than the order in which links are found), and to generate a site report automatically as it creates the WebMap. If you do not want Site Server Express to explore the entire site, you will be able to choose how many pages will be explored. When Site Server Express is done exploring the site, it will ask you for a name prefix for the summary report and (if you instructed it to generate a report) show you summary statistics for the Web site.

Site Server Express creates a summary report by default (unless you uncheck the Summary Report checkbox) and displays it in your Web browser when you create an initial WebMap. Microsoft Site Server (the commercial version, which is not included with Internet Information Server 4) has additional reports that can tell you more about your Web site. The summary report is divided into three parts:

Object Statistics   This part lists the number and size of the objects stored in your Web site, broken down by their type (such as HTML pages, Java classes, image files, and so on).

Status Summary   This part describes the links in your Web site, separated into on-site and off-site links, and shows the number of good links, bad links, missing links, and unverified links.

Map Statistics   This part gives you such information as when the map was made, how "deep" it got, and the average number of links on a page in the Web site.

A graphic view of your links is a neat tool, but the real benefit of Site Server Express is its ability to search your Web map for problems such as broken links, "not found" objects, images without ALT tags, and large objects (which can cause a page to take a very long time to download). The Tools menu gives you the option to do a quick search on the following objects:

- ▶ Broken Links
- ▶ Home Site Objects
- ▶ Images Without ALT
- ▶ Load Size over 32K
- ▶ Non-Home Site Objects
- ▶ Not Found Objects (404)
- ▶ Unavailable Objects
- ▶ Unverified Objects

When you search on any one of these objects, Site Server Express creates a search results window and lists those objects in it. When you click on the object in the search results window, the tree view and cyberbolic view automatically go to that object. You can then double-click the object (or its parent if it is a broken link or a not-found object) to view the problem object or HTML page.

Site Server Express makes finding broken links easy. Then it is just a matter of fixing that link with the software you used to create the page, or perhaps just editing the file with a text editor so that the link points to the correct location. You need to set Verify offsite links if you want Site Server Express to make sure links outside your site are valid, because it does not verify them by default.

NOTE

Site Server Express, unfortunately, does not give you the capability to search for user-defined text, including searching for the content of hypertext links, headings, or titles. If you want to search for these items you must purchase Site Analyst. Site Analyst is a feature of Microsoft Site Server 2 and Microsoft Site Server, Enterprise Edition 2.

Creating a WebMap from a File and Configuring Content Analyzer

To create a WebMap from a file and configure Content Analyzer:

1. Select Start ➤ Programs ➤ Administrative Tools ➤ Windows NT 4 Option Pack ➤ Site Server Express 2.0 ➤ Content Analyzer to start the Content Analyzer.

2. Click the New WebMap button.

3. Select File and click OK.

4. Enter the home page path and filename of the default Web site home page (`c:\inetpub\wwwroot\index.htm` for most installations).

5. Enter the domain site and root (the name of your server).

6. Enter the location of the Scripts directory for the location of the CGI Bin directory (`c:\inetpub\scripts` for most installations).

7. Click OK.

8. Click OK in the Generate Site Reports window.

9. Observe the Server Summary report and then close the report (browser) window.

10. Select View ➤ Program Options.

11. Click the Cyberbolic tab.

12. Check the Enable Snap Mode option.

13. Uncheck the Show Common Ancestor When Selecting In Tree View option.

14. Click Apply.

15. Click OK.

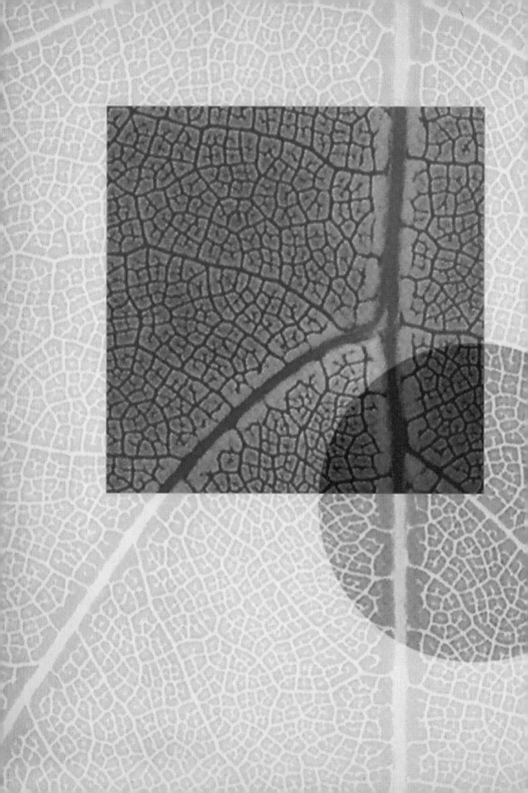

Chapter 12

TROUBLESHOOTING

A s a network administrator, you'll likely find that you spend the vast majority of your time troubleshooting problems on the network. Heck, if all you had to do was install some software and walk away, you'd be out of a job in no time. Solid troubleshooting skills are crucial for keeping your system up and running, and Microsoft has placed a significant amount of emphasis on this topic as it pertains to IIS.

MCSE Exam Notes:
INTERNET
INFORMATION
SERVER 4
EXAM 70-087
MATTHEW STREBE

Adapted from *MCSE Exam Notes: Internet Information Server 4* by Matthew Strebe

ISBN 0-7821-2303-1   320 pages $19.99

Resolve IIS configuration problems.

Very few errors apply just to the configuration of IIS itself—IIS installs automatically and very cleanly, so there's very little that can actually go wrong under normal circumstances.

Troubleshooting a Corrupted Installation

If, however, your IIS installation becomes corrupted, the following troubleshooting steps should be used in the order shown:

1. Delete and re-create problem Web sites. If the problem you're experiencing occurs only for a single Web site, and you've exhausted other troubleshooting measures, try deleting the site in the MMC and re-creating it. This often repairs metabase or registry corruption.

2. Reapply the latest service pack. Some software automatically installs older versions of system DLLs which can cause compatibility problems with applications like IIS that rely upon the services of the most recent system software. Reapplying the service pack generally resolves these problems.

3. Reinstall IIS4. Reinstalling IIS4 will restore missing files, registry keys, and metabase settings, automatically fixing a number of otherwise perplexing problems.

4. Remove IIS4 completely and reinstall. Sometimes registry or metabase settings become corrupt and the corruption persists through IIS4 installations. In these cases, you may have to completely remove IIS4 before reinstalling it to correct the problem.

 # Resolve security problems.

Web sites and FTP sites are easy to set up using IIS, and both IIS and NTFS security are very effective at protecting your data. You have to be careful when establishing security for your Internet site, however, because you can configure things so securely that even you can't access them.

Crucial Security Considerations

When setting up security for a site, keep the following in mind:

▶ Secure posting requires Secure Socket Layer, so you must have SSL configured and working on a Web site before you can use secure posting.

▶ Permissions for the anonymous user are controlled by adding NTFS permissions for the IUSR_*computername* account or the account specified in the Directory Security Anonymous Security and Authentication Control area of the Web site's properties.

▶ You can specify the anonymous user for each Web site through the Directory Security Anonymous Security and Authentication button in the Web site's properties.

▶ You can restrict access to or from a Web site by specific IP addresses or IP networks through the Directory Security IP Address and Domain Name Restrictions area of the Web site's properties.

▶ Service security restrictions control read access, write access, script execution, and application execution per site irrespective of user identity. When you need to control security for all users of a site, use service-based restrictions. Use NTFS permissions when various users will be allowed different levels of access.

▶ Restrict write access to Web, FTP, and NNTP sites that do not allow uploading or posting.

Security Troubleshooting Tips

Use the following pointers when troubleshooting security problems with an IIS installation:

▶ **Can't automatically submit a certificate request to Certificate Server.** Certificate Server must be installed and running on your computer (or on another computer in your network).

▶ **Can't require SSL communications on a Home Directory or Virtual Directory.** You must have a signed certificate installed in order to require Secure Socket Layer communications. You must have Windows NT Challenge/Response enabled to require Secure Socket Layer communications.

Part ii

▶ **Can't audit NTFS file and directory activity.** You must have auditing enabled in the User Manager or User Manager for Domains program.

▶ **IIS will not execute a script or DLL.** Script or Execute permissions must be enabled in a Home Directory or Virtual Directory before IIS will execute the program.

▶ **Users cannot log on using Basic Authentication but are able to using Windows NT Challenge/Response.** Basic Authentication must be enabled for users to log on using a specific account without using Windows NT Challenge/Response. In a multi-domain network, the default domain configured for Basic Authentication must be the domain from which all Basic users will be authenticated.

▶ **Users from outside your firewall cannot access Web sites on non-standard port addresses (such as the Administration Web site).** Your firewall must be configured to pass specific non-standard port numbers.

▶ **Users are confronted with a logon prompt even when they want to log on anonymously.** Logging on without a logon prompt or Windows NT Challenge/Response requires that Anonymous Authentication be enabled. The NTFS permissions for the files accessed must also include the anonymous user account.

▶ **Users report that they get a logon prompt when they attempt to access the Web site but access is denied after they enter an account name and password.** You must have an account defined for the users if Anonymous Authentication is disabled.

▶ **You can't log on to the IIS Administrative Web site.** You must have Windows NT Challenge/Response enabled to use the administrative Web pages.

▶ **The anonymous user cannot access any files.** The anonymous account defined in the Web site Authentication Properties sheet must exist, have the Log on locally user right, and have the same password as a Windows NT account. Ensure password synchronization is enabled. Anonymous accounts must be set to Password Never Expires.

▶ **Browsers other than Internet Explorer are unable to be authenticated by your Web site.** Web browsers other than Internet Explorer require Basic Authentication to be authenticated as anything other than an anonymous user.

▶ **Users can't access Web site data stored on UNC share.** Be sure that share permissions are set correctly, and that an account name and password are established for Web site access to the share.

With the myriad shares, groups, files, and directories that can be created in a network environment, some resource permission conflicts are bound to occur. When a user is a member of many groups, some of those groups may specifically allow access to a resource while other group memberships deny it. Also, cumulative permissions may occur. For example, a user may have Read access to a directory because he's a domain user and also have Full Control because he's a member of the Engineers group. Windows NT determines access privileges in the following manner:

▶ A specific denial (the No Access permission) always overrides specific access to a resource.

▶ When resolving conflicts between share permissions and file permissions, Windows NT chooses the most restrictive. For instance, if the share permission allows full control but the file permissions allow read-only, the file is read-only.

▶ When a user is a member of multiple groups, the user always has the combined permissions of all group memberships and any individual permissions assigned to the User Account.

Enabling Password Synchronization for a Web Site

Use the following procedure to enable password synchronization for a Web site:

1. Right-click the default Web site in the MMC and select Properties.

2. Select the Directory Security tab.

3. Click Edit in the Anonymous Access and Authentication Control area.

4. Check Allow Anonymous Access and click Edit.

5. Click Browse.

6. Select the IUSR_*computername* account for this server, or another account if you want to use a different account for anonymous access.

7. Check Enable Automatic Password Synchronization.

8. Click OK.

9. Click Yes to continue.

10. Click OK.

11. Click OK.

▶ Resolve resource access problems.

Access problems occur when a server can't be located or when security settings prevent authorized users from gaining access.

Common Access Problems

Access problems for Web sites fall into the following categories:

- ▶ **Connection problems** occur when no physical path to the destination server exists. These problems are quite obvious but beyond the scope of this book and the exam.

- ▶ **Routing problems** occur when TCP/IP packets cannot flow between the client and the server due to problems with routing tables, which are rare and outside the scope of this book and the exam.

- ▶ **Name resolution problems** occur when your browser cannot resolve the name provided in the URL to the IP address of the correct server. To find your Web site, the browser must be running on a computer that knows the IP address of a DNS server that can resolve your domain name, or a WINS server that knows your server's friendly name. To troubleshoot name resolution, make sure the client TCP/IP stack is set correctly to point to a WINS or DNS server, and make sure that the WINS or DNS server is properly providing your server's IP address.

▶ **Security problems** occur when the client cannot provide credentials that satisfy the server. To secure Web access from anonymous Web browsers and force Internet users to log in, remove the IUSR_*computername* account from the NTFS permissions for the Web site files. Make sure no groups that the IUSR account is a member of are in the permission list (such as EVERYONE). Anonymous users won't be able to log in unless you enter the correct password for the selected account or enable password synchronization in the Directory Security Anonymous Security and Authentication button in the Web site's properties.

Forcing a User to Log On

Use the following permissions to force a user to log on before using the default Web site:

1. Browse to `c:\inetpub\wwwroot` or its equivalent on your machine using the desktop Explorer.

2. Right-click on `default.asp` and select Properties.

3. Select Security.

4. Click Permissions.

5. Select the Everyone/Full Control permission and click Remove.

6. Select the IUSR_*computername* permission and click Remove.

7. Click Add.

8. Select Domain Users and click Add.

9. Select Full Control and click OK.

10. Click OK.

11. Click OK.

▶ Resolve Index Server query problems.

Index Server works very well and is almost completely automatic. However, its behavior may not be what you expect. Sometimes the results of a query can seem strange.

Common Index Server Problems

Index Server problems fall into four categories, all but one of which are actually optimization problems:

- ▶ **Queries return files that shouldn't be returned.** This problem can be caused by NTFS file permissions that are not correctly set up or by filtering files of all types when you should be restricting filtering to known types.

- ▶ **Queries don't return files that they should.** This problem can be caused because the catalog may be restricted to certain virtual directories, because not all files are being filtered and some extensions are not registered for filtration, or because file permissions are limiting the files that the query returns. This is almost the exact opposite of the above condition.

- ▶ **Queries take too long to fulfill.** You might be able to correct this optimization problem by forcing master merges more often. Or you may simply have too many users. Consider creating more catalogs if your data doesn't need to be searched in a single index or moving data to another server. Using more powerful server hardware or removing other applications such as a database or mail server function will also help.

- ▶ **Queries time out or fail to return any data.** If the cause of this problem is an overloaded Index Server, outright failure will be foreshadowed by queries that take too long to fulfill. Other causes of this problem are network connectivity problems or corrupted Index Server files. If you've verified the connection between the host and the server, try reinstalling Index Server.

If your server runs out of RAM, Index Server will pause its current indexing and merging so as not to load the system. Queries will still operate, but new pages will not be indexed until the service restarts when more RAM is available.

If your computer runs low on available hard disk space while Index Server is running, it will gracefully degrade as follows:

- ▶ Index Server will not start an indexing operation unless it determines that there is probably enough memory to complete the operation.

- ▶ Shadow merges in progress will be aborted and retried when disk space is freed up.

▶ Master merges will be paused until more disk space is available. A master merge pause event will be written to the event log along with a disk full error.

You can free up memory either by removing files from the corpus or by extending the volume set. In any case, you should not delete any files under the Index Server catalog directory in order to free up space. Index Server will detect additional space and resume indexing operations automatically.

▶ Resolve setup issues when installing IIS on a Windows NT Server 4.0 computer.

Most installations of IIS4 will proceed successfully and uneventfully. Most problems that occur during installation can be solved by repairing the computer or making sure Windows NT itself is correctly installed. IIS4 is included in Windows NT Server 4 Option Pack, downloadable for free from Microsoft. IIS4 is a complete upgrade to IIS3 with the exception that the Gopher service is no longer supported and will be removed if you install IIS4.

Common Installation Problems

If you have difficulty installing IIS4, the following checklist may help you figure out what is wrong:

▶ **Does the computer work?** IIS (and Windows NT) requires a stable hardware platform on which to run. Make sure that the computer is stable, without flaky memory or hard drive components, interrupt conflicts, or CPU bugs.

▶ **Is Windows NT installed correctly?** IIS needs a stable Windows NT platform on which to run. NT must also be informed of the actual configuration of hardware components. Ensure that NT is communicating with all of its components correctly.

▶ **Is the latest service pack installed?** IIS4 requires Service Pack 3. Install Service Pack 3 if it is not already present.

▶ **Does your computer have sufficient hard drive space?** IIS4 requires that your computer have at least 200MB of hard drive space, preferably much more. Check the free hard drive space on your server.

> ▸ **Is your computer powerful enough?** Microsoft recommends a Pentium 90 or faster microprocessor.

> ▸ **Does your computer have sufficient memory?** NT requires at least 32MB of memory and should have much more (see Chapter 7 for details) in order to run without performance degradation. Upgrade the memory in your server if it has less than 32MB.

After you troubleshoot the failed installation, determine the problem, and are ready to continue with the installation, the best thing to do is simply to restart the installation process. This will overwrite any previously installed files and produce a correct, complete installation of IIS4 on your server.

▶ Use a WebMap to find and repair broken links.

The Site Server Express component of IIS provides a wealth of interesting information. For troubleshooting purposes, the real benefit of Site Server Express is its ability to search your Web map for problems such as broken links, "not found" objects, images without ALT tags, and large objects (which can cause a page to take a very long time to download).

Content Analyzer's Tools menu gives you the option to do a quick search on the following objects:

- ▸ Broken Links
- ▸ Home Site Objects
- ▸ Images Without ALT
- ▸ Load Size Over 32K
- ▸ Non-Home Site Objects
- ▸ Not Found Objects (404)
- ▸ Unavailable Objects
- ▸ Unverified Objects

When you search on any one of these objects Site Server Express creates a search results window and lists those objects in it. When you click the object in the search results window, the tree view and cyberbolic view automatically go to that object. You can then double-click the object (or its parent if it is a broken link or a not-found object) to view the problem object or HTML page.

Site Server Express makes finding broken links easy. Then it is just a matter of fixing that link with the software you used to create the page, or perhaps just editing the file with a text editor, so that the link points to the correct location. Figure 12.1 shows the results of a link search.

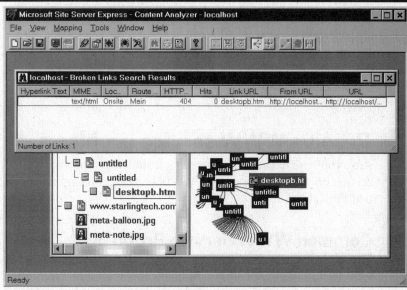

FIGURE 12.1: Finding broken links with Content Analyzer

Finding Broken Web Links in a Web Site

1. Launch the Content Analyzer.

2. Open or create a WebMap based on a Web site on your server.

3. Select Tools ➢ Quick Search ➢ Broken Links.

4. Record each file containing a broken link and the page to which the broken link refers.

5. Launch a text editor such as Notepad.

6. Open an HTML file containing a broken link.

7. Search for the name of the page to which the broken link refers, using the text editor's search menu option.

8. Change the found text to the name of an existing page.

9. Repeat steps 7 and 8 for each broken link in the file.

10. Repeat steps 6 through 9 for each file containing broken links.

11. Close the text editor.

12. Close all Content Analyzer documents.

13. Select File ➤ New ➤ Map From File.

14. Specify the same Web site as before.

15. Repeat this procedure from step 3 to verify that no broken links remain.

▶ Resolve WWW service problems.

After you've exhausted the preceding troubleshooting tips, the following section on ways to solve unique WWW service problems may provide additional help.

Common WWW Service Problems

The following lists some commonly encountered problems and suggests ways to solve them. This list is by no means exhaustive but may give you a nudge in the right direction when you are perplexed.

- ▶ **Can't find your Web server.** No DNS entry. In order for Web browsers to find your Web site, your IIS computer must have a domain name entry in the DNS server responsible for your network. Use the command line NSLOOKUP.EXE tool to check for name records for any machine on the Internet.

- ▶ **Can't create a virtual Web site.** You must specify a unique port number, IP address, or host header for the Web site.

- ▶ **Can't require SSL.** You must have a certificate installed to require SSL for your Web site.

- ▶ **Can't select another IP address.** You must configure Windows NT Server to respond to additional IP addresses. This is done through the Network control panel.

▶ **Can't find server by other name.** In order for Web browsers to find your Web site, your IIS computer must have an entry corresponding to that name in the DNS server responsible for your network.

▶ **Browser can't find virtual site.** If you are using host headers, the browser must support host headers or you must use the CGI/ISAPI workaround. If you are using a port other than 80 on your Web site, any reference to that Web site must explicitly reference the port in the URL.

▶ **Browsers with plug-ins for multimedia data files or other types of data ask if you want to save the file to disk rather than displaying the data.** A MIME type must be defined for data types other than those already defined in the IIS default setup.

▶ **Site has moved and browsers can't find it.** You can redirect browsers to the new location of a Web site using the URL option in the Home Directory tab of the Web site's Properties sheet.

▶ **Users report that they get a logon prompt when they attempt to access the Web site but access is denied after they enter an account name and password.** You must have an account defined for the users if Anonymous Authentication is disabled.

▶ **You can't log on to the IIS Administrative Web site.** You must have Windows NT Challenge/Response enabled to use the administrative Web pages.

▶ **The anonymous user cannot access any files.** The anonymous account defined in the Web site Authentication Properties sheet must also exist and have the same password as a Windows NT account.

▶ **Browsers other than Internet Explorer are unable to be authenticated by your Web site.** Web browsers other than Internet Explorer require Basic Authentication to be authenticated as anything other than an anonymous user.

▶ **Users can't access Web site data stored on UNC share.** Be sure that share permissions are set correctly, and that an account name and password are established for Web site access to the share.

Adding a MIME Type

Use the following procedure to add a MIME type:

1. Right-click the server's icon in the scope pane of the MMC and select Properties.

2. Click the File Types button.

3. Click New Type.

4. Enter **non** in the Associated Extension input box.

5. Enter **non-existent type** in the Content Type (MIME) input box.

6. Click OK.

7. Click OK.

8. Click OK.

Use the following procedure to install a digital certificate on your Web site using Certificate Server:

1. Right-click the Web site you want to install a certificate on and select Properties.

2. Click the Directory Security tab.

3. Click the Key Manager button.

4. Right-click the WWW service and select Create New Key....

5. Accept Automatically Send the Request to an On-Line Authority and click the Next button.

6. Enter **test key** in the Key Name field.

7. Enter **test** in the Password field.

8. Enter **test** again in the Confirm Password field.

9. Click the Next button.

10. Enter **test company** in the Organization field.

11. Enter **test division** in the Organizational Unit field.

12. Enter the fully qualified domain name that will be used by Web browsers to access the Web site in the Common Name field.

13. Click the Next button.

14. Enter your country in the Country field.

15. Enter your state or province in the State/Province field.

16. Enter your city or locality in the City/Locality field.

17. Click the Finish button. The certificate will be automatically submitted to the Certificate Server on your IIS computer if you installed Certificate Server. Click OK.

18. Click the Add... button.

19. Accept the Any Unassigned IP Address and Any Unassigned Port options and click the OK button.

20. Click OK again.

21. Select Commit Changes Now from the Computers menu.

22. Select Exit from the Computers menu.

23. In the Properties tab for the Web site, click the Secure Communications Edit... button again.

24. Check the Require Secure Channel When Using This Resource button.

25. Click OK.

26. Click Apply.

27. Click OK.

▶ Resolve FTP service problems.

Most FTP service problems fall under the general troubleshooting steps already covered for the other services. The process for troubleshooting FTP service problems is pretty much the same as for any other service.

FTP Troubleshooting Tips

When you have FTP service problems and you've gone through normal troubleshooting procedures, test your installation against the following questions:

▶ Is the IIS installation complete, uncorrupted, and running?

▶ For directory- or access-related problems, are directory permissions set the way they should be on both the home directory and the directory in question?

▶ For access problems, are the IUSR_*computername* account permissions and rights (especially the Log on locally user right) set correctly?

▶ Have you stopped and started the FTP service after adding a virtual directory?

▶ For custom client connection problems, have you set the directory listing style to UNIX?

▶ If certain clients can't attach to your FTP site running on an unusual port, is the client capable of attaching to an FTP server that is not running on port 21? You must specify the FTP port number when attaching with a client if your FTP service is not running on port 21.

You may also need to limit the bandwidth the IIS service uses if you use the same server for other functions, such as file service. You may find that IIS traffic is consuming an inordinate amount of network bandwidth if (for example) you share a T1 connection to the Internet for remote connectivity to another site.

Specifying UNIX as the Directory Listing Style

Use the following procedure to specify UNIX as the directory listing style:

1. Select Start ➣ Windows NT 4 Option Pack ➣ Microsoft Internet Information Server ➣ Internet Service Manager.

2. Expand the Internet Information Server node to show the active sites on your server.

3. Right-click on the test FTP site you created earlier and select Properties.

4. Select the Home Directory tab.

5. Select UNIX in the Directory Listing Style.

6. Click OK.

7. Right-click on the test FTP site and select Stop.

8. Right-click on the test FTP site and select Start.

9. Close the MMC.

Use the following procedure to limit service bandwidth for all IIS traffic:

1. Select Start ➤ Windows NT 4 Option Pack ➤ Microsoft Internet Information Server ➤ Internet Service Manager.

2. Expand the Internet Information Server node to show your server.

3. Right-click on your server.

4. Select Properties.

5. Check Enable Bandwidth Throttling.

6. Enter **10** in the Maximum network use input box.

7. Click OK.

8. Close the MMC.

Part ii

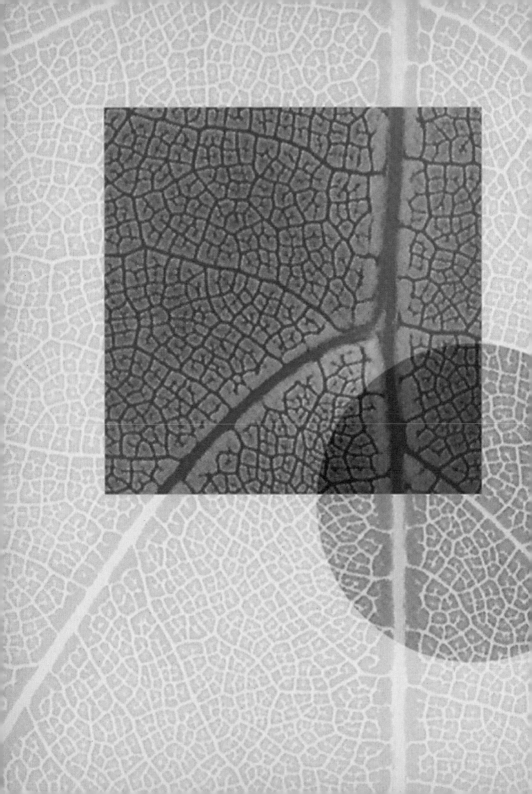

PART II

INTERNET INFORMATION SERVER 4 PRACTICE EXAM

Exam Questions

1. You want to see when your site is most often accessed during the week. Which tool should you use?

   A. Report Writer

   B. Index Server

   C. Content Analyzer

   D. Performance Monitor

2. You want to measure how much bandwidth your Web service consumes. Which counter should you monitor?

   A. Memory: Page Output/Sec

   B. IIS Global: Measured Async Bandwidth Usage

   C. Web Service: Bytes Total/Sec

   D. Active Server Pages: Transactions/Sec

3. You've set up an MS SQL Server application for workflow control and created a client based on ActiveX and Active Server Pages that runs over your company's intranet. After a few weeks of operation, users complain that some duplicate entries are appearing in certain databases. These duplicate entries are causing some customers to be overbilled. After debugging, you find that some work-at-home users are frustrated with the speed of their connection and click the Back button on their browsers to re-post information to the server when it's slow. This causes some records to be added to the database while other related records are interrupted. Which of the following solutions actually solves this problem?

   A. Re-implement the application to use Transaction Server.

   B. Increase the speed of your home users' Internet links.

   C. Upgrade your server hardware so the application is more responsive.

   D. Use Data Access Components to ensure data integrity.

4. How do you configure a Web site to use an ISAPI DLL?

   A. In the Home Directory tab of the Web site click Configuration and add an extension and a path to the file in the App Mappings tab.

   B. In the HTTP Headers tab of the Web site click Configuration and add an extension and a path to the file in the App Mappings tab.

   C. With the Registry Editor add an extension and a path to the file in the ScriptMap registry key.

   D. With the Registry Editor add an extension and a path to the file in the MimeMap registry key.

5. You have an ISAPI DLL that provides encrypted communications to your Web site using the Triple DES cipher. You want that DLL to run in a separate memory space from other DLLs for security reasons and so you can start and stop that DLL separately from other IIS applications. How can you most easily achieve your objective?

   A. Re-implement the DLL as a CGI script.

   B. Run multiple copies of IIS.

   C. Start IIS from the Run... item in the Start menu. Check the Run in Separate Memory Space option.

   D. Check the Run in Separate Memory Space option in the Home Directory tab of the Web site.

6. You want to limit the scope of queries from within the /Products/Software/Downloads section of your Web site to just that section of your Web site. You want to be able to query your whole site from the home page, however. How can you do this most easily?

   A. Set the CiScope value in the `.idq` file to `/Products/Software/Downloads`.

   B. Remove Read permission for the IUSR_SEARCH user from all directories except for the `/Products/Software/Downloads` directory.

C. Disable indexing on all virtual directories except for the `/Products/Software/Downloads` virtual directory.

D. You cannot limit the scope of a query.

7. You have an Active Server Pages program that interacts with an ActiveX control to accept query parameters and feed them to the Internet Database Connector for a bibliography search of technical papers authored by professors at your university. The search process works great but you would like to liven up the format of the resulting output Web pages by adding some graphics and links back to your home page. Which file should you modify?

A. `Query.asp`

B. `IDC.DLL`

C. `Bibform.htx`

D. `Query.idc`

8. You have embedded a small routine to count the number of times a page has been accessed (using <% and %> to enclose the JScript program) in the file `summary.html`. Rather than executing the program, however, IIS just returns the program as you typed it in the resulting Web page. You verify that the directory has Script access enabled. What is wrong?

A. You must remove the Read access for the directory.

B. You must enable Execute (including Script) access for the directory.

C. You must install a JScript interpreter ISAPI DLL.

D. You must rename the file to have an `.asp` extension.

9. You want to monitor the number of connections made to your IIS computer in real time. Which tool would you use?

A. Report Writer

B. Index Server

C. Content Analyzer

D. Performance Monitor

10. Index Server queries are taking too long. You've already restricted queries to the file types you actually want queried, but because of heavy usage, the Index Server is still not able to keep up. Using the Performance Monitor, you determine that shadow merges and master merges are happening far too often because new documents are being updated frequently. Which optimizations will help? (Choose all that apply.)

   A. Increase the amount of disk space allocated for shadow merges.

   B. Change the default master merge time to occur at 4:00 A.M. when the network is less loaded.

   C. Increase the amount of disk space allocated to catalogs.

   D. Implement bandwidth throttling to limit the number of simultaneous queries.

   E. Install more RAM and increase the amount of memory reserved for word lists to decrease frequency of shadow merges and master merges.

   F. Move the catalog to a disk different than the corpus to reduce the time that merges take to execute.

11. Your company will be creating a Human Resources site for internal use so employees can check their accrued vacation hours and other benefits. You want to provide a customized Web page for each employee that is generated when they access the site. Which solution will take the least effort to implement simple animation?

   A. Develop a WIN-CGI executable.

   B. Develop an ISAPI application.

   C. Develop an ASP script.

   D. Develop an ISAPI filter.

12. You wish to efficiently extend IIS to support encrypted communications for all Web pages using the BLOWFISH cipher. Which environment best fits your needs?

   A. JScript

   B. An ISAPI application

    C. CGI

    D. An ISAPI filter

13. Create an FTP virtual directory called `results` with the physical path `d:\results` with read/write access in an FTP site from a running MMC console. Choose the appropriate steps:

    A. Right-click the FTP site, select New ➤ Site, type **results** in the site description input box, click Next, type **d:\results** in the Path input box, check Allow Read Access, check Allow Write Access, click Finish.

    B. Right-click the FTP site, select New ➤ Virtual Directory, type **results** in the Alias input box, type **d:\results** in the Path input box, check Allow Read Access, check Allow Write Access, click Finish.

    C. Right-click the host computer, select New ➤ FTP Site, type **results** in the site description input box, click Next, type **d:\results** in the Path input box, check Allow Read Access, check Allow Write Access, click Finish.

    D. Right-click the FTP site, select New ➤ Virtual Directory, type **results** in the Alias input box, type **d:\results** in the Path input box, click Finish.

14. You've installed an IIS server at your Internet Service Provider's site so that it can participate on their high-speed Internet backbone directly, rather than being at the slow end of your T1 circuit. You need to determine how you will perform administrative functions like creating new sites remotely. The solution must be secure so that your IIS server can withstand hacking attempts from the Internet. You can configure your firewall to pass any network traffic you want between your site and the remote server.

Proposed Solution #1: Install the remote server. Enable Windows networking so that you can connect to the server using the MMC. Open the firewall to allow Windows networking protocols to pass.

Proposed Solution #2: Install the remote server. Use the HTML service managers to manage the Web sites and disable the Workstation, RPC, and Server services on the remote IIS server.

Choose the best answer:

   A. Neither will work.

   B. Both will work, but Solution #1 is preferable.

   C. Both will work, but Solution #2 is preferable.

   D. Both will work equally well.

15. What tool do you use to generate keys?

   A. User Manager

   B. Key Manager

   C. Certificate Server

   D. Microsoft Management Console

16. Choose the sequence that enables SMTP service transaction logs to create a new log every month using the Microsoft IIS Log File Format:

   A. Select the Default SMTP Site, select Action ➤ Properties, check Enable Logging, click OK.

   B. Select the local host, select Action ➤ Properties, select SMTP Service in the Master Properties pick box, check Enable Logging, select Microsoft IIS Log File Format, click OK.

   C. Select the default SMTP Site, select Action ➤ Properties, select SMTP Service in the Master Properties pick box, check Enable Logging, select Microsoft IIS Log File Format, click Properties, select Monthly, click OK, click OK.

   D. Select the local host, select Action ➤ Properties, select SMTP Service in the Master Properties pick box, check Enable Logging, select Microsoft IIS Log File Format, click OK.

17. Create a virtual directory for the NNTP service to store the test.results newsgroup in the g:\results directory. Choose the correct sequence:

A. Right-click the NNTP site, select New ➤ Virtual Directory, enter **test.results** in the Newsgroup Name, click Next, enter **g:\results**, click Finish.

B. Right-click the NNTP site, select Properties, select the Directories tab, click New, enter **test.results** in the Newsgroup Name, click Next, enter **g:\results**, click Finish.

C. Right-click the NNTP site, select Properties, select Groups, click Create New Newsgroup, enter **test.results** in the Newsgroup Name, click OK.

D. Right-click the NNTP site, select Properties, select Groups, click Create New Newsgroup, enter **test.results** in the Newsgroup Name, enter **g:\results** in the path input box, click OK.

18. Enable NNTP Service logging using W3C Extended Log File Format. Choose the correct sequence:

A. Right-click Default NNTP site, select Properties, check Enable Logging, click OK.

B. Right-click your Internet Server, select Properties, click Edit, check Enable Logging, click OK, click OK.

C. Right-click your Internet Server, select Properties, click Edit, check Enable Logging, select W3C Extended Log File Format, click OK, click OK.

D. Right-click Default NNTP site, select Properties, check Enable Logging, select W3C Extended Log File Format, click OK.

19. You've noticed a number of broken links while browsing your company's Web site. What tool will help you fix these broken links the fastest? (Choose all that apply.)

A. Report Writer

B. Content Analyzer

C. Usage Import

D. Microsoft Management Console

20. You want to tune the bandwidth settings of your various Web sites to keep some from overwhelming other, more important sites that sustain lower usage. What tool will help you determine how Internet browsers are using the several Web sites on your server? (Choose all that apply.)

A. Report Writer

B. Content Analyzer

C. Usage Import

D. Microsoft Management Console

21. You've implemented a Web site on your file server and intend to use NT file system security to secure the site. When you right-click the directory that you intend to secure and select Properties, you notice that there's no Security tab so you can't set file system security. What's wrong?

A. The volume is formatted with the FAT file system.

B. You haven't turned on file auditing.

C. You haven't enabled file system security in the Internet Service Manager.

D. You aren't logged in as the administrator so you can't change security permissions.

22. Your Web site is secured using the following permissions:

IUSR_*computername*	Read
Everyone	No Access
Domain Users	Change

Additionally, you've set IIS access permissions to Read, and you've disabled anonymous access through the Directory Security tab. Users complain that they cannot access the Web site through their browsers. How can you correct the problem?

   A. Enable anonymous access using the Microsoft Management Console.

   B. Set the IUSR_*computername* permission to Change using the desktop Explorer.

   C. Delete the Everyone ACE using the desktop Explorer.

   D. Set the Domain Users permission to Read.

23. Increased reliance on your corporate intranet has caused the site to grow larger than originally anticipated. You install another hard disk in your Web server, format it with the NT file system, and copy your site files to the new volume. You then configure the IIS services to point to the new locations using the virtual directory feature, making sure that your directory access settings are exactly the same as before. Suddenly, all users have access to the formerly secured financial directories. Why did this happen?

   A. You've used the wrong file system on the new hard disk drive.

   B. You've improperly configured IIS directory access security for the virtual directories in the Microsoft Management Console.

   C. The new site is allowing anonymous access.

   D. NTFS permissions were reset when you copied the files between volumes.

24. How do you redirect a Web browser that requests a Web site that has moved to another computer on the Internet (not a part of your domain)?

   A. Set the Local Path of the Web site to the UNC path of the new host computer (e.g., `\\IP address\share name`). Enter a valid username and password for the share.

   B. Change the default document to a document that informs the user that that site no longer exists.

   C. Click the button for a share located on another computer and then set the Network Directory of the Web site to the UNC path of the new host computer (e.g., \\IP address\share name). Enter a valid username and password for the share.

D. Click the button for a redirection to a URL and enter the new URL to the home site in the Redirect to: field.

25. You want anonymous access to your new virtual Web site to be done through a different anonymous access account than the default Web site uses, so you enter a new anonymous account name and password in the Directory Security portion of the Web site's Properties window. After you do this users are no longer able to access the Web site anonymously. What is wrong?

A. You must reboot your Web server computer for the changes to take effect.

B. The default anonymous account name and password for all Web services is overriding the password you have selected for that specific Web site. Remove the account name and password from the anonymous account settings at the computer level.

C. The account must be one of those listed in the Operators tab for the Web site.

D. You must also create the anonymous account using the User Manager or User Manager for Domains program and assign it the same password that you used in IIS. The account must also have Log on locally rights.

26. Select the correct sequence of actions to create a virtual Web site called Human Resources in the D:\HR directory from the MMC with the distinct IP address of 10.1.1.7 (assuming this address has already been added to the TCP/IP protocol on your machine). (Choose all correct answers.)

A. Right-click the server and select New ➤ Web Site. Type **Human Resources** and press Enter. Select 10.1.1.7 in the Select IP Address list box. Click Next. Click Next. Click Finish.

B. Right-click the default Web site and select New ➤ Site. Type **Human Resources** and press Enter. Select

10.1.1.7 in the Select IP Address list box. Click Next. Type **D:\HR** and press Enter. Click Finish.

C. Right-click the server and select New ➤ Web Site. Type **Human Resources** and press Enter. Select 10.1.1.7 in the Select IP Address list box. Click Next. Type **D:\HR** and press Enter. Click Finish.

D. Right-click the server and select New ➤ Web Site. Type **Human Resources** and press Enter. Click Next. Click Next. Type **D:\HR** and press Enter. Click Finish.

27. You want to use Content Analyzer to map a Web site that contains password-protected Web pages. The pages are in a directory that has only Windows NT Challenge/Response enabled. Content Analyzer fails to map those pages when you make the map using a URL. What is the problem?

A. You must enable the "Allow Content Analyzer to Scan Directory" permission in the Web site's Properties panel.

B. You must enable Basic Authentication for that directory.

C. You must enable Secure Socket Layer communications for that directory.

D. You must provide a correct default domain for basic authentication in the Web directory Security tab for that directory.

28. You have a 56K connection to the Internet. You've noticed that some very large files are being sent to your SMTP server by clients who are attaching pictures to their mail messages. You want to reject e-mail messages larger than 32K. Choose the method that will enable you to close connections when messages are too large:

A. Select Default SMTP Site, select Action ➤ Properties, select Messages, enter **32** in the Maximum Message Size input box.

B. Select Default SMTP Site, select Action ➤ Properties, select Messages, enter **32** in the Maximum Session Size input box.

  C. Select Default SMTP Site, select Action ➤ Properties, select Delivery, enter **32** in the Maximum Message Size input box.

  D. Select Default SMTP Site, select Action ➤ Properties, select Delivery, enter **32** in the Maximum Session Size input box.

29. You've established a single Index Server for your company that actually searches four different Web servers. Index Server won't return pages for the two Web servers on different domains. What should you do? (Choose all correct answers.)

  A. Establish trust relationships between the domains.

  B. Establish a user account with the necessary permissions to scan directories in the other domains.

  C. Stop and start the Content Index service.

  D. Add virtual directories that match the Web shares on the remote machines.

30. Which answer describes the steps necessary to delete the default catalog, assuming the Management Console is already running and the Index Server snap-in is loaded?

  A. Select Index Server on Local Machine, select Action ➤ Stop, select Action ➤ Delete.

  B. Select Index Server on Local Machine, select Action ➤ Stop, Expand Index Server on Local Machine, Expand Web, select Directories, select `c:\inetpub\wwwroot` (or its equivalent on your machine), select Action ➤ Delete.

  C. Select Index Server on Local Machine, select Action ➤ Stop, Expand Index Server on Local Machine, select Web, select Action ➤ Delete.

  D. Expand Index Server on Local Machine, select Web, select Action ➤ Delete ➤ Catalog, click OK.

Part ii

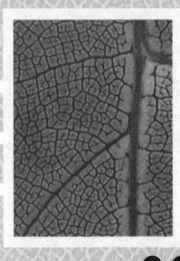

PART iii

EXCHANGE SERVER 5.5

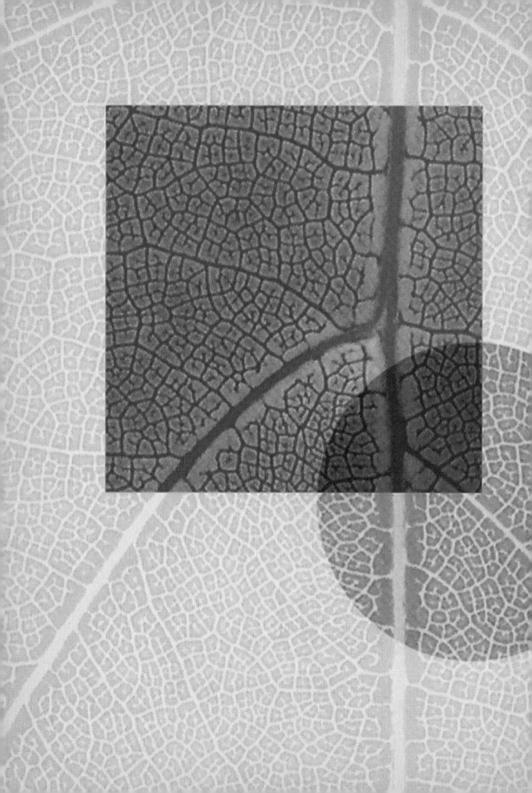

Chapter 13

PLANNING

T he objectives covered in this chapter are concerned with the aspects of Microsoft Exchange that you need to understand *before* you sit down at a computer and install the software. I have an uncle who is a carpenter; he has a favorite saying that sums up my philosophy towards networking—"Measure twice; cut once." Before you install your first Exchange server you need to analyze the needs of your company, the current network, and the capabilities of Exchange 5.5. The MCSE planning objectives will test your ability to analyze these needs and make good decisions about how to implement Exchange.

Adapted from *MCSE Exam Notes: Exchange Server 5.5*
by Robert King
ISBN 0-7821-2302-3   368 pages $19.99

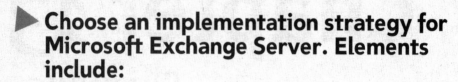

Choose an implementation strategy for Microsoft Exchange Server. Elements include:

- ▶ Server locations
- ▶ Address space

The MCSE Exchange Server 5.5 exam will test your knowledge of planning issues relating to where Exchange servers should be located within a system and how they should communicate. Before you begin the installation and configuration of individual Exchange servers, you need to decide where those servers will be physically located, where they will be defined within your Exchange environment, and how they will communicate with each other. These decisions can have a large impact on the efficiency of your overall messaging system.

Where the servers should be located and what mechanism they should use to communicate are two of the more critical design decisions that you need to make when planning an Exchange system. In order to make these decisions, you need to understand how Exchange servers are used and what types of communication will occur between them. The exam will test your knowledge on these issues.

The Exchange Hierarchy

Configuration information for an Exchange system is stored in a hierarchical, X.500-compliant database known as the Exchange Directory. You need to know how this database is organized in order to successfully configure an Exchange environment.

Don't let the terms "hierarchical" and "X.500" scare you. X.500 refers to an international committee that is responsible for the development of an industry-standard way of naming resources. Imagine that all of the computers in the world were connected to one network. In such an environment there would need to be a methodology for uniquely identifying each component on the network—that's what the X.500 standards are all about.

As for the term "hierarchical," you are probably already familiar with one hierarchical system—the DOS file system. Hierarchical refers to a system that stores data in a tree-like structure. The X.500 standards define a series of containers and subcontainers used to organize data—much like directories and subdirectories in DOS. The Exchange Directory is organized into a series of containers that hold configuration information about your Exchange environment.

There are numerous containers in the Exchange Directory. For this objective, you need to be able to define the major containers because they have an impact on server placement, and server placement affects your choice of address spaces.

Organization Container   At the top of the Exchange tree is the Organization container. It acts as the root of your structure, logically combining the various Exchange sites that you create into one structure. Normally each company has only one Organization. Microsoft Exchange does not support multiple-organization configurations.

If configured to do so, all servers in an organization can share information. Servers in different organizations are limited in the types of information that they can share. Because of this, it is recommended that all Exchange servers within a company be members of the same organization. You can define Exchange sites to control network traffic and the sharing of information.

Site Containers   Within an organization, you will need to define sites. Each *site* represents one or more Exchange servers that work together as a unit to route messages and configuration information. Because of the amount of network traffic generated between servers within a site, it is important that all servers within a site be connected on a LAN (local area network) or high-speed, reliable WAN (wide area network). This rule usually dictates the creation of sites within an Exchange organization, and is critical information on the exam!

Sites can be configured and maintained as a unit. This reduces the amount of redundant management that must be performed on each server—many parameters can be configured at the site level for all servers within the site.

Server Containers   Within a site is the Server container. This container holds configuration information about each individual server within that site. While it is convenient to configure your environment at the site level, there are times when individual servers need specific configurations. Since each server within the site is represented in the servers'

Part iii

container, you have the ability—on a server-by-server basis—to override the parameters set at the site level.

Recipient Containers   Each site also has at least one Recipient container. These containers are used to organize the various types of objects that can act as mail recipients within an Exchange site.

NOTE

The various types of recipients are covered in Chapter 14.

By default, one Recipient container is created for each site. By creating multiple Recipient containers, an Exchange administrator can separate recipients by department or location to ease administration.

There are numerous other containers in the Exchange hierarchy. Each of the containers is critical to an Exchange environment, and we will discuss them further as they relate to subsequent exam objectives. For now, though, we have enough information to discuss server placement within an Exchange system.

Server Placement

There are two aspects to server placement within an Exchange environment: physical location on the network and logical placement within the Exchange Directory. Both are governed by a fairly straightforward set of guidelines.

Physical Placement of Exchange Servers   The general rule of thumb to use when planning the physical location of Exchange servers is that servers should be placed near the users who need to access them. Try to avoid situations where users have to cross WAN links to retrieve their e-mail. Even within a LAN, try to place servers so that the majority of users do not have to cross routers to access their e-mail. The closer users are to the mail server which holds their e-mail, the faster the response times for those users.

Logical Placement of Servers within the Exchange Hierarchy

This is really a discussion of creating sites within an organization. Remember that all servers within a site should be connected on a LAN or across a high-speed, reliable WAN link with enough available bandwidth to accommodate the server-to-server traffic generated within an Exchange site.

Address Space

As discussed earlier in this chapter, an Exchange organization might be divided into multiple sites. Two components must be configured to allow communication between sites: a connector and an address space.

Connectors Microsoft Exchange uses a component known as a *messaging connector* as the physical definition of how sites communicate. There are four main connectors available:

1. Site Connector

2. X.400 Connector

3. Dynamic RAS Connector

4. Internet Mail Service

Each type of connector defines a different methodology of communication between sites.

NOTE
Chapter 14 covers each of the connectors in detail.

Address Space An *address space* defines a group of addresses. These addresses all reference a particular e-mail destination. All e-mail directed to a particular Microsoft Mail post office, for instance, consists of one or more sites. This address space is associated with a particular connector or gateway to be used to deliver the messages to that e-mail system.

Another way of thinking of this is to consider the address space as the path that e-mail should take to reach a set of recipients.

Microsoft Exchange uses the address space information to pass the messages to a component capable of delivering the mail to the appropriate destination.

▶ Develop the configuration of an Exchange Server computer.

The MCSE Exchange Server 5.5 exam will test your knowledge of the minimum system requirements and the recommended requirements for an Exchange server system. While knowing the minimum configuration

Part iii

is important, in real life there is a lot more to the configuration of an Exchange environment than just knowing the numbers.

To prepare for the exam, you should start by making sure you have the suggested minimums down, and then make sure you understand the other considerations that are involved in developing a configuration.

System Requirements for an Exchange 5.5 Server

The absolute minimum physical requirements for an Exchange 5.5 server are a Pentium 60 (or supported RISC-based) microprocessor with 24MB (32MB for RISC-based systems) of RAM and at least 150MB of available hard disk space for the Exchange server software after Windows NT server has been installed.

Microsoft recommends the following minimum hardware configuration as more realistic: Pentium 133 or faster (or a supported RISC-based) microprocessor with at least 32MB (48MB for RISC-based systems) of RAM and sufficient hard disk space for both the Exchange server software and the user e-mail and public folders that will be stored on the computer. Microsoft also suggests that multiple physical disks should be configured and that there should be enough disk space to increase the size of the paging file to at least 100MB plus the amount of physical RAM in the computer.

Other Considerations Involved in the Configuration of an Exchange 5.5 Server

While there are no set rules that govern what type of server hardware you should purchase or how you should configure your messaging environment, there are certain aspects of your network that can influence these decisions. Some of these are:

- ▶ Message volume
- ▶ Message storage
- ▶ Message traffic patterns
- ▶ The location and size of public folders

Each of these things has an impact on the design of your Exchange environment and the hardware that you purchase for your servers.

Message Volume Every user on any e-mail system uses that system in ways that are unique and specific to their needs. However, users can generally be grouped into one of three classifications based upon the amount of messaging traffic that they generate. These classifications can be used to estimate the impact that Exchange will place on your servers and on the network. Table 13.1 defines the three classes of user: light, medium, and heavy.

TABLE 13.1: Classes of Exchange e-mail users

CLASS	MESSAGES SENT/DAY	MESSAGES READ/DAY
Light	6.7	20.4
Medium	19.8	55.9
Heavy	38.6	118.9

(Source: Microsoft instructor-led course 973A: Microsoft Exchange Server 5.5 Series— Design and Implementation)

When planning an Exchange system, it is important for you to take the time to classify the various groups of users on your network. There are a few ways to make this determination:

Interview/watch users. While this is the least scientific method available, it is the most often used. Spend some time interviewing users about their plans for usage. Ask what Exchange would be used for, what types of messages would be sent, what plans are in place for using public folders, and how often they would access their e-mail software. Based upon this, you should be able to estimate the number of messages that an average user will generate and read each day.

Use the tools available in the current e-mail solution. If you are migrating from another e-mail system use its tools to quantify usage. Many e-mail packages have utilities that measure e-mail usage by user or groups.

Use the StoreStat utility. If you are currently using Microsoft Exchange, you can use the StoreStat utility provided in the Microsoft BackOffice resource kit to generate reports.

Message Storage   The storage of Exchange messages on public folders can have a large impact on the performance of an Exchange server. There are numerous types of data that must be stored on an Exchange server: everything from e-mail messages, to the Exchange directory, to whatever information is stored in public folders. Each of these items takes space on a hard drive and must be accessible when needed.

Public folders are stored on the server. Private mail folders can either be stored on the server or in personal folders (.PST) on the client's computer or both. There are benefits and drawbacks to each configuration.

Server-Based Storage Only

Advantages:

▶ All e-mail can be backed up from one location.

▶ Since e-mail is stored in a central location it is available to roving and mobile users.

▶ Less overall space is used to store e-mail because Exchange only stores one copy of a message, even if it is addressed to multiple users.

Disadvantages:

▶ Demands a large amount of storage on the server.

▶ The overhead of e-mail access can degrade the performance of the server.

Personal Folders Only

Advantages:

▶ Less storage required at the server.

▶ Server performance can be improved due to less client access.

Disadvantages:

▶ Users must back up their own e-mail.

▶ E-mail will not be available to roving or mobile users unless they are using the computer that stores their e-mail.

▶ More storage is needed as e-mail sent to multiple users will be stored in multiple locations.

A Combination of Personal and Server-Based Storage

Advantages:

▶ Allows e-mail storage to be configured to meet individual users' needs.

Disadvantages:

▶ It can become difficult to keep track of where each user is storing his or her e-mail.

▶ Users who store their e-mail locally will need to back up their own e-mail.

Remember that administrative policies can be set to limit the amount of e-mail that users can store.

Message Traffic Patterns   When you are doing your research to classify your users, you should also make note of which groups are most likely to send e-mail to each other. You can use this information to control the impact of Exchange on your network by placing the mailboxes of users who communicate often on the same Exchange server. This eliminates the need for their messages to travel across the network from server to server.

The Location and Size of Public Folders   Another consideration is the use of public folders within your Exchange system. You need to evaluate three aspects of public folders:

▶ The amount of new information that is generated each day—the number of messages and their average size.

▶ How long that data needs to remain on the server.

▶ The average number of users who access that data each day and how often they need to do so. You should also take into account how they use the data. Will they search, sort, or change views when accessing it?

NOTE
We will discuss the creation of public folders in Chapter 14 and their management in Chapter 15.

Part iii

For the planning objectives covered in the exam, be aware of the following:

▶ Public folders do not have to be stored on the same server as the users' mailboxes.

▶ An Exchange server can be dedicated to the task of holding public folders. This configuration can reduce the overhead on servers that hold user mailboxes.

▶ Public folders can be replicated to multiple servers to spread the workload across servers.

Revisiting the Physical Requirements

Earlier we discussed the physical minimums and a recommended minimum configuration for an Exchange server. We have also discussed a series of items that might influence those minimums. Now we can discuss particular components of an Exchange server.

System Memory   Server processes are multithreaded, and each process can dynamically allocate system memory and can use as much memory as the system has available.

NOTE
You can control aspects of memory allocation by using the Performance Optimizer utility that will be discussed in Chapter 16.

As with any NT server, it is best to have enough RAM available so that the system is not constantly using virtual memory.

Disk Usage   An Exchange server can place heavy demands on a server's hard disks. There are certain steps that an administrator can take to limit the impact of data storage on an Exchange server:

▶ Implement storage limits on all users to limit the amount of personal e-mail that they can store.

▶ Limit the maximum age of information stored in public folders.

▶ Limit the size of public folders.

▶ Limit the maximum message size.

Microprocessors   Exchange is a multithreaded application. This means that it can benefit from additional processors in the server. If the processor is the bottleneck on an Exchange server you should consider upgrading to a faster processor or moving the Exchange server software to a multi-processor computer, or adding processors to the computer. When analyzing an Exchange server remember that the server needs to handle requests from multiple users, might have additional components installed such as gateways or connectors, and might be used for other non-Exchange related functions.

Network Connections   Analyzing a network is well beyond the scope of this examination. On the server-side, if the network is the bottleneck, upgrade to multiple, high-speed network interface cards.

There is one more decision that you have to make regarding the physical configuration of your Exchange servers—how many will you have. There are two basic strategies available:

▶ Multiple, distributed, less powerful servers

▶ Fewer, more powerful servers

Multiple, Distributed, Less Powerful Servers

Advantages:

▶ The failure of any given server affects fewer users.

▶ Each server can be configured as needed for the users who access it.

▶ Hardware is usually less expensive and easier to configure.

▶ Many off-the-shelf configurations are available.

Disadvantages:

▶ There is more hardware to maintain.

▶ The hardware may not be extensible to meet system needs as the number of users increases.

▶ More network traffic is generated as the servers communicate with each other.

▶ More hardware means more administration.

Fewer, More Powerful Servers

Advantages:

▶ Specialized hardware is usually designed to facilitate later upgrades.

▶ There is less network traffic generated since there are fewer servers.

▶ Less overall disk storage is required since only one copy of each message is stored on a server.

▶ Most high-end servers have fault-tolerant systems built in.

▶ Less hardware means less administration.

Disadvantages:

▶ Specialized hardware is offered by fewer vendors, reducing the number of choices available.

▶ More data on each server increases the amount of time to back up and restore.

▶ The network must be able to handle the number of requests processed by each server.

▶ There is a single point of failure—a server failure will affect more users.

▶ Identify strategies for migration from previous versions of Exchange Server to Exchange Server 5.5.

Microsoft has created a very straightforward method for upgrading earlier versions of Exchange Server to version 5.5. There are few choices to be made, and you will have already made the big one—the choice to upgrade in the first place.

For the exam, you need to be clear on the steps involved in upgrading to Exchange 5.5. To upgrade an earlier version of Exchange Server to version 5.5, access the Exchange Server 5.5 setup program on the CD-ROM. When the startup program is started, it detects any Exchange Server components that are installed on the computer. If a previous version exists, the setup program will automatically update its database.

If the previous version installed was version 5.0, the setup program will immediately upgrade its database to the version 5.5 format. If the installed software was version 4.0, the setup program will first upgrade the database to version 5.0, and then upgrade it to version 5.5. In either event, remember that the first rule of LAN administration is to back up the system before making any major changes—and this upgrade is a major change.

Since the setup program for Exchange 5.5 upgrades all previous versions, there is really not much of a strategy required. You will, however, need to make a few choices. The issues you need to consider include the following:

- ▶ Deciding between an in-place upgrade or an upgrade to another location

- ▶ Updating the key management databases

- ▶ Upgrading multiple sites

- ▶ Security issues

Upgrade In-Place or to Another Location

The upgrade procedure will prompt the user to specify whether an in-place upgrade of the Exchange databases should take place or if the databases should be upgraded to another directory on the server. You cannot substitute a network drive for the local directory due to network latency. If you choose to upgrade to another location, the server must have adequate disk space to hold both the original and the new databases.

Updating the Key Management Server Database

Key Management Server is an advanced security service that can be installed as an Exchange component. A discussion of Key Management Server is beyond the scope of this examination. You should, however, be aware that the Key Management Server database must be upgraded to the Exchange 5.5 format. This process occurs automatically if the setup program detects that Key Management Server has been enabled. The Key Management Server administrator must be present to provide the appropriate passwords.

Part iii

Upgrading Multiple Sites

While no strategy is required, it is recommended that any bridgehead servers be upgraded first in both sites. Then you can proceed to upgrade the other servers in each site in any order.

WARNING

Be aware that intersite directory replication will halt until the bridgehead servers at both sites have been upgraded.

Security Issues

When upgrading an Exchange server you must be aware of the following two security issues:

1. The site service account must be granted the right to "Act as part of the operating system."

2. Security in Microsoft NT 4.0 has been changed so that only members of the administrators group can access the Registry of a remote computer. Since the setup program must access the Registry of a remote Exchange server when joining a site, the account you are using when performing the upgrade must be the account of a member of this group.

▶ Develop a long-term coexistence strategy. Protocols include:

- ▶ IMAP
- ▶ LDAP

The MCSE Exchange Server 5.5 exam will test your knowledge of the protocols that allow users to access their e-mail through Exchange. Communication in today's complex business environments requires a LAN administrator to have a flexible outlook. Users need to be able to access information in many different ways, depending upon circumstances. Some users only need to access their messages from their desktop computers in the office; other users need to access the Exchange system using a dial-up connection; still others need to access information across the Internet. No matter what the need, Exchange Server 5.5 can provide access to the data that is critical to success.

In order to provide the connectivity necessary for all of the various methods that can be used to access Exchange, an administrator needs to understand the protocols supported by an Exchange server. This objective lists two of those protocols: IMAP and LDAP. While these are two of the more current protocols supported there are others that you have to understand for the MCSE examination. We are going to add the following protocols to our list:

▸ POP3

▸ Active Server and HTTP

▸ NNTP

Coexistence with foreign e-mail systems is critical to success in today's business world. Chapter 14 discusses Exchange Server components that are used to connect to specific environments such as Lotus cc:Mail and Microsoft MS Mail. While these connectors are useful, it is important to have a generic solution available for those situations where there is no specific solution for connectivity. In those cases, administrators can utilize industry-standard protocols that are supported by most e-mail software packages on the market today. For the exam you need to have a thorough understanding of the following protocols.

POP3 (Post Office Protocol 3)

POP3 is an industry-standard protocol designed specifically to provide clients with the ability to retrieve e-mail messages from an e-mail server. There are numerous POP3 clients available on the market, including Microsoft Outlook Express. (Microsoft Outlook can also be configured to act as a POP3 client.)

POP3 is described as a mail-drop service: the POP3 server acts as a repository for e-mail until the recipient can retrieve it. You should be aware of the following limitations of the POP3 protocol:

▸ E-mail can only be retrieved from the Inbox folder of an Exchange server mailbox. E-mail stored in any other folder is not accessible.

▸ POP3 does not support the retrieval of encrypted e-mail.

▸ POP3 is *only* a retrieval protocol. It is designed to work with some other application that provides the ability to send e-mail.

POP3 functionality is integrated into the Exchange Server Information Store. This design streamlines the process for faster, easier access.

Part iii

POP3 Functionality   POP3 is a simplistic protocol. It relies on a short list of commands to provide its functionality. POP3 was designed to allow users access to their e-mail through an Internet connection, but its simple set of commands does not allow for many complex actions.

NOTE
The POP3 commands will be discussed in Chapter 14.

Active Server and HTTP

Users often need to access their e-mail from a computer that does not have the Exchange client or Outlook installed and configured. One of the easier methods of providing this access is to use a combination of IIS (Internet Information Server) and Exchange. With this combination, users can use any browser that supports both Java scripts and frames to access their e-mail across the Internet.

The user accesses the IIS server and requests a particular page, usually something like:

```
http://www.royal-tech.com/exchange
```

This page is an ASP (Active Server Page) script which allows the user to authenticate to the Exchange system using their NT user name and password. Once authenticated, the user requests their e-mail. The appropriate active server functions convert the e-mail into an HTML file that can be downloaded by the client's browser.

This method of access allows the user to access their e-mail from any computer that has access to the Internet. No special configuration is required at the client computer (other than that necessary to access the Internet).

Active Server and HTTP Functionality   To take advantage of Active Server and HTTP access to e-mail, IIS version 3.0 or later must be installed. This version is automatically installed during the installation of Windows NT Service Pack 3. You must also install the Active Server Pages as a separate process. This enables the Active Server Pages on the IIS server.

Once the server is configured, users can log on and access their e-mail by using the following process:

1. The user attempts to access the Exchange Server at `http://<web-server-URL>/exchange`.

2. The EXCHFILT.D11 file queries the browser to determine the language it requires. This process is transparent to the user. Based upon this step, the user's browser is sent a default logon page.

3. On the default logon page the user submits their logon name and password.

4. This information is used to authenticate the user. This authentication can use any of the following methods:

    ▶ Basic (clear text)

    ▶ Basic with Secure Sockets Layer (SSL)

    ▶ Windows NT Challenge/Response

    ▶ Windows NT Challenge/Response with SSL

5. Once the user is successfully authenticated, the request is passed to a library of functions that convert the user's mailbox contents into HTML pages that can be downloaded to the client.

Like POP3, the combination of Active Server Pages and HTTP allows a user access to their e-mail from a remote location. In Exchange 5.5 this combination allows access to more than just the user's Inbox—additional folders can also be accessed. It also provides access to additional functions such as the user's calendar and to-do lists. The biggest drawback to using this configuration is that it is not designed to download the e-mail to a local folder for offline use.

NNTP (Network News Transport Protocol)

The Internet News Service uses NNTP as a method to provide Exchange clients with access to the many Usenet newsgroups available on the Internet. Usenet newsgroups have been in use for many years providing a public forum for discussions on more than 20,000 topics. Many of these discussions are concerned with topics that are of interest to many businesses—everything from marketing strategies in a particular market to technical help on most software packages.

Newsgroups are stored on a group of servers. These servers allow users to post and retrieve messages to and from a particular thread of conversation. The Internet News Service allows an Exchange server to join as a member of one or more newsgroups. This can decrease user access times since the information is stored on their local server rather than on a server somewhere out on the Internet.

In an Exchange environment the Internet News Service uses the NNTP protocol to download the newsgroups to the Information Store. Users can then access those newsgroups as public folders on the Exchange server.

NNTP Functionality   Downloading the messages stored in a newsgroup is accomplished through a process called a *feed*. There are two configuration options available: a *push feed* or a *pull feed*. In either configuration you will need to list which of the newsfeeds available from your Internet service provider should be downloaded to your server.

The terms "push" and "pull" define which side of the partnership should initiate the download of information. Both terms are defined from the perspective of your Exchange server. In a push feed configuration, your Internet service provider initiates the connection based on its own schedule. In a pull feed configuration, you determine when the transfer should occur.

The Internet news service can also be used to publish Exchange public folders as newsgroups, either as an internal resource for your company or as a public forum on the Internet. Many companies use this type of configuration as a form of technical or product support.

IMAP4 (Internet Message Access Protocol)

IMAP acts quite a bit like the POP3 service. Users with an IMAP4-enabled client can access their e-mail and submit e-mail to an SMTP service for delivery. The big difference between the two is that IMAP has more functionality than POP3. This means that clients using an IMAP-enabled client can accomplish tasks that a POP3 client cannot, including the following:

▶ Access multiple folders (not just the Inbox)

▶ Search the contents of a mailbox without downloading those contents

▶ Leave a copy of the e-mail on the server

▶ Download only the headers of messages and determine which actual messages should be downloaded to the local machine

▶ Download only certain parts of a message (an attachment, for instance)

POP3 was developed to allow user access to their e-mail through an Internet connection. IMAP4 was developed later (for the same purpose) and was specifically designed to correct the major weaknesses of the POP3 specifications.

LDAP (Lightweight Directory Access Protocol)

In the past there was no standard way to store configuration information for a network service. Each vendor created their own methods of creating objects, accessing that information, and managing configurations. Recently there has been a definite trend toward standardizing the format of this information in a hierarchical, attribute-based, X.500-compliant database.

Given this "standard" method of storing data, it makes sense that a standard method of accessing and managing that information would be developed. The Lightweight Directory Access Protocol (LDAP) is that method. Clients with the appropriate permissions can access, delete, add, and modify objects within an X.500-compliant database. Users can, for instance, use LDAP-enabled client to search the Exchange database for information such as phone numbers or e-mail addresses. Given the appropriate permissions, they can also perform management functions such as adding users or changing the attributes of a recipient. LDAP relies on a very simple (yet powerful) set of commands to perform these functions. LDAP can allow remote access to the information stored in the Exchange Directory.

▶ Develop an infrastructure for Exchange Server.

- ▶ Identify public folders, including server-side scripting.
- ▶ Identify private information stores.
- ▶ Plan Internet connectivity and access.

This objective identifies the concerns that you need to take into account when planning for the workload placed on your Exchange server and your network by the messaging system. For this objective, there are three critical issues that you need to understand.

There are many types of overhead that can be generated, but the three main sources of overhead are public folders, Private Information Stores, and Internet access protocols.

Identify Public Folders, Including Server-Side Scripting

A public folder is a repository for shared information that is managed through Exchange. Administrators often think of Exchange public folders as only holding e-mail, but the truth is that many kinds of data can be stored—everything from e-mail to voice mail.

NOTE
We'll discuss the creation and management of public folders in Chapter 14.

You need to consider a few issues during the planning of your Exchange environment. Those issues include:

▸ Deciding whether you should distribute public folders on servers throughout your entire organization or dedicate a few servers to the task of holding them

▸ Deciding the number of replicas of each folder that should exist

▸ Deciding where those replicas should be physically located

Dedicated Public Folder Servers   Placing a public folder on an NT server can place the same pressures on that server as hosting any shared resource. That server must have the capacity to handle the extra network connections and the disk space to hold the data, and the network must have the bandwidth to handle the extra traffic that will be generated. In large environments it might be difficult to find servers that meet all of these requirements. In such an environment it is often preferable to dedicate servers to the task of holding public servers, thereby moving the overhead from servers that hold users' mailboxes.

Deciding the Number of Replicas of Each Public Folder
Exchange allows the administrator to configure multiple copies, or replicas, of each public folder. There are two reasons that you might decide to have more than one copy of your information: fault tolerance and controlling network or server overhead.

Fault tolerance   If the data contained in a public folder is of a critical nature, creating replicas of that data ensures that the loss of a single server does not imply the loss of the data.

Network or server overhead   If many users will need access
to the data you might decide to create multiple replicas to
spread the workload over many servers or network segments.

There are other reasons for creating replicas. Geographically separated
areas may dictate a need for multiple replicas. Or you might want to set
different age limits on different replicas to create an archive-like setup.

Deciding Where Replicas Should Be Physically Located   In many
ways this is the easiest of the three decisions—place a copy of the data
physically near the users who will need to access it. While this doesn't
reduce the total amount of traffic generated (users still have to access the
same amount of data no matter where it is placed), it does allow you to
control where that traffic will occur, and thereby also ensure quicker
access time. Proper placement can reduce the amount of traffic that has
to cross your routers or expensive WAN links, thereby decreasing the
impact of public folder access on your overall network.

Server-Side Scripting   Many companies use public folders to store
information that is critical to their success. Often an action needs to be
taken when a change is made to the contents of the folder. For example,
perhaps a company has a public folder used to store customer contacts.
When a contact is added to the folder, the company would like an e-mail
sent to the client informing them that their communication has been
received and is being acted upon. One way to ensure that this e-mail is
sent is to have a person who is responsible for monitoring the public
folder. This person can then send the response in a timely manner. The
problem with this solution is it relies on human intervention.

Exchange allows an administrator to create a server-side script that
automates actions that should occur based on changes to the contents of
a public folder. These scripts can be created in Notepad using a simple
scripting language, or by using one of many other tools available:
Microsoft Visual Basic, Microsoft JScript, or Microsoft Visual Studio in
conjunction with Outlook 8.03.

Server-side scripts can be activated on a set schedule (every hour, day,
week, etc.) or when one of the following events occurs:

▶ A new item is added to the folder.

▶ An existing item is changed.

▶ An item is deleted.

Part iii

Identify Private Information Stores

The Private Information Store is that area of the Exchange environment where users' mailboxes are stored. When planning the placement or configuration of Private Information Stores within your Exchange system you should consider the following:

- ▶ Numerous low-end servers versus fewer high-end computers

- ▶ Physical location of servers

Numerous Low-End Versus Fewer High-End Computers   There are two philosophies regarding the type of hardware that should be purchased to act as Exchange servers. The advantages and disadvantages of each were discussed earlier in this chapter.

Physical Location of Servers   As with any network server, it is usually best to place the computer physically near the users who will access it. This is true of servers that hold user mailboxes as well. Try not to have users cross a router or, worse, a WAN link in order to access their e-mail. Controlling this aspect of the Exchange environment can have a large effect on the impact of Exchange on your network.

Plan Internet Connectivity and Access

Earlier in this chapter we discussed the various technologies that users can use to access the Exchange environment through the Internet. At this point in the planning of your system you should choose which of those methods you are going to implement. For review, your choices are:

- ▶ POP3

- ▶ IMAP4

- ▶ NNTP

- ▶ Active Server Pages and HTTP

- ▶ LDAP

You should base your choices upon the needs of your users.

▶ Choose Microsoft Exchange Client installation and integration strategies. Elements include:

- ▶ Network installation
- ▶ Client computer installation
- ▶ Scripted client installation
- ▶ Forms interoperability
- ▶ Schedule+ interoperability
- ▶ Calendar interoperability

There are two sides to an Exchange environment: the server side and the client side. For this objective, you need to understand client-side issues.

For this objective, you need to understand the issues surrounding client software installation—including compatibility issues.

For the examination, Microsoft concentrates on Outlook as the client software to be used to connect to an Exchange 5.5 server. The first few topics of this objective address the various ways that Outlook can be installed.

Network Installation

Many administrators prefer to have clients run a shared copy of Outlook. This configuration offers the following advantages:

- ▶ Less disk space is used at each client.
- ▶ Since there is only one copy of the program, upgrades and other maintenance tasks are simplified.
- ▶ Since the program is stored in a central location, backing it up is centrally controlled.

Users still need to run the Outlook setup program, but in a shared installation environment they will see the option to "Run from Network Server" on their list of installation options. When chosen, this option will copy a minimum number of files to their local disk, leaving the bulk of the program on the server. We'll look at the process for setting up a network-shared installation in the "Necessary Procedures" section.

Part iii

Client Computer Installation

When configuring Outlook so that it runs from a local drive the administrator must decide how the application will be installed. One way, of course, is to carry the Outlook software to each computer and run SETUP.EXE from the local CD-ROM drive. While this method certainly works, it might not be convenient in a large environment. On a larger network, the administrator often creates an installation share point on an NT server and installs the software from there.

Scripted Client Installation

You can create a set of scripts that will automate the installation of Outlook. You will need to have a different set of scripts for each client hardware and software configuration in your environment. The scripts are stored in the OUTLOOK.STF and OUTLOOK.PRF files. These files are added to an installation share point to automate the process.

In many installations users will be using a variety of client software to access their Exchange e-mail. While Microsoft is certainly pushing the use of the Outlook client, many systems are still using the older Exchange client software. When this is the case, special consideration must be given to ensure compatibility and interoperability between the various versions.

Forms Interoperability

Exchange allows users to create customized forms for the submission of information to Exchange folders. These forms can be used to control how information is entered and to ease the data-entry process. Unfortunately, the older Exchange client used a process for the creation and use of custom forms that is different from the process that Outlook uses.

Clients using Outlook can use forms created by both Outlook and the Exchange client. Users using the Exchange client can only use forms created using the Exchange Forms Designer.

If your users are using a mixture of client software, you need to be aware of this limitation. There are two options available to you: either upgrade all of your users to Outlook or create all forms in the older Exchange Forms design tool.

Schedule+ Interoperability

In an environment that includes both MS Mail post offices as well as Exchange servers the administrator should install the MS Mail connector so that these users can exchange e-mail. Most users who are still using the older client software will also be using version 1 of Schedule+. Along with the MS Mail connector, the administrator can install the Schedule+ Free/Busy connector, which connects the schedule information in Exchange with that of Schedule+. This allows users to check schedules of users using both programs.

Calendar Interoperability

The Schedule+ Free/Busy connector also allows users from the MS Mail system to access calendars stored in Exchange and vice versa. There is overhead associated with installing and maintaining this connector so, in most cases, it should be considered an interim solution during an upgrade process.

There are many procedures for this objective—we mostly discussed the why rather than the how of client setup. You should, however, practice setting up Outlook a few times before taking the exam.

Creating a Network Installation Point

To create a shared installation point on a server, run the UCSETUP.EXE program found on the Outlook CD-ROM. This program will ask you which clients should be set up. Your choices are:

- ▶ Windows 95 or NT Client
- ▶ Windows 16-bit Client
- ▶ DOS Client

The program will copy the appropriate files to the server and create the share for you.

Installing Outlook from a Network Installation Point

Users will need to run the SETUP.EXE program found in the shared folder. They will be presented with the three choices: Typical, Custom, and Run from Network Server. In most cases, the typical installation is recommended—it includes the components needed by most users.

Installing Outlook to Use a Network Copy of the Program

Users will run the SETUP.EXE program found on the share point. To use a shared copy of Outlook they should choose "Run from Network Server" as the type of installation. The user will need to know the path to the shared copy of Outlook on the server.

Setting Up a Shared Copy of Outlook

From any computer on the network run the Outlook SETUP.EXE program with the /A command parameter. This instructs the set-up program to copy the program to a shared location. During the installation you will need to provide the following information:

▶ Your organization's name. As with any Windows program, you will be asked for the name of your organization.

▶ The product ID printed on the back of the CD-ROM package.

▶ The name and path to the directory where you want to store the Outlook program files.

▶ The name and path to the directory where you want to store any shared components.

When users install the Outlook client, they will choose the "Run from Network Server" type of installation. They will be asked for the location to install Outlook program files that are shared with other applications.

▶▶ Develop long-term administration strategies.

▶ Plan a backup strategy.

▶ Plan a disaster recovery strategy.

▶ Plan information store maintenance.

▶ Plan remote administration.

▶ Plan information retrieval strategies.

Many administrators make the mistake of planning only for the short-term. They worry about today's budget for hardware instead of thinking about what hardware will be needed in a few months. They worry about how they will install client software on all of the computers without thinking about which client software should be chosen. They worry about which backup software should be used instead of thinking about how they would recover from a major disaster.

This objective is concerned with the options available for long-term management of an Exchange environment. Knowing what is available can help you plan for future needs.

The MCSE Exam will test your knowledge of planning issues concerned with backup strategies and information retrieval strategies. You need to understand the choices available.

NOTE

The procedures involved in implementation of the backup strategy are the subject of later chapters.

Plan a Backup Strategy

There are four different types of backup to choose from for your Exchange system: Full, Copy, Incremental, and Differential.

Full   The entire system is backed up. Because all information is backed-up, this type of backup takes the most time. It is, however, the easiest to use in the event of a disaster—only one backup-set (the last set) is needed to recover.

Copy   This type of backup is usually only used in special circumstances. A copy backup is basically the same as a full backup except that no marking takes place. A full backup marks the information stores and log files so that the next incremental or differential backup can back up the correct files. A copy backup is usually used to get a full copy of the system without affecting the sequence of an incremental or differential schedule.

Incremental   A full backup is performed and then only the data that has changed since the preceding full backup or incremental backup is backed up. This is usually the quickest type of backup each night, but it can also be the most complex to restore from. To restore from an incremental set, you first restore the full backup and then restore each incremental tape until all have been restored.

Differential   A full backup is performed. A differential backup then backs up all of the data that has changed since that full backup. This method will result in the backup taking longer as time passes since the full backup and more changes are made to the data. At some point (usually once a week) you run another full backup and start the process again. While the differential type of backup might take longer than the incremental, it is usually easier to restore— only the full backup and the last differential tape sets are needed.

There are a few other considerations when planning your backup strategies:

Location of the tape devices   Many companies purchase a tape drive for each server. This reduces the amount of network traffic generated by the backup process. Other companies buy a high-end tape system and back up all servers to that device. Be aware of the overhead that this can place on the network and the server on which the tape drive is located.

Capacity of the backup system   Purchase a backup system that can handle the workload that will be generated by your system. You can estimate the amount of data that will need to be backed up each day. Knowing this, you can then compare that value with the average bytes/minute that your device can back up. Ensure that your tape drive can back up the required amount of data in an acceptable amount of time.

Using circular logging   Circular logging automatically overwrites the log files—reducing the amount of disk space required on your Exchange servers. Incremental and differential backups cannot be performed with circular logging enabled.

Setting a backup schedule   Backing up can place a lot of overhead on both the server and the network. Make sure that your backups are performed at a time when this overhead will not affect your users.

Off-site tape storage   Backups are an important part of your disaster recovery plan. Store your backups off-site so that a physical disaster (fire or flood, for instance) that damages your facilities will not also damage your backup tapes.

Plan a Disaster Recovery Strategy

There are various considerations when planning a recovery strategy. Here are a few.

▶ How you recover from a disaster will be determined by the backup strategy you are using for your backups and upon the configuration you are using for your log files.

▶ Exchange Server uses a series of databases to store system configuration information, user mailboxes, and data stored in public folders. These databases use the Joint Engine Technology (JET) format that uses log files to track and maintain data. There are four main databases that contain this data:

   ▶ Directory Service: Contains organization-wide configuration information, such as recipient information and configuration information for each server.

   ▶ Private Information Store: Contains user mailboxes.

   ▶ Public Information Store: Contains all data stored in public folders.

   ▶ Directory Synchronization Database: Maintains information about what has been synchronized with other e-mail systems such as MS Mail.

▶ The JET database technology uses a series of transaction logs to ensure that the main database does not become corrupted in the event of a hardware failure. All transactions are written to these log files before they are committed to the actual database. This allows the system to roll back to the point of the last complete transaction in the event of a hardware failure. If possible, the system will use the information in the log file to complete the transaction that was interrupted. If this is not possible, it can remove the incomplete transaction from the database. Log files can also be used to recover data in the event of a disaster.

▶ By default, Exchange is configured to use circular logging. This means that as transactions are committed to the database, the system can overwrite the log files. While this configuration saves disk space, it does limit their functionality for recovery.

Log Files   Exchange server uses various types of log files in the management of its databases. Log files are 5MB in size and are stored in two directories: \EXCHSRVR\DSADATA and \EXCHSRVR\MDBDATA. Table 13.2 summarizes the various types of log files and their function.

Part iii

TABLE 13.2: Exchange log files

Log file type	Description
Transaction logs	Hold transactions before they are written to the database
Previous logs	Older copies of transaction logs. These log files are maintained only if circular logging has been disabled.
Checkpoint files	A pointer file that keeps track of which transactions in the transaction log have been committed to the database
Reserved logs	Two log files that are used to reserve space on the disk in case it fills up. This extra reserve space ensures the database can shut down in a consistent state if the disk fills up.
Patch files	Temporary files used to track changes during a backup. These files are deleted by the backup software as it completes its process.

If the system is left at the default of circular logging, log files cannot be used during the recovery process. If circular logging has been disabled, the log file will be renamed when it becomes full and a new one will be created. The Windows NT backup software manages the previous log files.

During a full or incremental backup, the old log files are backed up and then purged from the hard disk. Since these log files contain all changes to the database, they can be used to reconstruct the database during a recovery.

All of this information leads us to the actual test objective—planning a disaster recovery plan. The first decision is whether or not to use circular logging.

WARNING
Microsoft suggests that circular logging be disabled in environments where data recovery is of high importance.

Placement of the Log Files   You will need to carefully consider the placement of the log files on your Exchange server. Placing the log files on the same physical disk as the actual database is not the optimum design. Placing them on another disk offers two advantages.

1. It spreads the workload over multiple disks. Writing to the database and to the log file on the same disk can create a performance bottleneck.

2. In the event that the disk that contains the database dies, you can restore from backup and the system will use the current log files to restore changes that have occurred since that backup.

Plan Information Store Maintenance

Like all other databases, the Exchange databases require regular maintenance. Three utilities should become a part of your regular Exchange server maintenance. The three tools are described in Table 13.3.

TABLE 13.3: Exchange maintenance utilities

UTILITY	DESCRIPTION
ESEUTIL	Checks the consistency of and defragments both the Information Store and Directory Services databases. (Exchange defragments the Information Store on a regular basis.)
ISINTEG	Checks the consistency of the Information Store database. It does this at the message level which is a higher order check than ESEUTIL performs.
MTACHECK	Checks the consistency of information in the MTA database (connector information and e-mail messages stored in queues).

One of the biggest concerns for administrators is the size of the Information Store databases. These databases store all of the users' e-mail as well as the data stored in public folders. As such, they can use a lot of disk space. There are a few steps you can take to control or limit the size of these databases:

▶ Limits can be set on the entire Information Store or on individual mailboxes.

▶ The administrator can manually clean mailboxes on a regular basis, deleting e-mail based on certain thresholds such as size or date.

▶ The Mailbox Cleanup agent (found in the BackOffice Resource Kit) can be used to clean up e-mail automatically based on thresholds.

Part iii

Plan Remote Administration

If you plan to manage Exchange servers at remote locations, you will need to install and configure a RAS (Remote Access Server) at each location. You will also need to configure the RAS client on those computers that will be used to call in and perform the management.

Plan Information Retrieval Strategies

An e-mail system is not worth much if users can't access their mail. You need to consider the technologies available and implement those that are relevant to your environment.

Different types of users need different technologies to access the information in an Exchange system. Earlier in this chapter we introduced the various connectivity options available. The next step in the planning of an Exchange environment is to decide which of those technologies will be needed in your environment.

The first step is to analyze your users' connectivity needs. Some of the questions you will need to ask are as follows:

- ▶ Which users connect only from their workstations at work?

- ▶ Do any users need access from remote locations?

- ▶ Which users carry laptops, and which of those have access to the Internet while traveling?

- ▶ Do your users need access to Internet newsgroups?

- ▶ How do your users find information (such as phone numbers) of other users?

Exchange offers technologies that can handle each of these needs:

- ▶ Users at the office are usually the easiest to configure. Install the client software and they are ready to go. Your major decision will be whether or not to give a user access to a shared client installation.

- ▶ Traveling users will need more thought. If your traveling users have access to the Internet, perhaps setting up a Web server and using HTTP and Active Server Pages for access would make sense. If, however, those users need to read their e-mail while offline, perhaps POP3 or IMAP4 would be more appropriate.

- ▶ If your users need access to Internet newsgroups you might want to add NNTP functionality to your server so that they can gain access to the information locally (as opposed to accessing the Internet themselves). This option provides faster response time for the users and also gives you more control over what information they have available.

▶ Lastly, remember that LDAP can be used to access information stored in the Exchange Directory, such as phone numbers. This might be a convenient way to offer a company-wide phone book to your users.

▶ Develop security strategies.

Messaging systems have become a critical part of many businesses. Securing the messaging environment from malicious or accidental changes is a major part of Exchange administration. The MCSE exam will test your knowledge of security issues.

Exchange 5.5 has an integral security system capable of controlling who can access or change the configuration of the environment. You need to determine which users should be able to make changes and implement security accordingly.

Permissions are a set of rights granted to a user or group that control access to the objects defined in the Exchange directory. A security context defines the boundaries in which permissions apply. The Exchange database follows a hierarchical structure of containers within containers, used to organize the information. A security context defines the containers to which a set of permissions pertains.

There are three security contexts in the Exchange hierarchy, described in Table 13.4.

TABLE 13.4: Exchange security contexts

Context	Containers Affected
Organization	Permissions only apply to the Organization container.
Site	Permissions apply to the Site container and all objects in the Site container except the Configuration container.
Configuration	Permissions apply to the Configuration container and all objects within it.

Part iii

There are a series of predefined roles that can be assigned to each user to control what actions they can take within the Exchange system. Each role is a combination of the rights to perform specific types of actions. Table 13.5 describes the permissions and Table 13.6 describes the predefined roles available in Exchange.

TABLE 13.5: Exchange permissions

Right	Description	Example
Add Child	Allows the creation of child objects in the container	A user with this right to the recipient container could create mailboxes in that container.
Modify User Attributes	Allows the modification of user-level attributes	A user with this right to a DL (distribution list) could change the membership of that list.
Modify Admin Attributes	Allows modification of administrator-level attributes	A user with this right could change the display name of a given object.
Delete	Allows deletion of objects	A user with this right to the recipient container could delete mailboxes.
Logon	Provides access to the directory	Administrators need this right to be able to run the administrator program.
Modify Permission	Allows modification of permissions	A user with this right could add another user as an administrator.
Replication	Replicates directory information with other servers	This right is required by the Site Service Account.
Mailbox Owner	Allows a user to read and delete messages in a mailbox	This right is given to the primary user of each mailbox (typically there is only one user per mailbox).
Send As	Allows a user to send messages that contain their return address	Users can be granted the right to send as another user, a process called *delegating*.

Each defined role grants a combination of these rights. Table 13.6 shows which rights are associated with each role.

TABLE 13.6: Roles in Exchange

	Admin	Permission Admin	Service Account Admin	View Only Admin	User	Send As
Add Child	X	X	X			
Modify User Attribute	X	X	X		X	
Modify Admin Attributes	X	X	X			
Delete	X	X	X			
Logon	X	X	X	X		
Modify Permission		X	X			
Replication			X			
Mailbox Owner			X		X	
Send As			X		X	X

Your job during the planning stage is to decide which users should have which permissions on each object.

▶ Develop server-side scripting strategies.

Exchange has the ability to create and manage collaborative applications. Unlike traditional applications that usually consist of a single executable file, Exchange collaborative applications are made up of various components. The exam will test your understanding of these components.

Exchange collaborative applications are made up of the following components:

- ▶ Folders store the data gathered by the application.
- ▶ Forms define how data should be entered into the application.

▶ Views determine how information is displayed. For instance, a view might sort the data so that it is more informative.

▶ Fields contain simple information. You might, for instance, have a field that stores the user's birthday.

▶ Databases provide an ordered structure for the storage of data.

This test objective is concerned with developing a strategy for server-side scripting. Server-side scripting is using scripted applications to store and manage data. Your strategy should define how you use this tool and what administrative tasks will be necessary.

There are many reasons for using server-side scripting. A few examples are as follows:

▶ To replace paper forms with a graphical user interface and electronic storage. For instance, you might create a vacation request form.

▶ To control the structure used when submitting data. By creating an Exchange form, you can control the structure of data. You might, for instance, create a Help Desk report form that asks for a specific set of information. This also simplifies the data-entry process by providing a standard interface.

▶ To simplify the routing of documents through your organization. Rather than sending paper documents from office to office, you can have a form routed automatically to the correct users.

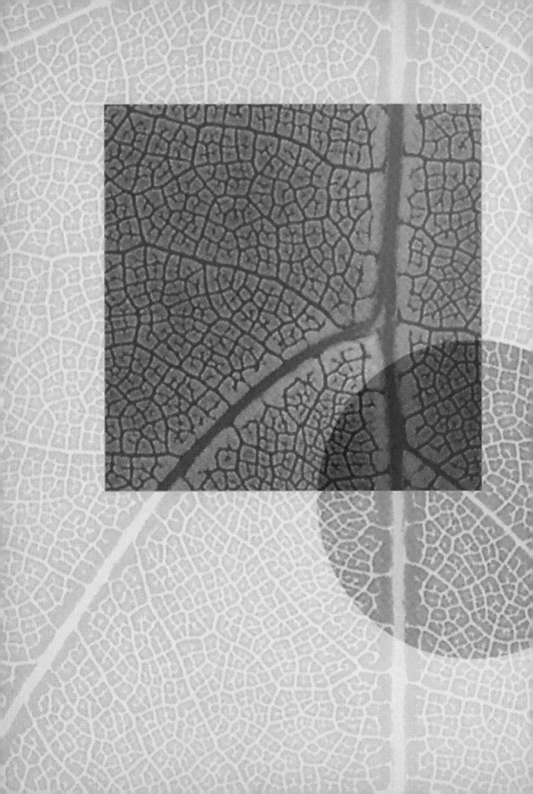

Chapter 14

INSTALLATION AND CONFIGURATION

In Chapter 13, we discussed many of the options available in an Exchange Server environment. This chapter concentrates on the procedures used to install and configure those options.

Planning is important, but knowing how to implement your plan is even more important. Microsoft wants MCSEs to be able to implement and maintain their products in the field, and the tests are written accordingly.

One of the best things you can do to prepare for the MCSE exam is to find a pair of computers, set up a lab, and practice, practice, practice!

MCSE Exam Notes:
EXCHANGE SERVER 5.5
EXAM 70-081
ROBERT KING

Adapted from *MCSE Exam Notes: Exchange Server 5.5* by Robert King
ISBN 0-7821-2302-3   368 pages $19.99

Install an Exchange Server computer.

After purchasing your hardware and software and planning your environment, your next step is to sit down at a computer and install Exchange Server 5.5. First, make sure you are familiar with the information you need in order to carry out the installation.

Types of Installations

During the installation you will be asked what type of installation you wish to perform. Your choices are:

Typical   Sets up an Exchange server which is fully functional, including the Administrator program. Choose this option on servers that are joining an existing site, but which will not participate in intersite communication.

Complete/Custom   Displays a list of optional components that can be installed. Those options include: Microsoft Mail Connector, Connector for cc:Mail, X.400 Connector, Exchange Server Administrator program, Books Online, and the Collaboration Data Objects used to provide services to World Wide Web clients.

Minimum   Only the core components are installed. This does not include the Administrator program.

Directory Structure

By default, the installation creates a directory named EXCHSRVR. Under this directory a series of subdirectories are also created. Table 14.1 lists these directories and indicates the share name of any that are automatically shared.

TABLE 14.1: Exchange directory structure

NAME	SHARED AS	DESCRIPTION
Add-ins	Add-ins	Subdirectories for various Exchange Server extensions such as the MS Mail Connector
Address	Address	Contains e-mail address proxy DLLs used to create e-mail addresses
BIN		Exchange Server components and Administrator program

TABLE 14.1 continued: Exchange directory structure

NAME	SHARED AS	DESCRIPTION
CCMCDATA		Temporary holding place for e-mail exchanged between Exchange and a cc:Mail system
Connect	connect$	Components for various connectors
DSADATA		Holds directory service databases
DXADATA		Holds directory synchronization database for MS Mail
IMCDATA		Directories for Internet Mail Service
INSDATA		Directories for Internet News Service
MDBDATA		Holds the Private and Public Information Store databases
MTADATA		Files used by the Message Transfer Agent
RES	Resources	File for use by the Event Viewer and Performance Monitor
SAMAPPS		Sample applications
TRACKING.LOG	TRACKING.LOG	Log files for message tracking
WEBDATA		Outlook Web Access components

Optimizer

The last step of an Exchange installation is to run the Exchange Optimizer. This software analyzes the configuration of your server to find the number of hard disks and the amount of memory and compares this analysis with the answers to a few questions. It then suggests changes to your configuration to improve performance and fault tolerance.

You need to provide the following information:

- ► The number of users that this server will support

- ► The services that this server will provide: Private Store, Public Store, connectors, and directory import; whether it is in a multi-server site, or will limit its function to POP3, IMAP4, or NNTP

- ► The number of users in the organization

Part iii

The actual installation of Exchange Server 5.5 is fairly straightforward. To prepare for the exam, make sure you have committed these steps to memory.

Starting Installation

If your CD-ROM is set up for autoplay, inserting the Exchange CD will bring up the opening screen. If you need to manually start the process, run LAUNCH.EXE located at the root of the CD-ROM.

From here you can start the installation, read any last minute news in the Release Notes, access the online documentation, or find out about the online resources that are available.

Choosing Setup and Server Components

Choose "Setup Server and Components" and you will move to a list of available components. Your choices include Microsoft Exchange Server 5.5, Chat Services, Applications and Authoring Tools, Internet Location Services, the Resource Kit, and a few specialized connectors. Choosing "Microsoft Exchange Server 5.5" starts the installation.

Read the software license and click the Accept button. You will be presented with a choice of type of install to perform. If you choose Complete/Custom, you will be presented with a list.

Choose the options that you wish to install and click Continue. If Internet Information Server is running, it will be stopped during the installation. Enter the CD key (found on the back of your CD case). You must then agree to the licensing agreement before you can continue.

Now you must decide whether your server should join an existing site or if a new site should be created. Give careful consideration to your answer because the only way to change it is to reinstall Exchange.

Assigning the Site Service Account

The next step is to assign the site service account. Be careful here, because the software will default to using the account you are logged in as. You should have already created an account specifically for this purpose. This account will be granted the following rights:

▶ Log on as a service

▶ Restore files and directories

▶ Act as part of the operating system

The installation program will verify that you have provided a valid account and password. At this point, SETUP copies the Exchange Server files to the appropriate directories, makes necessary changes to the Registry, and starts the services.

Running Optimizer

The next dialog box asks if you would like to run the Optimizer. In general, it is advisable to run the Optimizer and let it analyze your Exchange server. You will have to provide some information about how your server will be used, as shown in Figure 14.1. Optimizer will analyze your server and make suggestions as to the placement of files. It is usually best to accept these suggestions.

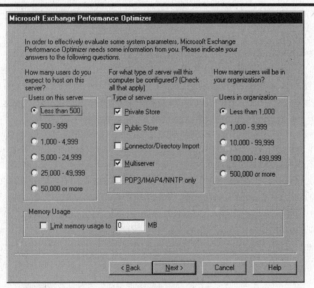

FIGURE 14.1: Performance Optimizer

▶ Configure Exchange Server for message recipients.

- ▶ Configure mailboxes.
- ▶ Configure custom recipients.
- ▶ Configure public folders.

▶ Configure distribution lists.

▶ Configure site addressing.

▶ Configure container-level search controls.

▶ Configure Address Book views.

The MCSE exam will test your knowledge of the procedures involved in configuring message recipients. Once your Exchange server is up and running, you will need to populate it with mailboxes, distribution lists, and the other objects that are necessary in a messaging environment. This objective concerns the process of populating your Exchange Directory.

This objective is concerned with the creation and configuration of various objects in the Exchange Directory.

Mailboxes

There are two ways to create mailboxes: using "User Manager for Domains" or using the Exchange Administrator program. When the Administrator program is installed on an NT server, extensions are added to User Manager for Domains so that, as a new user account is created, a mailbox can be automatically created for that user.

Custom Recipients

Custom recipients are used to represent destination addresses that are not part of your Exchange environment. You might, for instance, create a custom recipient to represent the Internet e-mail address of a vendor to whom your employees send a lot of e-mail. When creating a custom recipient, you must choose the type of address (Internet, X.400, Microsoft Mail, etc.) and then enter the address correctly. You must also have an address space defined. This defines a path to the recipient's e-mail system.

Public Folders

Public folders act as share points for data that are managed through Exchange Server. Public folders are created through the Outlook client. On the file menu, choose New, and then Folder. Give the folder a name and choose where it should be created (somewhere within the All Public Folders hierarchy).

Once created, you can manage the folder from within the Exchange Administrator program. Your folder will be located in the Folders container. Highlight it and choose Properties on the File menu.

One of the most important configuration decisions you have to consider is public folder replication. Exchange can be configured to automatically create copies of the public folder on multiple servers. You should do this for three primary reasons: to split the workload across servers, to provide a fault-tolerant copy of the data, and to decrease access time for clients. (For clients on each side of a slow WAN link, it improves access times if you have a replica stored on a local server.)

Distribution Lists

A distribution list (DL) acts as an "Exchange group," allowing a user to address e-mail to one recipient but have that e-mail delivered to multiple mailboxes. There are two critical areas of configuration that you need to be familiar with for the exam: DL owner and expansion servers.

DL Owner   You can set a user or group as the owner of the distribution list. The designated user(s) can change the membership of the list. This allows you to delegate some of the administrative tasks involved in managing a DL.

Expansion Server   When a message is addressed to a DL, the server must expand the membership list to determine where the message must be sent. The act of processing this expansion is a processor-intensive activity at the server. In large environments you might designate a particular server to act as the expansion server, thereby moving all the overhead to that server.

Site Addressing

In the Configuration container you will find the Site Addressing object. This object allows you to control the format of e-mail addresses as they are generated for recipients. This object also controls the calculation of the routing table used to route messages to recipients. You can determine how often the routing table will be regenerated.

Container-Level Search Controls

In Chapter 13, we discussed the LDAP protocol and its configuration. LDAP is designed to allow users access to the information stored in the directory. While this can be convenient, you might want to control which information is accessible.

Part III

Exchange Server allows you to control which attributes will be accessible through an anonymous or an authenticated connection.

Address Book Views

Address Book Views allow you to configure how addresses are presented to clients. You might, for instance, want to give managers the ability to view recipients by department. You can create a view that groups users by the value of their department property.

You can specify up to four properties to group by in each Address Book View. In our example, the managers might need to see all employees by department, and then grouped by state.

Creating the Address Book View creates a series of subcontainers under the Address Book Views container, one subcontainer for each grouping. Once the containers are created, you can use the container-level search controls to determine who can access the view.

Each of the procedures described in this section is critical to your success both in the exam and in your workplace. You should practice each process until it is second nature.

Creating Mailboxes

During the creation of a new user account in the NT accounts database, User Manager for Domains can automatically create a mailbox for that user. Another way to create a user is to use the Exchange Administrator program. From the File menu, choose New Mailbox.

There are numerous properties that you might have to configure on a user's mailbox: everything from names to phone numbers. Not all of the information is mandatory, but the more time you spend here, the more useful the directory will be to your users. The Lightweight Directory Access Protocol (LDAP) can be used to access this information, turning your Exchange Directory into an employee phone book. (Most of the Web browsers on the market today can use LDAP to access the Exchange Directory.)

Creating Custom Recipients

A custom recipient acts as an entry in your Global Address List that points to a foreign recipient. In the Exchange Administrator program, choose New Custom Recipient on the File menu. Choose the appropriate address type as shown in Figure 14.2.

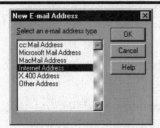

FIGURE 14.2: New E-mail Address

You will then enter the address in its native format. Exchange allows you to define the same properties for the custom recipient as for a normal Exchange mailbox.

Configuring Public Folders

Each tab on the property pages offers several configuration options.

General   Each public folder is a recipient and can be represented in the Global Address List. Configure how that object will appear, as well as assign permissions to users.

Replicas   Public folders can be configured to automatically replicate to other servers. Configure which servers should receive a copy.

Folder Replication Status   Displays information regarding the replication of the folder for each server on which it exists.

Replication Schedule   Configure when replication will occur. You have the following choices of when to use the Information Store Schedule:

- ▶ Never
- ▶ Always
- ▶ Selected times

Distribution Lists   Since a public folder can act as a recipient, it can also be a member of distribution lists. Configure this membership from this tab.

E-mail Addresses   Like any other recipient, a public folder is given various e-mail addresses for different e-mail systems.

Custom Attributes You can define custom attributes for recipients to store specific properties that are not defined in the normal Exchange properties.

Limits Set limits on how long information should stay in the public folder before aging out.

Advanced Set a trust level for replication to Microsoft Mail and choose the server that acts as the home for the folder.

NOTE
Advanced options are covered in more detail in Chapter 15.

Configuring Distribution Lists

To create a distribution list, choose New Distribution List from the File menu in the Administrator program. There are numerous configuration tabs for a distribution list. Each tab manages a different aspect of the object.

General Configure the list's display name and owners and designate an expansion server for the list.

Distribution Lists Modify the list of DLs of which the DL is a member.

E-mail Addresses Since a DL is a recipient, e-mail addresses must be generated for it.

Delivery Restrictions You can control from whom that DL will accept or reject messages.

Custom Attributes You can define custom attributes for recipients to store specific properties that are not defined in the normal Exchange properties.

Advanced Here you can set trust levels for replication to MS Mail systems, limit the size of messages that the DL can receive, and set DL options such as:

- ▶ Report to message originator
- ▶ Allow out-of-office messages to originator
- ▶ Hide from address book
- ▶ Hide membership from address book

Configuring Site Addressing

To configure the Site Addressing object, double-click its object. This object is found in the Configuration container. Each tab allows configuration of a different aspect of the object. The tabs are:

General   Designate a server to be used to calculate the routing table.

Permissions   Assign administrative permissions to users.

Site Addressing   Configure how specific e-mail addresses should be created for recipients within the site.

Routing Calculation Schedule   Configure how often the routing table should be recalculated.

Routing   Displays the routing table and allows you to force an immediate recalculation.

Configuring Container-Level Search Controls

To configure which attributes will be accessible to users, access the property pages of the DS Site Configuration object. This object is located in the Configuration container of your site. On the Attributes tab, highlight either "Anonymous Requests" or "Authenticated Requests" and then select those attributes that you wish to be made available.

Configuring Address Book Views

To create an Address Book View, open the Administrator program. On the File menu, choose New Other, and then choose Address Book View.

Give your view a descriptive name and then choose the properties by which you would like the recipients grouped.

If you wish to limit who can view the Address Book View, go to the Permissions tab and assign the search role to the appropriate users. They can now access the view in their Global Address List in Outlook.

▶ Configure connectivity to a mail system other than Exchange Server. Connector types include:

▸ X.400 Connector

- ▶ Microsoft Exchange Connector for Lotus cc:Mail

- ▶ Microsoft Mail Connector

In a perfect world, your messaging environment would be made up entirely of Microsoft Exchange servers. In the real world, however, you are often faced with the challenge of creating your messaging system using components provided by multiple vendors. The MCSE exam will test your knowledge of the procedures for connecting Exchange servers to other systems.

NOTE

Many companies are standardizing with Exchange for all new e-mail servers, but do not want to walk away from the investment they have in older legacy systems. In this situation, it will be your responsibility to ensure that information can flow among the various types of e-mail systems your company has in place.

Exchange Server uses address spaces and connectors to facilitate the flow of messages between Exchange and foreign e-mail environments. An address space defines a path to a group of recipients. If you want to connect to a Microsoft Mail postoffice, for instance, you would need to define an address space to that postoffice's server. Exchange would use that address space as the definition of how e-mail should be routed to get to that postoffice. An address space is created during the creation of a connector to the foreign system. We'll take a closer look at address spaces later in this section.

In general, connectors define the mechanism to be used when attempting message transfer between two systems or between two sites within an Exchange environment. For this objective, we will concentrate on connectors to foreign systems and their configurations.

X.400 Connector

When creating and configuring an X.400 Connector, you need to understand a few X.400 concepts. X.400 is an industry standard that defines message handling. This standard definition is widely recognized and accepted throughout the messaging industry and is used by most of the public e-mail carriers in the world. Because of its wide acceptance, most e-mail packages have the ability to send and receive e-mail using some sort of X.400 Connector. Exchange is no exception. The X.400 standards define both the messaging transport methods and the physical format that messages should take.

X.400 systems are made up of two basic components, each of which defines an area of responsibility. These areas are known as domains. At the top of the messaging structure are Administrative Management Domains (ADMD). ADMDs define the uppermost level of addressing. ADMDs are usually managed by large public providers such as AT&T, Sprint, and MCI.

Within an ADMD, there are multiple Private Management Domains (PRMD). Each PRMD defines a specific message destination, such as an Exchange e-mail system or cc:Mail postoffice. The easiest way to understand how these two domain levels are used is to look at how an X.400 address is created.

X.400 names are called O/R (Originator/Recipient) addresses. They are made up of a series of fields which, when combined, create a unique e-mail address. There are numerous fields defined by the standard. Some are mandatory and some are optional, but the combination of fields must uniquely identify the recipient. A name is created by filling in various values until a unique address is created. This means that X.400 names can look quite different from one system to another. The system administrator will usually define which fields are used in an environment so that addresses look the same for all of the recipients in that system. Table 14.2 lists the various fields available and how they are used in an address.

TABLE 14.2: X.400 fields

FIELD	ABBREVIATION IN NAME
Given name	G
Initials	I
Surname	S
Generation qualifier	Q
Common name	CN
121 address	121
UA numeric id	N-ID
Terminal type	T-TY
Terminal identifier	T-ID
Organization	O
Organizational unit 1	OU1
Organizational unit 2	OU2

TABLE 14.2 continued: X.400 fields

FIELD	ABBREVIATION IN NAME
Organizational unit 3	OU3
Organizational unit 4	OU4
PRMD name	P
ADMD	A
Country	C
Domain defined attribute	DDA

An X.400 name will be a combination of a number of these fields. While there are no strict rules as to which should be used (the only rule is that the end result be a unique identifier), the following example shows a typical name.

```
C=US;A=ATT;P=Royal-Tech;O=Education;OU=MS;S=KING;G=BOB
```

Compare the name to the fields in Table 14.2. As you can see, this address represents a user named Bob King who works in the MS Education Department of a company named Royal-Tech. This company is located in the United States and uses AT&T for its e-mail services. In an X.400 environment, e-mail is routed based on the X.400 address of the recipient. In our example, e-mail destined for Bob would need to make its way into the AT&T ADMD. Once there, the e-mail would have to be routed to the particular server or servers which accept e-mail addressed to the Royal-Tech PRMD. This routing is performed by X.400 Message Transfer Agents (MTA). This brings us to the topic at hand—configuring the X.400 Connector on an Exchange server.

► Configuring an X.400 Connector

The first step involved in creating and configuring an X.400 Connector is to determine which type of physical connection will be used and install the appropriate MTA transport stack. There are four transport stacks available:

- ► Eicon X.25
- ► RAS

▶ TCP/IP

▶ TP4

Each is used for a different type of connection. The Eicon X.25 transport stack is used when the physical connection will involve an X.25 packet switched network. The RAS transport stack is used for dial-up connections, the TCP/IP transport stack uses the TCP/IP protocol for communication (here the physical nature of the connection is not an issue), and the TP4 transport stack uses the TP4 protocol.

Once the transport stack is installed you can begin the installation of the X.400 Connector. You should be aware of the following configuration options.

Remote MTA Name   You will be asked to provide a Remote MTA name for the server to which this connector will communicate. This is usually the computer name of the remote computer. If applicable, you will also need to provide the password for the remote MTA.

These two values are set during the creation of an X.400 Connector. You will set the values for the connector you are creating and the administrator of the remote system will set these values for the connector on the remote computer. It is critical that you communicate with the remote administrator so that this information is available as you install the connector.

OSI Addressing   During the creation of your X.400 Connector you must provide the IP address or host name of the remote e-mail server. If you use the host name, make sure that the name can be resolved before configuring the connector.

NOTE

Use PING.EXE to determine if the remote host name can be resolved. At a command prompt, type **PING <FQDN>** where FQDN is the fully qualified domain name of the remote host.

You can also provide values for the T, S, and P OSI addresses. These addresses can be seen as "passwords" for layers of the OSI model. While these values are optional, if used they must match the values set at the remote server.

Global Domain Identifier (GDI)   The GDI is made up of the three topmost fields in your X.400 addresses: the PRMD, ADMD, and country

Part iii

fields. If the remote server is located in the same GDI as your system, you don't have to retype the GDI because it can be read from the Site Addressing settings. If not, you will have to provide these values during the creation of the connector.

Scheduling Activity   One of the benefits of using the X.400 Connector is the amount of control you have over its functions. You have the option of specifying when the connector should attempt to deliver e-mail. Your options are outlined below:

Remote Initiated   This connector will never attempt to open communication with a remote server. This option is most often used when using the RAS transport stack. This connector will wait indefinitely for the remote system to open communication. Note that if both sides are set to this option, e-mail will never be delivered.

Never   This option effectively disables the connector.

Always   This connector will attempt to open communication whenever messages need to be transferred.

Selected times   You can determine exactly when the connector should open communication with remote servers. This option allows you to schedule the connection during non-peak hours on your network, for example.

Microsoft Exchange Connector for Lotus cc:Mail

The Connector for Lotus cc:Mail allows the transfer of messages and directory information between an Exchange server and a Lotus cc:Mail postoffice. This connector is installed by default when you choose to perform a custom installation.

Lotus cc:Mail is a shared directory e-mail system, much like Microsoft Mail. Since there are no active processes on a cc:Mail server, all transfer activity must be initiated by the Exchange server. This activity can be divided into three processes:

cc:Mail Connector Service   Transfers e-mail between the Information Store and a Connector Store.

IMPORT.EXE   Uses a Lotus cc:Mail program that imports messages and directory information into the cc:Mail postoffice.

EXPORT.EXE   Uses a Lotus cc:Mail program that exports cc:Mail messages and directory information into a text file.

Before you can configure this connector, you need to understand the process used to transfer information.

Message Flow: Exchange Server to cc:Mail   Knowing how messages are routed between components can help you make decisions about how to configure the process. The following list explains the steps involved in sending a message from an Exchange server to a cc:Mail postoffice.

1. The Exchange Information Store receives a message addressed to a recipient in the cc:Mail postoffice. Because the address is not local, it is passed to the MTA (Message Transfer Agent).

2. The MTA checks the routing table and (based upon the address of the recipient) chooses the Connector for Lotus cc:Mail.

3. If the connector is on another Exchange server, the message will be routed to the MTA on that server. If not, the message is transferred to the Connector for Lotus cc:Mail queue to await retrieval by the connector.

4. The connector retrieves the message and converts it into a text file. This file is known as a *scratch* file.

5. On a set schedule, the connector moves the file to an Import directory in the cc:Mail Information Store (a directory maintained by the CCMC on the Exchange server).

6. The connector uses an IPC (inter-process communication) to start the IMPORT.EXE program (which is run on the Exchange server, but directed at the postoffice using a command line parameter).

Message Flow: cc:Mail to Exchange   Messages flowing from cc:Mail to Exchange take the following route:

1. The cc:Mail postoffice receives a message destined for an Exchange recipient.

2. On a set interval, the Exchange Connector for Lotus cc:Mail uses an IPC to start the EXPORT.EXE program (which is run

on the Exchange server, but directed at the postoffice using a command line parameter). This program converts the message into a text file and places it in the export directory on the Exchange server of the connector.

3. The connector retrieves the text file and converts it into an IPM (Interpersonal Message, the message format used within Exchange).

4. The connector places the message into a queue to await pickup by the MTA.

5. The MTA routes the message to the Exchange server upon which the user's mailbox exists.

Now that you have an understanding of how messages are routed between the two environments, there are a few particulars that you need to understand to properly configure the connector.

Scratch Files   While messages are in transit between Exchange and cc:Mail, they are converted into text files known as scratch files. These files are placed in one of two folders in an area known as the Connector Store. The Connector Store is a folder named CCMCDATA and a series of subdirectories. You need to be very aware of user permissions to these directories. Since the messages are stored as text files, anyone with access to the directory can read the content of the messages.

Connector for cc:Mail Registry Settings   There is a series of Registry settings that can be used to control and optimize the Connector for Lotus cc:Mail. All of the parameters discussed in Table 14.3 are located in the following Registry key:

```
HKEY_LOCAL_MACHINE\SYSTEM\CurrentControlSet\
Services\MSExchangeCCMC\Parameters
```

TABLE 14.3: cc:Mail Connector Registry settings

VALUE (AS IT APPEARS IN REGISTRY)	DEFAULT	DESCRIPTION
Seconds to wait before EXPORT	15 seconds	How often the EXPORT.EXE program is run
Seconds to wait before IMPORT	15 seconds	How often the IMPORT.EXE program is run

TABLE 14.3 continued: cc:Mail Connector Registry settings

VALUE (AS IT APPEARS IN REGISTRY)	DEFAULT	DESCRIPTION
Maximum number of messages to EXPORT	16	The number of messages requested from cc:Mail each time EXPORT.EXE is run
Maximum number of messages to IMPORT	5	The number of messages sent to cc:Mail each time IMPORT.EXE is run
cc:Mail to Exchange queue size	64	The maximum number of messages allowed to wait for conversion. When this value is reached the EXPORT.EXE program will not be run until the number of messages has decreased.
Exchange to cc:Mail queue size	64	The maximum number of messages allowed to wait for conversion. When this threshold is reached, outbound messages to cc:Mail will be held in the Information Store until the number has decreased.

Microsoft Mail Connector

The Microsoft Mail Connector provides the mechanism to transfer messages between an Exchange server and a Microsoft Mail postoffice. On the Exchange server, two components are involved in the process: the Exchange MTA and the Microsoft Mail Connector itself.

The connector has three components:

1. The Mail Connector interchange passes messages from the connector to the Exchange MTA.

2. The Mail Connector postoffice is a temporary storage area for messages passing between the two environments. It is also known as the *shadow postoffice*.

3. The Microsoft Mail Connector MTA passes messages to and from the MS Mail postoffice to the Mail Connector postoffice.

Before you can configure this connector you need to understand the process used to transfer information.

Message Flow: MS Mail to Exchange Server   Knowing how messages are routed between components can help you make decisions about how to configure the process. The following list explains the steps involved in sending a message from an MS Mail postoffice to an Exchange server.

1. The MS Mail Connector MTA places messages from the MS Mail postoffice into a queue in the Mail Connector postoffice (shadow postoffice).

2. The Mail Connector interchange periodically scans the shadow postoffice for messages and transfers them to the Exchange server MTA.

3. The Exchange server MTA delivers the messages to the Exchange server Information Store for delivery.

Message Flow: Exchange Server to MS Mail   The reverse flow is as follows:

1. The Information Store receives the message addressed to a MS Mail recipient. Since the address is not local, the message is given to the MTA for routing. The MTA checks the routing table and passes the message to a queue.

2. The MS Mail Connector interchange periodically checks the MTA queue for messages. It reads them, converts them into the proper format, and places them in the shadow postoffice.

3. The Mail Connector MTA scans the shadow postoffice for messages and sends them to the MS Mail postoffice. The messages are then deleted from the shadow postoffice.

Configuring a Transport Stack

Before you can install the X.400 Connector, you must install and configure a transport stack. On the File menu in the Exchange Administrator program, choose New Other. Click on the MTA Transport Stack and you will be given the choice of which stack to install. Your choices are the following:

Eicon X.25 MTA transport stack   Used to communicate across an X.25 network.

RAS MTA transport stack   Used across dial-up connections.

TCP/IP MTA transport stack   The most generic stack—it can be used across any IP network.

TP4 MTA transport stack   Uses the TP4 protocol (which must be installed first) to communicate.

Configuring the X.400 Connector

To create the X.400 Connector, choose New Other on the File menu in Exchange Administrator. Choose X.400 Connector on the submenu that follows. You will be asked which transport stack to use for this connector—choose one from the list. If you are not currently working in the Connections container, you will be prompted to move to that container.

Each tab allows configuration of a different aspect of the connector.

General   Configure the display and directory name of the connector object in the Exchange Directory. You also must provide the MTA name and password for the remote server (as configured by the administrator of that system).

Permissions   Configure which users are able to administer this connector.

Schedule   Configure how often this connector should attempt to attach to the remote system. The options are Remote Initiated, Never, Always, and Selected times.

Stack   Configure the IP address or host name of the remote server. You can also set the OSI address information.

Override   Set the local MTA name and password and configure parameters to optimize the communication between the servers. If the local MTA name is not specified here, the local NT computer name is used.

Connected Sites   When the connector is used to connect to another Exchange site, this tab is used in the configuration of Directory Replication (discussed later in this chapter).

Address Space   Allows you to enter the X.400 address space that the connector will handle for outgoing messages.

Delivery Restrictions   Build a list of users from whom to accept or reject message. This tab can be used to restrict which users can send messages over this connector.

Advanced   Configure which X.400 standards should be used, limit message size over this connector, and define the GDI for the remote site.

Part iii

Configuring the Connector for Lotus cc:Mail

The Connector for Lotus cc:Mail is installed by default when you choose to perform a custom installation. It is placed in the Connections container. To configure the connector, use the Exchange Administrator program. In the appropriate Site container, expand the Configuration container. Within the Configuration container, choose the Connections container. Double-click the Connector for cc:Mail object.

Each tab allows configuration of a different aspect of the connector.

Post Office   Configure the name, password, and path to the cc:Mail postoffice directory. This information is mandatory and the path will be confirmed before you can continue. Also set the version of cc:Mail that will be used for message conversion.

General   Limit the size of messages that can be transferred using this connector.

Permissions   Configure which users are able to administer this connector.

Dirsync Schedule   Used to configure the replication of directory information (address books) between the two environments (discussed later in this chapter).

Address Space   Create an address space that defines the destination cc:Mail system. If only one connector is created, use * to indicate that all cc:Mail messages should be routed through this connector.

Delivery Restrictions   Build a list of users from whom to accept or reject messages. This tab can be used to restrict which users can send messages over this connector.

Import Container   Used to define the recipient container to which cc:Mail account information should be replicated (discussed later in this chapter).

Export Containers   Used to define the recipients' container(s) which should be replicated to the cc:Mail system (discussed later in this chapter).

Queues   Allows you to view the contents of the connector's queues.

Diagnostics Logging   Configure the level of logging on various components of the connector.

Configuring the Microsoft Mail Connector

The MS Mail Connector is automatically created during a custom installation. To configure this connector, use the Exchange Administrator program. In the Connections container, found in the Configuration container of the appropriate site, double-click the MS Mail Connector.

Each tab allows configuration of a different aspect of the connector.

Interchange   Choose an administrator's mailbox to receive management messages.

Local Postoffice   Configure the names and password for the MS Mail postoffice (shadow postoffice).

Connections   Configure the physical connection to be used to connect to the MS Mail postoffice. You can also check the contents of the queue for any connection to determine the number of messages awaiting delivery.

Connector MTAs   Configure MTAs to each group of MS Mail postoffices to which you will connect.

General   Set message size limits.

Address Space   Define the address space(s) of the MS Mail system(s) to which this connector will deliver messages.

Diagnostics Logging   Configure the logging level for the various MS Mail-related categories.

▶ Configure synchronization of directory information between Exchange Server and other mail systems. Types of directory synchronization include:

- ▶ Manual
- ▶ Automatic

In the preceding objective we discussed the configuration of various connectors that allowed the exchange of messages between Exchange and foreign e-mail systems. While this functionality is important, it is not the complete picture—often you will want to exchange address book information as well. Otherwise your users will have to type in the e-mail address of recipients in the foreign system manually, which is sure to generate some Help Desk calls.

For this objective, you should understand the components needed to synchronize directory information with other e-mail systems. We will look at two different foreign e-mail systems—Lotus cc:Mail and MS Mail—and discuss the options available for directory exchange.

Directory synchronization (DS) is the act of exchanging addresses between an Exchange Server organization and a foreign e-mail system. Later we will see that MS Mail uses a particular protocol to perform this function—the Dirsync protocol. The two terms, Directory synchronization and Dirsync, are not interchangeable.

Directory Synchronization with a Lotus cc:Mail System

Directory synchronization using the Connector for Lotus cc:Mail is fairly straightforward. During the configuration of the connector, you define an Import Recipients container to hold the cc:Mail addresses that are imported. They are stored as Exchange custom recipients. You also define one or more Export containers from which Exchange recipient addresses will be exported to the cc:Mail system. You also configure the schedule of when the synchronization should occur.

Trust Level   One of the properties of each Exchange recipient is its trust level. The directory synchronization process uses this value to determine which accounts should be included in the process.

The trust level is a numeric value from 0–100. The default value for all types of recipients is 20, except public folders which default to 0. Each connector that performs directory synchronization is also given a trust value, the default value being 100. During the DS process the trust of the connector is compared to the trust of each recipient. If the recipient's trust value is less than that of the connector, the recipient is included in the DS process.

NOTE
The default values indicate that unless you make a change, all recipients in the Export container(s) will be exported to the cc:Mail system.

Directory Synchronization with an MS Mail Postoffice

Microsoft Mail has its own process for distributing recipient addresses throughout its postoffices. This process uses the Dirsync protocol. Before we can look at synchronization with an Exchange organization, you must first understand the MS Mail Dirsync process.

Dirsync within an MS Mail System   MS Mail postoffices are configured with one of two roles in the Dirsync process: Requestor or Server. The Dirsync Server acts as the master source of the system-wide address book for all other postoffice servers that are configured as Requestors.

The Dirsync process is divided into three phases:

T1   All Requestor postoffices send their address list to the Dirsync Server.

T2   The Dirsync Server compiles the list to build the Global Address List.

T3   Each Requestor postoffice rebuilds its postoffice address list with the Global Address List requested from the Dirsync Server.

Each process is configured to occur once every 24 hours. The only tricky part is ensuring that each process is complete before the next process begins. An Exchange server can be configured to act as either the Dirsync Server or as a Requestor by installing the appropriate Directory Synchronization Server (DXA).

Exchange Server as a DXA Server   If you install and configure the DXA Server component on your Exchange server, the following will occur:

T1   All MS Mail Requestors send in the changes that have occurred to the Exchange server DXA service.

T2   The Exchange server incorporates all Requestor information and all changes to Exchange recipients into a Global Address List.

T3   All Requestors ask for a list of changes to the Global Address List.

Exchange Server as a DXA Requestor   If your Exchange server is configured to act as a DXA Requestor, the following will occur:

T1   Your server sends a list of all changes in the Exchange Global Address List to the MS Mail Dirsync server.

T2   The MS Mail Dirsync server compiles all changes into a Global Address List.

T3   Your Exchange server requests all changes from the Dirsync server.

Having the addresses of foreign recipients automatically added to your Exchange address list and vice versa is a great convenience for your users. It is also a critical part of the interoperability of Exchange. This topic is tested upon heavily in the MCSE exam. Ensure that you are very familiar with the procedures before taking the exam.

Setting the Trust Value for a Recipient

The trust level is configured in the same way for all recipient types. In the Exchange Administrator program, double click the recipient. On the Advanced Properties tab you will find a Trust Level box. Enter the value you wish to set.

Configuring the cc:Mail Connector Import Recipients Container

In the Exchange Administrator program, move to the appropriate site and expand the Configuration container. Highlight the Connections container and access the properties of the Connector for cc:Mail object. On the Import Container tab, you can assign the Recipients container where cc:Mail accounts should be placed.

You can also configure a filter to accept or reject e-mail addresses that match a pattern. You might, for instance, only want to accept addresses from a particular cc:Mail postoffice.

This tab also contains a button that allows you to force an immediate synchronization. Most systems are configured to synchronize once every 24 hours. You can use this manual method if you need changes to be synchronized immediately.

Configuring the cc:Mail Connector Export Recipients Container

In the Exchange Administrator program, move to the appropriate site and expand the Configuration container. Highlight the Connections container and access the properties of the Connector for cc:Mail object. On the Export Containers tab you can specify which Recipients containers should be included in the directory export process. You can also set the trust level of the connector on this page.

Scheduling the cc:Mail Connector Directory Synchronization Process

In the Exchange Administrator program, move to the appropriate site and expand the Configuration container. Highlight the Connections container and access the properties of the Connector for cc:Mail object. On the Dirsync Schedule tab you can set the schedule for how often the directory synchronization process should occur.

Performing the cc:Mail Connector Directory Synchronization Process Manually

In the Exchange Administrator program, move to the appropriate site and expand the Configuration container. Highlight the Connections container and access the properties of the Connector for cc:Mail object. On the Export Containers tab click the Run Dirsync Now button.

Configuring an Exchange Server as a DXA Server

To install the DXA Server component, choose New Other on the File menu in the Exchange Administrator program. On the submenu, choose Dirsync Server.

Provide a name for the service and, if desired, configure an administrative account to receive management messages. On the Schedule tab, you can then schedule the Dirsync T3 process. The default is that the Dirsync process will update all Requestors at midnight each night.

Configuring an Exchange Server as a DXA Requestor

To install the DXA Requestor component choose New Other on the File menu in the Exchange Administrator program. On the submenu, choose Dirsync Requestor.

Each tab pertains to a different area of configuration.

General   Name the object and choose what types of addresses to request from the Dirsync Server.

Permissions   Determine which users should be able to manage the service.

Import Container   Choose the Recipients container to which MS Mail addresses will be added as custom recipients. You can also set the trust level for incoming recipients.

Export Containers   Select which Exchange Recipient containers should be exported to the MS Mail system and set the trust level for the export process.

Settings   Set some advanced parameters that control how this server will participate in the process, such as whether it should send updates, receive updates, or both.

Schedule   Determine when the DXA Requestor service should send changes to the Dirsync server.

▶ Configure directory replication.

In a multiple-server environment it is important that all servers have an up-to-date copy of the Exchange Directory. Directory replication is the process used to ensure that all servers contain the same information. The MCSE exam will test your knowledge of the procedures for setting up directory replication.

Within a site, replication is automatic. Changes to the directory are replicated to all servers within the site approximately five minutes after the change is made. Directory replication within a site, or *intrasite communication*, is handled directly by the Exchange Directory component of the Exchange servers in the site. Between sites, the Exchange Directory places all changes in e-mail messages and the MTA is responsible for routing them to servers in each site using the Site Connectors that are configured.

Changes are replicated at the object level. This means that if any property of an object is changed, the entire object must be replicated to all servers. Exchange Server uses update sequence numbers (USN) to determine which objects have been changed and replication lists to determine which servers should be notified of changes.

Update Sequence Numbers and Replication Lists

When a server is added to a site, it must obtain a current copy of the directory. During the installation you are asked for the name of a server within the site. The installation program will contact this server and request a copy of the directory database. In this information will be two critical lists: the REPS-TO and REPS-FROM lists. These lists contain the names of all servers to which the directory should be replicated and from which replication information should be accepted.

WARNING

Under normal circumstances the REPS-TO and REPS-FROM lists should be identical. If they are different this indicates a replication problem. You can access these lists by running the Administrator program in RAW mode. Start the program with the /RAW command line switch.

Each server keeps a USN for the copy of the directory database that it stores. Servers also keep track of what their USN was the last time they replicated with each server in the site. Each time a change is made to the directory, the local USN is incremented. Each object within the directory also has a USN. When an object is changed, its USN is incremented.

To determine what changes need to be replicated, each server compares its current USN with the stored value of the USN from the last time replication occurred. This comparison is done for each server in the site. If the current USN is higher than the stored USN, there are changes that need to be replicated. The server then searches the database for all objects with a USN higher than the old value. These are the objects that need to be replicated.

There really is no configuration of directory replication within a site. Configuration is necessary only for replication between sites.

Directory Replication Connector

Before a Directory Replication Connector can be created, you must first have a messaging connector configured to a remote site. The MTA routes messages bound for remote sites, including directory replication messages, to the messaging connector designated to transfer messages to the appropriate site. A messaging connector provides the information necessary to route messages to the remote sites.

Once the messaging connector has been created, you can create and configure a Directory Replication Connector to that site. This connector acts as the logical path that changes will take as they are replicated throughout the sites in your organization. It is very important that you plan this path carefully—no site can receive updates about another site from more than one place. In other words, there can be only one directory replication path from any site to any other site.

As an example, let's plan the directory replication connectors between three sites in an organization. Our sites will be named: Reno, St. Paul, and Tampa. You need to ensure that there are paths that allow changes in any one site to be replicated to all other sites. One plan would be to create a Directory Replication Connector (DRC) between Reno and St. Paul and another DRC between St. Paul and Tampa. Tampa would have a *transitive* connection to Reno. This means it would be informed of changes to the Reno site by the St. Paul site. Configuring another connector between Reno and Tampa is not allowed and would cause major replication problems.

WARNING

Most of the time Exchange will not allow you to make the mistake of creating redundant paths. But if you create a new path before an existing one has been replicated, you might inadvertently create a redundant path. This would cause serious replication problems in the future. Plan directory replication carefully!

Replication traffic between sites is routed by the MTA and the messaging connectors between the sites. This traffic is funneled to a bridgehead server at each site. There is a local bridgehead server which is responsible for routing outgoing changes and a remote bridgehead server which is the destination for those changes. Once the changes have been delivered, the normal intrasite directory replication process ensures that all servers in the site are aware of them.

Creating and Configuring a Directory Replication Connector

In the Exchange Administrator program, open the File menu and choose New Other. On the submenu, click Directory Replication Connector. A dialog box will appear asking you for the name of a server in the remote site. You are also asked if the server is available or not and whether both sides of the connector should be configured at this time.

Each tab of the object pertains to the configuration of a different aspect of the connector.

>   **General**   Name the connector and provide the local and
>   remote bridgehead server names.

Permissions   Configure which users are able to manage this object.

Schedule   Configure how often the connector will query the remote bridgehead server for changes. Your choices are:

Never   This option disables the connector.

Always   Every 15 minutes.

Selected times   This is the default setting. By default the connector will check for changes every three hours.

Sites   Allows you to configure with which sites the connector will communicate. There is also a Request Now button which allows you to initiate an immediate update.

▶ Import directory, message, and scheduling data from existing mail systems.

When a company moves from another e-mail system to Exchange Server, users' mailboxes, messages, address books, and other resources need to be converted from the old system to Exchange format. Exchange includes the tools necessary to accomplish this task. The MCSE exam will test you for a basic knowledge of the Migration Wizard in Exchange and other tools used.

There are three main tools used to perform a migration.

Source extractors   These programs copy the information from an existing e-mail system and convert it into a format that can be imported into an Exchange system.

Migration Wizard   This wizard exports information from foreign systems and imports information into an Exchange organization. It includes extractors for Microsoft Mail and Lotus cc:Mail, among others.

Directory Import and Export   These are options found in the Exchange Administrator program, used to extract account information from an existing Exchange organization and write it to a text file that can be modified, and to import a text file (usually the same file after modification) into an Exchange organization.

Part iii

Source extractors can extract the following from an existing messaging system:

- ▶ Address information
- ▶ Distribution lists
- ▶ Mailboxes
- ▶ Messages
- ▶ Folders
- ▶ Schedule information

Exchange Server ships with extractors for the following environments:

- ▶ Microsoft Mail for PC Networks v3.*x*
- ▶ Microsoft Mail for AppleTalk Networks v3.*x*
- ▶ Lotus cc:Mail (database versions 6 and 8)
- ▶ DEC All-In-One versions 2.3 and later
- ▶ IBM PROFS and OfficeVision
- ▶ Verimation MEMO MVS version 3.2.1 and later
- ▶ Novell GroupWise
- ▶ Collabra Share

There are two types of migration procedures available: one step and two step. In a one step migration the extractor gathers information from the existing e-mail system and imports it directly into an Exchange organization. In a two step migration, the extractor places the information in a CSV file. This file can be imported at a later date. The two step procedure allows the administrator to edit the CSV file to make any necessary changes. You might, for instance, want to change the mailbox names to match a company standard.

The Migration Wizard presents various options relating to the extraction and importation of the information.

Selecting mailboxes to export   You can select which mailboxes will be exported from the foreign system.

Creating mailboxes   You can decide whether to use existing mailboxes or create new ones during the import process.

Recipients container   You can choose the container in which the new accounts will be created.

Passwords   If the Migration Wizard is creating new NT accounts for the mailboxes, you can configure it to use random passwords or to use the alias of the mailbox as a password.

Messages and folders   You can import all of the data or only data within a specified date range.

Shared folders   Shared folders can be migrated to the Public Information Store.

Calendar files   Calendar information from the old system can be imported into Exchange.

▶ Install and configure Exchange Server client computers.

A messaging system is worthless if clients can't access their e-mail. This objective concerns the procedures involved in the installation of client software. The MCSE exam will test your ability to install the Outlook client.

We discussed client installation strategies in Chapter 13. The different methods of installation are:

Network installation   This method involves creating a shared copy of the program to reduce the amount of disk space used on each client computer.

Client computer installation   This method involves installing the client software on each computer.

Scripted installation   This method involves creating the scripts necessary for an unattended installation.

Installing Outlook

Place the Outlook CD-ROM in the drive and run the SETUP program. During the installation you will be asked for your name and the name of your organization. You will then be asked which of the following types of installation you wish to perform:

Typical   Installs the components used by most users.

Part iii

Custom   Presents a list of all components during the installation. You are given the opportunity to decide which components should be installed.

Laptop   Installs only the minimum required components.

Your last decision is to choose to which folder the files should be copied. The installation program does the rest.

After you have installed the client, you must create a profile. The first time you run Outlook you will be asked for the information needed to attach to your e-mail server and retrieve e-mail. This information is stored in your profile.

▶ Configure address lists and accounts by using the Administrator program.

Once your clients have access to the Exchange server, you must begin configuring your environment to meet their needs. There are many tasks involved in this, but this objective concerns only two of them: configuring address book lists for convenience and management, and configuring mailbox objects.

An address list is really not a server-based concept. Address lists are more readily recognized from the client's perspective. When a client sends a message they can either enter the recipient's address manually or they can choose the address from a list. The better this list is organized, the more convenient it is for the user to send e-mail.

The two most common address lists are the Global Address List and the Personal Address Book. The Global Address List contains addresses for all recipients in the Exchange Organization. These addresses are further organized by Site and Recipient container. Creating multiple Recipients containers with descriptive names can make the task of finding a Recipient easier for your users. Later in this chapter, we'll discuss the process for creating Recipients containers and placing mailboxes in them.

Managing mailboxes will also be discussed later, but first, there are a few topics of which you should be aware.

Display Name Versus Alias

Each recipient must have a display name that will appear in the Exchange Address Books. Each recipient also receives an alias that is used in the creation of various types of address for the mailbox. Both of these names are generated automatically as you configure a recipient. You can control how they are created by defining an Auto Naming standard.

E-Mail Addresses for Recipients

As each recipient is created, a series of addresses is created for it. These addresses are used when communicating with foreign e-mail systems. By default each recipient is given the following types of addresses (although your list might differ depending upon what types of connectors and gateways you have configured):

► cc:Mail

► MS Mail

► SMTP

► X.400

Delegating Access

For each user, you can grant another user the ability to send e-mail as the first user. This is most commonly used when an administrative assistant needs to be able to read and send e-mail on behalf of their supervisor.

Protocol Control

As discussed in Chapter 13, there are many ways to contact an Exchange server. Some of the more common protocols used are HTTP (through a Web site interface), IMAP4, LDAP, NNTP, and POP3. Most of these methods are only necessary for traveling or remote users. Exchange allows the administrator to enable or disable the ability to use each of these protocols to access e-mail at various levels: site, server, and recipient. We'll discuss this in more detail later in this chapter, but, for this objective, just be aware that you can control which protocols can be used to access a particular mailbox.

Creating a Recipients Container

In the Administrator program, on the File menu, choose New Other. Click on the Recipients Container option.

Configuring Auto Naming

To configure the format that display names and aliases will take, click on Options on the Tools menu in the Administrator program.

Part iii

Here you can control what format display names will take during recipient creation. Most are straightforward and require no further explanation. There is one option, however, that merits discussion: Custom. Using a series of variables (which can be found in Books Online) you can have your names created to match just about any pattern you like.

The same options are available for the creation of alias names and the changes are performed on the same properties page.

Configuring Address Generation (Site Addressing)

Each recipient is given a series of e-mail addresses for use when communicating with foreign e-mail systems. You might wish to change how these addresses are configured. A perfect example is the generation of SMTP (Internet) mail addresses. By default the address will be:

```
<mailbox alias>@Site.Organization.Com.
```

This probably does not match the domain information you are using on the Internet. You would need to configure the addresses to match the domain names you have registered on the Internet.

To change the generation of e-mail addresses, move to the Configuration container of the appropriate site in the Administrator program. Access the properties of the Site Addressing object. On the Site Addressing tab you have the opportunity to edit the format used to create recipient e-mail addresses.

Configuring a Mailbox

There are numerous parameters available to configure a mailbox. The properties are divided into 13 different pages.

Each page contains parameters that pertain to a different area of configuration.

General   Configures information that uniquely identifies the user. This is also where you assign a particular Windows NT account to the mailbox.

Organization   Allows optional information about the user's management role—who this user reports to and who reports to this user. This information will be available to any program that can access the Address Book.

Phone/Notes   Allows entry of multiple phone numbers for the user.

Permissions   Configures who can manage this object in the directory.

Distribution Lists   Displays and allows you to change the distribution lists of which this mailbox is a member.

E-mail Addresses   Displays the e-mail addresses assigned to this mailbox.

Delivery Restrictions   Allows configuration of lists of recipients from whom this mailbox will accept or reject messages.

Delivery Options   Allows assignment of "Send on Behalf of" permissions.

Protocols   Allows you to control which protocols can be used to access the messages in this mailbox.

Custom Attributes   The administrator can assign properties to these fields, allowing the system to store information specific to the environment.

Limits   Configures the maximum message size for incoming and outgoing messages. Also configures the amount of space the mailbox can use in the Information Store and at what size thresholds the user will receive a warning or be prohibited from sending e-mail.

Advanced   Sets the mailbox home server, the Recipients container, and the trust level.

▶ Configure the message transfer agent within a site.

The Message Transfer Agent (MTA) is responsible for all message traffic between servers within a site. Without proper configuration, messages might not make it to their destination—definitely not a desired result!

This objective is concerned with a series of parameters that can be used to optimize MTA traffic. There are four areas of configuration.

▶ Reliable Transfer Service (RTS) parameters determine how often the data being transferred is verified, how long to wait after an

Part iii

error before attempting to resend data, and how much data can be sent before an acknowledgment is expected from the destination server. (See Table 14.4.)

▶ Association parameters are concerned with the establishment of connections between servers. (See Table 14.5.)

▶ Connection retry values control how many times and at what interval a connection should be retried after an error. (See Table 14.6.)

▶ Transfer timeouts allow you to adjust how each message priority should be handled. There are three different priorities of messages. Each priority should be handled differently in the event of a communication problem. (See Table 14.7.)

TABLE 14.4: Reliable Transfer Service (RTS) parameters

PARAMETER	DEFAULT VALUE	DESCRIPTION
Checkpoint size	30KB	The amount of data that should be transferred before a checkpoint is inserted into the transmission
Window size	5	The number of checkpoints that can be unacknowledged before data transfer is stopped
Recovery timeout	60 seconds	The amount of time after an error that the MTA will wait for a reconnection before starting the transfer from the beginning

TABLE 14.5: Association parameters

PARAMETER	DEFAULT VALUE	DESCRIPTION
Lifetime	300 seconds	The amount of time to keep an association open to a remote server after all data has been sent.
Disconnect	120 seconds	The amount of time to wait for a response to a disconnect request before terminating the connection.
Threshold	50 messages	The maximum number of queued messages to a remote system. When this value is reached the MTA opens another association.

TABLE 14.6: Connection retry values

PARAMETER	DEFAULT VALUE	DESCRIPTION
Max. open retries	144 attempts	The maximum number of times the system will attempt to open a connection before generating a non-deliverable report
Max. transfer retries	2 attempts	The number of times the MTA will attempt to transfer a message over an open connection
Open Interval	600 seconds	The amount of time to wait after an error before attempting to reopen a connection
Transfer interval	120 seconds	The amount of time to wait before attempting to resend a message over an open connection after a failed attempt

TABLE 14.7: Transfer timeouts

PARAMETER	DEFAULT VALUE	DESCRIPTION
Urgent	1000 sec/KB	The maximum amount of time that an Urgent message can wait in a queue before a non-deliverable report (NDR) is generated
Normal	2000 sec/KB	The maximum amount of time that a Normal message can wait in a queue before a non-deliverable report (NDR) is generated
Non-urgent	3000 sec/KB	The maximum amount of time that a Non-urgent message can wait in a queue before a non-deliverable report (NDR) is generated

Part iii

The MTA inserts a checkpoint after every 30KB of data. The destination responds to each checkpoint with an acknowledgment. This lets the sending MTA know what data has successfully been transferred. The MTA will only allow 5 unacknowledged checkpoints to be outstanding—at that point it will stop sending and will wait for an acknowledgment. If no acknowledgment is received in 60 seconds, the MTA will delete checkpointed information (data already sent and acknowledged) and start the transmission from the beginning.

An *association* is a path opened to another system by the MTA. The MTA might open multiple associations to the same server on a single connection. The more associations there are, the more messages sent simultaneously and the more bandwidth the MTA will use. When a connection is made to another system the MTA starts sending messages. If there are more then 50 messages, the MTA will open multiple associations to the remote server. (The MTA can have up to 40 associations open at one time.) When all of the queues are empty the MTA will wait 300 seconds before issuing a disconnect request. It does this to allow the remote system the opportunity to use the connection to send messages back. After the disconnect request the MTA will wait 120 seconds for an acknowledgment of the request. If no acknowledgment is received in that time, the MTA will disconnect from the remote server.

When the MTA fails to send a message over an open connection, it will wait 120 seconds before attempting to resend the message. It will try to send the message twice over an open connection. The MTA will make 144 attempts to open a connection before deciding to mark the message as undeliverable. Between each attempt, the MTA waits 600 seconds before attempting to reopen the connection.

There are different priorities of messages available in Exchange. Each priority of message should be handled differently if there are communication problems. As you can see from the default values listed in Table 14.7, the more urgent the message, the sooner an NDR will be generated. Also note, however, that the larger the message, the longer it can wait. Rather than flooding your network, large messages are allowed to wait in a queue a little longer.

Setting the MTA Parameters

To access these values, find the MTA Site Configuration Object in the Configuration container of your site. Access its property pages and click on the Messaging Defaults tab.

▶ Configure the message transfer agent among sites.

Because most sites are connected by relatively expensive WAN links, configuring the MTA between sites is more critical than within a site. This objective is concerned with the parameters available to optimize intersite MTA communication.

This is a very short objective—all of the critical information was discussed for the last objective. The exact same parameters are available to configure the MTA between sites as are available within a site.

NOTE

What is new for this objective is that setting the parameters correctly becomes even more important, since message transfer between sites is prone to more problems than message transfer within a site.

The definition of an Exchange site is a group of Exchange servers connected by a high bandwidth, reliable link—most often all of the servers are on the same LAN. The implication of this definition is that servers in different sites will most likely be connected by slower, less reliable, and more expensive WAN links. When WAN links are involved there will be more timeouts, retries, and failed communication attempts. The parameters discussed for the last objective all had to do with configuring how Exchange should react to these types of problems.

Configuring the Message Transfer Agent among Sites

To configure the MTA between sites access the appropriate connector (X.400 or Dynamic RAS) in the Connections container. The Connections container will be found in the Configuration container of your site. Access the property pages of the connector and click on the Override tab in the X.400 Connector or the MTA Override tab in the Dynamic RAS Connector. You will see the same parameters discussed in the previous objective.

▶ Configure Internet protocols and services. Protocols and services include:

- ▶ POP3 and IMAP4
- ▶ Active Server and HTTP
- ▶ NNTP
- ▶ LDAP

We discussed the functionality of each of these protocols and services in Chapter 13. This objective relies upon that underlying knowledge to help configure and optimize them for your environment.

Before we begin looking at configuration options, let's review the functionality of the protocols and services.

- ▶ POP3 is a service that allows a user to connect to and retrieve mail from their Inbox using Internet protocols.

- ▶ IMAP4 is a service that allows a user to connect to and retrieve e-mail from an e-mail server. The user can access private folders (including their Inbox) and public folders.

- ▶ HTTP is a protocol used to access information on a World Wide Web server. For the purposes of our discussion, HTTP works in concert with Active Server pages and Exchange to turn a user's folders and messages into HTML pages that can be viewed with Web browser software.

- ▶ LDAP is a protocol used to access directory information.

- ▶ NNTP is the protocol used to access Internet newsgroups.

Each of these items can be configured to optimize their service in a particular environment. One of the most basic controls is to control which users can use each service. In general, protocols can be managed at three different levels within the Exchange hierarchy: site, server, and mailbox. Not all protocols, however can be managed in all three locations.

- ▶ POP3, IMAP4, LDAP, NNTP and HTTP can be managed at the site level.

- ▶ POP3, IMAP4, LDAP, and NNTP can be managed at the server level.

- ▶ POP3, IMAP4, LDAP, NNTP, and HTTP can be managed on a per-mailbox basis.

NOTE

To avoid confusion, just remember that HTTP is the only protocol that cannot be managed at the server level. This is because some management of this protocol must be done through the Web server software on a Web server.

The first level of control is to enable or disable each protocol. You have the following three choices: enabling them at the site level and then disabling them at selected servers; disabling them at the site level and then enabling them on selected servers; or enabling them at both the site and server levels and then disabling them on a per-mailbox basis.

Remember that if a protocol is disabled at the server, it doesn't matter what is done at the site or mailbox level—if the server won't service the protocol the user can't use it to access messages.

Many of the protocols require a user to authenticate before they can access information. There are numerous ways that authentication can be accomplished—each has its advantages and disadvantages.

Basic (Clear Text)   Authentication uses an unencrypted username and password.

> **Advantages**   Most client software will support basic authentication. It is simple and not prone to problems.

> **Disadvantages**   All traffic travels across the network in clear text format. This is the least secure method of authentication.

Basic (Clear Text) Using SSL (Secure Sockets Layer)   Uses SSL to encrypt the authentication on Port 993.

> **Advantages**   Provides a more secure channel of traffic.

> **Disadvantages**   Slower authentication process. Requires client software that is SSL-aware.

Windows NT Challenge/Response   Authentication uses Windows NT Security. Password is encrypted.

> **Advantages**   Most Microsoft software is aware of this method. It's fast and fairly secure.

> **Disadvantages**   While the password is encrypted, the username is not.

Windows NT Challenge/ Response Using SSL   Uses an SSL encrypted channel for authentication traffic.

> **Advantages**   The entire process is encrypted.

> **Disadvantages**   Slower authentication process. Requires client software that is SSL-aware.

MCIS (Microsoft Commercial Internet System) Membership System   Identifies the client using an MCIS Membership account database.

> **Advantages**   Secure technology. Can be used with very large databases of users (millions).

> **Disadvantages**   An MCIS Membership account database must be maintained separate from the Windows NT account database (SAM).

MCIS Membership System Using SSL Identifies the client using an MCIS Membership account database and encrypts the transmission.

Advantages Very secure technology. Can be used with very large databases of users (millions).

Disadvantages Same as for plain MCIS, plus the encryption slows the authentication process.

Idle connections

Another aspect of each protocol that must be configured is how the server should react to idle connections. An idle connection is a connection that is open but not being used. This might happen if a user connects to retrieve their e-mail but does not properly disconnect from the e-mail server. In this case, you can have Exchange close the connection after it has remained idle for a specified time.

Now let's discuss parameters that are specific to each protocol or service.

POP3

Other than choosing the authentication method and setting the idle time-out threshold, there are no special configuration issues.

IMAP4

IMAP4 is basically POP3 with a few more options. Since IMAP4 has the ability to access multiple folders (rather than just the Inbox) it is conceivable that you would want to allow anonymous access to public folders. You can allow this form of access and choose an account to use to set permissions for anonymous connections.

HTTP and Active Server Pages

Much of the HTTP and Active Server environment will be managed through the Web server software. There are, however, a few parameters controlled through the Exchange Administrator program. The first choice to make is whether the Exchange system should be accessible from an anonymous connection. If you are going to make public folders available through your Web site, this will be required. Next you need to decide if an anonymous user should be able to browse your Global Address List. Lastly, if you are going to make public folders available to anonymous users through the HTTP protocol, you will have to add each folder to the Folders Shortcut list.

NNTP

The only unique parameters for the NNTP protocol are concerned with the content of the newsgroups themselves.

LDAP

LDAP is a protocol designed to retrieve information stored in a directory services database. The LDAP specific parameters are concerned with the search process. You can control how much of each property is searched for a match to the search criteria submitted. Your choices are:

Treat "any" substring as "initial" substring searches (fast)   This option looks only at the beginning of each property value for a match (an "initial" substring search) even if the user was looking for something located anywhere in a property value (an "any" substring search). If the user requests to search the end of strings (a "final" substring search), the search is not performed. While this option is fast, it sometimes doesn't return all the data the user requests.

Allow only "initial" substring searches (fast)   This option configures the server only to perform searches on the beginning of properties. Any other type of search will not be performed.

Allow all substring searches (slow)   The server will perform any kind of search requested (initial, final, or any).

You can also create a referrals list. This list is made up of servers that the server can refer the client to if the server does not contain the requested information. As an example, a user might request information about a user named Katie King from Server A. If that information is part of another organization, the server will tell the client to request the information from another server.

You will need to know how to access the appropriate properties and what each property represents. As discussed earlier, there are three places within the directory that protocols may be managed: site, server, and mailbox.

Configuring Protocols at the Site Level

To configure protocols at the site level, open the Exchange Administrator program, move to the appropriate site and expand the Configuration container. Within the Configuration container highlight the Protocols container. Within the Protocols container access the properties of the appropriate protocol.

Part iii

Configuring Protocols at the Server Level

To configure protocols at the server level, open the Exchange Administrator program and move to the appropriate site container. Expand the Configuration container and then the Servers container. Highlight the server you wish to configure and move to its Protocols container. Access the property pages of the appropriate protocol.

Configuring Protocols at the Mailbox Level

To configure protocols at the mailbox level, move to the appropriate Recipients container and access the properties of the user that you wish to configure. On the Protocols tab you can enable or disable each protocol.

At the site and server level each protocol has configuration parameters. In the next few subsections, we first show the property pages of each protocol and then describe the options found on each tab.

Configuring POP3

Access the property pages of the POP3 object to change parameters.

General   Configure the display name, view the directory names for the object, and enable the protocol.

Permissions   Configure which users should have the ability to manage this object in the directory.

Authentication   Choose the authentication methods that will be supported: Basic, Basic with SSL, Windows NT Challenge/Response, Windows NT Challenge/Response with SSL, MCIS, and MCIS with SSL.

Message Format   Should messages use MIME or UUENCODE formatting?

Idle Time-out   How long should the server wait to close idle connections?

Configuring IMAP4

Access the property pages of the IMAP4 object to configure parameters.

General   Configure the display name and view the directory names for this object. Enable the protocol and whether to include public folders when folders are listed.

Permissions   Configure which users should have the ability to manage this object in the directory.

Authentication   Choose the authentication methods that will be supported: Basic, Basic with SSL, Windows NT Challenge/Response, or Windows NT Challenge/Response with SSL, MCIS, and MCIS with SSL.

Anonymous   Allow anonymous access.

Message Format   Should messages use MIME or UUEN-CODE formatting?

Idle Time-out   How long should the server wait to close idle connections?

Configuring HTTP

Access the property pages of the HTTP object to configure parameters.

General   Configure display name and view the directory names for this object. Enable the protocol, and configure anonymous access to public folders and the Global Address List.

Permissions   Configure which users should have the ability to manage this object in the directory.

Folder Shortcuts   Add public folders to the list that will be available through your Web server to anonymous users.

Advanced   Configure the number of address book entries that will be returned to a client.

Configuring NNTP

Access the property pages of the NNTP object to configure parameters.

General   Configure display name and view the directory names for this object. Enable the protocol and client access.

Permissions   Configure which users should have the ability to manage this object in the directory.

Newsfeeds   View the properties of newsfeeds you have created.

Control Messages   Newsfeeds send control messages regarding the content of the newsgroup. Here you can access those messages and accept or decline them.

Authentication   Choose the authentication methods that will be supported: Basic, Basic with SSL, Windows NT Challenge/Response, or Windows NT Challenge/Response with SSL, MCIS, and MCIS with SSL.

Message Format   Should messages use MIME or UUENCODE formatting?

Idle Time-out   How long should the server wait to close idle connections?

Anonymous   Allow anonymous access.

Configuring LDAP

Access the property pages of the LDAP object to configure properties.

General   Configure the display name and view the directory names of this object. Configure the port used by this protocol and enable its use.

Permissions   Configure which users should have the ability to manage this object in the directory.

Authentication   Choose the authentication methods that will be supported: Basic, Basic with SSL, Windows NT Challenge/Response, or Windows NT Challenge/Response with SSL, MCIS, and MCIS with SSL.

Anonymous   Allow anonymous access.

Search   Configure how searches should be performed.

Referrals   Build a list of referral servers.

Idle Time-out   How long should the server wait to close idle connections?

▶ Configure message tracking.

When messages are en route to their destination you will need a mechanism that allows you to follow their progress through your e-mail system. On an Exchange server that mechanism is message tracking.

Message delivery between servers is primarily the responsibility of the Message Transfer Agent (MTA). An Exchange server can be configured so that the MTA creates a log file which documents the path that messages take through the messaging system. This log file is located in the EXCHSRVR\TRACKING.LOG directory and named *YYYYMMDD* .LOG (where *YYYY* is the year, *MM* is the month, and *DD* is the day that the log was created).

Once the MTA has been configured to track messages, you can use the Message Tracking Center to access the information stored in the log file. The Tracking Center will display all of the messaging components that were involved in the delivery of the message.

There are two procedures involved message tracking: first you must turn message tracking on and then you must use the Message Tracking Center to use the information gathered.

Enabling Message Tracking

To enable message tracking, start the Exchange Administrator program and move to the Configuration container for the appropriate site. Access the property pages for the MTA Site Configuration object. On the General tab, ensure that the Enable message tracking option is selected.

Using the Message Tracking Center

The Message Tracking Center (MTC) acts as your interface to the information stored in the log file. Access the MTC by choosing the Track Message option on the Tools menu in the Administrator program. The opening dialog box allows you to search for messages from a certain user, or to a certain user, and to limit the age of messages displayed. The MCT will display a list of messages that match your search criteria. Double-click any message in the list to view more detailed information (see Figure 14.3).

Part iii

▶ Configure server locations.

Deciding where your Exchange server should be placed within the physical boundaries of your network requires an understanding of both the Exchange message delivery process and the underlying network infrastructure. This objective assumes a basic understanding of both of these topics.

TIP

Most of the exam questions that concern this objective do not ask about it directly. Most are scenario-based questions. They will describe an environment and ask you to choose the best solution from a list.

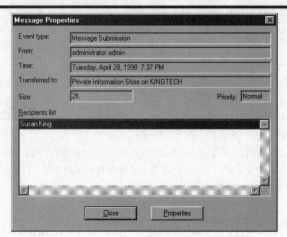

FIGURE 14.3: Message Properties

Some of the considerations that you must take into account when planning server location are the following:

Available bandwidth   If many users are going to access a particular server for their messages you must ensure that the server is placed on a network segment that has enough available bandwidth to handle the traffic that will be generated.

Local access   Users will usually see the best performance if their mail server is on the same network segment as they are. One of the most basic rules in networking is "Place resources near the users that use them." If users have to cross routers or expensive WAN links to access their e-mail, performance will usually suffer.

Fault tolerance   Many administrators like to spread multiple servers throughout the network. Not only does this increase performance for the users, but it also provides a degree of fault tolerance. If one server goes down a limited number of users will be affected.

Site boundaries   When determining the number of Exchange sites to create in your organization, remember that servers within a site should be connected by a fast and reliable network with plenty of available bandwidth. The intrasite network configuration must support RPC.

Configure security.

E-mail has become a critical part of the business world. Many businesses rely upon their e-mail for communication between employees, providing information to customers, and placing orders with vendors. Ensuring the security and integrity of messages as they are routed through various private and public networks has become an important concern for many administrators. This issue has become especially critical as companies start to use the Internet as a delivery mechanism.

Microsoft Exchange includes a Key Management (KM) component that enables encryption of both messages and electronic signatures that can help determine if a message has been tampered with during the delivery process. By default, the Key Management components are not installed on an Exchange Server. The Key Management components can either be installed during the initial setup by performing a Complete/Custom installation or they can be manually installed at a later time.

The Key Management security process revolves around a series of software keys used to encrypt and decrypt messages. Within an Exchange Organization there will be only one server responsible for the management of these keys—the Key Management Server. This server should be in the NT domain that you use for central management of your network, it should be backed up regularly, and it should use the NTFS file system. Once Key Management is installed on this server, a password must be provided each time the system restarts.

WARNING

The startup of the Key Management server might not be fully automatic. You must provide the Key Management password each time the computer restarts. This can be done manually by typing it in at a dialog box, or it can be read off a floppy disk. In both methods, however, someone must be present to provide the password.

The setup of Key Management will create two objects in the Configuration container. These objects are named CA and Encryption. The KM password is used to access and configure these objects. By default this password is **password**. You should change this password immediately after installation.

Since this objective is concerned with the configuration of KM, be sure and study the procedures used to accomplish this task. There are a few other details of which you should be aware.

Part iii

Encryption

The system administrator can configure the level of encryption used by KM security. There are three levels of encryption available: CAST-64 (the default), DES, and CAST-40. Due to export regulations, only CAST-40 can be used in locales outside of North America.

KM Administrators

Because multiple administrators could be involved with the management of the KM system, Exchange allows each administrator to have a different password to access the KM objects in the Exchange Directory.

Installing Key Management

Installing the KM components is done through the Exchange Server SETUP program. When prompted, choose the Complete/Custom installation option. Change the Exchange Server default components to include Key Management Server.

During the installation you will be asked for the site service account password. You will also be asked how you wish to receive the KM password. You can either have the password displayed for you to document or have it written to floppy (this option requires two formatted floppies).

The Key Management service is not configured to start automatically at system boot, nor is it started automatically during its installation. You must run the Services applet found in Control Panel, and double-click the Microsoft Exchange Key Management Server service and set the Startup Type option to automatic. You will also need to enter the KM password in the startup parameters box to manually start the service.

Configuring the KM Environment

There are two objects to configure on the KM service: CA and Encryption. Both are found in the Configuration container of the site in which the KM server is located.

The Encryption object allows you to set the encryption level used for your Exchange organization. The Algorithms page allows you to choose the encryption levels used within North America and in other locales.

To configure the CA object you must provide the administrative password for the KM system. By default this password is **password**. Each tab refers to a different set of parameters that can be configured (see

Figure 14.4). You must again provide an administrative password to access the Administrators and Passwords property pages.

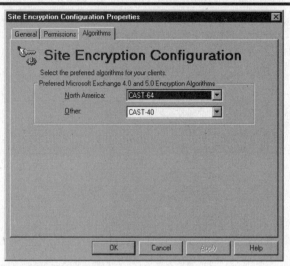

FIGURE 14.4: Site Encryption Properties

> **General** Change the display name of the CA object in the directory.
>
> **Permissions** Configure which users should have management permissions to this object.
>
> **Algorithms** Allows you to configure the level of encryption you will use for communication within your organization.

Enabling Advanced Security on a Mailbox To enable advanced security on a mailbox, access the properties of that mailbox. On the Security tab, click the Enable Advanced Security button. You will be given the option of mailing their temporary key to them via an Exchange message or displaying the key. If you choose to display the key you must document it and give it to the user.

Configuring the Client Software to Use Advanced Security

Users must enable advanced security on their client software. They should start Outlook, and choose Options on the Tools menu. On the

Options dialog box click on the security tab. Here they should click on the Set Up Advanced Security button.

They will be asked for the temporary key that was either e-mailed to them or provided by the administrator. They will also be required to enter a password that will be used to access the advanced security tools in Outlook. The user will receive a message from the KM server stating the advanced security has been successfully enabled.

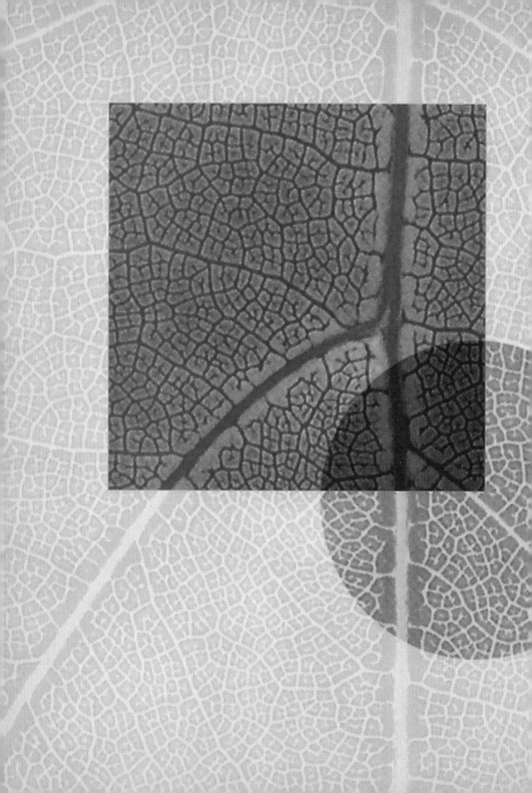

Chapter 15

CONFIGURING AND MANAGING RESOURCE ACCESS

I n Chapter 13, we discussed the planning of an Exchange Server organization and looked at many of the capabilities of Exchange Server 5.5. In Chapter 14, we discussed the installation of Exchange Server software and the creation and configuration of objects in an organization. The next logical step is to consider the management of your messaging system— how to ensure that your Exchange Server organization is secure, stable, and able to withstand a catastrophic failure. For the MCSE exam you need to have a thorough understanding of the tools available in Exchange to help you manage your system.

Adapted from *MCSE Exam Notes: Exchange Server 5.5* by Robert King

ISBN 0-7821-2302-3   368 pages $19.99

▶ Manage site security.

There are two areas of site security that you need to understand: the impact of Windows NT domain security and the importance of securing the Exchange Directory itself. Both of these topics play a major role in providing an environment in which messaging can be trusted with sensitive information.

Before you can begin securing the Exchange organization, you must first concern yourself with your Microsoft Windows NT domain structure. While NT domains are not examined directly in this examination, a complete understanding of this topic is prerequisite knowledge.

The Effect of Domain Structure on an Exchange Server Organization

A domain can be defined as a logical grouping of users and computers *managed through a shared database*. For our purposes, the italicized portion of the definition is critical. You need to understand how the shared accounts database, known as the Security Accounts Manager (SAM), affects our Exchange organization.

From the perspective of Windows NT, one of the purposes of the SAM is to authenticate users to resources. Each time a user logs on to a domain, the SAM is used to create a set of credentials which act as a security key. These credentials control access to the various resources in the domain. Without this key, a user cannot read data, use printers, or perform any other functions within the domain. Collectively, the permissions that a user account has are known as that user's security context.

TIP

If you log in as the Administrator account and attach to a resource, you are attaching within the security context of that account. This seems like a lot of words to describe a simple concept, but it is important that you understand the use of the term "context" in relation to security.

Exchange servers need to transfer data among themselves on a regular basis. They attach to each other within the security context of the site service account (SSA). This account is granted the following rights:

▶ Log on as a service

- ▶ Restore files and directories
- ▶ Act as a part of the operating system

This combination of rights allows the SSA to start Exchange Server services and access the necessary files and directories.

WARNING

This combination of rights is mandatory. It can also be rather dangerous. Make sure that you create an account specifically to act as the SSA and assign it a password that is difficult to guess.

When two Exchange servers communicate, they do so using the security context of the SSA. In other words, Exchange servers use the SSA, defined in the accounts database (SAM), to connect to each other.

Let's look at the relationship between your Exchange organization and your NT domain model.

Within a site, all servers must use the same site service account to communicate. In a single domain environment, this is simple to configure. Just create one SSA during the installation of your first Exchange server, and provide the name and password of this account during the installation of subsequent Exchange servers. (SETUP provides the name by default when you are adding additional servers into an existing site.) In this way, all of your servers will use the same SSA. Unfortunately, most environments that need more than one Exchange server are also divided into multiple NT domains.

With multiple NT domains, the SSA requirements are more complex. If you have Exchange servers that are part of the same Exchange site but are members of different NT domains, you are forced to choose between two configurations. Remember that Exchange servers within the same site must use the same site service account. With multiple domains you need to build a trust relationship between the two domains and use the account from one of the domains.

Communication between Exchange sites is not as complex. Between sites, you can provide the username and password of the SSA of the second site and use the SSA override property of the connector of the first site to connect the two sites.

Part iii

Securing the Site Using Exchange Directory Permissions

Just as NT has permissions to control access to resources, Exchange Server has its own set of permissions to control access to objects in the organization. Within the Exchange hierarchy, there are three levels of permissions: organization, site, and configuration. These three levels define security contexts within the hierarchy through which permissions are assigned and inherited.

When permissions are assigned to the Organization object, those permissions are inherited only by that object itself. When permissions are assigned at the site level, those permissions apply to the Site container, the system public folders, and the default Recipients container and any additional Recipients containers created in that site. Lastly, when permissions are assigned to the Configuration container, they are inherited by all objects within that container. With careful planning, you have the ability to delegate management responsibility of various areas within your Exchange organization.

NOTE
Table 13.5 in Chapter 13 describes the rights that are available within the Exchange Directory as well as their functions. Be sure and review this table as you prepare for the exam.

Assigning these rights to users allows you to manage the actions they can take within your messaging environment. You could take the time to individually assign these rights, but there is an easier way. The Exchange Directory includes a set of predefined security roles. Assigning a role to a user effectively assigns the set of rights necessary to perform a set of tasks.

NOTE
Table 13.6 in Chapter 13 describes the roles and the rights that each set of permissions includes. Make sure you are familiar with these roles before taking the exam.

Enabling the Permissions Page for All Objects

While all objects have a Permissions page, by default this page will not be visible on most objects in the Administrator program. To enable this page, start the Administrator program, and choose the Options choice on the Tools menu. Ensure that the Show Permissions Page for All Objects box is checked.

Using the Default Roles

Choose the object that you wish to manage and access its property pages. Access the Permissions page. Click the Add button and choose the appropriate user or group from the list. Then choose the role you would like this user to have from the Roles submenu as shown in Figure 15.1.

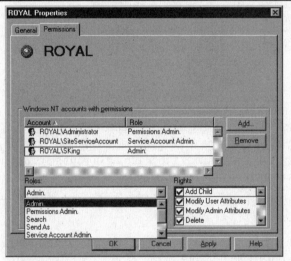

FIGURE 15.1: Permissions page with the user's role set to Admin.

Creating a Custom Role

There are times when a predefined role does not fit the function of a user. For these occasions, you can create a custom role that fits your needs exactly. To create a custom role, click the Add button, add the user to the permissions list, and then choose the appropriate rights from the submenu while that user is selected (see Figure 15.2).

Notice that as soon as you select a specific list of rights (as opposed to choosing a predefined role) the role is listed as Custom.

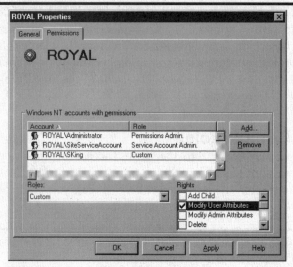

FIGURE 15.2: Custom permissions role

▶ Manage users.

A messaging system is one of the most user-based applications that can be placed upon a network. The whole point of e-mail is to facilitate communication between users. During the planning of your system, you considered various aspects of your environment:

▶ You purchased server hardware based on the expected number of users.

▶ You purchased hard disks based on an estimate of the amount of e-mail that users would store.

▶ You hired administrative staff based on an estimated workload.

▶ You planned a public folder strategy based on historical use of data.

This list can go on and on. The bottom line is that you planned an Exchange organization for a certain type of environment. Unfortunately, very few environments are static. Your company will grow, your users will begin to use their e-mail for more than just simple messaging, or your company will want you to provide a more organized method of presenting critical data. No matter what the change, you need to manage your environment during these changes. The MCSE exam will test your knowledge of the tools provided within Exchange to help you manage user mailboxes.

Of all of the types of objects in the Exchange Directory, none requires as much ongoing management as user mailboxes. You will need to add mailboxes for new employees, delete mailboxes for employees who are leaving, move mailboxes from one server to another, clean up mailboxes that have grown past a reasonable size, and sometimes make sweeping changes to many mailboxes at once. This objective is concerned with the various management tasks associated with mailboxes.

Using Templates to Create Mailboxes

In Chapter 14, we discussed the process of creating and configuring mailboxes on a one-by-one basis. While this process is fairly straightforward, it can take a lot of time to create a large number of mailboxes. One way to reduce data entry is to create a template mailbox with all of the desired default values entered. This template can then be used as the starting point when creating new mailboxes.

There is nothing special about a template mailbox. It is created like any other mailbox in the directory. When creating a template, enter those values that are common across your environment or for a particular type of user. You then copy the template when creating new mailboxes. Depending on your needs, you might create one template to be used when creating all mailboxes or a number of templates, each set up for a particular type of user.

While any mailbox can be used as a template, it is best to create specific mailboxes that will only be used in the creation of new accounts. These mailboxes should be named in such a way that their purpose is apparent. For example, you might create a template to be used when creating mailboxes for accounting personnel and name that mailbox "Accounting_template".

TIP

When you are viewing accounts in the Recipients container, these are presented in alphabetical order. While this is convenient for finding a specific user, it can be inconvenient when trying to find a template mailbox. One way to group your templates at the beginning of the list is to place a number at the beginning of the name. Using the example in the text, you might name the account "1_Accounting_template".

When you are using a template, all attributes are copied to the new mailbox except the first name, initials, last name, display name, alias name, directory name, and e-mail addresses.

Finding a Recipient

As the number of recipients in your organization grows, it can become difficult to locate a particular mailbox. The Exchange Administrator program includes a tool to help locate a recipient based upon the values of various attributes.

This tool allows you to limit your search by the value of various attributes such as first name, last name, department, or title, and even to limit your search to a particular Recipients container.

Moving a Mailbox

When planning your Exchange servers, you considered the number of users each server would support and the amount of e-mail that each user would have in their mailbox. As your e-mail system grows, it is not uncommon for the actual figures to exceed your planned values. When this happens you can move mailboxes from one server to another to distribute the workload evenly.

A user's mailbox physically resides on their home server. When moving a mailbox from one server to another, consider the amount of e-mail that it contains. Remember that all of the e-mail will have to be moved from one computer to another. For large mailboxes, this process can be lengthy and can generate a large amount of traffic on your network. Before moving a mailbox, either use the Clean Mailbox tool or ask the user to delete any unnecessary messages. Another option is to have the user move their e-mail to an offline folder, move the mailbox, and then have them move their e-mail to the new server-based mailbox.

Many administrators are surprised when a mailbox is larger after the move than it was before. The mailbox can grow because when a message is sent to multiple mailboxes on the same home server, Exchange stores only one physical copy of it. This is called *single-instance storage*. When a mailbox is moved, each message is moved to the new location, regardless of whether a copy already exists on the new home server.

Cleaning a Mailbox

While it is often best to train users to clean up their own mailboxes, deleting or archiving old e-mail, you are sometimes forced to perform this task for them. The Administrator program includes the Clean Mailbox tool to facilitate this process. The Clean Mailbox tool allows you to delete messages in a chosen mailbox based on age, size, and sensitivity. You can also limit what is deleted based upon its status. For instance, you can choose to delete only messages that have been read or only messages that are unread.

Modifying Recipients in Batches

There are times when you need to modify the attributes of a large number of recipients. For instance, your company might move, forcing you to change the address attribute of all mailboxes. You could manually edit this field on each recipient but, in a large environment, this would take a long time. The Exchange Administrator program has the ability to export the contents of a container to a .CSV (comma-separated value) file. This file can be edited using any text editor, and then imported back into the directory with the changes made.

Hiding a Template Mailbox from the Global Address List

The mailbox template is a normal mailbox object. This means that users can send e-mail to it. Messages sent to this mailbox are never deleted since no one actually uses the mailbox. To avoid this problem, hide the mailbox from the Global Address List. To accomplish this, access the properties of the recipient. On the Advanced tab, select Hide from Address Book.

Finding a Recipient

To search for recipients, choose Find Recipients from the Tools menu in the Administrator program. Enter the values for which you wish to search and click the Find Now button.

Moving a Mailbox

To move a mailbox, start the Exchange Administrator program. Highlight the recipient you wish to move and choose Move Mailbox on the Tools menu. The Move Mailbox dialog box will appear. Choose the destination server from the list, and click OK. Note that you can only move mailboxes to servers within the same site and you cannot move mailboxes to different Recipients containers.

Exporting/Importing Directory Contents

To export the contents of the directory, choose Directory Export from the Tools menu in the Administrator program. Name the export file, choose a container to export from, and choose the types of recipients to export. You can also have the contents of subcontainers exported and include hidden recipients.

 # Manage distribution lists.

Distribution lists (DLs) are a great convenience for users. Users can choose a DL and have e-mail sent to all of its members, rather than having to pick individuals from the Global Address List.

Most administrators think that managing a distribution list consists of adding and deleting users from the member list. The reality is that because they represent multiple recipients as one object, there are a few unique management tasks associated with DLs. Properly configuring your distribution lists can greatly reduce their impact on your servers and reduce the amount of time you spend managing them.

Setting an Expansion Server

When a message is sent to a DL, the MTA on the Exchange server must expand the membership list to determine where the message should be sent. The MTA must determine the home server of each member, and then sort these recipients so that only one copy of the message is sent to each server. This process places a heavy load on the originating Exchange server. As the administrator, you can designate an *expansion server* for the DL. An expansion server is responsible for routing messages addressed to the DL.

When a server receives a message addressed to a DL, the MTA will deliver the message to the MTA on the server designated as the expansion server. This MTA will then expand the member list and route the message to the appropriate servers. Setting up an expansion server allows you to move the processing to a less busy Exchange server.

Choosing a Distribution List Owner

The membership of some DLs changes on a regular basis. Keeping the membership list up to date can take a lot of time. Typically, only administrators can change the membership of a DL using the Administrator program. One way to delegate some of this workload is to assign an owner to the DL. The owner can modify the membership of the distribution list from their client software.

Trust Levels

As mentioned in Chapter 14, an Exchange server can be configured as a DXA participant (either Server or Requestor). The goal of this configuration is the exchange of recipient information between the Exchange Directory and the MS Mail postoffices. Trust levels are used to control which recipients will be included in the exchange.

The connector is configured with a trust level between 0 and 100. Each recipient is also configured with a trust level between 0 and 100. Only those recipients with a trust level lower that that of the connector will be included in the address list exchange.

TIP

Most administrators ignore the trust level feature of DLs. But it can be used to prevent users in the MS Mail system from flooding your Exchange environment with messages sent to large DLs (such as the Everyone in the Company distribution list). Do this by setting the trust levels on these DLs high enough so they won't be synchronized to the MS Mail system.

Controlling Message Size

You can set a size limit on the messages that will be accepted by a distribution list. Sending large messages to a DL with a long membership list can adversely affect server performance.

Setting Options Specific to Distribution Lists

There are a few management options that are unique to distribution lists. Table 15.1 lists these options and describes their purposes.

TABLE 15.1: Distribution list options

OPTION	DESCRIPTION
Report to DL Owner	Sends notifications to the DL owner when a message sent to the DL has requested delivery notification or is undeliverable.
Report to Message Originator	When delivery notification is requested for a message sent to the DL or when a message is undeliverable, this option allows notification to be sent to the message originator. When this option is not set, the originator receives a confirmation from the DL, not from each member.

Part iii

TABLE 15.1 continued: Distribution list options

OPTION	DESCRIPTION
Allow Out of Office Messages to Originator	Allows member's out-of-office messages to be returned to the message originator.
Hide from Address Book	The DL will not appear in the address book.
Hide Membership from the Address Book	The DL will appear in the address book, but users will not be able to view the recipients that are members of the DL.

WARNING

If the Hide Membership from Address Book option is selected, it will override the Report to Message Originator and Allow Out of Office Messages to Originator options, to ensure the secrecy of the member list of the DL.

Managing a Distribution List

To configure a DL, start the Exchange Administrator program, move to the appropriate Recipients container, and access the properties of the DL.

Each page of the property pages represents a different aspect of DL management.

General   Configure the display name and alias, owner, and expansion server of the DL.

Permissions   Configure the management roles assigned to users for this object.

Distribution Lists   Add this DL as a member of other DLs.

E-mail Addresses   Since the DL is a recipient, e-mail addresses must be created for it.

Delivery Restrictions   If needed, you can create a list of users who can or cannot send messages to this DL.

Custom Attributes   Enter the values for any custom attributes you have configured.

Advanced   Set the trust level for replication through the MS Mail Connector or cc:Mail Connector, limit the size of messages that can be delivered to this DL, and configure any of the unique DL options listed in Table 15.1.

▶ Manage the directory.

The Exchange Directory is basically just a database. Like any other database, it requires periodic maintenance. This objective is concerned with both the automatic and the manual maintenance required by the Exchange Directory.

The maintenance of the Exchange Directory can be divided into two types: online and offline. Online maintenance is performed on the directory while it is up and running, and offline maintenance is performed with the service stopped.

Online Maintenance

Because the directory exists on multiple Exchange servers, there must be a mechanism that lets all Exchange servers know when an object has been deleted from the directory. When an object is deleted, it is marked with a *tombstone*. This tombstone is replicated to all other Exchange servers in the organization so that all servers know to delete the object from their copy of the directory database. By default, Exchange Server lets tombstones live for 30 days to ensure that they have been replicated throughout the environment.

Once a tombstone has reached its life span, another process, called Garbage collection, deletes the object and reclaims the space in the database. By default, Garbage collection is performed every 12 hours.

Both of these time periods, the tombstone lifetime and the Garbage collection interval, can be changed.

WARNING

Changing the tombstone life span or the Garbage collection interval is not something you should do lightly. If you decrease the life span of tombstones you could end up with orphaned objects—objects that have been deleted on one server but for which a tombstone was never received at another server. Changing the Garbage collection interval can affect disk space recovery on your Exchange server.

Another online process is the IS/DS consistency check. This process compares information held in the Information Store against information held in the directory database. If the two don't match, the process places a time stamp on the inconsistent information. When run subsequently, if it finds an inconsistency with a time stamp over a particular age (e.g., one day), it will repair the inconsistency. An example of an inconsistency would be a mailbox in the Information Store that does not have a corresponding entry in the directory.

Offline Maintenance

Under normal circumstances, the online maintenance processes should be sufficient. Occasionally, however, you need to use a more direct approach. Exchange Server includes an offline maintenance tool called ESEUTIL.EXE. (This tool replaces the EDBUTIL.EXE used in earlier versions of Exchange.) The database (Directory Store or Information Store) must be stopped before this tool can be used. ESEUTIL.EXE performs the following tasks:

Defragments the database   Over time the database can become fragmented, which means that the data is not stored in contiguous areas on the disk. This can cause slower access times since the drive must read data from multiple areas on the disk. Due to the way that data is physically stored on the drive, this can also waste disk space. ESEUTIL.EXE will defragment the database, thereby increasing performance and possibly decreasing its size.

Integrity check   ESEUTIL.EXE examines the information in the database to ensure that there are no references to objects that no longer exist.

Recover a database   If the problem is severe enough, ESEUTIL .EXE can be used to rebuild the database. The tool will reconstruct each entry in the database.

Upgrade a database   ESEUTIL.EXE can be used to upgrade a copy of the database created by an earlier version of Exchange Server.

File dump   Used for advanced troubleshooting of the database, this option generates a formatted text file of various database file types.

Repair   This option will attempt to repair a corrupted database.

WARNING

There are two considerations when using ESEUTIL to recover a database. First, ESEUTIL rebuilds the database in a temporary file. This file will be at least as large as the original database, so ensure that you have enough disk space available. Second, if it finds a record that cannot be rebuilt, it deletes that record. Make a backup of the database before performing this task.

Configuring the Tombstone Lifetime and Garbage Collection Interval Parameters

Within the Exchange Administrator program, move to the Configuration container for your site. Access the property pages of the DS Site Configuration object. On the General page, enter times for Tombstone Lifetime and Garbage collection.

Scheduling Automatic Maintenance

Access the property pages of your server. On the IS Maintenance tab, you have a choice of selecting specific times or choosing Always. The Always setting causes maintenance to be performed every 15 minutes. By default, maintenance will be performed every day between 12:00 midnight and 6:00 A.M.

Using ESEUTIL.EXE

ESEUTIL.EXE is a command line tool and hence must be run from a command prompt. There are two steps involved: first stop the database and then run ESEUTIL.EXE. To stop the service, access the Services applet found in the Control Panel. Highlight Microsoft Exchange System Attendant and click the Stop button. When you are warned of the other services that are dependent on the System Attendant, choose OK.

To run ESEUTIL.EXE, change to the `<system_root>\system32` directory at a command prompt. Type **ESEUTIL /?** for help with the options available.

▶ Manage public information stores. Elements include:

- ▶ Server locations
- ▶ Rehoming of public folders

Part iii

Public folders can be a very important part of any Exchange Server environment. Public folders offer a secure, centrally managed, efficient way to share and collaborate on various types of data.

Once you have created and configured a public folder, created any server-side scripting or collaborative programs necessary, and determined how data should be presented in your public folders, the next task is to determine where those public folders should be physically located. This objective concerns the various tasks and decisions you need to consider when placing public folders within your organization.

Replication

An Exchange Server public folder can exist on multiple servers within your organization. As the administrator, you need to decide which servers should hold a copy of each public folder and how many copies should exist.

The first decision to make is whether to create multiple instances of a folder. Each copy is known as a replica of the folder and the process of keeping those copies synchronized is known as replication. You might create multiple replicas of a given folder for various reasons, including:

Load balancing   If you expect a particular folder to be heavily accessed, you might create replicas to balance the workload over multiple servers. This way no single server must support all client access to the folder.

Fault tolerance   Creating multiple replicas provides fault tolerance to the data in the folder. The failure of a single server will not make the information in the folder inaccessible.

Control network traffic   If you have WAN links in your network, you might place replicas on each side of the link to prevent user access across a slow or expensive line.

WARNING

Having a replica on each side of a WAN link can increase response time for users and can give you a certain amount of control over the traffic generated across the link. But the folders must be synchronized. This means that changes to the data must be sent across the link so that both copies contain the same information.

There are two aspects of public folders that must be replicated throughout your organization: the folder hierarchy and folder content. The hierarchy is a description of the organization of public folders and where they are stored. This information must be synchronized to all Exchange servers that contain a Public Information Store. The folder content is the actual data held within a folder. The folder content is only replicated to servers which are designated to hold a replica of the folder.

Placing a replica of a public folder on a server can be accomplished in two different ways. One way is to push the folder from one server to another. The other is to pull a replica from a source server. The terms *push* and *pull* are used to describe how the replica is placed on a particular server. In a push configuration, one server sends the contents to another. In a pull configuration, one server requests the contents from another. While this might seem like a small distinction, it can be important.

TIP

The terms push and pull can be confusing. They refer to which computer initiates the transfer of data. In a push relationship, the server that stores the data initiates the transfer by sending a change notification to the target. In a pull relationship, the target asks its partner for replication. The bottom line is the same: data is transferred from one copy of the folder to another.

By default, only administrators of the home server of the public folder can create a replica on another server. This gives you control over who can add replicas of a public folder to your organization. You can, however, configure a public folder so that anyone can place a replica on a server to which they have administrative privileges.

Once replicas have been placed, the data must be replicated and kept synchronized between all copies. You can control when this replication traffic is generated. By default, synchronization occurs every 15 minutes. You can set the interval or configure a set schedule for replication of changes.

Client Access

Once public folders have been placed on servers, your next task is configuring which replica users will access. As an example, let's consider a small company using Exchange public folders to hold their employee handbook. The company has defined two sites within the Exchange organization as shown in Figure 15.3. Each site has two servers that will hold a copy of the handbook.

The administrator would like users to access replicas that are located physically near them, both to increase client access performance and to control network traffic. Users don't choose or even know which server's replica they are accessing when they view public folders in their client. There are a number of variables involved in which copy of a public folder a user will access.

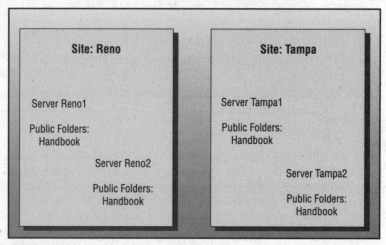

FIGURE 15.3: An example Exchange organization

Server Locations   The administrator can define a logical grouping of servers known as a location. When a user attempts to access a public folder, the client software will first try to access that folder on a server in the same location as the user's home server. This setting allows the administrator to control which users will use which replicas of public folders.

Site Affinity   If a user cannot locate a copy of a public folder within their home site, they may still be able to access a copy stored on a server in another site. To do this, the administrator must have defined an affinity value to the site that contains the public folder. The administrator can associate a different affinity value to each site as a method of controlling which site will be accessed first.

TIP

If an affinity value has not been associated with another site, users from a different site cannot access replicas of public folders located on servers in that site. You can use this fact to eliminate public folder access traffic across your slow or expensive WAN links.

The Process of Choosing a Public Folder

Once the public folder environment has been configured, users will begin to access the data stored in the public folders. The following describes the process used by the client software when determining which replica will be accessed.

1. The public folder server for the client is checked. The public folder server is determined by checking the value of the Public Folder Server attribute of the Private Information Store object of the user's home server.

2. The value of the Server Location attribute of the user's home server is checked, and servers in that location are checked next.

   ▶ If the user has an existing connection to a server in the same location, it is tried first.

   ▶ Then any other servers in the same location are tried in a random order.

3. All other instances within the same site are checked in a random order.

4. Instances in other sites are checked in an order based upon the affinity value associated with each site. The servers in the site with the lowest value are checked first.

   ▶ The servers in each site are randomly selected, until all have been attempted.

   ▶ If two sites have the same affinity value, all of the servers in both sites are pooled together and attempted in a random order.

Rehoming of Public Folders

Each public folder has a home server attribute. This attribute can be used to control which administrators can create replicas of the public server. *Rehoming* a public folder is the process of changing this attribute from one server to another. You must be an administrator of both the home server object and the new home server object within the Exchange Directory to rehome a public folder.

The process is straightforward. Just place a replica of the public folder on the new home server and change the value of the home server attribute for the folder.

Placing a Replica Using the Push Method

To push a replica of a public folder to another folder, access the property pages of that folder. Within the Administrator program, double-click the folder. The folder will be found in the Public Folders container located in the Folders container of the organization.

On the Replicas tab, highlight a server in the Servers list and click Add.

Placing a Replica Using the Pull Method

To pull a replica of a folder to a server, access the property pages of the Public Information Store of that server, found in the Servers container of the appropriate site.

On the Instances tab, highlight the public folder in the Public Folders list and click Add.

Limiting Replica Placement to Administrators of the Home Site

To limit who can create new replicas of a public folder to administrators of that public folder's home site, access the property pages of the public folder within the organization's Public Folders container. On the General tab, select Limit Administrative Access to Home Site.

Setting the Location Value for a Server

To set the value of the location attribute for a server, access the property pages for that server. In the Server Location submenu, either choose an existing location or type in a new one.

Setting Affinity Values to Alternate Sites

Access the property pages for the Information Store Site Configuration object located within the Configuration container of the site. On the Public Folder Affinity tab, choose the site in the left listbox and click Add. Then highlight the appropriate site in the right listbox and enter an affinity value in the Connected Site Cost: field, and click Set Value.

▶ Manage private information stores.

The Private Information Store (IS) contains messages addressed to users. It holds recipient mailboxes and all of their contents. As such, managing the Private Information Store is critical to your organization.

Exchange Server automatically performs the following maintenance tasks on the IS:

▶ Defragmentation

▶ Removal of expired messages

▶ Deletion of indices used to cache folder views

Defragmentation

There are two types of fragmentation that can occur in a database. File fragmentation occurs when the database grows. If no contiguous disk space is available, the file will be fragmented, or placed in different locations on the disk. The file can also become fragmented internally. When a user deletes a message, this frees up space within the file. Exchange will attempt to use the space, but occasionally an area will be so small that it is unusable.

Exchange Server defragments the file on a daily basis by default. The defragmentation process attempts to place the file in contiguous areas of the disk, and cleans up those areas within the file that are unused.

Removal of Expired Messages

When a user deletes a message, Exchange Server can retain the message for retrieval. At a regular interval, Exchange Server will search through the deleted messages for those which have exceeded the Deleted Item Retention Time. By default, this time is set to zero days. Be careful when setting this parameter because a long retention time can result in a large IS database.

Deletion of Indices Created to Cache Folder Views

When a user creates a view to sort the items in a folder, Exchange creates an index of the items for that view. When users switch views frequently, or create complex views of folders, the cached indices can take up considerable space. At a regular interval, the Exchange server deletes the oldest cached indices.

ISINTEG.EXE

Exchange Server includes a command line utility used to repair the IS database. Since the maintenance tasks described earlier are performed

Part iii

automatically based on the IS Maintenance schedule set in Exchange Administrator (by default once each day), you should seldom need to use the ISINTEG.EXE utility.

Use ISINTEG after performing a full restore from backup of the IS database, or if the IS database becomes corrupted so that users are unable to access their messages.

Scheduling the Information Store Maintenance Schedule

The IS maintenance can put a heavy load on your server. You should schedule maintenance at times when your server is not performing some other intense task (like a backup).

Access the properties of the appropriate server using the Administrator program. On the IS Maintenance tab, set the schedule. See Figure 15.4.

If you select Always, the maintenance process will occur every 15 minutes. This option is not recommended because of the overhead it places on the server.

Notice that the default schedule is between 12:00 midnight and 6:00 A.M. each morning. If this overlaps your normal backup time, change the schedule so that maintenance and backups do not occur simultaneously.

Setting the Deleted Item Retention Time

Access the property pages of the Private Information Store object for the appropriate server. On the General tab, enter a time in days that deleted messages should be retained.

Running ISINTEG.EXE

From a command prompt, type **ISINTEG −PATCH** after a full restore from backup.

To fix a damaged IS database, stop the Information Store service, then type **ISINTEG −FIX** at a command prompt.

▶ Back up and restore the Exchange Server organization.

In Chapter 13, we discussed the various methods and techniques of backing up your Exchange server. We also mentioned the various types of databases and log files that make up the Exchange environment and how they affect your backup and restore process.

For this objective, you need to understand the tools and procedures used to back up and restore an Exchange organization.

In Chapter 13, we discussed the four types of backups and what each method backs up. Table 15.2 summarizes this information.

TABLE 15.2: Backup methods

METHOD	ARCHIVE ATTRIBUTE	DESCRIPTION
Full	Reset	All data is backed up each time the backup is run.
Incremental	Reset	A full backup is performed, then for each subsequent backup, all data that has changed since the preceding backup is backed up.
Differential	Reset at full, not reset each day	A full backup is performed, then all data that has changed since the last full backup is backed up for each subsequent backup.
Copy	Not changed	Backs up all data without affecting normal Incremental or Differential rotation. Usually used before making changes to the system or to archive data for specific needs.

We also discussed the various log files used to protect your Information Store databases: Transaction logs, Previous logs, Checkpoint files, Reserved logs, and Patch files.

NOTE

To review backup methods and log files in detail, refer to the Chapter 13 objective "Develop long-term administration strategies." Note especially Table 13.2, which summarizes log files and their uses.

The NT Backup software is used to back up the Exchange organization. To automate the procedure, you can use a series of batch files and the AT.EXE command line utility.

Automating the Exchange Backup Process

By adding switches to the NT Backup tool, you can automate the backup of the Exchange Server services. Creating batch files and using the AT.EXE utility can automate the entire process.

When the Exchange Administrator program is installed on an NT server, the NT Backup utility is extended to support an Exchange Server backup. This extension provides the additional startup switches described in Table 15.3.

TABLE 15.3: NT Backup startup switches

SWITCH	DESCRIPTION
\is \\<server_name>	Backs up the Information Stores on the specified server
\ds \\<server_name>	Backs up the Directory Store on the specified server

WARNING

If you back up your network from central NT servers, you must install the Exchange Administrator program on those computers. This replaces the original Backup utility with one that is Exchange aware. Otherwise, you will not be able to perform an online backup of the Exchange environment.

You can use these command line switches in batch files in combination with the AT.EXE command to fully automate the backup of your Exchange environment. The AT.EXE command allows you to schedule commands and programs to run on an NT computer at a specified time and date. The syntax is as follows:

    AT [\\<computer_name>] time "command"

Where <computer_name> is the NetBIOS name of the computer where you wish the command to run, time is the time at which you wish the command to run, and command is the program you wish to run.

The easiest way to have the backups run every day automatically is to combine the AT command with a batch file.

NOTE

The Scheduler service must be started for the AT command to work. You can have the service start automatically by editing its startup parameters in the services applet, or start it manually from a command prompt by typing NET START SCHEDULE.

Using the Backup Utility

1. In Windows NT, choose Start ➤ Programs ➤ Administrative Tools ➤ Backup.

2. Select any sites you wish to back up. (You can also expand each site and choose which components to back up.)

3. Click Backup. The Backup Operations dialog box will appear.

4. In the Operations box, select Append to add this backup set to the end of the tape or Replace to overwrite what is on the tape.

5. In the Tape Name box, type a name for the tape (this is optional).

6. If you want the backup software to confirm that files were backed up properly, select Verify After Backup.

7. If you want the local Registry backed up, select Backup Local Registry.

8. To secure the tape by limiting access, select Restrict Access to Owner or Administrator.

9. Click Hardware Compression if you want the tape drive to compress the data on the tape.

While the backup is running, the Backup Status dialog box is displayed showing statistics about the current backup.

Using Batch Files and the AT.EXE Command to Automate Backups

To automate the backup process, first create a batch file that starts the process. The sample batch file is shown below:

```
BCK.BAT
```

```
ntbackup backup \is \\<computer_name> /t normal
ntbackup backup \ds \\<computer_name> /t normal
```

This batch file will back up both the Information Stores and directory service on the specified computer.

Then use the AT.EXE command to automatically run the batch file:

```
AT \\<computer_name> time /EVERY:M,T,W,Th,F "<path>\bck.bat"
```

That command will run the backup batch file Monday through Friday at the specified time.

TIP

The AT.EXE command must be reentered each time the computer is restarted. You might want to put it in a batch file and place it in the computer's startup group.

▶ Manage connectivity.

In Chapter 14, we discussed Exchange components used to connect Exchange sites to each other and to foreign e-mail systems. Once installed, these connectors require very little management. There are, however, a few configuration considerations you should know for this objective.

In Chapter 14, we discussed the following connectors:

- ▶ X.400

- ▶ Lotus cc:Mail

- ▶ Microsoft Mail Connector

- ▶ Directory Replication Connector

Each of these connectors is used to transfer information from one server to another or between different e-mail systems. As such, each can impact your network and inter-network infrastructure. This objective concerns the configuration of connectors to reduce the impact on your network and the management of connectors to ensure that your system is operating smoothly.

Managing the Directory Replication Connector

The Directory Replication Connector is responsible for keeping the Directory Services on your Exchange servers synchronized. The administrator can determine which sites will be included and schedule when this synchronization will occur. The administrator can also request an immediate update from remote sites to ensure that the local directory is synchronized with that of the remote site.

Determining Which Attributes to Include in the Synchronization

Each type of recipient in the Exchange hierarchy has a different set of attributes. A mailbox, for instance, includes such attributes as phone numbers, secondary phone numbers, and managers. Often, it is not necessary, or even desirable, to replicate all of this information to remote sites. The Administrator program allows the local administrator to control which attributes will be replicated to remote sites within the Exchange organization.

Determining Which Sites to Include in the Directory Replication Process

In the Exchange Administrator program, access the property pages of the Directory Replication Connector object. It will be found in the Directory Replication container within the Configuration container of the appropriate site.

On the Sites tab, add the sites from which you wish to accept updates to the Inbound Sites list. Add the sites to which you wish to send updates to the Outbound Sites list.

Requesting an Immediate Update from Inbound Sites

In the Exchange Administrator program, access the property pages of the Directory Replication Connector object. It will be found in the Directory Replication container within the Configuration container of the appropriate site.

On the Sites tab, highlight the inbound site you wish to request an update from and click the Request Now button.

Scheduling the Directory Replication Process

In the Exchange Administrator program, access the property pages of the Directory Replication Connector object. It will be found in the Directory Replication container within the Configuration container of the

Part iii

appropriate site. On the Schedule tab, choose the type of schedule you wish to configure.

Your choices are:

Never   This disables the Directory Replication Connector.

Always   An update will be performed every 15 minutes.

Selected times   Highlight the times you wish an update to be performed.

TIP

Avoid the Always choice if possible. It can place a heavy load on both the server and the network due to the frequency of the process. When selecting times, balance your need for an up-to-date address list with available bandwidth.

Controlling the Attributes Included in the Update Process

In the Exchange Administrator program, access the property pages of the DS Site Configuration object. It will be found in the Configuration container of the appropriate site.

On the Attributes tab, you can determine which attributes will be replicated for all e-mail recipients, or configure the list for each type of recipient by using the Show Attributes For: submenu.

To change the list for replication between sites, highlight Inter-site Replication on the Configure list, and select those attributes you wish to replicate.

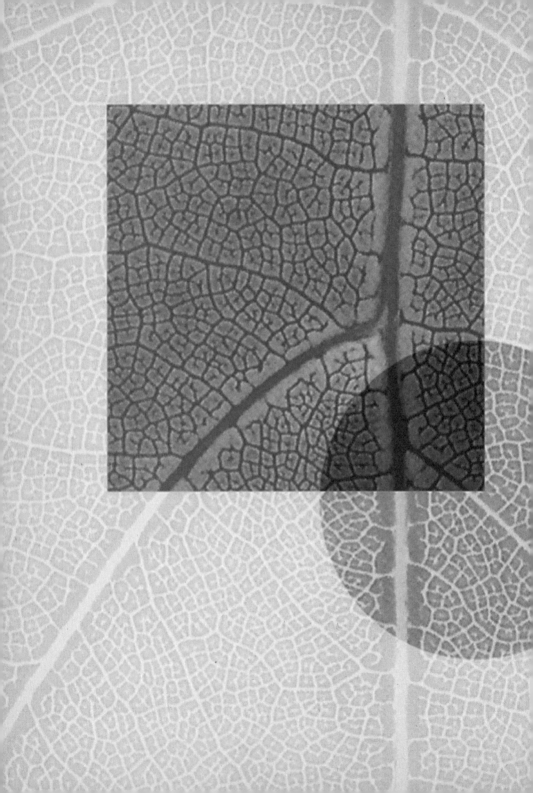

Chapter 16

MONITORING AND OPTIMIZATION

O nce you add Exchange to your company's system, you'll soon find that it becomes critical to the way your company does business. The many advantages that Exchange offers can also be its biggest drawback, as the company becomes dependent upon Exchange for much of its business communication.

E-mail becomes the primary method of communication (both internally and with external customers), public folders become the primary source of employee information, and the Internet becomes a major path of contact with traveling users. All in all, the loss of a single Exchange server can affect the productivity of hundreds of employees.

Given the importance of your messaging system, it is no wonder that one of your primary job functions will be the monitoring and optimization of your Exchange servers. You need to

Adapted from *MCSE Exam Notes: Exchange Server 5.5* by Robert King

ISBN 0-7821-2302-3   368 pages $19.99

ensure that your servers are up and running, and that they are performing at peak efficiency.

The objectives of this chapter concern the tools available both to monitor your Exchange environment and to optimize its performance.

▶ Configure a link monitor and a server monitor.

For a messaging system to be worthwhile, it must be up and running and able to communicate with all of its components. On the MCSE exam, this objective concerns the tools available to test these two conditions.

Link monitors and server monitors are two very basic tools for monitoring and optimizing your Exchange environment. Link monitors are used to check the connections between Exchange servers as well as the connections with foreign e-mail systems. Server monitors are used to check periodically that the Exchange services are running on a server.

Link Monitors

Link monitors can be used to ensure that the message transport is working between two Exchange servers or between an Exchange server and a foreign e-mail system. The link monitor periodically sends a message to the system being monitored. If a response is received, then the link is functional. All in all, this is a simple process.

When a link monitor is configured between two Exchange servers, the MTA sends a message to the MTA of the remote server. The remote MTA will recognize the purpose of the message and return a message to the MTA of the originating server. If a link monitor is configured to test the connection between an Exchange server and a foreign messaging system, you must provide an e-mail address for a nonexistent recipient on the foreign system. If the foreign system receives the message it will return a non-delivery report (NDR). If an NDR is received, it can be assumed that the communication channel is operational.

While setting up a link monitor is a straightforward process, there are a few configuration parameters that you need to know.

Polling Interval   The polling interval can be set to control how often the monitor sends messages to check connections. There are two intervals that can be set: normal and critical. The normal interval is the amount of time (in minutes) between messages sent to check the connection. If no response is received in a specified time the connection enters a warning or critical state. (These states will be explained later in this section.) Once a connection has entered the warning or critical state, the frequency of messages switches to the critical interval.

Bounce Return Time   The link monitor waits for a response to a message for a specified time before changing the state of the connection from normal to either warning or alert. The default bounce message return times are 30 minutes to enter the warning state and 60 minutes to enter the alert state.

Notification   The link monitor can be configured to take an action when a connection has been in either the warning or critical state for a specified period of time. There are three types of actions available:

Launch a process   You can select a file to execute. You might, for example, have the link monitor run a program that pages you.

Mail message   You can choose a recipient to receive an Exchange e-mail message.

Windows NT Alert   You can have an NT Alert message sent to a particular computer.

Server Monitors

Server monitors are used to check the condition of servers in a site. Problem notification occurs if a service fails to start or shuts down, if clients cannot connect to the server, or if the server is not on the network. Server monitors can be configured to take an action when an alert state is reached, such as restarting the computer with the problem. Server monitors can also synchronize the clocks of two servers.

The server monitor periodically checks the status of configured services on Windows NT servers within your organization. There are no special permissions necessary to check the status, but the appropriate permissions must be granted to the site service account in order to restart the computer or synchronize its clock.

Configuring a server monitor is straightforward, but there are a few configuration parameters that you should understand.

Polling Interval   The polling interval can be set to control how often the monitor checks a server. By default, configured servers will be checked at 15-minute intervals. You can configure a different interval for servers that have entered the critical state.

Notification   The server monitor can be configured to take an action when a connection has been in either the warning or critical state for a specified period of time. The three types of actions available to server monitors are the same as those available on link monitors: Launch a process, Mail message, and Windows NT Alert.

Actions   You can configure the server monitor to take an action when a service has been stopped on a configured server. The server monitor can respond in one of the following ways:

Take no action   This is basically a wait state. The server monitor will take no action when it discovers that a service is not responding.

Restart the service   The server monitor will attempt to restart the service on the monitored server.

Restart the computer   The server monitor will attempt to restart the monitored computer.

You have the option of configuring one of these actions on the first failed attempt to communicate with the monitored service, the second attempt, and each subsequent attempt.

A typical scenario would be to configure the monitor to take the following steps:

▶ Take no action on the first failed attempt. The server or service might have been too busy to respond in a timely manner or might be automatically correcting the problem.

▶ Restart the service on the second failed attempt. This option might not affect other processes running on the server.

▶ Restart the server on subsequent attempts. If the service does not respond to three attempts you can have the server monitor restart the server to reinitialize it.

You can create a restart message that will be displayed on the computer which is about to be restarted by the server monitor and you can set the length of time that the message will be displayed before the computer is restarted.

Time Synchronization   Certain Exchange functions are time critical. Each message, for instance, receives a time stamp. For time-critical functions, it is important that servers be set to the same time. A server monitor can synchronize the clocks of remote servers to that of the server hosting the server monitor. You can choose whether to have the server monitor place itself in a warning or critical state (and perform the action specified for these states), or to have the server monitor attempt to synchronize the clocks if they differ by a specified amount of time.

Configuring a Link Monitor

To create a link monitor, choose New Other from the File menu in the Exchange Administrator program. On the next menu, choose Link Monitor. Link monitors must be created in the Monitors container. If you are not already working in this container, you will be asked if you want to switch to that location in the hierarchy.

There are six property pages for a link monitor: General, Permissions, Notification, Servers, Recipients, and Bounce. Each page (tab) allows the configuration of a different aspect of the link monitor.

Configuring the General Page   On the General page, you configure the directory name, display name, and the location of the log files that contain the log, status information, and resulting notifications.

You also configure the polling interval from this page. The polling interval controls how often a message is sent to test the link.

Configuring the Permissions Page   On this page, you configure which users can manage the link monitor object in the Exchange hierarchy.

Configuring the Notification Page   On the Notification page, you configure who will be notified and how they will be notified in the event of a problem. There are three actions that can be configured: Launch a Process, Mail Message, or Windows NT Alert. In each case, there is an Alert Only option. If this option is selected, the action only takes place if the link is in an alert state. If it is not selected, the action occurs when the link goes into either a warning or an alert state.

> ▶ **Configuring the Launch Process Option**   The Launch Process page is shown in Figure 16.1. The following options must be entered on the Launch Process page:

Time Delay   Enter the length of time the link should be in the alert or warning state before activating the process.

Launch Process   Enter the path to the executable (or browse to it using the File button).

Command Line Parameters   Enter any parameters needed by the executable.

Append Notification Text to Parameter List   Adds notification text to the command line parameters.

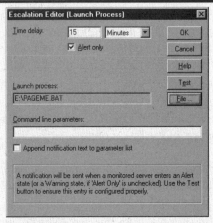

FIGURE 16.1:   Escalation Editor (Launch Process)

▶ **Configuring the Mail Message Option**   This option will send an Exchange e-mail message to a selected mailbox. The only new option is to choose the recipient of the message.

▶ **Configuring the Windows NT Alert Option**   The Windows NT Alert page is shown in Figure 16.2. An NT administrative alert (a pop-up dialog box) will be sent to the selected computer. Enter the NetBIOS name of the computer to which the alert should be sent.

Configuring the Servers Page   Configure which servers should be monitored by the link monitor. The servers must be in your organization but can be in different sites. Add the servers by highlighting them and clicking on the Add button.

Configuring the Recipients Page   Configure the link to check other Exchange organizations or foreign systems. The monitor will check for replies to the message. Specify a recipient that does not exist on the other system so that a non-delivery report will be generated.

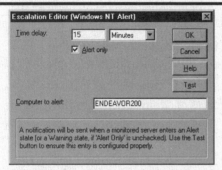

FIGURE 16.2: Escalation Editor (Windows NT Alert)

Configure a recipient using the Message Subject Returned From list, if you know that the system will return an NDR with the original subject text in the reply subject field. Use the Message Subject or Body Returned From list if you are not sure what format the NDR will take.

Using the Message Subject Returned From list is quicker since the entire message does not need to be scanned.

Configuring the Bounce Page   This page allows you to configure the maximum acceptable time for a return message to be sent back in reply to a link monitor message.

Configuring a Server Monitor

To create a server monitor, choose New Other from the File menu in the Exchange Administrator program. On the next menu, choose Server Monitor. Server monitors must be created in the Monitors container. If you are not already working in this container, you will be asked if you want to switch to that location in the hierarchy.

There are six property pages for a server monitor: General, Permissions, Notification, Servers, Actions, and Clock. The General, Permissions, and Notification pages for a server monitor are identical to the corresponding property pages of a link monitor. The Servers page includes an additional option. And, in place of the Recipients and Bounce pages on the link monitor, the server monitor includes an Actions page and a Clock page. The configuration of all six pages is summarized below.

General page Configure the directory name, display name, location of the log file, and the polling intervals.

Permissions page Configure which users can manage the server monitor object in the Exchange hierarchy.

Notification page The notification options available for a server monitor are the same as those available for a link monitor: Launch a Process, Mail Message, and Windows NT Alert.

Servers page The process of adding a server to the list to be monitored by a server monitor is identical to the process for a link monitor. There is the additional option of choosing a service to monitor on the target server. Click the Services button, and then add or remove services from the Monitored Services list.

Actions page Configure the action that should be taken in the event that a service has stopped. There are three options available: take no action, restart the service, and restart the computer. You can also configure a message to appear on the screen of the target server in the event that the server monitor must restart it.

Clock page Configure the allowable time differences between the server running the monitor and the target server. You can have the monitor either enter a warning or alert state depending on the time difference and also, if desired, have the monitor synchronize the clocks of the two servers.

NOTE

Be sure you are very familiar with the procedures involved in configuring these two monitors. These skills are mandatory knowledge for both the MCSE examination and your career.

▶ Optimize Exchange Server. Tasks include:

- ▶ Hardware optimization
- ▶ Operating system optimization

In Chapter 13, we discussed the hardware necessary for an Exchange server. For this objective, you use that information and an optimization tool named PERFWIZ.EXE to optimize your use of the hardware and the NT operating system.

The MCSE exam questions on this objective concern the use of a PERF-WIZ administrative wizard to optimize both the use of your hardware and the operating system to improve the performance of your Exchange server.

Before you can really optimize your hardware or operating system you must understand the components that have the greatest effect on your Exchange server environment. While every component of your hardware has some effect on performance, certain components have a greater effect than others.

CPU   The type and number of CPUs dictate, to a large extent, your Exchange server performance. Obviously, the better the processor, the better the overall performance. Exchange is a multithreaded application so it can take full advantage of multi-processor servers.

Memory   Microsoft Windows NT uses a virtual memory system in which data can be swapped between physical memory and hard drive space. The process of moving data between the two is known as demand paging. When a process, such as an Exchange service, needs more memory than is available, NT will swap data between memory and a temporary paging file located on a hard disk. If most of the frequently used data can't fit in physical memory, excessive paging can occur. Excessive paging, or *thrashing,* can cause unacceptable performance. One way to reduce the amount of paging is to add more RAM to the server. Another is to optimize the placement of the temporary paging file. Placing the file on a physical disk that is not overly utilized or splitting the paging file across multiple disks can also enhance performance.

I/O subsystem   The type and number of disk controllers and drives, and the choices you make for fault tolerant configuration can greatly affect the performance and the recoverability of your Exchange environment. In Chapter 15, we discussed the various log files used by Exchange Server to protect its databases. Moving these files to a physical disk, other than the one the database is stored on, can make restoring after a disaster easier.

Network hardware   Since clients access Exchange services through the network and Exchange servers use the network to communicate with each other and with foreign e-mail systems, the efficiency of your network can have a large effect on the overall performance. Consider the adapter types, cabling, routers and all of the other components that make up the network.

Other factors   Remember that all of the processes running on your Exchange servers affect overall performance. If your Exchange server also acts as a DHCP, WINS, or DNS server, consider moving those services to another NT server in your network.

Performance Optimizer (PERFWIZ.EXE)

Now that we have considered the various components that have an effect on the performance of your Exchange server, we can discuss a tool available to optimize your Exchange server automatically. The Performance Optimizer is an administrative wizard that analyzes your server's hardware and then makes suggestions to improve performance.

The Performance Optimizer should be run as part of the Exchange installation process (it can be started automatically at the end of the installation) and any time you change a server's hardware configuration. For example, you should run the Performance Optimizer after changing the amount of RAM, adding a disk controller, adding a microprocessor, changing the disk configuration, adding or removing any component on the server, or changing the number of users that a server will support.

Before running the Performance Optimizer, optimize your disk subsystem. Microsoft recommends the following disk configuration for an Exchange server:

▶ A physical disk containing the operating system and page file

▶ A physical disk for the Exchange transaction log files

▶ A stripe set consisting of multiple physical disks for all other Exchange server components

So that it can correctly analyze the hardware on the server, Performance Optimizer must stop the Exchange Server services. By default, PERFWIZ.EXE asks for certain information:

▶ The number of users that the server will support

- ▶ The services that will run on the server

- ▶ The number of users in the entire Exchange organization

- ▶ The amount of memory the Exchange Server software should use

The Performance Optimizer will test the speed and capacity of your hard drives and confirm the amount of memory available. It will combine this analysis with the information you provided to suggest changes to your configuration to increase performance.

The Performance Optimizer can also be run in a verbose mode which allows you to provide more information about how you want your system configured. While a complete discussion of all of the configuration parameters available is beyond the scope of this text, you should be familiar with the following:

- ▶ Threads are considered processes. The more threads a service has, the more tasks it can perform.

- ▶ Buffers are temporary holding places for data.

- ▶ Caches are similar to buffers, although they usually hold data for a specific amount of time.

Running PERFWIZ.EXE

The Performance Optimizer is located in the BIN subdirectory of the Exchange Server directory. In the Run dialog box, type:

```
<DRIVE:>\EXCHSRVR\BIN\PERFWIZ
```

(Add the −V parameter for more configuration options.)

This can also be run from the startup shortcut: Start ➤ Programs ➤ Microsoft Exchange ➤ Microsoft Exchange Optimizer.

You will be presented with a welcome screen. Click Next to continue. The program will then stop your Exchange services. You will be presented with the dialog box shown in Figure 16.3.

In this dialog box, you provide an estimate of the number of users on this server, select the services that the server will perform, and provide an estimate of the total number of users in your organization. When you click Next, the Performance Optimizer will analyze your hard disk drives in order to determine the best locations for the Exchange Server files. You will be presented with a dialog box informing you that Performance Optimizer has completed its analysis. Click Next to continue.

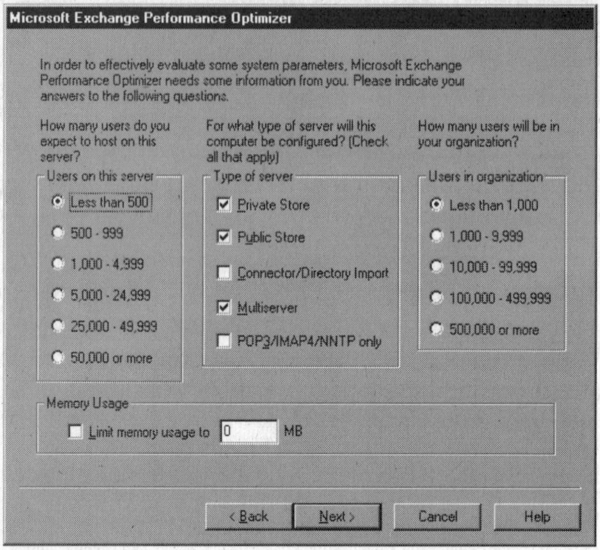

FIGURE 16.3: Microsoft Exchange Performance Optimizer questions

Based upon the analysis, Performance Optimizer will make suggestions as to the placement of various Exchange files.

Click Next and you will be presented with another dialog box asking if the files should be moved automatically. Click Next to continue. Lastly, you will be asked if the Exchange services should be restarted.

Using the –V Command Line Switch

If you use the –V command line parameter when starting Performance Optimizer, you will be asked to provide more information. Before the disk analysis, for instance, you will be presented with a list of the hard drives on your system. You can exclude drives from consideration during the optimization.

After the disk analysis is complete, you will be presented with a detailed report of disk performance.

The items included in the report are:

RA   The average time for random disk access

SEQ   The average time for sequential disk access

Smaller numbers mean better performance.

You will also be presented with six screens filled with various advanced parameters that you can configure to optimize your Exchange server. A full discussion of the options is beyond the scope of this examination.

► Optimize foreign connections and site-to-site connections.

This objective is a reinforcement of the materials covered in the following two objectives from Chapter 14:

- ► Configure the message transfer agent within a site.

- ► Configure the message transfer agent among sites.

Review the materials presented in Chapter 14, paying close attention to the parameters discussed in Tables 14.4–14.7.

► Monitor and optimize the messaging environment.

There are two distinct parts to this objective: monitoring the various components that make up the messaging environment and optimizing the connections between servers, sites, and foreign e-mail systems.

Monitoring is done through a process called *diagnostic logging,* and optimization is accomplished through a series of configuration parameters on connectors.

The critical information for this objective is divided into two parts: monitoring and optimization.

Monitoring the Messaging Environment

Many Exchange components offer the option of monitoring their activities by performing diagnostic logging. Once enabled, diagnostic logging will begin documenting events in the Windows NT Event Log. The following Exchange components include the ability to log their activities:

- ► Directory Service

- ► Directory Synchronization

- ► Information Store

- ► Internet Mail Service

- ▶ Key Management Server

- ▶ Message Transfer Agent

- ▶ Microsoft Exchange Connector for Lotus cc:Mail

- ▶ Microsoft Mail Connector

- ▶ Microsoft Schedule+ Free/Busy Connector

- ▶ IMAP4

- ▶ NNTP

- ▶ POP3

Each component offers different categories of actions that can be logged. In most cases you will probably not want to log all events generated by a particular category of a specific service. You can set the level of events that will be logged to one of four settings:

None   Only critical events, error events, and events with a logging level of zero are logged. This is the default logging level for all categories of all services.

Minimum   Logs events with a logging level of 1 or lower. These are usually significant events such as the failure of the component to carry out its regular tasks.

Medium   Logs events with a logging level of 3 or less. These are usually moderately important events such as the receipt of messages across a gateway.

Maximum   Logs events with a logging level of 5 or less. Many of these events will only be of interest to developers or support technicians.

Categories of Logged Events   Tables 16.1–16.4 summarize the categories of events that can be logged on a few of the Exchange components that include a logging option.

These tables are included as a guide to the types of parameters that can be tracked. Do not try to memorize each of them. You are not required to know any particular diagnostic parameters—just to have a general feel for them.

TABLE 16.1: Diagnostic categories for the Directory Service

CATEGORY	DESCRIPTION OF TYPES OF EVENTS LOGGED
Knowledge Consistency Checker	Events related to replication links between servers and sites
Security	Events related to Windows NT security
EXDS Interface	Communication between the directory and the Information Store, MTA, and Administrator program
MAPI Interface	Communication between MAPI clients and the directory
Replication	Events related to the Directory Replication process
Garbage Collection	Events related to the deletion of objects
Internal Configuration	Events related to the Registry and configuration variables
Directory Access	Events related to reads and writes of directory objects
Internal Processing	Events related to the internal operation of Exchange. Errors in this category are indicative of a serious problem.
LDAP Interface	Events related to clients accessing the directory using LDAP
Initialization/Termination	Events related to starting and stopping the directory
Service Control	NT Control Panel service events
Name Resolution	Resolution of addresses and directory names
Backup	Backup and restoration of the directory database
Field Engineering	Internal debugging events
Address Book Views	Events related to the validity of the entries in each Address Book view

Part iii

TABLE 16.2: Diagnostic categories for the Internet Mail Service

CATEGORY	DESCRIPTION OF TYPES OF EVENTS LOGGED
Initialization/Termination	Events related to the starting and stopping of IMS
Addressing	Address resolution
Message Transfer	Message queue operations
SMTP Interface Events	Interactions with SMTP hosts
Internal Processing	Operation of the IMS service
SMTP Protocol Log	Monitors the protocol conversations that occur during SMTP connections
Message Archival	Archives the text of messages

TABLE 16.3: Diagnostic category for Directory synchronization

CATEGORY	DESCRIPTION OF TYPES OF EVENTS LOGGED
MSExchangeDX	Events generated by directory synchronization with MS Mail

TABLE 16.4: Diagnostic categories for the Message Transfer Agent

CATEGORY	DESCRIPTION OF TYPES OF EVENTS LOGGED
X.400 Service	X.400 protocol events
Resource	MTA resources
Security	Security violations
Interface	Communication among MTA components and between MTAs
Field Engineering	Internal debugging
MTA Administration	Administrator program access to MTA queues and routing information
Configuration	Internal parameters
Directory Access	MTA's use of the directory
Operating System	MTA's use of NT functions
Interoperability	Logs the binary content of protocol messages

Optimizing the Messaging Environment

This topic was discussed in Chapter 14 for the two objectives concerned with configuring the Message Transfer Agent. In that chapter, we looked at the various parameters for configuring the MTA between servers and between sites.

NOTE

As you prepare for the MCSE exam, be sure and review the parameters discussed in Tables 14.4–14.7 of Chapter 14.

As shown in Figure 16.4, there are four main categories of parameters available for MTA configuration.

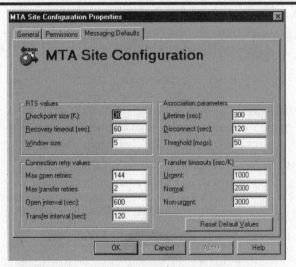

FIGURE 16.4: MTA configuration parameters

Reliable Transfer Service (RTS) values Control the verification of data during a transfer.

Association parameters Used to configure the associations, or paths, opened to other systems.

Connection retry values Control how many times the system should attempt to reopen failed connections.

Transfer timeouts Control how different priorities of messages are handled.

Enabling Diagnostic Logging

For each of the services, access the property pages in the Exchange Administrator and click on the Diagnostics Logging tab. Highlight a category of event and choose a logging level. You can select multiple categories (Shift-select or Ctrl-select) to change the logging levels of all of them at once.

► Monitor server performance by using SNMP and MADMAN MIB.

As your network grows and you add more services to your environment (like Exchange Server), management becomes more and more complicated. The Simple Network Management Protocol (SNMP) was created to allow remote management of network devices and software.

While a complete understanding of SNMP is not necessary for this examination, you should be familiar with a few of the basic concepts of the protocol.

SNMP Concepts

SNMP is aptly named: *Simple* Network Management Protocol. The protocol defines four actions that management tools can take against a target device:

Get   Query the device for information.

Get next   Query the device for the next piece of information.

Set   Change the value of a configuration parameter.

Trap   Set a threshold for a parameter and send a message to a management console if that threshold is met or exceeded.

Using these four actions, SNMP management software can perform some sophisticated management functions.

Each SNMP device or piece of software has a defined list of parameters that can be accessed using the SNMP protocol. These parameters are defined in a database known as a Management Information Base (MIB). MIBs follow an industry-standard format and are the backbone of SNMP functionality. Microsoft Exchange Server complies with RFC 1566, which defines the MIB format for SNMP Mail and Directory Management (also known as the MADMAN MIB).

Microsoft Exchange Server supports the MADMAN MIB in a unique manner. Exchange Server includes a series of tools which make the various Exchange-specific Performance Monitor objects and counters available as MIB objects. The technique actually exceeds the specifications defined in RFC 1566. What this means is that any Exchange counter which you can track using Performance Monitor can also be tracked using an SNMP management utility.

MIB Concepts

You can use any SNMP version 1 compatible management console to view the Exchange Server MIB. For some consoles, you may need to load the MIB file for object descriptions. This file is located on the Microsoft Exchange Server compact disk in the SUPPORT\SNMP\<PLATFORM>\ EXCHANGE.MIB file.

As explained earlier, MIBs define the parameters available to an SNMP management console. Each parameter is given a unique identification value, known as its object ID, which is used to access it. Object IDs are registered with the International Standards Organization (ISO). The ISO Object ID of the Exchange MIB is:

```
.ISO.ORG.DOD.INTERNET.PRIVATE.ENTERPRISES.MICROSOFT.SOFT-
WARE.SYSTEMS.OS.WINNT.PERFORMANCE.MSEXCHANGEMTA
```

Your SNMP management software will use a numeric interpretation of this ID to communicate with your Exchange server. The numeric representation is:

```
.1.3.6.1.4.1.311.1.1.3.1.1.1
```

The object ID above identifies the overall MIB—each parameter available appends a unique value to this ID. The Performance Monitor counters that map to the MIB objects described in RFC 1566 are detailed in Table 16.5.

RFC 1566 also describes a concept of MTA groups. In Exchange, each connection maintained by the MTA (e.g., to the Private Information Store, Public Information Store, or external connectors) is considered to be an MTA group for SNMP monitoring purposes. MTA group values are exposed through the MTA Connections Performance Monitor object. Table 16.6 lists the counters within the MTA Connections Performance Monitor object and how they are mapped to the RFC 1566 MTA group MIB objects.

TABLE 16.5: Exchange Performance Monitor MTA and IMS Object counters and their corresponding RFC 1566 MIB objects

MIB Object	MSExchangeIMS Counter	MSExchangeMTA Counter
MTAReceivedMessages	Inbound Messages Total	Inbound Messages Total
MTAStoredMessages	Total Messages Queued	Work Queue Length
MTATransmittedMessages	Outbound Messages Total	Outbound Messages Total
MTAReceivedVolume	Inbound Bytes Total	Inbound Bytes Total
MTAStoredVolume	Total Bytes Queued	Work Queue Bytes
MTATransmittedVolume	Outbound Bytes Total	Outbound Bytes Total
MTAReceivedRecipients	Total Recipients Inbound	Total Recipients Inbound
MTAStoredRecipients	Total Recipients Queued	Total Recipients Queued
MTATransmittedRecipients	Total Recipients Outbound	Total Recipients Outbound
MTASuccessfulConverted-Messages	Total Successful Conversions	Total Successful Conversions
MTAFailedConvertedMessages	Total Failed Conversions	Total Failed Conversions
MTALoopsDetected	Total Loops Detected	Total Loops Detected

TABLE 16.6: Exchange MTA Connections Performance Monitor object counters and their corresponding RFC 1566 MTA group MIB objects

MIB Object	MSExchangeMTA Connections Counter
MTAGroupReceivedMessages	Inbound Messages Total
MTAGroupRejectedMessages	Inbound Rejected Total
MTAGroupStoredMessages	Queue Length
MTAGroupTransmittedMessages	Outbound Messages Total
MTAGroupReceivedVolume	Inbound Bytes Total
MTAGroupStoredVolume	Queued Bytes
MTAGroupTransmittedVolume	Outbound Bytes Total
MTAGroupReceivedRecipients	Total Recipients Inbound
MTAGroupStoredRecipients	Total Recipients Queued

TABLE 16.6 continued: Exchange MTA Connections Performance Monitor object counters and their corresponding RFC 1566 MTA group MIB objects

MIB OBJECT	MSEXCHANGEMTA CONNECTIONS COUNTER
MTAGroupTransmittedRecipients	Total Recipients Outbound
MTAGroupOldestMessageStored	Oldest Message Queued (seconds)
MTAGroupInboundAssociations	Current Inbound Associations
MTAGroupOutboundAssociations	Current Outbound Associations
MTAGroupAccumulatedInbound-Associations	Cumulative Inbound Associations
MTAGroupAccumulatedOutbound-Associations	Cumulative Outbound Associations
MTAGroupLastInboundActivity	Last Inbound Association (seconds)
MTAGroupLastOutboundActivity	Last Outbound Association (seconds)
MTAGroupRejectedInbound-Associations	Rejected Inbound Associations (seconds)
MTAGroupFailedOutbound-Associations	Failed Outbound Associations
MTAGroupInboundRejectionReason	Outbound Connect Failure Reason
MTAGroupScheduledRetry	Next Association Retry

Installing the Windows NT SNMP Agent

Run the Network applet found in Control Panel. On the Services tab, click the Add button. In the Select Network Service dialog box, highlight SNMP Service and click OK.

You will be presented with the Microsoft SNMP Properties dialog box. Here you can configure various aspects of the SNMP service.

The SNMP Agent can be configured to send traps to a particular SNMP community and host ID. You can also set security options that limit which hosts may manage the server.

WARNING

If your server has any service pack installed, remember that any time you add a new service, you must reinstall the service pack.

Part iii

Adding the Exchange MIB

If you have not added any other MIB on your server other than those included with Windows NT, run the batch file included on the Microsoft Exchange Server CD-ROM.

At a command prompt run:

```
<D:>\Support\SNMP\<platform>\Install.bat
```

(where D: is your CD-ROM drive and <platform> represents the type of hardware you are using).

If you have already installed an MIB on your server you must perform the following procedure instead of using the batch file:

1. At a command prompt, run the PERF2MIB command to create the PERFMIB.MIB and PERFMIB.INI files. This creates the files necessary to add the Exchange Performance Monitor counters available to SNMP access.

2. Run the MIBCC command to create a MIB.BIN file. This will add the parameters from the PERFMIB.BIN and PERFMIB .INI files to your current MIB.BIN file.

3. Copy PERFMIB.Dll, PERFMIB.INI, and MIB.BIN to the System32 directory.

4. Run the REGINI command to configure the registry with the SNMP values.

5. Restart the SNMP service by using the Services applet in Control Panel.

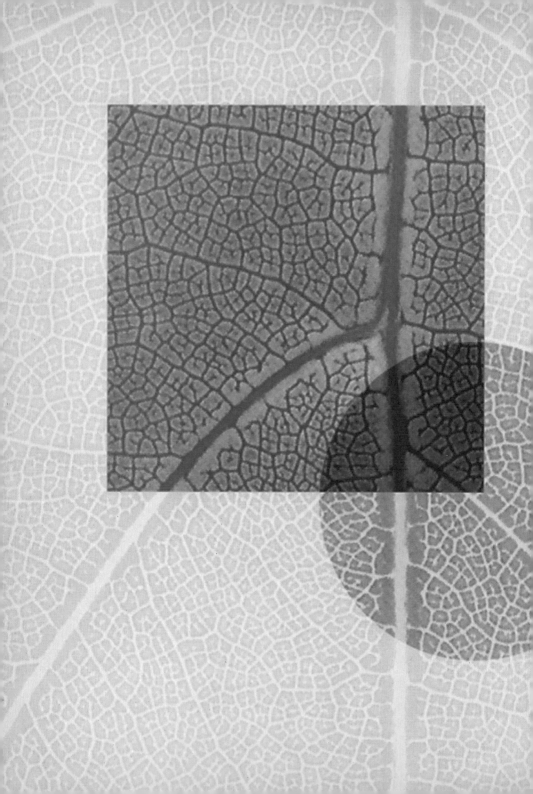

Chapter 17

TROUBLESHOOTING

No matter how carefully you carry out all the procedures covered in previous chapters—planning your Exchange environment in detail, installing and configuring your servers and Exchange organization precisely to plan, controlling access to resources, and studiously monitoring and optimizing your Exchange system—you will still have to troubleshoot problems!

The objectives for this chapter consist of a series of small sections, each of which pertains to a particular type of troubleshooting skill.

No one becomes a great troubleshooter overnight. Half the battle, however, is knowing the correct methods for troubleshooting the problems that can occur. The skills covered in this chapter are skills that will serve you well, both on the test and in your career.

Adapted from *MCSE Exam Notes: Exchange Server 5.5* by Robert King

ISBN 0-7821-2302-3   368 pages $19.99

Diagnose and resolve upgrade problems.

Upgrading your Exchange servers from an earlier version of Exchange to version 5.5 is a fairly straightforward process, if you follow the procedures outlined in Chapter 13. There are, however, a few common problems that you might encounter.

Odds are you will need to perform an Exchange upgrade at some point in your career. Microsoft is continually improving the Exchange Server software and you need to keep your environment up to date with the latest releases of software. From a sales perspective, Microsoft would also like to see you purchase and install the latest releases of all of their products. The MCSE exam reflects this philosophy. In other words, you need to know the available upgrade options to be successful on the test.

WARNING

Before implementing any major change to your environment you should perform and verify a complete backup of your Exchange system. An upgrade definitely qualifies as a major change. With a good backup set in hand, you can always return to the original configuration while you are troubleshooting any upgrade problems you might encounter.

Interference from Other Processes

Before beginning the upgrade process, ensure that you have unloaded any other programs that might be running on the server you are upgrading. Other programs can (and often do) interfere with the upgrade program. If your server also acts as your Web server, for instance, you should stop all Web services before upgrading the Exchange software. Another example would be any programs that run continuously in the background, such as anti-virus programs.

Server Monitor Problems

As discussed in Chapter 16, server monitors can be configured to check various services loaded on an Exchange server and to take action if those services are not running. The server monitor can be configured to attempt to restart the service or to restart the computer if a particular service does not respond.

The upgrade program stops Exchange Server services as it upgrades the software. If a server monitor has been configured to take an action on that server, it could attempt to restart those services (or to reboot the server) during the upgrade process. At best this would cause the upgrade process to fail, but it is conceivable that files could be corrupted if it were to occur at the wrong point in the upgrade process.

Disable any server monitors that are configured to monitor the Exchange server that you are upgrading.

Schema Mismatch

As discussed earlier, the Exchange Directory is a hierarchical database. The structure of that database is defined in a *schema*. The schema defines the list of properties for each object that can exist in the database. If for some reason the schema did not match between all servers, one server might contain configuration information that another server did not understand.

There are some major differences between the schema of Exchange 4.0 and Exchange 5.5. Before an upgrade can be performed, the schema of all Exchange 4.0 servers must be updated to match that of Exchange 5.5. This is accomplished by applying the Exchange Server 4.0 Service Pack 2 (SP2). There are two ways to accomplish this task.

The preferred method is to install the service pack to all of your Exchange 4.0 servers before beginning the upgrade process. This ensures that the directory database is consistent across your entire organization. The service pack also installs new versions of various other tools on all of your older servers.

Another method is to install SP2 on your bridgehead servers for each site and then to wait until directory replication has occurred before beginning your upgrades. During the directory replication process the new schema are applied to each server in the site.

Insufficient Disk Space for Fault-Tolerant Upgrade

When upgrading from Exchange Server 5.0, you have two upgrade options available: standard and fault tolerant. The standard upgrade option upgrades your Exchange databases in the current location. If the upgrade fails, you will have to restore those databases from your backup.

The fault-tolerant upgrade option backs up each database before the upgrade and then upgrades those backup files. If the upgrade process fails, the Exchange databases are untouched in their original locations. While this method of upgrade is safer, it does require at least twice as much disk space as the original size of your Information Store on the local server.

NOTE

The fault-tolerant upgrade method is not available when upgrading from version 4.0.

When the disk space is available, the fault-tolerant upgrade method is the preferred upgrade option.

Insufficient Hardware

Exchange Server 5.5 has many options that were not available in version 4.0. Before beginning the upgrade process, review the hardware requirements listed in Chapter 13 and ensure that your existing hardware will meet your needs.

▶ Diagnose and resolve server installation problems.

As with upgrades, most Exchange Server installations are quick and painless. On those rare occasions where problems do occur, you need to know the common fixes and tools used for troubleshooting.

For this objective, we will discuss two of the more common problems that can develop during an Exchange installation and two important tools for troubleshooting more complex problems.

Site Service Account Problems

The most common problem encountered during an Exchange installation is an incorrectly configured site service account. Remember that all servers within a site must use the same site service account and that this account must be granted the following set of rights:

- ▶ Act as part of the operating system.

- ▶ Log on as a service.

- ▶ Restore files and directories.

The installation program should make these security assignments automatically, but if there is a problem this is one area to check. Make sure that any other network administrators are aware of these needs and are instructed not to make changes to this account.

The site service account should also be configured so that its password never expires and so that the user cannot change the password. Also remember to clear the User Must Change Password at Next Logon box when creating the account.

Exchange Share Point Problems

As discussed in Chapter 14, the Exchange installation process creates a series of share points on your server. Exchange may not function properly if these share points are disabled. If Exchange seems to install correctly, but not all functions seem to work correctly, check to ensure that all of the share points were created correctly.

Checking That Exchange Server Services Are Running

Use the Services applet (found in the Control Panel) to ensure that all of the Exchange services have started properly. If not, try starting the stopped service manually. If it still doesn't start, read the error message and check the event log for additional clues to the problem.

Diagnostic Tools

When the installation process does not go as planned, you need to know which tools are available to help in diagnosing the problem. Two tools are available: the NT Event Viewer and a SETUP log file created by the installation process.

NT Event Viewer   If there are any problems with the Exchange boot process, alert messages will be written to the NT event log. These messages can be extremely helpful when troubleshooting an Exchange problem. When using the event log to diagnose an Exchange problem, keep the following in mind:

- ▶ Exchange writes its messages to the Application Log.

- ▶ Don't stop reading after the first error—many Exchange components are dependent upon other components. You should continue reading messages until you find the source of the problem.

- ▶ Some Exchange components are dependent upon other NT services loading properly. If the Exchange messages do not make the problem clear, check the System and Security Logs for other clues.

Exchange SETUP Log   The Exchange Server installation program creates a text file named Exchange Server SETUP.LOG and places it in the root of the drive onto which you are installing the Exchange Server software. While a complete discussion of the contents of this file is beyond the scope of this examination, you should be aware that it exists and have a general idea of what it contains.

The SETUP log file contains detailed information about what the installation program has accomplished. As you can see in Figure 17.1, the SETUP log file is extremely complex, but also extremely detailed.

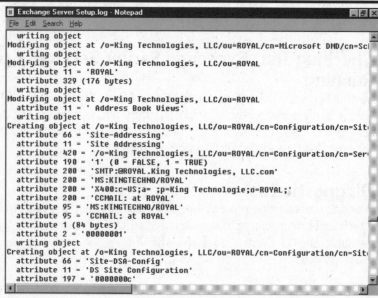

FIGURE 17.1: The Exchange Server SETUP.LOG file

▶ Diagnose and resolve migration problems.

Migration allows an existing non-Exchange e-mail system to be moved to an Exchange organization. Depending on the e-mail system being migrated, there may be tools for moving mailboxes, addresses, messages, folders, or schedule information. The ability to migrate users to Microsoft Exchange from some other e-mail system is a very important skill, both in your real-world job and on the MCSE examination.

Like any other major operation, migrations can sometimes run into problems. When this occurs, the Windows NT event log and the Migration

Wizard error-summary log file can usually point you to the source of the problem. There are a few common problems that you might encounter:

▶ The account used to perform the migration does not have administrative privileges in the existing system.

▶ The account used to perform the migration does not have administrative privileges on the Exchange server.

▶ One or more of the necessary files has been deleted.

▶ One or more of the necessary files has been renamed.

▶ Network problems occurred during the migration.

▶ The Private Information Store ran out of disk space during the migration.

While not specifically troubleshooting techniques, there are also a few migration considerations that you might want to take into account:

▶ The migration process can put a heavy load on your Exchange server. You might want to add RAM before performing the migration.

▶ Most of the foreign e-mail systems include a tool to clean up mailboxes. You might want to limit the size of the mailboxes being migrated by deleting old messages.

▶ When migrating a Lotus cc:Mail system, remember that e-mail of remote users (stored on their personal computers) will not automatically be migrated. Have those users copy their e-mail to a temporary postoffice so that you can run the migration against those files.

▶ When migrating from a Novell GroupWise system, the account used to perform the migration must have been granted proxy rights to the mailboxes being migrated. These rights can be configured to allow another user the ability to read, delete, or modify existing e-mail as well as send e-mail on behalf of (or as) the user.

▶ Diagnose and resolve connectivity problems. Elements include:

▶ Foreign connectivity

▶ Site-to-site connectivity

▶ Internet connectivity

▶ Connectivity within a site

One of the more crucial components of any Exchange server is its ability to connect to other servers (both foreign and other Exchange servers). Knowing how to diagnose and resolve connectivity problems is critical to your success, both on the job and on the examination.

Each of the different types of connections mentioned for this objective has its own tools and techniques for troubleshooting problems. You should be aware of the techniques used for each.

Foreign Connectivity

The most important troubleshooting tip for foreign connectivity is to be sure you have a full understanding of the process involved in connecting. Review the information presented in Chapter 14 about connecting to foreign systems.

For the exam, be aware of the following:

▶ Most problems that occur when connecting to MS Mail systems are related to the directory synchronization process. Remember that your Exchange server can be configured as either a Dirsync Server (which means that it will correlate the address books from your MS Mail postoffices into a Global Address Book and disburse that book back to them) or as a Dirsync Requestor (which means that your Exchange server will send its Global Address List to an MS Mail postoffice for inclusion into the MS Mail Global Address Book). In either case, remember that timing and the ability to communicate are critical.

▶ When connecting to a Lotus cc:Mail system remember that two programs must run on the Exchange server: IMPORT.EXE and EXPORT.EXE. These programs transfer messages to and from a temporary directory (where messages are stored as text files). Many cc:Mail connectivity problems are concerned with the proper functioning of these programs.

Site-to-Site Connectivity

Each of the connectors used to connect Exchange sites includes a series of parameters for optimizing communication. These parameters were discussed in detail in Chapter 14 and have been mentioned for numerous objectives throughout this book. This should be a strong indication that these parameters are very important on the test. If you haven't done so already, go back to Chapter 14 and review the RTS, connection retry, association, and transfer timeout parameters available for configuring connectors.

Before diagnosing a problem, you must be aware that a problem exists. One way to be informed of problems is to wait for user complaints. While this is effective, it is probably not the best method available. For a more proactive approach, configure link monitors between servers in your sites. These monitors can be configured to inform you if the link is not functioning.

Once you have determined that a problem exists, diagnose a site-to-site communication problem using information available in the Message Transfer Agent object for each server. The MTA object includes two useful properties: diagnostic logging and the ability to view the contents of the MTA queues.

We discussed diagnostic logging in Chapter 16. The MTA object Diagnostic Logging property pages include numerous categories of information. A full discussion of these options is beyond the scope of this examination.

You can also view information about each of the MTA queues on an Exchange server as shown in Figure 17.2. As you can see from the figure, it is fairly easy to determine which connector has a backlog of items.

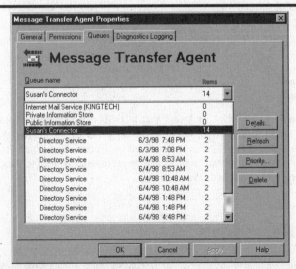

FIGURE 17.2: MTA queues

Part iii

Double clicking on any message in the queue will display information about that message. Included is the name of the originator of the message, the time of submission, and its priority.

Internet Connectivity

Troubleshooting the Internet Mail Service (IMS) involves the same steps as troubleshooting site-to-site connectivity. The IMS Connector includes three queues. You can view the number of messages in each queue by accessing the Queues property page of the IMS Connector. The three queues are described in Table 17.1.

TABLE 17.1: IMS queues

Queue	Description
MTS Out	Receives messages from the MTA on the Exchange server that is running the IMS Connector. These messages are from Exchange users sending e-mail to SMTP recipients.
OUT	Messages are sent from this queue to SMTP recipients.
IN	This queue receives messages from an SMTP system. These messages are converted to Exchange format and passed to the Information Store.

Double clicking on any message in a queue will display detailed information for that message. The administrator can also delete any message in a queue by highlighting it and clicking the Delete button. Often a corrupted message in a queue can hinder the operation of the queue.

WARNING

Beyond the IMS Connector, be aware that Internet e-mail is dependent upon numerous underlying services working correctly. TCP/IP must be configured properly and host names must be resolved to IP addresses. Your first step should be to ensure that host names can be resolved by trying to Ping a few sites by their Fully Qualified Domain Name.

Connectivity within a Site

Diagnosing communication problems within a site is essentially the same as diagnosing communication problems between sites. Use a link monitor to warn you of problems, and then check the MTA queues to determine which queue is the problem. You can then enable diagnostic logging to provide more information about the problem.

▶ Diagnose and resolve problems with client connectivity.

Messaging systems exist to allow users the ability to communicate. If clients are having problems connecting to their e-mail server, then the system is not doing its job. Understanding the common client connectivity problems is critical information for any Exchange administrator.

When clients cannot connect to their e-mail server, the problem usually lies in one of two areas: either in the configuration of the protocols in use or in the configuration of their profile. In either case, diagnosing the problem is very straightforward.

Protocol Problems

If a client is having problems connecting to their e-mail server, you should first determine if they are able to see the server in their Network Neighborhood. If not, the problem is network-related rather than Exchange-related. Troubleshooting network problems is beyond the scope of this examination, but it's still useful to know a few of the more common problems (and their solutions).

- ▶ Ensure that the client is using the same protocols as the Exchange server. If your server is using TCP/IP and the client is configured with only IPX, communication cannot occur.

- ▶ If you are using TCP/IP, ensure that the client is configured properly. Each client must have a unique IP address and must have the correct subnet mask configured. If the Exchange server is across a routed network, ensure that the client is configured with the correct address for their default gateway.

- ▶ If you are using TCP/IP, ensure that the client can resolve the host name into the appropriate IP address for your Exchange server. Either check the HOSTS file or the IP address of their DNS server.

- ▶ If you are using NWLink (or another implementation of IPX/SPX), ensure that the client is configured to use the correct frame type.

Part iii

NOTE

A complete discussion of troubleshooting network-related problems is beyond the scope of both this book and the exam it covers. For more information, see the Sybex Study Guides.

Profile Configuration Problems

Determining if the user's profile is incorrectly configured is fairly straight-forward. First, ensure that the user's account information and e-mail server name has been entered correctly. If the user's computer is connected to the network, ensure that the profile is not configured to work offline.

Checking the Profile for a User

Checking the profile for a user is a simple process. Access the Mail and Fax (or Mail in Windows NT) applet in the Control Panel. Ensure that the Microsoft Exchange Server service is included in the profile as shown in Figure 17.3.

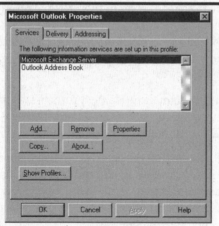

FIGURE 17.3: Microsoft Outlook properties

Highlight the Microsoft Exchange Server service and click the Properties button. If the mailbox name and server information have been confirmed, they will be underlined in the dialog box. If not, ensure that they have been entered correctly and click Check Name.

Also ensure that the Connect with the Network option is selected under When Starting.

TIP

One way to force name resolution is to retype the mailbox name and click the Check Name button. If the name is underlined, then a connection has been made.

▶ Diagnose and resolve information store problems.

Since the Information Store databases are the storage location for all messages, problems with them can affect all users on a server. Knowing the appropriate actions to take is extremely important during such a crisis.

Exchange Server performs general maintenance tasks on the Information Store databases on a regular schedule. Since this process can place a high load on a server, the administrator should ensure that this maintenance does not occur during peak times or during a period when the server is busy carrying out some other task, such as performing a backup.

During the maintenance period, Exchange performs the following:

▶ Defragments the Private and Public Information Stores

▶ Removes expired messages based on configured age limits

▶ Deletes indices created to cache folder views

This daily maintenance should be sufficient. There are, however, a few situations that might require administrator intervention.

▶ If the server's disk becomes full, causing the IS service to automatically stop

▶ In the event of a power failure, if the IS service does not restart properly

▶ Any time the Information Store service does not start correctly

In these situations, you may need to run a utility named ISINTEG .EXE. This tool is designed to check the IS databases for consistency and correct any problems.

Scheduling Daily Maintenance Tasks   To schedule the daily maintenance tasks, access the property pages of your server in the Exchange Administrator program. On the IS Maintenance tab you can set the times that maintenance should occur.

Part iii

Highlight those times when you would like Exchange to perform its maintenance.

To run the ISINTEG.EXE utility, you must first stop the Information Store services. Access the Services applet (found in the Control Panel) and stop the Microsoft Exchange Information Store service. You may be warned that other Exchange services are dependent upon the Information Store. If so, click OK to continue.

Your next step is to access a command prompt and move to the \EXCHSRVR\BIN directory. From this directory you can run the ISINTEG utility. To perform a repair, type `ISINTEG -FIX`. For a complete list of options, type `ISINTEG -?`.

▶ Diagnose and resolve server directory problems.

The directory service manages the objects in your Exchange organization. When problems occur they can result in your entire organization being (at best) unmanageable or (at worst) unavailable.

There are two major maintenance tasks that must be performed on the Exchange directory on a regular basis: tombstone collection and consistency checking. Under normal circumstances, both tasks are performed automatically.

Tombstone collection is the process of deleting information about objects that have been deleted. As you may recall from Chapter 15, deleted objects are marked with a tombstone. This tombstone is replicated to all other servers so that all copies of the directory remain consistent. After a period of time, objects marked with a tombstone are physically deleted from the directory.

Consistency checking allows the directory to check for references to objects that no longer exist. The consistency checking process cleans up these references.

As mentioned earlier, under normal circumstances, the automatic maintenance should be sufficient. When the Exchange directory services will not start, you might need to use the ESEUTIL.EXE utility. The ESEUTIL.EXE utility can be used to carry out the following tasks.

Defragment the database   Over time the information stored within a database can become fragmented. The ESEUTIL.EXE utility can rearrange the data within the database.

Consistency check   Compares the information within the database to make sure there are no references to nonexistent objects.

Recover a database   If the directory becomes so corrupted that normal maintenance cannot fix it, ESEUTIL.EXE can attempt to fix the problem by rebuilding each record in the database.

Changing the Tombstone Lifetime   Access the properties of the DS Site Configuration object in the appropriate site. On the General page, change the tombstone lifetime.

Running ESEUTIL.EXE   First you must stop the Exchange services on your server using the Services applet in the Control Panel or a NET STOP command from a command prompt. Next access a command prompt and change to the \<WINNT>\SYSTEM32 directory. Type **ESEUTIL** for a list of available options.

▶ Diagnose and resolve server resource problems.

As discussed in Chapter 13, Exchange Server can place a heavy load on an NT server. You must be able to diagnose and resolve any physical resource problems in order to optimize your Exchange environment.

The tool most commonly used to diagnose problems with physical resources is the NT Performance Monitor tool. When Exchange Server is installed on an NT server, a series of additional Exchange- specific counters are added to the Performance Monitor tool. Some of these counters are detailed in the following tables.

Table 17.2 shows the Message Transfer Agent counters.

TABLE 17.2: Message Transfer Agent counters

OBJECT	COUNTER	DESCRIPTION
MSExchangeMTA	Message/sec.	Average number of messages the MTA sends and receives each second
	Work queue length	Current count of the messages in MTA queues awaiting processing
MSExchangeMTA-Connections	Queue length	Number of objects in MTA queues

Part iii

Table 17.3 shows the Exchange directory counters for the MSExchange-DS object.

TABLE 17.3: Directory counters

COUNTER	DESCRIPTION
Pending Replication Synchronization	Current count of unanswered synchronization requests
Remaining Replication Updates	Current count of changes waiting to be applied to the directory

Table 17.4 shows the Information Store counters for the MSExchange-ISPrivate and MSExchangeISPublic objects.

TABLE 17.4: Information Store counters

COUNTER	DESCRIPTION
Average delivery time	Average amount of time the last 10 messages waited in the IS queue for the MTA
Average local delivery time	Same as above but for local delivery involving the local IS only
Client logons	Current number of users logged on to the IS
Active client logons	Current number of users logged on to the IS who have initiated some server activity in the last 10 minutes
Messages Delivered/Min.	Average number of messages delivered by the IS per minute
Message Recipients Delivered/Min.	Above value divided by the number of recipients to which they were addressed
Messages Sent/Min.	Average number of messages sent from the IS to the MTA per minute

Table 17.5 shows the Microsoft Mail Connector counters.

TABLE 17.5: Microsoft Mail Connector counters

OBJECT	COUNTER	DESCRIPTION
MSExchangeMSMI	Messages Received	Total number of messages received by the Exchange server from the MS Mail Connector
MSExchangePCMTA	File contentions/hour	The rate at which multiple clients try to read and write exclusively to key MS Mail and MS Mail Connector postoffice files
	LAN/WAN Messages Moved/hour	Checks MS Mail connector overall performance

Table 17.6 shows the Internet Mail service counters for the MSExchange-IMC object.

TABLE 17.6: Internet Mail Service counters

COUNTER	DESCRIPTION
Queued MTS-IN	Current count of messages awaiting delivery within the Exchange environment
Bytes queued MTS-IN	The size of messages that have been converted to Exchange format and are awaiting delivery
Messages Entering MTS-IN	Converted messages entering the MTS-IN folder per hour
Queued MTS-OUT	Current count of messages waiting to be converted to Internet Mail format
Bytes Queued MTS-OUT	The size of the messages awaiting conversion to Internet Mail format
Messages Leaving MTS-OUT	Number of messages converted for delivery to the Internet per hour
Connections Inbound	Current count of SMTP connections made to the IMS by other SMTP hosts
Connections Outbound	Current count of connections made by the IMS to other SMTP hosts
Connections Total Outbound	Count of successful SMTP connections established to other SMTP hosts by the IMS since it was started
Connections Total Inbound	Count of successful SMTP connections accepted from other SMTP hosts by the IMS since it was started

Part iii

TABLE 17.6 continued: Internet Mail Service counters

COUNTER	DESCRIPTION
Connections Total Rejected	Total number of connection requests that IMS has rejected since it was started
Connections Total Failed	Total number of connections IMS tried and failed to establish to other SMTP hosts
Queued Outbound	Current count of messages awaiting delivery to the Internet
Queued Inbound	Current count of messages received from the Internet and awaiting processing
NDRs Total Inbound	Total number of NDRs generated for inbound messages
NDRs Total Outbound	Total number of NDRs generated for outbound messages
Total Inbound Kilobytes	Total size of messages transferred to the Exchange server
Total Outbound Kilobytes	Total size of messages transferred from the Exchange server
Inbound Messages Total	Total number of inbound messages since the IMS was started
Outbound Messages Total	Total number of outbound messages since the IMS was started

Table 17.7 shows the counters for the Connector for Lotus cc:Mail object (MSExchangeCCMC).

TABLE 17.7: Connector for Lotus cc:Mail counters

COUNTER	DESCRIPTION
NDRs to Microsoft Exchange	Number of NDRs sent to Exchange users since the connector was started
NDRs to Lotus cc:Mail	Number of NDRs sent to cc:Mail users since the connector was started
Messages sent to Microsoft Exchange/hour	Average number of messages sent per hour
Messages sent to Lotus cc:Mail/hour	Average number of messages sent
Microsoft Exchange MTS-IN	Number of messages in the MTS-IN queue
Microsoft Exchange MTS-OUT	Number of messages in the MTS-OUT queue

TABLE 17.7 continued: Connector for Lotus cc:Mail counters

COUNTER	DESCRIPTION
Messages sent to Microsoft Exchange	Total number of messages sent to Exchange users since the connector was started
Messages sent to Lotus cc:Mail	Total number of messages sent to cc:Mail users since the connector was started
Dirsync to Microsoft Exchange	Total number of changes sent to the Exchange Directory since the last Dirsync cycle started
Dirsync to Lotus cc:Mail	Total number of changes sent to the cc:Mail address list since the last Dirsync cycle started

As you can see from these tables, Performance Monitor can provide a lot of detailed information about what is happening on your server. Along with the Exchange-specific counters, you should also watch the following generic NT counters, as shown in Table 17.8.

TABLE 17.8: Generic Performance Monitor counters

OBJECT	COUNTER	DESCRIPTION
Logical-Disk	%Disk Time	The percentage of time the disk spends reading or writing. A sustained rate of over 90% indicates a disk bottleneck.
Memory	Pages/sec	Measures paging of memory from or to the hard disk. A high average could indicate that the server needs more RAM.
Processor	%Processor Time	The percentage of time the processor is busy. An average value consistently over 90% indicates that the server is overburdened.
Process	Elapsed Time	The number of seconds a process has been running. Allows you to check if a process has recently been restarted without having to look through the event log.
Redirector	Bytes Total/sec.	The number of bytes per second sent and received by the network redirector.
Redirector	Network Errors/sec.	Measures the number of network errors encountered. If this number is above zero, check the system event log for details.

▶ Diagnose and resolve message delivery problems.

When messages are not being delivered properly, you must know how to diagnose and resolve the problem quickly. E-mail has become too critical to many companies for delivery problems to be tolerated.

This objective is concerned with the configuration of message tracking. Make sure you have a good understanding of the materials presented for the objective entitled "Configure Message Tracking" in Chapter 14.

TIP

Review the material presented in Chapter 14 carefully. Message tracking is an important administration skill on the job even though it is not heavily tested on the exam!

▶ Diagnose and resolve backup problems and restore problems.

A backup can only be considered successful if the information can be restored. Many administrators forget this basic rule. When there are problems with your backups you must be able to correct them so that you are covered in the event of system failures.

Most problems involved in the backup and restore procedures are hardware based. Some of the problems you might encounter include: your backup device does not have an NT 4.0 driver, the write heads are dirty and need to be cleaned, or you have used a tape too many times and it is no longer storing data dependably. In any event, these problems are outside the scope of this examination.

Once the hardware is working correctly, backup and restore problems are usually fairly simple. For backups the most common problems are:

▶ The batch file that you are using to automate the backup is not correct.

▶ The account used to back up the system does not have the appropriate permissions.

▶ Some other process is competing for system resources while the backup is running.

More problems are encountered during the restore process than during the backup process. These are the worst of all problems because they happen at a point where time is critical—your system is down and you need to restore it as quickly as possible. The biggest mistake is to forget to run the ISINTEG utility with the –PATCH option after performing a restore from a backup that was made while the Information Store was offline. This is a required step that ensures that messages will have unique identifiers going forward.

▶ Diagnose organization security problems.

Configuring and maintaining the Key Management Server components of an Exchange Server environment was discussed in Chapter 14. This objective is concerned with diagnosing and resolving problems with that component.

Review the information presented in the "Configure security" objective of Chapter 14. Table 17.9 summarizes the most common Key Management security problems and their fixes.

TABLE 17.9: Common advanced security problems

PROBLEM	FIX
KM Server will not start.	Remember that the password must be provided each time the KM Server restarts. This can either be done manually or from a floppy disk.
KM service is not running after installation of the software.	The KM service must be started manually after its installation.
A user cannot use the advanced security features in Outlook.	The administrator must enable advanced security on each mailbox before the user can take advantage of advanced security features. The administrator provides a password to the user and then the user must configure advanced security on their Outlook client software.
A user forgets their security password.	The administrator must recover that user's password from the KM database.
The user's password expires.	The KM administrator must perform a renewal of that user's KM security keys.

Part iii

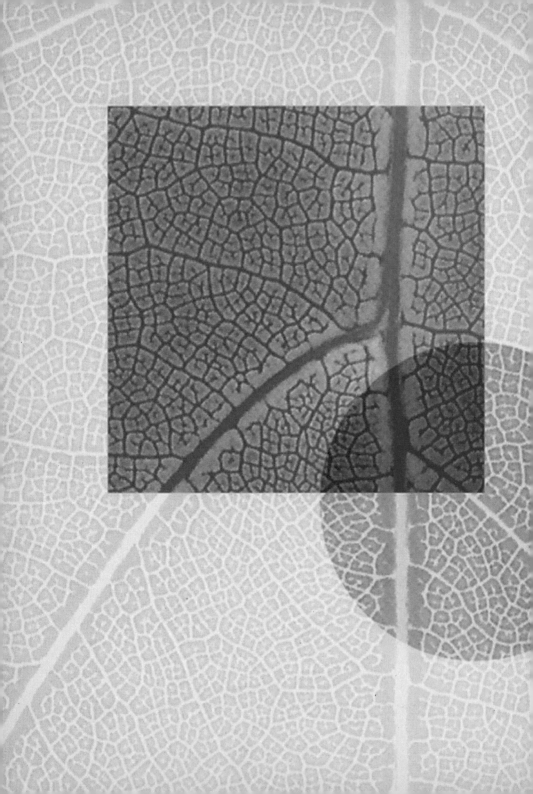

PART III

EXCHANGE 5.5 PRACTICE EXAM

Exam Questions

1. Which of the following MIBs defines the parameters available for management on an Exchange server?

   A. EXCH.MIB

   B. MADMAN MIB

   C. MIBCC.MIB

   D. PERFMON.MIB

2. You have just added the SNMP service to your Exchange server. You are already using an SNMP management console to manage other services on your server and you have previously customized your MIB.BIN file. Which of the following would you run to configure the Exchange SNMP parameters?

   A. Run the INSTALL.BAT file located in the SUPPORT\ SNMP\<PLATFORM>\ directory of your Exchange server compact disk.

   B. Run the PERF2MIB and MIBCC commands from a command prompt.

   C. Nothing; installing the SNMP service is all that is needed.

   D. Installing the SNMP service installs a new version of Performance Monitor that answers SNMP calls from a management console.

3. You are upgrading an Exchange server to version 5.5. The upgrade fails within the first 15 minutes every time you attempt it. You've watched the screen and it fails at a different point in the process each time. Which of the following would you try first?

   A. Try a different Exchange Server 5.5 CD-ROM to see if you have a bad disk.

   B. Ensure that the network connection is functional.

   C. Disable any server monitors that might be checking the server you are upgrading.

   D. Check to see that you have sufficient disk space available for the upgrade.

4. You are upgrading your older Exchange 4.0 software to Exchange 5.5. The upgrade process fails with an error message that mentions the schema. Which of the following is the most likely cause?

   A. Exchange 4.0 cannot be upgraded directly to version 5.5. You must purchase version 5.0 and upgrade to that first.

   B. You have not installed SP2 on your Exchange 4.0 servers.

   C. Your bridgehead servers are not communicating between sites.

   D. Your Exchange databases have become corrupted and you must restore them from tape before continuing.

5. Your installation of Exchange Server 5.5 went just fine on your first Exchange server. Everything seemed to be working until the first time you restarted the computer. At that point, none of the Exchange Server components started correctly. Upon examining the event log you find errors that indicate a failed logon. Which of the following would you do first?

   A. Call a few individuals to determine if anyone else is having problems logging on to the system.

   B. Reinstall Exchange to recreate the security information.

   C. Check the site service account to determine if the User Must Change Password at Next Logon box is checked.

   D. Turn on auditing to audit failed logon attempts.

6. Server A in your site has a current USN of 10. The last time Server B communicated with Server A the USN was 5. Which of the following will occur?

   A. Server A will request changes from Server B.

   B. Server B will request changes from Server A.

   C. No replication will occur.

   D. Both servers will query a third server to determine what the value should be.

7. Users are reporting errors when trying to send e-mail to other users on their home Exchange server. Which of the following would you do first?

A. Check to ensure that they have the appropriate permissions to the Exchange Directories.

B. Check the installation of the Outlook client for those users to determine if it is configured properly.

C. Check the recipients' configuration to determine if a faulty rule has been configured that is denying receipt of e-mail.

D. Check to see if the users are members of the Mail Users global group.

8. You are migrating a foreign e-mail system into your Exchange environment. Which of the following would help speed up the process?

A. Add RAM to the Exchange server performing the migration.

B. Migrate users in groups. This way only a few mailboxes would be migrated during any given migration process.

C. Delete unnecessary messages in the mailboxes on the existing system before performing the migration.

D. Delete any unused mailboxes in the existing e-mail system before performing the migration.

9. After migrating a Lotus cc:Mail system into your Exchange organization, you discover that some users' messages were not migrated. Which of the following is the most likely cause?

A. Those users had not granted proxy rights to the account performing the migration.

B. Mail over 30 days old cannot be migrated from a cc:Mail system.

C. Users whose account name is over 12 characters long are not migrated.

D. Those users are probably remote users with e-mail stored locally.

10. Your users are complaining that they are unable to receive e-mail from clients over the Internet. Which of the following actions would you take?

A. Call the administrator at one of the client sites and ask if their Internet e-mail system is configured properly.

B. Place a packet analyzer on your network and check to see if the e-mail is reaching the router.

C. Attempt to Ping a remote server by using its FQDN.

D. Check the IMS queues to see if e-mail is becoming backlogged in a queue.

11. E-mail has become critical to your company. Rather than wait for user complaints, you want to know about connectivity problems in a timely manner. Which of the following actions would you take?

A. Configure a series of link monitors between your servers, configuring them to e-mail you in the event of a problem.

B. Designate one person in each department to call you as soon as anyone has a problem.

C. Configure a packet analysis tool to alert you in the event of line problems.

D. Configure your client to send a message to a nonexistent account on each server every 15 minutes.

12. A client calls and complains that they cannot access their e-mail. Upon further discussion, you discover that their Outlook client is displaying an error message that states that the e-mail server cannot be found. Which of the following should be your next step?

A. Ensure that the user's mailbox has not been deleted.

B. Replace the network cable to their computer.

C. Check their profile to ensure that their account information has been entered correctly.

D. Have them click their Network Neighborhood to ensure that they can see the server on the network.

13. After installing Exchange Server on one of your existing NT servers, you find that backups are taking an extremely long time to complete. Which of the following corrective actions would you perform first?

    A. Move the tape device to another server and perform the backup across the network.

    B. Set the IS maintenance schedule so that it does not overlap with the backup schedule.

    C. Move some data to another server to reduce the overall amount of time necessary to back up the server.

    D. Limit the space allowed for each mailbox.

14. Your company had a power failure last night. When the system restarts, Exchange does not seem to be working. Upon checking the Services applet, you notice that the IS service has not started properly. Which of the following troubleshooting tasks would you perform?

    A. Run a disk utility to clean up your file structure.

    B. Run the NT PROB.EXE utility to check for problems in the registry.

    C. Restore your Exchange environment from backup.

    D. Run ISINTEG –FIX to fix the problem.

15. You have determined that your Exchange directory has become badly corrupted. Which of the following tools would you use to correct this problem?

    A. EDBUTIL.EXE

    B. ESEUTIL.EXE

    C. DBMAINT.EXE

    D. DIRFIX.EXE

16. You would like to ensure that objects are deleted from your directory database soon after they are marked for deletion. Which of the following parameters would you change?

    A. RTS Checkpoint value

    B. Tombstone lifetime

    C. Deletion interval

    D. DIRFIX timeout

17. You suspect that an Exchange service has recently been restarted. Which of the following methods would confirm your suspicion?

    A. Check the date on the appropriate file in the \EXCH-SRVR folder.

    B. Look through the NT event log.

    C. Check the "time of service" statistics in the Exchange Administrator program.

    D. In Performance Monitor, check the Process: Elapsed Time statistic for the service.

18. While performing your regular maintenance you notice that the Performance Monitor counter Processor: %Processor Time is consistently over 90%. What does this indicate?

    A. The processor is not being used for 90% of the time.

    B. The processor is being used over 90% of the time.

    C. You should add more services to this server to use the free time available.

    D. You should move processing to another server to take the load off this server.

19. You are attempting to track the route of a message sent by one local user to another. The list comes up empty. What is the probable cause?

    A. You have not enabled message tracking on the appropriate components.

    B. You do not have the permission to track another user's e-mail.

    C. The message was lost before it was received by the Exchange server.

    D. The message was never sent—the user is lying.

20. The message tracking information for a particular message says that it was delivered to the Internet Mail Service and forwarded on. It was never received by the recipient. Which of the following would you do next?

Part iii

    A. Check the IMS outgoing queue to see if the message is awaiting delivery.

    B. Call the administrator of the other e-mail system and have them confirm that their Internet Mail system is configured properly.

    C. Have the user resend the message and see if it goes through this time.

    D. Uninstall IMS and reinstall it.

21. You have performed a restore using your backup tapes. Upon restarting the Exchange server, you notice that the IS service has not started properly. Which of the following is the most likely problem?

    A. Your tape backup was corrupted.

    B. Your tape device is not supported by Windows NT 4.0.

    C. The Windows NT backup utility cannot backup Exchange.

    D. You need to run the ISINTEG utility with the −PATCH option.

22. You back up all of your servers from a central location. You notice that you cannot back up the Exchange Server environment. What is the likely cause of this problem?

    A. The network is too slow to perform a backup.

    B. You have not installed the extensions to the backup utility on the backup server.

    C. Your tape is not large enough to hold the Exchange databases.

    D. You do not have the permissions necessary to perform an Exchange backup.

23. After a restart, the KM Server will not finish the boot process. What is the probable cause?

    A. The KM service is RAM-intensive. The server probably does not have enough RAM.

    B. The KM Server requires a password to complete its boot process.

    C. The KM service has become corrupted and needs to be reinstalled.

    D. After a restart, the KM Server must be reinitialized using the Exchange 5.5 CD-ROM.

24. You recently purchased a tape jukebox system to back up all of the NT servers on your network. On the first backup attempt, you find that everything except Exchange is backing up properly. Which of the following is the most likely problem?

    A. Exchange Server can only be backed up to a local tape drive.

    B. The backup program must be configured to back up remote systems.

    C. You must stop the Exchange Server services manually before backing them up.

    D. You must install the Exchange Administrator program on the central computer so that the NT Backup program is replaced with the Exchange-aware version.

25. Which of the following are advantages of a server-based message store configuration?

    A. Central location for backups

    B. Mail is available to roving and mobile users.

    C. Lower overhead at the server

    D. Less overall disk space used

26. Your company wants to ensure that the time stamps on all e-mail messages are consistent. Which of the following solutions would you suggest?

    A. Use the AT.EXE utility to schedule a process on remote servers to set the time.

    B. Configure your link monitor to include the system time in its message to remote servers.

    C. Configure your server monitor to synchronize time between the target server and the server upon which it is running.

Part iii

D. Add a manual timecheck to your daily maintenance tasks.

27. You wish to run the Exchange Performance Optimizer to optimize your Exchange server. You also want to mandate some advanced configuration parameters. Which of the run commands would suit your needs?

    A. `<DRIVE:>\EXCHSRVR\BIN\PERFWIZ.EXE`

    B. `<DRIVE:>\EXCHSRVR\BIN\ADVOPT.EXE`

    C. `<DRIVE:>\EXCHSRVR\BIN\PERFWIZ.EXE -V`

    D. `<DRIVE:>\EXCHSRVR\BIN\PERFWIZ.EXE -ADVANCED`

28. Which of the following are disadvantages of using fewer, more powerful Exchange servers?

    A. Fewer vendor choices are available.

    B. Backup time increases.

    C. Server failure affects more users.

    D. Less network traffic is generated.

29. Which of the following would be a valid user account to use when installing an Exchange server into an existing site?

    A. Any user account

    B. None. Since Exchange supports anonymous access, you do not need to be logged in.

    C. The account of any member of the administrators group

    D. The hidden recipient site service account created during the Exchange installation

30. Which of the following are required to access e-mail using an Internet browser?

    A. Active Server Pages

    B. Internet Information Server

    C. POP3 services

    D. A browser which supports JavaScripts and frames technologies

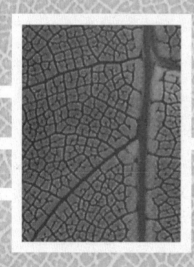

PART iV

SQL Server 7 Administration

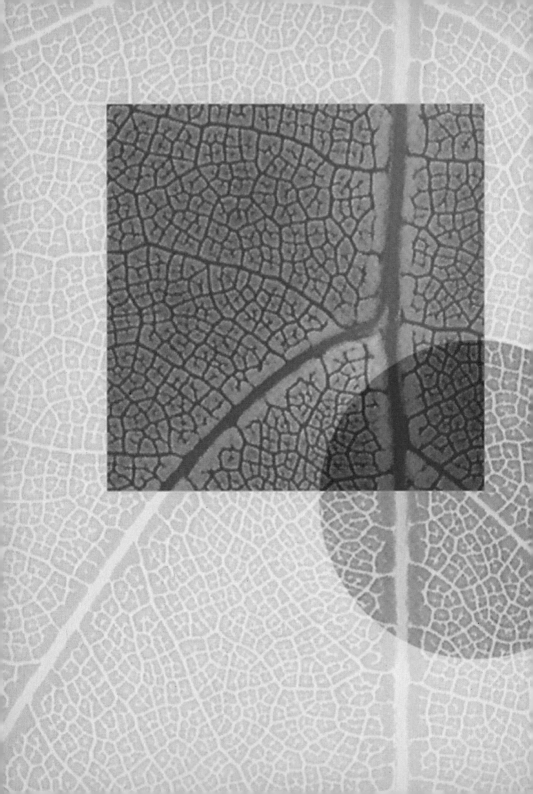

Chapter 18

PLANNING

Y ou cannot just start installing SQL and then expect it to work right when you are done; the installation must be planned. That is what will be discussed here—planning SQL Server installation. You'll start by planning the security systems that you'll need to put in place to keep prying eyes out of sensitive material. Then, you'll read about capacity planning, so that all of your users can access your data efficiently and avoid running out of space.

After security and capacity have been discussed, you can develop a data availability plan, deciding what types of backups to use so that you can bring your data back online quickly in the event of a disaster. Then, just in case you are migrating from another database server, you will set up a migration plan. Finally, a replication plan will be hashed out, so that all of your users can access data locally if you have more than one server.

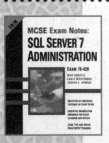

Adapted from *MCSE Exam Notes: SQL Server 7 Administration* by Rick Sawtell, Lance Mortensen, and Joseph L. Jorden

ISBN 0-7821-2477-1   368 pages $19.99

Develop a security strategy.

- ▶ Assess whether to use Microsoft Windows NT accounts or Microsoft SQL Server logins.

- ▶ Assess whether to leverage the Windows NT group structure.

- ▶ Plan the use and structure of SQL Server roles. Server roles include fixed server, fixed database, and user-defined database.

- ▶ Assess whether to map Windows NT groups directly into a database or to map them to a role.

- ▶ Assess which Windows NT accounts will be used to run SQL Server services.

- ▶ Plan an *n*-tier application security strategy, and decide whether to use application roles or other mid-tier security mechanisms such as Microsoft Transaction Server.

- ▶ Plan the security requirements for linked databases.

Hackers are running rampant today; people are using their knowledge of computer systems to access sensitive data, steal corporate secrets, or just be malicious. SQL Server is especially prone to such attacks since it is where many companies store their sensitive data. To keep hackers out, you must have a good security plan.

In this section, the components of a good security plan will be examined. First, you'll figure out whether to use Windows NT accounts or SQL Server logins to grant access to your users. If you go with Windows NT accounts, you should read about the benefits of leveraging the group structure in Windows NT.

After your users have access to the server, you need to know how to limit what they are capable of doing with the data on your server; that is why the various roles at your disposal will be discussed. Then, you'll figure out which Windows NT accounts the SQL Server services will run under. After that, the security requirements for *n*-tier applications and linked databases will be covered.

Since you don't want just anybody accessing your data, these security concepts are going to be very important to you in the real world. Anything that is this important in the real world is also very important on the exam, so watch closely as the secrets of security are uncovered.

Assessing Whether to Use Windows NT Accounts or SQL Server Logins

The type of accounts you use depends a great deal on your authentication mode. An *authentication mode* is how SQL processes user names and passwords. There are two such modes in SQL 7: Windows NT Authentication mode and Mixed mode.

In Windows NT Authentication mode, a user can simply sit down at their computer, log on to the Windows NT domain, and gain access to SQL Server. Here's how it works:

1. The user logs on to a Windows NT domain; the user name and password are verified by NT.

2. The user then opens a trusted connection with SQL Server.

3. SQL will then try to match the user name or group membership to an entry in the syslogins table.

4. Since this is a trusted connection, SQL does not need to verify the user password; that is, SQL trusts NT to perform that function.

The main advantage to Windows NT Authentication mode is that users do not have to remember multiple user names and passwords. That will vastly increase security since there is less danger of users writing their passwords down and storing them in an unsafe place (such as a sticky note on their monitor). This mode also gives you tighter reign over security, since you can apply NT password policies that will do such things as expire passwords, require a minimum length for passwords, keep a history of passwords, and so on.

One of the disadvantages is that only users with a Windows NT network account (created in User Manager for Domains) can open a trusted connection to SQL Server. For example, that means that a Novell client running the IPX Net-Library cannot use Windows NT Authentication mode. If you have such clients, you will need to implement Mixed mode.

Mixed mode allows both NT Authentication and SQL Authentication. In SQL Authentication:

1. The user logs on to their network, NT or otherwise.

2. The user opens a nontrusted connection to SQL Server using a user name and password other than those used to gain network access.

3. SQL then matches the user name and password entered by the user to an entry in the syslogins table.

The primary advantage here is that anyone can gain access to SQL using Mixed mode, regardless of the network they log on to. This means that Mac users, Novell users, Banyan Vines users, and the like can gain access. You could also consider this to be a second layer of security, since hacking into the network in Mixed mode does not mean that someone has automatically hacked into SQL at the same time.

Ironically, multiple passwords can be a problem as well as an advantage. Consider that users will have one user name and password to log on to the network and a completely separate user name and password to gain access to SQL. When users have multiple sets of credentials, they tend to write them down and thus breach the security system you have worked so hard to set up.

Assessing Whether to Leverage the Windows NT Group Structure

While standard logins can be used by only one user, a Windows NT login can be mapped to one of the following:

▶ A single user

▶ A Windows NT group that an administrator has created

▶ A Windows NT built-in group (e.g., Administrators)

Before you create a Windows NT login, you must decide to which of these three you want to map it. Generally, you will want to map to a group that you have created. This will help you a great deal in later administration. For example, suppose you have an Accounting database to which all 50 of your accountants require access. You could create a separate login for each of them, which would require you to manage 50 SQL logins. On the other hand, if you create a Windows NT group for these 50 accountants and map your SQL login to this group, you will have only one SQL login to manage.

Planning to Use Server Roles and Map Groups

Once your users have access to SQL as a whole, they need to be limited in what they can do. That is what fixed server roles are used for. Some users may be allowed to do whatever they want, whereas other users may only be able to manage security. There are seven server roles to which you can assign users. The following list starts at the highest level and describes the administrative access granted:

Sysadmin: Members of the sysadmin role can do whatever they want in SQL Server. Be careful whom you assign to this role; people who are unfamiliar with SQL can accidentally create serious problems. This role is only for the database administrators (DBAs).

TIP

Built-in\Administrators is automatically made a member of the sysadmin server role, giving SQL administrative rights to all of your NT administrators. Since not all of your NT administrators should have these rights, you may want to create a SQLAdmins group, add your SQL administrators to that group, and make the group a member of the sysadmins role. Afterward, you should remove Built-in\Administrators from the sysadmin role.

Serveradmin: These users can set server-wide configuration options, such as how much memory SQL can use or how much information to send over the network in a single frame. If you make your assistant DBAs members of this role, you can relieve yourself of some of the administrative burden.

Setupadmin: Members here can install replication and manage extended stored procedures (these are used to perform actions not native to SQL Server). Give this to the assistant DBAs as well.

Securityadmin: These users manage security issues such as creating and deleting logins, reading the audit logs, and granting users permission to create databases. This, too, is a good role for assistant DBAs.

Processadmin: SQL is capable of *multitasking;* that is, it can do more than one thing at a time by executing multiple processes. For instance, SQL might spawn one process for writing to cache and another for reading from cache. A member of the processadmin group can end (called *kill* in SQL) a process. This is another good role for assistant DBAs and developers. Developers especially need to kill processes that may have been triggered by an improperly designed query or stored procedure.

Dbcreator: These users can create and make changes to databases. This may be a good role for assistant DBAs as well as developers (who should be warned against creating unnecessary databases and wasting server space).

Diskadmin: These users manage files on disk. They do things such as mirroring databases and adding backup devices. Assistant DBAs should be members of this role.

Once your users have access to a database through a database user account, you must limit what they can do in that individual database by assigning them to a database role. Fixed database roles have permissions already applied; that is, all you have to do is add users to these roles and the users inherit the associated permissions. (That is different from custom database roles, as you will see later.) There are several fixed database roles in SQL Server that you can use to grant permissions:

Db_owner: Members of this role can do everything the members of the other roles can do as well as some administrative functions.

Db_accessadmin: These users have the authority to say who gets access to the database by adding or removing users.

Db_datareader: Members here can read data from any table in the database.

Db_datawriter: These users can add, change, and delete data from all the tables in the database.

Db_ddladmin: Data Definition Language administrators can issue all DDL commands; this allows them to create, modify, or change database objects without viewing the data inside.

Db_securityadmin: Members here can add and remove users from database roles, and manage statement and object permissions.

Db_backupoperator: These users can back up the database.

Db_denydatareader: Members cannot read the data in the database, but they can make schema changes.

Db_denydatawriter: These users cannot make changes to the data in the database, but they are allowed to read the data.

Public: The purpose of this group is to grant users a default set of permissions in the database. All database users automatically join this group and cannot be removed.

There will, of course, be times when the fixed database roles do not meet your security needs. You might have several users who need Select, Update, and Execute permissions in your database and nothing more. Because none of the fixed database roles will give you that set of permissions, you can create a custom database role. When you create this new role, you will assign permissions to it and then assign users to the role; then, the users will inherit whatever permissions you assign to the role. That is different from the fixed database roles, where you did not need to assign permissions, but just added users.

NOTE

You can make your custom database roles members of other database roles. This is referred to as *nesting roles.*

Suppose that your human resources department uses a custom program to access their database, and you don't want them using any other program for fear of damaging the data. You can set this level of security by using an *application role*. With this special role, your users will not be able to access data using just their SQL login and database account; they will have to use the proper application.

Once you've created an application role, the user logs on to SQL, is authenticated, and opens the approved application. The application executes the `sp_setapprole` stored procedure to enable the application role. Once the application role is enabled, SQL no longer sees users as themselves; it sees users as the application and grants them application role permissions.

You may have noticed, though, that these roles are just a way of grouping users together to grant similar permissions; Windows NT groups serve the same purpose. Which is better, having Windows NT groups directly in the database or mapping users to roles? Here's a quick rule of thumb: If you have a use for the group other than SQL database access (and permission to do so), you should create a Windows NT group and map it to the database role. If you have no other reason to group these users together besides SQL database access, you are probably better off creating separate accounts and adding them to the role individually.

Choosing Accounts to Run the SQL Server Services

As a security precaution, the SQL services log on with one of two types of user accounts. The first is a local system account, which allows SQL to start but not access any network resources. The second type is a domain user account; this is just like any other user account with extra rights (specifically *log on as a service* and *act as part of the operating system*). If you intend to perform replication, use multiserver jobs, or have SQL send e-mail, you must have the services log on with the domain user account (called a *service account* when used by a service).

When you create a service account for SQL Server, you can create a single account for all SQL Server services to use, or you can create separate accounts for the individual services.

While the service account assigned to the SQLAgent needs administrative rights (on both Windows NT and SQL Server), the account assigned to the other SQL Server services doesn't. You may want to create and assign separate accounts to limit the rights of the accounts assigned to the MSSQLServer service and also to help in auditing security issues. No matter how you do it, though, any service account you create needs rights to the \MSSQL7 folder and user rights on the domain.

Configuring *N*-Tier Security and Linked Databases

When your resources are spread across multiple SQL Servers, your users may need access to resources on multiple, or *n* number of, servers. This is especially true of something called a *distributed query* (see Figure 18.1), which returns result sets from databases on multiple servers.

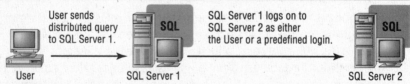

User sends distributed query to SQL Server 1.

SQL Server 1 logs on to SQL Server 2 as either the User or a predefined login.

User   SQL Server 1   SQL Server 2

FIGURE 18.1: Distributed query

Although you might wonder why you would want to perform distributed queries when you could just replicate the data between servers, there are practical reasons for doing the former. Don't forget that because SQL Server is designed to store terabytes of data, some of your databases may grow to several hundred megabytes in size—and you really don't want to replicate several hundred megabytes under normal circumstances.

The first step is to inform SQL that it will be talking to other database servers by running the `sp_addlinkedserver` stored procedure. The procedure to link to a server named AccountingSQL looks something as follows:

```
sp_addlinkedserver @server='AccountingSQL', @provider='SQL
Server'
```

Your users can then run distributed queries by simply specifying two different servers in the query. The query `select * from SQLServer .pubs.dbo.authors, AccountingSQL.pubs.dbo.employees` would access data from both the SQL Server (the server the user is logged in to, or the sending server) and the AccountingSQL server (the remote server) in the same result set.

The security issue here is that the sending server must log in to the remote server on behalf of the user to gain access to those data. SQL can use one of two methods to send this security information: security account delegation or linked-server login mapping. If your users have logged in using Windows NT Authentication, and all of the servers in the query are capable of understanding Windows NT domain security, you can use account delegation. Here's how it works:

1. If the servers are in different domains, you must make certain that the appropriate Windows NT trust relationships are in place. The remote server's domain must trust the sending server's domain.

2. Add a Windows NT login to the sending server for the user to log in with.

3. Add the same account to the remote server.

4. Create a user account for the login in the remote server's database and assign permissions.

5. When the user executes the distributed query, SQL will send the user's Windows NT security credentials to the remote server, allowing access.

If you have users who access SQL with standard logins, or if some of the servers do not participate in Windows NT domain security, you will need to add a linked login. Here's how to do it:

1. On the remote server, create a standard login and assign the necessary permissions.

2. On the sending server, map a local login to the remote login using the `sp_addlinkedsrvlogin` stored procedure. To map all local logins to the remote login RemUser, type `sp_addlinkedsrvlogin @rmtsrvname='Account-ingSQL', @useself=FALSE, @locallogin=NULL, @rmtuser= 'RemUser', @rmtpassword='password'`.

3. When a user executes a distributed query, the sending server will log in to the AccountingSQL (remote) server as RemUser with a password of *password*.

▶ Develop a SQL Server capacity plan.

- ▸ Plan the physical placement of files, including data files and transaction log files.

- ▸ Plan the use of filegroups.

- ▸ Plan for growth over time.

- ▸ Plan the physical hardware system.

- ▸ Assess communication requirements.

Imagine that one of the sales people in your company asks you why they are unable to add that huge new customer to the sales database, and the only answer you can give is, "We ran out of disk space; we'll have a new disk in tomorrow." This would reflect very poorly on you and your future with the company, so you need to make sure it doesn't happen. The way to avoid this is by creating a capacity plan—figuring out how big your databases are going to be and allocating resources accordingly.

In this section, where your data and transaction log files should be placed for maximum performance and space will be discussed. You'll also read about using filegroups for managing your data, especially VLDBs (very large databases). You then get to engage in the fine art of prognostication (foretelling the future)—you'll plan for growth over time. Finally, the physical hardware that you need for all of this, and the communication links that are needed to maintain it all, will be discussed.

If you don't want to have to tell your boss that no one can work because the databases are full, you need to read this section carefully. Even though this information is not heavily tested, it will make your life much easier.

To know where to put your database files, you need to understand a little bit about them. When you create a database, you are allocating hard-disk space for one of three file types: database files, secondary database files, and transaction log files. Database files, which store data and system tables, have a default extension of .MDF. The transaction log is stored in one or more files, with a default .LDF extension. If you create a database that spans multiple database files, the additional database files have a default filename extension of .NDF. With that understanding, it is easier to answer the question of placement.

Physical Placement of Files

No one can actually tell you where to place your files; that is hardware dependent. Here, though, you will get some advice and some things to consider about where the files should go. The most important things to consider are disk space (present and future), speed, reliability, and fault tolerance. A RAID (Redundant Array of Inexpensive Disks) array takes all of this into consideration. There are four types you should consider.

RAID 0   RAID 0 uses disk striping; that is, it writes data across multiple hard-disk partitions in what is called a *stripe set*. This can greatly improve speed because multiple hard disks are working at the same time. RAID 0 can be implemented through the use of Windows NT software or on third-party hardware. While RAID 0 gives you the best speed, it does not provide any fault tolerance. If one of the hard disks in the stripe set is damaged, you lose all of your data.

RAID 1   RAID 1 uses disk mirroring. Disk mirroring actually writes your information to disk twice—once to the primary file and once to the mirror. This gives you excellent fault tolerance, but it is fairly slow, because you must write to disk twice. Windows NT includes the ability to mirror your hard disks. RAID 1 requires only a single hard-disk controller.

RAID 5   RAID 5—striping with parity—writes data to the hard disk in stripe sets. Parity checksums will be written across all disks in the stripe set. This gives you excellent fault tolerance as well as excellent speed with a reasonable amount of overhead. The parity checksums can be used to re-create information lost if a single disk in the stripe set fails. If more than one disk in the stripe set fails, however, you will lose all your data. Although Windows NT supports RAID 5 in a software implementation, a hardware implementation is faster and more reliable—it is suggested that you use it if you can afford it.

RAID 10   RAID 10 (sometimes referred to as RAID 1+0) is the "big daddy." This level of RAID should be used in mission-critical systems that require 24 hours a day, 7 days a week uptime and the fastest possible access. RAID 10 implements striping with parity as in RAID 5 and then mirrors the stripe sets. You still have excellent speed and excellent fault tolerance, but you also have the added expense of using more than twice the disk space of RAID 1. Then again, RAID 10 is for a situation in which you can afford no SQL Server downtime.

Some other issues that you should keep in mind when planning your database file placement are as follows:

▶ All data and log files that a particular SQL Server manages must reside on that SQL Server machine. They cannot be over the network.

▶ Only one database is allowed per data file, but a single database can span multiple data files.

▶ Transaction logs must reside on their own file, but they can span multiple log files.

▶ Database files fill up their available space by striping across all data files in the filegroup. In this manner, you can eliminate hot spots and reduce contention in high volume OLTP (Online Transaction Processing) environments.

▶ Transaction log files do not use striping, but fill each log file to capacity before continuing to the next log file.

▶ For communication, backup devices can be created across a network. Databases must be on the local machine.

NOTE

It is strongly suggested that you place your transaction logs on separate physical hard drives. In this manner, you can recover your data up to the second in the event of a media failure. If you are using RAID 5 (striping with parity), this is not an issue.

Space Requirements and Growth

Another very important factor to consider in planning your data storage and placement requirements is growth. However, to plan for growth, you must understand how SQL stores data. There are two main types of storage structures in SQL Server 7: extents and data pages.

Extents and Pages   At the most fundamental level, everything in SQL Server is stored on an 8KB page, which is the smallest unit of I/O in SQL. The page is the one common denominator for all objects in SQL Server. There are many different types of pages, but every page has some factors in common. Pages are always 8KB in size and always have a header, leaving about 8092 bytes of usable space on every page.

There are five primary types of pages in SQL Server:

Data pages: Data pages hold the actual database records. Although 8092 bytes are free for use on a data page, records are limited in length to no more than 8000 bytes. This is because records cannot cross rows, and approximately 52 bytes are used for transaction log overhead in the transaction log entries. Transaction logs are held on standard data pages.

Index pages: Index pages store the index keys and levels making up the entire index tree. Unlike data pages, there is no limit to the total number of entries that can be made on an index page.

Text/image pages: Text and image pages hold the actual data associated with text, ntext, and image data types. When a text field is saved, the record will contain a 16-byte pointer to a linked list of text pages that hold the actual text data. Only the 16-byte pointer inside the record is counted against the 8000-byte record-size limit.

Statistics pages: Every index has a statistics page that tracks the distribution of values in that index. The statistics page is used by the query optimizer in choosing the most appropriate index for any given query request.

Pages are combined into *extents,* which are blocks of eight pages totaling 64KB in size. Because the extent is the basic unit of allocation for tables and indexes, and all objects are saved in a table of some kind, all objects are stored in extents. When an object needs more space, SQL allocates it another extent. This is done because it is much faster to allocate a lump of pages all together rather than each one separately, and it keeps the database from being horribly fragmented.

Estimating Required Space for Tables   Now that you understand how space is allocated, you can ask yourself the age-old question, How large should the databases be? If they are too large, you will waste space, yet if they are too small, you will be constantly expanding them. To find a balance, you must be able to accurately estimate the required space. To estimate that space, you need to do as follows:

1. Calculate the space used by a single row of the table.

2. Calculate the number of rows that will fit on one page.

3. Estimate the number of rows the table will hold.

4. Calculate the total number of pages that will be required to hold these rows.

To calculate the space used by a single row in a table, you need to add the storage requirements for each field in the table plus an additional 2 bytes per row of overhead. This will give you the total space that is occupied by a single row. For example, if a table in a database has three fields defined as Char(10), Int, and Money, the storage space required for each row could be calculated as follows:

▶ Char(10)=10 bytes

▶ Int=4 bytes

▶ Money=8 bytes

▶ Overhead=2 bytes

▶ Total=24 bytes

WARNING

A row is limited to 2 bytes of overhead only when no variable-length data types (varchar and varbinary) have been used and no columns allow nulls. If variable-length columns are used or nulls are allowed, additional overhead must be added. The amount will depend on the data type and number of columns.

Once you know how much space is taken by each row in your table, you will be able to calculate the number of rows that can be contained on a single 8KB page; well, actually about 8092 bytes are free for storing data because of the header on each page. The total number of rows per page can be calculated as 8092÷*row size*. The resulting value will be rounded to the nearest whole number because a row cannot span pages. In the example above, each row requires 24 bytes of space to store. You can calculate the rows per page as follows:

8092÷24=337

In addition, the number of rows that can fit on one page may also depend on a fill factor that is used for the clustered index. *Fill factor* is a way of keeping the page from becoming 100 percent full when a clustered index is created. For example, if a clustered index is built on your table with a fill factor of 75 percent, this means that the data would be reorganized so that the data pages would be only 75 percent full. This means that instead of 8092 bytes free on each page, you could use only 6069 bytes.

Now that you know how to calculate the number of rows on a single page, you need to estimate the total number of rows that will be in your table. To do that, you have to know your data to estimate how many rows your table will eventually hold. When you make this estimate, try to consider as well as possible how large you expect your table to grow. If you do not allow for this growth in your estimates, the database will need to be expanded.

Once you have estimated the number of rows in your table, you can calculate the number of pages your table will take up by using the following equation:

number of rows in table÷number of rows per page

Here, the result will be rounded up to the nearest whole number.

In the example above, you saw that 337 rows would fit in a single page of the table. If you expect this table to eventually hold 1,000,000 records, the calculation would be as follows:

▶ 1,000,000÷337=2967.4

▶ Round the value to 2968 pages

Now, you can extend your calculation to determine the number of extents that must be allocated to this table to hold these data. Since all space is allocated in extents, you again need to round up to the nearest integer when calculating extents. Remember that there are eight 8KB pages per extent. Our calculation would be as follows:

2968÷8=371

Part iv

Since a megabyte can store 16 extents, this table would take about 23.2MB of space to store. Now you are ready to estimate your index space.

Estimating Index Storage Requirements   Indexes in SQL Server are stored in a B-Tree format; that is, you can think of an index as a large tree. You can also think of an index as a table with a pyramid on top of it. The ultimate concept here is that for every index, there is a single entry point: the root of the tree or the apex of the pyramid.

When estimating storage requirements, the base of this pyramid can be thought of as a table. You go through the same process in estimating the "leaf" level of an index as you would in estimating the storage requirements of a table. Although the process is very similar, there are a couple of issues that are important to consider:

▶ You are adding the data types of the index keys, not the data rows.

▶ Clustered indexes use the data page as the leaf level. There is no need to add additional storage requirements for a clustered-index leaf level.

The toughest part of estimating the size of an index is estimating the size and number of levels you will have in your index. While there is a fairly long and complex series of calculations to determine this exactly, you will usually find it sufficient to add an additional 35 percent of the leaf-level space estimated for the other levels of the index.

Working with Filegroups

Filegroups are used for explicitly placing database objects onto a particular set of database files. For example, you can separate tables and their nonclustered indexes onto separate filegroups. This can improve performance because modifications to the table can be written to both the table and the index at the same time. This can be especially useful if you are not using striping with parity (RAID 5).

Another advantage of filegroups is the ability to back up only a single filegroup at a time. This can be extremely useful for a VLDB because the sheer size of the database could make the backup an extremely time-consuming process. Another advantage is the ability to mark the filegroup and all data on the files that are part of it as either READONLY or READWRITE.

There are really only two disadvantages to using filegroups. The first is the administration that is involved in keeping track of the files in the filegroup and the database objects that are placed in them. The other disadvantage is that if you are working with a smaller database and have RAID 5 implemented, you may not be improving performance.

The two basic filegroups in SQL Server 7 are the primary, or default, filegroup that is created with every database and the user-defined filegroups that are created for a particular database. The primary filegroup will always contain the primary data file and any other files that are not specifically created on a user-defined filegroup. You can create additional filegroups using the ALTER DATABASE command or the Enterprise Manager.

Filegroups have several rules that you should follow when you are working with them:

▶ The first (or primary) data file must reside on the primary filegroup.

▶ All system files must be placed on the primary filegroup.

▶ A file cannot be a member of more than one filegroup at a time.

▶ Filegroups can be allocated indexes, tables, text, ntext, and image data.

▶ New data pages are not automatically allocated to user-defined filegroups if the primary filegroup runs out of space.

▶ Develop a data availability solution.

▶ Choose the appropriate backup and restore strategy. Strategies include full database backup; full database backup and transaction log backup; differential database backup with full database backup and transaction log backup; and database files backup and transaction log backup.

▶ Assess whether to use a standby server.

▶ Assess whether to use clustering.

Most systems administrators don't realize the full extent of the damage that can come from a downed system. Think about this example: You have 20 sales people that cannot do any work without the SQL Server running, so when it goes down, they don't work and you lose money. How much money, though? You probably pay an average of $25 per hour for sales people, which means that you are losing $500 an hour in labor—this is the extent of some administrators' calculations, but there is more.

Part iv

In this section, you will read about how to prepare for a database system crash. You will look at how to effectively combine full, differential, filegroup, and transaction log backups to minimize downtime when a crash occurs. The value of a standby server and clustering so that your users don't even know when one of the systems goes down will also be discussed.

All of this information is going to prove extremely valuable both in your own networks and on the test that you are preparing for, so pay close attention.

As a database administrator, you need to be prepared for anything, from hardware failures to malicious updates. You need to be able to bring your data back to a consistent state, which requires a good backup strategy. To devise this strategy, you will need to answer a few questions, such as:

► What type of backup will you use?

► How often will the backups occur?

► Will backups be on hard disk or tape?

► Who will be responsible for the backups?

► How will the backups be verified?

► What are the policies for backing up nonlogged operations?

► Does a standby server make sense for the installation?

SQL Backup Types

There are four types of backups that you can use to back up your data. Most often, you will use a combination of the following:

Full database backups: With full database backups, the entire database is backed up. Although they are the easiest to implement and restore from, full database backups may not be practical because of the amount of time required for very large databases.

Transaction log backups: Because the transaction log records all changes made to a database, backing up the log (after performing an occasional full database backup) allows you to re-create the database without having to do a full database backup every time.

Differential database backups: New with SQL 7, differential backups back up only data that have changed since the last full backup. These could be more efficient than transaction log back-ups for databases with existing data that change often. For example, if a person's bank account changes 10 times in one day, the transaction log backup would contain all 10 changes, while the differential backup would contain just the final amount.

Filegroup backups: Also new with SQL 7, filegroup backups allow you to back up different pieces of the database, based on the various files that make up the database. Usually, filegroup backups are done when the time required to perform a full database backup is prohibitive.

How Often Will the Backups Occur?

The frequency of your backups is directly proportional to the amount of data loss you can tolerate in the event of a system crash. For example, if you back up only once a week on Sunday, and then have a system crash on Friday, you would lose the entire week's work. Conversely, if you were to back up the transaction log every hour, the most data you will lose will be an hour's worth.

For your user databases, you may want to consider a combination of the four types of backups. If, for example, you have a database that does not change very much, perhaps containing archive data, you may just want to do a full backup once a week. If you have a database that changes throughout the day, though, you will want to use a different strategy.

For a database that changes regularly, you could perform a full backup once a week, then transaction log backups every day. That would give you recovery up to the day before the crash.

If you need more protection than that, you could perform a full backup once a week and transaction log backups every two hours. This would get you good recovery, but the restoration is slow because you must restore the full backup and then each transaction log backup in sequence.

For a faster restoration, you could do the full backup once a week, transaction log backups during the day, and differential backups at night throughout the week. With this final strategy, your restorations would be much faster because you need to restore only the full backup, the differ-ential from the night before, and the transaction log backups up to the time of the crash.

If you are working with a very large database (VLDB), you may not be able to back up the entire database at one time. In that instance, you can

Part iv

back up certain files of the database by using a filegroup backup. First, you would perform a full database backup, then during the day perform regular transaction log backups and at night perform a filegroup backup, getting a different filegroup each night. With this strategy, you would then need to restore only the full backup, then the filegroup backup for the failed file and any transaction log backups that occurred since the filegroup backup of the restored filegroup.

For your system databases, consider the following suggestions:

Master database: Schedule it for weekly backups and perform a manual backup after major modifications to your databases, devices, or users.

MSDB database: Schedule it for weekly backups and perform a manual backup after major changes to tasks, events, operators, or alerts.

Tempdb database: Don't bother backing it up, because it is automatically cleared every time SQL Server is stopped and started.

Model database: You should make a baseline backup of this, and then manually back it up whenever it changes (which won't be very often).

Pubs and Northwind databases: Don't bother backing these up, because they are simply sample databases that give you live data to practice on.

To What Medium Will the Backups Be Made?

SQL Server can back up databases to tape or a dump device (a file). If a tape drive is used, it must be on the Windows NT HCL (hardware compatibility list) and installed in the computer running SQL Server.

Who Is Responsible for the Backups?

If there is only one DBA in your company, you have no problem deciding who gets to perform the backups, but if there is more than one, you must decide who does what. You need to have a plan in place to make sure that one of the administrators is performing the backups on a regular basis and that when that administrator goes on vacation, another can take over in their place.

How Will the Backups Be Verified?

More than likely, you have a fire extinguisher in your home or office—have you ever looked at the top of it? There is a gauge that tells you whether it is full. If you don't check that gauge on your extinguisher regularly, it may not work for you when you need it. The same is true of your backups—you must verify that they are good before you need to use them.

You could have SQL verify each backup for you, or you could play it safe and verify them yourself by restoring them to a separate computer. Not only does this verify the integrity of your backups, it helps prepare you in case you have to bring up a spare server quickly.

What Are the Policies for Backing Up Nonlogged Operations?

While most transactions are logged by SQL Server in the transaction log, some are not. This means that if a database has to be restored, any and all of the nonlogged operations that happened since the last backup would be lost. You need to back up your databases immediately after you perform any of the following tasks:

- ▸ Fast bulk copies when Select Into/Bulk Copy is enabled

- ▸ Select Into commands when Select Into/Bulk Copy is enabled

TIP

Back up the database before starting a nonlogged operation, in case you need to restore the database to its previous state.

NT Clustering

You can obtain an additional component for Windows NT Server 4 called Cluster Server that allows you to have two separate computers using the same SCSI hard drive. Using this product, if one server fails for any reason, the backup system can take over all of the functions of the failed system, and the users won't even notice what happened. The only drawback to this solution is the expense—you need to purchase two computers instead of one, and you need to purchase Cluster Server separately.

Standby Servers

A standby server is the budget version of clustering. It can easily be set up to receive periodic copies of the data from the primary server. If the primary server goes down, the standby server can be renamed as the primary server and rebooted; it will then look and act like the primary server. Making a standby server work correctly involves a few steps:

1. Create the primary server as usual.

2. Create the secondary server with a unique name.

3. Do periodic full backups of the databases on the primary server.

4. Restore the backup files to the standby server.

5. Do frequent backups of the transaction log on the primary server.

6. Restore the backups of the transaction log to the standby server using the Standby switch if you wish to make the standby database read-only, or with the No Recovery switch otherwise.

7. If you have the time to prepare to switch servers, perform a transaction log backup of the primary server and a restoration on the standby server, and take the primary server offline.

8. Set the databases on the standby server for real use by using the Recover switch.

9. Rename the standby server as the primary server and reboot the standby server.

10. Use the standby server normally until the primary server is ready to come back online; then, simply follow steps 1 through 9 again.

▶ Develop a migration plan.

▶ Plan an upgrade from a previous version of SQL Server.

▶ Plan the migration of data from other data sources.

You may be one of hundreds, if not thousands, of people who have SQL 6.5 server in place right now, but since you found out what SQL 7 is capable of, you've decided to install this latest version. Can you imagine the chaos if there were no upgrade path? You would need to manually rebuild all of your data—Microsoft would probably not sell many copies of SQL 7 that way. Fortunately, there is not only an upgrade path from older versions of SQL, but there is a migration path from other database applications as well. In this section, you will read about what you need to do to prepare for a successful upgrade or migration to SQL 7.

SQL Server 7 allows you to upgrade databases and entire servers from SQL Server 6 and 6.5 using the Upgrade Wizard, but it does not support upgrades directly from earlier versions (4.21). Since the upgrade process is irreversible, you will need to carefully consider the following questions before you can run the Wizard successfully.

The first question to consider is whether you meet the following upgrade requirements:

- ▶ Service Pack 4 for Windows NT

- ▶ Internet Explorer 4.01 Service Pack 1

- ▶ 32MB of RAM

- ▶ 180MB of free hard-drive space (for full installation), plus free space equal to about 1.5 times the size of the databases being upgraded

- ▶ If upgrading SQL 6.5, Service Pack 3 (or higher) for SQL 6.5 is required

- ▶ If upgrading SQL 6, Service Pack 3 (or higher) for SQL 6 is required

- ▶ Named Pipes installed with the default pipe name `Pipe\SQL\Query`

Once you meet the hardware and software requirements, you can move into the deeper questions.

WARNING

If you are upgrading servers involved in replication, you must upgrade the distribution server first, because SQL Server 7 has support for SQL Server 6.*x* replication tasks. The reverse is not necessarily true.

One-Computer vs. Two-Computer Upgrades

One of the first questions to answer is whether to leave the old SQL Server in place and migrate the data to a new server, or upgrade the original 6.x server to SQL Server 7.

The main advantage of using a second box is that the original server is untouched during the upgrade and can quickly be brought back online if there is a problem with the upgrade. The major disadvantage here is that a second server at least as powerful as the original 6.x server must be purchased or leased.

Upgrading vs. Side-by-Side Installation

If you decide to go with the one-computer upgrade, you have one more decision to make. You can perform a live upgrade by installing SQL 7 in the same folder that 6.x occupied, or you can install 7 in a different folder.

The advantage of installing SQL 7 on top of 6.x is that the conversion is quick and painless, and all functions and settings of 6.x are carried into 7. The disadvantage is that if the upgrade fails for any reason (such as a power interruption), there is no 6.x server to go back to.

The advantage of installing 7 in a different folder than 6.x is that the SQL 7 installation can be thoroughly tested before converting your databases to the 7 format. Not only that, but you can preserve your old databases, which would allow you to switch between SQL 6.x and 7 by running a simple program (Switch to SQL 6.5/Switch to 7). The disadvantage of installing SQL 7 in a new folder is that it will take significantly more hard-drive space (because you have two copies of each database) and requires manually converting your databases and settings.

Migrating from Other Data Sources

The Upgrade Wizard will not handle an upgrade from any other vendor's database system. This means that if you are running Oracle, Sybase, or even Access, you will need to migrate the data using other tools provided by SQL. Those tools are discussed in detail in Chapter 4.

▶ Develop a replication strategy.

> ▶ Given a scenario, design the appropriate replication model. Replication models include single Publisher and multiple Subscribers; multiple Publishers and single Subscriber; multiple Publishers and multiple Subscribers; and remote Distributor.

▶ Choose the replication type. Replication types include snapshot, transactional, and merge.

If you have a very popular database, perhaps a catalog database used by all your sales people, do you want them all to access the data from a single server? In a small organization, that may work fine, but if you have hundreds or thousands of users spread out across a wide area, that single server will become a bottleneck that will bring your server to its knees. With replication, you can make copies of the data on remote servers so that all of your users can access the data they need locally, without going over a WAN link to your server.

In this final section, the fine points of replication will be examined. The proper model to use for a given scenario as well as which replication type would be best will be discussed. The concepts you are about to read about will be tested heavily and will save you from endless support calls when you have too many users for one server, so pay close attention.

You use replication to put copies of the same data at different locations throughout the enterprise. The most common of the many reasons why you might want to replicate your data include:

▶ Moving data closer to the user

▶ Reducing locking conflicts when multiple sites wish to work with the same data

▶ Allowing site autonomy so that each location can set up its own rules and procedures for working with its copy of the data

▶ Removing the impact of read-intensive operations such as report generation and ad-hoc query processing from the OLTP database

To describe and implement replication, SQL Server 7 uses a Publisher/Subscriber metaphor. Your server can play different roles as part of the replication scenario: It can be a Publisher, Subscriber, Distributor, or any combination of these. The data that is replicated is published in the form of an article, which is stored in a publication. These publications can be pushed to Subscribers, meaning that the subscription is initiated at the Publisher, or pulled, meaning that the subscription is initiated at the Subscriber.

NOTE

One of the major differences between push and pull subscriptions is that with push subscriptions, the replication agent runs on the distribution server; with pull subscriptions, it runs on the Subscriber. There will be more discussion of the agents in Chapter 4.

Here is a list of key terms used as part of the Publisher/Subscriber metaphor:

Publisher: This is the source database where replication begins. The Publisher makes data available for replication.

Subscriber: The Subscriber is the destination database where replication ends and either receives a snapshot of all the published data or applies transactions that have been replicated to it.

Distributor: This is the intermediary between the Publisher and Subscriber. The Distributor receives published transactions or snapshots, and then stores and forwards these publications to the Subscribers.

Publication: The publication is the storage container for different articles. A Subscriber can subscribe to an individual article or an entire publication. If they subscribe to an individual article, they are actually subscribing to the whole publication, but just reading one article.

Article: An article is the data, transactions, or stored procedures that are stored within a publication. This is the actual information that is going to be replicated. Articles can be partitioned vertically, in which only a subset of columns is replicated; horizontally, in which a subset of records is replicated; or a combination of both.

Two-phase commit: Two-phase commit (sometimes referred to as *2PC*) is a form of replication in which modifications made to the Publishing database are made at the Subscription database at exactly the same time. This is handled through the use of distributed transactions. As with any transaction, either all statements commit successfully or all modifications are rolled back. To accomplish this task, two-phase commit uses the Microsoft Distributed Transaction Coordinator (MS-DTC), which implements a portion of the functionality of the Microsoft Transaction Server. In this chapter, the focus will be on replication as opposed to two-phase commits.

NOTE

A Publisher can publish data to one or more Distributors. A Subscriber can subscribe through one or more Distributors. A Distributor can have one or more Publishers and Subscribers.

Now that you have the lingo down, you are ready to look into the various replication models. There are four of them to consider here.

Single Publisher with Multiple Subscribers

As shown in Figure 18.2, both the Publishing database and the Distribution database are on the same SQL Server. This configuration is useful when modeling replication strategies for the following business scenarios:

- ▶ Asynchronous order processing during communication outages

- ▶ Distribution of price lists, customer lists, vendor lists, etc.

- ▶ Removal of MIS activities from the Online Transaction Processing (OLTP) environment

- ▶ Establishment of executive information systems

The main advantage of this model is the ability to move data to a separate SQL Server, thus allowing the publishing server to continue to handle online transaction-processing duties without having to absorb the impact of the ad-hoc queries generally found in MIS departments.

You can use any type of replication here—transactional, merge, or snapshot. If you do not have to update things such as text, ntext, and image data types, it is suggested that you use transactional replication here. MIS departments generally don't need to make changes to the subscribed data.

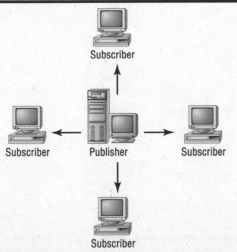

Subscriber

Subscriber   Publisher   Subscriber

Subscriber

FIGURE 18.2:   Single Publisher with multiple Subscribers

Part iv

NOTE

You can further reduce the impact of replication on your OLTP server by implementing pull subscriptions. This would force the distribution agent to run on each Subscriber rather than on the OLTP distribution server.

Multiple Publishers with a Single Subscriber

The model shown in Figure 18.3 is very useful in the following situations:

▶ Roll-up reporting

▶ Local warehouse inventory management

▶ Local customer order processing

You need to keep several things in mind when you attempt to use this model. Because multiple Publishers are writing to a single table in the database, you must take some precautions to ensure that referential integrity is maintained. If your New York office sends an order with a key of 1000, and your Milwaukee office also sends an order with a key of 1000, you would have two records with the same primary key. You could get bad data in your database, because the primary key is designed to guarantee the uniqueness of each record. In this situation, only one of those records would post.

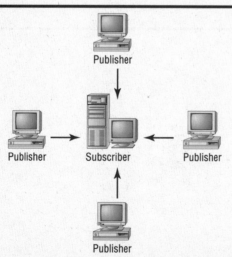

FIGURE 18.3: Multiple Publishers with a single Subscriber

To make sure that this doesn't become a problem, implement a composite primary key, using the original order ID number along with a location-specific code. You could, for example, give the New York branch a location code of NY and the Milwaukee branch a location code of MW. This way, the new composite keys would be NY1000 and MW1000. There would be no more conflicting records, and both orders would be filled from the Denver offices.

This scenario is especially suited to transactional replication, because the data at the Denver site is really read-only. Snapshot replication wouldn't work here, because that would overwrite everyone else's data. You could use merge replication if the other locations needed to be able to see all the orders placed.

Multiple Publishers with Multiple Subscribers

This model is used when a single table needs to be maintained on multiple servers. Each server subscribes to the table and also publishes the table to other servers. This model can be particularly useful in the following business situations:

- ▶ Reservations systems

- ▶ Regional order-processing systems

- ▶ Multiple warehouse implementations

To illustrate this model, think of a regional order-processing system as shown in Figure 18.4. Suppose you place an order on Monday and want to check on that order on Tuesday. When you call up, you may be routed to any of several regional order-processing centers, which is just fine, because with this model, each of these centers should have a copy of your order.

It is probably best to use transactional replication for this scenario, using some type of region code (as described in the previous scenario). Each order-processing center should publish only its own data, but it should subscribe to data being published by the other Publishers. In addition, each location should update only the data it owns. This scenario is also a good candidate for transactional replication with an updating Subscriber. In this case, each center could update data owned by another center; however, this update would take place at both servers and therefore maintain transactional consistency.

Part iv

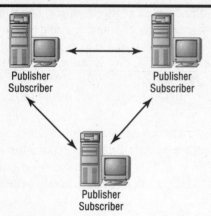

FIGURE 18.4:   Multiple Publishers with multiple Subscribers

Using a Remote Distributor

In this model, you remove the impact of the distribution process from your OLTP server, which gives you the best possible speed on the OLTP server. This model is useful in situations where you need the optimal performance out of your OLTP server. As discussed earlier, a single distribution server can work with multiple Distributors and multiple Subscribers. Figure 18.5 shows a representation of this strategy.

This calls for transactional replication and minimizing the impact of replication on the Publishing database. By moving just transactions, rather than moving snapshots or attempting to merge data at the Publisher, you can gain the most speed and have the lowest impact on the Publisher.

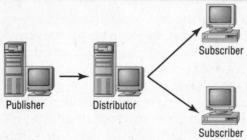

FIGURE 18.5:   Central Publisher with a remote Distributor

Heterogeneous Replication

In addition to the replication scenarios just discussed, it is possible to replicate data to non-Microsoft SQL Server databases. This is known as *heterogeneous database replication*. Currently, SQL Server supports replication to MS Access, Oracle, and IBM databases that conform to the IBM DRDA (Distributed Relational Database Architecture) data protocol. To replicate to an ODBC data source, the Subscriber must meet the following ODBC driver requirements:

- ▶ It must run in 32-bit mode.

- ▶ It must be thread-safe.

- ▶ It must allow updates.

- ▶ It must support the T-SQL DDL (Data Definition Language).

- ▶ It must fully support the ODBC Level 1 Conformance standard.

When you publish to these ODBC Subscribers, you need to keep the following rules in mind:

- ▶ Only push subscriptions are supported.

- ▶ ODBC does not support batched statements.

- ▶ The ODBC DSN (Data Source Name) must conform to the SQL Server naming conventions.

- ▶ Snapshot data will be sent using bulk copy's character format.

- ▶ Data types will be mapped as closely as possible.

Internet Replication

You can even configure your SQL Server to publish to the Internet. If you do, you must make some additional configuration changes to your SQL Server 7 computer. For either a push or pull style of replication, the following items must be configured:

- ▶ TCP/IP must be installed on the computers where the merge agent and distribution agents are running.

- ▶ The publishing server and the distribution server should be on the same side of the firewall.

- ▶ The publishing server and the distribution server should have a direct network connection to each other (rather than a connection across the Internet). This is for both security and latency concerns.

Part iv

Some additional configuration changes need to be made if you are going to allow pull subscriptions:

▶ Microsoft's IIS must be installed on the same server as your distribution server.

▶ Both the merge and distribution agents must be configured with the correct FTP address. This is done through the distribution agent or from a command prompt.

▶ The working folder must be available to your subscription servers.

▶ The FTP home folder on your IIS computer should be set to the distribution working folder. This is normally *ServerName*\ C$\MSSQL7\ReplData.

Distribution Types

Now that you have the models down, you are almost ready to choose a type; the two basic types are replication or distributed transactions. The main difference between the two types is in the timing. With distributed transactions, your data are 100 percent in synchronization, 100 percent of the time. When you use replication, there is some latency involved. It may be as little as a few seconds, or as long as several days or even weeks. Distributed transactions require that the replicated databases be connected at all times or they will fail, whereas replication is unaffected by this condition.

Before you choose a type, though, you should understand the factors that influence your decision. The three main items to consider are autonomy, latency, and transactional consistency:

Autonomy: This refers to how much independence you wish to give each Subscriber with regard to the replicated data. Will the replicated data be considered read-only? How long will the data at a Subscriber be valid? How often do you need to connect to the Distributor to download more data?

Latency: This refers to how often your data will be updated. Do they need to be in synchronization at all times? Is every minute enough? What if you are a salesperson on the road who dials in to the office once a day? Is this good enough?

Transactional consistency: Although there are several types of replication, the most common method is to move transactions from the Publisher through the Distributor and onto the

Subscriber. Transactional consistency comes into play here. Do all the transactions that are stored need to be applied at the same time and in order? What happens if there is a delay in the processing?

Once you understand these factors, there are a few more questions to answer before you can choose a distribution type:

- What are you going to publish? Will it be all the data in a table, or will you partition information?

- Who has access to your publications? Are these Subscribers connected, or are they dial-up users?

- Will Subscribers be able to update your data, or is their information considered read-only?

- How often should you synchronize your Publishers and Subscribers?

- How fast is your network? Can Subscribers be connected at all times? How much traffic is there on your network?

When you factor in latency, autonomy, and consistency, you actually end up with six different distribution types:

- Distributed transactions

- Transactional replication

- Transactional replication with updating subscribers

- Snapshot replication

- Snapshot replication with updating subscribers

- Merge replication

Distributed transactions have the least amount of latency and autonomy, but they have the highest level of consistency. Merge replication has the highest amount of latency and autonomy, and a lower level of consistency.

Using Distributed Transactions   When you use distributed transactions or 2PC to replicate your data, you have almost no autonomy or latency, but you do have guaranteed transactional consistency. With 2PC, either all changes are made at exactly the same time or none of the changes are made. Remember that all the affected subscribers must be in contact with the Publisher at all times.

This type of distribution is most useful in situations where Subscribers must have real-time data, as in a reservations system.

For example, think of a cruise line that has only so many rooms of a particular type available. If someone in Dallas wants the Captain's Suite and someone in California also wants the Captain's Suite, the first one to book the room will get it. The other booking won't be allowed, because that location will immediately show up as already booked.

Using Transactional Replication   When you use this distribution method, transactions are gathered from the Publishers and stored in the Distribution database. Subscribers then receive these transactions and must work with the data as if they were read-only. This is because any changes made to their local copy of the data might not allow newly downloaded transactions to be applied properly, which would destroy the transactional consistency.

The advantages to this approach include the fact that transactions are relatively small items to move through the system (unlike snapshot replication, which will be looked at shortly). The main disadvantage of using transactional replication is that Subscribers must treat the data as read-only.

Use this distribution method when Subscribers can treat their data as read-only and need the updated information with a minimal amount of latency, such as in an order-processing/distribution system with several locations where orders are taken. Each of those order locations would be a Publisher, and the published orders could then be replicated to a Subscription database at your central warehouse. The central warehouse could then accept the orders, fill them, and ship them out.

Using Transactional Replication with Updating Subscribers
This will probably become the most popular form of replication in SQL Server 7. When you use transactional replication with updating Subscribers, you are gaining site autonomy, minimizing latency, and keeping transactional consistency. This (in most cases) would be considered the best possible solution.

When you implement transactional replication with updating Subscribers, you are essentially working with all the tenets of transactional replication. The major difference is that when you change the subscription data, 2PC changes the Publishing database as well. In this fashion, your local Subscriber is updated at exactly the same time as the Publisher. Other Subscribers will have your changes downloaded to them at their next synchronization.

This scenario can be useful for a reservations system that needs to be updated frequently, but does not need total synchronization. Let's use a library as an example here. You wish to reserve a book on SQL Server 7. You go to the computer, look up the book you wish to reserve, and find that one copy is currently available. When you try to reserve the book, however, you might find that your data isn't 100 percent up to date and the book has already been checked out. In this example, when you try to reserve your book, the Subscriber automatically runs a 2PC to the Publisher. At the Publisher, someone has already checked out that last copy, and therefore the update fails. At the next synchronization, your Subscriber will be updated with the news that the last copy has been checked out.

Using Snapshot Replication   When you use snapshot replication as your distribution method, you are actually moving an entire copy of the published items through the Distributor and on to the Subscribers. This type of replication allows for a high level of both site autonomy and transactional consistency because all records are going to be copied from the Publisher, and the local copy of the data will be overwritten at the next synchronization. Latency may be a bit higher because you probably will not move an entire snapshot every few minutes.

OLAP (Online Analytical Processing) servers are prime candidates for this type of replication. The data at each Subscriber are considered read-only and don't have to be 100 percent in synchronization all the time. This allows your MIS departments to run their reporting and ad-hoc queries on reasonably fresh data without affecting the OLTP server (which is doing all of the order-processing work).

Keep in mind that administrators and MIS ad-hoc queries generally don't modify the data. They are looking for historical information, such as how many widgets they sold, etc., so that data that is a few hours or even a few days old will generally not make a difference to the results returned by the queries.

Using Snapshot Replication with Updating Subscribers   The initial portion of this distribution style works just as in snapshot replication, with the added ability for the Subscriber to update the Publisher with new information. The updates use the 2PC protocol as described above.

This maintains a high level of site autonomy, a high level of transactional consistency, and a moderate level of latency. The data may be downloaded to the Subscriber only once a day, but any updates the Subscriber tries to make to data must first be approved by the Publisher.

Part iv

This type of distribution is useful when you have read-only data that needs to be updated infrequently. If your data needs to be updated often, it is suggested that you use transactional replication with updating Subscribers.

Snapshot replication might be useful when auditing your database, downloading portions of the data, and double-checking that everything is being updated properly. The occasional mistake could then be quickly fixed and auditing could continue.

Using Merge Replication   Merge replication provides the highest amount of site autonomy, the highest latency, and the lowest level of transactional consistency. Merge replication allows each Subscriber to make changes to their local copy of the data. At some point, these changes are merged with those made by other Subscribers as well as changes made at the Publisher. Ultimately, all sites receive the updates from all other sites. This is known as *convergence*. That is, all changes from all sites converge and are redistributed so that all sites have the same changes.

Transactional consistency is nearly nonexistent here, because different sites may all be making changes to the same data, resulting in conflicts. SQL Server 7 will automatically choose a particular change over another change and then converge those data. To simplify: Sooner or later, all sites will have the same copy of the data, but those data may not necessarily be what you wanted.

For example, Subscriber A makes changes to record 100. Subscriber B also makes changes to record 100. While this doesn't sound too bad, suppose the changes that Subscriber A made to record 100 are due to changes that were made to record 50. If Subscriber B doesn't have the same data in record 50, Subscriber B will make a different decision. Obviously, this can be incredibly complex.

You might wonder why anyone would want to use merge replication. There are, however, many reasons to use it, and with some careful planning, you can make merge replication work to your advantage. There are triggers you can modify to determine which record is the correct record to use. The default rule when records are changed at multiple sites is to take the changes based on a site priority. Converge the results and then send them out. The exception to this general rule is when the main database is changed as well as all of the user databases. In this case, the user changes are applied first and then the main database changes.

For example, say you have a central server that you call Main and 20 salespeople who are using merge replication. If one of your salespeople modifies record 25 and you modify record 25 at the Main server, when the records are converged, the user changes will first be placed in the Main server, and then the Main server changes will overwrite them.

If you design your Publishers and Subscribers to minimize conflicts, merge replication can be very advantageous. Look at the highway patrol, for example. A patrol car might pull over a car and write up a ticket for speeding. At the end of the day, that piece of data is merged with data from other officers who have also written tickets. The data are then converged back to all of the different squad-car computers. It is unlikely that the same individual will be stopped by two different police officers on the same day. If it does happen, however, the situation can be remedied using either the default conflict-resolution triggers or custom triggers that the police departments can create themselves.

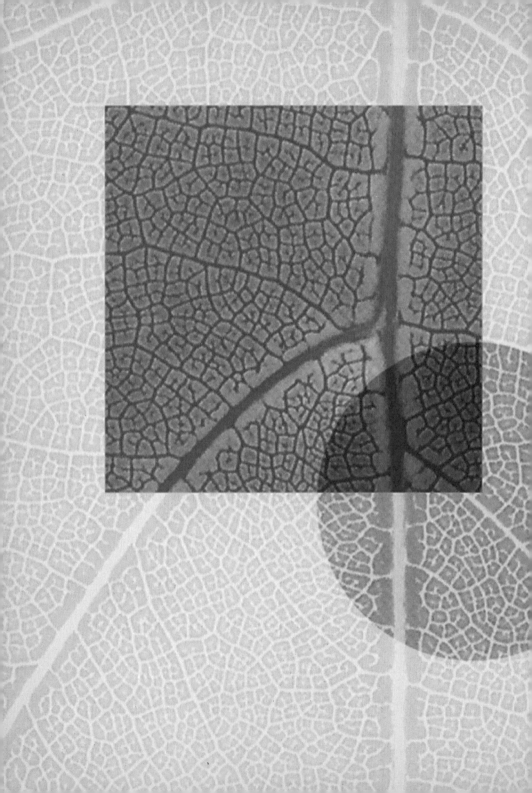

Chapter 19

INSTALLATION AND CONFIGURATION

Now that you have a plan for implementing SQL Server, you're ready to start the installation process—but be careful. More often than not, we click the Next key every time we see it and accept the default settings for our software, which can prove hazardous to SQL Server. Many options in setup will need your attention if you want SQL Server to function properly when you're done; in fact, if you misconfigure some of these options, you will need to reinstall SQL Server to make corrections.

Just to be sure you don't fall into that trap, each and every screen in the setup program and the various options on those screens will be analyzed. Pay close attention to those options—since Microsoft wants to be sure that SQL Server DBAs are capable of installing the software that they will be administering, these options can affect your performance on the exam as well as the performance of your server.

Adapted from *MCSE Exam Notes: SQL Server 7 Administration* by Rick Sawtell, Lance Mortensen, and Joseph L. Jorden

ISBN 0-7821-2477-1   368 pages $19.99

Install SQL Server 7.

- ▶ Choose the character set.

- ▶ Choose the Unicode collation.

- ▶ Choose the appropriate sort order.

- ▶ Install Net-Libraries and protocols.

- ▶ Install services.

- ▶ Install and configure a SQL Server client.

- ▶ Perform an unattended installation.

- ▶ Upgrade from a SQL Server 6.*x* database.

To use SQL, or any other product, you need to install it first. As with any other installation program, there are options to consider: Where will the files be stored, what options will be installed, etc. With SQL, these options become very important because if they are misconfigured, SQL may not function properly—it may just be slow, or it may not work the way you want it to at all. So, pay close attention to each screen, and each option on each screen—not only for the sake of your server, but for the sake of your exam score, since these options will be tested.

While the installation process is relatively painless, once your decisions are implemented, they can be difficult to change. Therefore, it is a good idea to carefully consider each of the options in the setup program, rather than just clicking the Next button. The first option you will need to know for the exam is the character set.

Choosing a Character Set

A *character set* defines how SQL sees the characters you type in. The first 128 characters in the set are defined by the first 7 bits of the byte used to store them—by using the 8th bit of that byte, you get 128 extended characters for a total of 256 characters in a set. The most important thing to remember here is that SQL supports only one character set at a time, and, once installed, that character set cannot be changed. To help overcome this limitation, SQL supports Unicode characters (as you will soon see).

It is crucial to pick a character set that will be recognized by the applications installed on the SQL Server. For instance, if an application wishes to store the character _, it will be able to do so only if certain character sets have been selected.

SQL Server supports the following character sets:

1252 (ISO 8859, ANSI):   This is the default character set for SQL Server 6.*x* and 7, and should be chosen when you are using Windows clients exclusively.

850 (multilingual):   This is the old default character set and is still in use in many databases, especially those upgraded from earlier versions of SQL Server. This would be a good choice for multinational companies.

437 (U.S. English):   Although this is a popular character set because it contains support for graphic characters not normally supported by databases, its compatibility with other languages is limited.

Selecting Unicode Collation

SQL Server 7 supports Unicode character types. Unicode characters are represented by 2 bytes (rather than a single byte), allowing 65,536 possible characters for a given field instead of the 256 allowed by a code page. In plain English, this means that Unicode makes it possible to store characters from multiple languages on one computer. The Unicode sort order is used to sort those Unicode data so that they are organized and neat.

The sort order for Unicode data, the default Unicode collation, is case-insensitive, width-insensitive, and Kana (Japanese)-insensitive. Use the default selection unless you have been specifically instructed to change it. If you need to support multiple languages, but have to use the 850 or 437 character sets, you can choose the Unicode data type when you create your columns.

Choosing the Right Sort Order

The *sort order* determines how data are stored, compared, and returned during queries. The available sort-order selections will be determined by the character set chosen. The main sort orders include the following:

Dictionary sort order, case-insensitive: This is the default sort order and treats upper- and lowercase characters the same for comparison purposes. This can improve performance since

SQL does not have to differentiate between upper- and lower-case characters when storing, retrieving, and indexing data.

Dictionary sort order, case-sensitive: This sort order retains and enforces all cases in the database when using SQL Server. This means that McDonald (with an uppercase *D*) and Mcdonald (with a lowercase *d*) are entirely different words in this sort order. Since SQL has to take the time to differentiate the characters, this sort order slows performance.

Binary sort order: The fastest and simplest sort order, binary sort order sorts everything by the binary representation of the data, not as a dictionary would sort characters.

Installing Network Libraries and Protocols

SQL Server doesn't automatically support every protocol that is installed on the computer—SQL has to be told that the protocols are there and how to use them. That is why you need to install Net-Libraries. SQL Server supports the following protocols and standards:

TCP/IP: Support for this industry-standard protocol is enabled by default using TCP port 1433. Since SQL relies on the operating system for TCP/IP configuration settings, such as address and subnet mask, connections to the SQL Server that do not function properly may be caused by TCP/IP configuration problems and not by SQL Server.

IPX/SPX: Support for this protocol, used by NetWare servers and clients, is not enabled by default. Installing IPX/SPX on the SQL Server allows NetWare clients to connect to the SQL Server even if they don't have a Microsoft client installed. If you enable support for IPX/SPX, you can also configure the name of the server that NetWare clients will see. Both NetWare and Microsoft clients should use the same server name to avoid confusion.

Named Pipes: Support for this networking standard is enabled by default. Named Pipes is a common method for connecting to a resource over a network. Note that Microsoft's NetBEUI, TCP/IP, and NWLINK (IPX/SPX) support the Named Pipes specification natively.

Multi-Protocol: Support for this standard is enabled by default. Multi-Protocol support allows clients to connect via two or more methods, allowing encryption across TCP/IP and IPX/SPX.

AppleTalk: Support for this protocol is not enabled by default. AppleTalk is used by Macintosh clients.

DecNet: Support for this protocol is not enabled by default. DecNet is used by some older Digital clients.

Installing the SQL Server Services

When you set up the full version of SQL, three separate services are installed: MSSQLSERVER, SQLAGENT, and MS-DTC. With the desktop version, you will not get MS-DTC. You can install a fourth service separately—MSSearch—which provides full-text indexes for SQL Server 7. Here is what these services do:

MSSQLSERVER: This is the actual database engine and is required for any computer you wish to be a SQL Server. To check whether the service has been installed, go to Control Panel ➢ Services and look for it by name.

SQLAGENT: SQLAGENT is a helper service designed to take care of the automation performed in SQL Server. Although this service is not technically required, you should not run without it. You can check on its installation by going to Control Panel ➢ Services.

MS-DTC: The MS-DTC (Database Transaction Coordinator) service is an optional service designed to take care of transactions that span multiple SQL Servers. When a transaction is performed across two or more servers, the MS-DTC service ensures that the transaction is performed on all servers; otherwise, the transaction is rolled back.

MSSearch: When you install full-text index support, you install the MSSearch service, which will allow you to perform English queries. It is basically the same service supported by Microsoft's Index Server engine.

Installing SQL Clients

When Microsoft speaks of a software client, they mean one of two things: ODBC or DB-Library and OLE-DB connections. Most of the applications you use to create custom front ends, such as Office 95/97 and IIS, install ODBC drivers for SQL Server. If client computers already have ODBC and SQL drivers installed, all you will need to do is configure the ODBC connections via the ODBC Data Sources applet of the Control Panel. Once inside the ODBC applet, you generally add one of two types of configurations:

▶ User DSN is usable only by the user who created it.

▶ System DSN is usable by any user and application contained on the computer.

When you install a SQL client (not ODBC), you can install just the client piece (which lets the client connect to SQL Server), or you can install the SQL Server management tools (Enterprise Manager, Query Analyzer, etc.). To install the Client Connectivity software and/or the management tools, choose a Custom installation and leave only the management tools selected.

Performing Unattended Installations

SQL Server can be installed without prompts by using various batch files and initialization files that are contained on the CD-ROM, as shown in Table 19.1.

TABLE 19.1: Sample Batch and Initialization Files for SQL Server 7

BATCH FILE	INITIALIZATION FILE	ACTION
Sql70cli.bat	Sql70cli.iss	Installs SQL Server administration tools
Sql70ins.bat	Sql70ins.iss	Installs a typical version of SQL Server
Sql70cst.bat	Sql70cst.iss	Performs a custom installation, which can be used to install all components
Sql70rem.bat		Uninstalls SQL Server

You can edit the sample initialization files to fit your site, or you can edit the initialization file that is created during an installation (stored as setup.iss in the \MSSQL7\install folder).

You can also run the SQL setup program as follows:

```
Setupsql.exe k=Rc
```

This will generate the script file in the \Windows or \Winnt folder. Choose Cancel when prompted to copy files, or a full installation will take place.

Upgrading from a SQL 6.x Database

Databases can be upgraded using the Upgrade Wizard. SQL Server 6 and 6.5 databases can be directly upgraded to SQL Server 7, while any SQL 4.21 databases must first be upgraded to SQL 6.x before you can upgrade them to SQL 7.

When upgrading SQL Servers and databases, you may run into problems, such as when objects in the old databases cannot be created in the new database. This happens when:

▶ The object has been renamed with the sp_rename stored procedure.

▶ The accompanying text in syscomments is missing.

▶ Stored procedures have been created within other stored procedures.

▶ The owner of an object's login ID is not created at the new server.

▶ The older server was using integrated security, but the new server is using mixed security, and the NT groups have not been created at the new server.

Other issues that you may encounter when upgrading servers and databases include the following:

▶ The upgrade process will fail if @@Servername returns NULL.

▶ Stored procedures that reference or modify system tables will not be converted.

Servers involved with replication should be upgraded in a certain order: The distribution server must be upgraded first. Many SQL 7 replication functions will not be enabled until all involved servers are upgraded.

WARNING

You may opt to have the Upgrade Wizard delete old SQL 6.x devices and databases. If you do, all devices and databases will be deleted whether or not they were upgraded. For this reason, if you have the Wizard delete old databases, you should upgrade all user databases at the same time.

The most important procedure in this chapter is the actual setup of SQL Server. In this section, each screen in the setup program and the available options will be examined. There is no need to memorize each and every option on each and every screen, but you should have a general familiarity with the setup program. The most important thing is knowing what will happen if any of these options are misconfigured—for example, if the sort order is set improperly.

Installing SQL Server 7

To successfully install SQL Server 7, use the following steps:

1. In User Manager, create the account that will be used as the service account.

2. Run the setup program from the SQL Server 7 CD-ROM.

3. Install the prerequisites (Windows NT SP4 and IE 4.01 SP1 if not already installed) by choosing the appropriate operating system from the main setup screen. Reboot after installing all prerequisites and rerun the setup program.

4. Select the appropriate version of SQL Server to install. Choose Desktop if on a workstation or Standard (full) if on a server. Choose Next.

5. Select Local installation if you are running the setup program on the computer you wish to become the SQL Server; otherwise, choose Remote and supply the name of the remote server. Choose Next.

6. Select Next at the Introduction screen.

7. Select the appropriate license information, enter your CD key, and select OK.

8. Enter your name and company name, then select Next.

9. At the Upgrade Wizard prompt, inform SQL whether or not to perform an upgrade (you can upgrade later via the Upgrade Wizard). Select Next.

10. Select an installation type. Select Next to continue.

11. If you selected Custom, then select the Server Components, Management Tools, Client Connectivity, and Books Online checkboxes. Select Next to continue.

12. Select the Sort Order, Character Set, Unicode Support, and Installation folders (note that it may be best to leave the default settings). Select Next to continue.

13. Select the network support to install. Note that Named Pipes, TCP/IP, and Multi-Protocol Net-Libraries are already selected. Select Next to continue.

14. Select the service account created in step 1 for the SQL services to use. Select Next to continue.

15. Click Next to go to the Licensing screen.

16. Enter your appropriate licensing information. Choose Continue, check the Agree box, and choose OK.

17. Review and adjust the installation settings as needed, then click Next to start the installation. The installation will take several minutes.

18. Choose OK when prompted that the installation has finished.

▶ Configure SQL Server.

> ▶ Configure SQL Mail.

> ▶ Configure default American National Standards Institute (ANSI) settings.

Thankfully, the terrors of SQL 6.5 have been vanquished. Gone are the days when you had to configure memory settings, user connections, and procedure cache just to get your system to function. These days, while you may need to configure some of those options, you are *required* to perform only some minor configurations.

One of the things you need to configure is SQL Mail so that SQL can send you an e-mail or a page if something goes wrong. You also need to be familiar with the ANSI settings—while they are not tested as much as SQL Mail, you need to be sure that SQL's ANSI compliance is set to your liking.

For the most part, SQL is self tuning. You may need to change memory settings or user connections, but it is not required. In fact, changing even the ANSI-setting defaults is not required (just highly recommended). One thing that does require your attention to work, however, is SQL Mail.

SQL Mail

Without SQL Mail, your server will be able to alert you of problems via only a net-send message that pops up on your computer screen—which is great, unless you are not in front of your screen. When you're not in front

Part iv

of your screen, you need an e-mail or a page, which is what SQL Mail is for. The main issues involved with SQL Mail are as follows:

- ▶ You must have a MAPI-compliant mail server (i.e., MS Exchange Server).

- ▶ You need to install Outlook on the SQL Server.

- ▶ If you want to be paged, you will need an alphanumeric pager that is capable of receiving pages via SMTP (Internet) mail.

ANSI Settings

SQL Server complies with the American National Standards Institute (ANSI) SQL-92 specifications. Because of this, you need to be aware of some options that will affect the ANSI-specific settings:

ANSI NULL default: This setting specifies whether new columns that are created have a default value of NULL. The default is NOT NULL.

ANSI NULL: When this is set to True, all comparisons with a NULL value will return a result of NULL (unknown). If it is set to False (the default), any non-Unicode comparisons against a NULL value will return True if the value is NULL (compare NULL to NULL) or False if the value is anything else (compare "Bob" to NULL).

ANSI warnings: If this is set to True, errors or warnings are issued when divide-by-zero errors occur or NULL values appear in aggregate functions. If this is set to False (the default), errors or warnings are not generated for these events.

If you want to know when there is a problem, you will need to configure SQL Mail to send you e-mail or page you over the Internet. You will also need to understand how to configure the various ANSI options.

NOTE

These procedures are placed in the order in which they are listed in the Microsoft exam objectives list—it does not matter in which order you configure them in real life. If you want to set up ANSI first, then SQL Mail, feel free to do so.

Configuring SQL Mail

To get SQL Mail up and running, use the following steps:

1. Ensure the availability of a MAPI-compliant server, such as MS Exchange Server.

2. Create a mailbox for the SQL service account on the mail server.

3. Install Microsoft Outlook on the SQL Server.

4. Log on to Windows NT on the SQL Server using the SQL service account.

5. In the Control Panel, double-click the Mail and Fax (or just Mail on some systems) icon.

6. Click the Add button to create a mail profile.

7. Be certain that Exchange Server support is installed.

8. Write down the profile name when you have finished creating it.

9. Open Outlook to test the new profile—you may be asked to verify the Exchange Server and mailbox names at this point.

10. Log off Windows NT and log back on using your normal account.

11. Open Enterprise Manager, right-click your server, and select Properties.

12. On the Server Settings tab, click the Change button and type in the name of the profile you wrote down in step 8.

13. Click the Test button to verify connectivity, then click OK and OK again.

Configuring ANSI Settings

To configure the ANSI settings, use the following steps:

1. Set the properties of SQL Server by opening Enterprise Manager, highlighting the server, and choosing Tools ➤ Properties, or by right-clicking and choosing Properties.

2. Go to the Connections option screen by clicking the Connections tab.

3. Set various options as desired. Choose OK to save your settings.

4. Set the desired database options by highlighting a database, right-clicking, and choosing Properties.

5. Go to the Options tab.

6. Set the various database options as desired. Choose OK to save your settings.

▶ Implement full-text searching.

It is probably safe to assume that when you store data in SQL, you would like to use it again later. That task becomes quite daunting if you can't find the data you are looking for, which is why Microsoft has developed the full-text search service. Full-text search is actually a modified Index Server engine that allows you to index and search entire character and text fields, as opposed to how searching functioned in earlier versions of SQL, which would search only the first 255 characters of a field.

While this new service will make it much easier for your users to find the data they are looking for, it makes SQL Server a little more challenging to administer. In turn, anything that makes SQL more challenging to administer will be tested—in this case, quite a bit. So, for the sake of your users' sanity and your certification, immerse yourself in the following information on full-text searching.

To make this service work, the first thing you need to do is install the MSSearch service, which is done by running a Custom setup and selecting the Full-Text Search option. When that is done, you can start creating catalogs and full-text indexes.

Each database has one (and only one) catalog, which is a collection of full-text indexes. A full-text index is a lot like a regular index, with a few small differences:

▶ While full-text indexes can be administered through the database, they are stored in the file system.

▶ Only one is allowed per table.

▶ They are not changed automatically with the addition of new data—they must be *repopulated* at scheduled intervals.

These catalogs and full-text indexes can be created through either stored procedures or Enterprise Manager. However, the easiest way is through the Full-Text Wizard (to be examined in the "Necessary Procedures" section). Before you jump in with both feet, consider a few caveats:

▶ Remember that while a catalog can contain multiple indexes, a full-text index cannot span catalogs.

▶ Tables containing a timestamp column can do incremental repopulations, while tables that do not contain a timestamp column will do full repopulations.

▶ Back up the catalog files occasionally. Catalog files, which contain the full-text indexes, are stored as separate files; by default, they are not backed up when the database is backed up.

▶ Periodically monitor the size of the catalogs by using Performance Monitor or by checking the size of the files using Explorer or My Computer.

Full-text searching is not installed by default—you must add it. Once it is installed, there are no default settings to rely on—you must configure it to make it work. The procedure that follows will help you install, configure, and subsequently administer the full-text searching capability.

Implementing Full-Text Searching

To implement full-text searching on a database, you need to do as follows:

1. Make certain that the Full-Text Search engine is installed, which can be done by running a Custom setup with the setup program.

2. Start Enterprise Manager.

3. Highlight the database you want to modify and go to Tools ≻ Full-Text Indexing. This will start the Full-Text Indexing Wizard. Choose Next to proceed.

4. Select a database and choose Next.

5. Select an available table and choose Next.

6. Select the default index and choose Next.

7. Select the columns to be indexed.

8. Create a new catalog (index) for the searches by entering a name for the new catalog. Note that if you have already

Part iv

created a catalog, you could have chosen to either use a previous catalog or create a new one. Choose Next when finished.

9. You can schedule the catalog for periodic updates by selecting the New Schedule button and entering a name and schedule.

10. Choose OK and Next to save the schedule and go to the summary page.

11. Choose Finish to create the index. You should now see a note that the Wizard completed successfully. Note that the catalog will not be populated until it is updated manually or as scheduled.

12. Choose OK to close the screen.

13. To populate the index, go to the Pubs database, highlight the Full-Text Catalogs folder, right-click, and choose Repopulate All Catalogs.

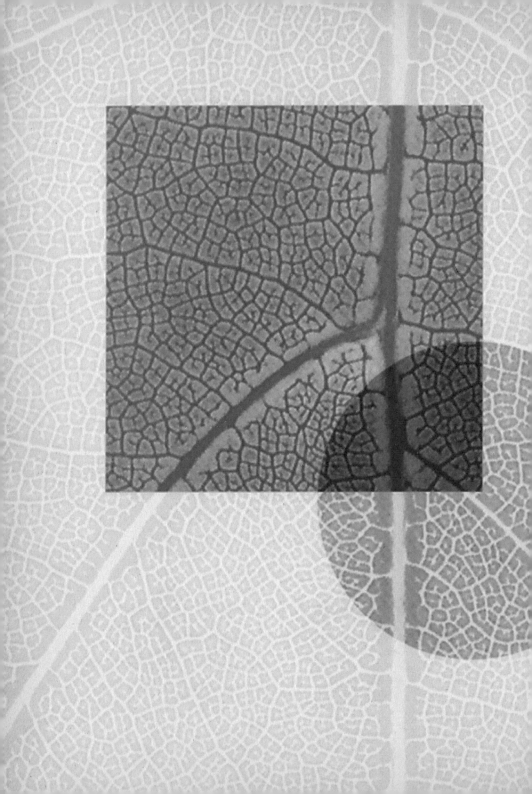

Chapter 20
CONFIGURING AND MANAGING SECURITY

In this chapter, you will get down to the mechanics of implementing your security plan, learn the methods for creating both Windows NT and standard logins, and examine the ways of easier user account administration.

No security system is complete without the capability to monitor the system, so Profiler will also be discussed. A full discussion of Profiler will come in Chapter 22; here, you will find just enough information to audit database activity to make sure your security plan is working as expected.

Adapted from *MCSE Exam Notes: SQL Server 7 Administration* by Rick Sawtell, Lance Mortensen, and Joseph L. Jorden

ISBN 0-7821-2477-1   368 pages $19.99

▶ Assign SQL Server access through Windows NT accounts, SQL Server logins, and built-in administrator logins.

If you own a business housed in your very own building, you do not want just anyone to be able to walk right in. Since you want only your employees to have access, you would give them keys to the front door. The same principle holds true with SQL Server—you need to give users a "key," called a *login* in SQL, so that they can gain access to the system as a whole.

Before logins can be discussed, though, authentication modes need to be examined, since the authentication mode you use will affect the type of logins you assign to your users. You will surely see these concepts on the exam, and not as simple questions either. Most likely, these questions will be presented as story questions that take you through a series of problems—for example, a user needs access, but can't log in—and the problems will all stem from the fact that the wrong login type was assigned or the wrong authentication mode was used, so make sure you understand these topics.

For the exam, you will need to know how to create the two types of logins (Windows NT and standard) and what the differences are between the two. You will need a firm grasp of the differences between authentication modes, which is how SQL processes user names and passwords. Finally, you will need to understand the role that the Windows NT Administrators group plays in SQL security.

Working with Windows NT Authentication

In Windows NT Authentication mode, a user can simply sit down at their computer, log on to the Windows NT domain, and gain access to SQL Server. This is referred to as a *trusted* connection because SQL trusts Windows NT to verify the user's password. SQL will need to verify only the user's login account, which it does by matching either the Windows NT user name or the group membership (an important exam concept) to an entry in the syslogins table in the Master database. This means that you could add 50 users to a local group in Windows NT (specifically in User Manager) and create a single Windows NT login for that group—all 50 users will have access using that one Windows NT login.

For the exam, it is important to know that only users with the Named Pipes, TCP/IP, or Multi-Protocol Net-Libraries can open a trusted connection to SQL Server. So, if you have clients that require other Net-Libraries (such as NetWare), you will need to implement Mixed mode.

Mixed Mode and Standard Logins

Mixed mode allows both NT authentication and SQL authentication. In SQL authentication, the user logs on to their network (Windows NT or otherwise), opens a nontrusted connection to SQL, and supplies a user name and password to gain access. In this method, SQL must verify both the user name and password by matching them with a record in the sys-logins table. When Mixed mode is used, anyone can gain access to SQL, regardless of the Net-Library used.

Built-In Administrator Logins

SA login is the first of two administrative accounts that are created as soon as SQL is installed. Short for System Administrator, SA is a standard login with a blank default password that is capable of doing anything on the system. It is a very good idea to change this password immediately after installation. For the test, remember that SA is not for everyday use—it is for backward compatibility only.

The second administrative account is the built-in administrator Windows NT group-type login. This login grants administrative access to your Windows NT Administrators local group. For the test and real life, it is a good idea to create a local Windows NT group (perhaps SQLAdmins) with all of your SQL administrators, create a Windows NT login for the new group, and grant it administrative access by adding it to the sysadmins server role. Once that is done, you can delete the built-in administrators login account (or at least remove it from the sysadmins role).

Since there is not a great deal of effort involved in creating login accounts, you will not see a great deal of it on the test—but it may be touched on, so you need to know how to do it through Enterprise Manager and via Transact-SQL (T-SQL). Here, you will find procedures for creating standard login accounts graphically and then with T-SQL. Then, the same sets of procedures for Windows NT accounts will be examined.

Creating Standard Logins

Creating a standard login via Enterprise Manager is a simple process; just follow these steps:

1. Open Enterprise Manager and expand your server by clicking the + sign next to the icon named after your server.

2. Expand the Security folder and click the Logins icon.

3. Choose Action ➤ New Login.

4. Type the name for your new user in the Name box.

5. In the Authentication section, select SQL Server Authentication.

6. In the Password text box, type **password**.

7. Under Defaults, select a default database—leaving this as Master will connect your users to the Master database.

8. Click the OK button.

9. Retype the password in the Confirm New Password text box.

10. Click OK to create your new standard login.

To create a standard login using Transact-SQL, you will use the `sp_addlogin` stored procedure:

```
sp_addlogin 'username', 'password', 'default_database'
```

Creating Windows NT Logins in Enterprise Manager

Creating Windows NT logins in Enterprise Manager is not much different than creating standard logins. The biggest difference is that the Windows NT account must already have been created in User Manager for Domains—if it has not, the creation of the new login will fail. Follow these steps to create a Windows NT login:

1. Verify that the Windows NT account (user or group) you are using exists in User Manager—if it does not, create it.

2. In Enterprise Manager, expand your server and click Logins in the Security folder.

3. Choose Actions ➤ New Login.

4. In the Name box, type a valid Windows NT account name (user or group).

5. Select Windows NT Authentication and select your domain from the Domain drop-down list.

6. Under Defaults, select a default database.

7. Click OK to create the new login.

Creating Windows NT Logins Using T-SQL

To create a Windows NT login using T-SQL, you will use the `sp_grant-login` stored procedure:

```
sp_grantlogin 'NTdomain\accountname'
```

Here, you will notice an immediate but subtle difference between creating standard and Windows NT logins with T-SQL—`sp_grant`login is for Windows NT logins, and `sp_add`login is for standard.

NOTE

With `sp_grantlogin`, you cannot assign a password (since that is done in User Manager), nor can you assign a default database.

▶ Assign database access to Windows NT accounts, SQL Server logins, the guest user account, and the dbo user account.

Back to the building analogy—just because your users have keys to the building it does not mean that they have access to the resources (such as file cabinets) inside. Similarly, in SQL, just because your users have login accounts it does not mean that they have access to the resources (such as databases) stored there.

For your users to be able to gain access to those resources, you need to create a database user account for them in each and every database to which they need access. In this section, you will read about not only how to create user accounts in the database, but also how to use the two accounts that already exist—dbo and guest. These two special accounts can prove useful if properly used, but very dangerous if improperly used—you can be sure to find these two accounts on the test.

For the test, it is important to know not only how to create the database user account, but also to know what it is used for. As mentioned, once you use a key to get in the front door of an office building, you don't automatically have access to all of the file cabinets in that office—you will need to be issued a separate key for each file cabinet.

In SQL, the key that gets you in the front door is a login, and the separate key for each file cabinet is a database user account. Once your user has a database account (and permissions applied to that account), they will be able to work with the data inside.

When you first look in the Users folder of one of your databases, you notice that two users already exist: dbo and guest. Members of the sysadmin fixed server role automatically become the dbo (database owner) user in every database on the system. In this way, they can perform all the necessary administrative functions in the databases, such as adding users and creating tables. *Guest user* is a catch-all term used for people who have a SQL login, but not a user account in the database. These users can log in to SQL as themselves and access any database where they do not have a user account. The guest account should be limited in function since anybody with a SQL login can use it.

NOTE

Whenever a member of the sysadmin fixed server role creates an object (such as a table), it is not owned by that login—it is owned by the dbo. If MorrisL created a table, it would not be referred to as `MorrisL.table`, but instead as `dbo.table`.

While there is not a great deal of effort involved in creating database user accounts, you need to know how to do it. The steps required to create a user account using Enterprise Manager will be discussed first, then the procedures for T-SQL will be examined.

Creating a Database User Account in Enterprise Manager

The process for creating a database user account in Enterprise Manager is as follows:

1. Open Enterprise Manager and expand your server.

2. Expand Databases by clicking on the + sign next to the icon.

3. Click the Database Users icon.

4. Choose Action ➢ New Database User.

5. In the Login Name box, select one of the available names; note that only logins that you have already created are available.

6. You can enter a name in the Login Name box. Then, SQL will see the user as whatever you type here instead of as their login name.

7. Click OK.

Creating a Database User Account with T-SQL

To create a database user account with T-SQL, you need to use the
`sp_grantdbaccess` stored procedure. The syntax is as follows:

```
sp_grantdbaccess 'login', 'name_in_db'
```

For example, by executing `sp_grantdbaccess 'Sales', 'Sales-Users'`, you would create a user account in your database called Sales-Users that would allow the Sales login to access your database.

▶ ## Create and assign SQL Server roles. Server roles include fixed server, fixed database, public, user-defined database, and application.

If you own a business, what should your users be able to do once inside? The managers probably have permission to do whatever they want; the janitorial staff has permission to do next to nothing. In a similar fashion, you need to limit your users' administrative access in SQL Server, both to the server as a whole and in each database where they have access.

In this section, limiting administrative access to the server as a whole by assigning users to fixed server roles will be discussed. Then, limiting access in a specific database by assigning users to a database role that can be fixed or user defined will be examined. Finally, limiting access on an application-specific basis by using application roles will be discussed.

Fixed server roles are used to limit the amount of administrative access that a user has once logged in to SQL Server. Some users may be allowed to do whatever they want, whereas other users may be able only to manage security. For the test, you do not need to memorize each permission for each role, but you should have a general understanding of what each role is capable of—for example, sysadmins can do whatever they want, whereas processadmins can only kill a process.

Available Fixed Server Roles

Here is a list of the fixed server roles:

Sysadmin: Members of the sysadmin role can do whatever they want in SQL Server. Be careful whom you assign to this role—people who are unfamiliar with SQL can accidentally create serious problems. This role is only for the database administrators (DBAs).

Serveradmin: These users can set serverwide configuration options, such as how much memory SQL can use or how much information to send over the network in a single frame. If you make your assistant DBAs members of this role, you can relieve yourself of some of the administrative burden.

Setupadmin: Members here can install replication and manage extended stored procedures (used to perform actions not native to SQL Server). Give this to the assistant DBAs as well.

Securityadmin: These users manage security issues, such as creating and deleting logins, reading the audit logs, and granting users permission to create databases. This, too, is a good role for assistant DBAs.

Processadmin: SQL is capable of multitasking; that is, it can do more than one thing at a time by executing multiple processes. For instance, SQL might spawn one process for writing to cache and another for reading from cache. A member of the processadmin group can end (called *kill* in SQL) a process. This is another good role for assistant DBAs and developers. Developers especially need to kill processes that may have been triggered by an improperly designed query or stored procedure.

Dbcreator: These users can create and make changes to databases. This may be a good role for assistant DBAs as well as developers (who should be warned against creating unnecessary databases and wasting server space).

Diskadmin: These users manage files on disk. They do things such as mirroring databases and adding backup devices. Assistant DBAs should be members of this role.

Available Fixed Database Roles

Database roles are used to limit what users can do inside a single database. If, for example, you do not want a user to be able to modify data, but you do want them to read data, then add them to the db_datareader role. Here is a list of the default database roles:

Db_owner: Members of this role can do everything the members of the other roles can do as well as some administrative functions.

Db_accessadmin: These users have the authority to say who gets access to the database by adding or removing users.

Db_datareader: Members here can read data from any table in the database.

Db_datawriter: These users can add, change, and delete data from all the tables in the database.

Db_ddladmin: DDL (Data Definition Language) administrators can issue all DDL commands; this allows them to create, modify, drop, or change database objects without viewing the data inside.

Db_securityadmin: Members here can add and remove users from database roles, and manage statement and object permissions.

Db_backupoperator: These users can back up and restore the database.

Db_denydatareader: Members cannot read the data in the database, but they can make schema changes.

Db_denydatawriter: These users cannot make changes to the data in the database, but they are allowed to read the data.

Public: The purpose of this group is to grant users a default set of permissions in the database. For the test, it is important to note that all database users automatically join this group and cannot be removed.

There will, of course, be times when the fixed database roles do not meet your security needs. You might have several users who need select, update, and execute permissions in your database and nothing more. Because none of the fixed database roles will give you that set of permissions, you can create a custom database role, assign permissions to it, and then assign users to the role. That is different from the fixed database roles, where you did not need to assign permissions, but just added users.

If you have a custom application for accessing data, you may even want to restrict access to your database to that one application. You can accomplish this with an application role, which will force your users to employ the proper application for data access.

Once you've created an application role, the user logs on to SQL, is authenticated, and opens the approved application. The application executes the `sp_setapprole` stored procedure to enable the application role. Once the application role is enabled, SQL no longer sees users as themselves; it sees users as the application and grants them application-role permissions.

For the test, one of the first things you need to know is how to add users to fixed server roles through Enterprise Manager or T-SQL. Once you have limited what the users can do at the server level, you need to restrict what they can do in each database by adding them to a database role. Finally, you will see the procedures for creating and activating an application role so that you can restrict which applications users are allowed to employ in manipulating data.

Adding Users to Fixed Server Roles in Enterprise Manager

The procedure for adding users to fixed server roles in Enterprise Manager is as follows:

1. Open Enterprise Manager and select Server Roles.

2. Double-click the fixed server role to which you want to add users.

3. Click Add, select the login you wish to add, and click OK.

Adding Users to Fixed Server Roles Using T-SQL

To add a user to a fixed server role using T-SQL, you will use the `sp_addsrvrolemember` stored procedure:

```
sp_addsrvrolemember 'login', 'server_role'
```

Adding Users to a Database Role in Enterprise Manager

The procedure for adding users to a database role in Enterprise Manager is as follows:

1. Open Enterprise Manager, expand your server and databases, then select the database with which you want to work.

2. Click Database Roles.

3. In the contents pane, double-click the role you want to modify.

4. Click the Add button.

5. Select a database user account and click OK.

Adding Users to a Database Role Using T-SQL

To accomplish this task using T-SQL, you need to use the sp_addrole-member stored procedure:

```
sp_addrolemember 'role_name' 'user_name'
```

If you create an application role, you will be able to force your users to access the database with only approved applications.

Creating an Application Role in Enterprise Manager

Here's how to create an application role with Enterprise Manager:

1. Open Enterprise Manager and select Database Roles in the database in which you want to create the role.

2. Choose Action ➤ New Database Role.

3. In the Name box, type the name of the new role.

4. Under Database Role Type, select Application Role.

5. Enter the password that will be used to activate the role in the Password box.

6. Click OK to get back to the Enterprise Manager.

7. To grant permissions to the new role, double-click it and click the Permissions button.

8. Click OK to get back to the previous dialog box, and click OK again to return to Enterprise Manager.

Creating an Application Role Using T-SQL

If you would rather use T-SQL to create an application role, you will need to use the sp_addapprole stored procedure:

```
sp_addapprole 'new_role_name', 'password'
```

Activating an Application Role

Once you've created the application role, you need to place some T-SQL code in your application to activate it. The stored procedure to use is `sp_setapprole`:

```
sp_setapprole 'rolename', 'password'
```

▶ Grant to database users and roles the appropriate permissions on database objects and statements.

Adding users to roles to grant them permissions is easy and saves time, but it doesn't work for every situation. It is very possible that a fixed database role will give a user too much or too little permission—in those instances, you will need to understand how to grant permissions and which permissions are available.

In this section, the available permissions, both statement and object, and how to apply them will be discussed. The three states of permissions and how these can affect your users will also be examined. You don't need to memorize each of these permissions for the test, but it is a good idea to have a general understanding of each of them and what they are used for. It is especially important to understand the effects of the three states of permissions: grant, revoke, and deny. In your own SQL Servers, if you don't grant users the right permissions or if you grant permissions at the wrong level, your users may have too much or too little access.

The first type of permissions you will need to understand is statement permissions, which have nothing to do with the actual data; they allow users to create the structure that holds the data. Do not grant these permissions haphazardly, however—it can lead to such problems as broken ownership chains (discussed later) and wasted server resources. It is best to restrict these permissions to DBAs, assistant DBAs, and developers. The statement permissions you have to work with are as follows:

- ▶ Create Database
- ▶ Create Table
- ▶ Create View
- ▶ Create Procedure

- ▶ Create Index
- ▶ Create Rule
- ▶ Create Default
- ▶ Backup Database
- ▶ Backup Log

NOTE

The Create Database permission can be granted only on the Master database.

Once the structure exists to hold the data, your users will require object permissions to start working with the data contained therein. Using object permissions, you can control who is allowed to read from, write to, or otherwise manipulate your data. Here is a list of object permissions and what they are used for:

Select: When granted, allows users to read data from the table or view. When granted at the column level, this will allow users to read from a single column.

Insert: Allows users to insert new rows into a table.

Update: Allows users to modify existing data in a table. When granted on a column, users will be able to modify data in that single column.

Delete: Allows users to remove rows from a table.

References: When two tables are linked with a foreign key, this allows the user to select data from the primary table without having Select permission on the referenced table.

Execute: This allows users to execute the stored procedure where the permission is applied.

It is also good to know that SQL understands the concept of ownership. When a user creates an object, they own that object and can do whatever they want with it. For example, if a user named JacksonR creates a table, she can assign permissions as she chooses, granting access only to those users she deems worthy. That is a good thing until you consider what is known as an *ownership chain*.

Suppose that GibsonH creates a table and grants permissions on that table to ThompsonA (see Figure 20.1). Then, ThompsonA creates a view based on that table and grants Select permission to SmithB. SmithB will not be able to select from the view because the ownership chain has been broken. SQL will check permissions on an underlying object (in this case, the table) only when the object owner changes. Therefore, if ThompsonA had created both the table and the view, there would be no problem since SQL would check only the permissions on the view. However, because the owner changed from accounting (which owned the view) to ThompsonA (who owned the table), SQL needed to check the permissions on both the view and the table.

The best way to avoid broken ownership chains is to make all the users who need to create objects members of either the db_owner or the db_ddladmin fixed database roles. Then, if they need to create objects, they can specify the owner as dbo (i.e., `create table dbo.table_name`). This way, the dbo would own all objects in the database, and since the ownership would never change, SQL would never need to check any underlying permissions.

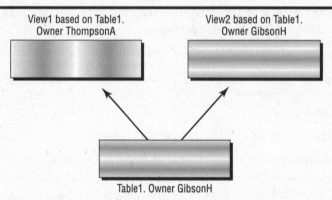

View1 based on Table1.
Owner ThompsonA

View2 based on Table1.
Owner GibsonH

Table1. Owner GibsonH

FIGURE 20.1: Example of a broken ownership chain (broken between Table1 and View2)

Finally, you should understand the three states of any permission: granted, revoked, or denied.

Grant: Granting allows users to use a specific permission. For instance, if you grant SmithB Select permission on a table, he can read the data within. A granted permission is signified by a black check mark on the Permissions tab.

Revoke: In this state, while users are not explicitly allowed to use a revoked permission, if they are a member of a role that is allowed, they will inherit the permission. That is, if you revoke the Select permission from SmithB, he cannot use it. If he is a member of a role that has been granted Select permission, SmithB can read the data just as if he had the Select permission. Revocation is signified by a blank check box on the Permissions tab.

Deny: If you deny a permission, the user does not get the permission—no matter what. If you deny SmithB Select permission on a table, then, even if he is a member of a role with Select permission, he cannot read the data. Denial is signified by a red X on the Permissions tab.

Since not much effort is required in actually assigning the permissions, you will not see a great deal of this information on the test, if any at all. Still, you need to know how to do it, both through Enterprise Manager and T-SQL.

Assigning Permissions with Enterprise Manager

The procedures for assigning object and statement permissions through Enterprise Manager are exactly the same:

1. Open Enterprise Manager and expand your server, then expand Databases.

2. Right-click the database you want to modify and select Properties.

3. In the Properties dialog box, select the Permissions tab.

4. From the Permissions tab, you may grant, revoke, or deny any of the available permissions.

Assigning Permissions Using T-SQL

Assigning object and statement permissions is a little bit different when using T-SQL. In either case, you use the same three commands. Here are some examples for statement permissions:

Grant: GRANT *permission* to *user name*

Revoke: REVOKE *permission* from *user name*

Deny: DENY *permission* to *user name*

Here are some examples of the same three commands for assigning object permissions:

Grant: GRANT *permission* on *object* to *user name*

Revoke: REVOKE *permission* on *object* from *user name*

Deny: DENY *permission* on *object* to *user name*

▶ Audit server and database activity.

Most people at one time or another have had to pass through a security checkpoint. At that checkpoint, a security guard sat watching monitors and searching packages. Why was this guard there? Because you can have the most advanced security system in the world, but without someone keeping watch, it will eventually fail. A thief would simply need to probe the system systematically for weak spots and, once they were found, take advantage of them to break in. With a guard watching, this becomes a great deal more difficult.

The same is true for SQL. You cannot simply put a security system in place and then leave it. You must keep watch to make certain no one is probing for weak spots and attempting to break in. This task of keeping watch has been delegated to Profiler, a tool that you will become friends with in the real world. Profiler is capable not only of monitoring security, but of tracking any event on the server—because of that power, you will find a number of questions on the exam that involve Profiler in some way. You should know when and how to use it.

Profiler is used to track and record activity on the SQL Server, which is done by performing a trace. A *trace* is a record of the data captured about events, which can be a stored in a database table, in a trace log file that can be opened and read in Profiler, or in both. Traces can be one of two types: *shared,* viewable by anyone, or *private,* viewable only by the owner. Security traces should be private so that only you have access.

The actions that are monitored on the server are known as *events,* and those events are logically grouped together in *event classes.* Not all of these events have to do with security; in fact, most of them have to do with optimization and troubleshooting. Table 20.1 lists the classes and events that are important from a security standpoint.

TABLE 20.1: Classes and Events

Event Class	Event
Misc	**Loginfailed:** This will tell you if someone has tried to log in unsuccessfully. If you notice someone repeatedly failing to log in, it means either the user forgot their password or someone is trying to hack in using the user's account.
	ServiceControl: This monitors SQL Server starts, stops, and pauses. If you note a stop or pause and you are the only administrator, it means there is a problem with the server itself—or someone has hacked in with an administrative account.
Objects	**Object:Deleted:** This will tell you if an object, such as a table, has been deleted. From a security standpoint, this is after the fact, since the damage may have already been done. By monitoring this, however, you should be able to catch the culprit if something is improperly deleted.
SQL Operators	**Delete:** This is logged just before a delete statement is executed. It does not stop delete statements from executing, it just records them. This event will be useful in catching a hacker if something is illicitly deleted.

For the purpose of the exam, it is a good idea to know how to create a trace and add the appropriate events.

Creating a Trace and Adding the Appropriate Events

To create a trace and add the appropriate events, follow these steps:

1. Open Profiler in the SQL Server 7 program group.

2. Choose File ➤ New ➤ Trace.

3. Enter a name for your trace in the Trace Name box.

4. For Trace Type, select Private.

5. To run the trace against your own machine, select Local.

6. Click the check box next to Capture to File and click OK to select the default filename.

7. Click the check box next to Capture to Table and fill in the subsequent dialog box:

   ▶ Server: Local

   ▶ Database: *Database_name*

   ▶ Owner: *Yourself*

   ▶ Table: *Table_name*

8. Click OK to return to the previous dialog box.

9. Select the Events tab.

10. Under Selected Events, remove any unneeded classes.

11. Under Available Events, select the events you want to monitor and click Add.

12. Click OK to start the trace.

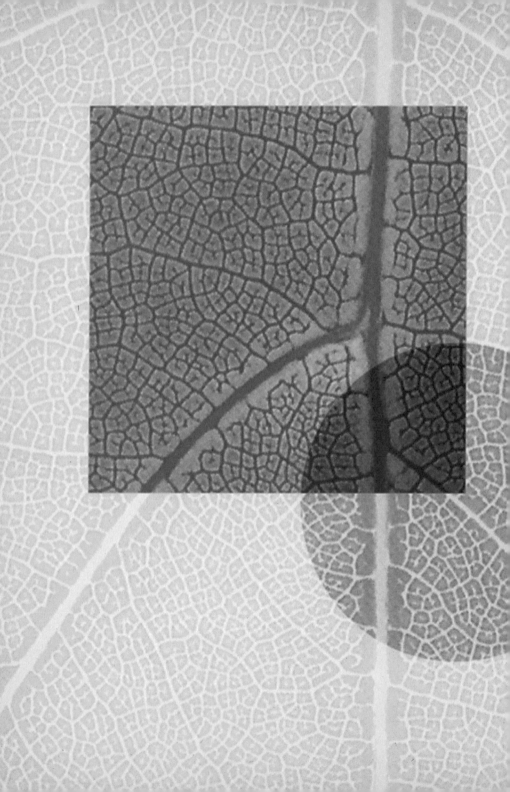

Chapter 21

MANAGING AND MAINTAINING DATA

Y ou have installed and configured SQL Server so that you can use it to store data, which means that you will need to create databases. This chapter will show you how to create the data files used for storing data and how to lump them all together in filegroups. You will also need to know how to load the database with data. The methods discussed in this chapter are INSERT, SELECT INTO, bcp, DTS, and BULK INSERT. Since the data you load into your database may get damaged or lost, the mechanics of backing up will be discussed. Then, the procedures for restoring them from those backups will be covered. Since bottlenecks slow system performance and should be avoided, how to replicate your databases to other servers in the organization so that your users can access a local copy will be discussed.

Adapted from *MCSE Exam Notes: SQL Server 7 Administration* by Rick Sawtell, Lance Mortensen, and Joseph L. Jorden
ISBN 0-7821-2477-1   368 pages $19.99

Finally, many companies today have multiple SQL Servers in their organization with different databases on each one. The caveat is that people need to access data from multiple servers in some of their queries. These queries are referred to as distributed queries—you will learn how to configure SQL Server to allow this process to happen.

▶ Create and manage databases.

▶ Create data files, filegroups, and transaction log files.

▶ Specify growth characteristics.

The first step in making your database server useful is to create databases. However, what do you do when you find that your database is running out of space or it is using too much space? To fix those problems, expanding and shrinking databases as well as dropping databases when you no longer require them will be discussed.

As with almost everything in SQL, there are two ways to create databases: graphically in Enterprise Manager and via Transact-SQL (T-SQL). When you employ the graphic method of creating databases, Enterprise Manager actually performs the T-SQL statements in the background for you. Bearing that in mind, most of the discussion will involve creating a database with T-SQL.

Creating Data and Transaction Log Files

When you create a database, you must specify the logical name of the database, the physical filename where the database file will reside, and the size of the database file. Optional parameters include the maximum size to which the database is allowed to grow, as well as the growth characteristics. Also, while it is not required, you can also specify the logical and physical filenames of the transaction log with maximum size and growth characteristics. If you opt not to specify the transaction log parameters, SQL will create a transaction log for you in the same directory as the data file. The basic syntax of the CREATE DATABASE statement is as follows:

```
CREATE DATABASE db_name
[ON {[PRIMARY]
(NAME = logical name,
 FILENAME = 'physical filename',
 [SIZE = initial size,]
```

```
    [MAXSIZE = maxsize,]
    [FILEGROWTH = [filegrowth MB | %])} [...n]]
[LOG ON
{(NAME = logical name,
 FILENAME = 'physical filename',
 [SIZE = initial size],
 [MAXSIZE = maxsize],
 [FILEGROWTH = filegrowth MB | %])} [...n]]
 [FOR LOAD | FOR ATTACH]
```

The following list explains the uses of the listed parameters:

db_name: This is the name that you are going to give this database. It must follow the rules for SQL Server identifiers.

PRIMARY: This parameter, the name of the filegroup, defaults to PRIMARY. (Filegroups are an advanced topic that will be covered later in this chapter.) In short, filegroups allow you to place individual database objects in separate files. For example, you might place a large table on one filegroup and the table's index on another filegroup. In this manner, writes to the table do not interfere with writes to the index. These filegroups are used with the ALTER DATABASE statement, not the CREATE DATABASE statement.

logical name: This is the logical name of the database file, which you will use to reference this particular database file while in SQL Server.

'physical filename':   Since the database file is stored on disk, you must provide a filename and complete path. Note that it is surrounded by single quotation marks.

initial size: This is the initial size of the database expressed in either kilobytes or megabytes. Keep in mind that this will allocate hard-disk space, just like any other file on disk.

maxsize: This is the maximum size to which the database can grow, specified in either kilobytes or megabytes. This is useful when you specify filegrowth options.

filegrowth: This option specifies the size of the increments by which a given database file should grow. It can be expressed

in either kilobytes or megabytes, or as a percentage. If not specified, the default is 1MB.

FOR LOAD: This option marks the database for dbo (database owner) use only and is used for backward compatibility
with SQL Server 6.5. This means that the database is not
marked online, but is waiting for data to be loaded into it
through a SELECT INTO/BULK COPY operation or through
the restoration of a backup.

FOR ATTACH: This option reattaches the files that make up
a database. It essentially re-creates entries in the system tables
regarding this database file.

The following listing is an example of how to create a database using
the CREATE DATABASE statement. In this example, you will create a
database that has data spanning two files and a transaction log. You will
also set the autogrowth and maxsize parameters.

```
CREATE DATABASE Complex
ON PRIMARY
(NAME = Complex_Data1,
 FILENAME = 'C:\MSSQL7\Data\Complex_Data1.mdf',
 SIZE = 5MB,
 MAXSIZE = 10MB,
 FILEGROWTH = 1MB)
(NAME = Complex_Data2,
 FILENAME = 'C:\MSSQL7\Data\Complex_Data2.ndf',
 SIZE = 2MB,
 MAXSIZE = 10MB,
 FILEGROWTH = 2MB)
LOG ON
(NAME = Complex_Log1,
 FILENAME = 'D:\Logs\Complex_Log1.ldf',
 SIZE = 2MB,
 MAXSIZE = 8MB,
 FILEGROWTH = 1MB)
```

This creates a database with an initial size of 9MB—5MB for the first
file, 2MB for the second file, and 2MB for the log. The database has a
maximum size of 28MB.

Now that you have successfully created a couple of databases, it is time to learn how to gather more information about them. Using the Enterprise Manager, you can gather a wealth of information about your database. This includes the size of the database, its current capacity, any options that are currently set, etc. If you click your database in the console tree, you will receive summary information in the right pane, as shown in Figure 21.1.

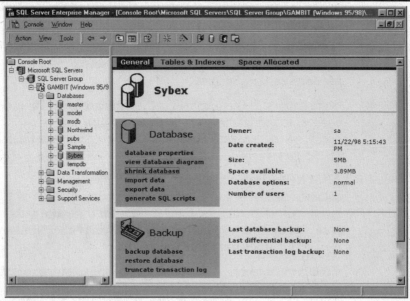

FIGURE 21.1: The Database Information pane

You can also use system stored procedures to gather information about your database. The sp_helpdb stored procedure used by itself will give you information about all databases in your SQL Server. You can gather information about a particular database by using the database name as a parameter.

Managing Database Options

The first step in managing databases is understanding the options that, when set, will change the way your database behaves in given situations. You can view and modify database options using the Enterprise Manager or the sp_dboption stored procedure, which includes options that are not available through the GUI.

To view the options on a database in Enterprise Manager, you right-click your database and choose Properties. From the Database Properties dialog box, click the Options tab.

The database options are broken into separate categories for Access and Settings. Here is what the different settings mean:

DBO Use Only: Only members of the db_owner fixed database role have access to this database. This option is frequently used when performing a restoration or other tasks where you do not want to allow nonowners in the database.

Single User: Only one user at a time can access the database and with only a single connection. This is useful when renaming or restoring a database.

Read Only: This option marks the database as read only. No changes to the database will be allowed. Since no locking occurs when Read Only is set, it is useful on databases where no changes are made to the data.

ANSI NULL Default: This option specifies that new columns created or added to tables have a default value of NULL. Although this is a default setting for the entire database, you can override this value by specifying either NULL or NOT NULL when you create your columns.

Recursive Triggers: This option allows recursive triggers to fire. *Recursive triggers* occur when one trigger fires a trigger on another table, which in turn fires another trigger on the originating table.

Select Into/Bulk Copy: This option allows you to perform nonlogged operations. This includes the use of the bcp (bulk copy) command-line program as well as statements that create or fill tables using the SELECT INTO SQL statements.

Truncate Log on Checkpoint: This option specifies that the inactive portion of the transaction log should be truncated at the checkpoint process. Every minute, the checkpoint process is activated and checks each database in SQL Server. If it finds a database with five minutes worth of changes, it flushes the modified data pages in cache to the hard disk. When dirty pages have been written to disk as well as to the transaction log, you have a known point of consistency. This option is useful if you do not want to keep an active transaction log. You use it often during the development stages of a database.

Torn Page Detection: This option allows SQL Server to detect when a partial-page write to disk has occurred. Because this is a form of data corruption that should be avoided, you should enable this option.

Autoclose: This option safely closes your database when the last user has exited from it. This can be a useful option for optimization. It decreases the amount of resources that SQL Server needs to consume to maintain user information and locks.

Autoshrink: This option will automatically shrink both data and log files. Log files will be shrunk after a backup of the log has been made. Data files will be shrunk when a periodic check of the database finds that the database has more than 25 percent of its assigned space free. Your database will then be shrunk to a size that leaves 25 percent free.

Auto Create Statistics: This option will automatically generate statistics on the distribution of values found in your columns. The SQL Server query optimizer uses these statistics to determine the best method to run a particular query.

Auto Update Statistics: This option works with the auto-created statistics mentioned above. As you make changes to the data in your database, the statistics will be less and less accurate. This option periodically updates those statistics.

Use Quoted Identifiers: This option allows you to use double quotation marks as part of a SQL Server identifier (object name). This can be useful in situations in which you have identifiers that are also SQL Server reserved words.

The `sp_dboption` stored procedure includes the following additional database options that are not available through the Enterprise Manager:

Concat Null Yields Null: This option specifies that anything you concatenate to a NULL value will return a NULL value.

Cursor Close on Commit: This option automatically closes any open cursors when the transaction that created the cursor completes. (*Cursors* are a subset of the results from a query.)

Default to Local Cursor: This option creates cursors that are local in nature and available only to the local batch, trigger, or stored procedure that generated the trigger. This option can be

Part iv

overridden by using the GLOBAL keyword when creating the cursor.

Merge Publish: This option allows a database to be a Publisher as part of merge replication.

Offline: This option takes a database offline and shuts it down. When a database has been taken offline, it can be placed on removable media such as a CD-ROM.

Published: This option specifies that the database is allowed to publish data for use in replication.

Subscribed: This option specifies that the database can participate in the Subscriber side of replication.

Managing Database Size

It is possible that your database may be so popular that it is filled with data much faster than anticipated and becomes too small. Fortunately, you can fix this problem by expanding the database. This expansion is accomplished by expanding the existing data file or adding secondary data files.

If you find that your database is taking up too much space on the disk, you can shrink it. In Enterprise Manager, this is done by right-clicking the database and selecting Shrink Database. The other way to do this is by running the DBCC SHRINKDATABASE command, which will attempt to shrink all files in the database, or the DBCC SHRINKFILE command, which will attempt to shrink a specific database file. When you run DBCC SHRINKDATBASE(*db_name*)by itself, it will tell you how much your database can be shrunk. Here is the syntax of the SHRINKDATABASE command:

```
DBCC SHRINKDATABASE {
(db_name,
[target_percent],
[{NOTRUNCATE | TRUNCATEONLY}])}
```

The following list presents the arguments and their meanings:

***db_name*:**   The logical name of the database that you wish to shrink.

***target_percent*:**   The percentage of free space left in the database after it has been shrunk. If, for instance, you have a

100MB database and wish to have 10MB of free space, you would enter 10 as the target percentage (10 percent of 100). The end result cannot be larger than the current database or smaller than the current data size.

NOTRUNCATE: This option just consolidates the data into one area and the free space into another area without releasing any free space back to the operating system. It is akin to defragmenting the database. For obvious reasons, NOTRUNCATE ignores the *target_percent* parameter.

TRUNCATEONLY: This clause will ignore the target_percent parameter and shrink the database to the size of data. Afterward, it releases all of the freed-up disk space back to the operating system.

When you no longer need a database, you can drop it from your server, freeing up disk space for other database files. Only the owner of a database has the authority to drop a database. Dropping a database is a very simple task, which can be accomplished through either Enterprise Manager or the T-SQL statement DROP DATABASE. Although the process is easy, you must remember that dropping a database is permanent. If you need to recover your database later, you will need to restore it from a backup.

NOTE

Master, Model, and Tempdb cannot be dropped.

WARNING

The MSDB database can be dropped, but doing so will render the SQLServer-Agent service and replication completely unusable. It will also cause errors whenever you do a backup or restoration, because the system will attempt to write information to the detail and history tables in the MSDB database.

Working with Filegroups

The two basic filegroups in SQL Server 7 are the primary, or default, filegroup that is created with every database and the user-defined filegroups created for a particular database. The primary filegroup will always contain the primary data file and any other files that are not specifically created on a user-defined filegroup. You can create additional filegroups using the ALTER DATABASE command or the Enterprise Manager.

Filegroups have several rules that you should follow when you are working with them:

▶ The first (or primary) data file must reside on the primary filegroup.

▶ All system files must be placed on the primary filegroup.

▶ A file cannot be a member of more than one filegroup at a time.

▶ Filegroups can be allocated indexes, tables, text, ntext, and image data.

▶ If the primary filegroup runs out of space, it will not automatically start using space from a user-defined filegroup.

When you use filegroups, you may find that just one file in the database has grown too large and must be reduced. You can shrink that one file using the SHRINKFILE command:

```
DBCC SHRINKFILE { (filename | file_id} [, target_percentage]
[, {EMPTYFILE | NOTRUNCATE | TRUNCATEONLY}])}
```

The *filename* or *file_id* parameters are used to specify the individual database file you wish to shrink. The *file_id* can be found by first running an sp_helpdb stored procedure.

The other new parameter is the EMPTYFILE option, which is used in conjunction with a filegroup. You can use this option to move all data stored on a particular file to other files in the filegroup. EMPTYFILE will then mark the file as empty. Once a file has been marked empty, you can remove it from the filegroup using the ALTER DATABASE command with the REMOVE FILE parameter.

You will need to know a few procedures for the exam. The first, how to create data files and the corresponding transaction logs, will not be hit very hard. Since the next procedure, managing filegroups, is new in SQL 7, you will need to understand it well for the exam. Finally, the procedures for managing filegrowth (which you should have a firm grasp of for the exam, since they have been completely revamped for SQL 7) will be explored.

Creating Data Files and Transaction Log Files

As with nearly everything in SQL, there are two methods to create these files: graphically and with T-SQL. Creating data and transaction log files in Enterprise Manager is done using the following steps:

1. Expand your Databases folder.

2. Right-click either the Databases folder in the console tree or the white space in the right pane, and choose New Database from the context menu.

3. On the General tab of the Database Properties dialog box, you can type in the name of your new database. When you enter the name, notice that the database filename automatically fills in.

4. Set the first data file's initial size.

5. If you want to have the file grow automatically, set the Automatically Grow File option to true (checked).

6. If your database will grow automatically, set the File Growth increment in either MB or percentage.

7. If your database will autogrow, you should set Restrict Filegrowth to the largest size you can afford. If you don't, the database will grow to take the entire hard disk.

8. Click the Transaction Log tab and set all of the same options. Note that the size of the transaction log should be 10 to 25 percent of the size of the data file.

9. When finished, click OK.

The alternate method for creating data and transaction log files is by using the CREATE DATABASE statement. To create a 4MB database named Sample that can grow to 10MB (in 10-percent increments) and a corresponding 1MB transaction log file that can grow to 4MB (in 10-percent increments), use the following code:

```
CREATE DATABASE Sample
ON [PRIMARY]
(NAME = 'SampleData',
 FILENAME = 'C:\MSSQL7\Data\SampleData.MDF',
 SIZE = 4,
 MAXSIZE = 10,
 FILEGROWTH = 10%)
LOG ON
(NAME = 'SampleLog',
 FILENAME = 'C:\MSSQL7\Data\SampleLog.LDF',
 SIZE = 1,
```

Part iv

```
MAXSIZE = 4,
FILEGROWTH = 10%)
```

Managing Filegrowth Characteristics

The time will come when you need to expand or shrink your database. There is not a great deal of work involved with this, and it should not happen very often, but it is still necessary to know how to do it.

Expanding Databases   To work this miracle through Enterprise Manager, you just right-click the database and select Properties. In the subsequent dialog box, you can add additional data and log files. Simply click in a new box and fill in the new logical name, physical location, initial size, and other properties.

Expanding databases using T-SQL is just as simple. In the following example, you will see how to add a secondary file to a database named Sample using the ALTER DATABASE statement. The secondary file here is 4MB with the capacity to grow to 10MB in 2MB increments:

```
ALTER DATABASE Sample
ADD LOG FILE
(NAME = Sample_Log2,
 FILENAME = 'C:\MSSQL7\Data\Sample_Log2.ldf',
 SIZE = 4MB,
 MAXSIZE = 10MB,
 FILEGROWTH = 2MB)
```

Shrinking Databases   Shrinking a database using the Enterprise Manager is not particularly intuitive. Right-clicking your way to the Properties sheet and entering a smaller value for the Initial Space option will not shrink the database. The following steps will shrink a database in Enterprise Manager:

1. Open the Enterprise Manager.

2. Drill down to the Database folder and click the database you want to shrink.

3. Right-click the Sample database in the console tree and choose All Tasks ➤ Shrink Database.

4. Click Shrink Database by (%) and change the value. If, for example, you want to shrink a 13MB database down to 7MB, you would enter 50.

5. Click OK when you are finished.

6. You should get a confirmation message that tells you that the database has been successfully shrunk.

To shrink a database with T-SQL, you need to use the DBCC SHRINK-DATABASE statement. To shrink a database named Sample leaving only 10 percent free space in the database, you would execute:

```
DBCC SHRINKDATABASE (Sample, 10%)
```

Working with Filegroups

Creating filegroups is a relatively straightforward task and will not be tested on a great deal. In fact, for the exam, it is better to understand what filegroups are used for rather than the mechanics of creating them. Nonetheless, it is still necessary to understand the procedures involved.

Creating Filegroups with the Enterprise Manager   You can create the filegroups when you create a new database or when you alter an existing database. The following steps outline the creation of a new filegroup with a new database file added to it:

1. Drill down in the console tree and right-click the database you want to modify, then choose Properties.

2. Just under the data file information, add a new data file, and then add a name for the new filegroup in the File Group box.

3. Click OK when you are finished.

Creating Filegroups with T-SQL   As you might expect, using T-SQL to create a filegroup is a bit trickier. To add a filegroup and then add data files to the filegroup, you need to use the ALTER DATABASE statement.

In this example, you will create a new filegroup called Testing on the Dummy database. You will also see the results of the query.

```
ALTER DATABASE Dummy
ADD FILEGROUP Testing
```

```
GO
```

```
The command(s) completed successfully
```

Then, once you have created the filegroup, you are ready to add files to it. The following code will create a new table called fgTable_Data2, which will be 2MB in size and a part of the Sales filegroup:

```
USE NewSample
GO
ALTER DATABASE Sample
ADD FILE
(NAME = fgTable_Data2,
 FILENAME = 'C:\MSSQL7\Data\fgTable_Data2.ndf',
 SIZE = 2MB)
TO FILEGROUP Sales
```

Removing a Filegroup   To remove a filegroup, you must first ensure that all the files that make up the filegroup have been removed. Once the files have been removed, you can remove the filegroup using the ALTER DATABASE statement. The following steps demonstrate how to do this:

1. Run the following query to remove the files from the filegroup:

```
USE Sample
GO
ALTER DATABASE Sample
REMOVE FILE fgTable_Data1
GO
ALTER DATABASE Sample
REMOVE FILE fgTable_Data2
GO
```

2. Now that the data files have been removed, you can remove the filegroups themselves. Run the following query:

```
USE NewSample
GO
ALTER DATABASE NewSample
REMOVE FILEGROUP Sales
GO
```

▶ # Load data by using various methods. Methods include the INSERT statement, the SELECT INTO statement, the bcp utility, Data Transformation Services (DTS), and the BULK INSERT statement.

Once you have successfully created your database, it is important to fill it with data. Several methods for filling your databases, each one having its own strengths—the INSERT statement, the SELECT INTO statement, the bcp utility, Data Transformation Services (DTS), and the BULK INSERT statement—will be examined.

Under ordinary circumstances, you will need to fill your databases with new data only when the database is first created—but not all circumstances are ordinary. Some databases will need to be completely cycled on a regular basis, such as a catalog database that needs to be updated with brand-new data every quarter. Because such circumstances are becoming so commonplace, Microsoft has deemed it necessary to make this topic an exam objective.

Not only will inserting massive amounts of data at one time be covered, but also how to insert small amounts—just one record. In this section, the various methods for loading data, either in vast amounts or one record at a time, will be discussed. How to enter vast amounts will be covered a little later on; first, let's discuss how to update small amounts of data with the INSERT statement.

Loading Data with the INSERT Statement

The INSERT statement is used to add a single row of data to your table. Before you can use the INSERT statement, you need to know the structure of the table into which the data are being inserted. Specifically, you should know the number of columns in the table, the data types of these columns, the column names, and any defaults or constraints (e.g., IDENTITY) that are on a particular column. You can gather this information by using the sp_help tablename stored procedure or by right-clicking a table in Enterprise Manager and choosing Properties.

The easiest way to work with the INSERT statement is to specify data for each column in the table that requires data, in the same order in which the columns were defined.

Part iv

NOTE

When you are inserting character data, you must enclose the characters in single quotation marks. When you are inserting numeric data, you do not use quotation marks.

There is much more information that could be covered regarding the INSERT statement, but that is useful much more to the SQL Server developer than it is to the administrator. For the exam, you really need to know when it is appropriate to use the INSERT statement rather than the SELECT INTO statement, DTS, bcp, and so on.

Remember these facts about the INSERT statement:

▶ It generally adds a single record at a time.

▶ The inserted record is a logged transaction.

▶ If there is an index, it will be updated as well.

▶ You must have INSERT permission on the table to which you wish to add records.

Copying Tables with SELECT INTO

Essentially a copy-table command, the SELECT INTO statement is used to create new permanent tables or new temporary tables filled with data from another table.

To use the SELECT INTO command to create a permanent table in your database, you must first enable the Select Into/Bulk Copy database option. This can be done either in the Enterprise Manager or through the sp_dboption stored procedure. When you set the Select Into/Bulk Copy database option, you are specifying that you are about to perform a nonlogged insert of data. This is very important to know because it means that as soon as you are done with the operation, your database is vulnerable and needs to be backed up right away.

Keep the following things in mind when you are working with the SELECT INTO statement:

▶ To create a permanent table, you must have the Select Into/Bulk Copy database option enabled.

▶ To create local temporary tables, you must prefix your table name with an octothorp (#).

- To create global temporary tables, you must prefix your table name with two octothorps (##).

- To run the SELECT INTO command, you must have CREATE TABLE permissions in the database.

- Running a SELECT INTO statement performs a nonlogged operation—you should ensure your data by backing them up.

Copying Data with bcp

Bulk copy, or bcp, is a lightning-fast command-line utility for moving data between a text file and your SQL Server 7 database. The upside of bcp is its speed and compatibility. If you do not have indexes created on your tables and you have the Select Into/Bulk Copy database option set, reading an ASCII file into your server is very quick (better than 2000 rows per second on average).

There are disadvantages, however. First, because bcp is a command-line utility, it requires you to remember a number of different switches and is case-sensitive. Another disadvantage is that bcp transfers data only, not other database objects such as tables, views, and schema. The last downside is the fact that bcp cannot do data transformations such as converting a text string to a numeric value or splitting a Name field into a FirstName and a LastName field.

To use bcp, you must have the appropriate permissions. When you wish to move data from a text file into SQL Server 7, you must have READ permissions on the file itself (if using NTFS), and you must have INSERT permissions on the SQL Server table into which you would like to move the data.

To use bcp to move data from SQL Server to a text file, you must have NTFS permissions for either Change or Full Control on the directory and the file. Within SQL Server, you must have SELECT permissions on the table or view from which you want to pull your data.

Here is the syntax for bcp:

```
Bcp [[dbname.]owner.]tablename | view_name | "Query"}
{in | out | queryout | format } datafile
[/6]
[/a packet_size]
[/b batchsize]
[/c]
```

```
[/C code_page]
[/e errfile]
[/E]
[/f formatfile]
[/F firstrow]
[/h "hint [,…n]"]
[/i inputfile]
[/k]
[/L lastrow]
[/m maxerrors]
[/n]
[/N]
[/o output_file]
[/P password]
[/q]
[/r row_term]
[/S server_name]
[/t field_term]
[/T]
/U login_id
[/v]
[/w]
```

The following list explains each parameter. Note that the only required parameters are `tablename`, `in/out/queryout/format`, `datafile`, and `login ID '/U'`.

> ***dbname.owner.tablename*** or ***view_name*** or ***query***:   Specifies the name of the table view or query you want to export from or import to. If you don't specify the database name or the owner, these values will default to the current database and the user name of the person who is running the bcp command.

> **in/out/queryout/format:**   Specifies whether you are loading data into SQL Server 7 or extracting data out to a file.

> ***datafile***:   Specifies the name of the file with which you wish to work. If you do not specify the full path name with your file, it will default to the local directory from which you run the bcp

program. If you do not specify a filename at all, bcp will go into Format File mode. This allows you to create a format file that can be reused later. The format file is simply a template for bulk copying data into or out of SQL Server 7.

/6: Specifies that you are working with data from a SQL Server 6.*x* file.

/a *packet_size*: Allows you to specify the size of the packets you are going to be transferring across the network. The default is 4096 bytes.

/b *batchsize*: Specifies how many records you are going to transfer in a single batch. SQL Server will treat each batch as a separate transaction. If this option is not specified, the entire file will be loaded as a single batch.

/c: Specifies that the data being moved will all be converted to the character data type rather than the internal SQL Server data types. When used for export, it will create a tab-delimited flat file.

/C *code_page*: This option (note the capital *C*) allows you to specify a code page for the data file. For example, you can generate a file with the code page 850, which was the default code page for SQL Server 6.

/e *errfile*: Creates a path and filename containing the rows of data that bcp could not import or export properly. This can be very useful when you are troubleshooting your bcp operation. If you do not specify an error file, none will be generated. It is suggested that you use the `.ERR` file extension.

/E: The capital *E* specifies that identity columns in your SQL Server 7 table should be temporarily turned off. This allows the values in the source file to replace the automatically generated identity values in the SQL Server table during the bulk copy. Identity columns are similar to the autonumber feature in Microsoft Access.

/f *formatfile*: Allows you to specify the path and filename of the format file you wish to use during an insertion to or extraction from SQL Server 7. If you do not specify the format-file portion of this option, bcp will prompt you for formatting information and then create a format file called `bcp.fmt`.

Part iv

/F *firstrow*: The capital *F* and firstrow value allow you to specify a row, other than the first row, to begin reading into SQL Server 7.

/h *"hint"*: Allows you to specify any hints you wish to use. For example, you might create hints about check constraints or sort orders.

/i *inputfile*: Allows you to specify all these input parameters and store them in a file. When you run bcp again, all you need to do is specify this input file—all the stored parameters will be used. As always, specify the full path and filename.

/k: Specifies that empty columns will retain their NULL values rather than having some default value applied to them.

/L *lastrow*: Specifies the last row to load from the data file into SQL Server. If this is not specified, SQL Server will load all rows from the data file.

/m *maxerrors*: Allows you to specify the maximum number of errors SQL Server will allow before the bulk copy process is canceled. You should specify this option if you are importing large data files. The default value is 10 errors.

/n: Specifies that the data being transferred are in native format. In other words, the data being moved around retain their SQL Server 7 data types. This option is especially useful when you are moving data from one SQL Server to another SQL Server.

/N: Specifies that you will be using Unicode for character data and native format for all noncharacter data.

/o *output_file*: Specifies the name of the file that will receive any messages generated by the bulk copy. This option is useful when you run bcp from a batch file and later want to review what was processed.

/P *password*: Specifies the password you wish to use when logging into SQL Server from bcp. If you do not specify a password, bcp will prompt you for one.

/q: Specifies that quoted identifiers are being used. When this option is set, all identifiers (table name, column names, etc.) must be specified within double quotation marks.

/r *row_term*:   Specifies the value that bcp will use to determine where one row ends and the next row begins. You can use the following common characters as either field or row terminators:

\0:   Specifies an ANSI NULL.

\n: Specifies a new line.

\r: Specifies a carriage return.

\t: Specifies a tab.

\\:   Specifies a backslash.

/S *servername*:   Specifies the SQL Server to which you are connecting. If you don't specify a servername, bcp will assume that it is the local SQL Server.

/t *field_term*:   Specifies the field terminator. In many cases, this will be a comma or tab character.

/T: This capital *T* specifies that the bulk copy utility will connect to SQL Server over a trusted connection.

/U *login_id*:   Specifies the login ID that you will use to gain access to SQL Server and is a required parameter.

/v: Reports which DB-Library version is being used for the bulk copy process.

/w: Specifies that the data will be transferred using Unicode.

You should keep a few other items in mind when you are using bcp. Character mode is the most flexible method of bulk copy because all data are treated as characters. This means that SQL Server and most other applications can work with the data. When you use Character mode to export data, they will be stored as an ASCII text file. Native mode uses the internal SQL Server data types and can be faster for data transfers from one SQL Server to another SQL Server database. In fact, when you use the Transfer Manager (discussed later in this chapter), it uses bcp to move data from one SQL Server 7 computer to another SQL Server 7 computer.

When you perform a bulk copy to import data, you can do it in Normal mode, which means every insert is logged, or in Fast mode, which means inserts are not logged. To operate in Fast mode, you must enable the Select Into/Bulk Copy database option and drop all indexes that are affected by the data transfer. Once you have done this, you can quickly add your data using bulk copy. When you do a bulk copy, you should also

Part iv

be aware that defaults and data types will always be enforced, and rules, triggers, and constraints will always be ignored.

Since rules, triggers, and constraints are ignored during a Fast bulk copy, you should check the validity of your data by running queries or other stored procedures. A simple way to check your constraints is to run an UPDATE statement and set a particular field equal to itself. This will force all constraints to be checked against the new data. It will also fire off any update triggers associated with the table.

Once you are happy with your data, you should re-create your indexes and then back up your database because it is now unrecoverable.

Using BULK INSERT

You can be sure to see a question or two on the test regarding BULK INSERT because it is new to SQL Server 7. The BULK INSERT command treats data files like OLE-DB recordsets. Since SQL Server thinks the file is an OLE-DB recordset, it can move multiple records per step. You can move the entire file in one batch or in several batches.

One major difference between bcp and BULK INSERT is that BULK INSERT cannot move data from SQL Server to a file. Essentially, BULK INSERT gives you bulk copy capabilities through the use of T-SQL. Since bcp is a command-line utility, it can be placed into batch files; BULK INSERT cannot. You must be a member of the sysadmin server role to use the BULK INSERT command.

It is important to read through the BULK INSERT syntax and parameters at least once before the exam:

```
BULK INSERT [[database_name.][owner].]{table_name
FROM data_file}[WITH (
[BATCHSIZE = batch_size]]
[[,] CHECK_CONSTRAINTS]fa
[[,] CODEPAGE [= 'ACP' | 'OEM' | 'RAW' | 'code_page']]
[[,] DATAFILETYPE [= {'char' | 'native'| 'widechar' |
    'widenative'}]]
[[,] FIELDTERMINATOR [= 'field_terminator']]
[[,] FIRSTROW [= first_row]]
[[,] FORMATFILE [= 'format_file_path']]
[[,] KEEPIDENTITY]
[[,] KEEPNULLS]
```

```
[[,] KILOBYTES_PER_BATCH [= kilobytes_per_batch]]
[[,] LASTROW [= last_row]]
[[,] MAXERRORS [= max_errors]]
[[,] ORDER ({column [ASC | DESC]} [,…n])]
[[,] ROWS_PER_BATCH [= rows_per_batch]]
[[,] ROWTERMINATOR [= 'row_terminator']]
[[,] TABLOCK])]
```

Here are the parameters:

database_name.owner.table_name: The fully qualified table into which you BULK INSERT data.

data_file: The path and filename from which you wish to import.

CHECK_CONSTRAINTS: Specifies that constraints will be checked during the BULK INSERT.

CODEPAGE: Specifies which codepage was used to generate the data file.

DATAFILETYPE: Specifies in which format the data in the file have been stored. This could be character data, bcp native, Unicode character, or Unicode native.

FIELDTERMINATOR: Specifies which character has been used as a field terminator. As with bcp, the default is a tab character (often shown as \t).

FIRSTROW: Specifies the row with which you want to begin the BULK INSERT process. The default is the first row.

FORMATFILE: Specifies the full path and filename of a format file to be used with BULK INSERT.

KEEPIDENTITY: Specifies that IDENTITY values copied from the file will be retained rather than having SQL Server generate new values.

KEEPNULLS: This option is similar to the KEEPIDENTITY option. It specifies that NULL values in the data file will remain NULL values when loaded into the table.

KILOBYTES_PER_BATCH: Allows you to specify the number of kilobytes to be moved in each step. By default, this is the size of the entire file.

LASTROW: Specifies which row you to want to use to end the BULK INSERT process. By default, it is the last row in the file.

ORDER: Allows you to specify a sort order in the data file. This can improve performance in situations where the data file and SQL Server use different sort orders.

ROWS_PER_BATCH: Specifies how many rows of data to move in each step of the batch. If you use the BATCHSIZE option, you do not need to use this option. By default, all rows are moved in a single batch.

ROWTERMINATOR: Allows you to specify the end of a single row of data. The default value is the new-line character (\n).

TABLOCK: Specifies that a table lock, which will lock the entire table, should be used during the BULK INSERT procedure. No other users may make changes to data in the table during the upload. This can improve the BULK INSERT performance, but it will decrease performance for the other users.

Using Data Transformation Services (DTS)

Most companies store their data in a variety of locations and formats. SQL Server can move data through any of them as long as they are OLE-DB or ODBC compliant, by using DTS. When you are working with data from two SQL Server 7 computers, you can even transfer database objects and schema, including stored procedures, views, permissions, table layouts, etc. DTS does this by running a package, which can be created through Wizards or the DTS Designer.

DTS Packages DTS packages are a set of tasks designed into a workflow of steps. These steps and tasks are then grouped together into a package. You can create packages using the Import and Export Wizards, through a scripting language, from the command line using dtswiz and dtsrun, or visually through the DTS Designer.

Once you have created a package, it becomes a completely self-contained COM object, which you can interact with through the Enterprise Manager Task Scheduler, the command line, or COM-compliant languages (such as VBScript). The components that compose a package are as follows:

Task objects: Each task in a package defines a particular action that should be taken or some type of processing that should be done. Task objects can be used to perform activities such as running a T-SQL statement or sending e-mail.

Step objects: Step objects are used to coordinate the flow of tasks, giving structure to the work flows. While task objects are self-contained units, a task object that does not have an associated step object will not be executed. Steps can run in parallel or one after the other.

Connection objects: DTS uses connection objects to connect to both a data source and a destination. All of the information necessary to make a connection, including the login IDs, passwords, filenames, locations of the data, format of the data, etc., is contained in a connection object. Connection objects can be either data file (a text file) or data source (a database).

Data-pump object: The DTS data-pump object is an OLE-DB service provider that takes care of importing and exporting, and the data transformation.

Once created, these DTS packages can be stored in one of three locations: the MSDB database, the SQL Server repository, or as a COM-based object. Each of these has advantages:

MSDB database: Packages stored here take less space than in the repository, and other SQL Servers can connect to the packages and use them.

Repository: Storing packages here makes them available to other SQL Servers and, unlike the MSDB database, tracks metadata. The metadata are a lineage, or history, of how many times a package has been run and the changes it has made to the data.

COM file: When saved as COM-structured storage, packages are stored as data objects and data streams. A data object is similar to a folder, while a data stream is similar to a file within that data object. Any COM-compliant programming language can manipulate the DTS package when it is stored as a COM file.

Since security is a very pressing issue, you will most likely get a question on how to secure your packages once they're created. Two levels can be set:

DTS Owner passwords: A user or application with the DTS Owner password has complete access to the package. By default, you store a package with an Owner password.

DTS Operator passwords: Any user or application with this password has the ability to execute the package, but cannot modify or view the package components.

DTS Import and Export Wizards   Perhaps the easiest way to create packages is by using the Import and Export Wizards. While these tools do not allow a great deal of complexity in the packages they create, you can use them to perform the following tasks:

- ▶ Copy tables

- ▶ Copy query results, including the ability to create queries with the Query Builder Wizard

- ▶ Specify data-connection objects for both the source and destination

- ▶ Create and schedule DTS packages

- ▶ Transform data

- ▶ Run scripting languages

- ▶ Save packages in SQL Server, the repository, and COM-structured storage

- ▶ Transfer database schema and objects using Transfer Manager from one SQL Server 7 database to another SQL Server 7 database

DTS Designer   If you want to create complex data-transformation packages, DTS Designer is the tool for you. DTS Designer is a GUI-based utility you can use to create and edit your DTS packages. If you are familiar with programming in Access or Visual Basic, you should have no problems picking up the interface for the DTS Designer. Due to the sheer magnitude of the Designer, all of its aspects can't possibly be covered here (in fact it should have its own book), but you should definitely take a look at it.

Using the INSERT Statement

Using the INSERT statement is so simple that it does not even require steps. To add a single row to a table, just use the following code:

```
Use database
GO
INSERT INTO table VALUES
('col_one_value', 'col_two_value', 'col_three_value')
```

Using the SELECT INTO Statement

To use this statement, the Select Into/Bulk Copy option must be set on your database. To set this option from Enterprise Manager:

1. Navigate through the console tree to the database of your choice.

2. Right-click the database and choose Properties.

3. From the Properties window, click the Options tab.

4. On the Options tab, check the box next to Select Into/ Bulk Copy.

You may also set this option via T-SQL code. Execute your SELECT INTO statement and immediately set the Select Into/Bulk Copy option to false again as follows:

```
USE database
GO


EXEC sp_dboption 'database_name', 'select into/bulkcopy',
True
GO


SELECT * INTO new_table_name
FROM existing_table_name
GO


EXEC sp_dboption 'database_name', 'select into/bulkcopy',
False
GO
```

Using bcp

Even though bcp is used primarily for backward compatibility, it is still advisable to know how to use it. Used from a command prompt, the following code will transfer data out of a database to a text file (it wraps here for readability only):

```
bcp database..table out
c:\mssql7\data\filename.txt -c -SServerName -Usa -P
```

Part iv

Using BULK INSERT

As with the other T-SQL commands that have been discussed thus far, the BULK INSERT statement is simple to use. The following T-SQL code can be used to insert data into a table from a text file:

```
BULK INSERT database.owner.tablename
FROM 'c:\mssql7\data\filename.txt'
```

Using the Import and Export Wizards

Since both of these Wizards look identical, only the Import Wizard needs to be discussed. The following steps can be used to import a table using the Wizard:

1. Open the Enterprise Manager and connect to your SQL Server.

2. Right-click the Data Transformation Services folder and choose All Tasks ➤ Import Data from the context menu.

3. You should now be at the Import Wizard welcome screen. Click Next to continue.

4. You are now presented with the Choose a Data Source screen. Choose the source server. Choose your authentication type (Windows NT or Standard) and the source database from which to import. If the database you want does not show up in the drop-down list box, click the Refresh button and try again.

5. Clicking the Advanced button will display the Advanced Properties that you can work with.

6. Click Next to work with the Choose a Destination screen. Fill in the options as you did earlier. Click Next to continue.

7. You are now presented with the Specify Table Copy or Query dialog box. If you choose Table Copy, it will move an entire table. The Query option will allow you to specify a query and use the query builder. If you selected a SQL Server 7 data source and destination, the Transfer Objects option will also be available. Click Next to continue.

8. If you selected the Query option previously, you are now presented with the Type SQL Statement screen. You can type in a query, use the Query Builder button, or load a query stored

in a file. Once a query has been added, you can check it for syntax by clicking the Parse button. Click Next to move on.

9. You should now see the Select Source Tables screen. Notice that the Source Table is Query and the Destination Table is called Results. You can change that if you like. There is also an ellipsis (...) in the Transform field, which takes you to the Transformation dialog box when clicked.

10. If you are making changes, you should now be presented with the Column Mappings and Transformations screen.

11. If you click the Transformations tab and then choose the Transform Information as It Is Copied to the Destination option, you can specify your own custom transformations using one of three scripting languages.

12. Click the OK button to return to the Select Source Tables screen. Click Next to continue processing.

13. You are now presented with the Save, Schedule and Replicate Package screen. The Run Immediately option will run the package as soon as it has completed. You can also choose to make the package available for replication and set up a schedule for automatic execution. When you are finished, click Next to continue.

14. You are now presented with the Save DTS Package screen. Fill in the package name and description. This is also the place to secure your package with Owner and Operator passwords. Click Next to continue.

15. Finally, you are presented with the finish screen. Click Finish. You will see the package executing. You may be prompted with another dialog box informing you that the package ran and completed successfully.

Using the DTS Designer

To access the Designer, follow the steps outlined here:

1. Open the SQL Enterprise Manager.

2. Drill down through the console tree into the Data Transformation Services folder.

Part iv

3. Click the Local Packages icon, right-click an existing package, then choose Design Package.

4. You should now see the DTS Designer screen.

5. Right-click any of the objects or connections to view their information.

6. Close the DTS Designer when you are finished.

▶ Back up system databases and user databases by performing a full database backup, a transaction log backup, a differential database backup, and a filegroup backup.

As an administrator, one of the most important duties of your career is backing up your data. Why is this so important? Imagine what would happen if your sales database went off-line for a few hours—you could lose thousands of dollars in revenue, not to mention operating costs. You need to be sure that doesn't happen by performing backups. Since this topic can, and will, save you from disaster, you need to pay special attention not only for the real-world application, but for the exam.

Four different types of backups will be examined here: full, transaction log, differential, and filegroup. Each of these has its own strengths and weaknesses that can be exploited to your benefit.

The first step in backing up your data is creating a *backup device* (called a *dump* in earlier versions), which is where SQL stores backups. Backup devices can be permanent, which are reusable, or temporary, which can be used only once. The temporary variety is useful for emergency backups or backups that need to be shipped off for storage off-site. Permanent backup devices will be discussed in this section. These backup devices can point to files, or you can back up directly to tape.

If you use a tape, you can leave a single tape in the computer for both SQL and Windows NT backups, since SQL Server 7 uses the same tape format as Windows NT Backup. The problem with using a tape is that it needs to be installed physically in the SQL Server computer—it cannot be remote.

Since the majority of people back up to a file and then back the file up to tape as part of their Windows NT backup, the focus in this section will be primarily on backing up to files. Most of the principles for backing up to tape are the same.

If you have multiple backup devices, you can perform what is called a *parallel striped backup.* This speeds up the backup process by backing up to multiple devices at the same time. For example, backing up a database to tape may take an hour. If you have three tape drives in the SQL Server box and back up the database across all three devices, the backup would take approximately 20 minutes.

Another feature of striped backups is that they don't have to be restored simultaneously. A database that has been backed up on three different tape devices can be restored onto a SQL Server that has only one tape drive. You would restore the tapes in order: first, second, and third.

Once you have created the backup device, you can start the backup process. There are four types: full, transaction log, differential, and file-group—all of which are dynamic and can be performed while users are accessing the database.

NOTE

A backup device is essentially a pointer that SQL Server uses so that it knows where to put the backup file when the backup is actually done. Because of this, files are not created until the backup is actually performed.

Performing Full Database Backups

When a database backup is started, SQL Server will first do a checkpoint of the database and bring it up to date with all the completed transactions. SQL Server then takes a *snapshot* of the database and backs up the entire database. If users are trying to update pages, they will be temporarily blocked by SQL Server as it jumps ahead of the updates.

Any transactions that were not completed when the backup started will not be in it. Because of this, even though backups can be done during normal business hours, backing up the databases at night will help ensure that there is a clear understanding of what is in the backup as well as what didn't make it.

Databases can be backed up by either issuing T-SQL commands or using Enterprise Manager. The syntax for the command that backs up databases is as follows:

```
Backup Database <name> to <device> (with init)
```

Backing Up Transaction Logs

If the database is not set to Truncate Log on Checkpoint, the transaction log can be backed up and restored apart from the database.

The transaction log is a running total of all the transactions that have occurred in that particular database. One of the features of SQL Server is that the transaction log is truncated (cleaned out) only after a successful backup of the log. Many companies have run SQL Server for two or three months with no problems, until they suddenly find that no new transactions can be recorded because the transaction log is filled up.

The good news is that the transaction log will be cleaned out by SQL Server as part of a normal transaction log backup. The bad news is that SQL Server doesn't do this by default—all backups (and thus the cleaning, or truncating, of the log) must be configured by the administrator.

WARNING

Although the Truncate Log on Checkpoint option will automatically keep the log clean, it is not recommended for production environments because you cannot recover transactions that happened between database backups. You will also not be able to perform transaction log backups. If you do use the Truncate Log on Checkpoint option, make sure you perform frequent (at least nightly) database backups.

Another advantage of backing up the transaction log is that it can be restored up to a certain point in time. For example, if you have a backup of the transaction log for Wednesday and you later discover a major error had occurred at 4:05 P.M., you could restore the data up to 4:04 P.M.

You can back up the log by issuing the following command:

```
Backup log <database> to <device>
```

This command backs up the log and cleans it out.

Various switches can be added to the command to change the way the backup works:

Truncate_Only: This switch is used to clean out the log without backing it up. If you perform a full database backup every night, maintaining a backup of the log would be redundant, yet the log still needs to be cleaned out. `Truncate_Only` would perform this task.

No_Log: Since a transaction log backup writes a record to the transaction log, it will fail if the log fills to capacity. This switch will not record the backup in the log.

No_Truncate: This switch does the opposite of the Trun-cate_Only switch—it backs up the log without cleaning it out. The main purpose of this switch is to make a new backup of the transaction log when the database itself is either too damaged to work or completely gone.

WARNING

Note that with SQL Server 7, you must have at least one .MDF file (database file) still working for the No_Truncate switch to back up data successfully from the transaction log.

Performing Differential Database Backups

SQL Server 7 adds the ability to create a differential database backup, which records the final state of any added, edited, or deleted rows since the last full database backup.

To perform a differential backup using T-SQL syntax, simply open a Query Analyzer window and issue the following command:

```
Backup Database <database> to <device> with differential
```

Performing Filegroup Backups

SQL Server 7 also allows you to back up files and filegroups independent of the database. For example, suppose you have three data volumes (N:, O:, and P:) and three filegroups (Employees, Customers, and Orders), each residing on a different data volume. If the entire database took too long to back up, you could back up the Employees files on Monday, the Customers files on Tuesday, and the Orders files on Wednesday. Because backing up files or filegroups does not back up the transaction log, make sure you also perform a transaction log backup after backing up the filegroup.

To perform the filegroup backup using T-SQL, issue the following command:

```
Backup database <database> file=<filename>,filegroup=<file-
group> to <device>
```

For the test, you will need to know how to perform backups using Enterprise Manager and T-SQL. Since you need to have a backup device before you can perform those backups, you will also need to know how to create backup devices. The mechanics of backups will not be tested a great deal—it is more important to spend time on what they can do as opposed to how to make them do it. Even so, these procedures are very important to you.

Creating Backup Devices

Backup devices can be created with the `sp_addumpdevice` command. The syntax for the command specifies the logical name for the device and the path to the file that will be created after the backup is completed:

```
Sp_addumpdevice 'type', 'logical name', 'path'
```

Another, perhaps easier, method for creating these devices is through Enterprise Manager. To create a backup device, follow the steps below:

1. Open the Backup folder (under Management) inside Enterprise Manager.

2. Right-click and choose New Backup Device, or choose Action ➢ New Backup Device.

3. Add a name for your new device and point it to a file on disk. Alternatively, you could create the device on tape.

4. Choose OK to make the device.

5. Verify that your device was made by looking in the Backup folder.

Performing Full Backups

Performing a full backup using T-SQL is quite simple—just use the following code:

```
Backup Database dbname to backup_device with init
```

The `with init` statement is used for overwriting any exisiting data in the backup device; if no switch is specified, the backup will be appended to any existing data.

To perform a full backup through Enterprise Manager, use the following steps:

1. Highlight the database you want to back up.

2. Go to the Backup screen by either right-clicking and choosing All Tasks ➢ Backup Database, or choosing Tools ➢ Backup Database.

3. In the Backup dialog box, select the database to back up, then enter a name and description for the backup.

4. For a full backup, you need to select the Database—Complete radio button under Backup.

5. Under Destination, select either tape or disk, then select a device. If your device is not listed, click Add.

6. If you wish to erase all other data in the device, select the Overwrite Existing Media option from the Overwrite portion of the screen. If not, select Append.

7. Select OK to start the backup. You should see blue bars go across the screen as the backup proceeds. The Pubs database should take only a few seconds to back up.

8. After the backup completes, choose OK from the confirmation screen to close the Backup screen.

Backing Up and Restoring Directly to or from Files

SQL Server 7 can back up or restore directly to or from a file without having to specify a backup device first.

The syntax in SQL Server 7 to back up directly to a file is an extension of the `Backup Database` command, using a To keyword in front of the specified path and file instead of the device name. For example, to back up Pubs2 to a file, enter the following line:

```
Backup Database Pubs2 to C:\MSSQL\Dumps\Pubs2.dmp
```

Enterprise Manager can also be used to back up to a file directly. Instead of selecting a backup device, simply enter the path of the file you wish to use.

Backing Up Transaction Logs

The following steps demonstrate how to back up transaction logs:

1. Go to the Backup screen by highlighting the database in Enterprise Manager; select Backup Database, or right-click and choose Backup Database.

2. Back up the transaction log by selecting Transaction Log for the backup type; select a device to back up to and click OK to start the backup.

Part iv

Performing Differential Backups

You can also use Enterprise Manager to perform differential backups, as demonstrated by the following steps:

1. Start Enterprise Manager and go to the Management/ Backup folder.

2. You should create a separate device for the differential backups using *differential* somewhere in the naming scheme (i.e., pubs_diff_backup).

3. Highlight the database you want to back up and choose Backup Database from the Tools menu.

4. Select Differential Backup, choose the backup device, and click OK to start the backup.

Performing Filegroup Backups

To perform filegroup backups through Enterprise Manager, do as follows:

1. Highlight the database to back up and choose Backup Database from the Tools menu.

2. Select To Do a File and Filegroup Backup and select the Primary (default) filegroup. Choose OK.

3. Select a backup device and click OK to start the backup.

4. Choose OK to close the Backup screen.

Backup Device Information

Once you have backed up your data, there are several different ways to get information about the backup devices and the dates and contents of the backups stored on them. One way is by using the sp_helpdevice command with the particular database device specified. You can also use Enterprise Manager to see the contents of backup devices, as shown here:

1. Start Enterprise Manager.

2. Go to the Management ➤ Backup folder.

3. Highlight a backup device, right-click, and choose Properties.

4. Select the View Contents button.

5. Choose Close and Cancel to go back to Enterprise Manager.

▶ Restore system databases and user databases from a full database backup, a transaction log backup, a differential database backup, and a filegroup backup.

In this section, the methods used to restore your data from backups will be discussed—how to restore from full, differential, transaction log, and filegroup backups. There will also be some discussion of how to restore your system databases, whether or not you have a valid backup.

This section is going to prove invaluable to you when you're out in the real world simply because of this: Bad things happen. Your power may go out, you may get a hacker, or your building may burn down. In any of these instances, you will need to know how to restore. You should watch for a few restoration questions on the exam—since this topic will one day save your databases, Microsoft has wisely decided that SQL DBAs need to be tested on these concepts.

The process of restoring SQL databases can be summed up in the following steps:

1. Attempt to back up the transaction log.

2. Find and fix the cause of the failure.

3. Drop all the affected databases.

4. Restore the database from a database backup, or from a file or filegroup backup.

5. Restore the transaction log from a log backup, or restore the differential database backup.

Attempting to Back Up the Transaction Log

You should always try to create a transaction log backup after a database failure to capture all the transactions up to the time of the failure. You should use the No_Truncate switch, which backs up the log when the database is unusable. If you successfully back up transactions to the point of the failure, simply restore this new transaction backup set after you restore the other transaction log backups.

Part iv

Finding and Fixing the Cause of the Failure

This step involves troubleshooting NT and/or SQL Server to determine the cause of the failure. There are two basic reasons for determining the cause—obviously, the first is to fix the problem, and the second is to take the appropriate steps to prevent it from happening in the future.

Dropping the Affected Databases

Before the database can be re-created, it must first be dropped. You can delete it using either Enterprise Manager or the T-SQL `Drop Database <database>` command.

Restoring the Database

Enterprise Manager can restore databases quickly. Simply highlight the database to be restored, select the backup, and choose Restore. You can also restore a database without having to re-create it, because the restoration procedure will create the database if it doesn't already exist. To automatically re-create the database, simply choose a backup set to restore from—if the database doesn't exist, it will be re-created. If a database by the same name as that in the backup set already exists, it will be overwritten. If you wish to restore a backup set to a differently named database, use the Replace option (discussed below).

Although the syntax to do a restoration starts out simple, many options let you control exactly what is restored from which backup set.

The syntax to do a restoration is as follows:

```
Restore Database <database> from <device> <options>
```

The most common options are as follows:

Dbo_only: Tags the restored database as read only.

Recovery: Recovers any transactions and allows the database to be used. This is the default if none is specified and should be used on the last file restored.

No_recovery: Allows additional transaction logs to be restored and does not allow the database to be used until the Recovery option is used. This should be used when you have other files to be restored to the database.

TIP

If you use this option by mistake (or end up not having any logs to restore), you can issue the command Restore Database *<database>* Recovery to activate the database.

Replace: Required when the name of the database being restored is different than the one that was backed up.

Standby: Allows the database to be read only between log restorations. This is used for standby servers or other special purposes, such as testing the data contained in each transaction backup set.

Restart: Usually used with tape backups. Restart allows you to restart an operation at the point of failure. For example, suppose you have five tapes, and on the last tape, you insert the wrong one. By using the Restart switch, you can simply insert tape five and quickly finish the job.

Restoring the Transaction Log

Enterprise Manager or the Restore Log command can be used to restore transaction logs. Restoring transaction logs can be thought of as reapplying all the transactions in the order they occurred.

The T-SQL command to restore the log is as follows:

```
Restore Log <database> from <device> <options>
```

All the options that apply to the Restore Database command also apply to the Restore Log command, with the exception of the Replace option, which is not supported for log restorations.

Unlike restoring the entire database, restoring transaction logs literally reapplies all the transactions that took place between the time of the full database backup and the time of the transaction log backup, appending any changes to the database. It is because of this that SQL Server can restore transaction log backups up to a certain point in time.

For example, suppose your accounting department comes to you and asks you to bring the accounting data back to the state it was in at 3:02 P.M. yesterday. With the point-in-time restoration capability given to you by the transaction log, you can do just what they ask. To make it happen, just choose a date and time from the Point in Time Restore window.

Part iv

Restoring Differential Backups

Restoring a differential backup works very much like restoring transaction log backups. You must first do a full database restoration, then select the most recent differential backup to restore.

The T-SQL syntax to restore a differential backup is the same as for restoring the entire database.

Restoring Filegroups

Restoring filegroups can be done by using either Enterprise Manager or T-SQL syntax. It is done in Enterprise Manager in much the same fashion as full database restorations.

The T-SQL syntax for restoring files and filegroups is as follows:

```
Restore Database <database> from <device> File=<logical file-
name> Filegroup=<logical filegroup name>
```

Restoring the Master Database

Because the Master database contains all the settings for SQL Server, restoring the Master database is not only more complicated, but impossible to do accidentally. To restore the Master database, you must start SQL Server with the –m switch, which causes SQL Server to start in Single User mode.

NOTE

When you rebuild the Master database, the MSDB, Model, and Distribution databases also are rebuilt (reset). You should restore these databases from your most recent backups so that the scheduled jobs, alerts, operators, and ongoing replication don't disappear.

If the Master database becomes corrupt and, much to your chagrin, a current backup is unavailable, there is a procedure that will allow you to re-create the Master database so that you can gain access to the system again. The steps are as follows:

Find and fix the cause of the failure: Just as noted above, you will need to find and fix the hardware or software failure that caused the Master database to become corrupted.

Rebuild the Master database: Use the Rebuildm.exe program to rebuild the Master database.

WARNING

Rebuilding the Master database does not fix the existing one; it creates a completely new Master database—just as though you reinstalled SQL Server.

Attach valid database files to the Master database by running the `sp_attach_db` command for each file: You can attach databases without losing the data therein by using the `sp_attach_db` procedure. Because a newly rebuilt Master database will not know about any of your previous databases, you will need to run `sp_attach_db` for each of them.

Re-create the settings for SQL Server: Because the rebuilt Master database holds all the settings for SQL Server, they will revert to the defaults. You will need to reconfigure SQL Server with its previous settings, and probably stop and restart SQL Server to have them take effect.

Re-create the users and security for each database: Because the rebuilt Master database will have only the default SQL logins, you will need to re-create all of the logins.

Restore the MSDB, Model, and Distribution databases: Rebuilding the Master database also rebuilds the MSDB database. Any tasks, alerts, and operators you have created will have to be re-created by hand if a current backup of the MSDB database is unavailable.

These procedures will save your data when disaster strikes—and don't think it won't strike. Many administrators are lulled into complacency, and they don't take the time to learn the procedures for restoring their data. Because of that lack of knowledge, the restoration time can be twice as long, if it happens correctly at all. In this section, the procedures for restoring from a full, differential, transaction log, and filegroup backup will be examined.

Restoring from a Full or Differential Backup

Since the steps for restoring from a full or differential backup are exactly the same, the following steps will guide you through the restoration process for both:

1.   Right-click the database you wish to restore and choose All Tasks ➤ Restore Database.

2. Select the backup you wish to restore from the list of available backups.

3. If this is not the last backup you will be restoring, go to the Options tab and make sure that the Recovery Completion State is set to Leave Database Nonoperational. If this is the last file you will be restoring, make the database operational.

4. Select OK to start the restoration. Select OK at the Restoration Confirmation screen.

5. Go back to the Databases folder. The database you are restoring should be grayed out with "Loading" next to it.

Restoring from a Transaction Log Backup

To restore transaction logs using Enterprise Manager, follow the steps below:

1. Restore the database in question by highlighting it and selecting Restore Database from the right screen, or by right-clicking and choosing All Tasks ➤ Restore Database.

2. Select the device to restore from—it should be the one containing the transaction log backups.

3. Make sure you select Transaction Log from the Restore Backup Set menu.

4. Select OK to restore the transaction log. Select OK to close the confirmation window.

Restoring the Master Database

In this set of steps, you will see the procedures for restoring the Master database when you have a valid backup available:

1. Stop SQL Server.

2. Open a command prompt.

3. Start SQL Server in Single User mode by opening a command prompt and issuing the following command:

   `SQLSERVR -m`

4. Minimize the command prompt.

5. Start Enterprise Manager (SQL Server will show a red stop-light, even though it is running).

6. Highlight the Master database.

7. Go to the Restore screen.

8. Select the device Master was backed up to and choose Restore Now.

9. After the Master database is restored, the command prompt should automatically stop SQL Server and return to a regular C:\ prompt.

10. Restart SQL Server normally.

▶ Manage replication.

▶ Configure servers, including Distributor, Publisher, and Subscriber.

▶ Create publications.

▶ Set up and manage subscriptions.

Many companies in today's world have multiple database servers in their organizations, and those servers require much of the same data. Rather than having everyone come to one server, you can replicate the data to other servers in the organization and have everyone gain access to a local copy.

In this section, the mechanics of setting up and managing replication will be discussed. The first thing you will need to do for the sake of replication is configure your Distributors, Publishers, and Subscribers. Once that is done, you can create publications, which is what the servers in your organization subscribe to in order to get the data they need. Before any of this can take place, you must first configure your SQL Server. The computer itself must meet the following requirements:

▶ All servers involved with replication must be registered in the Enterprise Manager.

▶ The replication agents use the same Windows NT account that the SQLServerAgent uses. This account must have administrative rights and be a member of the Administrators group.

▶ The SQLServerAgent account must have the Log On as a Service advanced user right (this should have been assigned during setup).

- If the servers are from different domains, trust relationships must be established before replication can occur.

- Any account that you use must have access rights to the Distribution working folder on the distribution server.

- The server must have a minimum of 32MB of RAM with 16MB allocated for SQL Server 7.

- You must enable access to the Distribution working folder on the distribution server. For an NT Server, this is the \\Server-Name\C$\MSSQL7\ReplData folder. On a Windows 95/98 computer, you must use the share name C$ for the defaults to operate properly. (The $ means that only accounts with administrative rights can access that particular share.)

TIP

It is suggested that you use a single Windows NT domain account for all of your SQLServerAgents. Do not use a LocalSystem account, because this account has no network capabilities and will therefore not allow replication.

Installing a Distribution Server

Since installing distribution and publication are taken care of through the same Wizard, the actual setup will be covered in the "Necessary Procedures" section to follow. Before you jump in and start swimming in the pool of replication, though, you should be aware of a few things. For example, before you can enable a Publication database, you must be a member of the sysadmin fixed server role. Once you have enabled publishing, any member of that database's db_owner role can create and manage publications.

Keep the following points in mind when you choose your Distributor:

- Ensure that you have enough hard-disk space for the Distribution working folder and the Distribution database.

- You must manage the Distribution database's transaction log carefully. If that log fills to capacity, replication will no longer run, which can adversely affect your Publication databases as well.

- The Distribution database will store all transactions from the Publisher to the Subscriber. It will also track when those transactions were applied.

- Snapshots and merge data are stored in the Distribution working folder.

- Be aware of the size and number of articles being published.

- Text, ntext, and image data types are replicated only when you use a snapshot.

- A higher degree of latency can significantly increase your storage space requirements.

- Know how many transactions per synchronization cycle there are. For example, if you modify 8000 records between synchronizations, there will be 8000 rows of data stored on the Distributor.

- Consider using a remote Distributor to minimize the impact of replication on your publishing servers.

Adding a Publication

Once you have enabled distribution and publishing, you can add publications and articles to your server. When you add a new publication, you need to determine the type of replication that will be used, the snapshot requirements, and Subscriber options such as updating or anonymous Subscribers. You can also partition your data and decide whether you will allow push or pull subscriptions.

You will be walked through the Create Publication Wizard, but before you get there, you need to consider a few options:

- You should consider how often to publish a new snapshot for refreshing the Subscriber databases.

- Consider which tables and stored procedures you wish to publish before running the Wizard.

- If you will be using two-phase commit or the Microsoft Distributed Transaction Coordinator, you may want to allow updating Subscribers.

- Think about whether to allow pull subscriptions. If you have a large number of Subscribers or Subscribers over the Internet, this will be the way to go.

- Replicate only the data you need. Use filters to send only the fields and records that you need.

▶ Use primary keys on replicated tables to ensure entity integrity. If you don't have primary keys, you can perform only snapshot replication.

Creating a Subscription

As part of the process of creating a subscription, you will be able to specify the Publishers you wish to subscribe to and a destination database to receive the published data, verify your security credentials, and set up a default schedule. While you will see more detail on this when you step through the Wizard in the "Necessary Procedures" section, you should check these points first:

▶ You can use pull subscriptions to off-load the work from the Distributors to each Subscriber.

▶ You should use updating Subscribers rather than merge replication if possible.

Managing Replication

Managing and maintaining replication can be very intensive work for an administrator. Fortunately, Microsoft SQL Server 7 has included many tools in the Replication Monitor to make this job a lot easier. Before the use of these tools is discussed, however, one of the most important tasks in replication administration—backing up—must be examined.

Replication Backup Strategies   When you perform backups of your replication scenario, you can make backups of just the Publisher, the Publisher and Distributor, the Publisher and Subscriber, or all three. Each of these strategies has its own advantages and disadvantages. The following list highlights these distinctions:

Publisher only: This strategy requires the least amount of resources and computing time, since the backup of the Publisher does not have to be coordinated with any other server backups to stay synchronized. The disadvantage is that restoration of a Publisher or Distributor is a slow and time-consuming process.

Publisher and Distributor: This strategy accurately preserves the publication as well as the errors, history, and replication agent information from the Distributor. You can recover quickly because there is no need to reestablish replication. The disadvantages of this strategy are the coordination of the backups, and the amount of storage and computing time necessary to perform a simultaneous backup.

Publisher and Subscriber(s):   This strategy significantly reduces the recovery time by removing the initialization process (running a snapshot). The main disadvantages of this strategy manifest themselves when you have multiple Subscribers. Every Subscriber will have to be backed up and restored.

Publisher, Distributor, and Subscriber(s):   This strategy preserves all of the complexity of your replication model. The disadvantages are storage space and computing time. This scenario also requires the most time for recovery.

WARNING

It is essential that the Distribution database and log do not get filled to capacity. When this database or log gets filled to capacity, it can no longer receive publication information. When this occurs, the logged transactions at the Publisher cannot be removed from the log (unless you disable publishing). Over time, your Publishing database's transaction log will also get filled to capacity, and you will no longer be able to make data modifications.

Using the Replication Monitor   Once you have installed distribution and publication, you will notice a new icon in the console tree of your SQL Server—the Replication Monitor icon. This tool will allow you to monitor and maintain each and every part of replication. You can look at agent properties and histories, and even set replication alerts.

The Replication Monitor resides on the computer where the distribution server has been installed and gathers replication information about the different replication agents. Through the Monitor, you can edit the various schedules and properties of the various agents. This includes the agent history, which keeps track of everything that has happened during the replication, including information about inserts, updates, deletions, and any other transactions that were processed.

After a successful log is read and moved to the Distributor and the Subscriber pulls the transaction, the distribution server needs to be cleaned up. Once a transfer has been successfully completed, a clean-up job will run.

Part iv

There is at least one clean-up job for every Subscriber. In other words, if you have 20 Subscribers to your database, you will have at least 20 clean-up jobs on the Distributor. If you click the Miscellaneous Agents folder in the console tree, you will see some of the clean-up jobs that have been created. These are explained below.

Agent History Clean Up: Distribution: This job cleans up the historical information in the Distribution Agents History tables after they have aged out.

Distribution Clean Up: Distribution: This job cleans up the distributor by removing transactions from the Distribution database after they have aged out.

Expired Subscription Clean Up: This job removes expired subscription information from the Subscription database.

Reinitialize Subscriptions Having Data Validation Failures: This job reinitializes all subscriptions that failed because of problems with data validation.

Replication Agents Checkup: This job watches for replication agents that are not actively adding information to their history logs.

Working with Replication Scripts   Now that you have replication set up and working properly, you may wish to save all your hard work in the form of a replication script. This can save you a great deal of time in the event of a system crash, since, with a script in hand, you will not need to completely re-create your replication setup. You can just run the scripts and have replication right back to the way it was. Here is a list of even more advantages that this brings you:

► You can use the scripts to track different versions of your replication implementation.

► You can use the scripts with some minor tweaking to create additional Subscribers and Publishers with the same basic options.

► You can quickly customize your environment by making modifications to the script and then rerunning it.

► Scripts can be used as part of your database recovery process.

Getting Information about Replication   There are many stored procedures that are used to create and install replication on your computer. Here is a short list of stored procedures that are at your disposal for gathering administrative information about your SQL Server replication configuration:

sp_helpdistributor: This gathers information about the Distribution database, the Distributor, the working directory, and the SQLServerAgent user account.

sp_helpdistributiondb: This gathers information about the Distribution database, its files, and their location as well as information regarding the distribution history and log.

sp_helppublication: This gathers publication information and configuration options.

sp_helpsubscription: This gathers information associated with a particular article, publication, Subscriber, or set of subscriptions.

sp_helpsubscriberinfo: This gathers information about the configuration settings of a Subscriber, including information regarding frequency of the subscription, retry delays, and much more.

Enabling Distribution and Publishing

To replicate your data, you need to enable distribution and publishing:

1. Using Enterprise Manager, connect to your SQL Server.

2. Highlight your SQL Server and then choose Tools ➤ Replication ➤ Configure Publishing and Subscribers.

3. You are now presented with a welcome screen. If you take a closer look at the welcome screen, you'll see that you can create your local computer as the Distributor. Click Next to continue.

4. You are now presented with the Choose Distributor screen. Here, you will decide where the distribution server is going to be installed. Only SQL Servers that are already registered in the Enterprise Manager will be available here.

5. Leave the defaults and click Next to continue.

6. You can now decide whether you want to use all the default settings for your Distributor. Under normal conditions, this is not a problem at all. Since you are seeing this for the first

time, let's take a look at the customizable settings. Choose the Yes, Let Me option and click Next to continue.

7. You are now presented with the Provide Distribution Database Information screen. You can supply a name for the Distribution database as well as location information for its database file and transaction log. Keep the defaults and click Next to continue.

8. The Enable Publishers screen shows all registered SQL Servers. You can pick and choose which servers you wish to configure as publishers. The ellipsis (...) allows you to specify security credentials such as login ID and password as well as the location of the snapshot folder. Be sure to place a check mark next to your local SQL Server and then click Next to continue.

9. You are now looking at the Enable Publication Databases screen. You can select the databases on the newly enabled Publisher from which you wish to allow publishing. Next to the database you wish to replicate, select the check box for the type of replication you desire and click Next to continue.

10. You are now presented with the Enable Subscribers screen. This is very similar to the Enable Publishers screen. For this example, you are going to use the same SQL Server for publishing, distribution, and subscribing. If you have additional SQL Servers, feel free to implement replication to them now.

NOTE

If your server isn't listed here, you can click the Register Server button to register another Microsoft SQL Server computer. You must set up non-Microsoft SQL Servers through the Configure Publishing and Distribution screen.

11. Click the ellipsis to modify the security credentials of the subscription server.

12. You are now looking at the General tab of the Subscriber Properties screen.

13. In the Schedules tab, you can specify the replication schedule for both the merge and distribution agents. The default for these values is Continuously, but you can set the schedule to anything you like (just as when creating and scheduling

SQL Server jobs). Click OK to return to the Enable Subscribers screen.

14. Click Next to continue. You are now given a summary of the configuration options you have chosen. Click Finish to implement these configurations and enable the distribution server.

Now that you have successfully installed the Distribution database and distribution server, you should see the Replication Monitor icon up in the Enterprise Manager console tree.

Creating a Publication

In the following walkthrough, you will create a new publication:

1. Connect to your SQL Server in the Enterprise Manager. If you expand the Databases folder, you will now see a hand icon on the database you have set up for replication. This indicates that the database has been marked for replication.

2. Highlight the database with the hand icon and then go to Tools ➤ Replication ➤ Create and Manage Publications. You will now be presented with the Create and Manage Publications dialog box.

3. Highlight the database to publish and click Create Publication.

4. The Create Publication Wizard now starts with a welcome screen. Click Next to continue.

5. You can now specify what type of publication you wish to create—Snapshot, Transactional, or Merge. For this example, select Transactional and click Next to continue.

NOTE

Transactional replication on the Desktop edition of SQL Server running on Windows 95/98 is supported as Subscriber only. This is because the server-side network libraries for Named Pipes are required for this type of replication and are not available on Windows 95/98. Windows 95/98 Named Pipes on the client side is supported, however.

6. You can now specify whether you wish to enable updating Subscribers. As you might recall, updating a Subscriber makes changes at both the subscription server and the publishing

Part iv

server, using a two-phase commit. Either both servers are updated or neither of them is. For this example, keep the default No, Do Not Allow and click Next to continue.

7. The following graphic shows the Specify Subscriber Types screen. When you were working on the Distribution database installation, you learned that you could specify only Microsoft SQL Servers as Subscribers. Although you can enable non-Microsoft SQL Servers as Subscribers from here, you are not going to do that in this walkthrough. Leave the default All Subscribers Will Be and click Next to continue.

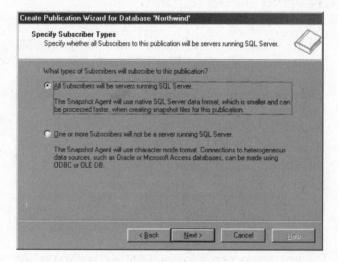

8. Here, you can determine which tables you wish to publish from. In essence, you are creating your articles. Click the check box next to the Categories table.

9. Selecting an article creates the ellipsis button. Click the ellipsis.

10. You are now presented with the Categories Properties pages. The General tab allows you to specify the Article Name, a Description, the Destination Table Name, and the Destination Table Owner. Change the Destination Table Name to rtblCategories and be sure to specify the owner as dbo.

11. The Snapshot tab allows you to specify what will happen during the snapshot process. Will you drop the existing table? Will you truncate the data in it? Leave the default options

and click OK to return to the Specify Articles screen. Once back at the Specify Articles screen, click Next to continue.

12. You are now presented with the Choose Publication Name and Description screen. When you are finished, click Next to continue.

13. You now see the Use Default Properties of the Publication dialog box. From here, you can accept the default filtering and partitioning options, or you can customize them. Although you will not make changes to these options, let's take a look at them. Click the Yes, I Will Define option and then click Next to continue.

14. When you see the Filter Data screen, you can choose to filter your data or leave them alone. Click the Yes, I Want to option, then click Next to continue.

15. From the Filter Table Columns screen, you can select which columns you wish to exclude from your replication. Click Next to continue.

16. You can now filter the rows. If you click the ellipsis, you can create a new filter by filling in a Where clause. When you are finished, click Next to continue.

17. You are now asked whether you wish to allow anonymous Subscribers. If you have many Subscribers or you are allowing subscriptions across the Internet, you may wish to allow anonymous Subscribers. Anonymous Subscribers reduce some of the administration of your replication. Note, however, that this choice does not compromise security. Leave the default No, Only Known and click Next to continue.

18. You are now presented with the Set Snapshot Agent Schedule screen. Remember that before replication can begin, a snapshot of your data must be moved to the Subscriber to set a baseline for all future replication. Click the check box to indicate that you want the Subscriber to create the first snapshot immediately. Click the Change button to set up your snapshot schedule. A snapshot schedule (formerly referred to as a *scheduled table refresh*) is useful when you have nonlogged operations running on the Publisher. If an operation is not logged, it won't be replicated. This can come in handy if you are replicating text, ntext, or image data types. Click Next to continue.

19. You are now at the finish screen. You can review the options you have chosen and, when you are ready, click Finish to complete the creation of your publication. After some processing takes place, you will return to the Create and Manage Publications screen, but with changes: Your new publication—Northwind_Categories—should be listed.

20. From here, you can push this publication to Subscribers, or you can look over its properties and subscriptions by clicking the Properties & Subscriptions button. When you do this, you will see much of the information you entered displayed in a set of pages. When you are finished, click OK to return to the Create and Manage Publications screen.

21. From the Create and Manage Publications screen, you can also delete your publications. Click Close to finish.

Creating Subscriptions

Once you have created a publication, the other servers in your organization can subscribe to the data you are publishing. Here are the steps for creating a pull subscription:

1. Connect to your SQL Server, highlight the server, and choose Tools ➤ Replication ➤ Pull Subscription to *Your Server Name*.

2. You are now looking at the Pull Subscription to *Your Server Name* dialog box.

3. Click the Pubs database and then click Pull New Subscription.

4. As always, you are presented with a welcome screen. Click Next to continue.

5. You can now see a list of Publishers. By expanding the Publishers, you can see the publications that they have made available. If you do not see your publishing server here, you can click the Register Server button to register another server. Expand the server you want to pull from and select a publication. Click Next to continue.

6. You must now specify the security credentials that your synchronization agent will use for the synchronization process. Fill in **sa** and no password. Click Next to continue.

7. You must now choose your destination database. This is where the subscribed data will be stored on your server. Click Next to continue.

8. If the schema and tables don't already exist at the Subscriber, they must be initialized there. Take the default value as shown below and click Next to continue.

9. You can now set the synchronization schedule. For snapshots, it might be wise to set up some type of regular schedule. For merge replication, you will most likely use a manual form of synchronization called *on demand.* Click Next to continue.

10. You are now looking at the Start Required Services screen. Because all your agents use the SQLServerAgent service to interact with the various servers, the SQLServerAgent must be running. If it is not, click the check box to force the service to start. Once you have it running, click Next to continue.

11. You are now at the finish screen again. As with other screens of this type, you can review your subscription. When you are satisfied, click Finish to create the subscription.

12. You should now be back at the Pull Subscription to *Your Server Name* screen, but this time your subscription should be displayed. Here, too, you can choose your subscription and look at its Properties pages. You can also delete the subscription or reinitialize it. When you are finished, click Close.

13. If you expand your destination database folder, you will notice that there is now a Pull Subscriptions folder in it. There is also a Publications folder under the published database. You can highlight these items and then double-click the publication or subscription in the right pane for additional information about them.

Working with Replication Monitor

Follow these steps to work with the various agents:

1. Open the Enterprise Manager on the SQL Server where the distribution server was installed.

2. Expand the Replication Monitor icon, then the Agents folder, and finally, highlight the Snapshot Agents.

3. If you right-click a publication in the details pane, you will see that you can view the agent history, properties, and profile. You can also start or stop the agent. There are options to modify the refresh rate and choose the columns to view. Right-click and choose Agent History.

4. You are now presented with the Snapshot Agent History. You can filter the list to show information based on all sessions; sessions in the last 7 days, the last 2 days, or the last 24 hours; or sessions with errors. You can also look at the Agent Profile and its settings as well as the Monitor Settings. The Monitor Settings allow you to specify how often the items in the Replication Monitor will be refreshed.

5. You can look at the details of a particular session. Session details include information about all the different processes that took place during the session.

6. Close the Snapshot Agent History. Right-click a publication and choose Agent Properties. You are now looking at the Properties sheets. These operate in the same fashion as the scheduled jobs that you have already worked with. When you are finished browsing, close the Snapshot Agent History.

Using Replication Scripts

In this walkthrough, you will create some replication scripts for your current setup:

1. Highlight your server in the console tree and then choose Tools ➤ Replication ➤ Generate Replication Scripts.

2. You are now presented with the Generate SQL Scripts pages. You can script the Distributor and the publications for the various replication items stored with this distribution server. The File Options tab allows you to save your script to several different file types. The default storage location for your scripts is `C:\MSSQL7\Install`. This particular folder holds many other scripts that are used to create and install your SQL Server and several databases.

3. The Preview button allows you to view the scripts themselves.

4. When you are finished viewing the scripts, click Close. You can now close the replication-scripting property pages.

Automate administrative tasks.

- ▶ Define jobs.

- ▶ Define alerts.

- ▶ Define operators.

- ▶ Set up SQLAgentMail for job notification and alerts.

Many years ago, if people wanted to wear clothes made from cotton, they had to pick and process the cotton by hand. This was an extremely time-consuming and repetitive process, almost mind numbing. That is why a rather creative man named Eli Whitney came up with the idea of the cotton gin to help automate the process. He wasn't the first to automate something, and he certainly wasn't the last—other people through the years have also seen the value of automating repetitive tasks so that they could be freed up to perform more complex and challenging duties.

Microsoft has followed suit by giving us automation in SQL Server. In this section, the discussion will involve not only how to automate repetitive tasks by defining jobs, but how to automatically warn someone when something goes wrong by defining alerts and operators. Finally, one of the handiest tools in SQL Server—SQLAgentMail, which allows you to send e-mail to operators when there is a problem—will be examined.

The information in this section is definitely going to save you time, lots of time. Learn this not just for the test, but for the real world. Let SQL take care of those repetitive tasks so that you can go home at a reasonable hour and come back in the morning to find your tasks have been completed by SQL Server automation.

To use SQL Server's automation capabilities, you must have the SQL-Agent properly configured. Here is a checklist to make sure this is done:

- ▶ SQLAgent must log on using a user account, with administrative rights.

- ▶ The service should be configured to start automatically (if it is set to manual, you will have to start it by hand every time you reboot your server).

- ▶ While most services don't require a user account assigned to them to function correctly, services that go beyond the physical box and connect to other servers on the network (as the SQLAgent may do) usually need a user account assigned. This is so they have an account with which to be authenticated on the remote server. Otherwise, they connect with NULL security credentials and by default will be denied access.

NOTE

When using the Desktop version of SQL Server with Windows 95/98, you cannot assign an account to the SQLAgent. Not assigning an account to the agent will not affect any jobs or alerts on the local computer. The major limitation on Windows 95/98 computers is that they cannot be assigned as job managers for other servers.

Defining Jobs

Earlier versions of SQL Server (4.21a and earlier) could schedule backups, but that was the extent of their scheduling capabilities. Beginning with version 6, SQL Server's scheduling capabilities have been greatly expanded. In SQL Server 7, you can define jobs to perform just about any task you can think of and schedule those jobs to run at regular intervals or when an alert is triggered. SQL Server supports four general types of jobs:

TSQL jobs: These jobs are written using T-SQL commands. They are often used to back up the database, rebuild indexes, and perform other various routine database maintenance activities.

CmdExec jobs: These jobs literally open a command prompt and run some sort of batch file or executable file. Common CmdExec jobs are those created by the Database Maintenance Plan Wizard or by the SQL Server Web Assistant.

Replication jobs: These jobs deal with replication. Normally, you would use the Replication Wizards and prompts to help set up replication jobs, although monitoring these jobs is an important step in maintaining replication.

Active Script jobs: These jobs can run Visual Basic or Java script at a regular interval.

These jobs that you create do not even have to be local. SQL Server 7 allows you to create what are called *multiserver jobs*. In a multiserver scenario, you have a master server, where the jobs are created, and target servers, where those jobs are run. Using this method, you can ease the administrative burdens of creating jobs since you need to create the job only once, at a single server, and have it run on multiple servers in your organization. Since the target servers upload the job status to the master server, you can even view the job history from one server (the master). To create multiple server jobs, you must do as follows:

- ▶ Ensure that all servers involved are running SQL Server 7 on Windows NT.

- ▶ Make certain that all SQLAgent services are logging on with a domain account.

- ▶ Designate one server as the master server (MSX).

- ▶ Designate a master server operator (MSX operator) to be notified in case a multiserver job fails.

- ▶ Designate one or more servers as target servers when you create the job.

NOTE

A target server can report to only one master server at a time.

When you actually create the job, you need to supply the name, schedule, and command to be executed during one or more steps. Once you've told SQL what to do, you need to tell it *when* by selecting one of four schedule settings:

When the SQLAgent starts: A job can be created that automatically executes whenever the SQLAgent starts. This would be good for an automated system of some kind.

When the CPU is idle: A job can be scheduled to start after the CPU has been idle a certain amount of time, which is configurable in the Properties screen of the SQLAgent.

One time only: A one-time-only job is usually created for a special purpose; it executes only once on its scheduled date and time.

Recurring: A recurring job happens on a regular basis. The job's frequency can be daily, weekly, or even monthly.

Defining Alerts

A SQL event that is written to the Windows NT application log can have an alert defined for it. When you define an alert, you are really telling

SQL to watch for errors in the Windows NT application log and match those errors to entries in the sysalerts table. If an event is matched to an entry in sysalerts, SQL follows whatever actions are prescribed by the alert, such as firing a job or sending an e-mail.

There are two types of alerts to create: SQL error-message and performance alerts. Error-message alerts are based on predefined messages that are stored in the sysmessages table—you can use the SQL messages (all 2000+ of them), or you can create your own. If you do create your own, you should call the new error message from within your T-SQL script or program by using the following command:

```
Raiserror (error_number, severity, state)
```

The performance alerts are used to warn you when one of the performance counters reaches a certain value; for example, when the transaction log of a database reaches 75 percent full. There are a few basic options to consider before creating an alert:

- ▶ If based on a SQL Server error message, define the error to look for. Alerts can be based on a generic error-message number, the error's severity, or an error happening in a specific database.

- ▶ Optionally, define the database in which the error must happen. An alert can filter error messages based on the database. For instance, an alert can be created to watch the Pubs database in case it fills up. This alert would operate only on the Pubs database; if any other database filled up, the alert wouldn't do anything.

- ▶ If based on a Performance Monitor counter, define which counter to monitor and the threshold that will trigger the alert.

- ▶ Define the response of the alert. Alerts can be set up to trigger jobs automatically and/or to warn operators that the alert was activated.

- ▶ Alerts are usually designed to perform a job when the alert is fired, so you need to define (or select) the job to be done. This is a standard job, so you are not limited in the tasks that it can perform.

- ▶ If the alert is meant to notify someone, define who will be notified and how this will be done. You can specify operators and whether they should receive an e-mail message and/or be paged when an alert is triggered.

- ▶ Activate the alert by selecting the Enabled box inside the Edit Alert dialog box (it is selected by default, but can be deselected to temporarily disable an alert).

If you have more than one system running SQL Server, you can define a central server that will receive from other servers events for which you have (or have not) defined alerts. The server that receives these events is called an *unhandled event forwarding server*. The server that is designated as the unhandled event forwarding server must be registered in Enterprise Manager.

NOTE

Windows 95/98 cannot forward events to, or act as, an unhandled events server.

Defining and Managing Operators

When you define an alert in SQL, it is probably because you want to notify someone that the alert has fired. The person that you will notify is called an operator in SQL Server. Operators can receive messages about alerts in one of three ways:

Net send: This a standard Windows NT net-send message that pops up a dialog box on the user's computer screen.

E-mail: This method will actually send a message to the user's mailbox. To use this, you must have SQLAgentMail configured and a MAPI-compliant messaging server (such as Exchange).

Pager: This will send the alert to an alphanumeric pager. The pager must be able to accept text messages sent over the Internet for this to work.

Configuring SQLAgentMail for Job Notification and Alerts

You may have figured out by this point that to define a fully functional operator, you must have SQLAgentMail configured. There are four basic steps to installing MAPI support for Windows NT 4:

1. Make certain that the SQLAgent service is logging on with a domain account (this step was most likely completed during setup).

2. Create a mailbox for the SQL user account on the MAPI-compliant mail server.

3. Log into the SQL Server computer as the SQL user account and create an Exchange profile that points to the Exchange Server and post office box created in step 2.

4. Assign the profile (created in step 3) to the SQL Mail portion of SQL Server. Start the SQL Mail session.

After you have configured and tested e-mail, you can start sending e-mails and pages to your operators whenever an alert fires or a job completes.

Defining Jobs

In this series of steps, you will create a job and make it recurring:

1. In Enterprise Manager, open the Management window and open the Jobs window. This should show you any jobs you have previously made.

2. Click the New button (it looks like a star) on the toolbar, or right-click the Jobs folder and choose New Job.

3. In the New Job Properties dialog box, enter a descriptive name for the job.

NOTE
You can pick target servers for this job if you have enlisted this server as a master server and have designated one or more target servers from the bottom right of the screen.

4. Go to the Steps tab.

5. Create a new step by selecting the New button at the bottom of the screen.

6. Enter a name for the step name, select the type (T-SQL, command, or Active Script), and then enter the command.

7. If the command is T-SQL, use the Parse button to check the command for syntax errors. You should get an OK box. If not, fix the command until it works.

8. Select the Advanced tab and change any necessary settings, such as what to do when the step fails, how many times to retry, etc.

9. Go to the Schedules tab in the New Job Properties dialog box.

10. Choose New Schedule.

11. Enter a descriptive name for the schedule.

12. Change the schedule for the job by selecting the Change button.

13. Set the schedule to whatever your needs may be—weekly, monthly, daily, hourly, etc. Choose OK to save the changed schedule.

14. Make sure the schedule is enabled and choose OK to save it.

15. Choose OK to save the new job. The job should now be listed in the Jobs folder.

Defining Alerts

There are two types of alerts to configure: error-message and performance alerts. The differences between the two are subtle, but enough to require two sets of steps.

Error-Message Alerts   This first set of steps will outline the method for creating an error-message alert:

1. In Enterprise Manager, open the Management window and open the Alerts window. You should see nine predefined alerts.

2. To add a new alert, click the New button on the toolbar, choose Action ➤ New Alert, or right-click and choose New Alert.

3. You'll see the New Alert dialog box. In the ID: New Name field, enter a name for the new alert.

4. In the Event Alert Definition section, select the Error Number option button and enter a number in the associated box—if you don't know the number you want, you can search for it by clicking the Find button next to the Error Number text box.

5. Select a specific database to report on or allow the message to be fired for all databases.

6. Go to the Response tab and select Execute Job if you wish to have a job run when the alert fires.

7. If you have operators defined, you may specify whether and how to alert them on the Operators tab at this time.

8. Click OK to save the alert. Your alert should now be listed with the default alerts.

Performance Alerts   This next series of steps will show you how to create an alert based on a performance counter:

1. In SQL Enterprise Manager, open the Management window and open the Alerts window. You should see nine predefined alerts (as well as any you have made).

2. To add a new alert, click the New button on the toolbar, choose Action ➤ New Alert, or right-click and choose New Alert.

3. You'll see the New Alert dialog box. In the ID: New Name field, enter a descriptive name for the new alert.

4. Change the Type to SQL Server Performance Condition Alert.

5. Select the object you want to monitor.

6. Select the appropriate counter.

7. Select whether the alert should fire if the value is equal to, over, or under the defined value.

8. Define a value for the alert to watch for.

9. Choose OK to save the alert.

Custom Error Message   If you find that the predefined SQL error messages don't suit your needs, you can create your own. In this set of steps, you'll do just that:

1. In SQL Enterprise Manager, highlight the server and select Action ➤ All Tasks ➤ Manage SQL Server Messages, or highlight the server, right-click, and choose All Tasks ➤ Manage SQL Server Messages.

2. Choose New to create a new message.

3. Add a custom message to an error number equal to or higher than 50,001 with the text you want to see when the alert is fired. You must also check the Always Write to Windows NT Eventlog box; otherwise, you will never receive an alert on the message.

4. Click OK, then OK again, to close the window.

5. To test the message, start the Query Analyzer.

6. Enter and execute the following query:

```
raiserror (50001,10,1)
```

The error message that you just created should appear in the Results window.

7. Open the Windows NT event log (select Programs ➢ Administrative Tools ➢ NT Event Viewer) and select Log ➢ Application to display the application log. The message that you entered should appear.

8. Double-click the message for more details. You should see the Event Detail dialog box with information about the error and your message.

Defining Operators

Here are the steps to create an operator:

1. In Enterprise Manager, go to the Operators folder under the SQL Agent and Management folders.

2. Click the New button, right-click and choose New Operator, or go to Action ➢ New Operator.

3. In the Edit Operator dialog box, enter an operator name, then the e-mail, pager, and/or net-send addresses for the person you want to notify.

4. If you have SQLAgentMail configured, you can click the Test button to send mail to the user. SQL Server should report that the message was sent successfully.

5. On the Notifications tab, select all the alerts you wish to have go to this operator.

6. Select OK to save the operator.

After you've set up your operators (defining their working hours), you can designate a fail-safe operator in case no other operators are on duty when an alert is triggered:

1. In Enterprise Manager, highlight the SQL Server Agent folder under the Management folder.

Part iv

2. Select Action ➤ Properties, or right-click and choose Properties to bring up the Properties screen.

3. Go to the Alert System tab. In the Fail-Safe Operator drop-down list box, select an operator you have already set up. Check the E-Mail box as well.

4. Click OK to save your changes.

Setting Up SQLAgentMail

In this series of steps, you are going to configure SQLAgentMail. This is very similar to the steps in Chapter 19 for configuring SQL Mail, but notice the subtle differences:

1. On your mail server, create a mailbox for your account if one does not already exist.

2. Log in to Windows NT as the user you created for the SQL-Agent account.

3. Go to Control Panel ➤ Mail and Fax, and select Add under the Profile section.

4. Assuming that you use Exchange Server for e-mail, leave Microsoft Exchange Server selected and clear all the other selections. Select Next.

5. Enter the name of the Exchange Server and the mailbox. Select Next.

6. Select No when asked if you travel with the computer. Select Next.

7. Take the default path to the Address Book. Select Next.

8. Do not choose to add Outlook to the Startup Group. Select Next.

9. Select Finish at the final screen.

10. Note the name of the profile. You will need to know this name for later steps.

11. Go to Enterprise Manager.

12. To configure the SQLAgentMail, right-click SQL Mail (under SQLAgent under Management) and select Configure.

13. Enter the name of the profile from step 10, then click OK.

14. To start the SQL Mail session, right-click the SQL Mail icon and choose Start. The session should start, and the arrow should turn green.

▶ Enable access to remote data.

▶ Set up linked servers.

▶ Set up security for linked databases.

When your users need access to data stored on multiple servers in one query, it is called a *distributed query*, which returns result sets from databases on multiple servers. Although you might wonder why you would want to perform distributed queries when you could just replicate the data between servers, there are practical reasons for doing the former.

Don't forget that because SQL Server is designed to store terabytes of data, some of your databases may grow to several hundred megabytes in size—and you really don't want to replicate several hundred megabytes under normal circumstances.

The first step is to inform SQL that it will be talking to other database servers by running the sp_addlinkedserver stored procedure. The procedure to link to a server named AccountingSQL looks something like this:

```
sp_addlinkedserver @server='AccountingSQL', @provider='SQL
Server'.
```

Your users can then run distributed queries by simply specifying two different servers in the query. The query select * from SQLServer .pubs.dbo.authors, AccountingSQL.pubs.dbo.employees would access data from both the SQL Server (the server the user is logged in to, or the sending server) and the AccountingSQL server (the remote server) in the same result set.

The security issue here is that the sending server must log in to the remote server on behalf of the user to gain access to the data. SQL can use one of two methods to send this security information: security account delegation or linked-server login mapping. If your users have logged in using Windows NT authentication and all of the servers in the query are capable of understanding Windows NT domain security, you can use account delegation.

Once you have configured this, it is essential to monitor your office to be sure that no one is trying to bypass security; this can be done with the SQL Profiler.

You should definitely understand how to make remote access work on your networks. The following steps will show you how to configure security account delegation:

1. If the servers are in different domains, you must make certain that the appropriate Windows NT trust relationships are in place. The remote server's domain must trust the sending server's domain.

2. Add a Windows NT login to the sending server for the user to log in with.

3. Add the same account to the remote server.

4. Create a user account for the login in the remote server's database and assign permissions.

5. When the user executes the distributed query, SQL will send the user's Windows NT security credentials to the remote server, allowing access.

If you have users who access SQL with standard logins, or if some of the servers do not participate in Windows NT domain security, you will need to add a linked login. Here's how to do it:

1. On the remote server, create a standard login and assign the necessary permissions.

2. On the sending server, map a local login to the remote login using the `sp_addlinkedsrvlogin` stored procedure. To map all local logins to the remote login RemUser, type:

```
sp_addlinkedsrvlogin @rmtsrvname='AccountingSQL', ~CA
@useself=FALSE, @locallogin=NULL, ~CA
@rmtuser='RemUser', @rmtpassword='password'
```

3. When a user executes a distributed query, the sending server will log in to the AccountingSQL (remote) server as RemUser with a password of *password*.

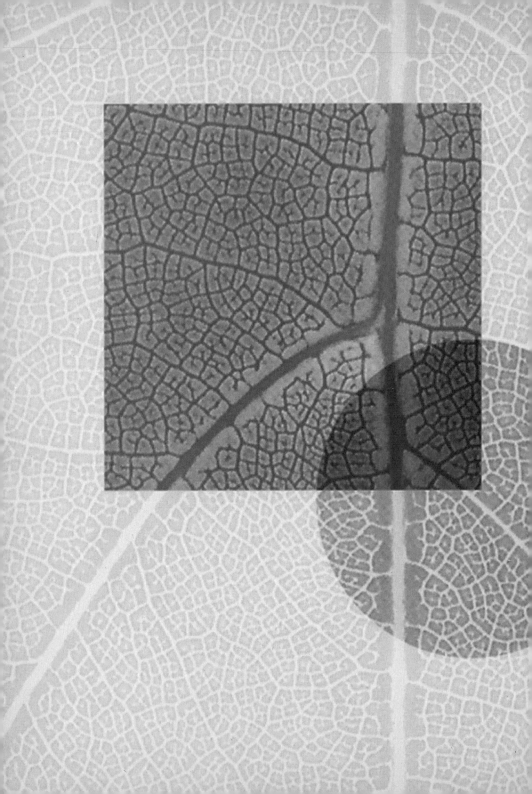

Chapter 22

MONITORING AND OPTIMIZATION

Most systems administrators spend their time fire fighting—that is, troubleshooting problems that have cropped up. It's safe to say that if they had taken the time to monitor and optimize the systems, those problems might never have arisen in the first place. That makes monitoring and optimization *proactive* troubleshooting, not *reactive,* as is the norm. Due to this fact, Microsoft hits this objective pretty hard on the test—they want to be sure that you are performing monitoring and optimization.

In this chapter, the various methods and tools for getting the reports you need from your SQL Server will be discussed. How to use Performance Monitor to check on not only SQL Server, but Windows NT as well, will be covered. Then, a great deal of time will be spent working with Profiler, which is a very powerful tool for monitoring. After the tools for monitoring have been discussed, how to optimize the system, specifically RAM and

Adapted from *MCSE Exam Notes: SQL Server 7 Administration* by Rick Sawtell, Lance Mortensen, and Joseph L. Jorden

ISBN 0-7821-2477-1   368 pages $19.99

CPU usage, will be examined. Then, the Query Governor, which will limit the resources that are used up by queries, will be introduced.

Monitor SQL Server performance.

This section will cover the tools available for monitoring and how to use those tools. Performance Monitor, which is useful for monitoring Windows NT as well as SQL Server, will be discussed. Then, Profiler, which is designed to monitor only SQL Server and therefore does a very comprehensive job of it, will be examined. A number of statistics as well as methodology for using the tools that you should become familiar with for the exam and your own edification will also be presented in this chapter.

SQL cannot function properly if it does not have available system resources, such as memory, processor power, fast disks, and a reliable network subsystem. If these subsystems do not work together, the system as a whole will not function properly. For example, if the memory is being overused, the disk subsystem will slow down because the memory will have to write to the pagefile (which is on the disk) far too often. To keep such things from happening, you will need to get reports from the subsystems; you can do this by using Performance Monitor.

Performance Monitor

Performance Monitor comes with Windows NT and is located in the Administrative Tools folder on the Start menu. Four views are available for your use:

Chart: This view displays a graph of system performance. As values change, the graph will spike or dip accordingly.

Report: The report view looks more like what you might get on a piece of paper, except that the values here change with system use.

Alert: With alert view, you can instruct Performance Monitor to warn you when something bad is looming on the horizon, perhaps when CPU use is almost—but not quite yet—too high. This type of warning gives you time to fix potential problems before they become actual problems.

Log: This view is for record keeping. With log view, you can monitor your system over a period of time and view the information later, as opposed to viewing it in real time (the default).

With each of these views, you monitor objects and counters. An *object* is a part of the system, such as the processor or the physical memory. A *counter* displays a number that tells you how much that object is being used. For example, the % Processor Time counter under the Processor Object will tell you how much time your processor spends working. Not only does Windows NT have several such objects and counters, the most common of which are listed in Table 22.1, but SQL Server provides some of its own. The SQL counters you will be using most often have been preset for you and can be accessed through the Performance Monitor icon in the SQL Server 7 menu on the Start menu. Table 22.2 describes each of the counters in the preset Performance Monitor.

TABLE 22.1: Common Counters and Values in Performance Monitor

OBJECT	COUNTER	RECOMMENDED VALUE	USE
Processor	% Processor Time	Less than 75 percent	Monitors the amount of time the processor spends working.
Memory	Pages/Sec	Fewer than 5	Monitors the number of times per second that data had to be moved from RAM to disk and vice versa.
Memory	Available Bytes	More than 4MB	Monitors the amount of physical RAM available. Since Windows NT uses as much RAM as it can for file cache, this number may seem low—as long as it is above 4MB, it is acceptable.
Memory	Committed Bytes	Less than physical RAM	Monitors the amount of RAM committed to use.
Disk	% Disk Time	Less than 50 percent	Monitors the amount of time that the disk is busy reading or writing.
Network Segment	% Network Utilization	Less than 30 percent	Monitors the amount of network bandwidth being used.

Part iv

NOTE

To see the Network Segment: % Network Utilization counter, you must install the Network Monitor Agent from Control Panel ➤ Network ➤ Services.

WARNING

If you don't enable the disk counters by executing diskperf -y (or -ye when using RAID), all disk counters will read zero.

TABLE 22.2: Preset SQL Counters in Performance Monitor

OBJECT	COUNTER	USE
SQLServer:Buffer Manager	Buffer Cache Hit Ratio	This tells you how much data is being retrieved from cache instead of disk. This number should be high.
SQLServer:Buffer Manager	Page Reads/Sec	Monitors the number of data pages that are read from disk each second.
SQLServer:Buffer Manager	Page Writes/Sec	Monitors the number of data pages that are written to disk each second.
SQLServer:General Statistics	User Connections	Monitors the number of user connections. Each of these will take some RAM.
SQLServer:Memory Manager	Total Server Memory (KB)	Monitors the total amount of memory that SQL has been dynamically assigned.
SQLServer:SQL Statistics	SQL Compilations/Sec	Monitors the number of compilation per second.

Profiler

Once the system is functioning efficiently, you can move up a rung and start monitoring the database engine by using Profiler. You will accomplish this by performing a *trace*, which is a record of data that has been captured about events. Stored in a table, a trace log file, or both, traces can be either shared (viewable by everyone) or private (viewable only by the owner).

The actions you will be monitoring, or tracing, are called *events* and are logically grouped into *event classes*. Some of these events are useful for maintaining security, and some are useful for troubleshooting problems, but most of these events are used for monitoring and optimization.

Possibly the easiest way to create a trace is by using the Trace Wizard, which is a very handy tool for creating a quick-and-dirty trace to get some standard information. You can create a total of six traces with this Wizard:

Find the Worst Performing Queries: This trace will help identify which queries are the slowest by grouping the output according to the duration of each query.

Identify Scans of Large Tables: This trace will identify scans of large tables. If you find such scans, you may need to create some indexes.

Identify the Cause of a Deadlock: Deadlocks, caused by multiple users trying to access the same data at the same time, can slow all users down. This trace will show the chain of events leading up to the deadlock and the object that was being accessed.

Profile the Performance of a Stored Procedure: Stored procedures are T-SQL code that is stored at the server for clients to access. Improperly written stored procedures can slow the system down. This trace will help find improperly written stored procedures.

Trace Transact-SQL Activity by Application: This trace will show you which applications are being used the most to access SQL Server.

Trace Transact-SQL Activity by User: This trace will help you see which of your users are accessing SQL Server the most and what they are doing while logged in.

One issue to be concerned with when you create and execute a trace is that it returns a great deal of data that you don't necessarily want or need to see. For example, a great deal of information about system objects is returned, and every application you use to access SQL (e.g., Enterprise Manager) will be recorded in the trace. To get rid of the extraneous data, you should consider filtering the trace, which will remove the excess data.

After you create and execute the trace, you can use it to re-create problem-causing events by replaying it. Loading your saved traces into Profiler will allow you to replay them against the server and, in this way, figure out exactly where the problem occurred. An especially nice touch is that you don't have to play the whole trace all at once; you can take it step by step to see exactly where the problem lies.

One final feature of Profiler is the Index Tuning Wizard, which is used to keep your indexes in top shape. Some circumstances that may require the services of the Index Tuning Wizard include wrong columns being indexed from the beginning, or users that have started querying different data over time, requiring the creation of new indexes.

To run the Index Tuning Wizard, you will need a workload, which you get by running and saving a trace in Profiler. It is best to get this workload during times of peak database activity to make sure that you give the Wizard an accurate load. If you aren't sure about which events to trace, you can base your trace on the Sample 1 Trace SQL definition, which defines a standard set of events to capture.

Tips and Techniques for Both Tools

If you want the best results from SQL Server's monitoring tools, you need to know and use the proper techniques. If you don't, the end result will not be what you are hoping for—or what you need.

Since you will never know if your system is running slower than normal unless you know what normal is, you will need a measurement baseline that shows you what resources (memory, CPU, etc.) SQL consumes under normal circumstances. You create the baseline before putting your system into production so that you have something to compare your readings to later on.

To create an accurate measurement baseline, you should have a test network with just your SQL Server and one or two client machines—this will limit the broadcast traffic on the network, which can throw off your baseline. If you don't have a test network, you may want to consider shutting down as many machines as possible and generating your baseline off-hours on your production network. You can then start your baseline. The Windows NT counters mentioned at the outset as well as the preset SQL counters should provide an accurate baseline with which you can compare future readings.

Once you have completed monitoring your system, you should archive the data (probably to tape). One of the primary reasons to do so is to back up requests for additional equipment. For example, if you ask for funds to buy more memory for the SQL Server, but don't bring any proof that the system needs the RAM, you are probably not going to get the money. If you bring a few months worth of reports, however, and say, "After tracking SQL for a time, we've found this...," management may be far more willing to give you the money you need. Using archived data in such fashion is known as *trend tracking*.

One of the most valuable functions of using your archived data for trend tracking is proactive troubleshooting—that is, anticipating and avoiding problems before they arise. Suppose you added 50 new users to your network about three months ago and are about to do it again. If you archived your data from that period, you would be able to recall what those 50 users had done to the performance of the SQL Server, and you could compensate for it. On the other hand, if you have thrown that data away, you might be in for a nasty surprise when your system unexpectedly slows to a crawl.

You should be familiar with several procedures for the test. The first thing you need to know is how to use Performance Monitor to check on the status of the server as a whole—how to use it to gather real-time data as well as log data to read later on. Then, we will cover how to use Profiler to the fullest, which includes creating traces manually and through the Trace Wizard. The final procedure is using the Index Wizard to optimize your system's indexes.

Using Performance Monitor

The following steps will help you monitor your system in real time using Performance Monitor:

1. From the Start menu, select Programs ➢ Administrative Tools ➢ Performance Monitor.

2. On the Edit menu, select Add to Chart to bring up the Add to Chart dialog box.

3. In the Object box, select the object you want to monitor (such as Processor).

4. In the Counter box, select a counter for the object.

5. Repeat steps 3–4 for any other objects you want to monitor.

6. Click Done and notice the graph being created on the screen.

7. Press Ctrl+H and notice the current counter turn white. This makes the chart easier to read.

8. On the View menu, select Report.

9. On the toolbar, click the + button to bring up the Add to Report dialog box.

10. Add the counters and objects that you wish to view, then click Done. Notice the report displayed on the screen.

11. On the View menu, select Alert View and click the + button on the toolbar.

12. Select the object and counter you wish to be warned about.

13. Under Alert If, select either Under or Over, and in the box next to it, type a corresponding value.

14. Click Add; then click Done.

Logging with Performance Monitor

The next series of steps will show you how to store your performance information in a log file so that you can read it at your leisure, rather than needing to watch the screen the entire time.

1. Open Performance Monitor in the Administrative Tools menu.

2. On the View menu, select Log.

3. On the Options menu, select Log to open the Log Options dialog box.

4. In the File Name box, type a log filename.

5. Under Update Time, set the seconds for Periodic Update (300 seconds, or 5 minutes, is average).

6. Click the Save button.

7. On the Edit menu, select Add to Log and notice that you are allowed to add only objects. All counters for each selected object will be logged.

8. On the Options menu, select Log to open the Log Options dialog box.

9. Click Start Log to start logging.

10. When you are done logging, on the Options menu, select Log. Then, click the Stop Log button.

11. On the View menu, select Chart.

12. On the Options menu, select Data From, then select Log File and enter the name of the log file in the text box.

13. On the Edit menu, select Add to Chart and notice that you are allowed to add only the objects that were logged.

14. Add your objects and click the Done button—notice the chart that has been created. Data is available for only the amount of time that you were logging.

15. Exit Performance Monitor.

Using Profiler

Now that you have mastered Performance Monitor, you are ready to move on to Profiler. The next few series of procedures will show you how to work with traces. You'll start by manually creating a trace with a filter applied:

1. From the Start menu, go to the SQL Server menu under Programs and click Profiler.

2. You may be asked to register a server—you must do so to create a trace.

3. On the File menu, select New, then click Trace to bring up the Trace Properties dialog box.

4. In the Trace Name box, type a name for your trace.

5. Select either Shared (accessible by all) or Private (accessible by the owner) as the Trace Type.

6. If you want to capture to a file on disk, check the Capture to File checkbox, and enter a name and location for the file.

7. To capture to a table, check the Capture to Table checkbox and fill in the server, database, owner, and table to capture to.

8. Click the Events tab.

9. Under Available Events, select the events you wish to monitor and click Add.

10. Click the Data Columns tab to change the data you see in the trace.

11. Click the Filters tab. You will notice that the only information filtered out is that which comes from Profiler.

12. To exclude system objects, select Object ID under Trace Event Criteria and check Exclude System Objects.

13. Click OK to start the trace.

Using the Trace Wizard

Fortunately, you don't have to create all of your traces manually—you can also use the Trace Wizard. This Wizard is great for creating a quick-and-dirty trace that can be fine-tuned later to your liking. You'll create a trace here for finding the worst performing queries:

1. Open Profiler, and on the Tools menu, select Create Trace Wizard.

2. In the Create Trace Wizard box, read through the checklist on the first screen and click Next.

3. On the next screen, select your server in the Server list.

4. In the Problem list, select Find the Worst Performing Queries, then click Next.

5. Select All Databases in the Database list.

6. In the Minimum Duration box, type a value for the number of seconds that a query must run to qualify to be shown.

7. On the next screen, select Choose to Trace One or More Specific Applications.

8. Check the MS-SQL Query Analyzer checkbox and click Next.

9. Leave the Trace Name set to Worst Performing Queries and click Finish. This will start the trace.

Using the Index Tuning Wizard

Now that you know how to create and filter traces both manually and through the Trace Wizard, you are ready to use the Index Tuning Wizard. Since this Wizard requires a workload, you need to create a trace first, then you can run the Wizard with the following steps:

1. Open Profiler.

2. On the Tools menu, select Index Tuning Wizard. This will open the welcome screen.

3. Click Next.

4. Select the local server in the Server drop-down list.

5. Select the database to tune.

6. Decide whether you wish to Keep All Existing Indexes.

7. Decide whether to Perform Thorough Analysis.

8. Click Next.

9. On the Identify Workload screen, select I Have Saved a Work-load File.

10. Click Next.

11. Click the My Workload File button.

12. In the File Open dialog box, select a trace created earlier and click OK.

13. When returned to the Specify Workload screen, click the Advanced Options button, note the defaults, and click OK.

14. Click Next.

15. Select the Tables to Tune.

16. Click Next—the Wizard will now start tuning your indexes.

17. You will now be asked to accept the index recommendations; click Next.

18. On the Schedule Index Update Job screen, select Apply Changes and Execute Recommendations Now, or schedule them for a later time.

19. Just below that, you can save the changes made to a script by checking Save Script File.

20. Click Next.

21. On the final screen, click Finish to apply the changes.

22. When you receive a message stating that the Wizard has completed, click OK.

23. Exit Profiler.

▶ Tune and optimize SQL Server.

In this section, the various methods for acting on those reports to optimize SQL Server will be examined. You'll see how to make SQL use RAM most efficiently, then you'll see how to optimize the CPU usage. Both of these configurations will be considered not only for a dedicated machine, but for shared machines (i.e., SQL and Exchange) as well. Finally, even though it is not listed as an exam objective, you will get hit pretty hard with RAID questions. So, you will learn how to optimize disk usage for your server.

SQL Server can dynamically adjust most of its settings to compensate for problems. It can adjust memory use, threads spawned, and a host of other settings. In some cases, unfortunately, those dynamic adjustments may not be enough—you may need to make some manual changes. A few specific areas that may require your personal attention will be discussed.

Manually Configuring Memory Use

While SQL is capable of dynamically assigning itself memory, it is not always best to let it do so. A good example of this is when you need to run another BackOffice program, such as Exchange, on the same system as SQL Server. If SQL is not constrained, it will take so much memory that none will be left for Exchange. The constraint you need to put in place is the Max Server Memory setting—by adjusting it, you can stop SQL Server from taking too much RAM. If, for example, you set Max Server Memory to 102,400 (100×1024 [the size of a megabyte]), SQL will never use more than 100MB of RAM.

NOTE

These concepts will be tested quite a bit, so become one with them.

You could also set Min Server Memory, which tells SQL never to use less than the set amount—this should be used in conjunction with Set Working Size. Windows NT uses virtual memory, which means that data in memory that has not been accessed for a while can be stored on disk. The Set Working Size option stops Windows NT from moving SQL data from RAM to disk, even if it is idle. This can improve SQL Server's performance, since data will never need to be retrieved from disk (which is about 100 times slower than RAM).

If you decide to use this option, you should set Min Server Memory and Max Server Memory to the same size, then change the Set Working Size option to one. This configuration should be used only on a dedicated SQL Server, since it will take RAM away from other programs and never give it back.

WARNING

For the amount of memory that SQL requires, you will want to have 1MB of Level 2 cache on your system. If you don't have enough L2 cache, your system may actually slow down when you add RAM.

Optimizing CPU Usage

Since SQL uses the CPU to the hilt, you may want to change the way SQL uses it. Each program on the system has a priority assigned to it by the operating system. Programs with a higher priority get more CPU time than programs with lower priorities. On a dedicated SQL server, you can change the priority that is assigned to SQL from the default 7 to 15 (or from 15 to 24 on a multiprocessor system) by using the `sp_configure` stored procedure. Setting the priority boost setting to 1 will make the priority higher. The boost can be set from Enterprise Manager on the Processor tab of the Server Properties dialog box, or by executing `sp_configure 'priority boost', '1'`.

WARNING

Priority boost is only for a dedicated machine—if you are running more than one program on the SQL Server, boosting the priority will take CPU time from the other programs.

Max Async I/O

It should go without saying that SQL needs to be able to write to disk, since that's where the database files are stored, but is SQL writing to disk fast enough? If you have multiple hard disks connected to a single controller, multiple hard disks connected to multiple controllers, or a RAID system involving striping, the answer is probably no. The maximum number of asynchronous input/output (Max Async I/O) threads by default in SQL is 32, meaning that SQL can have 32 outstanding read and 32 outstanding write requests at a time. Therefore, if SQL needs to write data to disk, it can send up to 32 small chunks of that data to disk at a time. If you have a powerful disk subsystem, you will want to increase the Max Async I/O setting.

The setting to which you increase it depends on your hardware. So, if you increase the setting, you must then monitor the server. Specifically, you will need to monitor the Physical Disk: Average Disk Queue Performance Monitor counter, which should be less than two (note that any

Part iv

queue should be less than two). If you adjust Max Async I/O and the Average Disk Queue counter goes above two, you have set it too high and will need to decrease it.

NOTE

You will need to divide the Average Disk Queue counter by the number of physical drives to get an accurate count. That is, if you have three hard disks and a counter value of six, you would divide six by three—which tells you that the counter value for each disk is two.

RAID

RAID (Redundant Array of Inexpensive Disks) is used to protect your data and speed up your system. In a system without RAID, data that is written to disk is written to that one disk. In a system with RAID, that same data would be written across multiple disks, providing fault tolerance and improved I/O. Some forms of RAID can be implemented inexpensively in Windows NT, but this uses such system resources as processor and memory. If you have the budget for it, you might consider getting a separate RAID controller that will take the processing burden off Windows NT. The types of RAID that you may want to consider for your SQL Server are listed here:

RAID 0 Stripe Set: This provides I/O improvement, but not fault tolerance.

RAID 1 Mirroring: This provides fault tolerance and read-time improvement. This can also be implemented as duplexing, which is a mirror that has separate controllers for each disk. This is the only way to provide fault tolerance for the operating system files and is best for the transaction logs.

RAID 0+1 Mirrored Stripe Set: This is a stripe set without parity that is duplicated on another set of disks. This requires a third-party controller, since Windows NT does not support it natively.

RAID 5 Stripe Set with Parity: This provides fault tolerance and improved read time. Since modifications to data are written initially in RAM and copied to disk later, you should not be overly concerned with write performance for the data files—that makes RAID 5 ideal for data files.

The ideal disk configuration is to have a combination of these forms. For instance, you may want to have your transaction logs on a mirrored (or duplexed) drive, and your databases on RAID 5 or RAID 0+1 array. No matter what fault tolerance you go with, you should consider getting a third-party RAID controller to take some of the burden off the system processor.

Setting Memory and CPU Usage

This series of steps will show you how to configure the Max and Min Server Memory settings as well as the Set Working Size setting:

1. In Enterprise Manager, right-click your server and select Properties.

2. Select the Memory tab to change the settings.

3. To manually set the minimum memory that SQL will use, move the Minimum (MB) slider to the desired position.

4. To manually set the maximum memory that SQL will use, move the Maximum (MB) slider to the desired position.

5. To set both Minimum and Maximum to the same setting, move the Use a Fixed Memory Size (MB) slider to the desired position.

6. To set the Set Working Size option, check the Reserve Physical Memory for SQL Server checkbox and set the amount of RAM in bytes that SQL is allowed to use.

Setting the CPU to a higher priority is so simple that there is not even a series of steps for it. You simply open the Properties dialog box for the server you want to boost, select the Processor page, and check the Boost SQL Server Priority on Windows NT checkbox.

NOTE

Any of the procedures you've just performed in Enterprise Manager can also be accomplished with T-SQL by using the sp_configure stored procedure.

 ## Limit resources used by queries.

Surprising as it seems, not all queries are properly written and optimized. It is because of this fact that you will need to know how to keep SQL from

Part iv

wasting system resources on poorly written queries. The Query Governor is designed to do just that.

Right out of the box, SQL will run any query you tell it to, even if that query is poorly written. You can change that by using the Query Governor. This is not a separate tool, but part of the database engine, and is controlled by the Query Governor Cost Limit.

The Query Governor Cost Limit setting tells SQL not to run queries longer than x (where x is a value higher than zero). If, for example, the Query Governor Cost Limit is set to two, any query that is estimated to take longer than two seconds would not be allowed to run. SQL knows how long a query will take to complete even before it is executed, because it keeps statistics about the number and composition of records in tables and indexes.

NOTE

If the Query Governor Cost Limit is set to zero (the default), all queries will be allowed to run.

The only thing you need to know here is how to set the Query Governor Cost Limit setting. The Query Governor Cost Limit can be set by using the command `sp_configure 'query governor cost limit', '1'` (the *1* in this code can be higher). It can also be set on the Server Settings tab of the Server Properties page in Enterprise Manager.

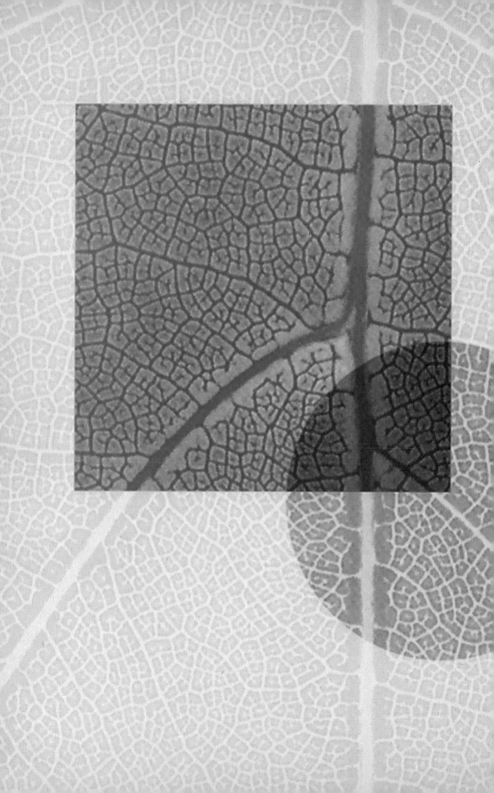

Chapter 23

TROUBLESHOOTING

You will need to be familiar with some tools to perform successful troubleshooting—the SQL error log and the Windows NT Event Viewer. The SQL Server error log is a group of ASCII text files located in the \MSSQL7\Log folder—the most recent is named ERRORLOG. When a new log is created, the old log is renamed ERRORLOG.1, which in turn is renamed ERRORLOG.2, and so on, for up to six history logs. Note that the oldest log file—ERRORLOG.6—is not renamed, but is overwritten by ERRORLOG.5.

The error log is not the only place where errors are stored, though; you would be remiss if you did not check the Windows NT Event Viewer, since SQL Server stores errors in the application log as well. Once you are familiar with these tools, you can perform successful troubleshooting.

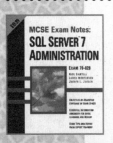

Adapted from *MCSE Exam Notes: SQL Server 7 Administration* by Rick Sawtell, Lance Mortensen, and Joseph L. Jorden

ISBN 0-7821-2477-1   368 pages $19.99

This troubleshooting knowledge will serve you well not only in the real world (where it will do the most good), but also for the test. The fact that the knowledge from this chapter will rescue you from disaster should assure you that there will be several questions on the exam designed to test your knowledge of these concepts. So don't take this chapter lightly!

▶ Diagnose and resolve problems in upgrading from SQL Server 6.x.

A lot of people out there will be upgrading from a previous version of SQL to version 7—you may even be one of them. Hopefully, you won't have any problems with your upgrade, but on the off chance that you do, this section can help you tremendously. You are going to read about the various problems that can occur when you upgrade a database to SQL 7 from a previous version and how to fix those problems. Since Microsoft is expecting a mass exodus from previous versions of SQL, you should be prepared for some questions on how to troubleshoot the upgrade.

The Upgrade Wizard will perform the actual work of morphing your 6.x databases into 7 databases. The first thing the Wizard needs to do is check the syscomments tables for inconsistencies, then it validates user permissions and logins. Once that is done, the Upgrade Wizard can transform your database schema and objects into a SQL 7 database, and fill that new database with your existing data.

If the Upgrade Wizard finds problems (heaven forbid) during the upgrade process, it will give you an error message saying, "One or more warnings have been logged. Please read the next screen carefully before you begin your upgrade." The Summary of Warnings screen is then displayed with the inconsistencies that the Wizard found. You can read about them right then or, if you want to view them later, you can read the error file. This is a text file with an `err.out` extension that is stored in the folder `\MSSQL\Upgrade\`*server name_date_time*. The error files themselves have a naming convention:

```
check65-<dbid><dbname>_err.out
```

For example, if the SQL Server is named Sybex and you did the upgrade on February 27, 1999, at 12:22:23 P.M. on the MySample database, the full path and filename for this output file would be as follows:

```
\MSSQL\Upgrade\Sybex_02-27-99_12:22:23\check65-
019MySample_err.out
```

While it is impossible to list every problem you could ever run into, the following list is a good summation of common problems and their associated solutions:

▶ If Tempdb is too small, you will have problems. For an upgrade, your Tempdb should be at least 10MB. However, it is recommended that you resize the database to 25MB or more for an upgrade.

▶ Ensure that the database users have valid SQL Server logins in the syslogins table on the Master database.

▶ If any objects have had their entries manually deleted in the syscomments table, you must drop and re-create the objects to re-create the syscomments entries.

▶ Since the upgrade process stops and restarts the SQL Server service, you should disable any stored procedures that are configured to execute at startup.

▶ If you have SQL Server 6.5 login accounts with a default database other than Master, that default database must exist in SQL 7; if not, the user accounts will not be upgraded.

▶ If you are using two computers to perform your upgrade, you cannot use the local system account, because it has no network capabilities. The user account that you do use should have administrative capabilities on both computers.

▶ Disable replication and clear the associated transaction logs.

▶ Do not try to upgrade to a different sort order or character set since SQL does not allow this.

▶ Diagnose and resolve problems in backup and restore operations.

Backups and restorations are designed to rescue you in case of disaster. That means if you are having problems with backups and restorations, you need to get them back online right away. In this section, you will read about some of the common problems with backups and restorations, and how to fix them.

Some database activities are not allowed during a backup. If one of these activities is going on when you try to start a backup, you will get

Error 3023. To fix this error, just wait until the illegal activity is complete and try your backup again. The activities that will cause this error are as follows:

- ▶ bcp
- ▶ CREATE INDEX
- ▶ Data file movement or resizing
- ▶ DBCC CHECKALLOC
- ▶ DBCC SHRINKDATABASE
- ▶ DBCC SHRINKFILE
- ▶ SELECT INTO

Two other errors that you may run into are Errors 3120 or 3149. These errors mean that you are trying to restore a database that was backed up from a server that is using a different character set or sort order than the system to which you are restoring. SQL Server can restore only databases that have the same character set and sort order as the backup. The best way to fix this error is to install another copy of SQL Server 7 on another computer that has the proper character set and sort order, and restore to that computer. Once your database has been restored, you can use Data Transformation Services to move the restored database from the second server to your permanent database.

One error that will become fairly common actually stems from an excellent new feature in SQL Server 7—the ability to share tapes with Windows NT Backup. Since SQL and Windows NT now use the same tape format, it is possible to accidentally try to restore a non-SQL backup into SQL Server—that is what generates Error 3143. By using the RESTORE HEADERONLY command, you will be able to tell whether you are actually looking at a SQL backup.

Some other common errors include attempting to back up a transaction log when you have the Truncate Log on Checkpoint database option enabled. With that option enabled, there is no log to back up, so the backup fails. It is also good to note that if you try to restore transaction logs out of sequence, or if you have gaps between the logs, your restoration will fail.

▶ Diagnose and resolve replication problems.

If you have a very popular database that all of the users in your company need access to, you are probably replicating that database. Databases are replicated so that users can access a local copy of the data without having to traverse slow WAN links and other bottlenecks to perform their queries. Once this replication is in place and working, your users come to depend on it for their data—if replication fails, your users will not be able to work.

Since so many companies today are finding use for replication and the employees are growing to depend on it so much, you need to know how to troubleshoot it when it fails. You will read about several areas where replication could break down, then you will look at some fixes. These areas will be covered quite extensively on the exam, so watch closely.

For replication to function the way it was intended, you need two SQL Servers connected via a network. Right away, you should see a potential problem: Since the SQLAgent takes care of replication, and that SQLAgent needs to talk to the SQLAgent on another computer, your SQLAgents need to be logged in using a domain account. Actually, all of the SQLAgents involved should be logging in with the *same* domain account, and that account should be an administrative account. Once SQL is configured properly, you can start working with replication.

Replication Will Not Run

Before replication can begin, an initial snapshot of the data must be copied to each subscriber. If the snapshot is not applied, replication cannot begin. If you suspect that the snapshot has not been applied, you need to first check that the snapshot agent is running; this can be done in Enterprise Manager under Replication Monitor.

If the snapshot agent is running, you need to check the agent history and look for any errors that may have occurred. One of the more common errors in this situation is security. If your snapshot agent is not doing anything at all, make certain that your distribution server is online and available, and that you have the appropriate permissions on the working folder at the distributor.

Part iv

No Subscribers Are Working

If none of your subscribers are getting replicated data, but the snapshot agent appears to be working, the problem is most likely with the logreader agent. If the logreader agent is not moving data from the transaction log of the Publishing database to the Distribution database, the distribution agent cannot move those records to subscribers. Since none of the subscribers are getting data, it is far more likely that the logreader, rather than the distribution agent, is not performing. To troubleshoot this, take a look at the history of the logreader agent in the Replication Monitor. Verify that the jobs are running as scheduled and that data is moving.

On the distribution server, you should verify that your Distribution database is large enough to hold the replicated transactions and that the Distribution-database transaction log is not full. Since this is a normal database, its transaction log can fill up just like any other if you do not perform transaction log backups regularly.

Several Subscribers of Many Are Not Working

When several subscribers of many are not working, it is almost definitely a problem with the distribution process. Because other subscribers are receiving replicated data, you know that the logreader process is working properly. You should check for the following problems:

- ▶ Check the distribution-agent histories for the failing servers.

- ▶ Ensure that the subscription server is online and has connectivity.

- ▶ Ensure that the Subscription database is available, not marked for DBO use only, and not set to read only.

- ▶ Ensure that the SQLAgent security credentials are set properly for the subscription servers; all SQLAgents should be using the same domain account.

- ▶ Ensure that the distribution agent is not waiting to perform a manual synchronization

Recovering Crashed Servers

Once you have repaired any other problems with replication, you can focus on another important area: recovery of crashed servers. When one of the servers in a replication scenario crashes, you need to know what to do to bring it back. Fortunately, in most cases, you don't need to do anything since SQL recovers itself well. Still, a time may come when SQL cannot recover itself and needs your help.

Recovering the Publishing Server   When your publisher goes down, your subscribers will not get updated data. SQL is actually pretty good at recovering from this, because the logreader agent places pointers (like bookmarks) in the transaction logs of published databases to track which transactions have been replicated already. If the publishing server crashes, the logreader agent will simply find the place where it stopped and continue once the system comes back online. If you have to restore the Publishing databases for some reason, your pointers and subscribers will be out of synch. To resynchronize them, you only need to run a snapshot, after which replication should proceed normally.

Recovering the Distribution Server   When your distribution server is down, replication halts. Since the distribution agent keeps track of which transactions have been applied to which subscribers, replication should continue from where it stopped when the system is brought back online. The real problem is when the distributor is down for an extended period. The distributor keeps transactions for only 24 hours (by default), then deletes them; this is known as the *retention period*. If this happens, just run a snapshot to resynchronize your subscribers.

Recovering the Subscription Server   When your subscription servers go down, you simply need to bring the servers back online. Replicated transactions on the distribution server will automatically be applied, and the subscriber will start running again normally. If the subscriber has been down for an extended period, you may want to run a snapshot just to be safe.

Reading Agent History

These steps will show you how to read agent history:

1. Open the Enterprise Manager and expand the Replication Monitor folder, then the Agents folder, and finally click the Snapshot Agents folder.

2. Right-click the agent in the right pane of the window and choose Agent History. This will give you information regarding how often the agent has run and what the agent accomplished.

3. Verify that the jobs are running as scheduled and that errors are not occurring.

Troubleshooting Security

This series of steps will show you how to test security between subscribers and distributors. First, if you are using a pull subscription, the distribution agent runs at the subscriber, so the subscriber must be able to log in to the distributor. Here's how to test it:

1. At the subscriber, log in to Windows NT as the SQLAgent service account.

2. Open Query Analyzer and connect to the distributor using Windows NT Authentication.

3. If you are successful logging in, your problem is not with security. If you fail, check your service account.

For a push subscription, the roles are reversed. All you need to do is follow steps 1 through 3, logging in at the distributor and connecting to the subscriber.

▶ Diagnose and resolve job or alert failures.

As an administrator, you are going to rely on jobs quite heavily to take over repetitive tasks such as backing up databases and performing routine maintenance. In fact, without the ability to schedule jobs, quite a bit of your time would be wasted doing menial work that could have been automated.

Alerts are another useful tool that warn you when something has gone wrong with your server and then fire a job to automatically fix whatever is wrong. Without alerts, you would have to get up from your chair, go to the server, and check for alerts yourself every few minutes just to be sure everything is OK; if there is a problem, you would need to repair it manually.

If you lose either of these capabilities, SQL Server administration is going to become a time-consuming nightmare, which is unacceptable. In this section, you will read about how to troubleshoot both jobs and alerts so that you do not lose automation capabilities.

For troubleshooting jobs, there are a number of important points to bear in mind:

▶ Ensure that the SQLServerAgent service is running.

▶ Ensure that the job, tasks, and schedules are enabled; this is especially true if you have made changes to an existing job.

▶ Ensure that the T-SQL or stored procedures in the job steps work.

▶ Ensure that the job owner has the appropriate permissions on all affected objects.

▶ Ensure that the steps operate as planned and fire in the correct order. For example, step two fires when step one completes successfully.

▶ If you are using e-mail or pager operators, ensure that SQL Mail is enabled and set up properly.

▶ Check the job history to see if the jobs are firing.

▶ Verify that the job is scheduled properly. SQL Server allows only one instance of a particular job to run at a time.

If you need to troubleshoot multiserver jobs, there are a few more areas to look at:

▶ Make certain that an operator named MSXOperator exists at the master server (MSX).

▶ The master server cannot be a Windows 95/98 system; it must be Windows NT.

▶ If the job will not download to the target server, check the download list at the master and the error log at the target for any problems that could block the download.

When you are troubleshooting alerts, many of the same cautions apply. In addition, you should verify the following items:

▶ Ensure that the alerts are being generated in the Windows NT application log. If the message is not sent to the application log, the alerts manager cannot see it.

▶ If you have alerts based on performance thresholds, ensure that the polling interval is set properly. SQL Server will poll the Performance Monitor every 20 seconds by default.

▶ If e-mail, pager, or net-send notifications are not timely, check that the delay between responses is not set too high.

Part iv

▶ Diagnose and resolve distributed query problems.

Many companies today have more than one SQL Server; in fact, some companies have large numbers of them. In such companies, users need to be able to access data that may be stored on more than one of those servers, which is what distributed queries are for. These queries will allow users to access remote tables just as if they were local tables in a standard T-SQL statement.

If you are using distributed queries, it is most likely that the tables in question are not replicated; if they were, there would be no need to use the distributed query. This means that if your distributed query setup fails, your users will have no way of accessing their data. When users cannot access data, they become irritable and cranky, and they like to make lots of support calls.

To make sure that this does not happen to you, some of the more common problems regarding distributed queries and how to fix them will be examined.

The two biggest problems you will run into when working with distributed queries are connectivity and security.

If your distributed queries have never worked for any of your users, your problem is most likely that you did not properly link the servers involved in the query. You should ensure that you have properly set up and configured the linked servers.

If your distributed queries are working fine for some users and not for others, the problem is more than likely incorrect permissions. If you are using Windows NT account-delegation security for your distributed queries, you will need to configure the security appropriately on the linked server; that is, your users will need logins and user accounts on the linked system with the appropriate permissions assigned.

▶ Diagnose and resolve client connectivity problems.

If your clients could not connect to your SQL Server, what good would it do to have a SQL Server? The answer is *none*—your system would be the equivalent of a large, beige paperweight. That makes your ability to troubleshoot client connectivity a very important issue.

A few areas will be examined here, including network connectivity, Net-Libraries, and DB-Libraries. The knowledge of how to troubleshoot these problems will prove invaluable to you in the office and the test center.

The best method for troubleshooting any problem is to start at the bottom and work your way up. If your clients cannot connect, you should make certain that the server is online, since another administrator may have shut it off, that the client is plugged in to the network, and that the hardware components are working.

The next step would be to check that the protocol is configured properly. There are a number of settings for the various protocols, so if you have just installed this machine, it is possible that some of those settings were misconfigured. Just try to find the server in Network Neighborhood (on a Windows machine) or the equivalent; if you don't see it on the network, your problem is with your operating system, not SQL.

Next, you need to check your Net-Libraries. SQL Server listens for client calls over any protocol that you have installed on your system, but for the client and server to talk, they must be running a common Net-Library. While you could use TCP/IP Multi-Protocol (which supports data encryption) or a host of other Net-Libraries, the default Net-Library is Named Pipes.

To test Named Pipes, you should first go to the server and open one of the graphic administration tools, or run OSQL from the command prompt—this will verify that Named Pipes are working locally. The next step would be to test Named Pipes from the client to the server using the makepipe and readpipe tools.

If that completes successfully, you know Named Pipes are working; if not, you have other network problems that have nothing to do with SQL, such as a corrupt protocol stack.

If Named Pipes come up successfully, but you still cannot connect, you probably have a DB-Library problem. You should verify that you have the same Net-Library and DB-Library on both the server and the client computer. This can be done with the Setup program or the Client Network utility.

Using Makepipe and Readpipe

The following series of steps will guide you through the use of makepipe and readpipe for testing Named Pipes connectivity. These tools are important—you will probably get a test question on them.

Part iv

1. To test Named Pipes, you will need a client and a server. On the server, go to a command prompt by selecting Start ➤ Programs ➤ MS-DOS.

2. At the command prompt, enter **makepipe**.

3. When the server starts waiting for a client to use the Named Pipe, you should see:

   ```
   Making PIPE:\\.\pipe\abc
   read to write delay <seconds>:0
   Waiting for Client to Connect. . .
   ```

4. From a client machine, enter the following:

   readpipe /Sserver name /Dstring

   For example, if your server's name is DBServ, and you want to send the message "testing123" to the Named Pipe, enter:

   readpipe /Sdbserv /Dtesting123

   You should get something like the following listing in response on the client machine:

   ```
   SvrName:\\DBServ
   PIPE: :\\DBServ\pipe\abc
   DATA: :Testing123
   Data Sent: 1 Testing123
   Data Read: 1 Testing123
   ```

5. On the server machine, you should see something similar to this:

   ```
   Waiting for client to send . . . 1
   Data Read:
   Testing123
   Waiting for client to send . . . 2
   Pipe closed
   Waiting for Client to Connect. . .
   ```

6. To close the Pipe, close the command-prompt window.

Using the Client Network Utility

You should also know how to check the DB-Library version and default Net-Library by using the Client Network utility.

1. Open the Client Network utility in the SQL Server 7 menu from the Start button.

2. Click the DB Library Options tab.

3. Notice the filename, version, date, and size of the library.

4. Click the General tab and notice that the default Net-Library can be changed.

▶ Diagnose and resolve problems in accessing SQL Server, databases, and database objects.

If your users can access the server and log in OK, but they cannot subsequently access the databases, your server is worthless to them. Your users must be able to access your data at all times without interruption; therefore, you must know how to keep this data online and accessible.

In this section, some time will be spent looking into the Database Consistency Checker (DBCC), which will allow you to fix database access problems. Then, you'll read about suspect databases and how to fix them. This will not be tested on extensively, but it is good to be familiar with this topic.

The first thing to check when your users cannot access a database or one of its objects is the permissions—wrong permissions can bar a user from accessing the object they need. If permissions are not the issue, you may be looking at a corrupt database. To check and repair a corrupt database, you need to become familiar with the Database Consistency Checker (DBCC). The DBCC acts as a collection of T-SQL statements that are used to check the physical and logical consistency of your database. Here are a few of the statements with which you should become familiar:

DBCC CHECKTABLE: You can run this command to verify that index and data pages are correctly linked and that your indexes are sorted properly. It will also verify that the data stored on each page is reasonable and that the page offsets are reasonable.

DBCC CHECKDB: This command does the same thing as the CHECKTABLE command, but it does it for every table in a database.

DBCC CHECKFILEGROUP: This command does the same thing as the CHECKTABLE command, except that it works on a single filegroup.

DBCC CHECKCATALOG: This command will check for consistency in and between system tables. For example, if there is an entry in the sysobjects table, there should be a matching entry in the syscolumns table.

DBCC CHECKALLOC: This command verifies that extents are being used properly and that there is no overlap between objects that should reside in their own separate extents. NEWALLOC performs the same function, but exists only for backward compatibility; use CHECKALLOC instead.

Since you should run these statements on a regular basis, it is best to schedule them. The easiest way to schedule them is to create a database maintenance plan and select all of the options for validating and repairing data.

Another particularly nasty problem is a database that is marked as suspect. This can happen to a database if one of the files becomes corrupted, deleted, or renamed. If the file is corrupted or deleted, you will need to restore from a backup. If it has been renamed, you only need to rename it to its original name and find the person who hacked in to your system and renamed it in the first place. Once you have restored the file to its original state, stop and restart the SQL Server—the automatic recovery process should unmark the suspect databases.

The only other thing that might cause a database to be suspect is a lack of permissions on an NTFS drive. You can fix this problem by logging on to Windows NT with an administrative account, taking ownership of the files in question, and granting the SQL service account read and write permissions to the file.

Finding a Suspect Database

In this section, you will mark the Northwind database as suspect to see what it looks like in Enterprise Manager:

1. Open the SQL Service Manager and stop the MSSQLServer service.

2. Open your C:\MSSQL7\Data (or whatever drive the file is on) folder and find the file named northwnd.mdf.

3. Rename `northwnd.mdf` to `northwnd.old`.

4. Restart the MSSQLServer service.

5. Open Enterprise Manager and notice that the Northwind database is grayed out and that the caption next to it says, "Suspect."

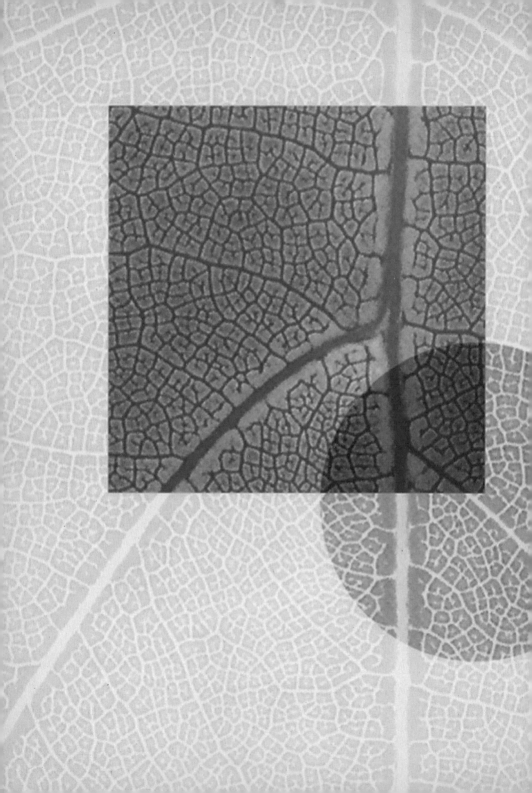

PART IV

SQL SERVER 7 ADMINISTRATION PRACTICE EXAM

Exam Questions

1. You have several Macintosh users on your network that require access to your SQL Server. Which type of account should they be assigned?

   A. Windows NT account

   B. SQL Server login

2. What is the smallest unit of allocation in SQL, and how large is it?

   A. Page; 2KB

   B. Page; 8KB

   C. Extent; 8KB

   D. Extent; 64KB

3. Your database crashes on Tuesday at 3:00 P.M. Using the following backup schedule, which backups would you have to restore to bring the database back up to date?

   ► Saturday at 1:00 A.M.; full backup

   ► Weekdays every two hours starting at 8:00 A.M.; transaction log backups

   ► Weekdays at 10:00 P.M.; differential backup

   A. Restore Saturday's full backup and all of the available transaction logs from Tuesday.

   B. Restore Saturday's full backup, all of the transaction log backups from Monday, then the Monday differential, and finally the transaction log backups from Tuesday.

   C. Restore Saturday's full backup, the differential from Monday, and the available transaction log backups from Tuesday.

   D. Restore the differential backup from Monday and the available transaction log backups from Tuesday.

4. True or false. The Upgrade Wizard is the best tool for upgrading from Access to SQL Server 7.

A. True

B. False

5. Which of the following types of replication makes a complete replicate of the published data on the Subscriber?

   A. Merge

   B. Transactional

   C. Copy

   D. Snapshot

6. Your company is based in New York with branches in Singapore, Paris, and Taiwan. All of these branches will need access to data stored on your server in their own language. How can you accomplish this?

   A. You can't.

   B. Choose a different sort order for each database.

   C. Choose the desired character set when you create the database.

   D. Choose the default Unicode character set, which allows different character sets in each database.

7. When SQL is first installed, what configuration is required for SQL to make use of the available RAM?

   A. Changing the Memory setting on the Configuration tab in the Server Properties dialog box

   B. Running `sp_configure 'memory', amount_of_ram`

   C. Setting min and max server memory settings

   D. None—SQL does this dynamically

8. True or false. To make the server easier to administer, you should create a single full-text catalog to contain all full-text indexes from all databases on your server.

   A. True

   B. False

Part iv

9. Your network comprises Windows 95, Windows 98, and Macintosh clients. Which authentication mode should you use?

   A. Mixed

   B. Windows NT Authentication

10. JohnsonK is a member of the sysadmins fixed server role. She creates a table in the Sales database called Customers. Who is the owner of the table?

    A. JohnsonK

    B. Sysadmins

    C. Administrators

    D. dbo

11. You want to grant administrative rights on the SQL server to some of your users. How should you do this?

    A. Add the users to the Windows NT Administrators local group.

    B. Add logins for each user separately and make each of them members of the sysadmins fixed server role.

    C. Add each of the users to a new Windows NT group called SQLAdmins, add a login for the new group, and make the new login a member of the sysadmins fixed server role.

    D. Create logins for each user and add each user to the db_owner database role in each database.

12. GibsonH is a member of the accounting and finance groups. Accounting has Select permission on the employees table in the accounting database. The Select permission has been revoked from finance on the same table. Can GibsonH select from the employees table?

    A. Yes

    B. No

13. SamuelsR owns a table and grants ChenJ Select permission. ChenJ creates a view and grants AdamsK Select permission.

What are the results when AdamsK tries to select from the view?

   A. AdamsK can select from the table since she has permission to do so.

   B. AdamsK cannot read from the table since she has not been given permission on the underlying table.

14. True or false. By tracking the Delete event under the SQL Operators event class, you can actually stop users from deleting objects.

   A. True

   B. False

15. When you use T-SQL to create a 100MB database, but do not specify the transaction log parameters, what happens?

   A. No transaction log is created.

   B. A 10MB transaction log is created in the same directory as the data file.

   C. A 25MB transaction log is created in the same directory as the data file.

   D. The CREATE DATABASE statement fails when the transaction log information is not specified.

16. Your company has just bought out a smaller company that is using an Access database to store critical information. You need to import this data into an SQL table for use by your users. What is the easiest way to do this?

   A. Export all of the data from the Access database to a text file, then import the text file into SQL using the INSERT statement.

   B. Export all of the data from the Access database to a text file, then import the text file into SQL using the BULK INSERT statement.

   C. Export all of the data from the Access database to a text file, then import the text file into SQL using bcp.

   D. Use the DTS Import Wizard.

Part iv

17. You have been performing full backups once a week and differential backups every night for the last two months. When is your transaction log cleared?

    A. Never.

    B. When the full backup is performed.

    C. When the differential backup is performed.

    D. SQL will clear it automatically when it gets too full.

18. One of your users has discovered some malicious updates to your data that occurred the day before at about 2:00. How can you bring the database back to the state it was in just before the update occurred?

    A. Perform a full database restoration with point-in-time recovery.

    B. Perform a differential database restoration with point-in-time recovery.

    C. Perform a transaction log restoration with point-in-time recovery.

    D. You cannot bring the database back to the previous state.

19. You have been successfully replicating data to several of your servers for over a month when suddenly replication stops functioning. What is the most likely cause?

    A. The distribution agent has been disabled.

    B. The transaction log on the Distribution database has filled to capacity.

    C. The Publication database has become corrupt.

    D. The Subscription database has become corrupt.

20. You have configured several operators that are scheduled to be paged throughout the week and on the weekend. There is, however, no one scheduled to be paged on Sunday morning from 12:00 A.M. to 8:00 A.M. What happens if there is a critical error during that time?

    A. SQL will page the last person who was on duty.

    B. No one will be paged.

    C. If there is a fail-safe operator, that person will be paged.

    D. The error message will be queued until the next operator is scheduled to be paged.

21. You have configured your servers to perform distributed queries using account delegation. Who can run the distributed query?

    A. Only people who are logged in using a standard login

    B. Only people who are logged in with a Windows NT login

    C. Anyone who has logged in and been validated

    D. Only members of the `db_execlinked` role

22. You need to know if your SQL Server can handle the load that your users are placing on it. When should you monitor your server?

    A. In the morning, when your users first start up.

    B. Just after lunch, when your users are getting back.

    C. There is no set time—monitor when activity is at its lowest.

    D. There is no set time—monitor when activity is at its highest.

23. You are running both SQL Server and Exchange Server on the same computer due to budget constraints. How should memory usage be configured so that both programs run efficiently?

    A. In SQL Server, adjust the Min Server Memory setting.

    B. In SQL Server, adjust the Max Server Memory setting.

    C. Set the Set Working Size option to one after setting both Min and Max Server Memory to the same size.

    D. Do nothing—SQL will detect Exchange and automatically assign RAM accordingly.

24. You are concerned that some of your users are writing queries that are wasting system resources because they take too long to complete (on average, more than three seconds). How can you stop SQL from running queries that take longer than three seconds to execute?

    A. Use `sp_configure 'query governor cost limit', '3'`.

    B. Use `sp_configure 'query governor', '3'`.

    C. Use `sp_configure 'query limit', '3'`.

    D. Use `sp_configure 'query governor limit', '3'`.

25. What steps should you take to prepare your server before running the Upgrade Wizard?

    A. Increase the size of Master to 25MB.

    B. Increase the size of Tempdb to 25MB.

    C. Disable automatic execution of stored procedures.

    D. Disable replication.

26. You want to restore a database to your server. Your server is using case-insensitive sort order, and the backup was made on a server using binary sort order. Will the restoration work?

    A. Yes, the restoration will work.

    B. Yes, the restoration will work, but there will be warnings.

    C. Yes, the restoration will work, but only the data will be restored—the schema must be created first.

    D. No, the restoration will fail.

27. The distributor has been offline for two days due to a systems failure. What do you need to do to update the subscribers?

    A. Nothing—they will resynchronize themselves.

    B. From the publisher, run a snapshot for each of the subscribers.

    C. From the distributor, run the `sp_resynch` stored procedure.

    D. Delete and re-create the subscription at each subscriber.

28. You have just created a new custom alert that does not seem to be firing. What is the most likely cause?

    A. The condition that causes the alert never occurred.

    B. The alert is not enabled.

    C. No operator is associated with the alert.

    D. The alert is not being written to the Windows NT application log.

29. True or false. All of the servers in a distributed query must be SQL Servers version 6.*x* or higher.

    A. True

    B. False

30. One of your users is complaining that they could access the SQL Server yesterday, but this morning, they can't seem to gain access to the databases. What should you do?

    A. Find out if the user can gain access to anything else on the network; if they can't, fix the connection.

    B. Check the DB-Library version and make sure it is the same as the server's.

    C. Make sure the client and server are running the same Net-Library.

    D. Have the user reboot the machine and try again.

Part iv

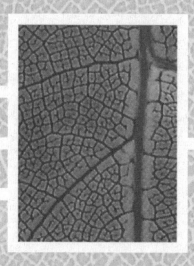

PART V

INTERNET EXPLORER 4
ADMINISTRATION KIT

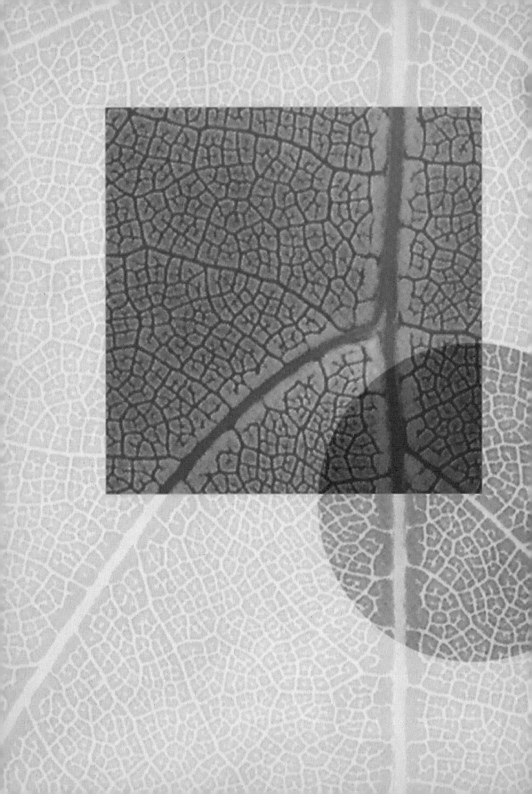

Chapter 24

PLANNING

Planning is the most important part of any successful rollout and is critical to its success. When network administrators want to distribute a new software package to users, time spent documenting, planning, and testing the package will save countless hours at the help desk.

When the tested package is viable enough to be distributed to users, many administrators will deliver the package only to a select group of test users first. The administrators will document and correct the errors encountered and then widen the scope of test users to include more users. This is called *a pilot roll out*. When a sufficient number of testers appear to be satisfied, the package is considered to be ready for distribution to the masses, or *end users*.

Once the package is ready for distribution, a media selection process begins. Choices include installing from CD-ROM, network, and floppy disks. Many factors can influence this decision, such as source and destination computers, cost, LAN and WAN connections, the time of day, and many others.

Adapted from *MCSE Test Success: Internet Explorer 4 Administration Kit* by Allen Jones

ISBN 0-7821-2333-3   416 pages $24.99

Using the Internet Explorer Administration Kit (IEAK) and sufficient planning, you can automate the delivery of Internet Explorer 4.01 using all of the above distribution methods.

▶ # In corporate administrator mode or Internet service provider mode, choose the appropriate installation of Internet Explorer 4.0, with or without the Windows Desktop Update.

When planning an installation of Internet Explorer, you must determine two things first. The first item to be determined is which IEAK organization type is the best fit for this Internet Explorer distribution. This decision is one of the first licensing decisions the administrator must make.

The next decision the administrator must make is determining which add-on components will be distributed. Many factors can influence this decision, including available hardware, user training, security, and functionality.

Licensing

The IEAK Wizard requires a customization code every time you start the program. You must register with Microsoft to get this code. In addition, you must agree to report your Internet Explorer (IE) distributions back to Microsoft quarterly.

Microsoft provides three distinct paths, called *modes,* to completing a distribution of IE. An administrator must choose which mode best fits their organization. The three modes are as follows:

- ▶ **Corporate administrator mode:** This is the most popular and most often used mode for businesses and corporations.

- ▶ **Internet service provider mode:** Also called ISP mode, it allows an Internet service provider to supply the end user with a single floppy disk, enabling them to download the browser from another site. Other methods of distribution are listed above.

- ▶ **Content provider mode:** Designed for hardware and software manufacturers, as well as anyone wishing to distribute HTML and IE applications.

NOTE

As we define the installation requirements for IE using the IEAK, we will be referring to the different modes using two and three letter designations. CA is Corporate Administrator Mode. ISP is Internet Service Provider Mode. ICP or CP is Internet Content Provider or Content Provider Mode.

Internet Explorer Add-on Components

One of the key features of the IEAK is the ability to develop customized installation packages for Internet Explorer. Administrators can choose between three predefined installation options: Minimal, Standard, and Full. If the predefined options are not suitable, you can alter the contents of the three existing options or add your own installation options to meet specific needs. You can then create an identity for this installation option. IEAK will support a total of 10 predefined sets of installation options. Each component is detailed in Table 24.1.

TABLE 24.1: IEAK's Three Default Installation Options and the Components Installed with Each

COMPONENT	MINIMAL	STANDARD	FULL
Internet Explorer 4.0	X	X	X
Java Support	X	X	X
Microsoft Internet Connection Wizard	X	X	X
Microsoft Outlook Express		X	X
Microsoft Wallet		X	X
NetMeeting			X
NetShow			X
FrontPage Express			X
Microsoft Web Publishing Wizard			X
Microsoft Chat			X
Disk space needed for installation*	56MB	72MB	98MB

*Disk space needed includes that for the required setup files and to run the installation program. Actual space needed for Internet Explorer will be somewhat less.

Internet Explorer 4.01   Supported in more than 20 languages. Using the Active Desktop, IE can become an integral part of the Desktop and make the browsing experience more productive for the end user.

IE 4.01 is considered to be a platform for other Internet-based products. Industry standards supported by IE 4.01 include:

- HTML
- Java
- ActiveX
- JScript
- Visual Basic Scripting Edition

Windows Desktop Update   The Windows Desktop Update provides seamless integration between the Web browser and the Windows Explorer, giving users a single interface with which to traverse file directories and surf Web pages.

The Update also allows users to integrate Active Channels and other HTML objects such as Web pages with the Desktop. Thus, frequently changing information, such as stock quotes or local weather conditions, can be presented to the Desktop on a regular basis.

Java Support   The Java support component installs the Java Virtual Machine (Java VM), which allows the browser to execute either Java applets or Java code. It also provides support for ActiveX controls, JavaBeans, VBScript, and MS JScript.

IE4 also includes a new package manager to help manage the storage of class libraries, and a new Internet Explorer object model, which allows dynamic updates of Web pages inside the browser.

NOTE

When someone refers to JScript or JavaScript, what he is really talking about is the implementation the same standard scripting language, ECMAScript. ECMA is the European Computer Manufacturers Association, a European-based association for standardizing information and communications systems. The standard recently approved, known as ECMA-262, is based on joint submissions from Microsoft and Netscape. JScript 3.0 is Microsoft's implementation of the new ECMA-262 scripting language. JavaScript is a scripting language written by Netscape that preceded the ECMA standard. The various implementations are simply marketed by different companies.

Microsoft Internet Connection Wizard   This wizard helps the end user set up an Internet connection. The wizard assists with modem detection, protocols, and creating a computer account. It can also assist in setting up Internet client software, including phone numbers, dial-up settings required by the ISP, and other internal configurations.

Microsoft Outlook Express   Every popular client browser has to support many Internet standards. Most include support for e-mail and Usenet newsgroups. Microsoft provides this functionality with an add-on component called Outlook Express, which can send and receive e-mail and manage address books for storing personal contacts. The ability to read and post to Usenet newsgroups is another feature.

Outlook Express supports many of the popular e-mail and news protocols in use today, including POP3, IMAP4, and NNTP. Microsoft Outlook Express will detect and migrate Netscape Mail, Eudora, Exchange/Inbox, Outlook, and Internet Mail, including the address books.

Microsoft Wallet   One of the emerging and rapidly changing technologies on the Internet is payment technology. Whenever a payment transaction crosses the Internet, security of the transaction is a real concern.

Microsoft implements payment technology with an add-on component called Microsoft Wallet. Wallet consists of two modules: one stores shipping and billing addresses, while the other stores credit information. All transactions are sent and stored securely; we use encryption technology.

NetMeeting   NetMeeting provides several multimedia capabilities, collobaration, remote application control (for meetings), video conferencing, etc. Another stand-alone program bundled with Internet Explorer, it provides the abilities for multiple users to have an audio or video conference, collaborate on documents, and share applications. These tasks can be done within an office intranet or across the Internet.

NetMeeting users connect to each other by way of the Internet Locator Service (ILS). ILS uses the Lightweight Directory Access Protocol (LDAP) to maintain a current directory listing of NetMeeting users. ILS is bundled with Exchange Server 5.5 and Site Server, or you can use one of many public servers.

NetShow   NetShow provides streaming multimedia support for Internet users. NetShow clients can be distributed with IE, allowing compressed video and audio broadcasts to be received. The feeds can be live broadcasts such as news events, or on demand such as viewing a music video at a record company's Web site. NetShow supports all the popular Intel Compression and Decompression, MPEG, AVI and MS Active Streaming Formats.

FrontPage Express   A limited version of FrontPage 97, FrontPage Express gives end users everything needed to create simple Web pages without having to learn HTML. It uses a WYSIWYG environment to provide full editing capabilities. It does not include Active Server Pages or WebBots, Front Page's server side objects.

Microsoft Web Publishing Wizard   This wizard automates the process of uploading newly created HTML files to any Web server. If you are responsible for several pages of Web content, the Web Publishing Wizard makes uploading easy.

Microsoft Chat   This graphical client adds Microsoft Internet Chat Server and Internet Relay Chat (IRC) support to IE 4.01. Two or more Microsoft Chat users communicate across the intranet or Internet using text conversations through a server.

▶ Develop custom installation strategies for Internet Explorer 4.0.

To create a custom package, you must use the IEAK Wizard. The wizard has five stages of configuration. Once the wizard finishes, the choices made by the IEAK administrator are written to a file called `INSTALL`. `INS`. The names of all the IEAK Wizard screens that are used to generate this file are listed below for your reference.

Stage One: Gathering Information

- ▶ Enter Company Name and Customization Code
- ▶ Select a Language
- ▶ Select Media to Distribute Your Browser

Stage Two: Specifying Active Setup Parameters

- ▶ Select a Microsoft Download Site
- ▶ Automatic Version Synchronization (AVS)
- ▶ Specify Custom Active Setup Components

▶ Specify Trusted Publishers

Stage Three: Customizing Active Setup

▶ Customize the AutoRun Screen for CD-ROM Installations

▶ Customize the Active Setup Wizard

▶ Custom Components Install Section

▶ Select Silent Install

▶ Select Installation Options

▶ Specify Download URLs

▶ Select Version Number

▶ Specify Where You Want to Install Your Browser

▶ Integrating the Web Desktop Update

Stage Four: Customizing the Browser

▶ Customize the Window Title and Toolbar Background

▶ Customize the Start and Search Pages

▶ Specify an Online Support Page for Your Browser

▶ Favorites Folder and Links Customization

▶ Customize the Welcome Message and Desktop Wallpaper

▶ Customize the Active Channel Bar

▶ Specify Active Desktop Components

▶ Customize Desktop Toolbars

▶ My Computer and Control Panel Web View Customization

▶ User Agent String Customization

▶ Automatic Browser Configuration

▶ Specify Dynamic Branding and User Customization Settings

▶ Specify Proxy Settings

▶ Site Certificate and Authenticode Settings

▶ Security Zones and Content Ratings Customization

Stage Five: Customizing Components (if Necessary)

- ▶ Specify Internet Mail Servers, Domain, and News Server
- ▶ Specify Lightweight Directory Access Protocol (LDAP) Server Settings
- ▶ Outlook Express Customizations
- ▶ Include a Signature
- ▶ System Policies and Restrictions
- ▶ Security Zones and Content Ratings Customization

Languages

Currently Internet Explorer supports more than 20 languages. You can create a package for each of these languages, but only one at a time. If you need other languages, you must create a separate package.

Distribution Disks

The installer files for Internet Explorer are automatically added to a package. These files are also customizable, including the AUTORUN.EXE file. You can customize the browser to fit your brand. You can also brand the Active Setup process to include your own company name and logo.

Installing from a Download Site

You can build a package to be distributed from a URL that your users enter into their current browser. They can download from up to 10 Web servers or local file servers, unless you are doing a silent installation. If you are doing a silent installation, you may have only one download URL.

Installing Additional Components

In addition to installing Internet Explorer and its add-on components, you have the option of installing up to 10 additional programs of your choice with the IEAK Wizard. You can add these programs to any of the predefined or custom installations during package creation.

Signing the .CAB Files

To prevent users from executing harmful code and scripts, some browsers may not allow users to download such material unless it is digitally

"signed." To sign programs, you must get a digital certificate from a recognized certificate authority. This digital certificate helps to show that
the code is original and comes from a recognized source. You should sign
all program files and .CAB files that you wish to distribute. You can get a
certificate from Verisign at http://www.verisign.com.

Creating a Silent Installation

If you want to distribute IE without intervention from the user, choose to
install the package silently. You can choose this option—Select Silent
Install—during Stage Three.

NOTE

If you choose the silent installation in the corporate administrator mode and
distribute from a URL, you can specify only one download URL.

User Agent String

The User Agent String is a way of uniquely identifying a distribution of
IE. The string consists of two parts: the browser identification, which
identifies the particular version of a browser, and a string that the IE
administrator can append. During package creation, you can enter a text
string during Stage Four: Customizing the Browser.

▶ In corporate administrator mode, develop appropriate security strategies for using Internet Explorer 4.0 for various sites. Sites include:

- ▶ Public kiosks
- ▶ End-user sites
- ▶ Business sites

You can configure Internet Explorer to serve in many environments with
several different input devices. When security is a concern, you can configure IE to ignore many Web sites, and you can configure browsers to reject
harmful content. The number of uses for Internet Explorer in public kiosk
environments for retrieving a set of specific data pages is growing.

Part v

Public Kiosks

Public kiosks are stand-alone terminals that are connected to another information source. They are designed to be easy to navigate and generally require little or no input from the end user. Internet Explorer 4.01 has a special kiosk mode that removes virtually all of the Windows 95 interface, including toolbars, menu bars, and the Start menu, allowing a user to maneuver through Web pages with only a mouse.

To use this special kiosk mode, use the following command line:

```
IEXPLORE -k start page
```

where *start page* equals the Web page that should first appear on the public kiosk.

While it is possible to navigate using only the keyboard, the kiosk mode can be quickly circumvented by pressing Alt+F4. This mode is best used when only a pointing device, such as a touch screen or a mouse, is required to navigate through content.

End-User Sites

Internet Explorer distributions for end users are the largest use of the IEAK. In the Internet service provider mode, the end user can install Internet Explorer with only one diskette. The diskette provides enough information to allow the end user's computer to dial the Internet service provider and download the rest of Internet Explorer. You can also distribute the browser to end users on CD-ROM.

Some end users may want to restrict the content they receive. You can accomplish this by setting up a proxy server to filter the Web sites that a user can access.

Business Sites

Business users have widely differing needs and requirements when it comes to setting up a browser. They may be blocked from accessing the Web directly because of a proxy server or a firewall, or they may not be networked at all, making it necessary to install from a CD-ROM rather than a network connection.

Businesses may also want to restrict or limit access to certain Web sites from the browser. This can be accomplished through the proxy server. You can limit what type of content is downloaded using security zones. Keeping harmful content, such as ill-designed Java, from the end user is also important.

▶ Choose Active Desktop items and develop Active Channels.

When using the Windows Desktop Update, you can distribute information to the Windows Desktop. For instance, you could develop an Active Desktop item that hosts a stock quote page on the Desktop, with the price changing every 15 minutes. Thus, it would be important to keep your Active Desktop page up to date. You can do this by configuring a Channel Definition File (CDF).

The Active Desktop is split in two layers: the Icon layer and the HTML layer. With these two layers, you can customize a Desktop to suit almost every need.

Icon Layer

The Icon layer provides the Desktop shortcuts to the user and contains the shortcuts for My Computer, Network Neighborhood, Recycle Bin, and other icons that would normally make up the Desktop. The Icon layer always sits on top of the HTML layer.

HTML Layer

The HTML layer is a single Web page that contains Desktop frames. These frames are capable of displaying Web-based content such as HTML, ActiveX, and Java.

▶ Develop strategies for replacing other Internet browsers. Other browsers include:

- ▶ Microsoft Internet Explorer 3.*x*
- ▶ Netscape Navigator

When you're upgrading from an existing browser, saving all of the end user's personalized settings is very important. Your end users have spent months or years creating a list of their favorite destinations. During the setup process on the client workstation, many of the settings will be migrated into Internet Explorer.

Internet Explorer 3.x

Internet Explorer 4 will upgrade over an existing installation, saving the proxy settings, favorites, and cookies. You must reinstall any plug-ins. However, if the plug-ins are compatible with IE4, you may be able to distribute them as part of the IE package.

Netscape Navigator

IE 4 will also import proxy settings, bookmarks, and cookies from Navigator 3.0. You must reinstall any plug-ins. If the plug-ins are compatible with IE4, you may be able to distribute them as part of the IE package. Both Netscape Navigator and Internet Explorer can coexist on the same machine.

▶ Develop strategies for replacing other Internet mail clients. Other mail clients include:

- ▶ Internet Mail and News
- ▶ Netscape Mail
- ▶ Eudora

When started for the first time, Microsoft Outlook Express will detect and migrate certain versions of Netscape Mail, Eudora, Exchange/Inbox, Outlook, and Internet Mail. Mail messages, address books, and news settings can be imported.

Importing Mail

Mail from the following programs can be imported into Outlook Express:

- ▶ Netscape Communicator v4
- ▶ Netscape Mail v3 and below
- ▶ Microsoft Exchange
- ▶ Microsoft Outlook
- ▶ Microsoft Internet Mail
- ▶ Microsoft Windows Messaging
- ▶ Qualcomm Eudora Pro v3.0 and below
- ▶ Qualcomm Eudora Light v3.0 and below

Importing Address Books

The following types of address books can be imported:

- ▶ Netscape Communicator v4
- ▶ Netscape Mail v3 and below
- ▶ Microsoft Exchange Personal Address Book
- ▶ Microsoft Internet Mail
- ▶ Qualcomm Eudora Pro v3.0 and below
- ▶ Qualcomm Eudora Light v3.0 and below
- ▶ Any comma-delimited text file (.CSV)

Importing Mail Accounts

When upgrading an existing mail client, you can also let Outlook Express import existing mail account settings. This prevents the user from having to reenter these settings.

▶ Choose the appropriate configuration strategy for Microsoft Outlook Express.

Configuring Outlook Express begins in Stage Five of the IEAK Configuration Wizard. You can also configure it later through the IEAK Profile Manager (if you enabled autoconfiguration in Stage Four) or the Outlook Express program itself under the Tools ➤ Accounts menu. Configuration consists of entering setup information for the mail, directory, or news services.

Mail and News Services

The two most popular protocols for client e-mail are supported under Outlook Express. The most popular one is Post Office Protocol (POP3). However, the Internet Message Access Protocol (IMAP4) is gaining support. Both have advantages and disadvantages in storage, security, and functionality.

Enter the incoming mail server's name and the SMTP server's name for outgoing messages. These server names may be the same. Then enter the name of the Internet newsgroup server that provides your NNTP service.

Part v

If you want to make Outlook Express the default client for mail or news, select the appropriate checkboxes. If your server requires the use of Secure Password Authentication, select that option.

Directory Services

After configuring the mail and news options, you are given the opportunity to preconfigure a directory server. Outlook Express supports the Lightweight Directory Access Protocol. This service allows the end user to validate names, and look up e-mail addresses and other directory-type information. Users can access the client by choosing Start ➤ Find ➤ People.

Friendly Name   Enter the name of the LDAP server in the Friendly Name field.

Directory Service   In this field, enter the URL of your directory service, such as `ldap.mycompany.com`.

Home Page   You can preselect the home page of the LDAP server (loaded whenever someone clicks the Web site button inside the LDAP client) by entering the LDAP server's URL into the Home Page field.

Search Base   The context of the LDAP search is predefined in the Search Base field. Valid options are referred to in Table 24.2.

TABLE 24.2: LDAP Search Contexts

SEARCH BASE	SEARCH DEPTH
Base (default)	Searches entire directory
One	Searches only the current directory
Sub	Searches only the current subtree

Service Bitmap   The service bitmap is an image that is displayed when a user chooses Start ➤ Find ➤ People, and is usually used to advertise the logo of the directory service. It must be 134 by 38 pixels in size and contain 16 colors.

You can use LDAP to validate e-mail addresses on outgoing e-mail. You can also require that an LDAP client provide a password, an encrypted password, or no password at all.

▶ Choose the appropriate configuration strategy for Microsoft NetMeeting. Elements include:

- ▶ Settings
- ▶ Restrictions

One of the traits of a successful application rollout is when an application works the same way across each of the platforms and desktops for which it is designed. To accomplish this, we need a method that ensures that the application is configured properly the first time and is not altered. NetMeeting is an example of such an application that needs common configurations across the company.

Nearly all the configuration settings needed for a distribution of Microsoft NetMeeting can be found in the IEAK Profile Manager. You can prevent users from using unneeded portions of NetMeeting, and you can configure the client with all of the necessary server and directory information.

Restricting the Use of File Transfer

You can prevent the user from receiving or sending files by checking the appropriate boxes.

Restricting the Use of Application Sharing

Aside from the ability to disable application sharing, you can prevent the user from sharing clipboards, MS-DOS windows, and Explorer windows, and from collaborating.

Restricting the Use of the Options Dialog Box

You may disable menu choices and specific configuration pages to prevent a user from changing the preconfigured settings. You can also restrict the user from answering calls and using the audio or video.

Other NetMeeting Restrictions

The remaining restrictions that you can apply to NetMeeting concern the setting of directory servers and bandwidth restrictions.

▸ Specify a default NetMeeting server (called an Internet Locator Server or ILS).

▸ Add your NetMeeting addresses to an Exchange server to assist in locating other NetMeeting users. Microsoft Exchange Server 5.5 provides an Internet Locator Server for NetMeeting users.

▸ Preset the User Information Category: Note that this option applies only to silent installs and cannot be changed. You must uninstall and reinstall NetMeeting if you decide to change this category later.

▸ Set the NetMeeting home page. Preset the page that is loaded when users select Help ➢ Product News.

▶ Choose the appropriate configurations for the NetMeeting client. Configurations include:

▸ Internet Locator Service (ILS) server connectivity

▸ IP connectivity

▸ Peer-to-peer networking

▸ Proxy server settings

▸ Proxy client settings

The responsibilities of an IEAK administrator will likely include the task of configuring NetMeeting. There are many options in this program; therefore, it is rarely configured correctly the first time by end users. The IEAK Wizard will allow a consistent installation of this client. Adding locator servers, configuring protocols, and restricting user options are just a few of the administrative challenges facing the IEAK administrator.

ILS Server Connectivity

You can specify a default ILS server in the IEAK Profile Wizard. This server will be the first server contacted when NetMeeting is started. You can either choose one from the list or enter the name of another ILS server.

IP Connectivity

NetMeeting supports the IPX/SPX and TCP/IP protocols. You can also dial from computer to computer (using a null modem cable). However, there are some restrictions with these methods. If you wish to use audio conferencing, you cannot use the null modem or IPX/SPX. Additionally, if you want to connect to other NetMeeting users through the Internet, you must use the TCP/IP protocol.

Peer-to-Peer Networking

NetMeeting supports the International Telecommunications Union H.323 standard for audio and video conferencing. Peer-to-peer networking is accomplished through the ILS. As clients register their locations (network addresses) with the server, clients wishing to initiate a call may query the ILS to get the user's current location. After the location is obtained, the two clients may initiate a conversation or share an application through a peer-to-peer connection.

Proxy Server Settings

To support all the features of NetMeeting, the ports referenced in Table 24.3 are necessary. You may need to reconfigure your Winsock Proxy before NetMeeting will operate correctly.

NOTE

Most of these services require TCP or UDP connections on ports between 1025 and 65535. If these ports are limited by a proxy or a firewall, you may not be able to utilize all of the features of NetMeeting with clients on the remote side of your proxy server firewall.

TABLE 24.3: Ports Required to Use NetMeeting and Associated Programs

Port	TCP or UDP	In- or Outbound	Service
389	TCP	Both	Internet Locator Service (LDAP)
522	TCP	Both	User Locator Service (NetMeeting 1.0 backwards compatibility)
1503	TCP	Both	T.120 protocol (multipoint data conferencing)

TABLE 24.3 continued: Ports Required to Use NetMeeting and Associated Programs

PORT	TCP OR UDP	IN- OR OUTBOUND	SERVICE
1720	TCP	Both	H.323 audio conference call setup and negotiation (TCP)
1731	TCP	Both	Audio call control (TCP)
Dynamic*	TCP	Both	H.323 call control
Dynamic*	UDP	Both	H.323 streaming (Real Time protocol)

*Dynamic ports are assigned randomly from 1025 to 65535.

Proxy Client Connections

In Internet Explorer, select View ➤ Internet Options. Then click the Connections tab. The Proxy Servers section contains the address and port to forward Internet traffic. You can also choose to bypass the proxy for local addresses.

▶ ## In corporate administrator mode or Internet service provider mode, choose strategies for managing automatic configuration by using the IEAK Profile Manager. Methods include:

- ▶ Microsoft JScript autoproxy
- ▶ .ins files
- ▶ .adm files

After the distribution is complete, the IEAK administrator may choose to make configuration changes from time to time. The changes can be pushed out easily to the users with automatic configuration files and autoproxy files. Most of these changes or updates will take place using the IEAK Profile Manager. With this utility, you can make changes and update your IE installations.

IEAK Profile Manager

The IEAK Profile Manager is a convenient way to manage the Internet Explorer installation after the package has been distributed and the software has been installed. You can select custom choices for individual groups and users.

Autoproxy with Microsoft JScript Files   The JScript autoproxy files assist the IE administrator by letting them dynamically configure advanced proxy settings. These files can provide the correct proxy configuration to allow newly installed browsers to quickly reach the Web and can block certain domain names or address ranges from reaching the browser.

The files are dynamic to allow fast updates and may appear with .JS, .PAC, or .JVS extensions. Optionally, you could also lock down the proxy settings within the browser. The autoproxy files could be stored in a central location, allowing the administrator to quickly update the proxy configuration for many browsers at once.

To configure autoproxy files, enter the name of the URL that points to a valid .JS, .JVS, or .PAC autoproxy file.

Autoconfiguration with .INS Files   After you've used the IEAK Wizard to create your package, the wizard creates a master or global settings file called INSTALL.INS when the package is built. The file contains the installation choices for Internet Explorer. It is also possible for users and groups to have their own .INS files. Simply name the .INS file after the user or group. Hence, Phil's custom .INS file would be called PHIL.INS; if he were a member of the sales group, his group .INS file would be called SALES.INS.

The group .INS file will override settings in an INSTALL.INS file. Both are overridden by settings in a user .INS file. To create specific user or group .INS files, open the INSTALL.INS (or other master) file and then choose File ➤ Save As. Name the new file with the user or group name. You will have to specify the location of the .CAB files.

NOTE   .INS files that were created in previous versions of IEAK are also compatible with IEAK4.

System Policies with .ADM **Files**   Windows NT manages user interface configuration through the use of system policies and .ADM files. Each .ADM file contains choices for registry settings to enforce consistent configurations between logins. Policies can mandate properties such as disabling the shutdown button when logging on. They can also dictate nearly every aspect of the Desktop, from the Start menu to the color scheme. Policies are edited with the System Policy Editor and the resulting .POL file (policy file) is stored in the NETLGON directory awaiting the next login. Policies are applied to the registry at every login.

The IEAK Profile Manager handles the .ADM files similarly to how the System Policy Editor handles them. The Profile Manager allows you to import the .ADM files to further customize the browser. You can then edit the additional options and setup choices for your own users. The .ADM files are incorporated into .INF files, which are then packaged into the .CAB files. When the .CAB files are unpacked, the policies chosen will then be applied.

Reconfiguration Settings   Reconfiguration settings determine the interval at which IE will reread the autoconfiguration files and update the browser. You can set this interval at which the browser reconfigures, preventing a wide variance in settings across the enterprise. Setting the value to zero or leaving it blank forces IE to reconfigure only at boot time.

▶ Develop a configuration plan for Active Setup components.

Internet Explorer will be installed with a compact installation program that can be customized, or branded, to fit your organization. You can use customized logos and bitmaps to identify IE with your company. You can also choose from a set of default images.

Advance Preparation

Prior to running the IEAK, you need to make a few preparations. A directory tree needs to be created, special bitmaps need to be added, and third-party programs need to be prepackaged into .CAB files.

Directory Structure   Create the following directory structure in your source drive:

Directory	Use
\CIE	IE distribution parent directory
\CIE\BITMAPS	Location of special bitmaps used during installation

Bitmaps   In the \CIE\BITMAPS directory, you may create your own special bitmaps to reflect your company logo. The user's computer must be able to display 256 colors for the special bitmaps to display correctly. You may include:

▶ A background bitmap for the AutoRun screen (CD packages only)

▶ CD-ROM button images (CD packages only)

▶ Custom 135-by-256-pixel bitmap used during Active Setup

▶ Custom background toolbar bitmap (can be any size, 256 colors or less)

Bundling Other Applications with IE   You can also include other software (custom components) with the distribution of IE, using a utility called IExpress. Options are available to bundle the component's files, and there's an option to run an installation command. You can also set the computer to reboot after the program is installed.

Installing IE with Active Setup

When Active Setup begins, it will extract the IE4 setup files into a temporary directory. Active Setup will then find the [String] section in IE4SETUP.INF and look for the URL location of IE4SITE.DAT. It will then open that URL location and display the available download site choices from which the user can select. After the user selects the download site, Active Setup downloads and decompresses the setup files (.CAB files).

After the setup files are decompressed, the selected components are installed, and if needed, the system will reboot. Upon reboot, the system may spend several minutes updating itself with the new IE settings.

▶ Develop strategies for using the Internet Connection Wizard in Internet service provider mode. Elements include:

- ▶ Modem detection
- ▶ Stack installation
- ▶ Configuration of dial-up connections

The Internet Connection Wizard helps your users configure their individual computers to be able to connect to the Internet. While some users access the Internet through local area networks, other users may have to use modems to get the resources they need. Some mobile users may connect using a combination of both. The Internet Connection Wizard appears just after installation, before the end user begins using their browser. The following three steps are performed:

- ▶ **Computer setup:** Checks for modems and will run the Modem Setup Wizard if installation is necessary. Also checks dialing settings, that the TCP/IP protocol (formerly known as TCP/IP protocol stacks in 16-bit operating systems without networking support) is installed properly and configured, and Dial-Up Networking.

- ▶ **Internet account creation:** Loads the IEAK-configured ISP sign-up Web page, or if a default does not exist, allows the user to choose an ISP.

- ▶ **Internet software setup:** If the account was created in the previous step, the Internet Connection Wizard will set up any necessary Internet software.

Configuring the `.ISP` File

The Internet service provider (ISP) mode provides a method for clients to connect to the ISP and create a computers account prior to installing IE. These `.ISP` files provide enough information to dial up the ISP and begin signing up for an account. `.INS` files are personalized with user-specific information.

Because no personalization information is included in the .ISP file, a single .ISP file will allow any client to connect and create an account. The sign-up process occurs in three phases:

1. The client connects to the ISP's sign-up server.

2. HTML pages collect the client's address and billing information.

3. The sign-up server then sends the client a custom .INS file that has been personalized for the client with browser branding information.

Part v

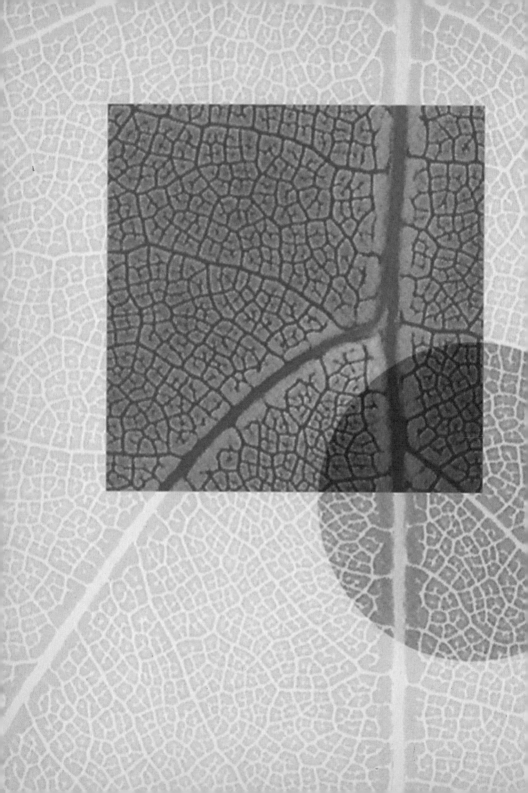

Chapter 25

INSTALLATION AND CONFIGURATION

After you have formed the groundwork for your installation, it is time to start putting the pieces together. By this time, you have forecasted your users' needs and gathered the appropriate software to generate the package.

This chapter covers the actual package creation from start to finish. We will concentrate on the IEAK Wizard, which involves many of the exam objectives in this portion of the exam.

Adapted from *MCSE Test Success: Internet Explorer 4 Administration Kit* by Allen Jones

ISBN 0-7821-2333-3   416 pages $24.99

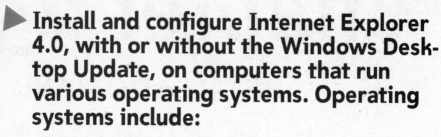

Install and configure Internet Explorer 4.0, with or without the Windows Desktop Update, on computers that run various operating systems. Operating systems include:

- Microsoft Windows NT Server 4.0

- Microsoft Windows NT Workstation 4.0

- Microsoft Windows 3.*x*

- Microsoft Windows 95

- Macintosh

Administrators who install IE are faced with a number of options during setup. Installing IE in a large environment becomes a challenge with many different hardware devices and operating systems in use. The factors and parameters for installation; hardware and operating system requirements; and the customization options for IE as provided by the IEAK are covered in this section.

Internet Explorer 4.01 Installation Requirements for the Intel x86 Platform

Before you can start to install IEAK, you need to successfully install Internet Explorer 4.01 or higher. The minimum installation requirements for the Intel x86 platform are outlined below and in Tables 2.1 and 2.2.

Hardware   The minimum hardware necessary to install Internet Explorer 4.01 on x86 platforms is as follows:

- 486/66 or Pentium-class processor

- Hard disk space as listed in Table 25.1

- Memory as listed in Table 25.2

- Mouse

- Modem

- CD-ROM

TABLE 25.1: Internet Explorer 4.01 Hard Disk Requirements

DEFAULT INSTALLATION OPTION	SPACE REQUIRED*
Minimum	40MB
Standard	47MB
Full	73MB

*You will need additional space for installation. For total space needed, please refer to Table 1.1

TABLE 25.2: Internet Explorer 4.01 Memory Requirements

OPERATING SYSTEM	OPTION(S)	MEMORY REQUIRED
Windows 3.1	Minimum installation	12MB
Windows 95	Standard installation	8MB
Windows 95	Browser only, Outlook Express	12MB
Windows 95	Standard or Full installations with Windows Desktop Update	16MB
Windows NT 4	All	24MB

Software   Some of the operating systems that will support Internet Explorer 4.01 are as follows:

- Windows NT Workstation 4 with Service Pack 3
- Windows NT Server 4 with Service Pack 3
- Windows 95
- Windows 98
- Windows 3.1

NOTE

When installing IE using Windows NT, you must use a user account that has administrative privileges on the local computer. Any user can install IE on Windows 95 or 98.

Encryption   Internet Explorer 4 is available in the standard 40-bit version. However, if secure transactions are a concern or private communications are a requirement, a 128-bit version is available for use in the United States and Canada.

Additional Windows 3.1 Installation Requirements   To install Internet Explorer 4.01, you must also have:

- A VGA-compatible monitor or higher
- An Internet connection
- An entry in CONFIG.SYS containing FILES=50

Internet Explorer 4.01 Installation Requirements for the Macintosh Platform

When planning an installation of Internet Explorer 4.01 on a Macintosh, you should consider the minimum hardware and software requirements.

Hardware   The minimum hardware necessary to install Internet Explorer 4.01 on a Macintosh is as follows:

- Macintosh with 68030 or higher processor
- System 7.1 or higher
- 8MB of RAM with virtual memory on
- 21MB of hard disk space

Software   You will also need the following items to install Internet Explorer 4.01:

- Open Transport 1.1.1 or higher, or MacTCP 2.0.6
- Valid PPP connection

Installing IE 4

To install IE4, you may choose from one of several installation options:

- From CD-ROM
- From the Internet
- From floppy disks
- From a file server

To successfully install IE4, use the following steps:

1. To install IE, click on `IE4SETUP.EXE` or visit `http://www`
   `.microsoft.com/ie/download/`. Once you have downloaded the file, you need to connect to (or remain connected
   to) your IE file source (server, Internet, or CD-ROM). Once
   you click on `IE4SETUP.EXE`, you have started Active Setup.

2. You will be presented with two options: Install, which downloads the installation files chosen and proceeds to install
   those files on your computer, and Download Only, which
   downloads the IE installation files, but does not execute
   them. With this option, you can download now and install
   later.

3. The default installation of IE presents three distribution
   package choices. Each choice contains specific packages of
   IE add-on components. You can have up to 10 installation
   options per package, unless you choose a silent installation,
   in which case you are limited to 1 installation option. The
   three default choices are Minimum, Standard, and Full. Refer
   to Table 24.1 to determine which choice is best suited for the
   installation. You can always add or remove components later
   from the installed Desktop.

4. The next choice during installation is whether to use Windows Desktop Update. If you will be using this option, click
   Yes. Otherwise, click No.

5. Now you must find a nearby download site. The user is presented with a list of choices, and a selection is made. IE will
   download installation files from this site. If you chose a silent
   installation, you are limited to only 1 download site rather
   than the usual 10 sites.

6. If this is a new installation, the user chooses the destination
   path during this portion of setup. If you have an existing
   installation of IE on your computer, the installed directory
   will appear in this field.

7. After you have chosen the destination path, Active Setup will
   begin downloading the selected components. If you chose to
   download now and install later, Active Setup will notify you
   once the download is finished.

8. If you chose to install IE now, Active Setup will notify you once the download is complete. After a few moments, installation will begin.

9. After the installation is complete, the system will reboot; then, Active Setup completes the installation by making the proper registry changes. This will take a few moments to complete for each IE add-on component.

10. Once the above steps are successfully completed, Internet Explorer 4 is installed and ready for use.

Installation Considerations

When considering the plan for Internet Explorer distribution, you may have several groups of users with similar needs. You can save time in building packages for these groups by copying the INSTALL.INS file (generated when you complete the IEAK Wizard) to a new, empty directory. When you restart the wizard and point to the new directory, the wizard loads the INSTALL.INS copy. As you build the new package, the displayed defaults will be the same selections you made in the previous run of the IEAK Wizard.

IEAK Installation Requirements

After you have successfully installed Internet Explorer 4, you may now install the Internet Explorer Administration Kit. The minimum requirements to install the Kit are listed in the following sections.

Hardware   The minimum hardware necessary to install and run the IEAK is as follows:

▶ **Processor:** 486/66 or greater

▶ **Memory:** IEAK has the following memory requirements:

Operating System	Memory Required
Windows 95	8MB
Windows NT	16MB

▶ **Disk space:** IEAK requires a large workspace. Calculate the space taken by the components. You will need four times that space on the destination drive and four times that space on a temp drive.

If the temp drive and the destination drive are the same, the space needed is the component space times eight. For instance, if the component space equals 30MB, you will need space as follows:

Drive	Space Needed
Destination	120MB
Temp	120MB

If the destination drives and the temp drives are the same, you would need 240MB. When creating multiple packages, you should also allow between 40MB and 100MB for each package you wish to create.

Software   The minimum software requirements to install the IEAK are as follows:

- ▶ Windows 95 or NT 4.

- ▶ If running Windows NT, the page file must be set to 40MB or greater.

- ▶ Customization code from Microsoft. For more info, visit `http://ieak.microsoft.com`.

- ▶ Internet Explorer 4.

NOTE

Even though this unit focuses on the x86 platform, IEAK can be run on the Sun and Compaq Alpha platforms. You must be running Solaris 2.5 or newer on Sun platforms.

▶ Specify and customize Active Setup components.

Active Setup is a small program that allows end users to install Internet Explorer, search for previous installations, and download installation files from the Internet. It can recover from failed downloads, thus preventing the user from having to download the entire package again. It can also check for newer versions of IE add-on components.

You can customize Active Setup to fit a user's needs. Organization logos and bitmaps can be used to brand IE to fit an organization.

Customization of Active Setup begins when the IEAK administrator runs the IEAK Wizard.

Selecting a Microsoft Download Site

This portion of the IEAK Wizard requires that you choose a Microsoft download site from a list of sites. However, this site is not to be confused with the download-site choices the user has when installing the package—it is for keeping up to date with the latest builds of IE add-on components for package distributions. Once the Microsoft download site is chosen, the IE add-on components are updated with the very latest releases through Automatic Version Synchronization (AVS).

Using Automatic Version Synchronization

After you select the IE download site, the IEAK Wizard will make sure that you have the updated versions of the add-on components, using the IEAK Automatic Version Synchronization (AVS).

After the IEAK Wizard checks the components you have already downloaded (this can take some time), a dialog box appears showing you the update status of each product. Three icons are associated with the status, as shown in Table 25.3.

TABLE 25.3: AVS Status as Shown by Icon Color

Icon	Color	Meaning
[T2501.TIF]	Red	You do not currently have this product.
[T2502.TIF]	Yellow	You have this product, but it is out of date—it needs to be synchronized.
[T0203.TIF]	Green	You have this product, and it is up to date.

You can choose to synchronize a single component or all out-of-date components (as shown in Figure 25.1).

Custom Active Setup Components

As you customize the Active Setup experience, you may wish to add other programs besides the add-on components provided. You may also wish to manually edit some of the setup files. Each of these procedures is explained for you in this section.

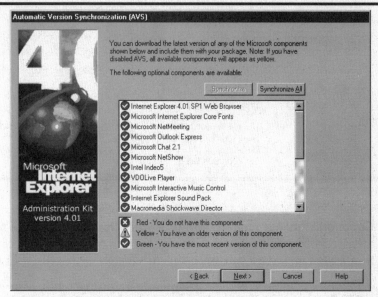

FIGURE 25.1:   Automatic Version Synchronization status

IExpress   You can package and distribute your own custom programs in addition to IE add-on components. These custom programs are packaged by a utility called IExpress, which will create a self-extracting package for installation from your custom program files. IExpress packages installation instructions by creating a self-extraction directive (. SED file).

After you have digitally signed and packaged your custom component, you may add it to the package through the IEAK Wizard, during Stage Two: Specifying Active Setup Parameters.

You must supply several pieces of information about your package to the IEAK Wizard, as referenced in Table 25.4.

TABLE 25.4: Options for Specifying Custom Programs

FIELD	INFORMATION
Component	Name of the custom component
Location	Path to location of custom . CAB or self-extracting . EXE file
Command	The command needed to execute the . CAB file (required when using . CAB files)
GUID	Global unique identifier—identifies a program

TABLE 25.4 continued: Options for Specifying Custom Programs

FIELD	INFORMATION
Parameter	Type any parameters you want to append to the .EXE file (if using .EXE)
Size	Program size
Version	Unique version number of your program—needed by IE to determine when an upgrade is available
Uninstall Key	For end users to be able to uninstall

Common Files Associated with IE Installation   A number of files are associated with the installation of Internet Explorer. In Table 25.5 below, a few important ones are detailed.

TABLE 25.5: Common Files Associated with Setting Up Internet Explorer

FILENAME	PURPOSE
IE4SETUP.EXE	.EXE program to start IE4 installation—extracts setup programs and then starts IE4WZRD.EXE
IE4SITES.DAT	Contains potential download sites for IE, created during Stage Three, Specify Download URLs
IE4WZRD.EXE	Setup file that connects to the download site chosen and retrieves the rest of the Internet Explorer distribution
IEREMOVE.EXE	Used to uninstall IE4 in case the Add/Remove Programs option from the Control Panel fails

 Customize the browser.

This section concentrates primarily on Stage Four of the IEAK Wizard: Customizing the Browser. You will be walked through each screen of Stage Four, and each dialog box and its impact on the IE distribution will be discussed.

While the other four stages of distribution development concentrate on add-on programs and how the browser is installed, this IEAK stage has more to do with personalizing the browser for the end user.

Customize the Window Title and Toolbar Background

You can customize the text that appears on the Windows title bar of Internet Explorer and Outlook Express. In this window, you can enter the name of the entity for which you are building the distribution in the Title Bar Text field. When customized, Internet Explorer's title bar will read, "Microsoft Internet Explorer provided by," followed by the value you entered in the field. Outlook Express's title bar, if also packaged, will read, "Outlook Express provided by," followed by the same value.

You can also provide a custom bitmap that will be used as a backdrop for the Internet Explorer toolbar. The bitmap should be the same size as the toolbar and should not contain a lot of dark colors—any button text would not be easily visible.

Customize the Search and Start Pages

You can specify the initial start and search pages for the user by entering values. Enter the appropriate URLs for a search page and a home page.

Specify an Online Support Page for Your Browser

You can provide a technical support page to assist in the support of your users. Whenever a user chooses Help ➤ Online Support from the IE menu bar, the URL that you specify in the dialog box will be loaded.

Favorites Folder and Links Customization

In this window, you can prepare all of the folders and links to be distributed with your browser. Favorites are found on the menu bar. Links are normally found just under the IE address bar.

You can add the favorites and links in this window by hand with the Add URL and Add Folder buttons, or you can import a set of favorites with the Import button. You can distribute up to 200 favorites.

Customize the Welcome Message and Desktop Wallpaper

When Internet Explorer is first started, a default welcome page is displayed. You can choose to keep this welcome page, select your own welcome page, or start with no welcome page at all. If you choose a custom page, there is a field for you to enter the appropriate starting URL. You can also disable the welcome window and work directly with the browser when it has been started for the first time.

You specify default wallpaper by entering a name and location of a .BMP, .GIF, or HTML file.

Customize the Active Channel Bar (CA Mode Only)

The IEAK administrator can create packages containing custom Active Channels. To distribute these channels using the corporate administrator mode, you must first configure the IEAK computer with all of the appropriate channel settings. Once you have configured these channels, you can import the channel settings into the IEAK. This import takes place during Stage Four. You can also delete a competitor's channel.

Select Channel or Category (ICP Mode or ISP Mode Only)

When setting up the default channels in Internet Explorer, the IEAK administrator can add or delete channels prior to distribution. You can tell IEAK whether to include a channel or channel category. If you choose to include a channel category, you can add multiple channels in the newly created category. You have three options from which to choose:

- ▶ **Do not add any channels:** With this option, the default channel bar will be used.

- ▶ **Add a channel category:** This option will allow you to create a new channel category in which you may add additional channels.

- ▶ **Add only one channel:** This option will allow you to add a single channel.

If you choose to add a category, you will be asked to include additional information about the category, such as a title, the category's URL, and image and icon information.

You will also be asked to include specific information about your channel(s), such as a title, the URL to the CDF file, paths to the channel's images and icons, and a subscription schedule.

Delete Competing Channels (ICP Mode or ISP Mode Only)

You can also delete any channels that belong to your competitors. On this screen, any default channel may be deleted. You can also restore the deleted channels at a later date by rerunning the IEAK Wizard and clicking Restore. This is helpful if you delete a channel and later realize that you need it.

Customize Software Update Channels

The IEAK administrator can completely customize software distribution channels. The IEAK administrator can also set up the channels, and have the IEAK Wizard import the settings and CDF/OSD files for distribution.

Add a Custom Desktop Component (ISP Mode Only)

IEAK administrators can include a single Active Desktop component, provided the Windows Desktop Update will be installed. The component could be a CDF file or an actual HTML component, such as a .GIF or .BMP file. Specify the URL of the component you wish to include.

User Agent String Customization

The User Agent String is a way of uniquely identifying a particular brand of browser or distribution. The string is sent from the client browser when it tries to request a document from the server. The string consists of two parts:

- ▶ The browser identification, which identifies the particular brand and version of a browser (this is hard-coded by Microsoft and cannot be changed).

- ▶ A string that the IE administrator can append to further identify this browser. During package creation, you can enter a text string that will be appended to the browser identification.

Automatic Browser Configuration

This screen will enable the IEAK administrator to configure IE to use automatic configuration files. The automatic configuration files can be used to reconfigure IEAK options and proxy settings. Enter the URL where the browser can find these configuration files.

When properly configured, these entries will permit the IEAK administrator to update the autoconfiguration and autoproxy settings without making a trip to the user's Desktop.

Specify Proxy Settings

The IEAK administrator can specify the proxy server that the browser will use to connect to the Internet. You can use different proxy servers for different services, or use the same proxy for everything. To use the same proxy for everything, enable the Use the Same Proxy Server for All Addresses checkbox.

Additionally, you can tell Internet Explorer to limit the use of the proxy. Specific protocols can be bypassed, as can specific domain names or Internet addresses.

Select a Sign-up Method (ISP Mode Only)

When users connect to the Internet for the first time, they need to create an Internet account. With IEAK, you have the following options for specifying an account to use:

- ▶ **Internet Sign-up Server:** This server is a stand-alone server that uses CGI scripting or Active Server Pages to create accounts on the fly. The scripts or pages are custom written by the ISP. When the user completes the sign-up process as custom written, a custom configuration file is downloaded to the computer, which completes the installation.

- ▶ **Serverless Sign-up:** This option allows the end user to specify any necessary parameters. With this process, the user must specify only the user name, password, and dial-up information to allow them to connect to the Internet.

- ▶ **No Sign-up Server:** This method asks for no account information and assumes that the end user will configure or has previously configured all necessary dial-up networking information.

▶ Configure built-in and custom components of Internet Explorer 4.0 by using the IEAK Wizard. Components include:

- ▶ Microsoft Outlook Express

► Microsoft NetMeeting

This section covers Stage Five of the IEAK Wizard: Customizing Components. This is the final stage before generating the package—any components that were chosen must be configured. These components include Outlook Express and NetMeeting. You can also supply configuration information to any LDAP servers and configure system policies for any components.

Specify Internet Mail Servers, Domain, and News Server

You can specify what type of mail server the end user will be receiving from (whether it will be a POP3 or IMAP4 server), the server's name, the outgoing mail server's name, and the Internet news server's name. You can also specify default clients and require the user of Secure Password Authentication to validate user passwords.

Specify LDAP Server Settings

You can also specify your directory server (LDAP server) settings by entering the appropriate values. For more information on these settings, refer to the "Directory Services" section of "Configuring Outlook Express" in Chapter 24.

Outlook Express Customizations

You can customize particular parts of Outlook Express to fit your organization's branding. For specific information on what to enter in this screen, please refer to the section "Customizing Outlook Express" later in this chapter.

System Policies and Restrictions

After you have successfully configured all of the built-in components of IE, such as Outlook Express and NetMeeting, you can set system policies for any other optional components. This gives the IEAK administrator an opportunity to make configuration changes.

You can specify policy settings for individual users, groups, or computers. The policies are in the same .ADM file format used in Windows NT system policies. Careful planning and testing of system policies in a controlled environment are required to ensure consistent administration.

WARNING

It is extremely important that planned changes to an installation be thoroughly tested in a protected test environment before being dispatched to the rest of your users. By testing and implementing strict change-control procedures in your environment, you will be able to cut down on the number of trouble calls you receive.

System policies are typically used to prevent users from making changes to component configurations and Desktop settings. It is recommended that changes to system policies take place after the package has initially been built and tested. The IEAK administrator should use the IEAK Profile Manager to update the package's system policies.

► Configure channels, software distribution channels, and site subscriptions.

Pushing content can be accomplished with IE using several different delivery methods. IE uses channels and site subscriptions to download the latest content to the hard drive without interrupting the user, or IE can just simply notify the end user that updated content is available. IE can also use e-mail to notify the user about the update.

IE also has the ability to push software updates for built-in and custom components. If a new update is available, the notifications listed above are available, and IE can update the software for the user.

Configuring Channel Subscriptions

A *channel* is a grouping of similar Web pages or content that can be transferred from the server to the client at the client's request.

A channel subscription permits Internet Explorer users to schedule regular updates of channels (sometimes called Active Channels) to the local disk for future viewing. The channel's content can include HTML, Dynamic HTML, and ActiveX technology.

To subscribe to a channel, perform the following steps:

1. The user starts the subscription by clicking on a hyperlink that points to a Channel Definition Format (CDF) file. The CDF file contains basic information such as location of the content and suggested frequency of the updates.

2. When the user subscribes, the CDF file and the current content are downloaded.

3. The user can then tailor the CDF file to suit their individual tastes, such as increasing the frequency of updates.

NOTE

Channel subscriptions (CDF files) are stored in the user's profile at Favorites\Channels.

Creating CDF Files

When planning or organizing the automated delivery of content, the IEAK administrator needs a mechanism to organize the flow of information. If the administrator were to configure 1,000 browsers to check for updated content at 9 A.M. tomorrow, users would have difficulty obtaining the information once a sufficient number of users connected to the download site. This is kept under control by using CDF files. An example of a CDF file is shown below.

```
<CHANNEL HREF="http://www.myfishhook.com/catchotheday.asp">

<TITLE>The Fishhook Network</TITLE>

<ABSTRACT>The Fishhook Network is a channel which displays
catches from the Gulf of Mexico on a daily basis. To show
your catch to the rest of the Internet, bring it by the
Internet Bay in Galveston, Texas and experience the best of
the web.</ABSTRACT>

<SCHEDULE>
<EARLIESTTIME DAY="1" HOUR="0" MIN="0"/>
<INTERVALTIME DAY="1" HOUR="0" MIN="0" />
<LATESTTIME DAY="1" HOUR="12" MIN="0" />
</SCHEDULE>

<LOGO HREF="http://www.myfishhook.com/directory/image.gif"
STYLE="IMAGE" />
<LOGO HREF="http://www.myfishhook.com/directory/icon.ico"
STYLE="ICON" />

</CHANNEL>
```

Customizing the CDF File for Channel Subscriptions   The CDF file can be edited either on the server or on the local client. The structure of the file follows the format of the Extensible Markup Language (XML), version 1.0.

NOTE

For more information on the Extensible Markup Language, visit the Web site `http://www.w3.org/TR/WD-xml`.

Some of the tags used in the creation of a CDF file are described below.

<SCHEDULE>   The <SCHEDULE> element is used to specify the frequency with which content is updated. Table 25.6 details the valid parameters of this tag.

TABLE 25.6: Parameters for Use within the <SCHEDULE> Tag

PARAMETER	USE*
STARTDATE	Specifies the day when schedule will commence
STOPDATE	Specifies the day when schedule will end
TIMEZONE	Specifies to which time zone the schedule refers
INTERVAL TIME	Specifies how often updating occurs
EARLIEST TIME	Specifies the earliest time (during the interval) the schedule can begin. If not present, defaults to INTERVAL TIME
LATEST TIME	Specifies the latest time (during the interval) for updates to the schedule. If not present, defaults to INTERVAL TIME

*Times are stated in 24-hour format.

The restrictions to the values that you can use with the parameters listed in the previous table are shown in Tables 2.7 and 2.8.

TABLE 25.7: Legal Values of Specific Points in Time for the <SCHEDULE> Tag (Used with Point-in-Time Elements Such As STARTDATE and STOP-DATE)

FIELD	LEGAL VALUES
Date	YYYY-MM-DD
Year (YYYY)	Between 0000 and 9999

TABLE 25.7 continued: Legal Values of Specific Points in Time for the <SCHEDULE> Tag (Used with Point-in-Time Elements Such As STARTDATE and STOPDATE)

FIELD	LEGAL VALUES
Month (MM)	Between 01 and 12
Day (DD)	Between 01 and 31
Hour	Between 00 and 23
Minute	Between 00 and 59

TABLE 25.8: Legal Values of Specific Values of Time for the<SCHEDULE> Tag (Used with Elements Such As INTERVALTIME)

FIELD	LEGAL VALUES
Day	Any natural number—a value of 1 would mean daily
Hour	Any natural number—a value of 1 would mean hourly
Minute	Any natural number—a value of 1 would mean once per minute

<TITLE>   This tag represents the general name of the channel.

<ABSTRACT>   Within this tag, place a description of the channel's content. Whenever a user holds the mouse over the channel inside the channel bar, this description will appear.

<CHANNEL>   This tag specifies the general location of Active content. It is also the parent container for any <ITEM> elements.

<ITEM>   This element denotes the location of something specific within the channel and is considered the child of a channel element.

<LOGO>   This tag specifies a logo and an icon to be used with the channel. The logo requirements are listed below.

Style Object	Format	Number of Colors	Size (in Pixels)	Special Notes
Image	.GIF or .JPG	256	80×32	Black background
Image-wide	.GIF or .JPG	256	32×194	Color background
Icon	.GIF or .JPG	16	32×32	None

Internet Explorer will use default icons and logos if none are specified.

Configuring Software Distribution Channels

After you have distributed the browser, you will want to set up a Web page to facilitate distribution of upgrades. For instance, you may wish to set up a download center for updating the Internet Explorer base code and any add-ons or custom programs that you have distributed.

Additional information regarding the construction of CDF and OSD files is available at `http://www.microsoft.com/workshop/delivery/cdf/reference/CDF.htm`. This is accomplished through subscriptions to software distribution channels, which are similar to regular content-based channels. The configuration of these channels is accomplished through files that also borrow from XML-based elements. These files are created using the Open Software Distribution (OSD) format. You do not need to create an OSD file if you will be using Active Setup to install your component.

The advantages to using OSD files are as follows:

▶ Can detect when new code is available, download new code, and install

▶ Can detect and replace missing components of programs

NOTE

Subscriptions to software distribution channels are located in the user's profile at `Favorites\Software Updates`.

Updating the Installation   Planning an update to a software distribution requires careful thought as to how you would like to install the software. You have many options for pushing out the new update.

- Send the user an e-mail message when new updates are available. The user must have enabled e-mail notification on the Receiving tab of the channel's Properties sheet.

- Download the files containing the new update to a local computer and notify users how to install at their own convenience.

- Automatically install updates on the user's computer, and notify the user of the successful update.

Additional OSD File Elements   OSD files are built upon the same XML specifications upon which CDF files are built. The OSD specification adds additional elements. These elements are detailed below.

NOTE

For more information on OSD and software distribution, visit http://www.microsoft.com/workshop/delivery/sdchannel/reference/software_channels.htm.

CHANNEL HREF   This tag represents the summary page for this channel.

HREF   Notification page that contains instructions and hyperlinks for downloading.

VERSION   Notes the major, minor, build, and custom version number of the update. You must change this with each new update.

AUTOINSTALL   A "Yes" in this field tells the system to update the installation without user intervention. This field overrides the PRECACHE value.

STYLE   Specifies which type of download is appropriate for this update. Two choices are detailed below.

Parameter	Function
MSICD	Uses Microsoft Internet Component Download to download the distribution package and look for instructions in the OSD file
Active Setup	Uses Active Setup to install the package—no OSD file is used

PRECACHE   If this field is set to "Yes," the software update is downloaded to the user's hard disk. A "No" in this field means the update will not be downloaded to the user's hard disk.

USAGE VALUE   Specifies the Web page that is e-mailed to the user if the user has enabled e-mail notification and IE has sensed a change in the subscribed page.

IMPLEMENTATION   Used to separate installations on different platforms and operating systems. You can have multiple instances of this element within the same file to permit downloads for multiple operating systems.

Distributing Custom Components Using Preconfigured Channels

To distribute custom components using software distribution channels, perform the following steps:

1. First you must create the CDF file on the local computer running the IEAK Wizard.

2. Configure the channel as you would expect it on the client browser.

3. Next, subscribe to the channel.

4. When you run the IEAK Wizard on the local machine, you can import the channel settings and distribute them to your users.

Configuring Site Subscriptions

Normally, a user will add a Web site to their favorites list for easy retrieval. They can retrieve the Web page by clicking on the Favorites menu and finding their menu choice. When the content changes, they have the option of downloading content and being notified of the change by e-mail. You can schedule the subscription to be updated hourly, daily, weekly, or monthly. You can also specify to update between certain hours or only on weekdays.

Site subscriptions are very similar to channel subscriptions. However, a channel subscription begins with the download of a CDF file; the site subscription does not require one.

Another difference is that the site subscription can download up to three levels of pages and links, whereas the channel subscription can be very specific about what content will be downloaded.

NOTE
Site subscriptions are located in the user's profile in a directory called `Favorites`.

▶ Configure Outlook Express for custom installations of Internet Explorer 4.0.

You can apply a few customizations to the Outlook Express package. These customizations provide a personal touch to the distribution and provide the organization with opportunities to distribute their branding or identity. This section explains how the IEAK administrator supplies these graphics and other customizations.

InfoPane

The InfoPane is a small, one-inch window (640×50 pixels) at the bottom of the Outlook Express screen that can be used to disseminate information and other links. It displays an HTML file that resides on the local machine (it can be part of the distribution) or points to a Uniform Resource Locator (URL).

Some potential uses for the InfoPane are the posting of company announcements and dissemination of help-desk tips.

Welcome E-Mail

You can also include a custom welcome e-mail in each new user's mailbox. Fill in the HTML filename containing the message in the HTML Path field. Then enter the appropriate Reply-To e-mail address and Sender name.

Signature

The final step in customizing Outlook Express is to include a standard signature. While you cannot include the individual user's name, you might want to include a quote or standard company address for further modification later.

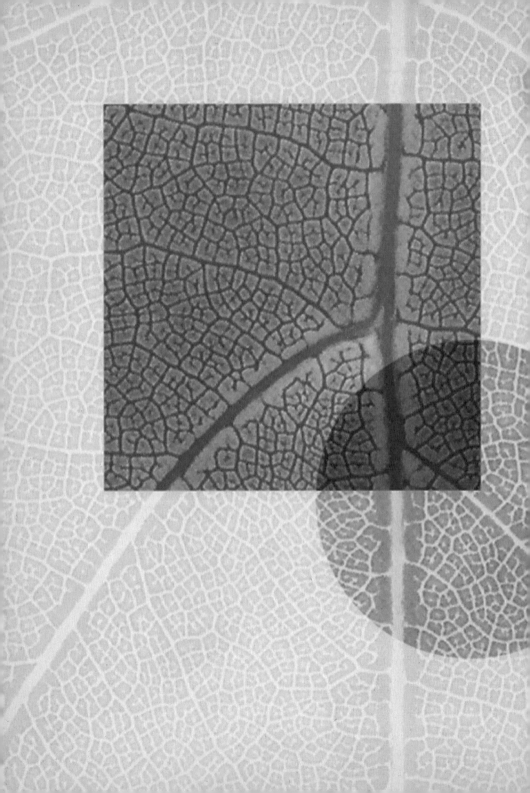

Chapter 26

CONFIGURING AND MANAGING RESOURCE ACCESS

Configuring security is an important responsibility of the IEAK administrator. IE provides several parameters that protect the user from harmful content using security zones and levels. These configurations can be implemented at the time of package creation or later with autoconfiguration.

NOTE

Most of the contents of this chapter refer to the corporate administrator mode of IEAK. This is due to the limitations imposed upon ISPs and ICPs when deliverying Internet Explorer as it pertains to security.

Configuration parameters sometimes change or new and upgraded equipment may become available. Proxy servers may move around, also demanding a change in the IE configuration. These changes to configurations can be tedious if approached through individual workstations. The IEAK Profile Manager is

Adapted from *MCSE Test Success: Internet Explorer 4 Administration Kit* by Allen Jones
ISBN 0-7821-2333-3   416 pages $24.99

the utility that the IEAK administrator uses to make configuration changes on the fly from a centralized location before or after distribution.

▶ Only in corporate administrator mode, create and assign various levels of security for security zones.

If exposed to the Internet, Web browsers can be the most vulnerable part of a network. End users who have become addicted to "point-and-click" can unwittingly introduce malicious programs and other undesirable content into the network. The threat could also come from an intranet as well, so caution here is well warranted.

Fortunately, there are some features built into modern browsers that allow the IEAK administrator to protect their network. Internet Explorer security is composed of two major components: zones and levels.

Security zones, shown in Figure 26.1, are logical groups in which the IEAK administrator can classify Web sites based on the amount of risk that site presents. Trusted local sites can provide programs and other content unhindered, while other less-trusted sites are restricted from supplying potentially dangerous content.

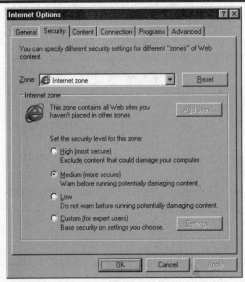

FIGURE 26.1:   Internet Explorer, the Internet zone, and the four security level choices

Security levels determine what each security zone can allow. Based on the IEAK administrator's choices, certain browser features (such as downloading files) can be restricted. By evaluating the available functions and features at each security level, the browser can be modeled to fit a particular security policy.

Security Zones

Four default security zones are supplied with Internet Explorer:

- ▶ Local intranet zone
- ▶ Trusted sites zone
- ▶ Restricted sites zone
- ▶ Internet zone

The IEAK administrator uses these zones to implement security. The proper way to establish the zones is for the IEAK administrator to decide beforehand the best divisions of Internet and intranet Web sites across the four zones.

When grouping sites, you can either add individual Web sites or use wildcards to include many sites. You cannot prevent users from viewing a site or group of sites with security zones (a proxy server or a firewall product can provide this functionality); however, you can limit what these sites can do by placing them in more restrictive zones.

Whenever the browser requests content from a particular site and that site is listed within a zone, the security levels from that zone will apply. You can add sites to any zone except the Internet zone. The security levels of the Internet zone are applied when the requested Web site is not listed in any of the other three zones.

All four zones are described in the following pages, along with their default security level and what is enabled by default.

Local Intranet Zone (Default IE Security Level: Medium) This zone can contain internal Web sites that are not found in any of the three other zones, sites that are not routed through the proxy server, and any UNC (Universal Naming Convention) paths, such as local or network drives. The following are some of the features enabled in this zone.

ActiveX Controls and Plug-ins

▶ Script ActiveX controls marked safe for scripting

▶ Run ActiveX controls and plug-ins

▶ Initialize and script ActiveX controls not marked as safe

▶ Download signed ActiveX controls

User Authentication

▶ Use current logon automatically for user authentication

Downloads

▶ Fonts

▶ Files

Java

▶ Java Permissions (High safety)

Miscellaneous

▶ Set software channel permissions (Medium safety)

▶ Launch applications and files in an <IFRAME>

▶ Install Desktop items

▶ Submit nonencrypted form data

▶ Drag-and-drop, or copy-and-paste, files

Scripting

▶ Allow Active Scripting

▶ Script Java applets

To further decide which intranet sites best fit your security policy, select View ➢ Internet Options and then select the Security tab. Choose Local Intranet Zone from the Zone drop-down list and click the Add Sites button. You can now further refine what constitutes a local intranet site. If you still wish to add or define other sites as intranet sites, click on the Advanced button to add them.

Trusted Sites Zone (Default IE Security Level: Low)   This zone contains Web sites with trustworthy content. Any sites listed here will permit downloading and execution of content without notifying the user. The following are some of the features enabled in this zone.

ActiveX Controls and Plug-ins

▶ Download unsigned ActiveX controls

▶ Script ActiveX controls marked safe for scripting

▶ Initialize and script ActiveX controls not marked as safe

▶ Download signed ActiveX controls

▶ Run ActiveX controls and plug-ins

User Authentication

▶ Use current logon automatically for user authentication

Downloads

▶ Fonts

▶ Files (can be downloaded and installed without user intervention)

Java

▶ Java Permissions (Low safety)

Miscellaneous

▶ Set software channel permissions (Low safety)

▶ Launch applications and files in an <IFRAME>

▶ Install Desktop items

▶ Submit nonencrypted form data

▶ Drag-and-drop, or copy-and-paste, files

Scripting

▶ Allow Active Scripting

▶ Script Java applets

Trusted sites are added by selecting View ≻ Internet Options , selecting the Security tab, and then choosing Trusted Sites Zone from the Zone drop-down list. Click on the Add Sites button. You can now add sites to the zone.

Restricted Sites Zone (Default IE Security Level: High)   This zone contains Web sites with content that you do not trust. Downloading and execution of content is prohibited. The following are some of the features enabled in this zone.

ActiveX Controls and Plug-ins

▶ Script ActiveX controls marked safe for scripting

User Authentication

▶ Prompt for user authentication

Downloads

▶ Files

Java

▶ Java Permissions (High safety)

Miscellaneous

▶ Set software channel permissions (High safety)

▶ Submit nonencrypted form data

▶ Drag-and-drop, or copy-and-paste, files

Scripting

▶ Allow Active Scripting

Restricted sites are added by selecting View ≻ Internet Options, selecting the Security tab, and then choosing Restricted Sites Zone from the Zone drop-down list. Click on the Add Sites button. You can now add sites to the zone.

Internet Zone (Default IE Security Level: Medium)   This site represents all other Web sites that do not currently belong in another zone. Normally, most Web sites will use the security assigned here. For detailed information on what features are available by default to this zone, see the "Local Intranet Zone" section earlier in this unit.

Security Levels

By adding sites to the individual security zones (except the Internet zone), you have the basis for a security model that you can apply to every site covered by the zone. All that is left is to determine the proper security level for each zone. If you are not satisfied with the default security levels applied to the zones, you may alter the level to high, medium, low, or custom. The custom level is one that you can use to permit or deny individual features.

In the custom level, certain features may be disabled, enabled, or simply left to the discretion of the end user. The security levels (high, medium, and low) provided with IE are listed along with their permissions in Table 26.1.

TABLE 26.1: Internet Explorer default security levels and feature setting summary

FEATURE	LOW	MEDIUM	HIGH
ActiveX controls and plug-ins			
Download unsigned ActiveX controls	P	D	D
Script ActiveX controls marked safe for scripting	E	E	E
Initialize and script ActiveX controls not marked as safe	P	P	D
Download signed ActiveX controls	E	P	D
Run ActiveX controls and plug-ins	E	E	D
User Authentication			
Use current logon for user authentication	Auto logon with current username and password	Auto logon only in the intranet zone	Prompt for user name and password
Downloads			
Fonts	E	E	D
Files	E	E	P

TABLE 26.1 continued: Internet Explorer default security levels and feature setting summary

FEATURE	LOW	MEDIUM	HIGH
Java			
Java Permissions (safety)	Low	High	High
Miscellaneous			
Set software channel permissions	Low	Medium	High
Launch applications and files in an <IFRAME>	E	P	D
Install Desktop Items	E	P	D
Submit nonencrypted form data	E	P	P
Drag-and-drop, or copy-and-paste, files	E	E	P
Scripting			
Allow Active Scripting	E	E	E
Script Java applets	E	E	D

Legend : E = Enabled, D = Disabled, P = Prompt User

Most of the features in Table 26.1 are self-explanatory, but a few merit further discussion. For instance, consider the Use Current Logon for User Authentication and Java Permissions options. Both break out further into other levels of permissions and are examined in detail below.

Use Current Logon for User Authentication   In addition to the three settings show in Table 26.1, the IEAK administrator can set user authentication to use an anonymous logon. The following are all the choices available for providing logon credentials to the Web site.

▶ **Anonymous logon**   Attempts to use guest account to log in if needed

▶ **Prompt for user name and password**   Asks end user for logon credentials; caches and continues to use these credentials for the rest of the session

▶ **Automatic logon only in the intranet zone**   Prompts for username and password in all other zones; caches and continues to use these credentials for the rest of the session

▶ **Automatic logon with the current username and password**   Tries current username and password to login; if this fails, prompts for valid username and password, then caches and continues to use these credentials for the rest of the session

Java Permissions   For the most part, the Java safety levels correspond directly to the Internet Explorer security levels. But the IEAK administrator can choose to forgo the default Java security choices and use the Custom level. If you choose this route, you can customize the Java permissions or disable Java completely. All five permissions settings available to Java content are shown below.

▶ **Custom**   Set permissions manually

▶ **Low Safety**   Applets run without hindrance

▶ **Medium Safety**   Applets run in their own memory space and have limited features outside it

▶ **High Safety**   Applets run in their own memory space

▶ **Disable Java**   Disable Java applets from running

Software Channel Permissions   Different choices will enable different security features in IE. When selecting software channel permissions, you must consider the following.

▶ **High Safety**   Disables all of the software distribution channel features

▶ **Medium Safety**   Allows e-mail notification and automatic downloads, but does not allow automatic installation

▶ **Low Safety**   Allows for e-mail notification, automatic downloads, and automatic installation. Note that this setting is required for updates without user intervention.

Certificates

Behind the scenes of Internet Explorer security are digital certificates, which are downloaded from a *publisher* to demonstrate that their code is authentic. The certificate is issued by a *certificate authority*, for example,

VeriSign. Individuals can also be issued certificates, to certify that e-mail sent by them is authentic or to allow them to gain access to a server when positive ID is required. You can distribute your own certificates with your package distribution, as shown in Figure 26.2.

Authenticode   After a publisher has received a digital certificate to show that the code is authentic, the publisher can sign the code to show that the code has not been tampered with.

Internet Explorer, by default, will not allow a user to download unsigned code without first being warned. In addition, Internet Explorer will check to make sure that the digital certificate is authentic and has not been revoked.

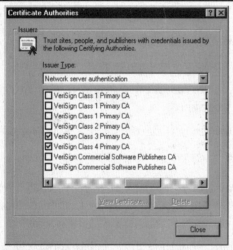

FIGURE 26.2:   Default Certificates Authorities registered with IE at installation. It is not recommended that you remove these certificates.

Impact on Roaming Users

Once you have chosen the appropriate security settings for your browser, you will want to decide who will be able to modify the settings. Users can always decide to alter the settings through the Internet Explorer menu, unless you specifically restrict it. *Roaming users* are those who may use more than one machine and whose common Desktop settings are stored in a centralized and shared location. These users must have their settings (including most IE settings) downloaded at each logon. The IEAK administrator has three choices when considering updates.

- ▶ Restrict user and profile changes

- ▶ Allow profile changes, but restrict user changes

- ▶ Allow both user and profile changes

To alter these settings and lock down the Desktops, use the IEAK Profile Manager to load the INSTALL.INS file, then select System Policies ➤ Restrictions ➤ Internet Restrictions ➤ Security. Note that this type of change will affect anyone who installs the package.

Content Advisor

The Content Advisor is the feature of Internet Explorer that prevents a user from retrieving content deemed inappropriate by the IEAK administrator during configuration. The IEAK administrator can help block access to inappropriate content by restricting availability to Web sites with certain ratings. Internet Explorer employs the PICS (Platform for Internet Content Selection) format of rating Web sites, which was developed by the World Wide Web consortium.

NOTE

For more information regarding PICS and content rating, point your web browser to http://www.w3.org/PICS/.

Web Site Ratings   Internet Explorer uses PICS with an Internet Content Evaluator called the Recreational Software Advisory Council (RSACi), which provides Web site rating information to client browsers. RSACi classifies sites in four areas, each ranked on a scale of 0 to 4 as shown below, with 4 being the most strongly worded caution. Table 26.2 details these ratings.

TABLE 26.2: RSACi method of rating Web site content.

AREA	RATING	DESCRIPTION
Language	0	Inoffensive slang; no profanity
	1	Mild expletives
	2	Moderate expletives
	3	Obscene gestures
	4	Explicit or cruel language

TABLE 26.2 continued: RSACi method of rating Web site content.

AREA	RATING	DESCRIPTION
Nudity	0	None; no nudity
	1	Revealing attire
	2	Partial nudity
	3	Frontal nudity
	4	Provocative frontal nudity
Sex	0	No sexual activity or romance
	1	Passionate kissing
	2	Clothed sexual touching
	3	Nonexplicit sexual touching
	4	Explicit sexual activity
Violence	0	No violence
	1	Fighting
	2	Killing
	3	Killing with blood and gore
	4	Gratuitous violence

NOTE

For more information regarding the RSACi method of content rating, point your web browser to http://www.rsac.org/ratingsv01.html.

Using Content Advisor   When setting up Web site restrictions with the Content Advisor, you as an IEAK administrator must decide what the user will be allowed to see, based on the ratings shown in Table 26.2. You can find the Content Advisor by selecting Internet Options from the View menu, and clicking the Content tab.

In the corporate administrator mode, during Stage Four, you will have an opportunity to assign default security modes and set other security options. You can use the IEAK Wizard to change content restrictions in your distribution before the package is created. Or, alternately, you can set restrictions later using the IEAK Profile Manager and autoconfiguration. See Figure 26.3.

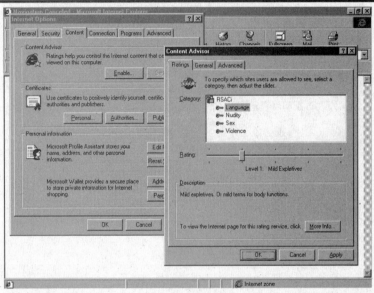

FIGURE 26.3: Changing the rating inside a category as specified by the Content Advisor. Moving the slider adjusts the permissible content.

Web Sites with No Rating   With Internet content so flexible and changing so rapidly, it is nearly impossible to classify or catalog it all. It is also impractical for all Web sites to be rated by the same rating service. If you take away users' ability to view unrated Web sites (see Figure 26.4), you may inadvertently prevent them from viewing useful content. This may cause unnecessary frustration for the users. When setting up the Content Advisor, a supervisor password is entered. This password can be used to temporarily bypass the restrictions and load the content.

Test your security configuration thoroughly prior to the distribution.

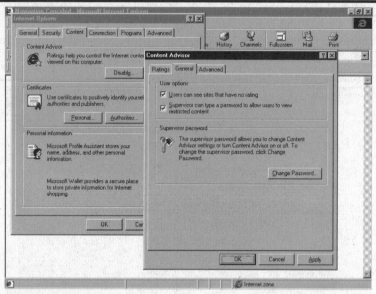

FIGURE 26.4: Preventing users from viewing unrated content may create problems for end users.

▶ In corporate administrator mode, manage proxy server support for custom installations of Internet Explorer 4.0.

With the spread of harmful content across the Internet, many organizations have begun to rely on the protection provided by firewalls and similar software products. Proxy servers can afford some of that protection.

As new proxy servers are brought online, security policies change, and connections to the wide-area network (WAN) improve, changes will have to be made to the browser's proxy configuration.

It would be impractical to require end users to change these proxy settings. Therefore, it is important to maintain a centralized proxy configuration that can be shared by all browsers and updated by the IEAK administrator.

What Is a Proxy Server?

A *proxy server* is a hardware- or software-based product that acts as a gatekeeper. It prevents unwanted content from the outside world (usually the WAN) from reaching the local-area network (LAN) and unnecessary internal LAN content from reaching the WAN. The proxy server actually has simultaneous network connections to both the LAN and the WAN on different network devices. It provides valuable security features and subtle performance improvements to the LAN side of the network (using web page caching; see performance features below).

While a software-based product cannot afford the same level of protection that hardware-based firewalls can, any such protection is better than none at all.

Security Features   The security features of proxy servers usually consist of one or more of the following.

- ▶ **Packet filtering**   Determines which types of traffic to permit in or out of the network

- ▶ **Masking**   Hides the true internal network addresses of your hosts from the external network.

- ▶ **Alerts**   Whenever an attempt to bypass the proxy is detected, the event can be logged. Some third-party products can page you if an attempt is detected.

Performance Features   Small performance improvements are sometimes available with proxy servers. They include the following.

- ▶ **Caching of frequently used content**   Most frequently and most recently downloaded content (such as Web pages and files acquired through FTP) are cached, making download times improve for the next user who requests it. This feature is usually quite hardware-intensive, requiring large amounts of disk space.

- ▶ **Support for multiple protocols**   This feature permits the use of other protocols (such as IPX with the standard Internet protocol) without modifying the client protocol stacks.

Autoproxy Files

IEAK supports the use of autoproxy files, which are written using JScript. These files are usually located in a common, centralized area and can be edited with any text editor.

The autoproxy file shown below, an example of the `isPlainHost-Name()` function, will test the host name passed to it. If the host name contains no dots ('.') in the address, as would a destination of a server found on the local intranet, then the browser is instructed to connect directly to the host. Otherwise, the browser is instructed to pass the request on to a proxy server named BIGPROXY on port 80.

```
function FindProxyForURL(url, host) {
    if (isPlainHostName(host))
    return "DIRECT";
    else return "PROXY BIGPROXY:80";
}
```

The following example of the isResolvable() function shows an auto-proxy script that will first try to resolve the host name. If it fails to resolve the name, then the request is passed to the proxy server BIGPROXY on port 80. If it successfully resolves the name, then it will instruct the browser to connect to the host using a direct connection.

```
function FindProxyForURL(url, host) {
    if (isResolvable(host))
    return "DIRECT";
    else return "PROXY BIGPROXY:80";
}
```

You can find many other examples of autoproxy files in IEAK Help, under the heading "JavaScript or JScript Auto-Proxy Example Files."

Proxy and Security Management Methods

If there are browsers that have already been distributed, and autoconfiguration is a requirement, then you can still require existing IE client browsers to use autoconfiguration. To require a previously-installed browser to begin using autoconfiguration, perform the following steps:

1. To require a previously-installed browser to begin using auto-configuration, click View ➤ Internet Options.

2. Select the Connection tab and look for the Automatic Configuration section.

3. Click the Configure button. You will be asked to provide the URL pointing to the autoconfigure INS file.

4. To require new packages to use autoconfiguration, specify the proper autoconfigure URL in the Automatic Browser Configuration screen.

5. To make changes happen immediately, click Refresh; otherwise, autoconfiguration will begin the next time you start the browser.

6. From that point on, the browser will follow the autoconfigure value specified in the Automatic Browser Configuration screen. This value is expressed in minutes. If the autoconfigure value is set to zero, the browser will check for new updates every time the browser is started.

▶ Manage automatic configuration by using the IEAK Profile Manager. Methods include:

- ▶ JScript autoproxy
- ▶ .INS files
- ▶ .ADM files

The IEAK administrator will use the IEAK Profile Manager after the IE distribution is complete to keep the installation up to date with the most current configurations. Companies sometimes change policies or relocate equipment. These types of changes are easy to manage with the IEAK Profile Manager.

WARNING

It is extremely important that any proposed changes to an installation are thoroughly tested in a protected test environment before they are dispatched to the rest of your users. By testing and implementing strict "change control" procedures to your environment, you will be able to cut down on the number of support calls you receive.

In short, autoconfiguration can save hours of configuration time in medium to large enterprises. It allows you to update a centralized configuration file on a shared network point rather than updating individual workstations.

JScript Autoproxy Files

Autoproxy files are small, dynamic text files that allow IE to quickly configure its own proxy client to point to the correct proxy server and satisfy a particular client request. There can be multiple proxy servers configured at once, allowing the proper proxy server to be selected depending on the destination.

You can also use the autoproxy files to block a domain or domain name. The JScript file usually sits on a Web server and can be retrieved at any time. The interval at which the autoproxy file (. INS file, . JS file, or . PAC file) is re-read is called the *Autoconfigure interval*.

IEAK Profile Manager

After you have successfully completed a distribution, you can manage the installation by using the IEAK Profile Manager. When you started the IEAK Wizard and named the directory where the distribution was to be built, a file was created called INSTALL . INS. Each time that you ran the IEAK Wizard, all of your choices during package creation were stored in that file.

After modifying the distribution, you can simply run IEAK Profile Manager and make your changes. The resulting . INS file is updated with your changes (and the package is updated as well). When clients' auto-configure values expire, the autoconfigure URL that you specified in the Automatic Browser Configuration screen will be re-examined for changes.

. INS Files   These files represent choices made using the IEAK Wizard and may also represent updates made with the IEAK Profile Manager. In the IEAK Profile Manager, you can update the . INS file by highlighting any of the pages under the Wizard Settings section.

. ADM Files   System policies provide strict control for user environments and software programs. Even though you can configure many options with the IEAK, you must depend on system policies to prevent end users from altering those configurations.

The IEAK Profile Manager provides system policy support to several IE add-on programs including the following.

- ▶ Microsoft Chat
- ▶ Microsoft NetMeeting
- ▶ Outlook Express

You can also configure system policies in your own bundled programs by telling the IEAK Profile Manager where to find the . ADM file for the custom program. Once you've updated the IEAK Profile Manager, you will be able to update the system policies.

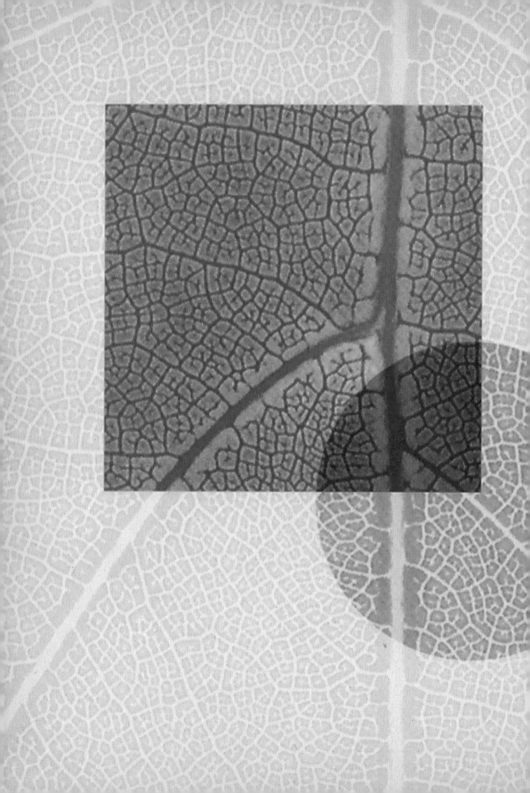

Chapter 27

INTEGRATION AND INTEROPERABILITY

After you've gone through the painstaking effort of developing and thoroughly testing your package, it is time to distribute the package to the masses. Distribution decisions are important and have wide-reaching effects. Method, time of day, and WAN connections all play an important part in the decision-making process.

Other decisions to be made include the upgrading and importing of valuable data including e-mail and newsgroups. Many people heavily depend on e-mail and cannot afford to lose weeks or months of historical electronic "paper trails."

This unit also covers the configuration of NetMeeting, including the ability to share applications and conduct video conferences.

Adapted from *MCSE Test Success: Internet Explorer 4 Administration Kit* by Allen Jones
ISBN 0-7821-2333-3   416 pages $24.99

▶ # In corporate administrator mode or Internet service provider mode, deploy a preconfigured version of Internet Explorer 4.0 by using the IEAK. Distribution methods include:

- ▶ Download
- ▶ CD-ROM
- ▶ Floppy disk

Deciding the best mode for delivering your package may be difficult or easy, based on your environment. Depending on your autoconfiguration choices, this may not be a one-time process, but an ongoing process to keep the latest components on the Desktop. Each of these factors affects the deployment decision.

IEAK gives you the choice of installing from several different sources—most common is the distribution by download. Moving the installable files to a common point for downloading either by Web site or by UNC is a very common practice. The IEAK administrator can also distribute by CD-ROM or multiple floppy disks. If the IEAK administrator chose the Internet service provider mode, they have the additional option of a single floppy disk for mailing. Each of these options is listed for you in Table 27.1.

TABLE 27.1: Available Distribution Options Based on the Organizational Mode Chosen

MODE	CD-ROM	MULTIPLE FLOPPY DISKS	SINGLE FLOPPY DISK
Internet Content Provider/Developer	X	X	
Corporate Administrator	X	X	
Internet Service Provider	X	X	X

You can choose which methods to use to distribute just after entering the correct customization code in the IEAK Wizard. The IEAK Wizard asked you during Stage One where you would like to place the installable files.

Corporate Administrator Mode/Internet Content Provider

The corporate administrator mode and the Internet content provider mode can distribute the installable files (called installables) by CD-ROM, by download, or by multiple floppy disks. The download method is the most popular, which requires very little assistance from the end user.

Internet Service Provider Mode

The Internet service provider mode can distribute the installables by CD-ROM or by multiple floppy disks. However, in this mode, you also have the option of downloading as in corporate administrator mode, but with a twist.

Since many ISPs are not reachable by network drive, as are many corporate installations, ISPs have the option of placing the Active Setup files on a single floppy disk. This single floppy disk contains everything needed to begin the installation, including the necessary portions of the Internet Connection Wizard to complete the modem connection.

Authenticode Technology

Before you can distribute your package to your users, you must take a few steps to assure your users that the package is indeed coming from you. The method of identifying the code as authentic is called *signing*. Signing is equivalent to bundling a package and shrink-wrapping it to show that no tampering has taken place. The default security model of IE will recognize *unsigned* code and warn the user before executing it.

Before you can sign code, you must go through an approval and validation process. You—the IEAK admin—must get a digital ID to sign your package before you can sign and distribute it. You will need to sign several files, each of which are detailed for you in this section.

Getting a Digital ID   You can purchase an inexpensive digital ID from a certificate authority, such as VeriSign. This will positively identify your code to the rest of your users. Depending on the type of ID that you purchase, you will need to provide some personal information to get your ID.

For instance, with an individual software publisher ID, VeriSign will compare the personal information you provide with a national consumer database, such as Equifax, before issuing the ID. This usually takes only a couple of minutes.

If you apply for a commercial software publisher ID, VeriSign will compare the business information you provide with several sources, such as directory information and financial information services, before issuing the digital ID. This could take a few days.

The ID consists of two parts. The first part is the Software Publishing Certificate (SPC) file, which contains the actual digital ID, or certificate. You can retrieve it across the Internet from VeriSign upon approval.

The second part is generated by your browser during the registration process—it creates a Private Key (PVK) file. The PVK file should be stored on a floppy diskette and kept in a secure location. It contains a password needed to use the certificate. Each time that you sign code, you will be asked for the password. If the key is lost or stolen, you should contact VeriSign to revoke your certificate and have the certificate replaced.

Depending on whom you use to generate your digital ID, somewhere during the process you will install the digital key into your browser, and then you will become a trusted publisher.

The end result of all of the checking, certificates, and authorizations is to be able to assure the user that the code they are about to download is still intact as the publisher intended. These IDs do not encrypt the information—they merely provide an electronic shrink-wrap to show that the software is still intact, packaged as intended, and unmodified.

Issuing Your Own Digital IDs   There are other sources from which to get a digital ID. Microsoft publishes a Certificate Server with the Windows NT Option Pack. This server is capable of acting as a Root Certificate Authority or participating in an existing Certificate Authority hierarchy. In either case, you can issue, revoke, and renew internal certificates for use within your own organization without having to purchase certificates from a third party.

Issuing your own certificates substantially increases the IEAK administrator's workload and is not usually practical unless certificates are already in use with other products such as Microsoft Exchange or Internet Information Server.

Signing the Files   After you have received your digital ID and have installed it, you can sign your distribution. You will use the SIGNCODE .EXE utility to sign the files. Table 27.2 details some of the usage parameters of this utility.

TABLE 27.2: Usage Parameters of the SIGNCODE.EXE Utility

SWITCH	DESCRIPTION
-v	PVK file containing the private key
-spc	SPC file containing software publishing certificates
-t	TimeStamp server's http address (optional)

The following listing is an example of SIGNCODE.EXE used to sign a 32-bit executable.

```
J:\CIE\DOWNLOAD\WIN95_NT\EN>signcode -v A:\pk.pvk -spc
A:\cred.spc -t
http://timestamp.verisign.com/scripts/timstamp.dll
ie4setup.exe
```

If the signing process was successful, you will see this message:

```
Succeeded
```

When you download this newly signed executable from a Web site, you will see something similar to Figure 27.1.

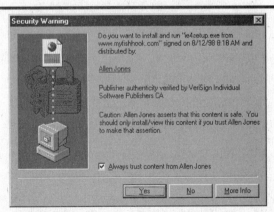

FIGURE 27.1: Example of a properly signed executable once it is downloaded. This was generated using an Individual Software Publishers certificate.

Determining Which Files to Sign   You don't have to sign every file in a distribution, but you should sign 32-bit executables, CAB files, DLL files, and OCX files. Here is a list of IE distribution files that you should sign just prior to distribution (the files may or may not exist, depending on the type of distribution):

- ► BRANDING.CAB

- ► DESKTOP.CAB

- ► IE40CIF.CAB

- ► IE4SETUP.EXE

- ► FOLDERx.CAB, where x could be any numeric character

- ► CHLxxx.CAB, where xxx could be any alphanumeric characters

Distribution Methods

Once you have successfully created the package for the distribution and signed the necessary components, it is time to move your installables to their new home on the Web site. After package creation, your file structure may look similar to Figure 27.2.

FIGURE 27.2:   Directory structure just after package creation

Download   Download sites for IE are created in two parts. In the default directory that you specified as the destination for your package, you will find two important directories, DOWNLOAD and IE4SITE. These directories contain everything you need to finish your download site.

> **Moving the Files**   When using the default IE security settings, users will be warned if they attempt to download and execute unsigned code. This usually falls under the Internet security zone, which is by default set to Medium security. To prevent these warnings, be sure to sign the appropriate installation files using a valid digital ID.

To establish a download site for your package, perform the following steps:

1. Move the `IE4SITES.DAT` file from the `IE4SITE` folder to the directory of a Web site you specified in Stage Three.

2. You will also want to move the subdirectory of the language you are building the package for into the above-named directory. For instance, if you are building in English, the subdirectory will be called EN.

3. If you specified more than one download site in the IEAK Wizard as being available, you will have to repeat these steps for each site. If you are in the corporate administrator mode and chose to do a silent installation in the IEAK Wizard, you will have only one site available from which to download. Otherwise, you may have up to 10 sites from which to download.

Finishing Touches   To summarize, the root of your Web-based installation site should contain the `IE4SITES.DAT` file and the appropriate language subdirectory. From this point, you can distribute the `IE4SETUP.EXE` file found in the DOWN-LOAD subdirectory as necessary. Once loaded, it will attempt to connect to the newly established download site and retrieve files. This file contains the installation engine and everything needed to finish the installation.

This type of installation is best suited when bandwidth is not an issue or when add-on components may change frequently. It is easy to change installations using this method.

CD-ROM   CD-ROM installations are a bit different than download installations. You do not necessarily need to have your code signed when installing software from a CD. Perform the following steps:

1. All that is necessary is to move the appropriate directory to the root of the CD-ROM drive.

2. At the root of the CD directory, you will find a file called `AUTORUN.INF`, which is used to autostart the CD at the time of insertion.

3. This directory should be the root of your CD-ROM. If you copy this directory and all subdirectories to your CD-ROM,

you will have a CD-ROM installation of your package that is capable of starting as soon as the CD is inserted.

This type of installation is best suited when distribution over the network is not feasible. Limited network bandwidth, slow WAN links, or other hindrances might make the CD-ROM installation more attractive.

Floppy Disk   A single or multiple floppy disk installation is also available. In certain cases, some older, legacy equipment may not have a CD-ROM drive. You can utilize either a single floppy disk or multiple floppy disks, depending on your needs.

Single Floppy Disk   A single floppy disk can be used in conjunction with the download site to retrieve and install Internet Explorer. The single floppy disk option is available only in the Internet service provider mode. It is intended to make the task of installing Internet Explorer as easy as inserting the floppy disk and starting a single program.

1. To create the single floppy, look in the content of FLOPPY\WIN95_NT.

2. You will find a subdirectory appropriate for the language that you are creating, such as EN for English.

3. Copy the contents of that directory to a floppy disk.

4. This floppy now contains everything needed to begin the installation.

5. When the user starts the IE4SETUP.EXE file, a version of the Internet Connection Wizard will establish a connection to the download server that you have provided and begin the installation.

Multiple Floppy Disks   In some cases, you may wish to create a set of floppy disks with which to install Internet Explorer. These might be used in extreme cases, where a CD-ROM and a network connection are unavailable.

1. Look in the subdirectory called MFLOPPY for the necessary installation files.

2. Note that the structure consists of Disk1, Disk2, and so on.

3. Make sure that the contents from each directory are copied to each appropriate disk.

▶ # Replace other Internet browsers. Other browsers include:

- ▶ Microsoft Internet Explorer 3.*x*
- ▶ Netscape Navigator

To make the user's first experience with Internet Explorer 4 a positive one, one of your goals should be to make the transition seamless. This includes taking into account what browser the user is currently using.

Microsoft Internet Explorer 3.*x*

Internet Explorer 4 will install directly on top of existing 3.*x* installations. During installation, proxy settings, favorites, and cookies will be retained with the new version. Any plug-ins that were installed in 3.*x* will need to be reinstalled. You may be able to distribute those plug-ins within a package. Explorer 3.*x* and 4.*x* cannot coexist on the same machine unless in a dual-boot environment (two segregated operating systems on different disk drives on the same machine).

Netscape Navigator

Internet Explorer 4 will also migrate the same proxy settings, bookmarks, and cookies from Netscape 3. Plug-ins will have to be reinstalled or distributed with a package. Navigator and Explorer can coexist on the same machine.

▶ # Replace other Internet mail clients. Other mail clients include:

- ▶ Internet Mail and News
- ▶ Netscape Mail
- ▶ Eudora

Many users today consider their e-mail to be the most business-critical application found on their computer. To damage or otherwise remove weeks and months of historical information will cause a lot of users grief and unhappiness, and make them unproductive. Properly migrating mail from an application to Outlook Express will certainly be a large critical-success factor in your distribution.

Outlook Express can migrate mail from several sources. In this section, we will examine the upgrade procedure for three sources: Internet Mail and News, Netscape Mail, and Eudora.

Internet Mail and News

Internet Mail and News was a Microsoft SMTP/POP3/NNTP client that was integrated as a component into Microsoft products, most notably Internet Explorer 3. Internet Mail and News has evolved into Outlook Express, which is now IE's default client for Internet e-mail and newsgroups.

Outlook Express can directly migrate the address book and e-mail from existing Internet Mail and News clients.

Netscape Mail

Outlook Express can migrate address books and existing e-mail from Netscape Mail, which is part of Netscape Navigator. While Outlook Express can migrate many other versions and other packages besides Navigator, we will concentrate just on Navigator. Perform the following steps:

1. Begin by importing Address Books. Outlook Express can import address books from Netscape Mail. In Outlook Express, select File ➤ Import ➤ Address Book, then select Netscape Address Book from the list.

2. Follow the steps as required by the wizard to complete the import of the address book.

3. Existing e-mail from Navigator can also be imported. In Outlook Express, select File ➤ Import ➤ Messages, then choose Netscape Mail from the window and click Next.

4. If the default Netscape folder contains mail, you can choose this folder from which to import mail. If not, select the proper Navigator mail directory.

5. Next, choose the folders that you wish to import. The default is to import all folders.

6. Once you have specified the folders you wish to import, click on Finish to complete the import. The migration of e-mail is now complete.

Eudora

Qualcomm's Eudora is another popular e-mail product that may need to be migrated. Just as in Netscape's case, several different versions of Eudora are in use today. We will concentrate on Eudora versions 3 and below.

1. Outlook Express can import address books from Eudora. In Outlook Express, select File ➢ Import ➢ Address Book, then select Eudora Pro or Light Address Book from the list.

2. The import will begin immediately. Dialog boxes will pop up with any import problems along the way, such as duplicated addresses.

3. Once the address book import is complete, you receive a message similar to Figure 27.3.

4. Existing e-mail from Eudora can also be imported. Simply choose Eudora as the program you wish to import from.

5. If the folders were found in their default location, the directory will be filled in for you. Otherwise, pick the location of the folders.

6. Next, choose the folders that you wish to import.

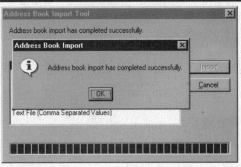

FIGURE 27.3: The address book import is complete.

7. Once you have specified the folders you wish to import, click on Finish to complete the import. The migration is complete.

▶ Configure NetMeeting for various tasks. Tasks include:

- ▶ Multi-point application sharing
- ▶ Transferring files
- ▶ Video conferencing

To properly deploy and use NetMeeting, it is important to properly configure the package. While some of the macro-level configuration can be accomplished with the IEAK Profile Manager, most of the micro-level configurations will take place on the Desktop.

General Configuration Options

Most NetMeeting configuration options are available from the Tools ➤ Options window (as shown in Figure 27.4). Each tab under this window will be covered in this section.

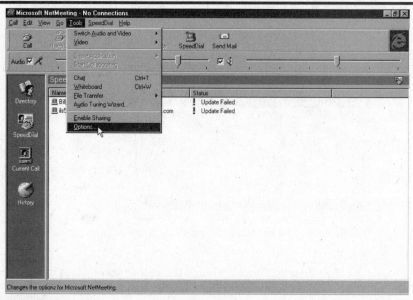

FIGURE 27.4: Most of the configuration options are available from the Tools ➤ Options window.

General   There are six tabs on the Options window. The first tab, General, contains several options.

Each option under this tab is explained below.

- ▶ **Show Microsoft NetMeeting Icon on the Taskbar**   Determines whether the NetMeeting icon appears on the Taskbar, located in the lower-right corner of the workspace. Default: Yes.

- ▶ **Run When Windows Starts and Notify Me of Incoming Calls**   Automatically starts NetMeeting when the computer starts and listens for incoming calls. Default: Yes.

- ▶ **Automatically Accept Incoming Calls**   Automatically accepts incoming calls from another party. Default: No.

- ▶ **Show the SpeedDial Tab When NetMeeting Starts**   When NetMeeting starts, the SpeedDial list is loaded rather than the default directory. The SpeedDial list is similar to a contact list or address book, containing frequently used names that the end user keeps current.

- ▶ **Show Intel Connection Advisor Icon on the Taskbar**   The Intel Connection Advisor reports statistics concerning the multimedia properties of the connection, such as audio and video loss rate, processor usage, and average delay rate.

You can also set NetMeeting to sample audio and video at a rate appropriate for the current connection to the Internet. For instance, if the user will be dialing in through a 28.8K modem, the "Network Bandwidth" value should be set to 28800 bps or Faster Modem. If the user is connected directly to the network, but is limited by an outgoing ISDN line to the Internet, the slower of the two connections should be chosen.

Finally, you can choose the destination of any files that you will be receiving. You can click on either View Files to load Explorer in the current directory or Change Folder to select an appropriate folder.

My Information   On this tab, you should enter personal information to be displayed by the directory server. You can enter information such as your first and last name, e-mail address, city and state, country, and optionally a few comments to be displayed in the directory entry.

You can also categorize your personal information as being for personal, business, or adult-only use.

Calling   On this tab, you can choose the default operation by the directory server at logon, whether you log on immediately, and to which server you log on. You can also select to log in to the directory server, but not publicly list your name in the directory server.

You can choose to have those who call you and those whom you call to automatically be added into the SpeedDial list. You can also choose the frequency of the SpeedDial updates.

Audio   The Audio tab contains the controls for the audio portion of NetMeeting. The Tuning Wizard assists in setting the speaker volume and microphone sensitivity levels.

If you have an H.323 gateway available, you can use NetMeeting to place a call to a regular telephone through the H.323 gateway. This is just one adaptation of a new technology called Voice over IP. While not quite a widespread industry standard yet, H.323 is gaining popularity as available bandwidth increases.

Video   On this tab, you can set the options involving the video portion of NetMeeting. You can set when to begin the sending or receiving of video, the image size, or the video priority—in other words, which is more important: slower, choppier images that are better in quality or faster, grainier images that are smoother in delivery. You can also alter the video capture device's properties.

Protocols   The last tab of the Options window allows you to select which protocol to use with NetMeeting. Choosing the correct protocol is important. Some protocols do not support all NetMeeting features. For instance, if you wish to use audio conferencing, you must use the TCP/IP protocol. The null modem and IPX/SPX protocols do not support this feature.

Multi-Point Application Sharing

Application sharing is one of NetMeeting's strong points. Any Windows-based application may be shared with conference participants. Only the person sharing the application needs to have the application installed. This host can also grant permission to conference participants to use the application remotely. Figure 27.5 demonstrates a conference that is sharing an application.

If the user shares the Program Manager application, the Desktop is effectively shared. Any program started with the shared Desktop will be available to the conference participants for collaboration. Users must exercise caution when sharing the Desktop because this can give complete control of the Desktop to the other user.

Transferring Files

During the conference, files can be shared among conference participants. The files can be transferred in the background as the conference continues. You can transfer files to several conference participants.

Video Conferencing

Video is the most exciting part of NetMeeting—it enables two users to conduct a video conference. If you need to broadcast images to multiple participants, you may need to investigate the capabilities of NetShow.

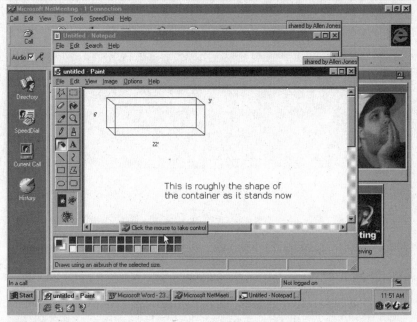

FIGURE 27.5: Application sharing using NetMeeting. Conference participants can see whatever the host sees and even contribute. Note that only one person at a time can control the application.

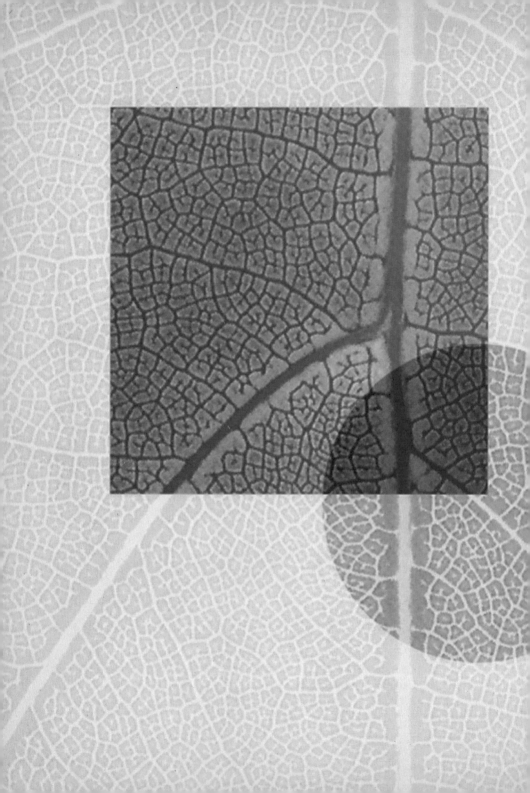

Chapter 28

MONITORING AND OPTIMIZATION

I n years past, users chose a pleasing background photo and
grew used to seeing such images as their family, favorite
pets, or favorite vacation spot, or just left the background
blank altogether. Internet Explorer allows users and administrators to use this otherwise unutilized space to communicate
dynamic information to the user.

In this unit, we turn our attention to this space and the
development and deployment of Active Content, comprising
Active Channels and site subscriptions. They both fit into a
much larger picture, the Active Desktop.

We also spend time on maximizing network resources and
the efficiency of the browser. We examine the best use and configuration of the caching abilities of Internet Explorer.

Adapted from *MCSE Test Success: Internet Explorer 4
Administration Kit* by Allen Jones
ISBN 0-7821-2333-3   416 pages $24.99

Customize Active Desktop items and Active Channels.

The Active Desktop is a method of distributing information and content to users' Desktops in a common and organized fashion, using HTML. Active Desktop turns the user's Desktop into a live workspace, taking advantage of the Desktop background and adding content to new foreground windows called Desktop items.

> **NOTE**
>
> The Active Desktop is available only if the Windows Desktop Update has been installed and is in use. You must also have selected View as Web Page under Start ➤ Settings ➤ Active Desktop.

The Active Desktop is divided into two layers, the Icon layer and the HTML layer. We will concentrate on customizing both in this section. We will also cover the customization of Active Channels.

Icon Layer

The Icon layer is the top layer that represents the shortcuts that are available on the Desktop and includes such default icons as My Computer, Network Neighborhood, and Recycle Bin. This layer can be customized several ways, including manual updates by end users, system policies, and user profiles.

End users can create new shortcuts on the Desktop by dragging and dropping a new icon on the Desktop or right-clicking on the Desktop and selecting New.

System policies can specify that the user's Desktop be replaced with a Desktop previously chosen by an administrator. By setting the appropriate permissions on the Desktop, the Desktop can be altered only by those who hold the proper permissions. This can supplement or replace the traditional roaming or mandatory user profile.

User profiles can also contain shortcuts and icons. In the case of roaming profiles, administrators can easily update the Desktop by updating the profile.

HTML Layer

The HTML layer is controlled by a single HTML page that is created and edited solely by Internet Explorer. The file is called DESKTOP.HTM and is located in the directory (replace the environment variables as appropriate to your system) *SYSTEMROOT*\Profile*USERNAME*\Application Data\Microsoft\Internet Explorer. This file contains the Desktop wallpaper and any Desktop items that will be displayed.

Viewing the Desktop as a Web Page   You can add any static HTML page that you wish to make a background page for the Desktop to the HTML layer by performing the following steps:

1.   While on the Desktop, right-click.

2.   Select Properties.

3.   Click the Background tab.

4.   From this window, you can change your Desktop's background and set it to any page available on your local machine or your intranet.

Desktop Items   A Desktop item is an instance of an HTML document or an image that sits on the Desktop. It can also be an ActiveX control. Desktop items are located in the HTML layer and are "floating" items—they always sit atop the background and just below the Icon layer.

Desktop items do not usually have navigational controls (though they have slider bars if the content is larger than the window), and they can point to any content source, whether it be on the intranet or Internet. They are resizable to fit the user's preference.

Desktop items are designed to convey dynamic information to users. They can contain routine, static Web pages or the more dynamic Active Channels. For instance, if an oil company wanted all of its employees to know the latest crude oil price, an Active Channel could be developed to display the very latest pricing information using a Desktop item without user intervention. For an example of Active Desktop items, notice the investment ticker on the Active Desktop shown in Figure 28.1.

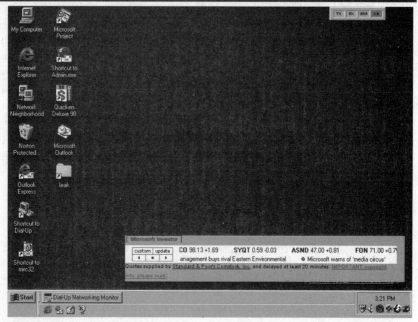

FIGURE 28.1:   An example of Active Desktop items on a Desktop with the Windows Desktop Update installed

Active Channels

In previous units, we've talked about subscribing to content—that is, downloading pages and pages of material for occasional perusal later. We've also talked about using Active Channels and CDF files to selectively pick the content we wish to see. This section touches on some examples of creating Active Channels to fit the user's needs.

An Active Channel is best described as a Web site or set of pages that have been grouped together for downloading on a predefined schedule. The group and schedule is set by a Channel Definition Format (CDF) file, which is downloaded by the user or distributed with the browser.

NOTE

CDF files are implemented by browsing to a CDF file—the Subscription Wizard then takes over, querying the user about subscription preferences. CDF files can also be distributed ahead of time with a browser to provide the functionality right out of the box.

Since we have covered the elements of a CDF file, let's concentrate on how we can use Active Channels to solve various business problems.

Delivery of Updated Content   We stated earlier in this unit that Active Desktop components were a good way to quickly distribute time-sensitive information to the Desktop. What if the information could not completely fit in the Active Desktop's small floating window? What if the contents were on multiple pages in the midst of thousands of other pages of data? We are now left with just two choices, the Web site subscription and the Active Channel.

Example

Real Estate Brokerage needs to update their current listings on each agent's Desktop. Three pages need to be distributed, containing the current listings, pending sales, and sold homes. Each page could have over 20–30 links to different homes, and the pages may change 8 or 10 times per day. Network traffic must be minimized.

In this example, a Web site subscription could be impractical. A site subscription could potentially download much more data than what is necessary and can take up too much bandwidth.

An Active Channel will work best here because the CDF file can be tailored to download only those three pages of data. Each page would contain the links for each house and maybe a thumbnail photo for each. The brokers can click on homes in which they are interested. The site can keep individual pages with larger photos for each home. You can set up the CDF file for a recommended subscription for your users.

```
<CHANNEL
HREF="http://www.myfishhook.com/homeschannelpage.htm">

<TITLE>The Fishhook Homesellers Network</TITLE>

<ABSTRACT>The Fishhook Homesellers Network is a private net-
work for real estate agents to display their homes for sale.
Homes which have a contract pending are listed on a different
page. Recently sold homes have their own page, too.
</ABSTRACT>

<SCHEDULE STARTDATE="1998-08-25">

<INTERVALTIME HOUR="1" />
<EARLIESTTIME HOUR="06" />
<LATESTTIME HOUR="18" />
</SCHEDULE>
```

```
<LOGO HREF="http://www.myfishhook.com/images/home.gif"
STYLE="image" />
<LOGO HREF="http://www.myfishhook.com/images/homeicon.ico"
STYLE="icon"/>

<LOGO HREF="http://www.myfishhook.com/images/homewideicon.gif
STYLE="image-wide">

<ITEM HREF="http://www.myfishhook.com/homes/forsale.htm"
PRECACHE="yes">

<ABSTRACT>Current Listings - All the homes we have for sale
in this big city</ABSTRACT>

<TITLE>Current Listings</TITLE>

</ITEM>

<ITEM HREF="http://www.myfishhook.com/homes/pending.htm"
PRECACHE="yes">

<ABSTRACT>Pending Listings - All the homes we have for sale
which have a contract pending at this time.</ABSTRACT>

<TITLE>Pending Listings</TITLE>

</ITEM>

<ITEM HREF="http://www.myfishhook.com/homes/sold.htm"
PRECACHE="yes">

<ABSTRACT>Sold Listings - All the homes we have for sale
which recently sold.</ABSTRACT>

<TITLE>Sold Listings</TITLE>

</ITEM>

</CHANNEL>
```

With this particular CDF file, all three pages will be cached to each agent's disk for offline viewing starting on August 25, 1998, and update the user's Desktop hourly every day between 6 A.M. and 6 P.M.

Screensavers   A screensaver is yet another element that can be specified in a CDF file and have the information cached. The screensaver will appear (if properly configured in the Desktop Properties) when instructed by the operating system.

Users can navigate through pages within the screensaver; however, if an external link is clicked, the screensaver closes, the Desktop is returned to its previous state, and a new browser instance is opened and directed to that external link. Here is a portion of a sample CDF file.

```
<ITEM HREF="http://www.myfishhook.com/homes/hotlistings.htm"
PRECACHE="yes">
<ABSTRACT>Hot Listings! - These are the homes which we think
are priced attractively.</ABSTRACT>
<TITLE>Hot Listings</TITLE>
<USAGE VALUE="ScreenSaver"></USAGE>
</ITEM>
```

▶ Use the IEAK Profile Manager to optimize network resources and components.

In the previous section, we discussed the practical application of Active Content. This section discusses the optimization of network resources for the Desktop and any selected components. It will show you how to use the IEAK Profile Manager to approach optimal performance for the Desktop you have created. We finish this section by summarizing how to lock down the Desktop to prevent future changes by end users.

WARNING

It is extremely important that any proposed changes to an installation be thoroughly tested in a protected test environment before being dispatched to the rest of your users. By testing and implementing strict change-control procedures to your environment, you will be able to cut down on the number of trouble calls you receive.

The actual value or benefit of these options is relative to your existing network, and should be evaluated and tested individually. Each topic heading in this section corresponds with a subcategory of the System Policies and Restrictions in the IEAK Profile Manager.

Each of these features can be enabled or disabled prior to distribution. For browsers that have already been distributed, the use of autoconfiguration is required and recommended.

Internet Restrictions

Network performance may be optimized in this section by preventing user changes to the Desktop.

Here are some of the policies and restrictions from the Internet Restrictions folder that may have an impact on your network resources.

Disable Changing Cache Settings A user might change the cache settings, causing more hits on a Web site and more network traffic. If they cache more content or the wrong content, outdated information may result.

Disable Changing History Settings Changing the history settings may cause interruptions with the AutoComplete feature, which heavily depends on the History folder.

Disable Changing Connection Settings Users may potentially disable their modem or change to inappropriate modem settings.

Disable Changing Proxy Settings Users may potentially disable their proxy settings, rendering them unable to get to the network. Changing the settings may also result in sending a proxy request to the wrong proxy server.

Disable Changing Automatic Configuration Settings Users could remove themselves from autoconfiguration. Outdated configurations are not always the most efficient.

User Profiles/Disable Roaming Cache Roaming profiles are cached on every Desktop the roaming user visits, depending on the value of this checkbox. Caching profiles for roaming users can significantly reduce the logon traffic on a network.

Channels Settings Each of the items in this section is important to the overall effectiveness of the network. Users may be tempted to increase the frequency of updates, raising the network loads. They may add additional subscriptions or remove themselves from a subscription.

Internet Settings

Network performance may be optimized in this section by preventing user changes to the connection configuration.

Here is an example of the policies and restrictions from the Internet Settings folder that may have an impact on your network resources.

Modem Settings Most of the these settings involve the modem connection to a remote host. You can specify options such as the number of dialing attempts, autodialing, and automatic disconnection if idle.

Subscriptions

The Subscriptions section likely has more effect on network resources than any other in the IEAK Profile Manager. These options can control the amount of content and when it can be downloaded, despite CDF file settings.

Listed below are the major settings that affect network performance.

Maximum KB of Site Subscription This limits the amount of content that a site subscription can supply. A value of zero removes the restriction altogether.

Maximum KB of Channel Subscription This limits the amount of content that a channel subscription can supply. A value of zero removes the restriction altogether.

Maximum Number of Site Subscriptions That Can Be Installed
Users cannot sign up for more site subscriptions than are allowed here. A value of zero removes the restriction altogether.

Minimum Number of Minutes between Scheduled Subscription Updates Too many updates from too many clients can clog the network. Limiting this will cut down on network traffic. A value of zero removes the restriction altogether.

Beginning (or End) of Range in Which to Exclude Scheduled Subscription Updates This is another opportunity to limit network traffic. Many companies run backups during the night. To reduce the backup efficiency while updating Desktops for employees that are at home isn't very practical.

Subscriptions/Maximum Site Subscription Crawl Depth The default crawl depth is three layers. To cut down on the size of subscriptions and reduce network traffic, you can limit the depth to which the crawls go, despite any other user preferences.

Protecting the New Desktop

After you have configured the perfect Desktop, IEAK administrators will use the IEAK Profile Manager to protect the Desktop. They may also use policies as part of the login process to keep other operating system restrictions in place. Putting together a solid, consistent Desktop for each user will be a large success factor in your distribution.

Establishing and sticking with a good change-control policy will be the key to sustaining your success and lowering your total cost of ownership. Having this management in place beforehand will require a dedicated, teamwork-style effort, but will be worth it after the distribution has taken place.

Here is a list of some of the major items that could have an impact on protecting the Desktop. They can be found under the Web Desktop folder, which resides in the System Policies and Restrictions section.

Desktop Page

▶ Do not allow changes to the Active Desktop

▶ Hide Network Neighborhood icon

▶ Disable adding any Desktop items

▶ Disable deleting any Desktop items

▶ Disable editing any Desktop items

▶ Disable closing any Desktop items

▶ Disable changing wallpaper

▶ Disable adding new toolbars

▶ Disable resizing all toolbars

Start Menu

▶ Remove Favorites from Start menu

▶ Remove Find menu from Start menu

▶ Remove Run menu from Start menu

▶ Remove the Active Desktop item from the Settings menu

▶ Remove the Folder Options item from the Settings menu

▶ Disable logoff

- ▶ Disable Shut Down command
- ▶ Disable changes to Printers and Control Panel settings
- ▶ Disable changes to Taskbar and Start menu settings
- ▶ Hide Custom Programs folder

Shell

- ▶ Disable File menu in shell folders
- ▶ Only allow approved Shell extensions
- ▶ Disable net connections/disconnections

Printers

- ▶ Disable deletion of printers
- ▶ Disable addition of printers

System

- ▶ Run only specified Windows applications
- ▶ Do not allow computer to restart in MS-DOS mode (Win95 only)

▶ Set up schedules for automatic updates. Locations include:

- ▶ Site subscriptions
- ▶ Channels
- ▶ The Active Desktop

One of the most exciting features in Internet Explorer is automatic content delivery. This feature depends upon scheduling, which ensures that the content is delivered with a frequency that is useful to the user. In this section, we cover this topic and the methods used to schedule and deliver the content, such as Web site subscriptions, Active Channels, and Active Desktop items.

Scheduling Content Delivery

We covered how to edit CDF files and preset the schedule for delivery in Unit 2. This section covers how the user can set up content delivery schedules without having to know complex CDF file parameters. Perform the following steps:

1. If you are subscribing to content for the first time, you have the same opportunity to set up the schedule as after you've already subscribed.

2. If the latter is the case, use Windows Explorer to go to *SystemRoot*\Subscriptions. All the subscriptions and channels for the system reside here.

3. This folder will tell you when the last time the channel or subscription was updated. This folder is also very helpful because it tells you when the next update is scheduled for, the URL, and what schedule the subscription is on.

TIP

To tell whether these are channels or subscriptions, expand the location field to see the file extension. If the location field contains a CDF file, you are subscribed to an Active Channel. Anything else is a Web site subscription.

4. To change these settings, highlight the entry, right-click, and click on Properties.

5. If you click on the Receiving tab, you can change the type of subscription and notification options.

6. You can have Internet Explorer notify you by e-mail that the content has been updated. The subscription type will specify whether the content will be downloaded for offline viewing. You can even specify a password for this site if one is required.

7. To change the delivery schedules, click on the Schedule tab.

8. You can have the subscription updated automatically or manually (at the end user's direction). Automatic subscriptions can be daily, weekly, or monthly.

9. You can even use a Custom Schedule specification to check only on weekdays and certain hours of the day. Updates cannot occur more frequently than once an hour.

Now that we've demonstrated the capabilities of using subscriptions with Internet Explorer, let's examine the different types of subscriptions and where they might be useful.

Site Subscriptions

Site subscriptions are defined as periodic examinations of Web site content for any changes since the last examination. They are initiated by the user without any assistance by the Web site administrator. A partial subscription means that the user is notified that changes have taken place. No content is downloaded in a partial subscription. A full subscription means that the content is downloaded for offline viewing.

When a site is subscribed to, the site is regularly visited on a predetermined basis. If the content of the site changes (up to three levels deep), the user is notified by e-mail or a small, red "gleam" to the subscription icon. If this is a full subscription, the new content is downloaded for offline viewing. Site subscriptions are the user's equivalent of "crawling" the Web site to look for changes. Site subscriptions have no CDF file.

Setting up schedules for site subscriptions takes place at the time of subscription or by using Windows Explorer as described previously.

Active Channels

As covered previously in this unit, Active Channels download specific content, as opposed to the Web-site-crawling nature of the site subscription. You can pick and choose which content to download. You can also download other objects with Active Channels such as screensavers and software updates. More scheduling options are available to Active Channels than to site subscriptions because of the flexibility of the CDF file.

Active Desktop Items

Active Desktop items are similar to screensaver objects—they can be specified using a CDF file and scheduled like any other Active Content. Here is a sample CDF file using our real estate example.

```
<CHANNEL>


<SCHEDULE STARTDATE="1998-08-25">

<INTERVALTIME HOUR="1" />
<EARLIESTTIME HOUR="06" />
<LATESTTIME HOUR="18" />
</SCHEDULE>


<ITEM
HREF="http://www.myfishhook.com/reports/salestodate.htm"
PRECACHE="YES">
```

```
<TITLE>Yearly Sales to Date</TITLE>
<USAGE VALUE="DesktopComponent">
<OPENAS VALUE="HTML" />
<HEIGHT VALUE="200" />
<WIDTH VALUE="200" />
<CANRESIZE VALUE="NO" />
</USAGE>
</ITEM>

</CHANNEL>
```

This CDF file will place a 200-pixel-by-200-pixel HTML window frame on the Desktop. Inside this frame, the `salestodate.htm` page will be loaded and updated on the same schedule as above—hourly from 6 A.M. to 6 P.M.; daily, starting on August 25, 1998. The user will not be able to resize this window once placed on the Desktop.

Optimize caching and performance.

The last topic for this testing objective concerns the overall performance from both sides of the street, the user browser's content cache and its effect on performance.

Checking for Newer Versions of Stored Pages

When a user browses to a new site, Internet Explorer saves all of the content downloaded into a special folder called *SYSTEMROOT*\Temporary Internet Files. The next time this site is browsed, this folder is available to supply the same content, depending on the settings.

If the browser is set to check for newer versions of stored pages every time you visit the page, Internet Explorer will not prefer the cache and will attempt to download every page. This will result in slower download times for the user.

If the browser is set to check every time you start Internet Explorer, the browser will check to see if the content exists in the cache before downloading—if it is present, the browser will prefer the cache. This is the default setting of Internet Explorer.

However, if the browser is set to never check for new pages, the browser will prefer using the cache over downloading. In this case, a new page can be added to the cache, and it will be retained between uses of Internet Explorer. It can potentially remain there unless the user clears the cache, presses F5, or clicks on Refresh to force a new download of the page. The chance of receiving outdated content and information is greater using this setting.

Temporary Internet Files Folder   The slider bar underneath the Temporary Internet Files Folder section allows you to change the amount of space reserved for the cache. If you increase the space allotted, you can improve the performance by allowing for more cached content.

The View Files button will allow you to examine the contents of the cache, while the View Objects button will allow you to examine what program components have been downloaded and installed on your system.

History Files

While you are visiting a site, a record is kept of your visit. Depending on the configuration, the user can use this history to their advantage. The AutoComplete function of Internet Explorer depends on this history. As you type fully qualified domain names (FQDNs) into the Address bar, the AutoComplete function of Internet Explorer searches back through the history and suggests sites previously visited.

You can increase the range of dates that AutoComplete has to work with by increasing the value of Days to Keep Pages in History, accessible by choosing View ➤ Internet Options. To clear the history, click on Clear History. Please keep in mind that clearing the history does not clear the cache nor does it prevent others from being able to reconstruct what sites you have viewed.

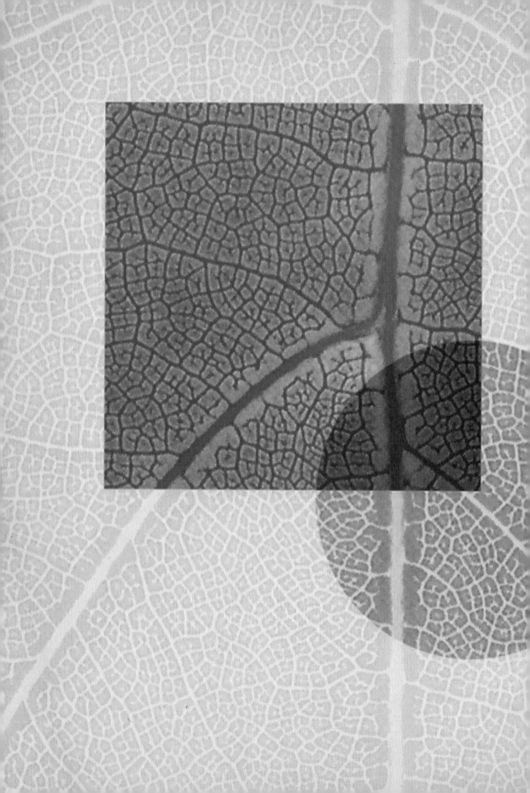

Chapter 29

TROUBLESHOOTING

The final unit in this text concentrates on troubleshooting. This unit examines the most common problems found before, during, and after the deployment of Internet Explorer, including setup, configuration, protocols, network topology, and user needs.

This particular unit is not meant as a complete troubleshooting guide, but is a high-level assessment of the top issues found in a few select areas of Internet Explorer.

Adapted from *MCSE Test Success: Internet Explorer 4 Administration Kit* by Allen Jones
ISBN 0-7821-2333-3   416 pages $24.99

▶ Diagnose and resolve the deployment failure of a preconfigured version of Internet Explorer 4.0.

Resolving Internet Explorer installation failures is not a small task. For instance, the installation may quit prematurely, leaving the operating system in an unknown state. The installation could also be interrupted by other events, prompting setup to halt. Fortunately, Internet Explorer creates and updates a few logs that help diagnose these issues. In this section, `Active Setup Log.txt`, which tracks and logs all changes made by Active Setup, and `IE4 Setup Log.txt`, which logs the IE4 installation process, will be described.

Active Setup Logs

This setup log is created by the Active Setup program, `IE4WZRD.EXE`, and details every step of the setup process. As a result, the file is very lengthy.

NOTE

You can find `Active Setup Log.txt` in the *SYSTEMROOT* directory; for example, `WINNT`.

As you interpret each line in the file, you will notice that some lines have result codes appended to the end of each line. The codes are interpreted by extracting the number from the colons that precede and immediately follow the number at the end of some of these lines. Compare the code to the result codes listed in Table 29.1. For example, the line

```
Setup mode selected :2:
```

means that the result code is 2, and the interpreted Active Setup message is "Downloading (Server to download folder)." Note that not every line will have a code.

TABLE 29.1: Possible Result Codes for Active Setup Log.txt

Result Code	Description
0	Initializing (Making a temp folder, checking disk space)
1	Dependency (Checking for all dependencies)
2	Downloading (Server to download folder)
3	Copying (Download folder to temp installation folder)
4	Retrying (Restarting download due to time-out or some other download error)
5	Checking trust
6	Extracting
7	Running (.INF or .EXE)
8	Finished (Installation complete)
9	Download finished (Downloading complete)

Part v

Installation Setup Logs

There is another log to be considered in troubleshooting Internet Explorer. When the download is complete and the actual installation of Internet Explorer begins, the installation process is tracked and logged into a file called IE4 Setup Log.txt. This log is a good source of information and an easy way to detect and resolve the problems surrounding the installation of Internet Explorer.

NOTE

You can find IE4 Setup Log.txt in the *SYSTEMROOT* directory; for example, WINNT.

Be sure to update your Windows NT Emergency Repair Disk (ERD) after installing Internet Explorer 4. If you attempt to restore the registry using the old ERD after installing IE, you will leave your system in an unusable state.

Administrator Rights

You must have local administrative rights on the system on which you wish to install Internet Explorer. Failure to do so will prevent the installation from creating the proper registry keys, and may leave your system in an unusable state.

Diagnose and resolve problems related to the IEAK Wizard.

The IEAK Wizard as configured has many potential places for the distribution to not happen as planned. In many cases, a new distribution or a change in the configuration files can resolve the problem. In this section, we examine the more common problems that arise from the IEAK Wizard and creating distributions.

Relocating Installation Servers

When thinking of moving or changing download servers, the IEAK administrator must consider that the Active Setup program will query the IE4SITES.DAT file in the download directory specified in the IEAK Wizard. This file contains up to 10 download sites for Internet Explorer. If a download site moves, the IEAK administrator must update every IE4SITES.DAT file that mentions that site.

Adding Other Languages to a Distribution

Internet Explorer can support additional languages within the browser or distribution packages with complete language support. The latter is usually called a *localized* version of the browser. English versions are usually found in EN directories.

Adding Language Support to Existing Browsers   If you wish to add support for other languages to a browser and still wish to retain the original language, you can do so through Internet Explorer. Perform the following steps:

1.   Choose View ➤ Internet Options and click on the Languages button.

2.   From this screen, you can click on Add.

This procedure would be used when you do not intend to change the operating system language and just want the browser to support foreign languages. This will permit content written in a foreign language to display correctly.

Creating Distributions in Other Languages   The proper way to change languages is to create a version of Internet Explorer in that language. You must complete the wizard again for every language for which you wish to create a package. For instance, if you created a package in English and wish to create another for Danish and German, you would be required to run the wizard and create two more packages.

Localized Versions and Windows Desktop Update   The language version of Windows Desktop Update (WDU) must match the language of the local machine's operating system. If the user attempts to install WDU from another language, only the browser will be installed. Note that this restriction does not apply to the browser.

Adding Other Components

If you distribute your browser and later realize that you have forgotten a component, you can either add the component individually through Control Panel ➤ Add/Remove Programs or build another package that includes the component.

If you wish to add a component to a package, you will want to rerun the IEAK Wizard, increment the package version number, add the new component, and redistribute.

For instance, if you forgot to add the Windows Desktop Update to the package and have distributed the package to 50 users, it would be a little impractical to visit 50 workstations. In this case, the package probably should be rebuilt.

However, if the package is not rebuilt, the IEAK administrator or their designee would have to log in to each machine and run setup manually.

Upgrading

When a new package is rebuilt with an upgrade, IEAK administrators will update the version number during Stage Three. This version number is important in the upgrade process because Active Setup will not allow an upgrade over a newer product. That is to say, version 2.0.0.1 cannot be upgraded to 1.1.2.1, but 1.1.2.1 can be upgraded to 2.0.0.1.

Part v

If you would rather use an eight-digit number instead of a version number, enter it in the Configuration Identifier field. The company name specified in Stage One must match in both versions for this feature to work.

Whenever someone selects Product Updates from the Internet Explorer Help menu, it will load ADDON95.HTM or ADDONNT.HTM from the download site. If you would like to specify another URL, enter that URL in the box at the bottom of the screen.

▶ Diagnose and resolve connection failures of Outlook Express.

More often than not, failing to connect after installing Outlook Express or NetMeeting is a result of improper configuration. After these two programs have been successfully installed and implemented within your environment, you can assume that a single-machine failure is a result of configuration or hardware problems. Multiple-machine failures could be from a loss of connectivity or a serious error in the distribution, barring any sudden changes to system policies or changes with the IEAK Profile Manager. We will concentrate on major configuration issues in this section.

Connection problems in Microsoft Outlook Express can take on many forms. For instance, the correct protocols on the client may or may not be loaded, and if they are, they may not necessarily be configured correctly. The wrong server information could be specified.

Let's take a closer look at some specific problems and their resolutions.

Unable to Send or Receive E-Mail   If an IEAK administrator is called to investigate why a computer is unable to send or receive e-mail, the following list may be able to assist in locating the problem:

- ▶ Is the TCP/IP protocol installed correctly?

- ▶ Is the Internet account set up in Outlook Express correctly?

- ▶ Are the incoming and outgoing e-mail servers specified correctly?

- ▶ Is the network cable or serial communication cable connected correctly to the computer?

- ▶ If a modem is used to connect, is the modem configured correctly?

- ▶ Is there a network event in progress, such as an outage?

We can troubleshoot some of these problems by examining the tools provided for you later in this chapter. These tools will not necessarily diagnose the problem completely; however, they can narrow down the possibilities.

Logging Options   Several logging options to Outlook Express can help diagnose connectivity problems. Perform the following steps to activate logging for Outlook Express.

1. Choose Tools ➢ Options and click on the Advanced tab.

2. Near the bottom of this screen, there are three checkboxes (as shown in Figure 29.1).

3. These three checkboxes will help diagnose many types of connection failures. Select the News, Mail, or IMAP Transport logging options to create any combination of the following logs: POP3.LOG, SMTP.LOG, INETNEWS.LOG, or IMAP.LOG.

POP3.LOG and SMTP.LOG will be generated whenever the mail log is active. With these logs, you can track and diagnose certain mail delivery and reception failures, newsgroup errors, and protocol issues. If Outlook Express is not the default e-mail client, some of the logging options will be grayed out.

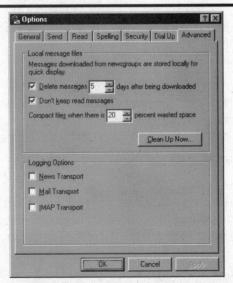

FIGURE 29.1: Logging different transports in Outlook Express. Not all logging options will be available, depending on how Outlook Express is installed and what other e-mail clients are on the system.

Diagnose and resolve connection failures of NetMeeting.

This application is difficult to optimize, yet it is rather easy to troubleshoot. Protocols and device configurations play a large part in the audio and video connectivity. Some of the more common connection problems are described below.

No Audio Features Available   Audio capabilities depend upon the use of the TCP/IP protocol and connecting through a LAN or an Internet connection. Null modems and other protocols are not sufficient to support audio connections.

If TCP/IP is installed and audio features are not available, check the TCP/IP configuration. If this is correct, the problem likely exists with the sound card. The sound card may not be configured correctly, or may be conflicting with another device. Full-duplex audio can sometimes cause the sound card to conflict with other devices in the same system.

NOTE

Service Pack 3 must be installed on Windows NT 4 for NetMeeting 2 to operate correctly, including sharing files.

Other Audio Problems   Audio can be difficult to manage. Many performance problems are solved using the Audio Tuning Wizard, which will permit the adjustment of audio recording levels and the audio speakers' sound volume. To get to the Audio Tuning Wizard from NetMeeting, choose Tools ➤ Audio Tuning Wizard. Follow the instructions in each dialog box.

Cannot Share Video   Video capabilities also depend upon the use of the TCP/IP protocol and connecting through a LAN or an Internet connection. Null modems and other protocols are not sufficient to support video connections.

If the local video portion of NetMeeting is not operational, check the source video device. NetMeeting can recognize only one video-input device at a time. Check the cabling and connection of the device, and make sure that the driver for the camera is loaded and configured properly.

▶ Diagnose and resolve failures of webcasting. Types of webcasting include:

- ▶ Site subscriptions
- ▶ Channels
- ▶ Active Desktop items

When you are resolving webcasting failures, there are a number of issues with which to be concerned. While this section will examine a few of those issues, there are many different configuration and system performance parameters besides those listed here.

Site Subscriptions

Subscriptions are always available by looking in *SYSTEMROOT* Subscriptions. You can right-click on any item in the list and get the details about the subscription. Some sites take steps to prevent Web crawls, thereby negating the benefit of site subscriptions.

E-Mail Confirmation

If e-mail notification is not taking place, perform the following steps:

1. Use Windows Explorer to visit *SYSTEMROOT*Subscriptions.

2. Right-click on the appropriate subscription and choose Properties.

3. In the Properties dialog box, click on the Receiving tab.

4. Then, click on Send an E-Mail Message to the Following Address and change the e-mail address to reflect where confirmations are supposed to be mailed.

5. Double-check the name of the outgoing e-mail server to be sure it is listed correctly.

Channels and Active Desktop Items

Channels fail most often when the CDF file has been edited and now contains a syntax error. Scheduling problems can also arise, and must be resolved. If the referenced URLs no longer exist, this can cause problems for the browser and ultimately the end user.

Active Desktop items can fail for a number of different reasons. Loss of connectivity is a common reason. Active Desktop components have regular schedules by which to look for updates.

▶ Diagnose and resolve failures of caching.

Caching problems will fall into one of two general categories, no matter the cause: either the cached pages have become outdated and the information being presented to the user is incorrect, or the browser is not configured to reach its full potential, creating performance issues for the end user.

Outdated Information

Let us examine the first scenario.

1. If a browser is presenting out-of-date pages from the cache, select View ➤ Internet Options in Internet Explorer.

2. Click on the Settings button from the Temporary Internet Files section.

3. If the radio button to never check for new pages is selected, the browser is set to retrieve your content from the cache and never download the content, even if it changes.

4. You can temporarily resolve the problem by clearing the cache by clicking on Delete from the Internet Options screen.

Poor Performance

The second major category of caching problems can result from a number of things. Most complaints about poor performance result from the cache underperforming. The cause can be several reasons.

If a browser's cache is set to check for new pages on every visit to the page, the browser is not relying on the cache for repetitive content. This means that the browser does not trust the cache, instead downloading each piece of content. This can result in poor performance to the end user.

Roaming Users and Caching

If the network has users with roaming profiles, the IEAK administrator will be faced with another challenge. When roaming profiles are used, the Temporary Internet Files folder is replicated back to the server, containing many megabytes of information. Moving these files and the rest of the profile across the network at each logon and logoff can saturate a network at peak times. It will also occupy large amounts of a hard disk.

To solve this problem, you may have to use the IEAK Wizard or Profile Manager.

1. Select the System Policies and Restrictions section (the last step in the IEAK Wizard) and Internet Settings.

2. Check the Delete Saved Pages When Browser Is Closed option.

▶ # Choose the appropriate tools for troubleshooting network connection failures. Tools for troubleshooting include:

▶ IP configuration

▶ PING

▶ Trace route

▶ Network Monitor

▶ NSLOOKUP

When users complain about connectivity issues, a good set of tools is needed to quickly troubleshoot and isolate the problems. Windows NT and Windows 95 have many of the tools needed to resolve problems with client networking. All of these tools are used to troubleshoot TCP/IP— they do not have any value with any other protocol. Likewise, proxy servers or Internet firewalls may interfere with the proper operation of these utilities.

IP Configuration

There are two utilities to examine the TCP/IP configuration. Though they serve the same purpose, they each work a little differently. Both report the TCP/IP configuration, and release and renew DHCP leases if the client uses DHCP. We will explain both utilities in this section.

WINIPCFG (Windows 95)   Primarily used in Windows 95, this utility will show you the TCP/IP configuration: the host name, what DNS servers the client will attempt to resolve Internet addresses from, what type of name resolution the client will perform, and some information about the IP routing, NetBIOS resolution, and WINS Proxy (as demonstrated in Figure 29.2).

FIGURE 29.2:   The WINIPCFG utility. It is primarily used in Windows 95.

The utility also shows the currently assigned TCP/IP address, the subnet mask, the default gateway, and to which WINS servers the client reports.

If your network uses DHCP, the DHCP server that assigned you the IP address lease will be shown. When the lease was obtained and when it expires are displayed at the bottom of this utility. The row of buttons at the bottom are important to DHCP, too. They control the renewal and release of the DHCP lease. If a user clicks on Renew, the client will attempt to renew the lease. If the user clicks on Release, the address lease is returned to the DHCP server so that another client can lease the address. The Renew All and Release All buttons are for multiple network interfaces. They can renew and release all leases on every network card, without having to select them individually.

IPCONFIG (Windows NT)   This utility is very similar to WINIPCFG. A text version of the TCP/IP configuration tool, this utility reports the same information as its graphical counterpart.

This command is available only in Windows NT. An example of the output is listed below.

```
C:\>ipconfig /all


        Host Name . . . . . . . . . : myhost
        DNS Servers . . . . . . . . : 206.134.133.10
                                      206.134.224.5
        Node Type . . . . . . . . . : Broadcast
        NetBIOS Scope ID. . . . . . :
        IP Routing Enabled. . . . . : Yes
        WINS Proxy Enabled. . . . . : No
        NetBIOS Resolution Uses DNS : No


Ethernet adapter EPRO8:


        Description . . . . . . . . : Intel EtherExpress PRO
        Adapter
        Physical Address. . . . . . : 00-AA-00-60-08-02
        DHCP Enabled. . . . . . . . : No
        IP Address. . . . . . . . . : 10.1.2.1
        Subnet Mask . . . . . . . . : 255.255.0.0
        Default Gateway . . . . . . :


Ethernet adapter NdisWan11:


        Description . . . . . . . . : NdisWan Adapter
        Physical Address. . . . . . : 00-01-D0-18-91-80
        DHCP Enabled. . . . . . . . : No
        IP Address. . . . . . . . . : 168.191.154.12
        Subnet Mask . . . . . . . . : 255.255.0.0
        Default Gateway . . . . . . : 168.191.154.12
```

This utility has four modes that affect its usage.

Command	Use
IPCONFIG	Reports only basic TCP/IP configuration
IPCONFIG /ALL	Reports TCP/IP configuration verbosely
IPCONFIG /RELEASE	Releases the DHCP address lease and returns IP address back to the address pool
IPCONFIG /RENEW	Attempts to renew the DHCP lease with the DHCP server

Potential Uses   These utilities might be used to test for the correct setup of TCP/IP. They can also be used to tell if the client is receiving leases from the correct DHCP server and if the DHCP server is handing out the correct lease information.

TRACERT

TRACERT (called trace route) is a utility to view the path that a packet travels in between two hosts. It can be used when a user complains that they cannot reach a particular Web site from their browser or they are having problems with any other program or network connection that relies on the TCP/IP protocol. Other sites may or may not be connecting correctly.

Trace route depends on Internet Control Message Protocol (ICMP) errors and messages to develop a report for the user. The user inputs the FQDN or IP address of the host that he would like to trace the route to, such as www.microsoft.com (as shown below).

```
C:\>tracert www.microsoft.com
```

This command depends on the ICMP protocol, as mentioned earlier. The protocol has a special message called ICMP_TIME EXCEEDED. It is used in trace route when a packet is generated with a short time-to-live (TTL) value. The TTL is the number of network devices the packet can cross before the packet expires. When the packet expires, the network device on which it expired sends an ICMP message back informing the source (the client who initiated the trace route) where the packet expired. This information (with a quick reverse lookup on DNS) helps generate the output of the trace route utility. Here is the first section of sample output in our trace route example.

```
Tracing route to www.microsoft.com [207.46.130.14] over a
maximum of 30 hops:

1 171 ms 170 ms 180 ms sdn-
  ar01txhous002t.dialsprint.net[168.191.154.2]

2 170 ms 180 ms 171 ms 168.191.154.129

3 180 ms 190 ms 181 ms sdn-fw-2-1-T1.dialsprint.net
  [207.143.150.8.1]
```

In this example, on line one, the first packet sent out expired on that network device. As soon as that ICMP message was received, the second packet was sent out, only this time the TLL value was incremented by one. After the packet reached the second network device, it expired, sending back a second ICMP message, which creates the second line in our trace route. This process repeats until the destination host is found, the client cancels the operation, or the TTL value exceeds 30 hops (the value of 30 could differ, depending on your network).

By starting at zero (the closest network device and the first hop) and incrementing the counter by one after each report back, we can develop a roadmap for the packet to its destination.

The times in each column represent up to three calculated destination times. If you see a star in a column, it means the packet was lost and not returned. Whenever you see several rows of stars, a network device or host is not responding. The packet also might have been trapped by a firewall or other similar filter, preventing its return.

PING

PING is another utility that is used to test for connectivity between two points. It can be used to send a test packet to a destination address. It also relies on ICMP messages, which report connection information back to the client. When a ping is sent to a destination host, it replies back using ICMP that the packet was received. The timestamp in the ICMP message will permit the PING utility to calculate the time to reach the destination.

In many cases, PING is used to verify that a client is configured properly and speaking correctly to the TCP/IP network. Using PING to troubleshoot requires an organized approach.

1. First, you must ping what is called the loopback address. A *loopback address* is a special address in every card that will allow the TCP/IP stack to send and receive the same packet.

2. The loopback address is assigned the IP address of 127.0.0.1.

3. Any packet sent to that address will be reflected back at itself.

4. If the ping returns a successful message, you can assume that you have a working IP stack.

5. You can ping the IP address with which the client is configured.

6. Next, ping the host name of the local machine.

7. If this fails, you may need to double-check the TCP/IP host name that is configured, or use NSLOOKUP as described below to verify name resolution.

8. The next step to take with PING is to verify that you can ping another host on the same network segment. It might be another workstation across the room or the network printer down the hall.

9. Send a test ping and see if it returns correctly.

If this ping fails and all the previous pings have been successful, check your physical connectivity to the network. Is the network cable plugged in? Is there a cabling problem between you and the hub? You might try two or three local workstations just to be sure.

If this ping was successful, it is time to ping the default gateway. The default gateway is the access point to the rest of your network. If you cannot ping the gateway, you can't reach the outside world. Ping the IP address of the gateway.

If the ping to the gateway was successful, try pinging a known working host on the Internet. Other network devices and Web servers are great test subjects, since they are running most of the time. If the ping is not successful, the default gateway is not always to blame—that particular route or path to that host could be down, or that host in general could be down.

In any of the above cases, if you have a successful, working TCP/IP stack, use the PING utility in conjunction with the trace route command. You will find that both complement each other in troubleshooting.

Network Monitor

Network Monitor is used to capture and examine packets sent from one host to another. Filters are used to restrict the display of packets to those that are selected from a host screen (as shown in Figure 29.3). The filter can restrict the display to any combination of a certain protocol, a certain machine, or the data transfer between two particular hosts.

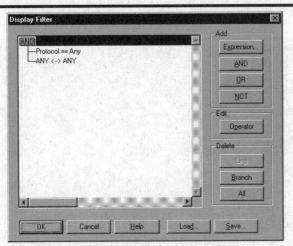

FIGURE 29.3: Using filters with Network Monitor

The filter as shown in Figure 29.3 is watching nearly all protocols and all addresses. The arrows shown in this example are meant to depict the direction or flow of packets moving either inbound or outbound from the device.

Using Network Monitor, you can watch the traffic between a host that is running the Network Monitoring Agent and any device on the network. This is ideal for monitoring remote subnets.

NSLOOKUP

NSLOOKUP is a client utility that will query a DNS server to convert an Internet host name to an IP address. Anyone can set up a DNS server, which leads to inaccurate information and other errors.

You can use NSLOOKUP to query a specific Internet host name and see the result. You could have the correct IP address or the wrong IP address, or maybe the server cannot resolve the address (Figure 29.4 shows the correct usage of NSLOOKUP and a positive result).

In most cases, if incorrect information is the result, the DNS admin will have to make adjustments to the DNS setup. This could take some time to propagate the new, corrected information.

If the server cannot resolve the address, either the incorrect name is given to NSLOOKUP or the machine is not properly registered. Also, Internet connectivity to the destination site could be down, with the DNS unavailable. Try running a trace route to confirm.

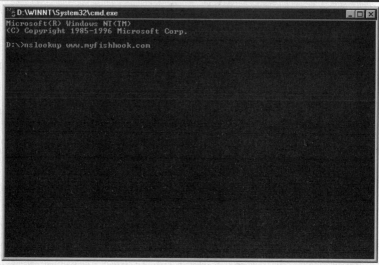

FIGURE 29.4: A positive result in NSLOOKUP

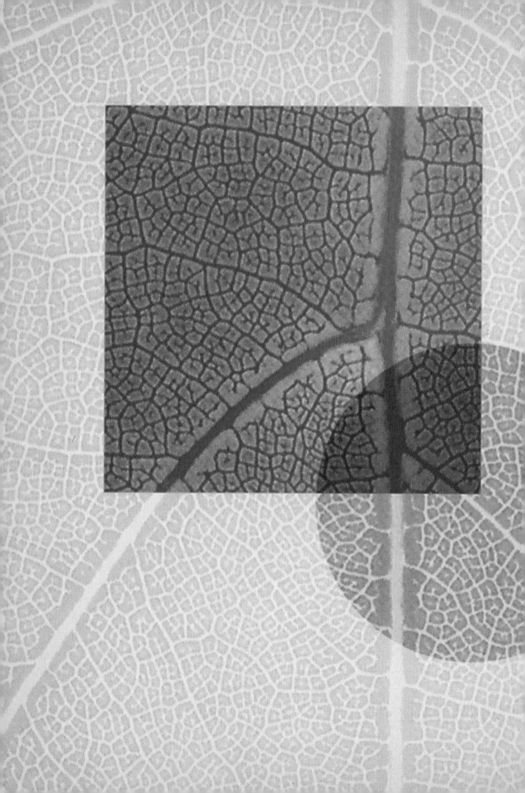

PART V

INTERNET EXPLORER 4 ADMINISTRATION KIT PRACTICE EXAM

Exam Questions

1. You have been asked to distribute a browser to several public kiosks. These browsers must be able to start using the kiosk mode and load a page found at the URL http://www.myfishhook.com/kiosk.htm. What command would you use in this situation?

   A. `iexplore -kiosk /url:`
   `http://www.myfishhook.com/kiosk.htm`

   B. `iexplore -kiosk -url:`
   `http://www.myfishhook.com/kiosk.htm`

   C. `iexplore -k -u`
   `http://www.myfishhook.com/kiosk.htm`

   D. `iexplore -k`
   `http://www.myfishhook.com/kiosk.htm`

2. Microsoft requires that you report the number of browsers distributed using the Internet Explorer Administration Kit. How often should you report?

   A. Monthly

   B. Quarterly

   C. Semi-annually

   D. Annually

3. Which organizational mode allows you to perform a silent installation?

   A. Corporate administrator

   B. Internet service provider

   C. Internet content provider

   D. Both corporate administrator and Internet service provider

4. Which installation provides a single floppy disk option for installation?

    A. Corporate administrator mode

    B. Internet service provider mode

    C. Internet content provider mode.

    D. Both corporate administrator and Internet content provider modes

5. Consider the following scenario:

A group of public relations executives have asked you to create a browser distribution that will permit them to collaborate on projects. File transfer is not allowed among the executives for security reasons. The existing environment is based on the IPX protocol.

Required result: Allow the executives to collaborate on projects.

Desired results:

    1. Prevent the executives from sending or receiving files.

    2. Provide streaming video capabilities on the Desktop.

Solution: Implement the TCP/IP protocol in the environment. Create a distribution that includes Microsoft Net-Meeting and NetShow. Use the IEAK Profile Manager to prevent file transfers using NetMeeting.

Does this solution:

    A. Meet the required result and both desired results

    B. Meet the required result and only one of the desired results

    C. Meet only the required result and none of the desired results

    D. Not meet the required result

6. What is the maximum number of download URLs that you can have while in the corporate administrator mode of IEAK doing a silent installation?

A. 1

B. 3

C. 10

D. None of the above

7. Which of the following file extensions would not be found on a file that is responsible for configuring proxy settings for the browser?

A. .JS

B. .PAC

C. .INS

D. .JVS

8. Which items of Internet Explorer 3.x will not be migrated to Internet Explorer 4?

A. Cache settings

B. Favorites

C. Cookies

D. Proxy settings

9. When using the Internet Connection Wizard, choose the statement that most closely matches the correct file descriptions.

A. All users can use the same .ISP file to connect to the sign-up server and receive a personalized .INS file.

B. All users can use the same .ISP file to connect to the sign-up server and receive the same .INS file that all users receive.

C. A single user may use a personalized .ISP file to connect to the sign-up server and receive the same .INS file that all users receive.

D. A single user may use a personalized .ISP file to connect to the sign-up server and receive a personalized .INS file.

10. Consider the following scenario:

You have been hired at a computer lab at a university. Your task is to upgrade the existing browsers and install news-group clients on every workstation. The department chair-person wants to make department announcements on every browser and newsgroup reader.

Required result: Upgrade existing browser and newsgroup reader.

Desired results:

1. Provide an announcement page in every Internet Explorer browser.

2. Provide an announcement page in every installation of Outlook Express.

Solution: Develop a package that uses Internet Explorer and Outlook Express. Give the IEAK Wizard the URL of the start page of the Web-based announcements. Also during the wizard, supply the URL of a 640-by-50-pixel html page for the InfoPane in Outlook Express.

Does this solution:

A. Meet the required result and both desired results

B. Meet the required result and only one of the desired results

C. Meet only the required result and none of the desired results

D. Not meet the required result

11. If a new Internet user has already received a user name, password, and dial-up information, which sign-up server is appropriate?

A. Internet sign-up server

B. Serverless sign-up server

C. No sign-up server

D. None of the above

12. When bundling your custom applications into CAB files, which utility will you use?

    A. IE4SETUP.EXE

    B. IE2CAB.EXE

    C. IEXPRESS.EXE

    D. IE4XPRES.EXE

13. Which utility would you use to restore a channel that had been previously deleted during package creation?

    A. IEAK Help

    B. IEAK Wizard

    C. Internet Explorer Setup, from Add/Remove Programs

    D. You cannot undelete a channel once distributed

14. Which one of the following <SCHEDULE> tags will result in downloading content every four hours between 2 A.M. and 10 P.M.?

    A.
```
<SCHEDULE>
        <INTERVALTIME DAY="1" />
        <EARLIESTTIME HOUR="0200" />
        <LATESTTIME HOUR="2200" />
</SCHEDULE>
```

    B.
```
<SCHEDULE>
        <INTERVALTIME DAY="1" />
        <EARLIESTTIME HOUR="02:00" />
        <LATESTTIME HOUR="22:00" />
</SCHEDULE>
```

    C.
```
<SCHEDULE>
        <INTERVALTIME DAY="1" />
        <EARLIESTTIME HOUR="2" />
        <LATESTTIME HOUR="22" />
</SCHEDULE>
```

D. `<SCHEDULE>`

```
<INTERVALTIME HOUR="4" />
<EARLIESTTIME HOUR="2" />
<LATESTTIME HOUR="22" />
</SCHEDULE>
```

15. Susan has created a distribution that includes the Full installation of the browser and the Windows Desktop Update. Which systems as shown below will support this package? (Choose all that apply.)

    A. 486/25 with 200MB free disk space, 16MB of memory

    B. 486/66 with 65MB free disk space, 24MB of memory

    C. Pentium 200 with 70MB free disk space, 64MB of memory

    D. Pentium 120 with 200MB free disk space, 64MB of memory

16. Which of the following are not custom options for Outlook Express?

    A. Common signature for appending to the end of each mail message

    B. Creating a welcome e-mail for the user's first time with the product

    C. Creating an InfoPane, which can contain HTML or another URL

    D. Personalized user signature for appending to each mail message

17. Consider the following scenario:

    You have been asked to develop an Internet Explorer distribution for a hospital. Administration has asked that the browser permit them to run ActiveX controls from sites they trust and to be prompted for a choice whenever the situation arises about sites they do not trust. They also want the ability to view live, streaming video events.

Required result: Provide a new browser distribution package that includes the ability to view live, streaming video events.

Desired results:

1. Allow the user the ability to run ActiveX controls from sites they trust without hindrance.

2. Prompt the user before running ActiveX controls from sites they do not trust.

Solution: Plan and create a distribution using the corporate administrator mode. Do not install the Windows Desktop Update. Accept all default zone permissions. Add the untrusted sites to the Restricted Sites zone. Install NetShow.

Does this solution:

A. Meet the required result and both desired results

B. Meet the required result and only one of the desired results

C. Meet only the required result and none of the desired results

D. Not meet the required result

18. Which of these are not Java Permission settings?

A. Low Safety

B. Custom

C. Disable Java

D. No Safety

19. Which of the following is not a benefit of using a proxy server?

A. Caching of frequently used content to increase performance

B. Masking the true address of the user's workstation

C. Crawling a Web site and caching the content to increase performance

D. Supporting multiple protocols

Part v

20. What will happen if a user attempts to download code that is signed using an expired certificate?

    A. Authenticode technology will prevent the download from occurring.

    B. Authenticode technology will permit the download, but would first prompt the user for action.

    C. Authenticode technology will permit the download and notify the IEAK administrator.

    D. Authenticode technology will prevent the download from occurring and notify the IEAK administrator.

21. If a zone is not listed in any other zone, in what zone is it considered to be?

    A. Restricted Sites

    B. Internet

    C. Trusted Sites

    D. Local Intranet

22. A customer has asked that you build a package that prevents the browser from displaying anything stronger than fighting. Which of the following settings will satisfy this requirement?

    A. Violence rating set to 0

    B. Violence rating set to 1

    C. Violence rating set to 2

    D. Violence rating set to 3

    E. Violence rating set to 4

23. When autoconfiguration takes place, where does it attempt to retrieve configuration information?

    A. From the URL supplied during package creation in the Automatic Configuration window

    B. From the URL specified during user installation

   C. From the URL supplied during package creation in the Automatic Browser Configuration window

   D. From the URL supplied during package creation in the Autoconfigure Setup window

24. Which of the software channels permissions will allow automatic download and automatic installations? Choose the best answer.

   A. High Safety

   B. Medium Safety

   C. Low Safety

   D. Medium and Low Safety

25. Choose two files that represent the parts of a digital ID.

   A. Software Publisher Certificate (SPC) file

   B. Software Encryption Key (SEK) file

   C. Public Key (PK) file

   D. Private Key (PVK) file

26. Which application will share the entire Desktop and comprise security at the installation?

   A. File Manager

   B. Program Manager

   C. Windows Explorer

   D. Internet Explorer

27. Which protocol supports audio conferencing in NetMeeting?

   A. NetBEUI

   B. IPX

   C. TCP/IP

   D. None of the above

28. Which of the following files does not have to be signed before packaging?

   A. BRANDING.CAB

   B. IE4SETUP.EXE

   C. IE40CIF.CAB

   D. DESKTOP.CAB

   E. Both B and C

   F. All of the above files must be signed before packaging

29. From where does the AutoComplete function get its information?

   A. Temporary Internet files

   B. History files

   C. The cache found in *SYSTEMROOT*\System32\Cache

   D. The cache found in *SYSTEMROOT*\System32\History

30. A user reports that her Web browser is returning pages and other Web content very slowly. You open up a browser on your Desktop, and the updated content is displaying just fine. What should you look for on the end user's machine?

   A. Check the settings under Temporary Internet Files—is it checking for new pages with every visit to the site?

   B. Check the settings under Temporary Internet Files—is it not checking for new pages, but instead preferring the cache?

   C. Check the settings under Temporary Internet Files—is it checking for expired pages in the cache?

   D. Check the settings under Temporary Internet Files—is it not checking for expired pages in the cache, and the cache is filling beyond capacity?

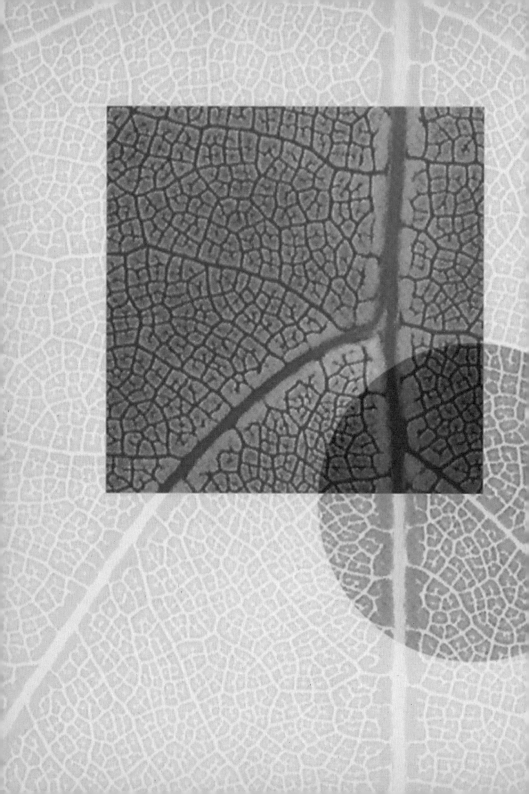

Appendix A

Exam Answers

Part i: TCP/IP for NT Server 4

1. Your computer network consists of 35 Windows NT Work-stations, each with one network interface card (NIC). In addition, it has four NT Servers with three interface cards each and four routers, each with three interface cards. How many IP addresses will you need?

   A. 43

   B. 47

   C. 59

   D. 94

   Answer: C. You will need 59 IP addresses, 35 for each of the workstations, 12 for the servers, and 12 for the routers.

2. Two address resolution protocols are

   A. DNS

   B. WINS

   C. DHCP

   D. IP

   Answer: A and B. DNS will resolve DNS names to IP addresses and WINS will resolve NetBIOS computer names to IP addresses.

3. Your network consists of three Windows NT Servers, 100 Windows NT Workstations, and 350 Windows 9x workstations. You are concerned about address resolution of Net-BIOS computer names. Given this scenario, which TCP/IP service should you use?

   A. DHCP

   B. DNS

   C. WINS

   D. RIP

Answer: C. DHCP is responsible for IP address assignments, not resolution. RIP is a routing protocol. That leaves DNS and WINS. By default, DNS host names are the NetBIOS computer name, but the Microsoft approved answer would be WINS. Look for a scenario with all Microsoft products and think WINS.

4. What is multilink?

   A. The ability to have two or more modems handling different calls at the same time

   B. The ability of two or more modems to call out at the same time

   C. The ability to use more than one communication channel for the same connection

   D. The ability to have two network interface cards in the same system at the same time

Answer: C. The ability to use more than one communication channel for the same connection.

5. The NT Server named NTSRV_1 is assigned five IP addresses to its single network card. It is a

   A. Router

   B. Multihomed system

   C. Multihomed computer

   D. DHCP server

Answer: C. It is a multihomed computer. If it had multiple network cards bound to separate networks, it would be a multihomed system.

6. When configuring a network card to communicate using TCP/IP, which two entries are mandatory?

   A. IP address

   B. Gateway

   C. WINS Server

   D. Subnet mask

Answer: A and D. You must enter the IP address and the subnet mask. If your network is small, you may not need a gateway or a WINS Server, but if you are communicating using IP, you will need unique IP addresses and a subnet mask.

7. Which term(s) would describe a DNS database?

    A. Distributed

    B. Dynamic

    C. Manually configured

    D. Hierarchical

Answer: A, C, and D. The DNS database is distributed over many sites; it is manually configured, even at the highest levels; and it is hierarchical.

8. TCP/IP protocol properties are found as part of which Control Panel selection?

    A. Modems

    B. Networks

    C. Devices

    D. TCP/IP protocol

Answer: B. TCP/IP protocol properties are found as part of the Network selection in the Control Panel.

9. By default, a DHCP client leases a DHCP address for

    A. One day

    B. Two days

    C. Three days

    D. Four days

Answer: C. DHCP addresses are leased for three days by default.

10. Your network consists of six subnets. On each subnet, you want IP addresses to be assigned dynamically. You must have

either a(n)_____ or a(n) _____ on each subnet.

  A. PDC, BDC

  B. DHCP server, DHCP relay agent

  C. NT 3.51 Server, NT 4.0 Server

  D. Windows 98 Workstation, Windows 95 Workstation

Answer: B. To accomplish this task, you should have either a DHCP server or a DHCP relay agent on each subnet.

11. Which of the following operating systems can host a WINS Server?

  A. NetWare 3.12

  B. Windows NT 3.5x Server

  C. Windows 98 Server

  D. Windows NT 4.0 Server

Answer: B and D. A WINS Server can run on computers configured with NT Server with a version of 3.5x or greater.

12. Your network consists of 10 Windows NT Servers, 100 Windows 9x workstations, 37 Windows NT Workstations, and a smattering of Windows for Workgroups workstations. What type of resolution system should you configure?

  A. DHCP

  B. WINS

  C. DNS

  D. ARP

Answer: B. Because the entire network consists of Windows products, the resolution method of choice is WINS.

13. The WINS Server database has become corrupt. The database has been configured so it will be backed up. What is the first way to try to restore the database?

  A. From a tape backup

B. From the registry backup

C. From the %systemroot%\system32\backup directory

D. By stopping and restarting WINS

Answer: D. The first way to try to restore the database is to stop and restart the WINS service. When WINS senses the corrupt database, it will try and restore the last backup.

14. You find that your workstation has an IP address of 129.16.15.24 with a subnet mask of 255.255.0.0. What is the network portion of that address?

    A. 129.0.0.0

    B. 129.16.0.0

    C. 129.16.15.0

    D. 129.16.15.6

Answer: B. Because this is a Class B address, with the default subnet, the network portion of the address would be 129.16.0.0.

15. How many hosts can you have on a network with the address of 205.46.15.0, with a subnet of 255.255.255.240?

    A. 62

    B. 30

    C. 14

    D. 6

Answer: C. A Class C address with a subnet of 255.255.255 .240 can have 14 subnets, each with up to 14 hosts.

16. The InterNIC has assigned you an IP address of 205.46.15.0. What is the default subnet mask for this address?

    A. 255.0.0.0

    B. 255.255.0.0

    C. 255.255.255.0

    D. 255.255.255.255

Answer: C. 205.46.15.0 is a Class C address. The default subnet mask for a Class C address is 255.255.255.0.

17. You are troubleshooting a TCP/IP problem and you find that the IP address is an invalid address. Which address below is the invalid address?

   A. 106.34.25.90

   B. 128.4.6.224

   C. 2.128.224.240

   D. 255.23.5.2

Answer: D. 255.23.5.2 is not a valid IP address.

18. The dynamic routing protocol that is provided with Windows NT Server is

   A. SAP

   B. RIP

   C. IPX

   D. SPX

   E. NetBIOS

Answer: B. Windows NT Server comes with the Routing Information Protocol or RIP.

19. What happens to the TTL when a packet crosses a router?

   A. The router adds 1 to the TTL.

   B. Nothing happens to the TTL.

   C. The router subtracts 1 from the TTL.

   D. The router adds a number equal to the metric to the TTL.

Answer: C. The router will decrease the TTL by 1 until it reaches 0. If the TTL is 0, the packet is discarded.

20. What two ways can Windows NT establish and maintain a route table?

A. Volatile

B. Dynamic

C. TTL

D. Static

Answer: B and D. NT route tables can be established and maintained either statically or dynamically.

21. How do you add static routes to a router table?

    A. Using the route command-line utility

    B. Using the Server Manager for Domains graphical user interface

    C. Using the Route Manager graphical user interface

    D. Using the table command-line utility

Answer: A. Static routes are added to an NT route table using the Route command-line utility.

22. Your company has experienced a sudden growth in the use of laptop computers. Users now want to dial up the company RAS server and access services using encryption. Which protocol(s) should you enable?

    A. PPP

    B. ISDN

    C. SLIP

    D. PPTP

Answer: D. The Point-to-Point Tunneling Protocol (PPTP) provides for encryption.

23. You have configured your RAS server to dial up your ISP to establish a connection. What gateway address should you put in the server's TCP/IP configuration for the dial-up connection?

    A. None, it should be left blank

    B. The IP address of the network interface connecting the server to the local network

   C. The IP address of the router that hooks into the ISP

   D. The IP address of the ISP server

Answer: A. The gateway address should be left blank.

24. Which utility is used to configure DHCP scopes?

   A. DHCP Manager

   B. Domain Manager

   C. TCP/IP Manager

   D. User Manager for Domains

Answer: A. DHCP Manager is used to configure scopes.

25. The first record created in a DNS database is a

   A. SOA

   B. PTR

   C. A

   D. NDS

Answer: A. The first record created in a DNS database is a Start of Authority record or SOA.

26. In the DNS database a "zone" is

   A. Another name for the root of the database

   B. The way the database is divided. COM and EDU are DNS Zones.

   C. The part of the database this server manages

   D. A scope of IP addresses

Answer: C. A DNS Zone is the part of the database managed by a particular server.

27. You are troubleshooting a host computer that is unable to connect to one particular host on the network. The rest of the computers appear to be communicating without a problem. You have checked the IP configuration running IPCONFIG.

You now want to test and see if the local computer can respond to IP commands. The command you would issue is

    A. WINIPCFG

    B. PING *local_ipaddress*

    C. PING *remote_IP address*

    D. PING 127.0.0.1

Answer: D. PING 127.0.0.1 or the local loopback will check the IP configuration to see if it will respond to IP commands.

28. What is the (#) pound sign used for in the HOSTS file?

    A. To designate a comment line

    B. To designate the end of a line

    C. To designate the end of page

    D. To designate a special tag

Answer: A. In a HOSTS file, the # (pound sign) is used for a comment.

29. To send a job to a remote TCP/IP printer, you would use which command-line utility?

    A. LPQ

    B. LPR

    C. Add Printer Wizard

    D. The Services tab in the Network dialog

Answer: B. To send a job to a remote TCP/IP printer, you would use the LPR command-line utility.

30. The LPR utility sends print jobs in what format, by default?

    A. Text

    B. PCL

    C. PostScript

    D. Binary

Answer: A. By default, the jobs are sent in a text format.

Part ii: Internet Information Server 4

1. You want to see when your site is most often accessed during the week. Which tool should you use?

   A. Report Writer

   B. Index Server

   C. Content Analyzer

   D. Performance Monitor

Answer: A. Report Writer will graph how your site has been accessed over a period of time.

2. You want to measure how much bandwidth your Web service consumes. Which counter should you monitor?

   A. Memory: Page Output/Sec

   B. IIS Global: Measured Async Bandwidth Usage

   C. Web Service: Bytes Total/Sec

   D. Active Server Pages: Transactions/Sec

Answer: C. Web Service: Bytes Total/Sec. Other answers are not specific to the Web service.

3. You've set up an MS SQL Server application for workflow control and created a client based on ActiveX and Active Server Pages that runs over your company's intranet. After a few weeks of operation, users complain that some duplicate entries are appearing in certain databases. These duplicate entries are causing some customers to be overbilled. After debugging, you find that some work-at-home users are frustrated with the speed of their connection and click the Back button on their browsers to re-post information to the server when it's slow. This causes some records to be added to the database while other related records are interrupted. Which of the following solutions actually solves this problem?

   A. Re-implement the application to use Transaction Server.

   B. Increase the speed of your home users' Internet links.

    C. Upgrade your server hardware so the application is more responsive.

    D. Use Data Access Components to ensure data integrity.

Answer: A. This problem is caused because the process is interrupted, leaving garbage records behind. Speeding up the server doesn't actually solve the problem, it just decreases the likelihood of occurrence.

4. How do you configure a Web site to use an ISAPI DLL?

    A. In the Home Directory tab of the Web site click Configuration and add an extension and a path to the file in the App Mappings tab.

    B. In the HTTP Headers tab of the Web site click Configuration and add an extension and a path to the file in the App Mappings tab.

    C. With the Registry Editor add an extension and a path to the file in the ScriptMap registry key.

    D. With the Registry Editor add an extension and a path to the file in the MimeMap registry key.

Answer: A. With IIS4 you no longer have to edit the registry to add an ISAPI DLL to a Web site.

5. You have an ISAPI DLL that provides encrypted communications to your Web site using the Triple DES cipher. You want that DLL to run in a separate memory space from other DLLs for security reasons and so you can start and stop that DLL separately from other IIS applications. How can you most easily achieve your objective?

    A. Re-implement the DLL as a CGI script.

    B. Run multiple copies of IIS.

    C. Start IIS from the Run... item in the Start menu. Check the Run in Separate Memory Space option.

    D. Check the Run in Separate Memory Space option in the Home Directory tab of the Web site.

Answer: D. You can cause the ISAPI DLLs for a directory to run in a separate memory space by clicking the option in that directory's tab.

6. You want to limit the scope of queries from within the /Products/Software/Downloads section of your Web site to just that section of your Web site. You want to be able to query your whole site from the home page, however. How can you do this most easily?

   A. Set the CiScope value in the .idq file to /Products/Software/Downloads.

   B. Remove Read permission for the IUSR_SEARCH user from all directories except for the /Products/Software/Downloads directory.

   C. Disable indexing on all virtual directories except for the /Products/Software/Downloads virtual directory.

   D. You cannot limit the scope of a query.

Answer: A. The CiScope value limits the scope of the query.

7. You have an Active Server Pages program that interacts with an ActiveX control to accept query parameters and feed them to the Internet Database Connector for a bibliography search of technical papers authored by professors at your university. The search process works great but you would like to liven up the format of the resulting output Web pages by adding some graphics and links back to your home page. Which file should you modify?

   A. Query.asp

   B. IDC.DLL

   C. Bibform.htx

   D. Query.idc

Answer: C. The .htx file specifies the format of the data resulting from the query. The .idc file specifies how the query should be presented to the database. The .asp file presents the original query form that the user enters search terms into. The .DLL is the executable extension to IIS that performs the queries as specified by the .idc and .htx files.

8. You have embedded a small routine to count the number of times a page has been accessed (using <% and %> to enclose the JScript program) in the file summary.html. Rather than executing the program, however, IIS just returns the program as you typed it in the resulting Web page. You verify that the directory has Script access enabled. What is wrong?

   A. You must remove the Read access for the directory.

   B. You must enable Execute (including Script) access for the directory.

   C. You must install a JScript interpreter ISAPI DLL.

   D. You must rename the file to have an .asp extension.

Answer: D. IIS will only scan the HTML page for scripts to execute if it has an extension, such as .asp, associated with a scripting DLL, such as ASP.DLL.

9. You want to monitor the number of connections made to your IIS computer in real time. Which tool would you use?

   A. Report Writer

   B. Index Server

   C. Content Analyzer

   D. Performance Monitor

Answer: D. Performance Monitor will graph the number of connections for you in real time and compare them to other operating system values.

10. Index Server queries are taking too long. You've already restricted queries to the file types you actually want queried, but because of heavy usage, the Index Server is still not able to keep up. Using the Performance Monitor, you determine that shadow merges and master merges are happening far too often because new documents are being updated frequently. Which optimizations will help? (Choose all that apply.)

   A. Increase the amount of disk space allocated for shadow merges.

   B. Change the default master merge time to occur at 4:00 A.M. when the network is less loaded.

   C. Increase the amount of disk space allocated to catalogs.

   D. Implement bandwidth throttling to limit the number of simultaneous queries.

   E. Install more RAM and increase the amount of memory reserved for word lists to decrease frequency of shadow merges and master merges.

   F. Move the catalog to a disk different than the corpus to reduce the time that merges take to execute.

Answer: B, **E**, and **F**. Increasing the amount of RAM allocated to word lists will increase time between merges, and moving the catalog will reduce the time that merges take to execute. Scheduling the master merge to occur in off hours also improves performance.

11. Your company will be creating a Human Resources site for internal use so employees can check their accrued vacation hours and other benefits. You want to provide a customized Web page for each employee that is generated when they access the site. Which solution will take the least effort to implement simple animation?

   A. Develop a WIN-CGI executable.

   B. Develop an ISAPI application.

   C. Develop an ASP script.

   D. Develop an ISAPI filter.

Answer: C. ASP provides the fastest and most customizable method for returning custom content.

12. You wish to efficiently extend IIS to support encrypted communications for all Web pages using the BLOWFISH cipher. Which environment best fits your needs?

   A. JScript

   B. An ISAPI application

   C. CGI

   D. An ISAPI filter

Answer: D. An ISAPI filter is an excellent way to control or extend how IIS handles its communications.

13. Create an FTP virtual directory called `results` with the physical path `d:\results` with read/write access in an FTP site from a running MMC console. Choose the appropriate steps:

    A. Right-click the FTP site, select New ➤ Site, type **results** in the site description input box, click Next, type **d:\results** in the Path input box, check Allow Read Access, check Allow Write Access, click Finish.

    B. Right-click the FTP site, select New ➤ Virtual Directory, type **results** in the Alias input box, type **d:\results** in the Path input box, check Allow Read Access, check Allow Write Access, click Finish.

    C. Right-click the host computer, select New ➤ FTP Site, type **results** in the site description input box, click Next, type **d:\results** in the Path input box, check Allow Read Access, check Allow Write Access, click Finish.

    D. Right-click the FTP site, select New ➤ Virtual Directory, type **results** in the Alias input box, type **d:\results** in the Path input box, click Finish.

Answer: B. A and C create a new FTP site; D does not implement access permissions correctly.

14. You've installed an IIS server at your Internet Service Provider's site so that it can participate on their high-speed Internet backbone directly, rather than being at the slow end of your T1 circuit. You need to determine how you will perform administrative functions like creating new sites remotely. The solution must be secure so that your IIS server can withstand hacking attempts from the Internet. You can configure your firewall to pass any network traffic you want between your site and the remote server.

    Proposed Solution #1: Install the remote server. Enable Windows networking so that you can connect to the server using the MMC. Open the firewall to allow Windows networking protocols to pass.

Proposed Solution #2: Install the remote server. Use the HTML service managers to manage the Web sites and disable the Workstation, RPC, and Server services on the remote IIS server.

Choose the best answer:

A. Neither will work.

B. Both will work, but Solution #1 is preferable.

C. Both will work, but Solution #2 is preferable.

D. Both will work equally well.

Answer: C. This solution prevents a wide range of hacking exploits and is optimized for low bandwidth connections. Solution #1 will work but opens your IIS server up to a wide range of security holes.

15. What tool do you use to generate keys?

A. User Manager

B. Key Manager

C. Certificate Server

D. Microsoft Management Console

Answer: B. The Certificate Server digitally signs keys created by the Key Manager.

16. Choose the sequence that enables SMTP service transaction logs to create a new log every month using the Microsoft IIS Log File Format:

A. Select the Default SMTP Site, select Action ➤ Properties, check Enable Logging, click OK.

B. Select the local host, select Action ➤ Properties, select SMTP Service in the Master Properties pick box, check Enable Logging, select Microsoft IIS Log File Format, click OK.

C. Select the default SMTP Site, select Action ➤ Properties, select SMTP Service in the Master Properties pick box, check Enable Logging, select Microsoft IIS Log File Format, click Properties, select Monthly, click OK, click OK.

    D. Select the local host, select Action ➤ Properties, select SMTP Service in the Master Properties pick box, check Enable Logging, select Microsoft IIS Log File Format, click OK.

Answer: C. Other options either don't work or do not complete the requirement.

17. Create a virtual directory for the NNTP service to store the test.results newsgroup in the `g:\results` directory. Choose the correct sequence:

    A. Right-click the NNTP site, select New ➤ Virtual Directory, enter **test.results** in the Newsgroup Name, click Next, enter **g:\results**, click Finish.

    B. Right-click the NNTP site, select Properties, select the Directories tab, click New, enter **test.results** in the Newsgroup Name, click Next, enter **g:\results**, click Finish.

    C. Right-click the NNTP site, select Properties, select Groups, click Create New Newsgroup, enter **test.results** in the Newsgroup Name, click OK.

    D. Right-click the NNTP site, select Properties, select Groups, click Create New Newsgroup, enter **test.results** in the Newsgroup Name, enter **g:\results** in the path input box, click OK.

Answer: A. C creates a newsgroup in the root directory, not in a virtual directory, and the other options won't work.

18. Enable NNTP Service logging using W3C Extended Log File Format. Choose the correct sequence:

    A. Right-click Default NNTP site, select Properties, check Enable Logging, click OK.

    B. Right-click your Internet Server, select Properties, click Edit, check Enable Logging, click OK, click OK.

    C. Right-click your Internet Server, select Properties, click Edit, check Enable Logging, select W3C Extended Log File Format, click OK, click OK.

    D. Right-click Default NNTP site, select Properties, check Enable Logging, select W3C Extended Log File Format, click OK.

Answer: D. A selects Microsoft logging format, and B and C modify Web site logging, not NNTP logging.

19. You've noticed a number of broken links while browsing your company's Web site. What tool will help you fix these broken links the fastest? (Choose all that apply.)

    A. Report Writer

    B. Content Analyzer

    C. Usage Import

    D. Microsoft Management Console

Answer: B. Content Analyzer is used to analyze Web site content.

20. You want to tune the bandwidth settings of your various Web sites to keep some from overwhelming other, more important sites that sustain lower usage. What tool will help you determine how Internet browsers are using the several Web sites on your server? (Choose all that apply.)

    A. Report Writer

    B. Content Analyzer

    C. Usage Import

    D. Microsoft Management Console

Answer: A, C, and **D**. Report Writer and Usage Import work together to create reports from IIS service logs, which must be configured using the Microsoft Management Console.

21. You've implemented a Web site on your file server and intend to use NT file system security to secure the site. When you right-click the directory that you intend to secure and select Properties, you notice that there's no Security tab so you can't set file system security. What's wrong?

    A. The volume is formatted with the FAT file system.

    B. You haven't turned on file auditing.

C. You haven't enabled file system security in the Internet Service Manager.

D. You aren't logged in as the administrator so you can't change security permissions.

Answer: A. FAT volumes have no security options.

22. Your Web site is secured using the following permissions:

IUSR_*computername*	Read
Everyone	No Access
Domain Users	Change

Additionally, you've set IIS access permissions to Read, and you've disabled anonymous access through the Directory Security tab. Users complain that they cannot access the Web site through their browsers. How can you correct the problem?

A. Enable anonymous access using the Microsoft Management Console.

B. Set the IUSR_*computername* permission to Change using the desktop Explorer.

C. Delete the Everyone ACE using the desktop Explorer.

D. Set the Domain Users permission to Read.

Answer: C. In this case, the specific No Access permission for Everyone overrides all other access permissions.

23. Increased reliance on your corporate intranet has caused the site to grow larger than originally anticipated. You install another hard disk in your Web server, format it with the NT file system, and copy your site files to the new volume. You then configure the IIS services to point to the new locations using the virtual directory feature, making sure that your directory access settings are exactly the same as before. Suddenly, all users have access to the formerly secured financial directories. Why did this happen?

A. You've used the wrong file system on the new hard disk drive.

B. You've improperly configured IIS directory access security for the virtual directories in the Microsoft Management Console.

C. The new site is allowing anonymous access.

D. NTFS permissions were reset when you copied the files between volumes.

Answer: D. Copying files between volumes causes those files to receive the NTFS permissions of the parent directory on the new volume.

24. How do you redirect a Web browser that requests a Web site that has moved to another computer on the Internet (not a part of your domain)?

A. Set the Local Path of the Web site to the UNC path of the new host computer (e.g., `\\IP address\share name`). Enter a valid username and password for the share.

B. Change the default document to a document that informs the user that that site no longer exists.

C. Click the button for a share located on another computer and then set the Network Directory of the Web site to the UNC path of the new host computer (e.g., `\\IP address\share name`). Enter a valid username and password for the share.

D. Click the button for a redirection to a URL and enter the new URL to the home site in the Redirect to: field.

Answer: D. With a redirection IIS simply tells the Web browser where to look for the files, rather than retrieving the files and sending them to the browser.

25. You want anonymous access to your new virtual Web site to be done through a different anonymous access account than the default Web site uses, so you enter a new anonymous account name and password in the Directory Security portion of the Web site's Properties window. After you do this users are no longer able to access the Web site anonymously. What is wrong?

A. You must reboot your Web server computer for the changes to take effect.

B. The default anonymous account name and password for all Web services is overriding the password you have selected for that specific Web site. Remove the account name and password from the anonymous account settings at the computer level.

C. The account must be one of those listed in the Operators tab for the Web site.

D. You must also create the anonymous account using the User Manager or User Manager for Domains program and assign it the same password that you used in IIS. The account must also have Log on locally rights.

Answer: D. The account must also exist as a Windows NT account, and IIS will not create it for you. Do *not* make the anonymous account also an operator for the Web site–that would allow anyone to change your Web site settings!

26. Select the correct sequence of actions to create a virtual Web site called Human Resources in the D:\HR directory from the MMC with the distinct IP address of 10.1.1.7 (assuming this address has already been added to the TCP/IP protocol on your machine). (Choose all correct answers.)

A. Right-click the server and select New ➤ Web Site. Type **Human Resources** and press Enter. Select 10.1.1.7 in the Select IP Address list box. Click Next. Click Next. Click Finish.

B. Right-click the default Web site and select New ➤ Site. Type **Human Resources** and press Enter. Select 10.1.1.7 in the Select IP Address list box. Click Next. Type **D:\HR** and press Enter. Click Finish.

C. Right-click the server and select New ➤ Web Site. Type **Human Resources** and press Enter. Select 10.1.1.7 in the Select IP Address list box. Click Next. Type **D:\HR** and press Enter. Click Finish.

D. Right-click the server and select New ➤ Web Site. Type **Human Resources** and press Enter. Click Next. Click Next. Type **D:\HR** and press Enter. Click Finish.

Answer: B and **C**. A does not specify the path; D does not specify the IP address.

27. You want to use Content Analyzer to map a Web site that contains password-protected Web pages. The pages are in a directory that has only Windows NT Challenge/Response enabled. Content Analyzer fails to map those pages when you make the map using a URL. What is the problem?

   A. You must enable the "Allow Content Analyzer to Scan Directory" permission in the Web site's Properties panel.

   B. You must enable Basic Authentication for that directory.

   C. You must enable Secure Socket Layer communications for that directory.

   D. You must provide a correct default domain for basic authentication in the Web directory Security tab for that directory.

Answer: B. Site Server Express uses Basic Authentication to connect to password-secured resources via a URL.

28. You have a 56K connection to the Internet. You've noticed that some very large files are being sent to your SMTP server by clients who are attaching pictures to their mail messages. You want to reject e-mail messages larger than 32K. Choose the method that will enable you to close connections when messages are too large:

   A. Select Default SMTP Site, select Action ➢ Properties, select Messages, enter **32** in the Maximum Message Size input box.

   B. Select Default SMTP Site, select Action ➢ Properties, select Messages, enter **32** in the Maximum Session Size input box.

   C. Select Default SMTP Site, select Action ➢ Properties, select Delivery, enter **32** in the Maximum Message Size input box.

   D. Select Default SMTP Site, select Action ➢ Properties, select Delivery, enter **32** in the Maximum Session Size input box.

Answer: B. Although A appears correct, the Microsoft SMTP service will still allow messages larger than the size specified there. Using a maximum session size, the connection will be dropped immediately if the message is larger than the size specified. C and D don't work.

29. You've established a single Index Server for your company that actually searches four different Web servers. Index Server won't return pages for the two Web servers on different domains. What should you do? (Choose all correct answers.)

    A. Establish trust relationships between the domains.

    B. Establish a user account with the necessary permissions to scan directories in the other domains.

    C. Stop and start the Content Index service.

    D. Add virtual directories that match the Web shares on the remote machines.

Answer: A, B, C, and **D**. All these steps are necessary for inter-domain indexing.

30. Which answer describes the steps necessary to delete the default catalog, assuming the Management Console is already running and the Index Server snap-in is loaded?

    A. Select Index Server on Local Machine, select Action ➤ Stop, select Action ➤ Delete.

    B. Select Index Server on Local Machine, select Action ➤ Stop, Expand Index Server on Local Machine, Expand Web, select Directories, select `c:\inetpub\wwwroot` (or its equivalent on your machine), select Action ➤ Delete.

    C. Select Index Server on Local Machine, select Action ➤ Stop, Expand Index Server on Local Machine, select Web, select Action ➤ Delete.

    D. Expand Index Server on Local Machine, select Web, select Action ➤ Delete ➤ Catalog, click OK.

Answer: C. Other options either are impossible or don't delete the catalog.

Part iii: Exchange 5.5

1. Which of the following MIBs defines the parameters available for management on an Exchange server?

   A. EXCH.MIB

   B. MADMAN MIB

   C. MIBCC.MIB

   D. PERFMON.MIB

   Answer: B. The MADMAN MIB defines the industry-standard e-mail and directory parameters available.

2. You have just added the SNMP service to your Exchange server. You are already using an SNMP management console to manage other services on your server and you have previously customized your MIB.BIN file. Which of the following would you run to configure the Exchange SNMP parameters?

   A. Run the INSTALL.BAT file located in the SUPPORT\ SNMP\<PLATFORM>\ directory of your Exchange server compact disk.

   B. Run the PERF2MIB and MIBCC commands from a command prompt.

   C. Nothing; installing the SNMP service is all that is needed.

   D. Installing the SNMP service installs a new version of Performance Monitor that answers SNMP calls from a management console.

   Answer: B. The PERF2MIB and MIBCC commands add the Exchange-specific parameters to your MIB.BIN file. They must be run manually if you have previously customized your MIB.BIN file.

3. You are upgrading an Exchange server to version 5.5. The upgrade fails within the first 15 minutes every time you attempt it. You've watched the screen and it fails at a different point in the process each time. Which of the following would you try first?

   A. Try a different Exchange Server 5.5 CD-ROM to see if you have a bad disk.

B. Ensure that the network connection is functional.

C. Disable any server monitors that might be checking the server you are upgrading.

D. Check to see that you have sufficient disk space available for the upgrade.

Answer: C. There could be many reasons for this problem but given our list of solutions, answer C makes the most sense. Perhaps there is a server monitor that is checking the Exchange services and forcing them to restart in the middle of the upgrade process.

4. You are upgrading your older Exchange 4.0 software to Exchange 5.5. The upgrade process fails with an error message that mentions the schema. Which of the following is the most likely cause?

A. Exchange 4.0 cannot be upgraded directly to version 5.5. You must purchase version 5.0 and upgrade to that first.

B. You have not installed SP2 on your Exchange 4.0 servers.

C. Your bridgehead servers are not communicating between sites.

D. Your Exchange databases have become corrupted and you must restore them from tape before continuing.

Answer: B. Remember that the schema changed from version 4.0 to version 5.x. Applying SP2 to your Exchange 4.0 servers will update the schema.

5. Your installation of Exchange Server 5.5 went just fine on your first Exchange server. Everything seemed to be working until the first time you restarted the computer. At that point, none of the Exchange Server components started correctly. Upon examining the event log you find errors that indicate a failed logon. Which of the following would you do first?

A. Call a few individuals to determine if anyone else is having problems logging on to the system.

B. Reinstall Exchange to recreate the security information.

    C. Check the site service account to determine if the User Must Change Password at Next Logon box is checked.

    D. Turn on auditing to audit failed logon attempts.

Answer: C. Remember that the site service account is used as the security context of the Exchange components. If it is forced to change its password, it will fail the logon and no Exchange services will load.

6.   Server A in your site has a current USN of 10. The last time Server B communicated with Server A the USN was 5. Which of the following will occur?

    A. Server A will request changes from Server B.

    B. Server B will request changes from Server A.

    C. No replication will occur.

    D. Both servers will query a third server to determine what the value should be.

Answer: B. Changes have occurred on Server A since the last time they replicated, as evidenced by the USN numbers.

7.   Users are reporting errors when trying to send e-mail to other users on their home Exchange server. Which of the following would you do first?

    A. Check to ensure that they have the appropriate permissions to the Exchange Directories.

    B. Check the installation of the Outlook client for those users to determine if it is configured properly.

    C. Check the recipients' configuration to determine if a faulty rule has been configured that is denying receipt of e-mail.

    D. Check to see if the users are members of the Mail Users global group.

Answer: A. First check to ensure that Exchange has been configured correctly.

8. You are migrating a foreign e-mail system into your Exchange environment. Which of the following would help speed up the process?

   A. Add RAM to the Exchange server performing the migration.

   B. Migrate users in groups. This way only a few mailboxes would be migrated during any given migration process.

   C. Delete unnecessary messages in the mailboxes on the existing system before performing the migration.

   D. Delete any unused mailboxes in the existing e-mail system before performing the migration.

Answer: A, C, D. The migration process can place a heavy load on the server. Adding RAM reduces the amount of paging and therefore improves performance. Cleaning up the old environment before migration reduces the amount of data that must be converted, thereby reducing the amount of time it takes.

9. After migrating a Lotus cc:Mail system into your Exchange organization, you discover that some users' messages were not migrated. Which of the following is the most likely cause?

   A. Those users had not granted proxy rights to the account performing the migration.

   B. Mail over 30 days old cannot be migrated from a cc:Mail system.

   C. Users whose account name is over 12 characters long are not migrated.

   D. Those users are probably remote users with e-mail stored locally.

Answer: D. Have those users save their e-mail to a temporary post office and run the migration against that post office.

10. Your users are complaining that they are unable to receive e-mail from clients over the Internet. Which of the following actions would you take?

   A. Call the administrator at one of the client sites and ask if their Internet e-mail system is configured properly.

B. Place a packet analyzer on your network and check to see if the e-mail is reaching the router.

C. Attempt to Ping a remote server by using its FQDN.

D. Check the IMS queues to see if e-mail is becoming backlogged in a queue.

Answer: C, D. Attempt the Ping first—if this doesn't work, the problem is TCP/IP related. If the Ping is successful, check the IMS queues.

11. E-mail has become critical to your company. Rather than wait for user complaints, you want to know about connectivity problems in a timely manner. Which of the following actions would you take?

A. Configure a series of link monitors between your servers, configuring them to e-mail you in the event of a problem.

B. Designate one person in each department to call you as soon as anyone has a problem.

C. Configure a packet analysis tool to alert you in the event of line problems.

D. Configure your client to send a message to a non-existent account on each server every 15 minutes.

Answer: A. Link monitors are designed to alert you in the event of communication problems.

12. A client calls and complains that they cannot access their e-mail. Upon further discussion, you discover that their Outlook client is displaying an error message that states that the e-mail server cannot be found. Which of the following should be your next step?

A. Ensure that the user's mailbox has not been deleted.

B. Replace the network cable to their computer.

C. Check their profile to ensure that their account information has been entered correctly.

D. Have them click their Network Neighborhood to ensure that they can see the server on the network.

Answer: D. If the user has accessed their e-mail in the past, check to ensure that the problem is not network-related before trouble-shooting their e-mail profile.

13. After installing Exchange Server on one of your existing NT servers, you find that backups are taking an extremely long time to complete. Which of the following corrective actions would you perform first?

   A. Move the tape device to another server and perform the backup across the network.

   B. Set the IS maintenance schedule so that it does not overlap with the backup schedule.

   C. Move some data to another server to reduce the overall amount of time necessary to back up the server.

   D. Limit the space allowed for each mailbox.

Answer: B. Since backups were finishing before the installation of Exchange, we can assume that the process is working correctly. This means that one of two things has occurred: the Exchange databases are so large that they are adding extra time to the back-up process, or some Exchange service is competing with the backup software for system resources. The easiest fix would be to ensure that IS maintenance is not competing for resources.

14. Your company had a power failure last night. When the system restarts, Exchange does not seem to be working. Upon checking the Services applet, you notice that the IS service has not started properly. Which of the following trouble-shooting tasks would you perform?

   A. Run a disk utility to clean up your file structure.

   B. Run the NT PROB.EXE utility to check for problems in the registry.

   C. Restore your Exchange environment from backup.

   D. Run ISINTEG –FIX to fix the problem.

Answer: D. ISINTEG is designed to fix inconsistencies in the Information Store databases.

15. You have determined that your Exchange directory has become badly corrupted. Which of the following tools would you use to correct this problem?

   A. EDBUTIL.EXE

   B. ESEUTIL.EXE

   C. DBMAINT.EXE

   D. DIRFIX.EXE

Answer: B. The ESEUTIL.EXE utility can attempt to recover the database by recreating each object.

16. You would like to ensure that objects are deleted from your directory database soon after they are marked for deletion. Which of the following parameters would you change?

   A. RTS Checkpoint value

   B. Tombstone lifetime

   C. Deletion interval

   D. DIRFIX timeout

Answer: B. The tombstone lifetime controls how long a deleted object remains in the directory before being physically deleted.

17. You suspect that an Exchange service has recently been restarted. Which of the following methods would confirm your suspicion?

   A. Check the date on the appropriate file in the \EXCH-SRVR folder.

   B. Look through the NT event log.

   C. Check the "time of service" statistics in the Exchange Administrator program.

   D. In Performance Monitor, check the Process: Elapsed Time statistic for the service.

Answer: B, D. Both B and D are correct although it might be easier to find the information in Performance Monitor rather than having to look through the entire event log.

18. While performing your regular maintenance you notice that the Performance Monitor counter Processor: %Processor Time is consistently over 90%. What does this indicate?

   A. The processor is not being used for 90% of the time.

   B. The processor is being used over 90% of the time.

   C. You should add more services to this server to use the free time available.

   D. You should move processing to another server to take the load off this server.

Answer: B, D. This server is working more than 90% of the time and is probably overburdened.

19. You are attempting to track the route of a message sent by one local user to another. The list comes up empty. What is the probable cause?

   A. You have not enabled message tracking on the appropriate components.

   B. You do not have the permission to track another user's e-mail.

   C. The message was lost before it was received by the Exchange server.

   D. The message was never sent—the user is lying.

Answer: A. Remember, message tracking is not enabled by default.

20. The message tracking information for a particular message says that it was delivered to the Internet Mail Service and forwarded on. It was never received by the recipient. Which of the following would you do next?

   A. Check the IMS outgoing queue to see if the message is awaiting delivery.

   B. Call the administrator of the other e-mail system and have them confirm that their Internet Mail system is configured properly.

    C. Have the user resend the message and see if it goes through this time.

    D. Uninstall IMS and reinstall it.

Answer: B. If other Internet e-mail messages are being properly delivered, and the message has left your Exchange system, you can feel confident that your IMS connector is configured properly.

21. You have performed a restore using your backup tapes. Upon restarting the Exchange server, you notice that the IS service has not started properly. Which of the following is the most likely problem?

    A. Your tape backup was corrupted.

    B. Your tape device is not supported by Windows NT 4.0.

    C. The Windows NT backup utility cannot backup Exchange.

    D. You need to run the ISINTEG utility with the –PATCH option.

Answer: D. Always run ISINTEG –PATCH after performing a restore of an IS that was backed up offline.

22. You back up all of your servers from a central location. You notice that you cannot back up the Exchange Server environment. What is the likely cause of this problem?

    A. The network is too slow to perform a backup.

    B. You have not installed the extensions to the backup utility on the backup server.

    C. Your tape is not large enough to hold the Exchange databases.

    D. You do not have the permissions necessary to perform an Exchange backup.

Answer: B. Remember that the NT backup utility as installed from the NT CD-ROM is not capable of backing up Exchange servers until the extensions are installed.

23. After a restart, the KM Server will not finish the boot process. What is the probable cause?

A. The KM service is RAM-intensive. The server probably does not have enough RAM.

B. The KM Server requires a password to complete its boot process.

C. The KM service has become corrupted and needs to be reinstalled.

D. After a restart, the KM Server must be reinitialized using the Exchange 5.5 CD-ROM.

Answer: B. The KM Server will not boot completely unless the KM password is provided.

24. You recently purchased a tape jukebox system to back up all of the NT servers on your network. On the first backup attempt, you find that everything except Exchange is backing up properly. Which of the following is the most likely problem?

A. Exchange Server can only be backed up to a local tape drive.

B. The backup program must be configured to back up remote systems.

C. You must stop the Exchange Server services manually before backing them up.

D. You must install the Exchange Administrator program on the central computer so that the NT Backup program is replaced with the Exchange-aware version.

Answer: D. The version of NTBACKUP that ships with NT cannot perform an online backup of Exchange.

25. Which of the following are advantages of a server-based message store configuration?

A. Central location for backups

B. Mail is available to roving and mobile users.

C. Lower overhead at the server

D. Less overall disk space used

Answer: A, B, D. Only answer C is incorrect. Since all e-mail is stored at, and therefore accessed from, the server, overhead at the server is increased.

26. Your company wants to ensure that the time stamps on all e-mail messages are consistent. Which of the following solutions would you suggest?

   A. Use the AT.EXE utility to schedule a process on remote servers to set the time.

   B. Configure your link monitor to include the system time in its message to remote servers.

   C. Configure your server monitor to synchronize time between the target server and the server upon which it is running.

   D. Add a manual timecheck to your daily maintenance tasks.

Answer: C. Server monitors can be used to synchronize time between servers.

27. You wish to run the Exchange Performance Optimizer to optimize your Exchange server. You also want to mandate some advanced configuration parameters. Which of the run commands would suit your needs?

   A. `<DRIVE:>\EXCHSRVR\BIN\PERFWIZ.EXE`

   B. `<DRIVE:>\EXCHSRVR\BIN\ADVOPT.EXE`

   C. `<DRIVE:>\EXCHSRVR\BIN\PERFWIZ.EXE -V`

   D. `<DRIVE:>\EXCHSRVR\BIN\PERFWIZ.EXE -ADVANCED`

Answer: C. The −V command line parameter causes PERFWIZ .EXE to offer additional configuration parameters.

28. Which of the following are disadvantages of using fewer, more powerful Exchange servers?

   A. Fewer vendor choices are available.

   B. Backup time increases.

C.   Server failure affects more users.

D.   Less network traffic is generated.

Answer: A, B, C. Only answer D is incorrect. Because more users' mailboxes reside on each server, fewer messages will need to be routed to another server. This is not a disadvantage but an advantage to your network.

29. Which of the following would be a valid user account to use when installing an Exchange server into an existing site?

A.   Any user account

B.   None. Since Exchange supports anonymous access, you do not need to be logged in.

C.   The account of any member of the administrators group

D.   The hidden recipient site service account created during the Exchange installation

Answer: C. The user installing Exchange must be a member of the administrators group because the setup program must access the registry of an existing Exchange server in the site.

30. Which of the following are required to access e-mail using an Internet browser?

A.   Active Server Pages

B.   Internet Information Server

C.   POP3 services

D.   A browser which supports JavaScripts and frames technologies

Answer: A, B, D.

Part iv: SQL Server 7 Administration

1. You have several Macintosh users on your network that require access to your SQL Server. Which type of account should they be assigned?

   A. Windows NT account

   B. SQL Server login

   Answer: B. Macintosh users require a SQL Server login since they do not log on to Windows NT networks.

2. What is the smallest unit of allocation in SQL, and how large is it?

   A. Page; 2KB

   B. Page; 8KB

   C. Extent; 8KB

   D. Extent; 64KB

   Answer: B. The page is the smallest unit of allocation; the extent (at 64KB or eight pages) is the largest.

3. Your database crashes on Tuesday at 3:00 P.M. Using the following backup schedule, which backups would you have to restore to bring the database back up to date?

   ▶ Saturday at 1:00 A.M.; full backup

   ▶ Weekdays every two hours starting at 8:00 A.M.; transaction log backups

   ▶ Weekdays at 10:00 P.M; differential backup

   A. Restore Saturday's full backup and all of the available transaction logs from Tuesday.

   B. Restore Saturday's full backup, all of the transaction log backups from Monday, then the Monday differential, and finally the transaction log backups from Tuesday.

   C. Restore Saturday's full backup, the differential from Monday, and the available transaction log backups from Tuesday.

    D. Restore the differential backup from Monday and the available transaction log backups from Tuesday.

Answer: C.   If you use differential backups during the week, you need to restore only the full backup, then the differential, and then the transaction log backups that occurred after the differential backup.

4. True or false. The Upgrade Wizard is the best tool for upgrading from Access to SQL Server 7.

    A. True

    B. False

Answer: B.   The Upgrade Wizard will only upgrade SQL 6.*x* to SQL 7.

5. Which of the following types of replication makes a complete replicate of the published data on the Subscriber?

    A. Merge

    B. Transactional

    C. Copy

    D. Snapshot

Answer: D.   Snapshot is the only type that copies the full database every time. Incidentally, copy is not a type of replication.

6. Your company is based in New York with branches in Singapore, Paris, and Taiwan. All of these branches will need access to data stored on your server in their own language. How can you accomplish this?

    A. You can't.

    B. Choose a different sort order for each database.

    C. Choose the desired character set when you create the database.

    D. Choose the default Unicode character set, which allows different character sets in each database.

Answer: D. Unicode makes it possible to store data from more than one language, no matter what character set is used.

7. When SQL is first installed, what configuration is required for SQL to make use of the available RAM?

   A. Changing the Memory setting on the Configuration tab in the Server Properties dialog box

   B. Running `sp_configure 'memory', amount_of_ram`

   C. Setting min and max server memory settings

   D. None—SQL does this dynamically

Answer: D. While you can set the min and max memory settings, you aren't required to do so—SQL can assign itself memory dy-namically. The first two options are valid in SQL 6.5, but not in 7.

8. True or false. To make the server easier to administer, you should create a single full-text catalog to contain all full-text indexes from all databases on your server.

   A. True

   B. False

Answer: B. You cannot create a single, giant catalog. Each database must have its own catalog.

9. Your network comprises Windows 95, Windows 98, and Macintosh clients. Which authentication mode should you use?

   A. Mixed

   B. Windows NT Authentication

Answer: A. Your Macintosh users will require Mixed mode since they are incapable of making a trusted connection.

10. JohnsonK is a member of the sysadmins fixed server role. She creates a table in the Sales database called Customers. Who is the owner of the table?

A. JohnsonK

B. Sysadmins

C. Administrators

D. dbo

Answer: D.   Whenever a member of the sysadmins group creates an object, it belongs to the dbo user.

11. You want to grant administrative rights on the SQL server to some of your users. How should you do this?

    A. Add the users to the Windows NT Administrators local group.

    B. Add logins for each user separately and make each of them members of the sysadmins fixed server role.

    C. Add each of the users to a new Windows NT group called SQLAdmins, add a login for the new group, and make the new login a member of the sysadmins fixed server role.

    D. Create logins for each user and add each user to the db_owner database role in each database.

Answer: C.   Answer A would work, but it lowers security, and B would increase administrative load. Answer D would give administrative rights only in the databases, not at the server level.

12. GibsonH is a member of the accounting and finance groups. Accounting has Select permission on the employees table in the accounting database. The Select permission has been revoked from finance on the same table. Can GibsonH select from the employees table?

    A. Yes

    B. No

Answer: A.   Since the permission was merely revoked from finance and not denied, GibsonH will be able to read from the employees table since he inherits the Select permission from accounting.

13. SamuelsR owns a table and grants ChenJ Select permission. ChenJ creates a view and grants AdamsK Select permission. What are the results when AdamsK tries to select from the view?

 A. AdamsK can select from the table since she has permission to do so.

 B. AdamsK cannot read from the table since she has not been given permission on the underlying table.

Answer: B. This is a prime example of a broken ownership chain—since the owner changed from the view (ChenJ) to the table (SamuelsR), SQL had to verify permissions at each level.

14. True or false. By tracking the Delete event under the SQL Operators event class, you can actually stop users from deleting objects.

 A. True

 B. False

Answer: B. While this event will tell you just before an object is deleted, it will not stop the delete statement from executing.

15. When you use T-SQL to create a 100MB database, but do not specify the transaction log parameters, what happens?

 A. No transaction log is created.

 B. A 10MB transaction log is created in the same directory as the data file.

 C. A 25MB transaction log is created in the same directory as the data file.

 D. The CREATE DATABASE statement fails when the transaction log information is not specified.

Answer: C. A transaction log that is 25 percent of the size of the data file will be created in the same directory as the data file.

16. Your company has just bought out a smaller company that is using an Access database to store critical information. You need to import this data into an SQL table for use by your users. What is the easiest way to do this?

A. Export all of the data from the Access database to a text file, then import the text file into SQL using the INSERT statement.

B. Export all of the data from the Access database to a text file, then import the text file into SQL using the BULK INSERT statement.

C. Export all of the data from the Access database to a text file, then import the text file into SQL using bcp.

D. Use the DTS Import Wizard.

Answer: D.   Answers B and C would have worked, but they require you to use Access to create the text file. The DTS Wizard will access the Access database for you via ODBC.

17. You have been performing full backups once a week and differential backups every night for the last two months. When is your transaction log cleared?

A. Never.

B. When the full backup is performed.

C. When the differential backup is performed.

D. SQL will clear it automatically when it gets too full.

Answer: A.   If you do not perform transaction log backups, your transaction log will not be cleared. The only way to have a transaction log cleared automatically is by setting the Truncate Log on Checkpoint option to true (which should be done only on a development system).

18. One of your users has discovered some malicious updates to your data that occurred the day before at about 2:00. How can you bring the database back to the state it was in just before the update occurred?

A. Perform a full database restoration with point-in-time recovery.

B. Perform a differential database restoration with point-in-time recovery.

    C. Perform a transaction log restoration with point-in-time recovery.

    D. You cannot bring the database back to the previous state.

Answer: C. Transaction log restorations can be restored up to a point in time. This means that you can bring the database right back to the state it was in just before the update.

19. You have been successfully replicating data to several of your servers for over a month when suddenly replication stops functioning. What is the most likely cause?

    A. The distribution agent has been disabled.

    B. The transaction log on the Distribution database has filled to capacity.

    C. The Publication database has become corrupt.

    D. The Subscription database has become corrupt.

Answer: B. Like any other database, the Distribution database has a transaction log that must be cleared through a regular transaction log backup. If that does not happen, the log will fill, and replication will cease.

20. You have configured several operators that are scheduled to be paged throughout the week and on the weekend. There is, however, no one scheduled to be paged on Sunday morning from 12:00 A.M. to 8:00 A.M. What happens if there is a critical error during that time?

    A. SQL will page the last person who was on duty.

    B. No one will be paged.

    C. If there is a fail-safe operator, that person will be paged.

    D. The error message will be queued until the next operator is scheduled to be paged.

Answer: C. If you have a fail-safe operator, they will be paged; otherwise, no one will be paged.

21. You have configured your servers to perform distributed queries using account delegation. Who can run the distributed query?

    A. Only people who are logged in using a standard login

    B. Only people who are logged in with a Windows NT login

    C. Anyone who has logged in and been validated

    D. Only members of the db_execlinked role

Answer: B.   Only users who have logged in with a Windows NT account will be able to access the distributed query when the servers are configured to use account delegation. Incidentally, D is a trick answer.

22. You need to know if your SQL Server can handle the load that your users are placing on it. When should you monitor your server?

    A. In the morning, when your users first start up.

    B. Just after lunch, when your users are getting back.

    C. There is no set time—monitor when activity is at its lowest.

    D. There is no set time—monitor when activity is at its highest.

Answer: D.   If you monitor when activity is at its highest, you will get an accurate reading of the stress your users place on the system.

23. You are running both SQL Server and Exchange Server on the same computer due to budget constraints. How should memory usage be configured so that both programs run efficiently?

    A. In SQL Server, adjust the Min Server Memory setting.

    B. In SQL Server, adjust the Max Server Memory setting.

    C. Set the Set Working Size option to one after setting both Min and Max Server Memory to the same size.

    D. Do nothing—SQL will detect Exchange and automatically assign RAM accordingly.

Answer: B. By adjusting the Max Server Memory setting, you can instruct SQL not to take all available RAM—then, some RAM will be left over for Exchange.

24. You are concerned that some of your users are writing queries that are wasting system resources because they take too long to complete (on average, more than three seconds). How can you stop SQL from running queries that take longer than three seconds to execute?

    A. Use `sp_configure 'query governor cost limit', '3'`.

    B. Use `sp_configure 'query governor', '3'`.

    C. Use `sp_configure 'query limit', '3'`.

    D. Use `sp_configure 'query governor limit', '3'`.

Answer: A. The other three options are all typos and would not function.

25. What steps should you take to prepare your server before running the Upgrade Wizard?

    A. Increase the size of Master to 25MB.

    B. Increase the size of Tempdb to 25MB.

    C. Disable automatic execution of stored procedures.

    D. Disable replication.

Answer: B, C, and D. Master cannot be less than 25MB in the first place; the other three options are requirements for upgrading.

26. You want to restore a database to your server. Your server is using case-insensitive sort order, and the backup was made on a server using binary sort order. Will the restoration work?

    A. Yes, the restoration will work.

    B. Yes, the restoration will work, but there will be warnings.

    C. Yes, the restoration will work, but only the data will be restored—the schema must be created first.

    D. No, the restoration will fail.

Answer: D.   You cannot restore a database that was backed up using a different sort order or code page.

27. The distributor has been offline for two days due to a systems failure. What do you need to do to update the subscribers?

    A. Nothing—they will resynchronize themselves.

    B. From the publisher, run a snapshot for each of the subscribers.

    C. From the distributor, run the `sp_resynch` stored procedure.

    D. Delete and re-create the subscription at each subscriber.

Answer: B.   Running a snapshot after the distributor has been down for an extended period will resynchronize your subscribers.

28. You have just created a new custom alert that does not seem to be firing. What is the most likely cause?

    A. The condition that causes the alert never occurred.

    B. The alert is not enabled.

    C. No operator is associated with the alert.

    D. The alert is not being written to the Windows NT application log.

Answer: D.   All errors must be written to the application log; if not, they will not fire.

29. True or false. All of the servers in a distributed query must be SQL Servers version 6.*x* or higher.

    A. True

    B. False

Answer: B.   Any ODBC database can be part of a distributed query.

30. One of your users is complaining that they could access the SQL Server yesterday, but this morning, they can't seem to gain access to the databases. What should you do?

    A. Find out if the user can gain access to anything else on the network; if they can't, fix the connection.

    B. Check the DB-Library version and make sure it is the same as the server's.

    C. Make sure the client and server are running the same Net-Library.

    D. Have the user reboot the machine and try again.

Answer: A. The very first step is to make sure the user can access the network; just because they logged on to the local machine, it does not mean they are on the network.

Part v: Internet Explorer 4 Administration Kit

1. You have been asked to distribute a browser to several public kiosks. These browsers must be able to start using the kiosk mode and load a page found at the URL `http://www.myfishhook.com/kiosk.htm`. What command would you use in this situation?

    A. `iexplore -kiosk /url:`
       `http://www.myfishhook.com/kiosk.htm`

    B. `iexplore -kiosk -url:`
       `http://www.myfishhook.com/kiosk.htm`

    C. `iexplore -k -u`
       `http://www.myfishhook.com/kiosk.htm`

    D. `iexplore -k`
       `http://www.myfishhook.com/kiosk.htm`

Answer: D.

2. Microsoft requires that you report the number of browsers distributed using the Internet Explorer Administration Kit. How often should you report?

   A. Monthly

   B. Quarterly

   C. Semi-annually

   D. Annually

Answer: B.   Quarterly reports regarding browser distribution are required.

3. Which organizational mode allows you to perform a silent installation?

   A. Corporate administrator

   B. Internet service provider

   C. Internet content provider

   D. Both corporate administrator and Internet service provider

Answer: A.

4. Which installation provides a single floppy disk option for installation?

   A. Corporate administrator mode

   B. Internet service provider mode

   C. Internet content provider mode.

   D. Both corporate administrator and Internet content provider modes

Answer: B.

5. Consider the following scenario:

   A group of public relations executives have asked you to create a browser distribution that will permit them to collaborate on projects. File transfer is not allowed among the executives for security reasons. The existing environment is based on the IPX protocol.

Required result: Allow the executives to collaborate on projects.

Desired results:

1. Prevent the executives from sending or receiving files.

2. Provide streaming video capabilities on the Desktop.

Solution: Implement the TCP/IP protocol in the environment. Create a distribution that includes Microsoft Net-Meeting and NetShow. Use the IEAK Profile Manager to prevent file transfers using NetMeeting.

Does this solution:

A. Meet the required result and both desired results

B. Meet the required result and only one of the desired results

C. Meet only the required result and none of the desired results

D. Not meet the required result

Answer: A.

6. What is the maximum number of download URLs that you can have while in the corporate administrator mode of IEAK doing a silent installation?

A. 1

B. 3

C. 10

D. None of the above

Answer: A.

7. Which of the following file extensions would not be found on a file that is responsible for configuring proxy settings for the browser?

A. .JS

B. .PAC

    C. .INS

    D. .JVS

Answer: C.

8. Which items of Internet Explorer 3.x will not be migrated to Internet Explorer 4?

    A. Cache settings

    B. Favorites

    C. Cookies

    D. Proxy settings

Answer: A.

9. When using the Internet Connection Wizard, choose the statement that most closely matches the correct file descriptions.

    A. All users can use the same .ISP file to connect to the sign-up server and receive a personalized .INS file.

    B. All users can use the same .ISP file to connect to the sign-up server and receive the same .INS file that all users receive.

    C. A single user may use a personalized .ISP file to connect to the sign-up server and receive the same .INS file that all users receive.

    D. A single user may use a personalized .ISP file to connect to the sign-up server and receive a personalized .INS file.

Answer: A.

10. Consider the following scenario:

You have been hired at a computer lab at a university. Your task is to upgrade the existing browsers and install newsgroup clients on every workstation. The department chairperson wants to make department announcements on every browser and newsgroup reader.

Required result: Upgrade existing browser and newsgroup reader.

Desired results:

1. Provide an announcement page in every Internet Explorer browser.

2. Provide an announcement page in every installation of Outlook Express.

Solution: Develop a package that uses Internet Explorer and Outlook Express. Give the IEAK Wizard the URL of the start page of the Web-based announcements. Also during the wizard, supply the URL of a 640-by-50-pixel html page for the InfoPane in Outlook Express.

Does this solution:

A. Meet the required result and both desired results

B. Meet the required result and only one of the desired results

C. Meet only the required result and none of the desired results

D. Not meet the required result

Answer: A.

11. If a new Internet user has already received a user name, password, and dial-up information, which sign-up server is appropriate?

A. Internet sign-up server

B. Serverless sign-up server

C. No sign-up server

D. None of the above

Answer: B.

12. When bundling your custom applications into CAB files, which utility will you use?

    A. IE4SETUP.EXE

    B. IE2CAB.EXE

    C. IEXPRESS.EXE

    D. IE4XPRES.EXE

Answer: C.

13. Which utility would you use to restore a channel that had been previously deleted during package creation?

    A. IEAK Help

    B. IEAK Wizard

    C. Internet Explorer Setup, from Add/Remove Programs

    D. You cannot undelete a channel once distributed

Answer: B.

14. Which one of the following <SCHEDULE> tags will result in downloading content every four hours between 2 A.M. and 10 P.M.?

    A.
```
<SCHEDULE>
    <INTERVALTIME DAY="1" />
    <EARLIESTTIME HOUR="0200" />
    <LATESTTIME HOUR="2200" />
</SCHEDULE>
```

    B.
```
<SCHEDULE>
    <INTERVALTIME DAY="1" />
    <EARLIESTTIME HOUR="02:00" />
    <LATESTTIME HOUR="22:00" />
</SCHEDULE>
```

    C.
```
<SCHEDULE>
    <INTERVALTIME DAY="1" />
    <EARLIESTTIME HOUR="2" />
    <LATESTTIME HOUR="22" />
</SCHEDULE>
```

D. `<SCHEDULE>`

        `<INTERVALTIME HOUR="4" />`

        `<EARLIESTTIME HOUR="2" />`

        `<LATESTTIME HOUR="22" />`

    `</SCHEDULE>`

Answer: D.

15. Susan has created a distribution that includes the Full installation of the browser and the Windows Desktop Update. Which systems as shown below will support this package? (Choose all that apply.)

    A. 486/25 with 200MB free disk space, 16MB of memory

    B. 486/66 with 65MB free disk space, 24MB of memory

    C. Pentium 200 with 70MB free disk space, 64MB of memory

    D. Pentium 120 with 200MB free disk space, 64MB of memory

Answer: D.

16. Which of the following are not custom options for Outlook Express?

    A. Common signature for appending to the end of each mail message

    B. Creating a welcome e-mail for the user's first time with the product

    C. Creating an InfoPane, which can contain HTML or another URL

    D. Personalized user signature for appending to each mail message

Answer: D.

17. Consider the following scenario:

You have been asked to develop an Internet Explorer distribution for a hospital. Administration has asked that the browser permit them to run ActiveX controls from sites they trust and to be prompted for a choice whenever the situation arises about sites they do not trust. They also want the ability to view live, streaming video events.

Required result: Provide a new browser distribution package that includes the ability to view live, streaming video events.

Desired results:

1. Allow the user the ability to run ActiveX controls from sites they trust without hindrance.

2. Prompt the user before running ActiveX controls from sites they do not trust.

Solution: Plan and create a distribution using the corporate administrator mode. Do not install the Windows Desktop Update. Accept all default zone permissions. Add the untrusted sites to the Restricted Sites zone. Install NetShow.

Does this solution:

A. Meet the required result and both desired results

B. Meet the required result and only one of the desired results

C. Meet only the required result and none of the desired results

D. Not meet the required result

Answer: B.   The untrusted sites were added to the Restricted Sites zone, which are by default set to high security. In the high-security model, running ActiveX controls are disabled. To make this scenario work, the Restricted Sites zone should have been set to Custom and specifically granted to prompt permission.

18. Which of these are not Java Permission settings?

A. Low Safety

B. Custom

C. Disable Java

D. No Safety

Answer: D.

19. Which of the following is not a benefit of using a proxy server?

   A. Caching of frequently used content to increase performance

   B. Masking the true address of the user's workstation

   C. Crawling a Web site and caching the content to increase performance

   D. Supporting multiple protocols

Answer: C.

20. What will happen if a user attempts to download code that is signed using an expired certificate?

   A. Authenticode technology will prevent the download from occurring.

   B. Authenticode technology will permit the download, but would first prompt the user for action.

   C. Authenticode technology will permit the download and notify the IEAK administrator.

   D. Authenticode technology will prevent the download from occurring and notify the IEAK administrator.

Answer: B.

21. If a zone is not listed in any other zone, in what zone is it considered to be?

   A. Restricted Sites

   B. Internet

   C. Trusted Sites

   D. Local Intranet

Answer: B.

22. A customer has asked that you build a package that prevents the browser from displaying anything stronger than

fighting. Which of the following settings will satisfy this requirement?

A. Violence rating set to 0

B. Violence rating set to 1

C. Violence rating set to 2

D. Violence rating set to 3

E. Violence rating set to 4

Answer: B.

23. When autoconfiguration takes place, where does it attempt to retrieve configuration information?

A. From the URL supplied during package creation in the Automatic Configuration window

B. From the URL specified during user installation

C. From the URL supplied during package creation in the Automatic Browser Configuration window

D. From the URL supplied during package creation in the Autoconfigure Setup window

Answer: C.

24. Which of the software channels permissions will allow automatic download and automatic installations? Choose the best answer.

A. High Safety

B. Medium Safety

C. Low Safety

D. Medium and Low Safety

Answer: C.

25. Choose two files that represent the parts of a digital ID.

A. Software Publisher Certificate (SPC) file

B. Software Encryption Key (SEK) file

    C. Public Key (PK) file

    D. Private Key (PVK) file

Answer: A, D.

26. Which application will share the entire Desktop and comprise security at the installation?

    A. File Manager

    B. Program Manager

    C. Windows Explorer

    D. Internet Explorer

Answer: B.

27. Which protocol supports audio conferencing in NetMeeting?

    A. NetBEUI

    B. IPX

    C. TCP/IP

    D. None of the above

Answer: C.

28. Which of the following files does not have to be signed before packaging?

    A. BRANDING.CAB

    B. IE4SETUP.EXE

    C. IE40CIF.CAB

    D. DESKTOP.CAB

    E. Both B and C

    F. All of the above files must be signed before packaging

Answer: F.

29. From where does the AutoComplete function get its information?

A.   Temporary Internet files

B.   History files

C.   The cache found in *SYSTEMROOT*\System32\Cache

D.   The cache found in *SYSTEMROOT*\System32\
     History

Answer: B.

30. A user reports that her Web browser is returning pages and
other Web content very slowly. You open up a browser on
your Desktop, and the updated content is displaying just
fine. What should you look for on the end user's machine?

A.   Check the settings under Temporary Internet Files—is
     it checking for new pages with every visit to the site?

B.   Check the settings under Temporary Internet Files—is
     it not checking for new pages, but instead preferring
     the cache?

C.   Check the settings under Temporary Internet Files—is
     it checking for expired pages in the cache?

D.   Check the settings under Temporary Internet Files—is
     it not checking for expired pages in the cache, and
     the cache is filling beyond capacity?

Answer: A.

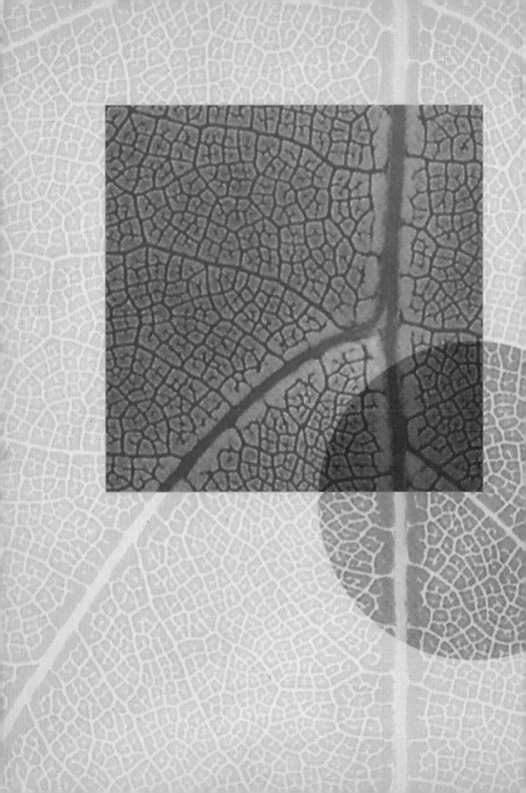

Appendix B

GLOSSARY

Access Control Entry (ACE)   A single account (group or user) associated with a permission such as Read, Write, Change, or No Access.

Access Control List (ACL)   A list of ACEs attached to an object. Every object has an ACL.

Account Delegation   The act of sending the current user's Windows NT security credentials to log in to a server; in this case, for accessing a SQL database.

Active Channel   A method for users to selectively receive content on their Desktops on a routine and scheduled basis. Active Channels are a method for authors to control Web-site crawling, reducing bandwidth requirements for their Web sites.

Active Desktop   A live palette for a user to display important dynamic information on the Desktop. It turns the usual background screen into a user workspace where content can be displayed to the user. It contains the background wallpaper and other Desktop items.

Active Server Pages   A server-side dynamic content technology that implements a scripting host like Visual Basic or JScript as an ISAPI filter DLL.

Active Setup   A small, downloadable program designed to detect setup problems automatically before they occur. It has features such as picking up a download from where it left off and detecting low disk space before downloading the installation files.

Active Setup Log.txt   A file that is generated by Active Setup that details the setup process. Success and errors are both recorded. This file is found in the *SYSTEMROOT* directory—for example, WINNT. Actual installation errors are recorded by IE4 SETUP LOG.TXT, also found in the *SYSTEMROOT* directory.

ActiveX Controls   ActiveX controls are frequently found in Windows applications and developed as DLLs. An example of an ActiveX control is the Channel bar, which sits on the Active Desktop and contains several Active Channels.

ActiveX   Another name for COM (Component Object Model)-based technologies, having a distant ancestry to OLE. A common example of ActiveX is called an ActiveX control.

. ADM Files   See *System Policies.*

Address List   A grouping of recipients created for ease of access or management.

Address Space   The path to a particular messaging system.

Administrative Management Domain (ADMD)   The topmost object in an X.400 e-mail transfer system, usually managed by a large corporation such as AT&T or MCI.

Alert   A response to an event in the database engine that is useful as a method of warning an administrator when something goes awry.

Alias   A name given to each recipient that is used in the creation of e-mail addresses. Also, the name used to refer to a virtual directory. The alias shows up as a subdirectory inside the Web site.

Anonymous Access   Allows access to a resource without a valid user name or password being provided.

ANSI Settings   These are settings in SQL that specifically affect ANSI SQL-92 compliance.

Append   Add the backup to the end of an existing tape, without overwriting what is on the tape already.

Application Role   This is used to apply permissions to a specific application so that only that application can be used to gain access to the data.

ARP (Address Resolution Protocol)   A command-line utility that shows IP address-to-hardware address resolution.

Article   The smallest unit in replication; this can be a full table or a subset of a table.

Association Parameters   Concerned with the establishment of connections between servers.

Association   A path opened between two systems by the MTA.

Attributes   Individual items of information stored about an object. Phone numbers, for example, are an attribute of mailboxes.

Authentication   A method used to verify the identity of a user. Various authentication methods exist, with various levels of secure information exchange and software compatibility.

Authenticode   Verifies that the code downloaded from the Internet has not been altered since it was published. The technology will verify and validate who published the software, giving the end user peace of mind that the software has not been tampered with.

Autoconfiguration   The process by which Internet Explorer reconfigures itself based on the autoconfiguration file found at the URL given. It repeats the process based on a time interval given to the browser.

Automatic Browser Configuration   See *Autoconfiguration*.

Automatic Version Synchronization (AVS)   Part of the IEAK Wizard that checks for the most recent versions of Internet Explorer 4 and any add-on components before the package is created. If IE or any add-on component is out of date, options are offered to download the most current product from the selected Microsoft download site.

Autoproxy File   Autoproxy files are small, dynamic text files that allow IE to quickly configure its own proxy client to point to the correct proxy server and satisfy a particular client request. There can be multiple proxy servers configured at once, allowing the proper proxy server to be selected depending on the destination. They can be found with file extensions like .JS, .JVS, and .PAC.

Backup Browser   A backup to the Master Browser of a subnet. It also responds to browser requests.

Backup Device   This is a pointer telling SQL where the backup files are stored. This can be either disk or tape.

Bandwidth Throttling   The apportioning of bandwidth among the various Web sites or services on an Internet server.

Basic (Clear Text) Using SSL (Secure Sockets Layer)   Uses SSL to encrypt the authentication on port 993.

Basic (Clear Text)   Refers to authentication that uses an unencrypted username and password.

Berkeley Internet Name Domain (BIND)   The most popular implementation of DNS used today.

Bottleneck   The single most limiting performance factor in a machine.

Broadcast Packet   A packet that is broadcast to each computer on the network.

Broken Ownership Chain   When not all objects in a chain are owned by the same user and SQL must check permissions on underlying objects, the ownership chain is broken.

Browser List   A list of all resources on your network. It is maintained by the designated browsers.

Buffers   Temporary data storage locations.

Cache   When specifically referring to Internet Explorer, the cache is a collection of all the recently downloaded content. Whenever a new site is visited, the content is stored in a folder called TEMPORARY INTERNET FILES. This content is displayed by the browser. The browser's default action is to reuse the content whenever it is needed, at least for the current browser session. Restarting the browser clears the cache.

Caching-only Server   When a DNS server is first configured, it only caches information it receives from other servers. It does not pass information to other servers. When a caching server receives information, it maintains that information in memory for use at a later time. This is a dynamic process and also a volatile process. If the server should come down for any reason, all the information stored in cache will be lost.

Carbon-unit Interface   The end user.

Catalog   The indexing data maintained by Index Server that contains the word list and the documents in which those words exist.

CDF File   A file based on the Extensible Markup Language (XML) format. Responsible for the setup and maintenance of channel subscriptions and Software Distribution Channels.

They are created and editable by the Web site administrator or an end user.

Certificate   A one-way encrypted hash that can be decrypted to prove the identity of the sender without providing the ability to forge the hash. Certificates are thus used as "digital signatures" to authorize transactions and prove identities in the absence of physical proof.

Channel Subscriptions   Initiated by a Channel Definition Format file, these are one of several methods of delivering content to end users. The CDF file can be authored or modified by the end user or the Web site administrator. These subscriptions can deliver specific content to the end users rather than depending on site-crawling methods.

Character Set   This defines how SQL sees the characters stored in your databases.

Checkpoint   Additional data added to a transmission that allows the destination server to acknowledge receipt of a given amount of data.

Cluster Server   This Microsoft product links two servers with a shared hard drive so that, in the event of a failure, one server can take over the functions of the failed system.

Collaborative Application   An application accessed and managed through Exchange.

Command Line Parameter   An option placed on the command line used to execute a program or batch file. These options can be used to configure how a program will execute.

Command Line Switch   Refers to parameters used to configure how a command line tool functions.

Connection Retry Values   Control how many times and at what interval a connection should be retried after an error.

Connector   An Exchange component used to connect an Exchange environment to a foreign mail system or to connect Exchange sites together.

Consistency Check   A process that checks that the Information Store and directory are consistent with each other.

Console File   A small file containing settings that control the snap-ins to be loaded and the display windows and their contents for an MMC administrative purpose.

Content Advisor   The Content Advisor is a feature of Internet Explorer that prevents a user from retrieving content deemed inappropriate by the IEAK administrator during configuration. The Advisor is based on the PICS (Platform for Internet Content Selection) format of rating Web sites.

Content Provider Mode   IEAK package creation and licensing mode designed primarily for hardware and software manufacturers.

Copy Backup   Essentially a full backup except that no file marking occurs. Usually used to acquire a "snapshot" of the system before a change is made.

Corporate Administrator Mode   IEAK package creation and licensing mode used primarily in businesses and other corporations. Supports up to 10 download sites and 10 installation options, unless the silent mode is used.

Corpus   The body of documents indexed by Index Server.

Counters   Each object in Performance Monitor has counters that report specific statistics of the object. For instance, the % Processor Time counter of the Processor object would report the percent of time during which the processor is busy.

.CSV Format File   A text file in which fields of data are separated by commas.

Customization Code   A licensing code obtained from Microsoft that allows you to distribute your browser as stated in your distribution agreement with Microsoft. This code is required to build a package or to use the IEAK.

Cyberbolic   A graphical view of Web page relationships that changes to display the relationships from the currently selected page.

Data File   The data file is where all database objects, such as tables and indexes, are stored.

Database   Stored sets of related information that can be retrieved using logical expressions (queries) that specify the set members desired.

Database Client   A program that queries, displays, and updates database information. Also called a front end.

Database Server   A program that stores databases and processes queries. Also called a back end.

Database User Account   A database user account is used for gaining access to a single database once a user is logged in.

DBCC   The Database Consistency Checker (DBCC) is used to ensure the physical and logical consistency of a database. Backups cannot be performed while it is running.

DB-Library   This is an Application Programming Interface (API) that developers can use to allow their applications to access data stored on SQL Server.

dbo   This is a powerful user in each database to which members of the sysadmins fixed server role are mapped.

Default Gateway   The IP address of a router to which all remote communication should be directed.

Defragmentation   A process that moves a file to contiguous disk space.

Department of Defense (DOD) Model   A four-level model that standardizes how communications occur between computers.

Desktop Items   A Desktop item is an instance of an HTML document or an image that sits on the Desktop. It can also be an ActiveX control. Desktop items are located in the HTML layer and are floating items—they always sit atop the background and just below the Icon layer.

DHCP (Dynamic Host Configuration Protocol)   Provides dynamic configuration of TCP/IP hosts by providing an IP address and other information, including the subnet mask, default gateway, and WINS Server.

DHCP Lease   The amount of time a workstation can keep an address.

DHCP Manager   Manages DHCP properties.

DHCP Relay Agent   DHCP requests cannot cross a router. Therefore, a relay agent must be configured on any subnet that does not have a DHCP server, but where hosts are using DHCP.

DHCP Scope   The range of addresses the DHCP server can manage.

Diagnostic Logging   The process of tracking events within an Exchange component by placing information in the NT Application event log.

Differential Backup   A backup method that starts with a full backup. Thereafter all of the data that has changed since the full backup is put to tape.

Digital ID   See *Certificate*.

Directed Packet   A packet that is addressed to a specific host.

Directory   A container for files and other directories in hierarchical namespace. Directories provide convenient objects to group and manage related files.

Directory Listing Style   The specific manner in which FTP directory contents are returned to the client. Two styles exist that mimic the command line displays of native directory commands: UNIX and MS-DOS. Of the two, UNIX is the far more widely used and compatible.

Directory Synchronization   The process of exchanging recipient lists across e-mail systems.

Dirsync protocol   The protocol used for all MS Mail directory synchronization communication.

Disk Fragmentation   Refers to the process in which files on a disk become broken into non-contiguous disk space. Defragmentation is the process of moving files to contiguous disk space.

Distributed Query   This is a query that returns data from tables stored on more than one server.

Distribution   A single bundle or package of software specifically prepared for dissemination and eventual installation to others. Can contain several programs ready for installation.

Distributor   All of the changes made on a published database are stored at the Distributor and then disseminated to all of the Subscribers.

Domain   A logical grouping of users and computers managed through a central database.

Domain Master Browser   Usually the Primary Domain Controller. It is the server that is responsible for maintaining the master browser list.

Domain Name Service (DNS)   A name resolution system that will equate a name, such as www.microsoft.com, to an IP address, such as 207.68.156.52.

DTS Package   This is a DTS object that defines a series of tasks to be executed in sequence for importing, exporting, and transforming data.

Duplicate Address   Two computers sharing the exact network and host address.

DXA   The Exchange service used to synchronize the Exchange Directory with MS Mail postoffices. There is both a Server DXA and a Requestor DXA.

Dynamic Link Library (DLL)   Separate code modules that can be independently loaded and executed to extend the functionality of a program.

Dynamic Router   A type of routing protocol that will determine the location of other routes and dynamically discover the routes available on the network.

E-mail   An addressed text message that is transmitted through a series of mail servers until it reaches its destination domain, where it is stored until retrieved by the intended recipient user.

Encryption   Applying an algorithm to a message to scramble or to code its content. The recipient must have the appropriate key or algorithm to decode the message.

End User   Someone who uses computers on a regular basis. They have varying levels of skill and will typically use a computer to accomplish one or more tasks. They do not normally perform system administrator tasks—they leave those to others.

Event   An action occurring on the server, such as a select statement or a user login failure.

Expansion Server   An Exchange server that has been designated to expand the member list of a DL and to route e-mail to the appropriate home servers.

Extent   A group of eight pages; this is the smallest unit that SQL will allocate for a table or index.

Fault Tolerance   Refers to a system that is designed with redundancy so that the failure of one component does not affect user access.

File Transfer Protocol (FTP)   A TCP/IP-based client/server service that allows the upload and download of files to and from a server running the FTP service to a client running an FTP client. FTP is one of the oldest useful TCP/IP services, and is widely supported.

File   Data stored on a file system that is located by a filename and associated with other parameters such as access permissions.

Filegroup   Filegroups are used for separating database objects into separate files; for example, a table could be on the primary filegroup while its index could be on a different physical disk in a different filegroup.

Filegroup Backup   This backup will back up a single filegroup of a database rather than the whole thing. This is typically used to speed up backups for VLDBs.

Filter   A specific ISAPI DLL that is inserted into the communications stream to process all information transmitted by a Web site or server.

Fixed Database Role   This is used to apply permissions to a group of users in a specific database.

Fixed Server Role   This is used to apply server-level permissions to groups of users.

Folder's Home Server   A server that holds a copy of a public folder. The folder can be configured so that only administrators of the site the home server is in can create new replicas.

FQDN (Fully Qualified Domain Name)   The full name of a host computer, complete with the full DNS name, for example, ntmail.corp.psconsulting.com.

Frame Type   A definition of how packets should be configured on an IPX/SPX network.

FTP Site (FTP Virtual Server)   A collection of related files stored in a directory tree that is served by the Microsoft FTP service on a specific TCP/IP address and port number with similar security requirements. One server may have multiple FTP sites, but they must all be on unique TCP ports.

Full Backup   A backup method that backs up the entire data structure.

Full-text Catalog   A catalog is a collection of full-text indexes; each database may have only one.

Full-text Index   This is the entity that makes full-text searching possible. It stores references to words in text and character fields. These may be defined only in a base table, not in temporary tables or views.

Garbage Collection   The process that deletes expired tombstones.

Gateway   A third-party Exchange component used to connect to non-Exchange messaging systems. Also, a Microsoft synonym for a router. A default gateway is the next address in the trip through the network.

Global Domain Identifier (GDI)   Usually consists of the three topmost levels of an X.400 address. Together they identify the location of the PRMD.

Guest User Account   This is a user account in each database that is used to grant access to users who have a login but no specific database user account.

H.323 Protocol   A set of standards that allows for a voice telephone call to take place over an Internet Protocol (IP) connection. NetMeeting can be used as a client to an H.323 gateway, allowing NetMeeting users to make telephone calls through the gateway. This technology is also known as Voice over IP.

Hierarchical   Describes a type of database that uses containers and subcontainers to divide information for ease of management.

Home Server   The Exchange server upon which a mailbox physically resides.

Hops   The number of routers a packet has to cross to get to its destination.

Horizontal Partitioning   This is publishing only a subset of records from a table.

Host Address   The portion of an IP address dedicated to the host.

Host Headers   A new technology introduced in the HTTP 1.1 specifications that allows Web servers to differentiate Web sites based on the host text contained in the initial connection negotiation. Prior to HTTP 1.1, the only way to differentiate Web sites was by TCP port or IP address. Host headers requires HTTP 1.1– compatible browsers such as recent versions of Netscape Navigator and Microsoft Internet Explorer.

HOSTS File   A text file that contains the host name and associated IP address of computers with which a client will communicate. This technology has been superseded by DNS.

HTML Extension (.htx) Files   Files used by the IDQ.DLL to format the returned data from a query as HTML files.

HTML Layer   Part of the Active Desktop—a Web page that contains the end-user frames that display content such as ActiveX, HTML, and Java. Sits in the background to the Icon layer.

HTML Service Managers   A set of Active Server Pages (ASP) applications organized as a Web site that provide the ability to control the metabase settings that make up a Web site.

HTTP (Hypertext Transfer Protocol)   The protocol used by most transactions on the World Wide Web.

HTTP Keep-Alives   An optimization that keeps the TCP connection open between a browser and a server between HTTP requests. Normally, the TCP connection is closed after each request. This optimization allows a server to respond faster to established clients, but requires more RAM and processor resources from the server.

Hypertext Markup Language (HTML)   A set of codes that can be embedded in normal text documents to delineate headers, text styles, embedded picture files, and hypertext links.

Hypertext   A specification whereby index links in a text document can be activated in order to move to a different location in the text document or to another document altogether. Hypertext is the enabling technology of the World Wide Web.

ICMP (Internet Control Message Protocol)   Handles error messages when datagrams or packets have been corrupted or discarded. The ICMP will also provide messaging in the case of systems that are overworked.

Icon Layer   Part of the Active Desktop; contains the icons that make up the Desktop, such as My Computer, Network Neighborhood, Recycle Bin, and others. Sits in the foreground to the HTML layer.

IE4SITES.DAT   Shows the download sites that are suitable to download installable software from. This file can be edited to reflect changes in the available servers.

IEAK Profile Manager   An easy way to manage a created package prior to or after distribution. You can also set policies and restrictions for users of the package. The Manager uses the INSTALL.INS file created during package creation.

IEAK Wizard   A key component of the IEAK, the wizard creates a full distribution of Internet Explorer suitable for publication.

Iexpress   Utility used to bundle your own add-on components as part of a package. You can supply an option to run an installation command and cause the computer to reboot once installed.

IIS (Internet Information Server)   Provides FTP server functionality.

IMAP4 (Internet Message Access Protocol)   An Internet protocol used to retrieve e-mail messages. It has more features than POP3.

Incremental Backup   A backup method that starts with a full backup. Thereafter, only the data that has changed since the preceding full or incremental backup is put to tape.

Indexing   The process of cataloging the location of words in a body of documents for cross-referencing.

InfoPane   A small, one-inch window at the bottom of the Outlook Express screen that can be used to disseminate information and other links. It displays an HTML file that resides on the local machine, or can point to a Uniform Resource Locator (URL).

Information Store   Refers to the Exchange databases that hold data. There are two: the Private Information Store that holds user mailboxes and the Public Information Store that holds public folder information.

.INS File Extension   Initially generated by the IEAK Wizard and maintained by the IEAK Profile Manager, the .INS file is used for a number of things, including autoconfiguration. Contains installation choices for Internet Explorer.

INSTALL.INS   The file that is created by the IEAK Wizard. Contains installation choices as determined by the IEAK administrator.

Internet Content Provider Mode   See *Content Provider Mode*.

Internet Data Query (.idq) Files   Files used by the IDQ.DLL to specify the scope and restrictions of a query.

Internet Database Administration (.ida) Files   Files loaded by the IDQ.DLL to specify global administrative parameters.

Internet Locator Server (ILS)   Uses LDAP to register, search, and report to other NetMeeting users who are online. Acts as a dynamic telephone directory, responding to new queries and registrations. Assists NetMeeting users in finding each other and connecting.

Internet Message Access Protocol (IMAP)   A protocol that expands upon the current industry remote e-mail client protocol standard of POP3. Allows for client-based or server-based storage of e-mail.

Internet Service Applications Programming Interface (ISAPI)   A Microsoft specification for creating IIS-compatible Web server extensions.

Internet Service Provider Mode   Also called the ISP mode, this mode allows Internet service providers to supply end users with a single floppy disk to install Internet Explorer.

Internet Sign-Up Server   A Web server that uses CGI scripting or Active pages to create Internet accounts on the fly. Users enter personal information and receive a configuration file to allow them to proceed with installation.

Internet Zone   This security zone is normally configured with the default security level of Medium. This zone represents all other Web sites that do not currently belong in another zone. Normally, most Web sites will use the security assigned here.

InterNIC   The body that regulates and assigns network addresses.

Inter-site Communication   Refers to messages sent from one site to another, as opposed to messages sent between servers in the same site.

Intrasite   Refers to any process that occurs within a site.

IP (Internet Protocol)   The routable protocol that computers use to communicate over the Internet.

IP Address Class   The InterNIC administers five address classes. Class A, Class B, and Class C licenses are most commonly used by computer networks today.

IP Address   A unique identifier for hosts on a TCP/IP network.

IPCONFIG   Primarily used in Windows NT, this utility will show you the TCP/IP configuration, the host name, what DNS servers the client will attempt to resolve Internet addresses from, what type of name resolution the client will perform, and some information about IP routing, NetBIOS resolution, and the WINS proxy.

IPX (Internet Packet Exchange Protocol)   A connectionless-oriented protocol; a Novell Netware standard.

ISAPI Filters   Dynamic Link Libraries written to the Internet Server Application Programming Interface (ISAPI) specification, which process the communication streams as they flow between the client and the server. ISAPI filters can be used to change Web data mid-stream in ways that enhance the functionality of

IIS–for example, to implement scripting languages like VBScript or JScript.

ISDN (Integrated Services Digital Network)   Provides communications over special phone lines using digital communications.

Java   An object-oriented programming language known for cross-platform compatibility and easier development. Internet Explorer 4 supports Java applets, JavaScript, and JavaBeans, among other standards.

JET (Joint Engine Technology)   The database format used by Exchange for its internal databases. JET databases use a series of log files to ensure data integrity.

Job   A series of tasks combined with associated schedules.

. JS File Extension   Autoproxy file responsible for dynamically configuring a browser to use the latest proxy server configuration. It can contain choices based on the name resolution request.

JScript   The Microsoft variant of JavaScript, a simple scripting language developed by Netscape based on the syntax of Sun's Java programming language.

Key Management Server   An optional component of Exchange that provides advanced security.

Keys   Digital files used as mathematical operators in the encryption process. The longer a key is, the stronger the encryption and the more difficult it is to crack.

Lightweight Directory Access Protocol (LDAP)   A protocol that allows users to validate names, and look up e-mail addresses and other directory information.

Line Printer (LPR)   Allows jobs to be sent to a printer that is serviced by a host running an LPD server.

Line Printer Queue (LPQ)   Allows a user to see what jobs are in a print queue on an LPD (Line Printer Daemon) server. It shows the state of the remote queue.

Link Monitor   An Exchange process used to confirm that a connection is functioning.

Link   A URL embedded in a hypertext document; when the link is clicked on, the document it references will be automatically loaded and displayed.

Linked Login   A login that allows users who are using standard security to perform distributed queries.

Linked Server   This is the remote server in a distributed query. This server does not need to be a SQL Server; it only needs to understand ODBC.

LMHOSTS   A text file that aids in the resolution of NetBIOS computer names to IP addresses.

Local Intranet Zone   A security zone that is set to the Medium level by default. Normally contains intranet Web sites added by the IEAK administrator or end users, depending on configuration.

Location Value   Refers to a method of logically grouping servers. When users access public folders, their client applications will first attempt to access the folder from servers in the same location as their home server.

Log File   In an Exchange DS, IS, or DXA database, all transactions are written to a log file before they are committed to the actual database. This allows recovery in the event of problems.

Logreader   This agent reads transaction logs on the publisher and moves transactions that are marked for replication to the Distribution database.

Loopback   A reserved IP address of 127.0.0.1 that is used to check the IP configuration on a local host.

MAC Address   A Media Access Control layer address is also referred to as the *hardware address*. This is a physical address of the network card, usually hard coded into the card at the manufacturer.

MADMAN MIB   The SNMP Mail and Directory Management MIB used to define the parameters available for management. MADMAN is defined in RFCs 1565–7.

Management Information Base (MIB)   An SNMP object that defines the parameters available for remote management.

Masquerade Domain   A name placed in the From field of an outbound e-mail message that is different than the domain name of the server actually originating the mail.

Master Browser   The primary browser for a subnet.

Master Index   The main index for all the documents indexed by the search engine.

Master Merge   An operation that merges the shadow index into the master index.

Master Name Server   A DNS server that passes its information off to a secondary name server. A master name server can either be a primary name server or a secondary name server.

MCIS (Microsoft Commercial Internet System) Membership System   Uses the MCIS Membership database to authenticate users.

Merge Replication   With this type of replication, all servers publish and subscribe to the same article, and all users can make changes.

Message   A text message with an addressed recipient in the form `user@server.domain`. SMTP forwards messages to the server specified after the @ symbol. The message server is then responsible for delivery to the user specified before the @ symbol.

Message Originator   Refers to the user who sent a particular message.

Message Tracking   A process that documents the path of messages through an Exchange messaging environment.

Message Transfer Agent (MTA)   The component of Microsoft Exchange that is primarily responsible for message delivery.

Messaging Application Program Interface (MAPI)   Messaging application interface authored by Microsoft and other third-party vendors. Developed to provide a common interface between dissimilar messaging systems. Assists users with exchange of messaging items such as calendaring, forms, and other workgroup applications.

Metabase   A speed-optimized hierarchical database of IIS settings, which is similar to the Windows NT Registry.

Metric   A parameter of the route command that specifies the number of hops between two network segments.

Microsoft Download Site   A site containing the latest version of Microsoft IE components that is chosen during package creation using the IEAK Wizard. This is a function of Automatic Version Synchronization. By contrast, an ordinary download site is where the IEAK administrator chooses to make their package available for downloading.

Microsoft Transaction Server (MTS)   A Microsoft product that provides the capability to bundle database operations as transactions.

Middleware   Software that performs protocol or data translation between the front end and the back end.

Migration Wizard   A wizard that exports information from foreign systems and imports information into an Exchange organization.

MIME Type   A method of identifying the type of data in a content stream to browsers so the browser can select the proper tool to present the information. MIME types in IIS4 consist of file extensions related to MIME application types.

Modem   From modulate/demodulate. Computer hardware that will turn a computer's digital signal into an analog signal that can be sent over a phone line. The modem at the receiving end will then turn the analog signal into a digital signal that the computer can understand.

Moderator   A person who determines which posts should become part of a newsgroup. Moderators are e-mailed the text of each post, and can either delete or return the post.

MTA Transport Stack   An Exchange component that defines the physical communication process.

Multihomed Computer   A computer with multiple IP addresses assigned to it.

Multihomed System   A multihomed computer with multiple network cards that are each bound to a different subnetwork.

Multilink   The ability of RAS to combine several serial signals into one, using either ISDN or modems.

Multiserver Job   This is a job that is designed to run on a remote server.

Multithreaded Application   An application that is specifically designed to take advantage of a computer with more than one processor.

Name Resolution   The process of resolving the network layer address of a computing device given its name. Domain Name Service looks the name up in a distributed database managed by name servers. NetBIOS-based networking protocols use broadcasts and dynamic discovery to record the names of computers participating in the same broadcast domain.

Named Pipes   This is an Interprocess Communications (IPC) mechanism that allows clients to talk to servers in a client/server scenario.

Namespace   A hierarchical view of controllable objects, which shows clearly how objects relate to one another. Snap-ins expose their namespace to the MMC, which is used to browse the various controllable objects.

NBTStat   A command-line utility that shows the effectiveness of the NetBIOS-to-IP address resolution.

Net News Transfer Protocol (NNTP)   A protocol for transferring message-based entries of a hierarchical database between servers called news servers.

NetBIOS   A protocol used on Windows networks to provide host identification by computer name.

Net-Library   This is a Dynamic Link Library (DLL) that SQL uses to communicate with a network protocol.

NetMeeting   An Internet Explorer 4 add-on component that supports audio and video conferencing, sharing applications, chat, and the transfer of files. Supports one-on-one discussions and large chats.

NetShow   Provides streaming audio and video support over the Internet. Used when the end-user application requires the use of live audio or video. Supports the use of multicast transmissions, enabling several clients at once to view the transmission.

Netstat   A command-line utility designed to show the status of the protocol and the network.

Network Address   An IP address is made up of a network address and host address. The network address uniquely identifies a network segment.

Network Monitor   Graphic utility used to capture and examine packets sent from one host to another.

New Technology File System (NTFS) Security   Protects objects like files and directories on an account-by-account basis, allowing users with sufficient permissions access while denying access to those without.

Newsgroup   A body of posts related by topic. Newsgroups are hierarchically related.

NNTP (Network News Transport Protocol)   An Internet protocol used to retrieve and post information to a Usenet newsgroup.

Non-Browser   A server on a subnet that does not participate in resolving NetBIOS names to IP addresses.

Non-Deliverable Report (NDR)   A message sent to the originator of a message when the message can't be delivered to its destination.

Nontrusted Connection   When a user connects over a nontrusted connection, SQL must validate the password.

N-tier   This is an application that is configured to use multiple, or *n* amount of, servers.

Object Permissions   These are permissions that allow users to manipulate the data in a database.

Object   In Windows NT Performance Monitor, an object is used to identify and monitor a system resource, such as the CPU or memory.

Open Database Connectivity (ODBC)   A database middleware product that provides a translation between clients and servers so that any ODBC-capable client can connect to an ODBC-compatible server.

Open System Interconnect (OSI) Model   This model is used to provide a reference point when discussing protocols.

Operator   The representation of an administrator's e-mail, pager, and net-send addresses in SQL Server.

Optimizer   A program that analyzes your server configuration and expected use and then can make changes and provide suggestions on how to optimize its configuration.

Option Pack   A suite of tools to enhance the Internet service functionality of Windows NT Server. You may not need to install an option pack if you don't need the functionality provided for your server.

Orphaned Record   A record in the database that references an object that has been deleted.

Outlook Express   Internet e-mail and newsgroup reader that is packaged as an add-on component to Internet Explorer 4. Supports the SMTP, POP3, and IMAP4 protocols.

.PAC File Extension   Autoproxy file responsible for dynamically configuring a browser to use the latest proxy server configuration. It can contain choices based on the name resolution request.

Package   See *Distribution*.

Page   The smallest unit of allocation in SQL Server; a single page is 8KB.

Password Synchronization   IIS's ability to automatically update the IIS services with the passwords of anonymous user accounts, thus preventing anonymous users from being denied Web pages if the IUSR_*computername* account password is changed.

Performance Monitor   A tool included with Windows NT that displays statistics for subsystems and components of an NT-based computer.

Permissions   A list of accounts and corresponding types of access attached to an object (e.g., shares, files, printers), which is used to determine the functions those accounts are allowed to perform on the object.

PING   PING is another utility used to test for network connectivity between two points. It can be used to send a test packet to a destination address and establish rough estimates of round-trip travel times.

Plug-in   An extension to a Web browser that handles the display of a specific MIME type. For instance, the Acrobat plug-in from Adobe displays the MIME type PostScript Display Format (.pdf) files.

Point-in-time Recovery   When restoring from transaction logs, this is the capability of SQL to restore data up to a certain date and time.

Polling Interval   A configuration parameter of link and server monitors that controls how often they refresh the status of the computers they are configured to monitor.

POP3 (Post Office Protocol version 3)   An industry-standard protocol used to retrieve e-mail.

Populate   To build a full-text index. The process of updating the full-text index is referred to as repopulating.

Port   A TCP/IP parameter that specifies which communication stream (or conversation) a packet belongs to. Services listen for connections on specific well-known ports when they provide a public service like FTP or WWW service.

Post   A public message hosted by the NNTP protocol.

Potential Browser   A server on a subnet that could become a browser.

POTS (Plain Old Telephone System)   The POTS is otherwise known as the phone company; expletives should be deleted!

PPP (Point-to-Point Protocol)   A Data Link layer transport that performs over point-to-point network connections, such as serial or modem lines. PPP can negotiate with any transport protocol used by both systems involved in the link. It can also realize data transfer efficiencies—such as software compression—and automatically assign IP, domain name service (DNS), and gateway addresses when used with Transmission Control Protocol/Internet Protocol (TCP/IP).

Primary Name Server   The server that hosts information for the Primary Zone.

Primary Zone   The first zone created in a DNS system, a management area.

Private Information Store   The database that contains messages in user mailboxes.

Private Management Domain (PRMD)   The object in an X.400 message transfer system that represents an actual destination, usually a particular company.

Protocol   A set of rules or standards that specifies how systems will communicate.

Proxy   Refers to rights granted to other users. In a GroupWise e-mail system, users can grant other users proxy rights to their mailboxes.

Proxy Server   A server that acts as a gateway between the local network and a larger network. Provides a packet filtering service for both inbound and outbound packets, thus protecting or masking a client's true identity from the larger network. A proxy server can also provide caching services for frequently downloaded content and Internet connectivity in other protocol environments where IP is not available.

.PST Files   Private mail folders stored on a local hard disk rather than on the server.

PSTN (Public Switched Telephone Network)   Another name for the phone company.

Public Folder   A folder used to hold shared data, managed through Exchange.

Public Role   A role in each database of which every user is a member. Users cannot be removed from this role.

Publication   This is a group of articles. A publication cannot span databases.

Publisher   This contains the original copy of the data to be replicated.

Pull Configuration   Refers to placing a replica of a public folder on an Exchange server by having that server request it from the home server.

Pull Replication   A way of configuring WINS database replication. Pull replication is used over slow links, and after initial startup it is triggered by time events.

Push Configuration   Refers to placing a replica of a public folder on an Exchange server by pushing it from the folder's home server.

PVK File   The Private Key file contains the password needed to use the certificate. This file is generated by your browser; therefore, if it's ever lost or stolen, you will have to create a new SPC and PVK file.

Query Governor   This is a setting that affects the database engine by not allowing SQL to run long queries.

Query   The process of retrieving documents based on the presence of specific keywords in the body of the document.

Querying   The process of retrieving documents based on the presence of specific keywords in the body of the document.

RAID   This is an acronym for Redundant Array of Inexpensive Disks. RAID arrays are a series of hard disks that are seen by the system as one disk. They are used to improve I/O and give fault tolerance.

RAS (Remote Access Service)   Allows other users to dial up the host computer and use the computer's resources, or use the computer as a gateway into the entire network.

Rebuilm.exe   This utility is used to re-create the Master, Model, MSDB, and Distribution databases when there is a system crash and no good backup is available.

Recipients Container   A container within the Exchange hierarchy that contains recipient objects.

Registry Corruption   Any state where conflicting registry information exists or where registry information is missing such that the proper operation of services is not possible. Often, reinstallation of software is required to properly restore registry settings.

Rehoming Changing the home server of a public folder.

Relay A mail host that simply forwards mail—it is neither the originating server nor the final recipient.

Reliable Transfer Service (RTS) Parameters Determine how often the data being transferred is verified, how long to wait after an error before attempting to resend data, and how much data can be sent before an acknowledgment is expected from the destination server.

Remote Execution (REXEC) Used to run a process on a remote host equipped with the REXEC server service. REXEC is password protected.

Remote Shell (RSH) Lets a user issue a command to a remote host without logging on to that host. A designated username must exist in the .rhosts file on a UNIX host running the RSH daemon.

Replica A copy of a public folder.

Replication The process of placing a copy of a public folder on a server and keeping it synchronized with other copies of the same folder located on other servers.

Replication Agents Scheduled tasks in SQL Server that perform the work of replication.

Replication List A list of servers that an Exchange server should replicate to and from.

Replication Scripts Transact-SQL scripts that can be used to completely re-create the replication scheme on a SQL Server.

Report Writer A utility of Site Server Express that summarizes the information contained in IIS logs in a concise human-readable form.

Reporting The process of condensing massive amounts of data into concise informative facts.

Repository This is a metadata storage container. When a DTS package is stored here, its data lineage is maintained.

Request for Comment (RFC) A series of articles that define how Internet-based services should function.

Resolver   Usually a client asking for a DNS name to be resolved to an IP address.

Resource Record   Added to a DNS database to indicate the function of the host or the purpose of the record.

Restricted Sites Zone   This security zone is configured with the default security level of High and contains Web sites with content that you do not trust. Downloading and execution of content is prohibited.

RIP (Routing Information Protocol)   Part of the TCP/IP protocol suite that provides IP routing across different subnets.

RISC (Reduced Instruction Set Computing)   A classification of microprocessors noted for high-speed, high-end servers.

Roaming Profiles   Designed for users that travel to more than one Desktop, roaming cache permits users to receive their Desktop consistently, no matter from where they log on. The profile and the user's Desktop are downloaded at each logon and updated at the end of each session.

Role   Roles are used to assign permissions to groups of users rather than individually.

Route   A command-line utility designed to print, add, and delete entries from a route table.

Route Command   Adds static routes to a route table.

Router   A hardware device that moves packets from one subnet to another.

Routing Table   A text file known as the GWART (Gateway Address Routing Table), used to determine the route that should be used to send a message to its recipient.

Schedule   A timer in a job that executes tasks.

Scheduler   An NT service that enables scheduling of events.

Schema   The definition of the structure of a database. For our purposes, the schema defines the objects (and their properties) that can exist in the Exchange Directory.

Scratch File   A temporary text file in which messages are stored during the transfer from Exchange to cc:Mail or vice versa.

Screensaver   Another CDF file element that allows for select information to be cached. This element permits a navigable screensaver to display cached information to the end user. It will appear on the Desktop depending on the settings of the operating system.

Script   A text file containing commands in a specific syntax that can be interpreted to perform a certain function.

Scripting Host   The environment in which a scripting language runs. The scripting host provides the objects that can be accessed by the scripting language to control the host environment. There are three scripting hosts provided with IIS: the Windows Scripting Host to control the operating system, Active Server Pages to automatically create HTML files and control the operation of IIS, and Internet Explorer, which interprets scripts on the client side.

Scripting Language   A simple interpreted language used to control discrete programmatic functions. JScript and VBScript are both scripting languages, as are Perl and BASIC.

Secondary Name Server   Provides DNS redundancy, load balancing, and faster client access. The secondary name server gets its information from the master name server. A Secondary name server cannot be used to manipulate the DNS database.

Secure Socket Layer (SSL)   A service used to encrypt data on the transmit end of a TCP stream and decrypt the data on the receive end. It provides a transparent method to secure communications between two-end systems.

Security Accounts Manager (SAM)   A database that contains user and computer account information.

Security Context   Refers to the total effective permissions of an account. When an Exchange server communicates with another Exchange server, it does so within the security context of the site service account.

Security Levels   Security levels determine what each security zone can allow. Based on the IEAK administrator's choices, certain browser features (such as downloading files) can be restricted.

Security Zones   Security zones are logical groups in which the IEAK administrator can classify Web sites based on the amount of risk that site presents. There are five security zones, four of which can be used by the IEAK administrator to configure security. The fifth zone is the local machine security zone, which has little or no security.

Server Monitor   An Exchange process used to check the status of services running on an Exchange server.

Serverless Sign Up   The Internet account sign-up method that requires the user to supply a user name, password, and dial-up information, permitting them to access the Internet. Users must have this information available prior to installation.

Server-Side Scripting   Refers to a script used by Exchange to fire an action based on an event in a public folder.

Service Account   This is a domain user account that is used by a service to log on.

Service Pack   A package of bug fixes and minor updates issued to strengthen the reliability and security of Windows NT. Service packs should be installed shortly after their release on all Windows NT Server computers.

Service Pack   Software used to update or fix a program.

Setup Script   Setup scripts are used in unattended installations to supply configuration values.

SETUP.LOG   A log file that contains information about what the installation program has accomplished.

Shadow Indexes   Disk buffers for word lists that have not yet been added to the monolithic master index.

Shadow Merge   An operation that combines all the shadow indexes and word lists into a single shadow index whenever the number of word lists or shadow indexes passes a certain threshold.

SIGNCODE.EXE   Utility used to sign 32-bit executables and other code. Uses the SPC and PVK files.

Signing a Message   Attaching a token to a message that includes information about its content. The token is encrypted and the recipient must have the appropriate key to decrypt it.

Once the token is decrypted its information can be used to determine if the message has been tampered with or corrupted during transit.

Silent Installation   A mode of installation in IEAK that allows an end user to complete the installation without intervention. Available using only the corporate administrator mode.

Simple Mail Transfer Protocol (SMTP)   A service used to exchange addressed text messages between Internet hosts. It is the transfer protocol for Internet e-mail systems.

Single-instance Storage   A method of message storage in which only one copy of a message sent to multiple recipients is stored on the server. This method of storage reduces the total amount of disk space required.

Site Affinity   A cost associated with an Exchange site that is used to control from which sites a public folder will be accessed.

Site Service Account   A Windows NT user account used by various Exchange services. This account must have the right to act as part of the operating system.

Site Subscription   Another method of delivering content to the end user, started when the user adds a favorite to the browser and configures the favorite to download the current page and those linked with it. Site subscriptions can download pages up to three levels deep. Site subscriptions depend on Web-site crawling methods, which could be blocked by some Web site administrators. They periodically check the original to see if changes have occurred. If so, the new content may be downloaded for offline viewing, depending on the subscription configuration.

Site   One or more Exchange servers that work together to route messages and configuration information.

Sites   Collections of HTML files, scripts, and applications with a consistent feel that together compose a coherent Internet property. A single server can host any number of sites.

SLIP (Serial Line Internet Protocol)   An implementation of Internet protocol (IP) over a serial line. SLIP has been replaced, by and large, by PPP.

Smart Host   A mail server to which all outbound mail is transmitted and all inbound mail is received. A mail proxy.

Snap-in   A special ActiveX control that controls a Windows NT service and exposes a namespace that can be controlled by the MMC.

Snapshot Replication   This type of replication copies the entire database to its Subscribers.

Snapshot   This is a complete copy of the database, copied from the Publisher to the Subscribers. It is used for initial setup and periodic refreshes.

SNMP (Simple Network Management Protocol)   The part of the TCP/IP protocol suite that allows users to manage the network. With SNMP you can keep track of what is being used on the network and how the object is behaving. SNMP is made up of two components, an SNMP agent and an SNMP manager.

SNMP Agent   A software piece running on the network to gather performance statistics. The SNMP agent is provided with Windows NT.

SNMP Community   A grouping of SNMP agents and SNMP managers for security purposes. SNMP agents can be configured to talk only to SNMP managers in the same community.

SNMP Manager   The software piece that can manage the network. It can request information from an SNMP agent.

SNMP Trap   Where the software agents send the information that has been gathered. Once the information has been trapped, the SNMP Manager can manage it.

Software Distribution Channel   Another adaptation of an Active Channel, this type of Channel allows for IEAK administrators to upgrade browser software and add-on components without user intervention. You can install immediately, or wait for the end user to approve the upgrade.

Sort Order   This defines whether SQL treats characters as case-sensitive, and whether they are sorted as binary values rather than character values.

Source Extractor   Software designed to extract information from an e-mail system and convert it into a format that can be imported to an Exchange organization.

.SPC File   The Software Publishing Certificate file—one of two parts of a digital ID. The SPC contains the actual IE distribution license and requires a password prior to use.

SQL Login   Also referred to as a standard login, a SQL login is an account used for gaining access to SQL Server where both the user name and password are verified by SQL.

SQL Mail   SQL Mail is used to send e-mail and pager alerts to administrators when problems arise.

SQL Switch   This is a program that will allow you to switch between SQL 6.5 and 7 if you have installed them in separate directories.

Statement Permissions   These are permissions that, when granted, allow users to create or modify objects in the database.

Static Router   A router that requires the manual input of the route table.

Stripe Set   A configuration of two or more disks that are seen as one logical drive. Data is written in "stripes" equally across all disks in the set. This configuration can increase disk subsystem performance and fault tolerance.

Subnet Mask   A 32-bit value that determines which part of a TCP/IP address specifies the network and which part specifies the unique host address.

Subnet   A network segment.

Subscriber   This server receives a copy of the data from a Publisher.

Substring Search   A search in which the user submits a string of data and requests any records containing that text.

Summary Report   An HTML page generated by Content Analyzer containing the details you need to optimize your Web site contents.

Suspect Database   This is a database that has gone offline due to being corrupted, deleted, or renamed.

Synchronization   A process that ensures that two or more copies of some data (in this case the Exchange Directory) are the same.

Synthetic Load   Activity of a fixed and known amount engaged in specifically for the purpose of measuring a computer's ability to respond to it.

Syscomments   This is a table stored in each database that contains the original T-SQL code used to define each view, rule, default, trigger, CHECK constraint, DEFAULT constraint, and stored procedure.

System Policies (.ADM Files)   Text files that contain registry keys and potential values. The values that are applied using Windows NT depend on the administrator's choices, the user name, group membership, and computer name. When you're using system policies under the IEAK Profile Manager, no concern is given to user name, group membership, and computer name.

Tag   A special feature of the LMHOSTS file to pre-load information into cache, designate a domain, or reference an external LMHOSTS file.

Task   A command, either T-SQL, command line, or active script, that occurs when it is scheduled to do so.

TCP (Transmission Control Protocol)   A connection-oriented communications protocol that is used by hosts on the Internet.

TCP/IP (Transmission Control Protocol/Internet Protocol)   The standard protocol suite of the Internet.

TDI (Transport Driver Interface)   A specification to which all Windows NT transport protocols must be written in order to be used by higher-level services, such as RAS.

Telnet   Establishes a terminal emulation session with a UNIX-based host running the Telnet service. Telnet, which requires a dependable connection, utilizes TCP.

Template   A recipient pattern used for the creation of additional recipients.

Temporary Internet Files   Directory name for Internet Explorer's cache to store all downloaded data.

Thrashing   Refers to excessive use of a hard disk. (The drive heads "thrash" across the disk.)

Threads   Processes running on an NT server.

Time Synchronization   A process that changes the time on a target server to match that of another.

Time to Live (TTL)   Each packet has a TTL. The default TTL is set to 16 and each time the packet crosses a router, the TTL is decremented by 1. If the TTL reaches 0, the packet is discarded.

Tombstone   A marker in the directory database that indicates that an object has been deleted.

Trace   A group of events that are recorded in Profiler and stored in a file, a table, or both.

TRACERT   A utility used to view the path that a packet travels in between two hosts. It can be used when a user complains that they cannot reach a particular Web site from their browser or any other program or network connection that relies on the TCP/IP protocol.

Transaction Log Backup   This backup will back up all transactions in the transaction log. It can be used to restore up to a certain point in time and is the only backup type that will clear the transaction log automatically.

Transaction Log File   Transaction log files are used to record transactions that make modifications to the data. They are used for up-to-the-minute recoverability in the event of a disaster.

Transaction   A package of discrete events that in sum represent a single operation that must either succeed in entirety or fail in entirety. Transactions are used whenever partial success would cause data corruption.

Transactional Replication   This type of replication copies transactions from the Publisher to the Subscriber as opposed to the full database.

Transfer Timeouts   Allows you to adjust how each message priority should be handled.

Transitive Connection   An implied connection where information about one site is gathered from another site.

Trivial File Transfer Protocol (TFTP)   FTP without the overhead. Because TFTP uses UDP instead of TCP, the inherent overhead in a connection-oriented protocol is removed. This means file transfer will be quicker, though the transfer may not be as reliable.

Trust Level   A value used to determine if a particular recipient should be included in the directory exchange with an MS Mail or cc:Mail system.

Trusted Connection   When a user connects to SQL over a trusted connection, SQL trusts Windows NT to validate the user's password.

Trusted Sites Zone   A security zone that is set to the Low security level by default. This zone contains Web sites with trustworthy content. Any sites listed here will permit the downloading and execution of content without notifying the user.

Unicode   Like a character set, this defines how SQL sees your characters—the difference is that Unicode understands 65,536 characters as opposed to the character set's 256 characters.

Uniform Resource Locator (URL)   The textual address of a document on the Web. A URL contains the protocol necessary to retrieve the document, the DNS name of the server upon which the document is stored, the path to the document, the document name, and any parameters required for the server to automatically generate the document if it is created dynamically upon request.

Universal Naming Convention (UNC)   A standardized method for referring to data located on foreign servers, taking the form *server**share**directorypath**data*, where *server* is the Windows name of the server, *share* is the share name of the directory that provides the data, *directorypath* is the path inside the share to the specific location being referenced, and *data* is the filename of the file referred to.

Update Sequence Number (USN)   A "change counter" used to control which objects are updated during directory replication.

Usage Import   A utility of Site Server Express that translates the log files into a database format understood by Report Writer and retrieves additional information, such as domain name from the IP address.

User Agent String   A series of characters supplied by the IEAK administrator that is appended to the browser identification that was already coded by Microsoft. This series of characters is designed to make distributions distinct to Web servers, which receive this code with every browser request.

User Datagram Protocol (UDP)   A connection-less method of delivery. A UDP packet makes a best effort to deliver a packet. If the packet is damaged in transit, it is up to the application to discover the problem and ask for a retransmission.

User Locator Service   This service is provided by the Internet Locator Server for backward compatibility with NetMeeting 1.0. See also *Internet Locator Server*.

Vertical Partitioning   This is publishing only a subset of columns from a table.

View   A definition of how data should be displayed or sorted.

View Indices   Type of index used to sort the information within a view based upon a user's needs.

Virtual Directory   An alias to a directory inside an FTP site that resides somewhere other than in the FTP site directory tree—for example, on another volume or another computer. Some security settings can be applied differently to virtual directories than they are applied to the FTP site as a whole.

Virtual Memory   A process that allows the operating system to use hard disk storage as an extension to RAM.

Virtual Server   Another term for a Web or FTP site on an IIS4 machine.

Visual Basic   A simple scripting language included in most Microsoft applications and operating systems. VBScript is the variant used by the Windows Scripting Host, Internet Explorer, and Internet Information Server.

Web Map   A graphical view of the relationships between HTML pages in a Web site.

Web Site   A group of interrelated Web pages with a unified purpose, a similar stylistic theme, and a distinct method of address (either by unique IP address, port, or host header).

Web Sites   A collection of related hypertext documents typically addressed from the same root URL and embodying a specific purpose. Web sites are an abstract collection used to apply similar security and administrative settings to a set of HTML documents.

WebMap   A cyberbolic map of a Web site that graphically shows pages connected by the links contained in them.

Windows Desktop Update (WDU)   End-user shell interface designed to provide seamless integration of the Windows Desktop with the Web browser. It allows end users to use the interface to traverse file directories and Web pages.

Windows Internet Naming Service (WINS)   Name registration service for NetBIOS names. Registers a NetBIOS name and its current IP address to prevent duplication. The database that is used to register is more frequently used to query to resolve the names into IP addresses, permitting hosts to communicate directly.

Windows NT Challenge/Response using SSL   Uses an SSL encrypted channel for authentication traffic.

Windows NT Login   An account used for gaining access to SQL Server where only the user name is verified by SQL—the password is verified by Windows NT.

WINIPCFG   Primarily used in Windows 95, this utility will show you the TCP/IP configuration of the operating system, the host name, what DNS servers the client will attempt to resolve Internet addresses from, what type of name resolution the client will perform, and some information about IP routing, NetBIOS resolution, and the WINS proxy.

WINS Proxy Agent   A computer configured to provide name caching or request forwarding on a network segment that does not have a resident WINS Server

Word List   A RAM buffer used to store indexed words until they are merged into the catalog.

Working Set   This is the amount of physical RAM an application is using at any given time.

World Wide Web (WWW)   A client/server file transfer and presentation protocol. Unlike FTP transfers, which are simply written to disk and stored when received, files transferred through the WWW service are opened by the receiving client (called a browser) and presented to the user by the method matching their MIME type. Common presentation types include text, hypertext, bitmapped graphics, sound, and video.

X.400   An industry-standard definition of how e-mail messages are addressed and formatted.

X.500   An industry-standard hierarchical database used to define and manage network entities.

Zone Properties   These are aspects of a zone that can be managed, including WINS integration. The zone properties that can be managed include the Time to Live feature of the WINS lookup. When a host name gets resolved via WINS, the address is cached for the WINS Cache Time-Out Value. If this address is ever forwarded to another DNS, the WINS Cache Time-Out Value TTL is sent.

Zone   An area of the DNS database that a particular server manages.

INDEX

Note to Reader: Throughout this index **boldfaced** page numbers indicate primary discussions of a topic. *Italicized* page numbers indicate illustrations. See also *Glossary*, pp. 958–995.

N

O

V

W

Sybex Books on the Web

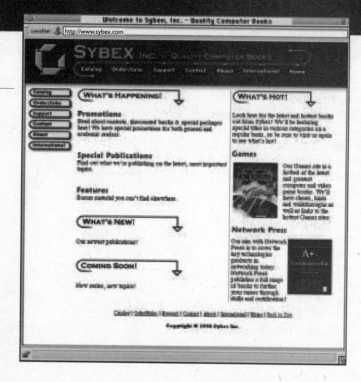

At the dynamic and informative Sybex Web site, you can:

- view our complete online catalog
- preview a book you're interested in
- access special book content
- order books online at special discount prices
- learn about Sybex

www.sybex.com

SYBEX Inc. • 1151 Marina Village Parkway
Alameda, CA 94501 • 510-523-8233

SYBEX

MCSE CORE REQUIREMENT STUDY GUIDES

Sybex's Network Press presents updated and expanded second editions
of the definitive study guides for MCSE candidates.

ISBN: 0-7821-2220-5
704pp; 7¹/₂" x 9"; Hardcover
$49.99

ISBN: 0-7821-2223-X
784pp; 7¹/₂" x 9"; Hardcover
$49.99

ISBN: 0-7821-2222-1
832pp; 7¹/₂" x 9"; Hardcover
$49.99

ISBN: 0-7821-2221-3
704pp; 7¹/₂" x 9"; Hardcover
$49.99

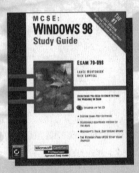

ISBN: 0-7821-2373-2
800pp; 7¹/₂" x 9"; Hardcover
$49.99

A $50.00 SAVINGS!

MCSE Core Requirements
Box Set
ISBN: 0-7821-2245-0
4 hardcover books;
3,024pp total; $149.96

Microsoft Certified
Professional
Approved Study Guide

www.sybex.com

NETWORK PRESS ®
SYBEX

STUDY GUIDES FOR THE MICROSOFT CERTIFIED SYSTEMS ENGINEER EXAMS